BARRON'S

MAT™

MILLER ANALOGIES TEST™

12TH EDITION

Karin Sternberg, Ph.D.
Sternberg Consulting, LLC

Robert J. Sternberg, Ph.D.
Professor of Psychology and Education, University of Wyoming

Andrew H. Body
Vice President, BWS Education Consulting

BARRON'S

MAT™ and Miller Analogies Test are trademarks, in the U.S. and/or other countries, of Pearson Education, Inc., or its affiliate(s), which was not involved in the production of, and does not endorse, this product.

© Copyright 2017, 2013, 2009, 2005, 2001, 1998, 1994, 1989, 1986, 1981, 1978,
1974 by Barron's Educational Series, Inc.

All inquiries should be addressed to:
Barron's Educational Series, Inc.
250 Wireless Boulevard
Hauppauge, New York 11788
www.barronseduc.com

ISBN: 978-1-4380-0954-4

ISSN: 1533-7715

Printed in the United States of America

9 8 7 6 5 4 3 2 1

10%
POST-CONSUMER
WASTE
Paper contains a minimum
of 10% post-consumer
waste (PCW). Paper used
in this book was derived
from certified, sustainable
forestlands.

Contents

Introduction

WHAT THIS BOOK CAN DO FOR YOU

This book is designed to help bring you to the point where your performance on the *Miller Analogies Test (MAT)* is the best of which you are capable. If the book succeeds in doing so, it has succeeded admirably, and so have you. Perhaps you are sitting for the *MAT* as a means to an end of being accepted into a graduate program. Perhaps your aim is to attain a high enough score to meet the minimum threshold for admission into a high or ultra-high I.Q. society. Perhaps yours is another aim entirely.

Regardless of your particular reason for motivation, it is evident that you already are amply motivated for success merely by the act of purchasing this book. You have made a commitment to excellence, and this book will be your steady, reliable chaperone as you prepare for the exam.

Many individuals do not reveal their true abilities on the *MAT* and other standardized tests. There are several reasons why this is so:

1. **The mystique of standardized tests.** One reason for underperformance stems from the aura of mystery that surrounds standardized tests. The mystique of standardized tests evolves from three common misconceptions. The first misconception is that the tests evaluate the whole person. In fact, the tests evaluate just a small segment of the person's behavior, and their evaluation of this small segment of behavior is, as we shall soon see, highly fallible. A second misconception is that there is nothing one can do to improve one's test performance, since the tests measure something that is innate rather than something that is learned. In fact, there is a great deal you can do to improve your test score, and in reading this book and in working on the practice tests, you are already doing it. The third misconception is an emotional one—it is the feeling of awe that people often have when faced with something they don't understand. By the time you are done with this book, however, you will understand the *Miller Analogies Test* very well, and what once seemed mysterious to you will be quite familiar.

   There are certain basic facts about the *MAT* that anyone who is to take the test ought to know. Some of these facts are readily available to the public through various pamphlets provided by the test publisher, but others are not. Many of the most important facts are among the least well known. Parts Two and Four of this book contain the basic facts that you ought to know about the *MAT*.

2. **Unfamiliarity with test-taking strategies and skills.** Many individuals never acquire the test-taking strategies and skills that would enable them to optimize their performance on the *MAT*. As a result, they make blunders that reflect their deficiencies in test-taking rather than in intellectual ability. Part Three of this book shows you just what an analogy is, the types of analogies that appear on the *MAT*, and the strategies you can employ to systematically approach *MAT* problems. Included are helpful hints that will prove useful to you in preparing for and then taking the actual test.

Part Five will help you in learning the words commonly used on the *MAT* and in reviewing some of the basic facts from the content areas used in the test. As you will see, the number of questions from each content area is small, and an extensive review of all possible areas is simply unfeasible.

3. **Lack of practice in taking *MAT*-type tests.** It is one thing to have developed a repertoire of test-taking strategies and skills, but it is another to readily apply them. Part Six of this book contains ten practice tests that are similar in difficulty, content, and form to the actual *MAT*. Like the actual test, each practice test has 120 items, is timed for 60 minutes, and requires a multiple-choice answer selection process from among four possible alternatives. As in the real test, answers are recorded on a separate answer sheet. By taking these tests, you will have an opportunity to utilize the test-taking strategies that you will acquire. You will build up a facility with *MAT*-type questions so that when you take the actual test, you will not have to waste time and points warming up to the types of questions that appear.

Before reading about the *MAT* and how to improve your performance on it, take the pretest in Part One to give yourself a sense of what the *MAT* is like. You will then stand to profit more from the suggestions that follow.

TIP

Although there are 120 items, only 100 are scored. The other 20 are experimental items. It is not possible to tell which items are scored and which are experimental.

HOW THIS BOOK IS ORGANIZED

This book is designed to help you study and strategize for the *MAT*. The manual presents you with the many types of analogies, how to achieve success on the test, and plenty of review. There are twelve practice tests, including a pretest that you can use as a diagnostic tool to find out what your strengths and weaknesses are and how to work toward improving your current score. Eleven additional tests are there to help you with even more practice! Review each section of this book and use it as a different test-taking strategy.

DON'T FORGET ABOUT THE ONLINE TESTS!

You can also take advantage of the *MAT* tests online that are user-friendly and include similar questions to those you will see on the actual exam. Each test (practice (untimed) and timed) contains answer keys and explanations. Use the online tests "after" you take all of the practice tests in the book, and try to take the timed test in one sitting. This is as close as you will get to test day.

Good luck!

Visit *barronsbooks.com/TP/MAT/* for access to two complete online practice tests, conveniently accessible on your computer, smartphone, or tablet.

ANSWER SHEET
Pretest

1. Ⓐ Ⓑ Ⓒ Ⓓ	31. Ⓐ Ⓑ Ⓒ Ⓓ	61. Ⓐ Ⓑ Ⓒ Ⓓ	91. Ⓐ Ⓑ Ⓒ Ⓓ
2. Ⓐ Ⓑ Ⓒ Ⓓ	32. Ⓐ Ⓑ Ⓒ Ⓓ	62. Ⓐ Ⓑ Ⓒ Ⓓ	92. Ⓐ Ⓑ Ⓒ Ⓓ
3. Ⓐ Ⓑ Ⓒ Ⓓ	33. Ⓐ Ⓑ Ⓒ Ⓓ	63. Ⓐ Ⓑ Ⓒ Ⓓ	93. Ⓐ Ⓑ Ⓒ Ⓓ
4. Ⓐ Ⓑ Ⓒ Ⓓ	34. Ⓐ Ⓑ Ⓒ Ⓓ	64. Ⓐ Ⓑ Ⓒ Ⓓ	94. Ⓐ Ⓑ Ⓒ Ⓓ
5. Ⓐ Ⓑ Ⓒ Ⓓ	35. Ⓐ Ⓑ Ⓒ Ⓓ	65. Ⓐ Ⓑ Ⓒ Ⓓ	95. Ⓐ Ⓑ Ⓒ Ⓓ
6. Ⓐ Ⓑ Ⓒ Ⓓ	36. Ⓐ Ⓑ Ⓒ Ⓓ	66. Ⓐ Ⓑ Ⓒ Ⓓ	96. Ⓐ Ⓑ Ⓒ Ⓓ
7. Ⓐ Ⓑ Ⓒ Ⓓ	37. Ⓐ Ⓑ Ⓒ Ⓓ	67. Ⓐ Ⓑ Ⓒ Ⓓ	97. Ⓐ Ⓑ Ⓒ Ⓓ
8. Ⓐ Ⓑ Ⓒ Ⓓ	38. Ⓐ Ⓑ Ⓒ Ⓓ	68. Ⓐ Ⓑ Ⓒ Ⓓ	98. Ⓐ Ⓑ Ⓒ Ⓓ
9. Ⓐ Ⓑ Ⓒ Ⓓ	39. Ⓐ Ⓑ Ⓒ Ⓓ	69. Ⓐ Ⓑ Ⓒ Ⓓ	99. Ⓐ Ⓑ Ⓒ Ⓓ
10. Ⓐ Ⓑ Ⓒ Ⓓ	40. Ⓐ Ⓑ Ⓒ Ⓓ	70. Ⓐ Ⓑ Ⓒ Ⓓ	100. Ⓐ Ⓑ Ⓒ Ⓓ
11. Ⓐ Ⓑ Ⓒ Ⓓ	41. Ⓐ Ⓑ Ⓒ Ⓓ	71. Ⓐ Ⓑ Ⓒ Ⓓ	101. Ⓐ Ⓑ Ⓒ Ⓓ
12. Ⓐ Ⓑ Ⓒ Ⓓ	42. Ⓐ Ⓑ Ⓒ Ⓓ	72. Ⓐ Ⓑ Ⓒ Ⓓ	102. Ⓐ Ⓑ Ⓒ Ⓓ
13. Ⓐ Ⓑ Ⓒ Ⓓ	43. Ⓐ Ⓑ Ⓒ Ⓓ	73. Ⓐ Ⓑ Ⓒ Ⓓ	103. Ⓐ Ⓑ Ⓒ Ⓓ
14. Ⓐ Ⓑ Ⓒ Ⓓ	44. Ⓐ Ⓑ Ⓒ Ⓓ	74. Ⓐ Ⓑ Ⓒ Ⓓ	104. Ⓐ Ⓑ Ⓒ Ⓓ
15. Ⓐ Ⓑ Ⓒ Ⓓ	45. Ⓐ Ⓑ Ⓒ Ⓓ	75. Ⓐ Ⓑ Ⓒ Ⓓ	105. Ⓐ Ⓑ Ⓒ Ⓓ
16. Ⓐ Ⓑ Ⓒ Ⓓ	46. Ⓐ Ⓑ Ⓒ Ⓓ	76. Ⓐ Ⓑ Ⓒ Ⓓ	106. Ⓐ Ⓑ Ⓒ Ⓓ
17. Ⓐ Ⓑ Ⓒ Ⓓ	47. Ⓐ Ⓑ Ⓒ Ⓓ	77. Ⓐ Ⓑ Ⓒ Ⓓ	107. Ⓐ Ⓑ Ⓒ Ⓓ
18. Ⓐ Ⓑ Ⓒ Ⓓ	48. Ⓐ Ⓑ Ⓒ Ⓓ	78. Ⓐ Ⓑ Ⓒ Ⓓ	108. Ⓐ Ⓑ Ⓒ Ⓓ
19. Ⓐ Ⓑ Ⓒ Ⓓ	49. Ⓐ Ⓑ Ⓒ Ⓓ	79. Ⓐ Ⓑ Ⓒ Ⓓ	109. Ⓐ Ⓑ Ⓒ Ⓓ
20. Ⓐ Ⓑ Ⓒ Ⓓ	50. Ⓐ Ⓑ Ⓒ Ⓓ	80. Ⓐ Ⓑ Ⓒ Ⓓ	110. Ⓐ Ⓑ Ⓒ Ⓓ
21. Ⓐ Ⓑ Ⓒ Ⓓ	51. Ⓐ Ⓑ Ⓒ Ⓓ	81. Ⓐ Ⓑ Ⓒ Ⓓ	111. Ⓐ Ⓑ Ⓒ Ⓓ
22. Ⓐ Ⓑ Ⓒ Ⓓ	52. Ⓐ Ⓑ Ⓒ Ⓓ	82. Ⓐ Ⓑ Ⓒ Ⓓ	112. Ⓐ Ⓑ Ⓒ Ⓓ
23. Ⓐ Ⓑ Ⓒ Ⓓ	53. Ⓐ Ⓑ Ⓒ Ⓓ	83. Ⓐ Ⓑ Ⓒ Ⓓ	113. Ⓐ Ⓑ Ⓒ Ⓓ
24. Ⓐ Ⓑ Ⓒ Ⓓ	54. Ⓐ Ⓑ Ⓒ Ⓓ	84. Ⓐ Ⓑ Ⓒ Ⓓ	114. Ⓐ Ⓑ Ⓒ Ⓓ
25. Ⓐ Ⓑ Ⓒ Ⓓ	55. Ⓐ Ⓑ Ⓒ Ⓓ	85. Ⓐ Ⓑ Ⓒ Ⓓ	115. Ⓐ Ⓑ Ⓒ Ⓓ
26. Ⓐ Ⓑ Ⓒ Ⓓ	56. Ⓐ Ⓑ Ⓒ Ⓓ	86. Ⓐ Ⓑ Ⓒ Ⓓ	116. Ⓐ Ⓑ Ⓒ Ⓓ
27. Ⓐ Ⓑ Ⓒ Ⓓ	57. Ⓐ Ⓑ Ⓒ Ⓓ	87. Ⓐ Ⓑ Ⓒ Ⓓ	117. Ⓐ Ⓑ Ⓒ Ⓓ
28. Ⓐ Ⓑ Ⓒ Ⓓ	58. Ⓐ Ⓑ Ⓒ Ⓓ	88. Ⓐ Ⓑ Ⓒ Ⓓ	118. Ⓐ Ⓑ Ⓒ Ⓓ
29. Ⓐ Ⓑ Ⓒ Ⓓ	59. Ⓐ Ⓑ Ⓒ Ⓓ	89. Ⓐ Ⓑ Ⓒ Ⓓ	119. Ⓐ Ⓑ Ⓒ Ⓓ
30. Ⓐ Ⓑ Ⓒ Ⓓ	60. Ⓐ Ⓑ Ⓒ Ⓓ	90. Ⓐ Ⓑ Ⓒ Ⓓ	120. Ⓐ Ⓑ Ⓒ Ⓓ

Pretest

Time: 60 MINUTES

> **Directions:** In each of the following questions, you will find three initial terms and, in parentheses, four answer options designated *a*, *b*, *c*, and *d*. You are to select from the four answer options the one that *best* completes the analogy with the three initial terms. To record your answers, use the answer sheet provided.

1. PEN : INK :: PENCIL : (*a.* limestone, *b.* graphite, *c.* talc, *d.* gypsum)

2. (*a.* probably, *b.* possibly, *c.* virtually, *d.* certainly) : 1 :: MAYBE : .5

3. HORRIFIC : HORROR :: SOPORIFIC : (*a.* joy, *b.* boredom, *c.* sleep, *d.* stupidity)

4. A/B : B/A :: (*a.* 1/15, *b.* 1/3, *c.* 2/3, *d.* 3/2) : 1.5

5. UNINTERRUPTED : (*a.* discrete, *b.* repeated, *c.* endless, *d.* likely) :: CONTINUOUS : CONTINUAL

6. PTOLEMY : EARTH :: COPERNICUS : (*a.* moon, *b.* sun, *c.* Jupiter, *d.* universe)

7. (*a.* sculptor, *b.* painter, *c.* poet, *d.* architect) : VENUS DE MILO :: AUTHOR : THE SCARLET LETTER

8. QUICK : RABBIT :: (*a.* sleepy, *b.* wise, *c.* hungry, *d.* angry) : OWL

9. PATRICIDE : (*a.* brother, *b.* sister, *c.* king, *d.* father) :: MATRICIDE : MOTHER

10. AMA : DOCTORS :: ABA : (*a.* athletes, *b.* miners, *c.* lawyers, *d.* historians)

11. WOODHULL : PELOSI :: ALBRIGHT : (*a.* Day O'Connor, *b.* Bush, *c.* Sebelius, *d.* Ginsburg)

12. MADISON : WAR OF 1812 :: (*a.* Reagan, *b.* G. H. Bush, *c.* Clinton, *d.* G. W. Bush) : GULF WAR

13. BULLET : (*a.* noose, *b.* head, *c.* force, *d.* blade) :: GUN : GUILLOTINE

14. (*a.* ·, *b.* ÷, *c.* **, *d.* undefined) : MULTIPLICATION :: + : ADDITION

15. PSYCHOLOGY : MIND :: PHYCOLOGY : (*a.* herbivores, *b.* carnivores, *c.* algae, *d.* cacti)

16. (*a.* Third Estate, *b.* House, *c.* Parliament, *d.* Commons) : LOWER :: LORDS : UPPER

17. BACTERIA : (*a.* bacteria, *b.* bacterium, *c.* bacterius, *d.* bacterion) :: MANY : ONE

18. SCURVY : VITAMIN C :: KWASHIORKOR : (*a.* vitamin A, *b.* vitamin B$_{12}$, *c.* protein, *d.* niacin)

19. CONVERSE : CONTRAPOSITIVE :: (*a.* B → A, *b.* A → B, *c.* not B → A, *d.* not A → B) : NOT B → NOT A

20. (*a.* New York, *b.* New Mexico, *c.* Missouri, *d.* Michigan) : LAKE :: MISSISSIPPI : RIVER

21. 0 PERCENT : (*a.* pressure, *b.* wind chill, *c.* THI, *d.* humidity) :: ABSOLUTE 0 : TEMPERATURE

22. OBTUSE : ACUTE :: (*a.* 0, *b.* 100, *c.* 180, *d.* 270) : 45

23. AB : AWAY :: (*a.* a, *b.* contra, *c.* ex, *d.* ad) : WITHOUT

24. UNCLE : (*a.* paternal, *b.* avuncular, *c.* uncial, *d.* uncinate) :: BROTHER : FRATERNAL

25. (*a.* women, *b.* marriage, *c.* falsehood, *d.* enlightenment) : MISOLOGY :: NOVELTY : MISONEISM

26. LIE : (*a.* lie, *b.* lay, *c.* laid, *d.* lain) :: LAY : LAID

27. HELTER : SKELTER :: HIGGLEDY : (*a.* niggledy, *b.* piggledy, *c.* spiggledy, *d.* wiggledy)

28. SPOOL : LOOPS :: (*a.* water, *b.* pools, *c.* dinghy, *d.* tools) : SLOOP

29. RILL : (*a.* stream, *b.* lake, *c.* ocean, *d.* lagoon) : NOVELLA : NOVEL

30. SONATA : SONATINA :: CONCERTO : (*a.* concertino, *b.* concertina, *c.* concert, *d.* concerto grosso)

31. NEW JERSEY : 8:00 :: OREGON : (*a.* 5:00, *b.* 6:00, *c.* 9:00, *d.* 10:00)

32. LINCOLN : 1 :: JEFFERSON : (*a.* 3, *b.* 5, *c.* 10, *d.* 25)

33. PLINY THE ELDER : (*a.* Carthaginian, *b.* Athenian, *c.* Milanese, *d.* Roman) :: THUCYDIDES : GREEK

34. (*a.* Uruguay, *b.* Argentina, *c.* Paraguay, *d.* Guatemala) : CENTRAL :: BRAZIL : SOUTH

35. ETHER : GENERAL :: NOVOCAINE : (*a.* specific, *b.* particulate, *c.* local, *d.* toxic)

36. D'ARTAGNAN : (*a.* Hugo, *b.* Mauriac, *c.* Dumas, *d.* Balzac) :: GATSBY : FITZGERALD

37. ARMY : LAND :: (*a.* Marines, *b.* Navy, *c.* CIA, *d.* Secret Service) : AMPHIBIOUS

38. TWO : (*a.* hydrogen, *b.* uranium, *c.* americium, *d.* deuterium) :: THREE : TRITIUM

39. YORK : N.Y. :: ORLEANS : (*a.* O.R., *b.* La., *c.* Fr., *d.* Miss.)

40. (*a.* Copland, *b.* Mendelssohn, *c.* Shostakovich, *d.* Bach) : 19th :: MOZART : 18th

41. MENELAUS : (*a.* Agamemnon, *b.* Priam, *c.* Achilles, *d.* Spartacus) :: HECTOR : PARIS

42. MAJORITY : MINORITY :: (*a.* Bolshevik, *b.* Maoist, *c.* Marxist, *d.* Trotskyite) : MENSHEVIK

43. FEIGN : FINE :: (*a.* right, *b.* writ, *c.* rate, *d.* rat) : WRITE

44. FATUOUS : (*a.* bright, *b.* prodigal, *c.* contemptuous, *d.* foolish) :: FASTIDIOUS : HARD TO PLEASE

45. (*a.* Ayer, *b.* Peirce, *c.* Santayana, *d.* Russell) : PRAGMATIST :: SARTRE : EXISTENTIALIST

46. ADDITIVE : (*a.* blue, *b.* red, *c.* green, *d.* white) :: SUBTRACTIVE : YELLOW

47. PROTON : NUCLEON :: MUON : (*a.* meson, *b.* electron, *c.* pion, *d.* positron)

48. BOARD : (*a.* fifteen, *b.* checkers, *c.* bridge, *d.* thirty-six) :: DECK : TWENTY-ONE

49. C# : Db :: B# : (*a.* Cb, *b.* Bb, *c.* C, *d.* Db)

50. SEVER : PERSEVERANCE :: CUT : (*a.* perseveration, *b.* perspective, *c.* pertinence, *d.* persistence)

51. FREUD : (*a.* Skinner, *b.* Allport, *c.* Murray, *d.* Erikson) :: KOHLBERG : PIAGET

52. (*a.* ellipsoid, *b.* semicircle, *c.* rhombus, *d.* angle) : PROTRACTOR :: RECTANGLE : RULER

53. BIPOLARITY : MONOLOGUE :: (*a.* dicotyledon, *b.* stamen, *c.* deciduous, *d.* pistil) : UNION

54. (*a.* patent medicine, *b.* adage, *c.* theory, *d.* heretic) : APOTHEGM :: DEXTERITY : ADROITNESS

55. FROM : TO :: (*a.* artery, *b.* ventricle, *c.* atrium, *d.* carotid) : JUGULAR

56. SOUSA : (*a.* waltzes, *b.* symphonies, *c.* marches, *d.* hymns) :: VERDI : OPERAS

57. INVOCATION : (*a.* benediction, *b.* recessional, *c.* prayer, *d.* vesper) :: START : FINISH

58. SASKATCHEWAN : REGINA :: (*a.* Quebec, *b.* Alberta, *c.* Ontario, *d.* Manitoba) : TORONTO

59. (*a.* obvious, *b.* latent, *c.* proximate, *d.* apposite) : MANIFEST :: COVERT : OVERT

60. DIRGE : REQUIEM :: GRIEF : (*a.* thanksgiving, *b.* mourning, *c.* penitence, *d.* joy)

61. (*a.* metropolitan, *b.* synod, *c.* district, *d.* diocese) : BISHOP :: PARISH : PRIEST

62. CONSONANT : VOWEL :: COMPOSITE : (*a.* prime, *b.* irrational, *c.* integer, *d.* zero)

63. IMPLODE : (*a.* explode, *b.* beseech, *c.* implicate, *d.* burst inward) :: IMPLY : HINT AT

64. EARTH : SUN :: PLANET : (*a.* heavenly body, *b.* sol, *c.* star, *d.* nova)

65. OCTOPUS : (*a.* six, *b.* eight, *c.* ten, *d.* twelve) :: PERSON : TWO

66. QUARTER : DOLLAR :: (*a.* season, *b.* day, *c.* month, *d.* decade) : YEAR

67. CAPTAIN : (*a.* admiral, *b.* ensign, *c.* commodore, *d.* midshipman) :: CORPORAL : SERGEANT

68. DAVID : VAN DYCK :: FRENCH : (*a.* Italian, *b.* German, *c.* Flemish, *d.* British)

69. (*a.* poulet, *b.* glacé, *c.* citron, *d.* entrecote) : SWEET :: CAFÉ : BITTER

70. WAIVE : WAVE :: (*a.* relinquish, *b.* relegate, *c.* remand, *d.* redress) : UNDULATE

71. WORK : (*a.* joule, *b.* ohm, *c.* ampere, *d.* coulomb) :: POTENTIAL DIFFERENCE : VOLT

72. PHILOLOGY : LANGUAGES :: MYCOLOGY : (*a.* flowering plants, *b.* ferns, *c.* weeds, *d.* fungi)

73. DEPENDENT : INDEPENDENT :: (*a.* autochthonous, *b.* canonical, *c.* anaclitic, *d.* irrecusable) : SELF-RELIANT

74. CX : (*a.* CXV, *b.* CL, *c.* CLX, *d.* CC) :: LV : LXXV

75. CAMEL : RHINOCEROS :: HUMP : (*a.* armor, *b.* snout, *c.* horn, *d.* hide)

76. ONTOLOGY : (*a.* being, *b.* metaphysics, *c.* growth, *d.* knowledge) :: DEONTOLOGY : ETHICS

77. (*a.* leukocytes, *b.* platelets, *c.* hormones, *d.* erythrocytes) : ANEMIA :: INSULIN : DIABETES

78. CALVIN : COOLIDGE :: (*a.* Alexander, *b.* Franklin, *c.* William, *d.* Robert) : PIERCE

79. PONTIUS PILATE : JESUS :: CREON : (*a.* Orestes, *b.* Oedipus, *c.* Antigone, *d.* Electra)

80. (*a.* bellicose, *b.* periphrastic, *c.* altruistic, *d.* nihilistic) : AGGRESSION :: IRENIC : PEACE

81. FIRST : LAST :: GENESIS : (*a*. Exodus, *b*. Deuteronomy, *c*. Leviticus, *d*. Numbers)

82. $\pi r^2 : 2\pi r ::$ AREA : (*a*. diameter, *b*. circumference, *c*. perimeter, *d*. volume)

83. BUCKINGHAM PALACE : XANADU :: ELIZABETH II : (*a*. Genghis Khan, *b*. Charles V, *c*. Citizen Kane, *d*. Donald Trump)

84. MONOGYNY : (*a*. life, *b*. religion, *c*. child, *d*. wife) :: MONOTHEISM : GOD

85. ESPRESSO : BLACK :: ORANGE PEKOE : (*a*. green, *b*. white, *c*. black, *d*. red)

86. DIANA : (*a*. Artemis, *b*. Minerva, *c*. Aphrodite, *d*. Hera) :: JUPITER : ZEUS

87. (*a*. B$_b$ major, *b*. E$_b$ major, *c*. F major, *d*. A major) : C MINOR :: G MAJOR : E MINOR

88. MAN : NAME :: (*a*. rig, *b*. appellation, *c*. maiden, *d*. woman) : GIRL

89. MANON LESCAUT : (*a*. wise, *b*. arrogant, *c*. promiscuous, *d*. wicked) :: TOM SAWYER : ADVENTUROUS

90. (*a*. Bull Moose, *b*. Whig, *c*. Socialist, *d*. Know-Nothing) : DEBS :: DEMOCRAT : STEVENSON

91. FIRST : CLERGY :: FOURTH : (*a*. nobles, *b*. commoners, *c*. children, *d*. journalists)

92. AMETHYST : GARNET :: PURPLE : (*a*. red, *b*. green, *c*. transparent, *d*. blue)

93. (*a*. loquacious, *b*. refractory, *c*. ostentatious, *d*. timid) : GARRULOUS :: AUDACIOUS : BOLD

94. FOUR : APRIL FOOL'S DAY :: (*a*. one, *b*. two, *c*. five, *d*. ten) : MAY DAY

95. STEEPLE : CHURCH :: (*a*. minaret, *b*. muezzin, *c*. imam, *d*. arch) : MOSQUE

96. VANILLA : (*a*. bean, *b*. Sussex, *c*. hasty, *d*. Brazil) :: RICE : YORKSHIRE

97. (*a*. Saint-Saëns, *b*. Strindberg, *c*. Bernstein, *d*. Rubinstein) : PLAYS :: FROST : POEMS

98. THERMO : HEAT :: ISO : (*a*. cold, *b*. pressure, *c*. humidity, *d*. same)

99. (*a*. Scotch, *b*. vermouth, *c*. gin, *d*. bourbon) : TOM COLLINS :: VODKA : BLOODY MARY

100. BELLEEK : (*a*. Scotland, *b*. Ireland, *c*. Holland, *d*. Belgium) :: LIMOGES : FRANCE

101. AMPERE : (*a*. current, *b*. magnetism, *c*. speed, *d*. gravity) :: WATT : POWER

102. BAIKAL : RUSSIA :: (*a*. Michigan, *b*. Superior, *c*. Ontario, *d*. Placid) : UNITED STATES

103. (*a.* Lady's Man, *b.* Black Beauty, *c.* Secretariat, *d.* Fortune's Fool) : MAN O' WAR ::
SEABISCUIT : WAR ADMIRAL

104. GAVRILO PRINCIP : ARCHDUKE FERDINAND :: (*a.* Robert E. Lee,
b. Lee Harvey Oswald, *c.* John Hinckley, *d.* John Wilkes Booth) : PRESIDENT LINCOLN

105. KILOGRAM : POUND :: 1 : (*a.* 2.2, *b.* 5, *c.* 0.2, *d.* 7.3)

106. ROSEMARY : (*a.* oregano, *b.* cumin, *c.* nutmeg, *d.* cinnamon) :: BASIL : SAGE

107. COBBLER : SHOES :: (*a.* tanner, *b.* smith, *c.* cooper, *d.* miller) : BARRELS

108. EXPECTORATE : (*a.* bite, *b.* spit, *c.* deliver, *d.* swallow) :: MASTICATE : CHEW

109. (*a.* net, *b.* hat trick, *c.* goalie, *d.* puck) : ICE HOCKEY :: SHUTTLECOCK : BADMINTON

110. ARMSTRONG : TRUMPET :: COLTRANE : (*a.* piano, *b.* saxophone, *c.* clarinet, *d.* trombone)

111. MOHAMMED : JESUS :: (*a.* Judea, *b.* Constantinople, *c.* Mecca, *d.* Jerusalem) : BETHLEHEM

112. RHOMBUS : HEXAGON :: 4 : (*a.* 8, *b.* 7, *c.* 6, *d.* 5)

113. RECORD PLAYER : (*a.* loudest, *b.* loud, *c.* quiet, *d.* quieter) :: SUPERANNUATED :
SUPERLATIVE

114. (*a.* feet, *b.* obedience, *c.* thought, *d.* memory) : ELEPHANT :: STRENGTH : ANT

115. DIAMOND : SAPPHIRE :: (*a.* Hope, *b.* Diana's, *c.* Indian, *d.* Pharoah's) : LOGAN

116. HEAVEN : ST. PETER :: HADES : (*a.* Lucifer, *b.* Scylla, *c.* Charybdis, *d.* Cerberus)

117. r-p-o-p-h-e-s-s-a-g-r : JABBERWOCKY :: CUMMINGS : (*a.* Milne, *b.* Cleary,
c. Carroll, *d.* Eliot)

118. X : (*a.* w, *b.* y, *c.* u, *d.* a) :: VERTICAL : HORIZONTAL

119. (*a.* nostalgia, *b.* kindness, *c.* loyalty, *d.* naiveté) : POLLYANNA :: DOUBT : THOMAS

120. MAASAI : EAST AFRICA :: LAPP : (*a.* Australia, *b.* Middle East, *c.* South Asia, *d.* Scandinavia)

ANSWER KEY
Pretest

1.	**B**	31.	**A**	61.	**D**	91.	**D**
2.	**D**	32.	**B**	62.	**A**	92.	**A**
3.	**C**	33.	**D**	63.	**D**	93.	**A**
4.	**C**	34.	**D**	64.	**C**	94.	**C**
5.	**B**	35.	**C**	65.	**B**	95.	**A**
6.	**B**	36.	**C**	66.	**A**	96.	**C**
7.	**A**	37.	**A**	67.	**C**	97.	**B**
8.	**B**	38.	**D**	68.	**C**	98.	**D**
9.	**D**	39.	**B**	69.	**B**	99.	**C**
10.	**C**	40.	**B**	70.	**A**	100.	**B**
11.	**A**	41.	**A**	71.	**A**	101.	**A**
12.	**B**	42.	**A**	72.	**D**	102.	**B**
13.	**D**	43.	**C**	73.	**C**	103.	**C**
14.	**A**	44.	**D**	74.	**B**	104.	**D**
15.	**C**	45.	**B**	75.	**C**	105.	**A**
16.	**D**	46.	**C**	76.	**A**	106.	**A**
17.	**B**	47.	**A**	77.	**D**	107.	**C**
18.	**C**	48.	**B**	78.	**B**	108.	**B**
19.	**A**	49.	**C**	79.	**C**	109.	**D**
20.	**D**	50.	**D**	80.	**A**	110.	**B**
21.	**D**	51.	**D**	81.	**B**	111.	**C**
22.	**B**	52.	**B**	82.	**B**	112.	**C**
23.	**A**	53.	**A**	83.	**C**	113.	**A**
24.	**B**	54.	**B**	84.	**D**	114.	**D**
25.	**D**	55.	**D**	85.	**C**	115.	**A**
26.	**B**	56.	**C**	86.	**A**	116.	**D**
27.	**B**	57.	**A**	87.	**B**	117.	**C**
28.	**B**	58.	**C**	88.	**A**	118.	**B**
29.	**A**	59.	**B**	89.	**C**	119.	**D**
30.	**A**	60.	**B**	90.	**C**	120.	**D**

ANSWER EXPLANATIONS FOR THE PRETEST

In the following, explanations concerning the correct responses are in roman font. Explanations regarding distracters (incorrect responses) that are not self-explaining or could be misinterpreted are in italics in order to highlight the explanations of the answers that are correct.

Note: You will see each *MAT* relationship type/content after the answer explanation in this Pretest; however, it will not be displayed in the Practice Tests. More on this in Part 3 of this book.

1. PEN : INK :: PENCIL : (*a.* limestone, ***b.* graphite**, *c.* talc, *d.* gypsum)

    (b) A pen writes with ink; a pencil writes with graphite.

    General Information—Association

2. (*a.* probably, *b.* possibly, *c.* virtually, ***d.* certainly**) : 1 :: MAYBE : .5

    (d) Something that is certainly true has probability 1 of occurrence; something that is maybe true can have probability .5 of occurrence.

    Language—Association

3. HORRIFIC : HORROR :: SOPORIFIC : (*a.* joy, *b.* boredom, ***c.* sleep**, *d.* stupidity)

    (c) Something horrific causes horror; something soporific causes sleep.

    Language—Semantic

4. A/B : B/A :: (*a.* 1/15, *b.* 1/3, ***c.* 2/3**, *d.* 3/2) : 1.5

    (c) $B/A = 1/(A/B)$; $1.5 = 1/(2/3)$.

    Logical—Mathematical

5. UNINTERRUPTED : (*a.* discrete, ***b.* repeated**, *c.* endless, *d.* likely) :: CONTINUOUS : CONTINUAL

    (b) Something that is uninterrupted is continuous; something that is repeated is continual.

    Language—Semantic

6. PTOLEMY : EARTH :: COPERNICUS : (*a.* moon, ***b.* sun**, *c.* Jupiter, *d.* universe)

    (b) Ptolemy believed that the earth is at the center of the planetary system; Copernicus believed that the sun is at the center.

    Natural Science—Association

7. (***a.* sculptor**, *b.* painter, *c.* poet, *d.* architect) : VENUS DE MILO :: AUTHOR : THE SCARLET LETTER

    (a) Venus de Milo was created by a sculptor (unknown); *The Scarlet Letter,* by an author (Nathaniel Hawthorne).

    Humanities—Classification

8. QUICK : RABBIT :: (*a.* sleepy, ***b.* wise**, *c.* hungry, *d.* angry) : OWL

    (b) A rabbit is reputed to be quick; an owl is reputed to be wise.

    General Information—Association

9. PATRICIDE : (*a.* brother, *b.* sister, *c.* king, ***d.* father**) :: MATRICIDE : MOTHER

    (d) Patricide is the murder of one's father; matricide is the murder of one's mother. *Fratricide stands for the murder of a brother; regicide refers to the murder of a monarch; sororicide stands for the murder of a sister.*

    Language—Association

10. AMA : DOCTORS :: ABA : (*a.* athletes, *b.* miners, ***c.* lawyers**, *d.* historians)

    (c) The AMA (American Medical Association) is an association of doctors; the ABA (American Bar Association) is an association of lawyers.

    General Information—Association

11. WOODHULL : PELOSI :: ALBRIGHT : (***a.* Day O'Connor**, *b.* Bush, *c.* Sebelius, *d.* Ginsburg)

    (a) Victoria Claflin Woodhull was the first woman to run for President; Nancy Pelosi was the first female Speaker of the U.S. House of Representatives; Madeleine Albright was the first woman to become U.S. Secretary of State; Sandra Day O'Connor was the first woman justice of the Supreme Court.

    Social Science—Association

12. MADISON : WAR OF 1812 :: (*a.* Reagan, ***b.* G. H. W. Bush**, *c.* Clinton, *d.* G. W. Bush) : GULF WAR

    (b) Madison was president during the War of 1812. G. H. W. Bush was president during the Gulf War.

    Humanities—Association

13. BULLET : (*a.* noose, *b.* head, *c.* force, ***d.* blade**) : GUN : GUILLOTINE

    (d) A gun kills by a bullet; a guillotine kills by a blade.

    General Information—Association

14. (***a.* ·**, *b.* ÷, *c.* **, *d.* undefined) : MULTIPLICATION :: + : ADDITION

    (a) A raised dot (·) can be used to signify multiplication; a plus sign (+) can be used to signify addition.

    Mathematics—Logical/Mathematical

15. PSYCHOLOGY : MIND :: PHYCOLOGY : (*a.* herbivores, *b.* carnivores, ***c.* algae**, *d.* cacti)

    (c) Psychology is the science of the mind; phycology is the science of algae.

    Language—Semantic

16. (*a.* Third Estate, *b.* House, *c.* Parliament, ***d.* Commons**) : LOWER :: LORDS : UPPER

    (d) The House of Commons is the lower house, and the House of Lords the upper house, of the British Parliament.

    Social Science—Classification

17. BACTERIA : (*a.* bacteria, ***b.* bacterium**, *c.* bacterius, *d.* bacterion) :: MANY : ONE

    (b) One refers to many bacteria (plural) or one bacterium (singular).

    Language—Association

18. SCURVY : VITAMIN C :: KWASHIORKOR : (*a.* vitamin A, *b.* vitamin B_{12}, ***c.* protein**, *d.* niacin)

    (c) Scurvy is caused by a deficiency of vitamin C; kwashiorkor is caused by a deficiency of protein. *Pellagra is caused by lack of niacin. One of the results of vitamin A deficiency is impaired vision. A lack of vitamin B_{12} causes macrocytic anemia and cognitive deficits like memory loss.*

    Natural Science—Association

19. CONVERSE : CONTRAPOSITIVE :: (***a*. B → A**, *b*. A → B, *c*. not B → A, *d*. not A → B) : (NOT B → NOT A)

(a) The converse of $A \to B$ is $B \to A$; the contrapositive of $A \to B$ is (not $B \to$ not A).
General Information—Logical/Mathematical

20. (*a*. New York, *b*. New Mexico, *c*. Missouri, ***d*. Michigan**) : LAKE :: MISSISSIPPI : RIVER

(d) Lake Michigan and the Mississippi River are bodies of water.
General Information—Classification

21. 0 PERCENT : (*a*. pressure, *b*. windchill, *c*. THI, ***d*. humidity**) :: ABSOLUTE 0 : TEMPERATURE

(d) 0 percent is the minimum possible humidity; absolute 0 is the minimum possible temperature.
Natural Science—Association

22. OBTUSE : ACUTE :: (*a*. 0, ***b*. 100**, *c*. 180, *d*. 270) : 45

(b) A 100° angle is obtuse; a 45° angle is acute.
Mathematics—Logical/Mathematical

23. AB : AWAY :: (***a*. a**, *b*. contra, *c*. ex, *d*. ad) : WITHOUT

(a) The prefix *ab-* means "away"; the prefix *a-* means "without." *The prefix contra- means "against." The prefix ex- means "excluding/without." The prefix ad- means "to/towards."*
Language—Semantic

24. UNCLE : (*a*. paternal, ***b*. avuncular**, *c*. uncial, *d*. uncinate) :: BROTHER : FRATERNAL

(b) Someone who is avuncular is like an uncle; someone who is fraternal is like a brother. *Someone who is paternal is like a father; uncial means written in capital letters; uncinate means that a tip is bent like a hook.*
Language—Semantic

25. (*a*. women, *b*. marriage, *c*. falsehood, ***d*. enlightenment**) : MISOLOGY :: NOVELTY : MISONEISM

(d) Misology is hatred of enlightenment; misoneism is hatred of novelty.
Language—Semantic

26. LIE : (*a*. lie, ***b*. lay**, *c*. laid, *d*. lain) :: LAY : LAID

(b) The past tense of lie is lay (or, in another meaning of lie, lied, but this is not an option); the past tense of lay is laid.
Language—Classification

27. HELTER : SKELTER :: HIGGLEDY : (*a*. niggledy, ***b*. piggledy**, *c*. spiggledy, *d*. wiggledy)

(b) Helter-skelter and higgledy-piggledy are synonyms.
Language—Association

28. SPOOL : LOOPS :: (*a*. water, ***b*. pools**, *c*. dinghy, *d*. tools) : SLOOP

(b) Spool spelled backward is loops; pools spelled backward is sloop.
General Information—Logical/Mathematical

29. RILL : (***a*. stream**, *b*. lake, *c*. ocean, *d*. lagoon) : NOVELLA : NOVEL

(a) A rill is a small stream; a novella is a small novel.
Language—Association

30. SONATA : SONATINA :: CONCERTO : (***a*. concertino**, *b.* concertina, *c.* concert, *d.* concerto grosso)

   (a) A sonatina is a small sonata; a concertino is a small concerto. *A concerto grosso is a baroque composition in which a small group of solo instruments play with an orchestra.*
   Humanities—Association

31. NEW JERSEY : 8:00 :: OREGON : (***a.* 5:00**, *b.* 6:00, *c.* 9:00, *d.* 10:00)

   (a) When it is 8:00 in New Jersey, it is 5:00 in Oregon.
   General Information—Logical/Mathematical

32. LINCOLN : 1 :: JEFFERSON : (*a.* 3, ***b.* 5**, *c.* 10, *d.* 25)

   (b) The head of Lincoln appears on a 1-cent piece; the head of Jefferson appears on a 5-cent piece. *Franklin Roosevelt is featured on a 10-cent piece. The regular 25-cent coin features George Washington.*
   General Information—Association

33. PLINY THE ELDER : (*a.* Carthaginian, *b.* Athenian, *c.* Milanese, ***d.* Roman**) :: THUCYDIDES : GREEK

   (d) Pliny the Elder was a Roman writer who wrote *Naturalis Historia.* Thucydides was a Greek historian who wrote *History of the Peloponnesian War.*
   Humanities—Classification

34. (*a.* Uruguay, *b.* Argentina, *c.* Paraguay, ***d.* Guatemala**) : CENTRAL :: BRAZIL : SOUTH

   (d) Guatemala is in Central America, Brazil in South America. Argentina, Uruguay, and Paraguay are in South America.
   Social Science—Classification

35. ETHER : GENERAL :: NOVOCAINE : (*a.* specific, *b.* particulate, ***c.* local**, *d.* toxic

   (c) Ether is a general anesthetic; novocaine is a local anesthetic.
   Natural Science—Classification

36. D'ARTAGNAN : (*a.* Hugo, *b.* Mauriac, ***c.* Dumas**, *d.* Balzac) :: GATSBY : FITZGERALD

   (c) D'Artagnan was a character created by Dumas in *The Three Musketeers*; Gatsby was a character created by Fitzgerald in *The Great Gatsby. Francois Mauriac wrote* Le Desert de l'Amour. *Honore Balzac wrote* La Comedie Humaine, *which contains about 100 novels and plays that describe French life after the fall of Napoleon. Victor Hugo wrote* Les Miserables.
   Humanities—Association

37. ARMY : LAND :: (***a.* Marines**, *b.* Navy, *c.* CIA, *d.* Secret Service) : AMPHIBIOUS

   (a) The Army is intended to engage primarily in land warfare; the Marines are intended to engage primarily in amphibious warfare. *The Navy is intended to engage primarily in sea warfare. The CIA is the intelligence agency of the United States that collects information about foreign governments and persons. The Secret Service protects leaders of the United States and visiting leaders from other countries. It also safeguards the payment and financial systems of the United States.*
   General Information—Association

38. TWO : (*a.* hydrogen, *b.* uranium, *c.* americium, ***d.* deuterium**) :: THREE : TRITIUM

   (d) Deuterium is an isotope of hydrogen with an atomic weight of 2; tritium is an isotope of hydrogen with an atomic weight of 3.
   Natural Science—Classification

39. YORK : N.Y. :: ORLEANS : (*a.* O.R., ***b.* La.**, *c.* Fr., *d.* Miss.)

(b) (New) York (the city) is in the state of New York (N.Y.): (New) Orleans is in the state of Louisiana (La.).
General Information—Classification

40. (*a.* Copland, ***b.* Mendelssohn**, *c.* Shostakovich, *d.* Bach) : 19th :: MOZART : 18th

(b) Mendelssohn was a 19th century composer (1809-1847); Mozart was an 18th century composer (1756-1791). *Copland (1900-1990) was a 20th century composer. Shostakovich (1906-1975) was a 20th century composer. J. S. Bach (1685-1750) was an 18th century composer.*
Humanities—Association

41. MENELAUS : (***a.* Agamemnon**, *b.* Priam, *c.* Achilles, *d.* Spartacus) :: HECTOR : PARIS

(a) Menelaus and Agamemnon were brothers, as were Hector and Paris. *Priam was the youngest son of Laomedon and king of Troy during the Trojan War. Achilles was the greatest warrior of the Greeks in the Trojan War. Spartacus was a Roman slave who led an unsuccessful slave uprising (the Third Servile War).*
Humanities—Classification

42. MAJORITY : MINORITY :: (***a.* Bolshevik**, *b.* Maoist, *c.* Marxist, *d.* Trotskyite) : MENSHEVIK

(a) In Revolutionary Russia, the Bolsheviks were the majority, or greater (*bolshe*), party, and the Mensheviks were the minority, or smaller, (*mensche*) party.
Humanities—Association

43. FEIGN : FINE :: (*a.* right, *b.* writ, ***c.* rate**, *d.* rat) : WRITE

(c) The pronounced vowel sounds are the same in feign and rate, and in fine and write.
General Information—Logical/Mathematical

44. FATUOUS : (*a.* bright, *b.* prodigal, *c.* contemptuous, ***d.* foolish**) :: FASTIDIOUS : HARD TO PLEASE

(d) Fatuous and foolish are synonyms, as are fastidious and hard to please.
Language—Semantic

45. (*a.* Ayer, ***b.* Peirce**, *c.* Santayana, *d.* Russell) : PRAGMATIST :: SARTRE : EXISTENTIALIST

(b) Peirce was a major philosopher in the pragmatist movement; Sartre was a major philosopher in the existentialist movement. *Ayer was a logical positivist; Santayana was an aphorist; Russell was one of the founders of analytic philosophy.*
Humanities—Association

46. ADDITIVE : (*a.* blue, *b.* red, ***c.* green**, *d.* white) :: SUBTRACTIVE : YELLOW

(c) Green is an additive (but not a subtractive) primary color in light; yellow is a subtractive (but not an additive) primary color. The subtractive color model involves pigments with colors that add up to black. The additive color model involves light with colors that add up to white.
Natural Science—Classification

47. PROTON : NUCLEON :: MUON : (***a.* meson**, *b.* electron, *c.* pion, *d.* positron)

(a) A proton is a nucleon; a muon is a meson (a fundamental particle responsible for the forces in the atomic nucleus).
Natural Science—Classification

48. BOARD : (*a.* fifteen, ***b.* checkers**, *c.* bridge, *d.* thirty-six) :: DECK : TWENTY-ONE

(b) Checkers is played with a board; twenty-one is played with a deck.
General Information—Association

49. C# : Db :: B# : (*a.* Cb, *b.* Bb, ***c.* C**, *d.* Db)

(c) C# and Db are played instrumentally as the same note, as are B# and C.

Humanities—Association

50. SEVER : PERSEVERANCE :: CUT : (*a.* perseveration, *b.* perspective, *c.* pertinence, ***d.* persistence**)

(d) Sever and cut are synonyms, as are perseverance and persistence.

Language—Semantic

51. FREUD : (*a.* Skinner, *b.* Allport, *c.* Murray, ***d.* Erikson**) :: KOHLBERG : PIAGET

(d) Freud, Erikson, Kohlberg, and Piaget were all prominent psychological theorists postulating stages of development. *Burrhus F. Skinner was a psychologist who is known for his work on operant conditioning. Gordon Allport is considered one of the founding fathers of personality psychology. Charles Murray is a political scientist and well known for writing* The Bell Curve *(with Richard Herrnstein) about the role of IQ in American society.*

Social Science—Classification

52. (*a.* ellipsoid, ***b.* semicircle**, *c.* rhombus, *d.* angle) : PROTRACTOR :: RECTANGLE : RULER

(b) A protractor is usually in the shape of a semicircle. A ruler is usually in the shape of a rectangle.

General Information—Association

53. BIPOLARITY : MONOLOGUE :: (***a.* dicotyledon**, *b.* stamen, *c.* deciduous, *d.* pistil) : UNION

(a) Bipolarity and dicotyledon refer to two of something; monologue and union refer to one of something.

Language—Semantic

54. (*a.* patent medicine, ***b.* adage**, *c.* theory, *d.* heretic) : APOTHEGM :: DEXTERITY : ADROITNESS

(b) Adage and apothegm are synonyms, as are dexterity and adroitness.

Language—Semantic

55. FROM : TO :: (*a.* artery, *b.* ventricle, *c.* atrium, ***d.* carotid**) : JUGULAR

(d) The carotid is an artery carrying blood away from the heart; the jugular is a vein carrying blood to the heart.

Natural Science—Association

56. SOUSA : (*a.* waltzes, *b.* symphonies, ***c.* marches**, *d.* hymns) :: VERDI : OPERAS

(c) Sousa (1854–1932) composed primarily marches; Verdi (1813–1901) composed primarily operas.

Humanities—Association

57. INVOCATION : (***a.* benediction**, *b.* recessional, *c.* prayer, *d.* vesper) :: START : FINISH

(a) An invocation starts a religious service; a benediction finishes it.

Humanities—Association

58. SASKATCHEWAN : REGINA :: (*a.* Quebec, *b.* Alberta, ***c.* Ontario**, *d.* Manitoba) :: TORONTO

(c) The capital of the Canadian province of Saskatchewan is Regina; the capital of Ontario is Toronto. Quebec City is the capital of Quebec. Edmonton is the capital of Alberta. Winnipeg is the capital of Manitoba.

Social Science—Classification

59. (*a.* obvious, ***b.* latent**, *c.* proximate, *d.* apposite) : MANIFEST :: COVERT : OVERT

    (b) Latent and manifest are antonyms, as are covert and overt.

    Language—Semantic

60. DIRGE : REQUIEM :: GRIEF : (*a.* thanksgiving, ***b.* mourning**, *c.* penitence, *d.* joy)

    (b) A dirge and a requiem both express grief and mourning.

    Language—Semantic

61. (*a.* metropolitan, *b.* synod, *c.* district, ***d.* diocese**) : BISHOP :: PARISH : PRIEST

    (d) A diocese is under the jurisdiction of a bishop; a parish is under the jurisdiction of a priest.

    Humanities—Classification

62. CONSONANT : VOWEL :: COMPOSITE : (***a.* prime**, *b.* irrational, *c.* integer, *d.* zero)

    (a) All letters are either consonants or vowels; all numbers are either composite or prime.

    Mathematics—Classification

63. IMPLODE : (*a.* explode, *b.* beseech, *c.* implicate, ***d.* burst inward**) :: IMPLY : HINT AT

    (d) To implode is to burst inward; to imply is to hint at.

    Language—Semantic

64. EARTH : SUN :: PLANET : (*a.* heavenly body, *b.* sol, ***c.* star**, *d.* nova)

    (c) The earth is a planet; the sun is a star. *A nova is a star that abruptly increases its light output and later on fades back to its normal state.*

    Natural Science—Classification

65. OCTOPUS : (*a.* six, ***b.* eight**, *c.* ten, *d.* twelve) :: PERSON : TWO

    (b) An octopus has eight arms; a person has two arms.

    Natural Science—Association

66. QUARTER : DOLLAR :: (***a.* season**, *b.* day, *c.* month, *d.* decade) : YEAR

    (a) There are four quarters in a dollar and four seasons in a year.

    General Information—Logical/Mathematical

67. CAPTAIN : (*a.* admiral, *b.* ensign, ***c.* commodore**, *d.* midshipman) :: CORPORAL : SERGEANT

    (c) In the Navy, a captain is immediately below a commodore in rank; in the Army, a corporal is immediately below a sergeant in rank.

    General Information—Classification

68. DAVID : VAN DYCK :: FRENCH : (*a.* Italian, *b.* German, ***c.* Flemish**, *d.* British)

    (c) David was a French painter; Van Dyck was a Flemish painter (Flanders is part of Belgium).

    Humanities—Classification

69. (*a.* poulet, ***b.* glacé**, *c.* citron, *d.* entrecote) : SWEET :: CAFÉ : BITTER

    (b) Glacé (ice cream) is sweet; café (coffee) is bitter.

    General Information—Association

70. WAIVE : WAVE :: (***a.* relinquish**, *b.* relegate, *c.* remand, *d.* redress) : UNDULATE

    (a) To waive is to relinquish; to wave is to undulate.

    Language—Semantic

71. WORK : (***a. joule***, *b.* ohm, *c.* ampere, *d.* coulomb) :: POTENTIAL DIFFERENCE : VOLT

(a) A joule is a unit of work; a volt is a measure of potential difference. *Ohm is the unit of electrical resistance. Ampere is a unit of electric current. Coulomb is the unit of electric charge.*
Natural Science—Association

72. PHILOLOGY : LANGUAGES :: MYCOLOGY : (*a.* flowering plants, *b.* ferns, *c.* weeds, ***d. fungi***)

(d) Philology is the study of languages; mycology is the study of fungi.
Natural Science—Semantic

73. DEPENDENT : INDEPENDENT :: (*a.* autochthonous, *b.* canonical, ***c. anaclitic***, *d.* irrecusable) : SELF-RELIANT

(c) Dependent and anaclitic are synonyms, as are independent and self-reliant.
Language—Semantic

74. CX : (*a.* CXV, ***b. CL***, *c.* CLX, *d.* CC) :: LV : LXXV

(b) The terms of the analogy are Roman numerals expressing the ratio 110 : 150 :: 55 : 75. In Roman numerals, I = 1, V = 5, X = 10, L = 50, C = 100, D = 500, M = 1,000.
Mathematics—Logical/Mathematical

75. CAMEL : RHINOCEROS :: HUMP : (*a.* armor, *b.* snout, ***c. horn***, *d.* hide)

(c) A camel may have one hump or two; a rhinoceros may have one horn or two.
General Information—Association

76. ONTOLOGY : (***a. being***, *b.* metaphysics, *c.* growth, *d.* knowledge) :: DEONTOLOGY : ETHICS

(a) Ontology is the study of being; deontology is the study of ethics.
Humanities—Semantic

77. (*a.* leukocytes, *b.* platelets, *c.* hormones, ***d. erythrocytes***) : ANEMIA :: INSULIN : DIABETES

(d) Anemia is characterized by a shortage of erythrocytes (red blood cells), diabetes by a shortage of insulin.
Natural Science—Association

78. CALVIN : COOLIDGE :: (*a.* Alexander, ***b. Franklin***, *c.* William, *d.* Robert) : PIERCE

(b) Calvin Coolidge and Franklin Pierce were both presidents of the United States.
Humanities—Association

79. PONTIUS PILATE : JESUS :: CREON : (*a.* Orestes, *b.* Oedipus, ***c. Antigone***, *d.* Electra)

(c) Pontius Pilate sentenced Jesus to death; Creon sentenced Antigone to death. *Orestes and Electra were the son and daughter, respectively, of Agamemnon. Oedipus was a king of Thebes in Greek mythology who killed his father and married his mother.*
Humanities—Association

80. (***a. bellicose***, *b.* periphrastic, *c.* altruistic, *d.* nihilistic) : AGGRESSION :: IRENIC : PEACE

(a) Someone who is bellicose fosters aggression; someone who is irenic fosters peace.
Language—Semantic

81. FIRST : LAST :: GENESIS : (*a.* Exodus, ***b. Deuteronomy***, *c.* Leviticus, *d.* Numbers)

(b) Genesis is the first book of the Torah; Deuteronomy, the last book.
Humanities—Association

82. πr^2 : $2\pi r$ :: AREA : (*a.* diameter, ***b. circumference***, *c.* perimeter, *d.* volume)

(b) πr^2 is the formula for the area of a circle; $2\pi r$ is the formula for the circumference of a circle.
Mathematics—Logical/Mathematical

83. BUCKINGHAM PALACE : XANADU :: ELIZABETH II : (*a.* Genghis Khan, *b.* Charles V, *c.* **Citizen Kane**, *d.* Donald Trump)

(c) Buckingham Palace is the abode of Elizabeth II; Xanadu was the abode of Citizen Kane (a fictitious character fashioned after William Randolph Hearst).

General Information—Association

84. MONOGYNY : (*a.* life, *b.* religion, *c.* child, *d.* **wife**) :: MONOTHEISM : GOD

(d) Monogyny is belief in one wife; monotheism is belief in one God.

Language—Semantic

85. ESPRESSO : BLACK :: ORANGE PEKOE : (*a.* green, *b.* white, *c.* **black**, *d.* red)

(c) Espresso (coffee) is black in color; orange pekoe (tea) is also black in color.

General Information—Association

86. DIANA : (*a.* **Artemis**, *b.* Minerva, *c.* Aphrodite, *d.* Hera) :: JUPITER : ZEUS

(a) Diana and Artemis are the Roman and Greek names, respectively, for the goddess of the moon and of hunting; Jupiter and Zeus are the Roman and Greek names, respectively, for the king of the gods. *Minerva was the Roman goddess of warriors, poetry, and medicine. Her Greek name was Athena. Aphrodite was the Greek goddess of love and beauty. Hera was the Greek goddess of women and marriage.*

Humanities—Semantic

87. (*a.* B♭ major, *b.* **E♭ major**, *c.* F major, *d.* A major) : C MINOR :: G MAJOR : E MINOR

(b) The keys of E♭ major and C minor both have three flats; the keys of G major and E minor both have one sharp.

Humanities—Association

88. MAN : NAME :: (*a.* **rig**, *b.* appellation, *c.* maiden, *d.* woman) : GIRL

(a) The letters in man form the first three letters in name reversed; the letters in rig form the first three letters in girl reversed.

General Information—Logical/Mathematical

89. MANON LESCAUT : (*a.* wise, *b.* arrogant, *c.* **promiscuous**, *d.* wicked) :: TOM SAWYER : ADVENTUROUS

(c) Manon Lescaut is a promiscuous literary character (by Francois Prévost); Tom Sawyer is an adventurous one (by Mark Twain).

Humanities—Association

90. (*a.* Bull Moose, *b.* Whig, *c.* **Socialist**, *d.* Know-Nothing) : DEBS :: DEMOCRAT : STEVENSON

(c) Eugene Debs was an unsuccessful Socialist candidate for president; Adlai Stevenson was an unsuccessful Democratic candidate for president.

Humanities—Classification

91. FIRST : CLERGY :: FOURTH : (*a.* nobles, *b.* commoners, *c.* children, *d.* **journalists**)

(d) The clergy formed the First Estate; journalists form what is sometimes called the Fourth Estate.

Language—Semantic

92. AMETHYST : GARNET :: PURPLE : (*a.* **red**, *b.* green, *c.* transparent, *d.* blue)

(a) An amethyst is purple; a garnet is red.

General Information—Association

93. (***a*. loquacious**, *b*. refractory, *c*. ostentatious, *d*. timid) : GARRULOUS :: AUDACIOUS : BOLD

(a) Loquacious and garrulous have similar meanings, as do audacious and bold.

Language—Semantic

94. FOUR : APRIL FOOL'S DAY :: (*a*. one, *b*. two, ***c*. five**, *d*. ten) : MAY DAY

(c) April Fool's Day is the first day of the fourth month; May Day is the first day of the fifth month.

General Information—Classification

95. STEEPLE : CHURCH :: (***a*. minaret**, *b*. muezzin, *c*. imam, *d*. arch) : MOSQUE

(a) A steeple protrudes from the top of a church; a minaret protrudes from the top of a mosque.

Humanities—Association

96. VANILLA : (*a*. bean, *b*. Sussex, ***c*. hasty**, *d*. Brazil) :: RICE : YORKSHIRE

(c) Four types of pudding are vanilla pudding, hasty pudding, rice pudding, and Yorkshire pudding.

General Information—Classification

97. (*a*. Saint-Saëns, ***b*. Strindberg**, *c*. Bernstein, *d*. Rubinstein) : PLAYS :: FROST : POEMS

(b) Strindberg wrote plays; Frost wrote poems. Leonard Bernstein was a conductor. Arthur Rubinstein was a pianist.

Humanities—Association

98. THERMO : HEAT :: ISO : (*a*. cold, *b*. pressure, *c*. humidity, ***d*. same**)

(d) *Thermo*- is a prefix meaning heat; *iso*- is a prefix meaning same.

Language—Semantic

99. (*a*. Scotch, *b*. vermouth, ***c*. gin**, *d*. bourbon) : TOM COLLINS :: VODKA : BLOODY MARY

(c) A Tom Collins is a mixed drink containing gin; a Bloody Mary is a mixed drink containing vodka.

General Information—Classification

100. BELLEEK : (*a*. Scotland, ***b*. Ireland**, *c*. Holland, *d*. Belgium) :: LIMOGES : FRANCE

(b) Belleek is a town in Ireland (and also a generic name for a type of porcelain). Limoges is a town in France (and also a generic name for a type of china).

General Information—Classification

101. AMPERE : (***a*. current**, *b*. magnetism, *c*. speed, *d*. gravity) :: WATT : POWER

(a) An ampere is a unit used to measure current just as a watt is a unit used to measure power.

Natural Science—Association

102. BAIKAL : RUSSIA :: (*a*. Michigan, ***b*. Superior**, *c*. Ontario, *d*. Placid) : UNITED STATES

(b) Lake Baikal is the largest lake in Russia just as Lake Superior is the largest lake in the United States.

General Information—Classification

103. (*a*. Lady's Man, *b*. Black Beauty, ***c*. Secretariat**, *d*. Fortune's Fool) : MAN O' WAR :: SEABISCUIT : WAR ADMIRAL

(c) Secretariat, Man o' War, Seabiscuit, and War Admiral are all famous race horses.

General Information—Classification

104. GAVRILO PRINCIP : ARCHDUKE FERDINAND :: (*a.* Robert E. Lee, *b.* Lee Harvey Oswald, *c.* John Hinckley, ***d.* John Wilkes Booth**) : PRESIDENT LINCOLN

(d) Gavrilo Princip assassinated Archduke Ferdinand in 1914 just as John Wilkes Booth assassinated President Lincoln (1865).

Humanities—Association

105. KILOGRAM : POUND :: 1 : (***a.* 2.2**, *b.* 5, *c.* 0.2, *d.* 7.3)

(a) There are 2.2 pounds in 1 kilogram.

Natural Science—Logical/Mathematical

106. ROSEMARY : (***a.* oregano**, *b.* cumin, *c.* nutmeg, *d.* cinnamon) :: BASIL : SAGE

(a) Rosemary, oregano, basil, and sage are all leafy herbs used to season food.

General Information—Classification

107. COBBLER : SHOES :: (*a.* tanner, *b.* smith, ***c.* cooper**, *d.* miller) : BARRELS

(c) The 18th century occupations cobbler and cooper worked on shoes and barrels respectively.

Language—Semantic

108. EXPECTORATE : (*a.* bite, ***b.* spit**, *c.* deliver, *d.* swallow) :: MASTICATE : CHEW

(b) To expectorate is to spit just as to masticate is to chew.

Language—Semantic

109. (*a.* net, *b.* hat trick, *c.* goalie, ***d.* puck**) : ICE HOCKEY :: SHUTTLECOCK : BADMINTON

(d) In the sports of ice hockey and badminton, the objects whose possession is passed between players and teams are the puck and shuttlecock, respectively.

General Information—Association

110. ARMSTRONG : TRUMPET :: COLTRANE : (*a.* piano, ***b.* saxophone**, *c.* clarinet, *d.* trombone)

(b) Louis Armstrong and John Coltrane are jazz musicians who played the trumpet and saxophone, respectively.

Humanities—Association

111. MOHAMMED : JESUS :: (*a.* Judea, *b.* Constantinople, ***c.* Mecca**, *d.* Jerusalem) : BETHLEHEM

(c) Religious tradition holds that Mohammed was born in Mecca and that Jesus was born in Bethlehem.

Humanities—Association

112. RHOMBUS : HEXAGON :: 4 : (*a.* 8, *b.* 7, ***c.* 6**, *d.* 5)

(c) A rhombus has four sides just as a hexagon has six sides.

Mathematics—Logical/Mathematical

113. RECORD PLAYER : (***a.* loudest**, *b.* loud, *c.* quiet, *d.* quieter) :: SUPERANNUATED : SUPERLATIVE

(a) The record player, used for playing music, is superannuated, or obsolete. The word loudest is superlative, the most extreme degree of the adjective.

Language—Classification

114. (*a.* feet, *b.* obedience, *c.* thought, ***d.* memory**) : ELEPHANT :: STRENGTH : ANT

(d) Elephants are known for their powers of memory just as ants are known for their feats of strength.

General Information—Association

115. DIAMOND : SAPPHIRE :: (***a. Hope***, *b.* Diana's, *c.* Indian, *d.* Pharoah's) : LOGAN

(a) The Hope Diamond and Logan Sapphire are famous examples of these gemstones.

General Information—Association

116. HEAVEN : ST. PETER :: HADES : (*a.* Lucifer, *b.* Scylla, *c.* Charybdis, ***d. Cerberus***)

(d) Various traditions hold that St. Peter guards the gates to heaven just as Cerberus, the three-headed dog, guards the gates to Hades. *Lucifer is the devil. In Greek mythology, Scylla and Charybdis were two monsters that lived on either side of a very narrow river. When sailors wanted to pass by, they got into reach of one monster when trying to avoid the other.*

Humanities—Association

117. r-p-o-p-h-e-s-s-a-g-r : JABBERWOCKY :: CUMMINGS : (*a.* Milne, *b.* Cleary, ***c. Carroll***, *d.* Eliot)

(c) e. e. cummings and Lewis Carroll wrote the somewhat nonsensical poems *r-p-o-p-h-e-s-s-a-g-r* and *Jabberwocky,* respectively.

Humanities—Association

118. X : (*a.* w, ***b. y***, *c.* u, *d.* a) :: VERTICAL : HORIZONTAL

(b) On two-dimensional graphs, the *x*-axis is vertical and the *y*-axis is horizontal.

Mathematics—Logical/Mathematical

119. (*a.* nostalgia, *b.* kindness, *c.* loyalty, ***d. naiveté***) :: POLLYANNA :: DOUBT : THOMAS

(d) To call someone Pollyanna calls attention to his/her naiveté, and to call someone Thomas calls attention to his/her doubt. These allusions are literary ones.

General Information—Association

120. MAASAI : EAST AFRICA :: LAPP : (*a.* Australia, *b.* Middle East, *c.* South Asia, ***d. Scandinavia***)

(d) The Maasai people are native to East Africa just as the Lapp people are native to Scandinavia.

Social Science—Association

PRETEST ITEM CLASSIFICATION CHART

<table>
<tr><th colspan="5">Relationship</th></tr>
<tr><th></th><th>Semantic</th><th>Classification</th><th>Association</th><th>Logical/
Mathematical</th></tr>
<tr><td>General Information</td><td></td><td>20, 39, 67, 94, 96, 99, 100, 102, 103, 106</td><td>1, 8, 10, 13, 32, 37, 48, 52, 69, 75, 83, 85, 92, 109, 114, 115, 119</td><td>19, 28, 31, 43, 66, 88</td></tr>
<tr><td>Humanities</td><td>76, 86</td><td>7, 33, 41, 61, 68, 90</td><td>12, 30, 36, 40, 42, 45, 49, 56, 57, 78, 79, 81, 87, 89, 95, 97, 104, 110, 111, 116, 117</td><td></td></tr>
<tr><td>Mathematics</td><td></td><td>62</td><td></td><td>4, 14, 22, 74, 82, 112, 118</td></tr>
<tr><td>Language</td><td>3, 5, 15, 23, 24, 25, 44, 50, 53, 54, 59, 60, 63, 70, 73, 80 84, 91, 93, 98, 107, 108</td><td>26, 113</td><td>2, 9, 17, 27, 29</td><td></td></tr>
<tr><td>Natural Science</td><td>72</td><td>35, 38, 46, 47, 64</td><td>6, 18, 21 55, 65, 71, 77, 101</td><td>105</td></tr>
<tr><td>Social Science</td><td></td><td>16, 34, 51, 58</td><td>11, 120</td><td></td></tr>
</table>

The row label column is headed vertically as **CONTENT**.

Remember: This chart shows the relationships and content for each analogy on the Pretest. You will not see this chart after other practice tests in this book. You can refer to this chart at any time as a reference.

Achieving Success on the *Miller Analogies Test*

2

- Facts about the *MAT*
- A word on computer-based tests
- How to solve analogies
- Practice in analogical thinking
- 30 helpful hints
- The 12 biggest mistakes test takers make
- Advice on preparing for the *MAT*
- Improving your intellectual skills

Success is a mindset—a way of life. Those who approach challenges with a dogged resolution almost always succeed, completely independent of talent, just as those who doubt themselves are often defeated before the task begins. One of the third author's favorite anecdotes involves a widely known story about the American basketball legend Michael Jordan—a man famous for his dedication to success and his hunger for competition. The exact details are often disputed (the most legendary moments almost always lack witness consensus), but the sentiment is the same, regardless of how the story is told.

One day during an NBA offseason in the early 1990s—nobody seems to recall exactly when—Michael was golfing against an opposing NBA player. It was a well-played, hard-fought match, but Michael was beaten by his opponent. Michael Jordan was not a man accustomed to defeat, and—though he accepted his loss graciously—he never forgot it.

Several years later, Michael's Chicago Bulls were playing his golfing opponent's team. His opponent almost certainly had forgotten the golf match ever occurred, but being the consummate competitor that he was, Michael recalled the moment vividly.

Michael—fed by his bitter remembrance of defeat in a meaningless golf round years ago—played a masterful game. Many, in fact, recall it as one of the finest of his career. Now, here is where we encounter the legend; late in the 4th quarter of what had been a decidedly one-sided affair, Michael made a very difficult shot. As he turned to run back toward the side of the court his team was defending, Michael turned to the man who had defeated him in golf all of those years ago. The man was sitting on the opposing team's bench, and some say he hadn't even played in the game.

"You!" Michael yelled, pointing at his golf opponent. "Don't you ever *bleeping* beat me in golf again!" And then he ran down the court, oblivious to his opponent's confusion, and proceeded to continue his domination.

Now, your opponent is not a golf player. Your opponent isn't a basketball player, or even really another person of any sort. Your opponent is the *MAT*, and in many senses, your opponent is yourself.

Perhaps the Pretest did not go so well for you, and that is perfectly okay. In fact, it is to be expected: the *MAT* is notoriously difficult and has swallowed up its share of victims over the years. But, just as Michael could do nothing about his golf match, you can do nothing about the first test. It is over. It is done.

At this point, your journey can proceed down either of two paths. On the one hand, you can allow yourself to be defeated. You can quit now and walk away from the test completely. Or, on the other hand, you can now turn to the *MAT* and declare: "Don't you ever *bleeping* beat me again." The choice is yours.

So, who do you want to be?

FACTS ABOUT THE *MAT*

History of the *MAT*

The *MAT* was developed for use at the University of Minnesota, where it was first administered in 1926. At the time, its use was restricted to this university. However, the test received a great deal of attention from psychologists and educators, and it was subsequently made more widely available on a restricted basis. Today, it may be administered only at licensed centers, and distribution of the test is carefully regulated. New forms of the test have been issued periodically over the years, each of which has test items of equal average difficulty and of similar content.

Description of the Test

The *MAT* is a 120-item, 60-minute verbal analogies test. All questions are in the form A : B :: C : D (A is to B as C is to D), with one of the four terms missing. Four possible options are given for the missing term. Of the 120 items, 100 count toward your score, and 20 are experimental and do not count. (This book occasionally refers to A as *Term one*, B as *Term two*.)

Your task is to select the option that best completes the analogy.

What the *MAT* Measures

According to the *Miller Analogies Test Manual* (1970), the "*Miller Analogies Test* (*MAT*) was developed to measure the scholastic aptitude at the graduate school level . . . The test items require the recognition of relationships rather than the display of enormous erudition [p. 3]."

As is often the case with standardized tests, theory is rosier than practice. While there is no question that the "recognition of relationships" is required, its importance relative to that of plain (and some not so plain) knowledge (or "enormous erudition," if you prefer) is probably overstated in the Manual.

Meer, Stein, and Geertsma (1955) investigated the relationship of *MAT* scores to scores on each subtest of the *Wechsler-Bellevue Intelligence Scale* (Wechsler, 1944), a former version of what has been among the most popular and highly respected intelligence tests (yes, some people actually do respect such things). These authors found by far the strongest relationship between scores on the *MAT* and scores on the Vocabulary subtest of the Wechsler-Bellevue. The second strongest relationship was with the scores on the Information subtest. The correlation between scores on the *MAT* and those on the verbal reasoning (Similarities) subtest of the Wechsler-Bellevue was not statistically significant!

Although this study was conducted on a restricted population, and therefore must be interpreted with caution, it points out something you will soon discover on your own: Vocabulary and, to a lesser extent, general information play an important role in determining *MAT* scores. No matter how good you are at reasoning, you first have to recognize and comprehend the concepts with which you are supposed to reason. You will probably find some (if not many) items on which your difficulty does not involve reasoning with the concepts, but of understanding them in the first place.

In one respect, all of this is not as bad as it sounds. Numerous studies have found that vocabulary is the best single predictor both of general intelligence and of performance in a fairly wide variety of tasks. This fact will probably be of more comfort to those who view themselves as walking dictionaries (or even better, walking encyclopedias) than to those whose vocabularies haven't kept up with their razor-sharp reasoning abilities.

Reasons for Taking the *MAT*

Most people who take the *MAT* do so for one of four reasons:

1. **Graduate study.** The most common reason for taking the *MAT* is to support an application for admission to a graduate level academic program at either the masters' or doctoral level.
2. **Scholarship aid.** A second common reason for taking the *MAT* is to support an application for financial aid in pursuing a graduate program.
3. **Business.** A third use of the *MAT* is as a selection or placement device in a business firm or agency. For example, an industrial organization may require the test of applicants to their management traineeship program.
4. **Guidance.** A fourth use of the *MAT* is for personal guidance by a college adviser or placement office.
5. **High I.Q.** High I.Q. societies like Mensa and ultra-high I.Q. societies like the Prometheus Society will accept an *MAT* score as an ample criterion for admission, should the result match each society's respective threshold.

If a school to which you are applying requires the *MAT*, you have no choice but to take it. But some schools offer you a choice of either the *GRE* or the *MAT*. In that case, you can take one or both. If you have the choice, here are the considerations that might incline you toward the *MAT*.

1. If you are weak in mathematics, the *MAT* is the preferred choice. One of three tests of the *GRE* is *Quantitative Reasoning*, whereas the *MAT* has just a few mathematically oriented items.
2. If you are particularly strong in vocabulary and general knowledge of the world, the *MAT* is the way to go. Although it is billed as a test of reasoning, vocabulary and general knowledge weigh heavily in the score, probably even more so than reasoning.
3. If you have difficulty taking tests that are long and grueling, the *MAT* is probably the better option. It is only 1 hour, versus 2½ hours of testing time for the *GRE*.
4. If you have found analogies to be a particular strength of yours, the *MAT* is also the way to go, as it is all analogies.
5. If you are weak in writing skills, you may wish to choose the *MAT* because, unlike the *GRE*, it does not require writing an essay.

More schools require the *GRE* than the *MAT*, so if you have the time or money only for one test, you may want to choose the *GRE*.

No matter the reason for taking the test, it is usually not taken before the senior year in college unless it is administered through special programs.

About the *MAT*

The following information is a summary of information contained in the Candidate Information Booklet, 2017, for the *Miller Analogies Test* (2017).

THE TEST

The test is administered in a computer-based format. It is usually administered through Controlled Testing Centers (CTC). Each CTC formulates its own schedule for testing, its own application process, and its own fee structure. Applications to take the test are made to the CTCs rather than to Pearson, except in rare cases described below. Today, there are more than 500 CTCs in the United States, Canada, and overseas. Locations of CTCs can be found in the Candidate Information Booklet, which can be downloaded from the Web.

There are different versions of the *MAT* to make sure that you won't be presented with the same items again if you take the test more than once.

A WORD ON COMPUTER-BASED TESTS

These days you do not have a choice between paper-and-pencil testing and computer-based testing anymore—when you take the *MAT*, you will need to do so at a computer terminal. The experience of taking a test on a computer may feel quite different from that of taking the same test in a paper-and-pencil version. But remember that it feels different for everyone else as well, so this does not put you at any disadvantage. And like most people today, you probably are also used to doing a lot of things on a computer. By the way, many studies show that even when people have a choice of how to take a test, their chosen medium does not have an impact on their performance: Scores from computer-based tests and their paper-and-pencil equivalents are usually comparable to each other (Karkee, Kim, & Fatica, 2010; Tsai & Shin, 2012; Wang et al., 2008).

The major difference between computer-based tests and paper-and-pencil tests is that you cannot get a grand overview of the test on the computer screen as conveniently as you can by skimming through paper pages. Going back to an item left unanswered is also different and may be a bit more time-consuming on the computer than on a paper test, but this is again true for anyone taking the test. So from our perspective, it is not worth worrying about the fact that the *MAT* now can be taken only by computer.

THE PUBLISHER

The publisher of the test is NCS Pearson, Inc. The company was founded in 1921 and is the oldest publisher of commercial tests in the United States. Pearson develops many of the tests used in the testing industry today, such as the *Wechsler Adult Intelligence Scales* and the *Metropolitan Achievement Tests*. It has a reputation for creating sound tests that are carefully researched and validated. However, like most testing companies, it tends to be rather conservative in the kinds of tests it publishes. The *Miller Analogies Test*, for example, is a very old test. It was already an old test when the first author worked at The Psychological Corporation (then the publisher of the *MAT*) during the summers of 1968 and 1969!

Testing Centers

At present, there are more than 500 testing centers in 50 states and in several foreign countries. Special arrangements can be made in foreign countries where there are no regular centers, but you should allow at least a month for arrangements of this kind to be made. If you reside more than 100 miles from a test center, or if you are not able to reach such a center within a month, special arrangements may also be made, but again you should allow ample time for these to be completed.

A complete list of testing centers may be obtained at *www.milleranalogies.com*, by calling 1-800-622-3231, or by writing to *MATscoring.services@pearson.com*. You should also contact them if you have made arrangements to take the *MAT* but have not received the bulletin of information regarding the test. The website for the test, which contains comprehensive information, is *www.milleranalogies.com*.

Alternative Testing Site

If you reside more than 100 miles from a CTC, you have the option of requesting an alternative testing site. In this case, you may actually find an individual to administer the test to you. The individual must be cleared by the company. It might be, for example, a faculty member at your college or university, an administrator at the school, or a U.S. Embassy administrator or consulate. The fee for such a testing is a stiff $149. The procedure for setting up such an alternative testing site is rather elaborate and is described in the Candidate Information Booklet.

SERVICE AND FEES

Normal Fees

Fees are set by each CTC. Generally, today they are around $65 to $90, on average. However, there are additional fees that can quickly add to the cost of taking the test.

Accommodations

Special accommodations can be made at most CTCs if you need them but the testing center must be notified in advance. Such accommodations include a Braille, large-print edition, or audio edition for the visually impaired. It is even possible to arrange for a reader. Other accommodations can be made as well for those with specific disabilities or disorders.

No Score Option

If you should decide during the test that you don't want the test scored, you can request this by clicking the **Do Not Process This Score** button. Once you click this option, your test will not be scored and consequently no scores will be reported to any score recipients. You will be sent a blank Official Score Report. Be aware, however, that once you click the **Do Not Process This Score** button, you cannot change your mind anymore—your fees will not be refunded, and you cannot request to have your test scored at a later time.

Retesting

You can repeat the *MAT* by applying for another test date at your testing center of choice. Of course, you also will have to pay the test fee again. It also may be worthwhile checking with the schools to which you plan to apply to learn whether they have a policy concerning scores from repeat exams.

Information for Those Who Speak English as a Second Language

You will not be permitted to use a dictionary or any other aids while taking the *MAT*. Although scores obtained by an individual for whom English is not a first language are always difficult to interpret, these scores would be completely uninterpretable if the test takers were allowed to use English-language aids. If your command of the English language does not reflect your true verbal abilities, you will obviously be at a competitive disadvantage in taking the test, although you will very likely find yourself at a similar disadvantage when entering the academic or employment situation for which the *MAT* is required.

Since there are no foreign-language editions of the *MAT*, you must take the test in English. However, any competent interpreter aware of your linguistic background will take into account the fact that English is not your native language when interpreting your score. It would be to your advantage to make this fact known to the appropriate official at any institution to which your score is sent.

Test Dates

The *MAT* is administered throughout the year by appointment. Since testing dates and times vary from one center to another, you will have to consult a local center for this information.

Score Reports

When you report for the test, you will be given an *Examinee's Report* to address to yourself. It will be returned to you with your score recorded on it in a few days after you take the test.

Scoring

NORMAL SCORING

Scoring is done electronically. You will receive a Preliminary Score Report when you have completed the test. Those scores still need to be verified by Pearson, however. It normally takes 10–15 days from the time you take the test until you receive your Official Score Report.

The following information is contained in the score report:

Scale Scores

On the *MAT*, scaled scores range from 200 to 600. The average score is 400. Percentile ranks range from 1 to 99.

Percentile for Intended Major

This tells you the percentage of people who scored below you in the major field in which you plan to concentrate.

Percentile for Total Group

This percentile is relative to all examinees who have taken the test, regardless of major.

The average score is 400 (cf. with the average on the GRE, which is 500). The theoretical range is 200 to 600, but extreme scores are very rare because the standard deviation is only 25 points, meaning that roughly two-thirds of all scores fall between 375 and 425, and roughly 95% of all scores fall between 350 and 450. Scores over 475 or under 325 will be extremely rare, each achieved by only a fraction of 1% of test takers. According to Meagher and Perez (2008), in the 2001–2003 normative sample (i.e., the sample on the basis of which raw scores were converted to standard scores), the range of scores was 231 to 563. However, the bottom and top scores were the extremes—no one scored lower than 231 or higher than 563 of more than 126,000 candidates.

NORMATIVE DATA

As noted above, scores on the *MAT* show a theoretical range of 200 to 600, but very few people score under 325 or over 475. Meagher and Perez (2008) have provided means (average scores) for different fields. They found averages of 397 for business applicants, 400 for education applicants, 414 for humanities applicants, 403 for applicants in the natural sciences, and 399 for applicants in the social sciences. In 2013, Pearson introduced new norms that better reflected the candidate population. The range of 200 to 600 currently remains the same.

VERIFYING YOUR SCORE

When you receive your score and believe there may be a mistake, you can write to Pearson within 60 days of your test date and request that your test be rescored manually. There is a $35 fee for this service. For the most part, such requests are not worth the bother. Machine scoring is typically accurate. But if your score appears totally off to you, it is probably worth the money, if only for the peace of mind.

REPLACEMENT SCORE REPORTS

If after four weeks from the date of testing you have still not received your score report, or if you receive a score report in a timely fashion but it is damaged, you can request a replacement at no charge if you send your request within six weeks of taking the test. Otherwise, there is a charge of $25. You can find the request form for your Score Report at *www.milleranalogies.com*.

SCORE RECIPIENTS AND TRANSCRIPTS

The fee for the test includes a score report to you as well as to as many as three institutions. However, for the institutions to be included in your official score report, they must be specified at the time you take the test. If you request them later, you will have to pay a fee of $25 per score report. Only accredited institutions of higher education and approved scholarship and fellowship organizations are entitled to receive score reports.

At the time of testing, you may list up to three addresses to which you want official score reports sent. It is essential that you know at this time the correct and complete address of any institutions to which you want the score sent. You cannot expect the testing center to supply this information. The charge for reporting scores at the time of testing to as many as three institutions is included in the test fee.

Should you later decide that you wish additional score reports sent out, you will have to make a request to Pearson. You can find the request form at *www.milleranalogies.com*.

The fee is $25 for each report.

Scores of tests taken more than 5 years ago will not be reported, since these scores may not be accurate reflections of current ability. You must therefore take the test again if you need a score reported but have not taken the test during the preceding 5 years. If you took the test more than 2 years but less than 5 years ago, the old score will be reported, but you are strongly urged to retake the test nevertheless. If you take the test twice within 2 years, both scores will be reported.

CANCELLATION OF SCORES

Pearson reserves the right to cancel scores. Scores may be cancelled for a variety of reasons. They include (a) repeating the same form of the *MAT* within a 1-year period, (b) the occurrence of an irregularity in the administration of the test, (c) questionable item responses or unusual answer patterns, or (d) a score gain that seems questionable. A questionable score gain is one that is 50 points or greater than the previous score. If your score is invalidated for reasons of questionable gain, you may take a third test at no charge. If your third score is within 25 points of the second one, the second score is validated. If it is not, no scores will be released. Exceptions can be made in special cases.

Practice Tests

You can take three practice tests offered by the publisher. At the time we are writing this book, the cost for each test is $30.00. The website to access for more information is *http://tpc-etesting.com/matopt/*. The tests will be scored for you by the test publisher.

What to Bring to the Test Center

All necessary forms and identifications   You will receive the necessary forms in the mail. Don't forget to bring them to the test, as well as other information you may want to supply, such as addresses of the universities to which you want the scores sent. Do not bring notes, dictionaries, or the like; they are not permitted.

Bring *two* forms of identification with you, at least one of which has a photo and your signature. The best forms of identification are government-issued ones, such as a driver's license or passport. Credit-card photos are not accepted as a form of photo identification. You will not be admitted to the testing until you show the two forms of identification.

A watch   There may not be a clock in the room, or it may not be easily visible. Having your own watch ensures that you will be able to check the time easily. A watch will also help you to pace yourself as you work on the test and will enable you to fill in any unanswered questions before the end of the testing period.

One or two pencils with good erasers   The testing center will provide scratch paper so you can write down any items you want to return to later. Note that no writing instruments other than pencils are allowed.

Your Retest Admission Ticket   If you are retaking the test, be sure to bring your Retest Admission Ticket. This is extremely important so that you do not risk the test score being invalidated.

What Not to Bring

Do not bring calculators, books, papers, notes of any kind, cell phones, digital personal assistants, cameras, or any other similar kinds of materials into the testing room. Also, do not bring food or beverages into the room where you will be tested. Visitors are not permitted in the testing room either, so leave your friends, loved ones, and chauffeurs outside!

When You Are at the Test Center

GUIDELINES FOR BEING AT THE CTC

When you go to the CTC, you should observe certain guidelines. First, you should arrive on time. If you arrive late, the policy is to not admit you. Thus, if you are traveling from a distance, be sure to leave more than enough time for your arrival.

Listen carefully to all the instructions you are given. You will be asked to provide various kinds of information, and it is important that you are prepared to provide it in order to ensure that your score is properly reported and validated. You will need to know your social security number, if you have one.

You must sign your name by clicking a signature box. If you do not sign, your scores will be held up.

Make sure that you ask any questions you have before the test begins, because you will not be allowed to ask questions after it has begun. Also, you cannot leave the testing room until after the test is over. So please—if you need to go to the bathroom, go before the testing starts. Do not plan to wait until afterward. You do not want to be spending the testing session thinking about these kinds of needs.

At the risk of stating the obvious, you are forbidden to give or receive aid during the test. If you do either, you will be required to terminate the testing session, your test will not be scored, and you will not receive a refund.

HOW TO SOLVE ANALOGIES

What Is an Analogy?

An analogy is a problem of the form A is to B as C is to D. For notational convenience, the problem is often written as

$$A : B :: C : D.$$

This is the way problems are presented on the *MAT*.

Processes Involved in Solving Analogies

Some years ago, the senior author did a detailed analysis of the mental processes people use to solve analogies (Sternberg, 1977). He found that, overwhelmingly, people use a common and fairly straightforward strategy.

Consider the analogy **Washington : 1 :: Lincoln : (a) 5, (b) 10, (c) 15, (d) 23** as an example.

STEP 1 *Encode the first analogy term.* You see the term "Washington," so you access meanings available to you in long-term memory, such as that Washington is the name of the first president, the name of a city, and the name of a state.

STEP 2 *Encode the second analogy term.* You see the term "1," and you access meanings available to you in long-term memory, such as that 1 is the first whole number, that it can be a unitary quantity of things, and that it is also often used to refer to something that is the best of a bunch.

STEP 3 *Infer the relation between the first and second analogy terms.* You try to figure out how Washington might be related to 1. You might now think of two possible relations, given your encoding: that Washington was the first (#1) president and that a bust of Washington appears on a $1 bill.

STEP 4 *Encode the third term of the analogy.* You see that the third term is "Lincoln."

STEP 5 *Map the relation between the first and second halves of the analogy.* You now can begin to relate the concept of *Lincoln* to the various relations between *Washington* and *1*. Of the inferred relations, both are still viable. Lincoln was also a president and also appears on a bill.

STEP 6 *Encode the answer options.* You see the terms "5," "10," "15," and "23," and know what each of the numbers is.

STEP 7 *Apply the relation you inferred* between *Washington* and *1* in the second half of the analogy. You now can try out the mapped version of the inferred relations on each of the options.

Note at this point the importance of knowledge to success on the *MAT*. To get this item correct, you had to know something about *Washington*. Now you have to know something about *Lincoln*. If you know that Lincoln is on the $5 bill, you have a possible answer, namely, (a). But unless you know that Lincoln was the 16th president, you may wonder whether one of the other options represents the ordinal position of his presidency. And if you do not know that Lincoln is on the $5 bill and you do not know that he was the 16th president, you may find any of the options potentially attractive. So in this item as in all *MAT* items, knowledge as well as reasoning are needed for a correct response.

STEP 8 **Discriminate** *among the answer options.* At this point, you decide which option best satisfies the constraints of the inferred relation. If you know both that Lincoln is on the $5 bill and that he was the 16th president, you can select (a) with confidence.

Sometimes there is an (optional) additional step after 7 and before 8. If you solve an analogy and believe that none of the answer options is correct, then you do that additional step.

STEP 8a **Justify** *one option as best although not optimal.* In this case, you choose the best answer, even if you believe it is not a perfect answer.

STEP 9 **Respond.** Select "(a)" or whatever your preferred answer is on the computer.

STEP 10 **Verify.** Make sure that the answer you selected is indeed the answer you intended to select. It is not uncommon to accidentally click another answer (especially if you are running behind on time and are forced to work quickly).

FOUR WAYS OF PRESENTING ANALOGIES

On *MAT* analogies, one of the four terms, A, B, C, or D, will be missing. In its place will be four options. Your task will be to select the option that best fits the analogy. The following analogy might be presented in any of four ways.

EXAMPLE

BLACK : WHITE :: DARK : LIGHT

1. BLACK : WHITE :: DARK : (*a.* gray, *b.* shaded, *c.* light, *d.* heavy)
2. BLACK : WHITE :: (*a.* somber, *b.* blue, *c.* gray, *d.* dark) : LIGHT
3. BLACK : (*a.* color, *b.* white, *c.* gray, *d.* coal) :: DARK : LIGHT
4. (*a.* gray, *b.* black, *c.* heavy, *d.* somber) : WHITE :: DARK : LIGHT

The correct options, of course, are *c*, *d*, *b*, and *b*, respectively.

Ways of Perceiving Relationships

You may conceive of the relationship between the terms of the above analogy in two ways. First, you may say to yourself something like "White is the opposite of black, and light is the opposite of dark." Instead, you may say "Black is dark and white is light." Either way you will arrive at the same answer.

The first way looks at the two terms on the left (A : B) as one unit and the two terms on the right as a unit (C : D). The second way looks at the first and third terms as a unit (A : C) and the second and fourth terms as another unit (B : D). The important thing is to discover a relationship that is the same between the two terms in each unit.

Sometimes it is more convenient to solve an analogy in one way, and sometimes in the other.

EXAMPLE

1. DOCTOR : PATIENT :: LAWYER (*a.* judge, *b.* jury, *c.* district attorney, *d.* client)

If the analogy is presented in this form, it is easier to consider the first and third terms as one unit, and the second and fourth terms as another.

A Common Mistake

A common mistake made by those who are relatively unfamiliar with analogies is to try to find a relationship between the first and fourth or the second and third terms. Don't do this. Often an incorrect answer option is waiting to be picked by those who use this kind of faulty reasoning.

In solving analogies, keep the following diagram in mind:

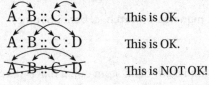

The analogy DOCTOR : PATIENT :: LAWYER : CLIENT is acceptable. The analogy DOCTOR : LAWYER :: PATIENT : CLIENT is acceptable. The analogy DOCTOR : PATIENT :: CLIENT : LAWYER is *not* acceptable. The third and fourth terms of an analogy may not be reversed, nor may the first and second terms. You can look for relations between A and B, C and D, A and C, and B and D in an analogy. You should **not** look for relationships between A and D or between B and C.

Errors Stemming from Reversals

Errors stemming from reversals are frequent.

EXAMPLE

BIRD : SPARROW :: (*a.* boy, *b.* species, *c.* mammal, *d.* phylum) : HUMAN BEING

The relationship is that a sparrow is a type of bird, and a human being is a type of mammal.

Someone might carelessly interpret the analogy as requiring him or her to infer that a sparrow is a type of bird and a boy is a type of human being. This relationship is correct, but it is not the one posed by the analogy.

Examples

It is important to realize that an analogy cannot be inverted. That is, in the analogy A : B :: C : D, the relationship of A to B must be the same as that of C to D. Or the relationship of A to C can be the same as that of B to D.

But the relationship CANNOT BE that A is to B as D is to C, or A is to D as B is to C. Inversions are not allowed. Consider some examples:

EXAMPLE

CAT : SIAMESE :: (*a.* animal, *b.* boxer, *c.* angora, *d.* pedigree) : DOG

The correct answer is *a*. The reason is that a Siamese is a kind of cat and a dog is a kind of animal. The tempting distracter is *b*. But note that if you were to choose *b*, you would be committing an inversion. View the analogy as taking the form A : B :: C : D. The relationship cannot be A (CAT) is related to B (SIAMESE) in the same way that D (DOG) is related to C (BOXER). Rather, it must be that A (CAT) is related to B (SIAMESE) in the same way that C (ANIMAL) is related to D (DOG). It cannot be that A is related to B as D is related to C.

EXAMPLE

PROTON : ATOM :: DIAL : (*a.* numeral, *b.* watch, *c.* band, *d.* time)

The correct answer is *b*. A proton is part of an atom and a dial is part of a watch. Note that the inverted form—PROTON is to ATOM as DIAL is to NUMERAL—does not work, because the analogy does not permit A to be related to B in the same way as D is related to C.

EXAMPLE

(*a.* tree, *b.* hemlock, *c.* maple, *d.* trunk) : DECIDUOUS :: SPRUCE : EVERGREEN

The correct answer is *c* because a maple is a kind of deciduous tree and a spruce is a kind of evergreen. Note that *a* does not work because it inverts the analogy. It would make a tree a superset of deciduous trees, but a spruce is not a superset but rather a subset of evergreen trees.

EXAMPLE

STREPTOCOCCUS : BACTERIUM :: HERPES : (*a.* type I, *b.* virus, *c.* bacteria, *d.* simplex)

The correct answer is *b* because streptococcus is a type of bacterium and herpes a type of virus. Note that one cannot invert the analogy. Thus, Type I is a type of herpes virus, but one is not allowed to have an analogy where A relates to B and D relates to C. Hence, the correct answer must be *b*.

What Makes an Analogy Difficult?

Miller analogies differ widely in difficulty. In general, one analogy may be more or less difficult than another analogy for any one or more of five reasons.*

1. **Difficulty of words.** You may simply be unfamiliar with the meanings of some or all of the words in the analogy. In this case, you may be stumped by vocabulary limitations before you even begin to figure out relationships. For example, the analogy IDOLATRY : IDOLS :: OPHIOLATRY : (*a.* icons, *b.* fire, *c.* serpents, *d.* darkness) would be easy for most people to solve if they knew that *ophiolatry* is serpent worship. The difficulty of the analogy resides in the unfamiliarity of a single word.

---

*Sternberg, R.J. Component processes in analogies reasoning. *Psychological Review*, 1977, 84, 353–378.
Sternberg, R.J. *Intelligence, Information Processing, and Analogical Reasoning: The Componential Analysis of Human Abilities.* Hillsdale, N.J.: Lawrence Erlbaum Associates, 1977.

2. **Difficulty of relation between A and B.** You may know the meanings of the A and B (first two) terms of the analogy, but be unable to figure out the relationship between them. Consider, for example, the analogy TRAP : PART :: TEN : (*a.* net, *b.* twenty, *c.* whole, *d.* lost). The terms are all easily recognizable. The difficulty of the analogy is in recognizing that the relationship between the first two terms is that the second is the first spelled backward.

3. **Difficulty of relation between A and C.** An analogy may be difficult because it is not immediately obvious how the A and C (first and third) terms match up. Consider, for example, the analogy GARMENT : WEAR :: POTION : (*a.* clothing, *b.* liquid, *c.* drink, *d.* magic). The terms *garment* and *potion* have little in common. Recognizing that one wears a garment does not immediately help you to decide what to do with *potion*. You must recognize that the rule that relates the first half of the analogy to the second half is that "B is what one does with A." One wears a garment, and drinks a potion.

4. **Difficulty of relation between C and D.** Sometimes you may be able to infer the relation between A and B, but have difficulty applying the analogous relation from C to D. Consider, for example, the analogy GOVERNOR : PRESIDENT :: LEGISLATURE : (*a.* Capitol, *b.* Congress, *c.* House, *d.* Speaker). The terms of the analogy are all familiar ones, and the relations between A and B and between A and C are straightforward. The difficulty of this analogy is in applying the analogy rule from *legislature* to the best answer. Options *a*, *b*, and *c* are all fairly plausible, but reflection will reveal that *b* is the best answer. Option *a*, *Capitol*, refers to a specific building; option *c*, *House*, refers to only one of two congressional bodies. *Congress* (option *b*) is the national legislative body, however, and a legislature is a state legislative body.

5. **Difficulty of relation between D and ideal answer.** Occasionally, you may come upon an analogy that for one reason or another seems to have no "perfect" answer. Consider, for example, the analogy MINUTE : HOUR :: FOOT : (*a.* yard, *b.* day, *c.* inch, *d.* length). The best answer is option *a*, although one could argue that this answer is far from perfect, since there are 60 minutes in an hour, but 3 feet in a yard. When none of the answer options seems quite right, you must either reconsider the way you have interpreted the analogy or else simply pick the answer that seems closest to the ideal one.

How to Select the Correct Answer

1. **Read all the options.** You must choose the best of the four alternative options presented. Keep in mind that item-writers make a deliberate (and usually successful) effort to make the incorrect options as plausible as possible. This fact has an important implication: *Read all the possible answer choices before selecting one.* Ace and Dawis (1973) found that analogies in which the last option is the correct one tend to be most difficult. A likely reason is that people sometimes don't bother to read through all the answers; they pick a plausible but incorrect option before they ever get to the last and correct option.

2. **Check the parts of speech.** In selecting an option, be systematic. When you don't know what all the terms mean, or when the relationship between them is not obvious to you, try to use context cues to figure things out. Remember that while not all terms of the analogy have to be of the same part of speech, they can be of no more than two parts of speech (except for nonsemantic analogies). Therefore, if an option you are considering introduces a third part of speech, it is probably incorrect.

3. **Infer the type of analogy.**

EXAMPLE

THRIFTY : (*a.* wasteful, *b.* economical, *c.* cheerful, *d.* wealthy) :: SLATTERNLY : UNTIDY

Suppose that you don't know what the word *slatternly* means. You need not give up on the analogy either by skipping it or by answering randomly. The first inference you can make is that this is a semantic relationship, which is an analogy involving the literal meanings of words. One important fact to note is that relationships involving synonyms are slightly more common on the *MAT* than antonym relationships. So a reasonable inference to make would be that *slatternly* means untidy, and that therefore option *b* is the correct answer, since *thrifty* means economical. Of course, you might not want to rule out the possibility of an antonym.

4. **Consider the sounds of words.** One thing you can do (and this really works on many occasions) is simply to look at the word *slatternly* and decide whether it *sounds* more like a word meaning tidy or one meaning untidy. Most people will choose *untidy*, and they will be correct. The answer to this problem is option *b*.

5. **Guess intelligently.** Suppose the item had been presented in this form:

EXAMPLE

THRIFTY : ECONOMICAL :: SLATTERNLY : (*a.* cheerful, *b.* quickly, *c.* circular, *d.* untidy).

The problem is now more difficult, with fewer context cues available. However, you can still approach the item systematically. First, you can reasonably eliminate option *b*. You know that *thrifty* and *economical* are adjectives, and three of the four answer options are also adjectives. *Quickly*, however, is an adverb, probably included as an incorrect option because it ends in *-ly*, as does *slatternly*. Next, you can reasonably eliminate option *c*. Although it is an *adjective*, it describes a property of an object, whereas *thrifty* almost always describes a characteristic of a person. You are now left with two options and have to make a choice, based on your past experience with words. When you finally choose an answer, you will still be guessing, but you will be guessing intelligently rather than blindly. Guessing can improve your score if you do it intelligently. Because there is no penalty for guessing, make an educated guess on any item when you are unsure of the correct answer. Try not to leave any items unanswered. Guessing intelligently can only improve your score.

6. **Use word association.** You will probably encounter some analogies on the *MAT* in which you find yourself simply unable to infer the relationship between the given terms. When all else fails, a strategy that is slightly better than wild guessing is to try word association. In using this strategy, you attempt to select the option that seems most closely related (in whatever way) to the given terms of the analogy.

The psychologist A. Willner had individuals take a form of the *MAT* as a word association test. Rather than try to solve the analogies, subjects were instructed to pick the answer option that seemed most highly associated to the given element. Willner found that on one of every four items, the correct answer (as keyed for the analogies test) was picked with greater than chance frequency. The indication is that, at least on some items, the word association technique will help you to do better than would random guessing. It is by no means a powerful strategy, however, and should be used only when your attempts to discover any kind of relationship have failed.

Allocating Your Time

A common problem in taking a test such as the *MAT* is one of time allocation. In particular, how much time do you allocate per item? You have 60 minutes for 120 items, meaning that you have to complete two analogies per minute, 30 seconds per analogy, in order to finish. And you really want to finish because items not answered are items lost. Moreover, looking at an item and getting an idea of what is on it provides a much better basis for taking a chance on an item than just answering at random!

First, always go in order because items are in order of difficulty. Your chances of getting items right are better on earlier than on later items. If you see an analogy and cannot answer it rather quickly—in 20 seconds or so—then make a notation somewhere of the item number. We recommend you use two different types of notations. One is for items for which you have an idea of what the correct answer is. The other is for items where you believe you pretty much have no idea of the correct answer. Then, when you go back, start with the items for which you have some idea of the correct answer. Do the items for which you have little idea last. But always answer the item once you have looked at it because you may not have time to go back. If you do have time, you can change your answer later. It is imperative to select an answer for every question. It is rare to encounter an analogy where you have zero familiarity with any of the four terms. Hopefully, you can at least eliminate one or two choices that is/are not logical. From there, if you were to definitively eliminate two choices, your probability of guessing and obtaining the correct answer is 50%, as opposed to the 25% success rate that can be expected with random guessing. Not guessing at all leaves you a 0% chance to attain the correct answer; you have given up and have effectively surrendered on that question.

Do not surrender. Granted, 25% is not a favorable probability, and random guessing should be avoided unless you are tightly time constrained. But, 25% is far superior to having no chance whatsoever.

A big mistake is to get hung up on a hard item. Sometimes, when taking a test, we lose track of the time. Losing track of time can be disastrous on a test such as the *MAT*. Each item counts the same, so it is absolutely not worth your time to spend a great deal of time on an item at the expense of other items. This is doubly true because, for all you know, the item may be one of the 20 experimental ones that do not count in any case. If you have answered all the other items, it is fine to spend that extra time. But if you haven't, be sure you answer all items to the best of your ability before you linger over any one item.

Sometimes, when people go back, they come up with a different answer than their initial one. A question they sometimes ask is whether to change the answer. We recommend you change the answer only if you are confident that the second answer is better than the first. There is some research to suggest that initial answers are better than revised answers.

> **Directions:** In each of the following, the first two terms are related, sometimes in multiple ways. The third term is like the first two terms in some way but different from them in another. See how the third term is (a) like the first two terms and (b) different from them.

1. LEMON : TANGERINE :: PEACH

2. JUICE : MILK :: PANCAKES

3. DANCE : LEAP :: TURNED

4. PLANETS : ASTEROIDS :: SUN

5. ¾ : 0.75 :: 0.25

6. CENTIMETER : MILLIMETER :: INCH

7. DEGAS : MONET :: COURBET

8. SATURN : MERCURY :: PLANETS

9. BRASS : TUBA :: PERCUSSION

10. MISSISSIPPI : HUDSON :: HURON

11. MORGAN : MUSTANG :: MALTESE

12. WHELK : LIMPET :: KELP

13. STAMP : PHILATELIST :: NUMISMATIST

14. PURPLE : GREEN :: RED

15. DISCOVERY : ATLANTIS :: VIKING

16. CALDECOTT : NEWBERY :: PULITZER

17. LIMESTONE : SANDSTONE :: MARBLE

18. PHALANGES : METATARSALS :: FEMUR

19. MILK : CHEESE :: WHEAT

20. VITAMIN A : VITAMIN D :: VITAMIN C

21. ARTERIOSCLEROSIS : MYOCARDIAL INFARCTION :: CARDIOVASCULAR DISEASE

22. CARBON MONOXIDE : NITROGEN OXIDE :: ASBESTOS

23. MONOPHONIC : HOMOPHONIC :: DUPLE METER

24. INCUS : STAPES :: PINA

25. PRESIDENT'S DAY : VALENTINE'S DAY :: MARTIN LUTHER KING, JR. DAY

26. WOOD-CARVED RELIEF : CORK INLAY :: TEXTURE DRAWING

27. WATERCOLOR : TEMPERA :: CHARCOAL

28. EQUILATERAL TRIANGLE : SQUARE :: RHOMBUS

29. SPAN : CUBIT :: STONE

30. PHAEDO : REPUBLIC :: POETICS

31. SOPHOCLES : ARISTOPHANES :: HIPPOCRATES

32. TUNDRA : TAIGA :: TROPICAL RAIN FOREST

33. DONATELLO : MASACCIO :: RAPHAEL

34. DADA : SURREALISM :: SOCIAL REALISM

35. LYMPHOCYTES : MONOCYTES :: ERYTHROCYTES

36. SPRUCE : PONDEROSA :: HICKORY

37. PECK : BUSHEL :: FLUIDRAM

38. TROPIC OF CANCER : ARCTIC CIRCLE :: INTERNATIONAL DATE LINE

39. STARS AND STRIPES : OLD GLORY :: STARS AND BARS

40. FLINT : MATCHES :: LIGHTNING

41. DOMINICAN REPUBLIC : CUBA :: CHAD

42. OFFSIDE : CLIPPING :: GOALTENDING

43. KENYA : BRAZIL :: AUSTRALIA

44. FILLMORE : VAN BUREN :: MARSHALL

45. TALLAHASSEE : COLUMBUS :: HOUSTON

46. IONESCO : BECKETT :: IBSEN

47. STIGMA : STYLE :: ANTHERS

48. CIRRUS : CIRROCUMULUS :: NIMBOSTRATUS

49. ORTHOCLASE : QUARTZ :: CALCITE

50. ST. PETER'S : SISTINE CHAPEL :: SANTA MARIA DELLA SALUTE

Answer Explanations

1. A lemon, tangerine, and peach are fruits. Lemons and tangerines are citrus fruits, but peaches are not.

2. Juice, milk, and pancakes are foods. Juice and milk are liquid; pancakes are solid.

3. *Dance*, *leap*, and *turned* are verbs. *Dance* and *leap* are present tense; *turned* is past tense.

4. Planets, asteroids, and the sun are heavenly bodies. Planets and asteroids revolve around a star (the sun), whereas the sun is a star.

5. $\frac{3}{4}$, 0.75, and 0.25 are numbers less than 1. $\frac{3}{4}$ equals 0.75, whereas 0.25 does not.

6. Centimeter, millimeter, and inch are units of measure. Centimeter and millimeter are units in the metric system; inch is a unit in the English system.

7. Degas, Monet, and Courbet were painters. Degas and Monet are considered impressionists; Courbet, a realist.

8. Saturn and Mercury are planets; planet is the superordinate category.

9. A tuba is an instrument in the superordinate category "brass." Percussion is a different category of musical instruments.

10. The Mississippi, Hudson, and Huron are all bodies of water. The Mississippi and Hudson are rivers; Huron is a lake.

11. Morgan, Mustang, and Maltese are all breeds. Morgan and Mustang are breeds of horses. Maltese is a breed of dog or cat.

12. Whelk, limpet, and kelp are found in the ocean. Whelk and limpet are marine gastropods that live in shells. Kelp is seaweed.

13. A philatelist and a numismatist are collectors. A philatelist collects or studies stamps; a numismatist, coins.

14. Purple, green, and red are colors. Purple and green are secondary colors; red is primary.

15. Discovery, Atlantis, and Viking are space vehicles. Discovery and Atlantis are space shuttles; Viking is a planetary probe.

16. The Caldecott, Newbery, and Pulitzer are awards given to literature. The Caldecott and Newbery are given specifically to children's books, whereas the Pulitzer is not.

17. Limestone, sandstone, and marble are rocks. Limestone and sandstone are sedimentary rocks; marble is a metamorphic rock.

18. The phalanges, metatarsals, and femur are bones. The phalanges and metatarsals are bones in the foot; the femur is a bone in the leg.

19. Milk, cheese, and wheat are foods. Milk and cheese are members of the dairy nutritional group; wheat is not.

20. A, D, and C are vitamins. Vitamins A and D are fat-soluble; C is a water-soluble vitamin.

21. Arteriosclerosis and myocardial infarction are examples of the superordinate category "cardiovascular disease"—a disease of the heart and blood vessels.

22. Carbon monoxide, nitrogen oxide, and asbestos are air pollutants. Carbon monoxide and nitrogen oxide are gases that contribute to outdoor air pollution. Asbestos is usually an indoor air pollutant; also, asbestos is not a gas.

23. Monophonic, homophonic, and duple meter are examples of basic musical elements. Monophonic and homophonic are examples of musical texture; duple meter is an example of musical rhythm.

24. The incus, stapes, and pina are parts of the ear. The incus and stapes are parts of the inner ear; the pina is part of the outer ear.

25. President's Day, Valentine's Day, and Martin Luther King, Jr. Day are observed as special days in the United States. President's Day and Valentine's Day are in February; Martin Luther King, Jr. Day is in January.

26. Wood-carved relief, cork inlay, and texture drawing are art techniques. Wood-carved relief and cork inlay are three-dimensional; a texture drawing is two-dimensional.

27. Watercolor, tempera, and charcoal are media of artwork. Watercolor and tempera are types of paints, but charcoal is not.

28. An equilateral triangle, a square, and a rhombus are polygons. An equilateral triangle and a square are regular polygons; a rhombus is not a regular polygon because its angles do not have the same number of degrees.

29. Span, cubit, and stone have been used as units of measure. Span and cubit are measures of length; stone is a measure of weight.

30. The *Phaedo*, the *Republic*, and the *Poetics* are literary works associated with Greek philosophy. The *Phaedo* and the *Republic* are Platonic dialogues, whereas the *Poetics* was written by Aristotle.

31. Sophocles, Aristophanes, and Hippocrates were Greek. Sophocles and Aristophanes were masters of dramatic art; Hippocrates is identified with science and medicine.

32. Tundra, taiga, and tropical rain forest are examples of biomes. Tundra and taiga are cold-climate biomes; tropical rain forests are warm-climate biomes.

33. Donatello, Masaccio, and Raphael were Italian painters. Donatello and Masaccio are associated with 15th century Italian art and are considered painters of the "Proto-Renaissance." Raphael's work is classified as 16th century, High Renaissance.

34. Dada, surrealism, and social realism are 20th century art movements. Dadaists and surrealists fought against conventional, accepted meanings in their art. Social realists believed that art has a social purpose and meaning.

35. Lymphocytes, monocytes, and erythrocytes are blood cells. Lymphocytes and monocytes are white blood cells; erythrocytes are red blood cells.

36. Spruce, ponderosa, and hickory are trees. Spruce and ponderosa are pines; hickory is a broad-leaf tree.

37. Peck, bushel, and fluidram are all units of measure. Peck and bushel are units of capacity (dry measure); fluidram is a unit of liquid measure.

38. The Tropic of Cancer, the Arctic Circle, and the International Date Line are divisions of the earth. The Tropic of Cancer and the Arctic Circle divide the earth horizontally; the International Date Line divides the earth vertically.

39. Stars and Stripes, Old Glory, and Stars and Bars are names given to American flags. Stars and Stripes and Old Glory denote the flag; Stars and Bars was a name for the Confederate flag.

40. Flint, matches, and lightning can start fires. Flint and matches are human means of starting a fire; lightning is a natural means.

41. The Dominican Republic, Cuba, and Chad are countries. The Dominican Republic and Cuba are in the Western Hemisphere; Chad is in Africa.

42. Offside, clipping, and goaltending are penalties imposed in sports. Offside and clipping are used in football; goaltending, in basketball.

43. Kenya, Brazil, and Australia are countries. Kenya and Brazil are located on the equator. Australia is in the Southern Hemisphere.

44. Fillmore, Van Buren, and Marshall have served as high officials of the U.S. government. Fillmore and Van Buren were presidents. Marshall was a Supreme Court judge.

45. Tallahassee, Columbus, and Houston are cities in the United States. Tallahassee and Columbus are capital cities; Houston is not.

46. Ionesco, Beckett, and Ibsen are playwrights. Ionesco and Beckett are considered modern playwrights (1944–1975). Ibsen preceded Ionesco and Beckett but is considered the "father of modern drama" because he introduced social problems into his plays.

47. Stigma, style, and anthers are all parts of a flower. Stigma and style are considered parts of the "female" flower (carpel); the "male" plant structure (stamen) is tipped with anthers that produce pollen.

48. Cirrus, cirrocumulus, and nimbostratus are clouds. Cirrus and cirrocumulus are high-altitude clouds; nimbostratus clouds often occur at low altitude.

49. Orthoclase, quartz, and calcite are minerals. Orthoclase and quartz are silicate minerals; calcite is a carbonate mineral.

50. St. Peter's, the Sistine Chapel, and Santa Maria Della Salute are cathedrals. St. Peter's and the Sistine Chapel are in Rome; Santa Maria Della Salute is in Venice.

30 HELPFUL HINTS

Certain strategies are effective for raising scores on the *Miller Analogies Test*. Here are 30 of the most important ones.

1. **Don't wait until the last minute to prepare for the test.** Research shows that you will do better if you spread your studying a little at a time over a longer period, rather than cramming all your studying into a shorter time right before the test. Therefore, start preparing at the earliest possible date!

2. **When you take practice tests, simulate actual testing conditions as closely as possible.** You best prepare yourself for the actual test if you take the practice tests under realistic conditions. Taking a standardized test means more than just answering a set of questions. It means you will be in an unusually stark testing room and will have to answer questions under time pressure. Actual testing conditions typically produce some degree of anxiety. Too much anxiety can hurt test scores, but so can too little anxiety. If you are too relaxed, you may find yourself not putting in maximal effort. Therefore, it is to your advantage to replicate actual testing conditions as closely as possible. When you take the practice

tests, it is important that you strictly observe the time limit. Simulate all aspects of the testing situation as closely as possible and don't allow distractions (such as phone calls or errands).

3. **Realize that you can improve your score.** One of the greatest sources of defeat is the belief that intellectual skills are fixed and hence unmodifiable. Once you believe that, it becomes true for you, because you make no effort to improve your intellectual performance.

Carol Dweck (1999) has studied thousands of students and found that they can be placed into two groups with respect to their beliefs about their abilities. One group believes that abilities are fixed; the other group believes that abilities are modifiable. When tasks are easy, the two groups of students do about equally well. But when tasks are difficult, the group that believes in the modifiability of abilities outperforms the group that believes that abilities are fixed. The reason is that the group that believes in the modifiability of abilities is willing to take on difficult challenges, whereas the group that believes in the fixedness of abilities is afraid to undertake tough challenges. People in this group are afraid they will look stupid if they try something hard. Believing that you can improve your intellectual skills is the first step toward improving them.

In fact, there is good evidence that intellectual abilities are modifiable (Grotzer & Perkins, 2000; Perkins & Grotzer, 1997; Sternberg, 1997; Ramey, 1994). It is to your advantage to act on this evidence.

4. **Be mindful when you take the test.** How many times have you gone over the results of a test and felt like kicking yourself because you missed easy questions—questions to which you knew the answer? People often find that a major proportion of the test items they answer incorrectly are answered incorrectly not because they did not know the answer, but because their attention slipped or they got careless. Ellen Langer (1989, 1997) has referred to such behavior as *mindless*.

When we behave mindlessly, we act as though we are on automatic pilot—doing things without thinking. Have you ever been driving for a while and then discovered that you missed making a turn, or that you have lost track of what you are doing? Or have you ever been reading and gotten to the end of a page or even a book chapter, only to realize that you have only the foggiest idea of what you have just read? These are examples of mindless behavior.

You might think that people would not show such behavior during tests, but they do. Sometimes people let their minds stray even when the potential stakes in the situation are very high. Think about the catastrophes that can result from being mindless when driving! Make the decision that for the 60 minutes you take the test, you will be completely *mindful* and will concentrate fully on the test.

5. **Take responsibility for your test score.** Julian Rotter (1990) has found that some people tend to be what he refers to as *internals*, whereas others tend to be *externals*. Internals take responsibility for their own successes and failures, whereas externals tend to blame other people or circumstances for their successes and failures. Research has consistently shown that *internals* tend to outperform externals in a variety of kinds of life tasks.

First, you need to take responsibility for your test preparation. There are always factors that will get in the way. You will have other things to do; perhaps you will have started preparing later than you should have; perhaps some catastrophic event has recently happened in your life or the life of a loved one. Whatever problems may emerge, it is essential that you take responsibility for preparing. This is the only way you can become truly prepared.

Second, you need to take responsibility for what happens the day of the test. The first author remembers that when he took the *Miller Analogies Test* some years ago, he was seated at a desk that was too small for him. It was uncomfortable, and he cursed his luck for getting stuck with such a small desk, not to mention the occasional noises of construction that came from outside. But then he realized that he had to take responsibility for his own performance. In many testing situations, *something* goes wrong. It may be different things on different days. Maybe you didn't sleep enough, or the room is too noisy. For the 60 minutes you take the test, put all of this out of your mind. Just focus on the test. The mark of the expert test taker is deciding that, for the time that the test is in progress, she will focus on the test and put other things out of her mind.

There is a wonderful scene in the film *For Love of the Game* based on the novel of the same name by Michael Shaara. The main character in the film is an aging professional baseball player in the last game of his career. At the beginning of the game, the director presents the world through the ballplayer's eyes and ears: fans jeering, opposing players taunting him, and the anonymous, indiscernible drone that comes with placing 40,000 people in an enclosed area. The cacophony is deafening, and the viewer wonders how anyone could focus with that sort of pandemonium.

But, as a professional, the main character is accustomed to the chaos. He whispers to himself, "clear the mechanism," and all of a sudden the noise disappears. Only silence remains. The main character has cleared his mind completely, and the only thing within his sphere of awareness is the task at hand: pitching a baseball game.

You, too, must learn to "clear the mechanism." During the hour of the *MAT*, shut off the droning of your personal life. The only things that matter are those 120 questions, and everything else is just background noise.

6. **Be motivated, regardless of the stakes.**

Several years ago, the undergraduates in the first author's department at the time (the Psychology Department at Yale) invited him to give a talk to a group of them. He was honored to have been asked to speak and showed up at the appointed time. Unfortunately, no one else showed up except the woman who had organized the talk. She was extremely apologetic and started to give him a number of possible explanations for why no one else showed up.

At first, the first author felt hurt, but then he started to laugh. He said that he was actually very grateful that only she had shown up. The reason was that he could expect (or, at least, hope) that any talk he ever gave in the future would have at least as good and probably a better turnout. He now would be able to motivate himself to give his best possible talk, if at least two people (the organizer plus one other person) showed up! If at least two people turned out, it would be better than the turnout that ill-fated day. And sure enough, whether he gets two people or two thousand, he gives it his best shot regardless of the stakes, remembering the time that only the organizer showed up.

Some of you will be taking the *Miller Analogies Test* for extremely high stakes. The test may play a pivotal role in your being admitted or not admitted to the graduate school of your choice, or it may determine whether or not you get financial aid. Others of you will be taking the test for lower stakes. Perhaps only schools you do not care so much about require this particular test, or perhaps you are not even sure you want to go to graduate school in the first place, so a low score will not bother you so much.

Remember the lesson from the speaking engagement, though. If it is worth your time to take the test, it is worth your time to give the test your best shot. You should prepare for the experience with whatever resources you can bring to bear. Too often, people sabotage themselves, telling themselves that something is not important. This way, if they do not do well on it, they do not feel so bad. Don't fall into self-sabotage. Give the *MAT* your best shot, regardless of the stakes. Successful people do nothing half-heartedly.

7. **Combat test anxiety with visualization and relaxation.** If you tend to be test anxious, there are steps you can take to help yourself combat your test anxiety. Spend some time each day imagining yourself in the actual testing situation, and try to relax while you visualize yourself actually taking the test.

If that image is too stressful, start with less threatening images and build up to the image of yourself taking the test. For example, you might first imagine yourself three weeks before the test, preparing for the test. That image should be less threatening. So try to relax. Then imagine yourself two weeks before, then one week before, then right at the test. In each case, try to relax as you construct your image.

This description is a simplification of a psychotherapeutic technique called *systematic desensitization*. If you find that this self-help technique does not enable you to relax, you might seriously consider going for a few sessions of therapy to a behavior therapist or a cognitive-behavioral therapist. These therapists can help you alleviate your anxiety.

There is a tenet within the ancient philosophy of Stoicism that is often quite useful when battling stress. It is known as "the premeditation of evils," and it has been used throughout history by many wise, powerful men, including the venerable Roman emperor Marcus Aurelius.

In the premeditation of evils, the concept is simple: *imagine the absolute, very worst that can possibly happen. Then notice that it really isn't all that bad.* For instance, imagine yourself failing miserably on this exam. What is the very worst that can happen—you can always take it again.

Would that really be so terrible?

Recognize that the *MAT* is important, but also recognize that doing poorly on it will never lead you to be hungry or homeless. Test anxiety, at its root, is merely a distortion of perspective.

8. **Eat something light before the test, avoiding large amounts of sugar.** Taking a standardized test consumes a great deal of your energy. The day of the test is not the day to fast or to skip breakfast. You need the energy you get from the meal. But don't eat a heavy meal right before a test. You want your energy directed toward the test, not toward digestion. Also, avoid large quantities of sugar. Sugar can give you an immediate high after you consume it, but often leads to a slump later. You cannot risk feeling the slump while you are taking the test.

9. **Go to the restroom before you start the *MAT*.** You also do not want to waste time getting up and going to the restroom—or needing to go! Make every effort to take care of your restroom needs before the test begins.

10. **Keep in mind that early items will tend to be easy while later items will be more difficult.** You should answer test items in the order that they are presented because they are in average order of difficulty. Thus, for the hypothetical "average" person, the items will be in exact order of difficulty. But because there really is no completely average person, each person will find the order of difficulty a bit different.

An important implication of the principle that items are in order of difficulty is that, if you find an early item to be very hard or a late item to be very easy, you may be misperceiving the point of the question. If you perceive an early item as very difficult, you may be reading things into the item that simply are not there. Ask yourself whether there might be some easier way to see the problem. If you see a later item as very easy, you may be failing to appreciate whatever it is that makes the item difficult, and you may choose a sucker response as your answer choice. Ask yourself whether you might be missing something important in the question. So keep in mind that early items ought to be, on average, relatively easy, and later items, on average, relatively difficult.

Consider two examples. Suppose the following analogy occurs relatively early in the test:

HIT : HIT :: TALK : (*a.* speak, *b.* lecture, *c.* talked, *d.* silent)

This analogy is a straightforward one but not a totally obvious one. At first glance, it might look like it is unbelievably simple, representing simply a repetition of a word. But it becomes obvious quickly that it does not involve merely a repetition, because none of the answer options is *talk*. It is not a synonym analogy either, because HIT is not a synonym for HIT, but, at first glance, the same word.

Option *c* should give the answer away. TALKED is the past tense of TALK, just as HIT is the past tense of HIT. That's all there is to the analogy. There is nothing more, nothing deep. Select option *c* and move on.

Now suppose the following analogy comes rather late in the test:

(*a.* France,   *b.* Russia,   *c.* Italy,   *d.* St. Helena) : NAPOLEON BONAPARTE :: ENGLAND : SIGMUND FREUD

The analogy at first appears to be straightforward. Napoleon was from France. But wait a minute. Sigmund Freud was not originally from England. He was from Austria. So the analogy is not about where a person was from, at least, not originally. The analogy requires you to know that Sigmund Freud, although he was born in Austria, died in England. Napoleon Bonaparte died on the island of St. Helena. The analogy, then, is quite difficult.

11. **Read every question completely.** Look at *all* the answer options presented for each question. Remember, distracters (wrong answers) are there, literally, to distract you. Sometimes, the first option (or the second or the third) may look good and you may be inclined to save yourself time by selecting it. *Don't do it.* The distracter may be a near miss. Consider an example:

PEN : INK :: PENCIL : (*a.* lead, *b.* eraser, *c.* paper, *d.* graphite)

A test taker in a hurry might quickly select option *a* because at first glance, it looks right. But in analogies, you are looking for the *best* answer, and you cannot know what the best answer is until you have read *all* the answer options. If you take the little additional time it requires to read *all* the options, you will discover that option *d* is graphite, which is a good competitor for being correct.

So which is the better option, "lead" or "graphite"? Well, in this case, ink is the substance contained inside the pen. The substance inside a pencil is graphite, not lead. The "lead" of a pencil is made of graphite. Thus, a pen uses (writes with) ink in the same way that a pencil uses (writes with) graphite, not lead. But if you do not read the whole test item, you may never get to choose the better answer.

12. **Read every question carefully.** You need to read every question not only completely, but carefully. Consider an example.

TERRIBLE : HORRIBLE :: INGENUOUS : (*a.* clever, *b.* sophisticated, *c.* naïve, *d.* foolish)

If you read this item carelessly, you may quickly choose *clever* as the correct answer, and end up getting it wrong. *Clever* would have been the best response had the third word in the stem of the analogy been INGENIOUS, but the word is INGENUOUS, not INGENIOUS. The best answer is thus the synonym for INGENUOUS, namely, NAÏVE. You need to read the words carefully.

Suppose you do not know what INGENUOUS means. In this case, you will have to guess. Use the process of elimination. If, at least, you read the question carefully, you will know that the word for which you need a synonym is *not* INGENIOUS, that *clever* probably is *not* the best answer, but rather, a distracter. At least you have eliminated one distracter and can choose from among the remaining three. It is also a good guess that *foolish* is wrong, because *foolish* is the opposite of *ingenious*; but we have now determined that the item most likely has nothing to do with being ingenious. Hence, your best bet is either option *b* or option *c*. As it turns out, option *c* is the best answer.

Here is another example:

FROWARD : (*a*. obedient, *b*. backward, *c*. disobedient, *d*. frontward) :: AHEAD : BEHIND

If read carelessly, the whole analogy appears to be about antonyms with respect to directions of movement. But that is not what the analogy is about. The first word is FROWARD, not FORWARD. And FROWARD means not easily controlled or contrary. The best answer is therefore *a*, because *obedient* is an antonym to FROWARD. Again, you must read each word carefully.

You may not know what FROWARD means. In this case, though, you can guess by using the process of elimination. Because you know that FROWARD is *not* FORWARD, it is a safe guess that you can eliminate the options pertaining to direction, namely, *b* and *d*. So *a* or *c* is probably the best answer. In fact, *a* is correct.

13. **Don't avoid questions just because they initially look difficult.** Sometimes, a question that looks difficult when you first glance at it proves not to be very hard at all. Therefore, before deciding to skip a question and come back to it, make sure that the question actually is difficult. Consider an example:

VENUS : BEAUTY :: PLUTO : (*a*. prosperity, *b*. underworld, *c*. war, *d*. hearth)

Maybe your first reaction is that you just don't remember all those Greek and Roman gods. But wait a minute. Look at the item. You may find that you remember a few of them, and the one you remember is that Pluto was supposed to be the god of the underworld.

14. **Watch out for reversals.** Remember that the direction of the relationship must be the same on both sides of the analogy. Do not trip yourself up by reversing directions. Consider an example:

METER : (*a*. millimeter, *b*. centimeter, *c*. decimeter, *d*. kilometer) :: YEAR : MILLENNIUM

It is very easy to trip yourself up on this analogy, because option *a*, *millimeter*, has the same initial letters, *mill*, as has the stem term MILLENNIUM. The option therefore sounds right if one is not sensitive to reversals. But a millennium is one thousand years. Because order counts, the second term must represent a thousand of the first term (METER), just as the fourth term (MILLENNIUM) represents a thousand of the third term (YEAR). The correct option thus must represent one thousand meters, not one-thousandth of a meter. The correct option therefore is *d*.

15. **Look for all valid relationships but only for valid relationships.** Remember that you can look for relationships either between the first and second and then the third and fourth terms, or between the first and third and then the second and fourth terms. All these relationships are *valid* for solving an analogy. But you *cannot* look for relationships between the first and fourth or between the second and third terms. These relationships are *invalid* for solving an analogy.

Consider the following analogy:

FOUR : 120/15 :: 32 : (*a*. 2^3, *b*. One hundred twenty-eight, *c*. Twenty-four, *d*. LXIV)

The basic analogy here is one of doubling. The second term is double the first and the correct option for the fourth term is double the third. Thus, removing differences of notation, 4 : 8 :: 32 : 64. But there is an option designed to trick test takers who might look for a relationship between the first and fourth or between the second and third terms. This option is *b*. The third term (32) is four times the second term (120/15), and option *b*, one hundred twenty-eight, is four times the third term (32). Note also that the second and third terms are in Arabic numerals, and that if one selects option *b* (One hundred twenty-eight) or even option *c* (Twenty-four), one will have the first and fourth as well as the second and third terms in the same system of notation. But these relations are irrelevant. The only relations that matter are between the first and second terms and the third and fourth terms, on the one hand, and the first and third terms and the second and fourth terms, on the other. The correct answer is *d*.

16. **Analyze item contents and relations carefully.** Remember that not all terms of the analogy have to be from the same content area. Do not be fooled by some associations just because they seem to be from the right content area. Also, analyze the relations carefully. Consider an example:

    ANNA KARENINA : LEO TOLSTOY :: (*a*. Scarlett O'Hara, *b*. Melanie Wilkes, *c*. Gone with the Wind, *d*. War and Peace) : MARGARET MITCHELL

    The analogy starts off with a name that is both the name of a character and the name of a book by Leo Tolstoy. At this point, one cannot tell whether the correct relation is about being a character in a book or about being the name of the book. The second half of the analogy clarifies the issue. The options contain two names of characters that are from *Gone with the Wind*, as well as the title of the book by Margaret Mitchell. Because options *a* and *b* cannot both be correct, the analogy must be about titles of books, so the correct option is *c, Gone with the Wind*.

    This analogy can be confusing. First, Scarlett O'Hara is so highly associated with *Gone with the Wind* that she can quickly appear to provide an attractive answer option. Moreover, it is quite possible that the correct relationship is one of characters in a novel. But the appearance of the name Melanie Wilkes, who is less closely associated with the novel, renders Scarlett O'Hara a less plausible option. The analogy thus appears to be about book titles, not about characters. Unless one carefully considers both the contents and the relations in the analogy, however, it is easy to get the analogy wrong.

17. **Examine parts of speech.** Remember that many words can serve as multiple parts of speech, and that you need to check the various meanings of a word to ensure that you are using the word in its proper meaning and part of speech. Check that parts of speech match properly. An option is wrong if it does not correctly match the needed part of speech, even though the option may be otherwise plausible. Consider an example:

    WAG : (*a*. tail, *b*. rattle, *c*. roll, *d*. joker) :: HARM : INJURE

    This is quite a difficult analogy that easily confuses the test taker. The most frequent use of the term WAG is as a verb, and the second half of the analogy contains two verbs, reinforcing the notion that, apparently, the entire analogy involves verbs. Because HARM and INJURE are synonyms, the relation must be one of synonymy. But the problem is that neither *rattle* nor *roll* is a good synonym for WAG. Both are somewhat related, but neither really comes anywhere close to being a synonym. So there is no option that fits WAG as a verb. The test taker must realize that WAG is being used as a noun and therefore that the synonym must also be a noun. A WAG is a joker.

18. **Be systematic.** Try to be systematic in selecting the correct option. Use word association only if all else fails.

Consider an example:

LIBERATE : FREEDOM :: LIAISE : (*a.* connection, *b.* captivity, *c.* limit, *d.* destine)

This analogy is difficult in part because many test takers will never have used or perhaps even seen the word LIAISE. It is an uncommon word, used primarily in Great Britain, and hence one can be forgiven for not knowing it. But you can be systematic and use your prior knowledge to try to solve the analogy.

First of all, LIAISE sounds like a verb, like LIBERATE. Because FREEDOM, the pair of LIBERATE, is a noun, you will want an option that is a noun. That removes option *d*, which is a verb. Because you know that liberating an individual or groups establishes a kind of freedom for that individual or group, you want to figure out what you would establish when you liaise. You probably know that a liaison is a person who establishes a connection. Therefore your best bet is to infer that to liaise is to establish a liaison, or a connection. You choose option *a*, which is the correct option.

19. **Pace yourself.** Because you will have 60 minutes to answer 120 items, you should average no more than 30 seconds per analogy. Some items will take more time, some less. Do not get bogged down on a few difficult items. This can be a tremendous waste of time. If an answer just does not come to you, come back to the particular question when (or if) you have time.

For example, suppose you come across the analogy:

K : POTASSIUM :: (*a.* So, *b.* Sd, *c.* Na, *d.* Hg) : SODIUM

You took chemistry and you are pretty sure that, if you really set your mind to it, you can retrieve the chemical symbol for sodium. The problem is that it just isn't coming to you. So you stare at the item and stare some more, and try to think of everything you learned in chemistry, hoping that the association will come to you.

You're wasting your time. You might wish to pick whatever answer looks the best to you, flag the item, and move on. You are much better off going on to other items, and coming back to this one if you have time. You could stare at the item for five minutes, and still not remember that the chemical symbol for sodium is Na.

20. **Use all the time you are allotted.** Never leave the test early. If you have time at the end of the test, review your answers, particularly to questions that you found to be difficult.

21. **Forget about other problems in your life.** If, while you are taking the test, you start thinking about anything but the test (e.g., a misunderstanding with a friend or a money problem), STOP! You can think about these other things later. Give the test 100% concentration.

22. **Answer every question.** If you have only a couple of minutes left and have not reached questions near the end, then fill in answers to these items anyway. If you left any items unanswered that you already looked at, fill in answers to those items too. There is no penalty for incorrect answers, and by leaving items unanswered you are wasting possible points.

23. **Write down the number of the items you need to go back to.** You may not be able to figure out the correct solution to every item right away. Remember you have only 30 seconds for each item. Move on to work on other items, but write down the items you think are difficult so you can return to them once you have finished the test.

24. **Don't panic.** If you find you don't know the answer to the first question, or to the second, or to the third, don't worry. Although items are arranged in order of difficulty, this ordering is of *average* difficulty. What is difficult for one person may be easy for another, and vice versa.

The test is tough to begin with, so you can expect to find questions you can't answer scattered throughout the test.

25. **Be self-confident.** Even if you're a notoriously poor test taker, after working through this book, you will have done pretty much all you can to ensure that you perform up to your full potential. That's the most you can ask of yourself.

26. **If you don't do as well as you had hoped, retake the test.** People typically do substantially better the second time they take a test. These "practice effects" are particularly notable on the *Miller Analogies Test*. Thus if things do not go as you had hoped, try again. Chances are you will do better the second time around.

27. **Remember that the test score is only one factor considered in admissions and financial aid decisions.** Decisions about admissions and financial aid are almost always based on many factors. Thus, you should not believe that your whole future will hinge on how you do on the *MAT*. After making your best effort, keep in mind that in most cases the test score is not the decisive factor in admissions and financial aid decisions.

28. **Don't confuse test scores with measures of intelligence.** Tests such as the *Miller Analogies Test* measure only a part—and arguably a relatively small part—of intelligence. These tests do not measure creative abilities or common-sense abilities, for example. These test scores account for only a relatively small proportion of the sources of individual differences that determine who succeeds in life (Gardner, 1983, 1999; Sternberg, 1997, 2000). Indeed, these tests account for only about 10% of the variation among individuals in their success. If you do well on the *MAT*, congratulations. If you don't, remember that there is much more to intelligence than what this or other similar tests measure.

29. **If you bought this book, then you have the right attitude toward life.** If you bought this book, then your attitude toward life is that you can do better if you work at it. Ultimately, that will probably count for a lot more than a test score. Albert Bandura (1997) has shown that one of the best predictors of success in life is a sense of *self-efficacy*, the belief that one can do what one needs to get done. Your buying this book shows that you believe that you can do better with hard work. And that is the attitude that will help you succeed in life.

30. **Practice with purpose.** The common perception is that taking practice tests is the best way to study. There is a good amount of truth to that maxim, which is why we have placed such a focus on practice tests in this book and even online. However, the statement "you must take practice tests" is not a comprehensive assessment of the process; merely completing test after test is of no benefit to you if you do not take the time to *review* each completed test and diagnose the types of errors that you are commonly making. Take the time to thoroughly examine each missed question, closely analyzing the structure and content of the analogy, while also dissecting the flaw in your thinking. Incorrect answers are the single greatest didactic tool for the test taker, because the mistakes present opportunities to recognize a weakness and correct that weakness. A musician can play the same song hour after hour, day after day, and never improve if she repeats the same error time after time: recitation has value, but only insofar as it promotes comfort with the process. True improvement requires an additional commitment to diligence.

References to Helpful Hints

Bandura, A. *Self-efficacy: The Exercise of Control.* New York: W. H. Freeman and Company, 1997.

Dweck, C. S. *Self-theories: Their Role in Motivation, Personality, and Development.* Philadelphia: Psychology Press, 1999.

Gardner, H. *Frames of Mind: The Theory of Multiple Intelligences.* New York: Basic, 1983.

Gardner, H. *Intelligence Reframed: Multiple Intelligences for the 21st Century.* New York: Basicbooks, 1999.

Grotzer, T. A., and D. A. Perkins. Teaching of intelligence: A performance conception. In R. J. Sternberg (Ed.), *Handbook of Intelligence* (pp. 492–515). New York: Cambridge University Press, 2000.

Karkee, T., D. Kim, and K. Fatica. *Comparability study of online and paper and pencil tests using modified internally and externally matched criteria.* Paper presented at the annual meeting of the American Educational Research Association, Denver, CO, April 2010.

Langer, E. J. *Mindfulness.* New York: Addison-Wesley, 1989.

Langer, E. J. *The Power of Mindful Learning.* Needham Heights, MA: Addison-Wesley, 1997.

Perkins, D. N., and T. A. Grotzer. Teaching intelligence. *American Psychologist*, Vol. 52, 1125–1133, 1997.

Ramey, C. T. Abecedarian Project. In R. J. Sternberg (Ed.), *Encyclopedia of Human Intelligence* (Vol. 1, pp. 1–2). New York: Macmillan, 1994.

Rotter, J. B. Internal versus external control of reinforcement: A case history of a variable. *American Psychologist*, Vol. 45, 489–493, 1990.

Sternberg, R. J. *Successful Intelligence.* New York: Plume, 1997.

Sternberg, R. J. Successful intelligence: A unified view of giftedness. In C. F. M. van Lieshout & P. G. Heymans (Ed.), *Developing Talent, Across the Life Span* (pp. 43–65). Hove, UK: Psychology Press, 2000.

Tsai, T., and C. D. Shin. A score compatibility study for the NBDHE: Paper-pencil versus computer versions. *Evaluation and the Health Professions* (published online before print; doi: 10.1177/0163278712445203), 2012.

Wang, S., H. Jiao, M. J. Young, T. Brooks, and J. Olson. Comparability of computer-based and paper-and-pencil testing in K-12 Reading Assessments: A meta-analysis of testing mode effects. *Educational and Psychological Measurement*, Vol. 68(1), 5–24, 2008.

THE 12 BIGGEST MISTAKES TEST TAKERS MAKE

1. **Believing that test scores are the measure of a man or woman.** All societies share certain "conventional wisdom." Some of it is true; some of it is not. For example, in 1787, a "three-fifths compromise" was enacted that, for determining political representation in the House of Representatives, would count each slave as three-fifths of a person. This was silly, and yet it was actually written into law. Societies do things at times that later seem odd. Our society believes, properly, we think, that tests have a useful role in high-stakes educational decisions, but some people start to view tests as measuring the worth of a person. Your worth as a person is *not* determined by your test scores. Many people with lower test scores go on to do great things. Some with higher test scores go on to do little.

2. **Believing the hype that the tests measure all they are supposed to measure.** People are either analytical thinkers or not analytical thinkers. And can't someone be a good analytical thinker without having the vocabulary and general information to do well on this particular test? Certainly. And how about those for whom English is a second language? Our society hypes various products, including tests. Don't get sucked in. No test is perfect. No test identifies analytical or any other kinds of thinkers in a foolproof way. The test is a means

to help you get into graduate school or to help you get a scholarship or fellowship. It's not a whole lot more than that.

3. **Believing that test scores cannot be improved.** Many students believe the statements that test publishers sometimes make that using books or taking courses to improve scores really cannot make much of a difference in test scores. Not so. Test-taking is a learnable skill, just as is riding a bicycle or using a word-processing program on a computer. Almost every skill is learnable and modifiable. Test-taking is no exception. At the same time, it is better to expect reasonable gains than unreasonable ones. If your goal is to increase your score 10 or 15 points out of 100, that is quite reasonable, and you may attain this goal. If your goal is to increase your score 30 or 40 points, for most people, that will not be a realistic goal.

4. **Being overconfident or underconfident.** People who are overconfident set themselves up for a fall. They do not take the challenge of the test seriously enough, thinking that without hard work and preparation they will ace the test. Often, they end up being disappointed. People who are underconfident often choke when they take this test or any other. They become so nervous that they cannot perform at their optimum level. So they create for themselves a self-fulfilling prophecy.

   You must find the right balance between adrenaline and panic. Much like a runner who can run more quickly with an adrenaline boost, you can achieve a higher level of mental clarity with a touch of nervousness.

   However, too much adrenaline is crippling. A runner's legs will fill with lactic acid, and he/she will become paralyzed by the hormone. A test taker will be equally paralyzed by too much adrenaline, albeit mentally instead of physically. The questions will be indecipherable, your thought processes will be incoherent, and the thumping heart within your chest will prevent you from doing your best on the *MAT*.

   Balance is the key to life. Find your personal equilibrium and use your body's natural stress reactions in a way that is advantageous instead of injurious.

5. **Taking the test close to the deadline for which the score must be submitted.** All tests have a standard error of measurement. That means that sometimes you will do better than you could have expected to do, and other times you will do worse. If you do worse, you can always retake the test. But you cut off your chance of doing that if you take the test too close to when the score is due. In that case, if you get a score that is lower than you had hoped for, you do not allow yourself the option to take it again. Don't wait until the last minute. Take the test early so that if you need to take it again, you will have time.

6. **Drinking a lot of caffeine before taking the test.** Research shows that caffeine can help mental performance. So a little coffee or tea before the test may actually help your score. But do not consume too much caffeine. First, it may make you jumpy and actually hurt your performance. Second, it may leave you wanting to go to the bathroom, and you will not be permitted to go during the testing session. Third, if you are not used to it, you may have side effects such as feeling restless, irritable, or trembling of the hands—the last things you need when you take a test.

7. **Cramming at the last moment.** Just don't. Research shows that last-minute cramming is not helpful and can actually hurt you. Don't study in the last 24 hours before the test. Just get plenty of rest and go to the test refreshed. You need to have a study plan that starts early and not at the last moment.

8. **Spending too much time on hard items.** If you get stuck on an item, move on. You then can later return to it. There are 120 items to be completed in 60 minutes. That is two per minute. You cannot afford to waste lots of time on hard items.

9. **Not reading items carefully.** Don't waste points on sloppy reading of items. Many people, on later finding out the answers to a test, feel like kicking themselves for getting items wrong for which they knew the answer, because they did not read the item carefully. You cannot afford to waste points on sloppy reading of items.

10. **Leaving items blank.** There is *no* penalty for wrong answers. Do *not* leave any blanks. When time is soon going to be up, make sure you answer every question, even if you answer at random.

11. **Not budgeting time.** You have 30 seconds per item. That's it. So you have to keep budgeting your time so as not to waste time. Don't let yourself get behind. If an item is too hard, move on. Near the end, fill in an answer at random if you cannot get back to it.

12. **Eliminating answer options that are correct.** Distracters—wrong answers—are chosen on the Miller Analogies Test to be attractive. That means it may be tempting to eliminate as incorrect an answer option that is actually correct. Unless you are confident that an option is wrong, do not eliminate it. If you cannot eliminate even one answer option *for sure,* guess at random. You will have a 1 out of 4 chance of getting the item right.

References

www.MillerAnalogies.com

http://harcourtassessment.com/haiweb/Cultures/en-US/dotCom/milleranalogies.com.htm

ADVICE ON PREPARING FOR THE *MAT*

That the *MAT* is not just a test of your reasoning abilities is probably evident to you from doing the Pretest in this book. The *MAT* also assesses your vocabulary and your knowledge of general information, as well as specific information in diverse areas. A person whose native language is not English and whose culture is not mainstream will find the *MAT* extremely difficult, even if the aid of a dictionary were allowed. The level of vocabulary on the test is high; in addition, the definition used for a particular word is not always the most salient or obvious.

In using this book, you are strongly advised to keep a notebook of words you don't know along with their definitions. Use a dictionary to look up words you're not sure of. Study these words regularly, and use them as much as possible, in order to add them to your vocabulary. Also study the vocabulary given in this book as well as the words in the practice tests. The vocabulary on pages 75–92 contains words often used in graduate-level tests and, in addition, provides you with useful synonyms and antonyms.

Five other techniques are also useful in learning new words:

1. Use mnemonics as much as possible, visualizing the words and their meanings as vividly as you can.
2. Group together similar words to study. Also, put together words with similar roots and related meanings.
3. Make flashcards with words on one side, definitions on the other. Study the cards during any free time you have.
4. Whenever possible, study the words with their antonyms and synonyms.
5. Read a good newspaper regularly, such as *The New York Times* or *The Wall Street Journal,* to reinforce the vocabulary you have learned.

Not all these techniques work for everyone; some are better than others for different people. But the benefits of increasing your vocabulary are enormous—you will raise not only your *MAT* scores but other test scores as well.

Fighting Test Anxiety

Almost everyone is familiar with test anxiety. You walk into the examination room and your heart starts beating rapidly, you start sweating, and you start thinking about how poorly you are about to do on the exam. This is detrimental to your test-taking. You may know all there is to know, but if you go into the exam overly anxious, you will not do as well as you should. It is normal for a test taker to have a mild amount of anxiety; it's what gets a person through an exam. However, too much anxiety can have a crippling effect when a person focuses on negative thoughts and ignores positive ones.

Causes of an individual's test anxiety may be one's exaggeration of the consequences of the exam, the demands one has placed on oneself, or the evaluation of oneself in terms of one's performance on the exam. The most effective way to handle test anxiety is with professional help (e.g., a clinical psychologist). Psychologists have found several techniques, most of which are based on relaxation, to be effective in battling test anxiety. One such technique is systematic desensitization.

Systematic desensitization teaches an individual to be able to relax in the presence of whatever causes the anxiety—in this case, an exam. The individual seeking this therapy is initially taught to relax while imagining anxiety-producing scenarios. The scenarios are graded. Some produce mild amounts of anxiety, whereas others produce extreme amounts of anxiety. Individuals work their way up from the least to the most anxiety-producing scenarios. The client begins by imagining the scenario that produces the least amount of anxiety while relaxing, and if that does not cause anxiety, the person imagines the next scenario on the scale. If it does cause anxiety, the client repeats imagining scenarios until he or she can do so without experiencing anxiety. The client gradually works through all of the scenarios until all of them can be imagined without a great deal of anxiety. It typically takes weeks or even a few months to get through all of them.

For example, a woman seeking treatment for test anxiety may first be told to imagine herself driving to the test center. If she does not feel anxiety while imagining this, she may then imagine getting out of the car, then imagine walking to the building, then imagine walking to the examination room, etc. She will go through this progression of scenarios until she can imagine herself picking up her pencil and taking the test without too much anxiety. At this point, her anxiety about taking tests should diminish.

Although this process works best when it is done with professional help over many sessions, you can learn from it. Its greatest lessons are that you should acquaint yourself with the testing process, and you should relax before an exam, not just a few minutes before sitting down to take it, but weeks in advance. Imagine all the details about the examination day that you can think of. For example, picture how you will get ready to go to the testing center, how you will get there, and how you will get through the paperwork. You should also take the practice tests in this book very seriously; they are very comparable to the real *MAT*. Take the practice tests under real test-taking conditions. For instance, find a quiet place, do not allow any distractions, set a time limit, and pretend you are in the examination room taking the real test. If you take all the practice tests in this book in that manner, when it comes time to take the real one, you will feel more comfortable with the test and the procedures.

Other recommendations that you may want to consider are the following:

1. Do not wait until the last minute to study. If you wait, you will get flustered by all the studying there is to do, and you will not be able to study as effectively. Study with a positive attitude. Of course there will be information you don't know—no one knows everything—but learn as much as you can, and remember that there is a lot that you do know already.

2. As you go to the test center, keep a positive attitude. Do not panic. You have done all the preparing you could do. Remember, the *MAT* is only one part of your entire portfolio. You have accomplished a great deal to get to where you are today, including higher education or

employment. Those taking your *MAT* score into consideration will also take into consideration everything else you have accomplished. Think ahead to after the exam. When the exam is over, and it is no longer looming over your head, you will still be the same person. This exam will not drastically change your life.

3. When you take the *MAT*, try to put aside other problems in your life. Give this exam your full concentration. Continue to relax. Have self-confidence. Answering a question you know should fuel your confidence. When you come to a question you don't know, as everyone does, do not let it discourage you. Make an educated guess and then move on.

IMPROVING YOUR INTELLECTUAL SKILLS

Recommended Reading

Most people read this book in order to attain as high a score as possible on the *Miller Analogies Test*. Many readers are also interested in improving the general level of their intellectual skills. Whereas the material in this book is aimed primarily at raising your score on the *MAT*, and only secondarily at improving your general intellectual skills, other books with the primary aim of improving your general intellectual skills are available. Although such books are not intended to improve your score on any one particular test, sharpening your intellectual skills can help you on a large variety of tests, including the *MAT*.

> **Successful Intelligence**
> By Robert J. Sternberg, published as a paperback by Plume, 1997. This book contains further ideas about mind improvement based on the author's triarchic theory of human intelligence.

Also, you will find it profitable to read high-quality literature. There are often questions about literary classics that require a knowledge of specific books. If you have *read* the books the test asks you about, then you will be at a tremendous advantage on those questions.

Moreover, high-quality literature (especially that from previous centuries) utilizes vocabulary that one normally doesn't encounter during daily life. Literature is a wonderful way to expand your familiarity with the difficult, obscure words that will appear on the *MAT*.

Other Test Preparation Books

Numerous other books containing problems of various kinds, including other test preparation books, can be quite helpful in improving general thinking skills. Thus, for the person whose goal is general improvement in thinking, Barron's other test preparation books, such as *GRE, 22nd Edition*, are recommended as supplements as well as taking advantage of the online exams provided by Barron's (*www.barronsbooks.com/TP/MAT*).

Kinds of Analogies Found on the *Miller Analogies Test*

3

- ■ Content of *MAT* analogies
- ■ Practice in recognizing content areas
- ■ Relationships used in *MAT* analogies
- ■ Practice in using and recognizing relationships
- ■ Distribution of categories

CONTENT OF *MAT* ANALOGIES

Success on the *MAT* requires familiarity with a broad range of subjects. There are different ways of classifying the subject areas. The following list of the general content areas covered by the *MAT* shows just one way to group these areas conveniently.

I Vocabulary

II General Information

III Humanities

- A. History
- B. Literature
- C. Mythology
- D. Philosophy
- E. Religion
- F. Art
- G. Music
- H. Grammar

IV Social Sciences

- A. Psychology
- B. Sociology
- C. Economics
- D. Linguistics
- E. Anthropology
- F. Political Science

V Natural Sciences

    A. Biology

    B. Physics

    C. Chemistry

VI Mathematics

VII Nonsemantic

The following examples will give you an idea of what each area covers:

1. VOCABULARY

STRIDENT : (*a.* wide, *b.* shrill, *c.* confident, *d.* rigid) :: TURBULENT : AGITATED

Answer: (**b**). This analogy deals with similarities in meaning. *Strident* and *shrill* are synonyms, as are *turbulent* and *agitated*.

2. GENERAL INFORMATION

JAPAN : ORIENT :: FRANCE : (*a.* Europe, *b.* Continent, *c.* Paris, *d.* Occident)

Answer: (**d**). This analogy concerns locations of countries. Japan is a country in the Orient. France is a country in the Occident.

3. HISTORY

(*a.* T. Roosevelt, *b.* F. Roosevelt, *c.* Wilson, *d.* Eisenhower) : SQUARE DEAL :: TRUMAN : FAIR DEAL

Answer: (**a**). This analogy involves presidential programs. T. Roosevelt introduced what he called the Square Deal. Truman introduced what he called the Fair Deal.

4. LITERATURE

NAPOLEON : FRENCH ARMY :: MAJOR BARBARA : (*a.* Salvation Army, *b.* English Army, *c.* American Army, *d.* Children's Army)

Answer: (**a**). This analogy is about army affiliations of officers. Napoleon was an officer in the French Army. Major Barbara, in Shaw's play by the same name, was an officer in the Salvation Army.

5. MYTHOLOGY

ZEUS : HERA :: JUPITER : (*a.* Venus, *b.* Minerva, *c.* Juno, *d.* Diana)

Answer: (**c**). This analogy requires recognition of two different names for the same god. Zeus was the Greek name and Jupiter the Roman name for the king of the gods. Hera was the Greek name and Juno the Roman name for his wife.

6. PHILOSOPHY

LOCKE : INDUCTION :: (*a.* Berkeley, *b.* Bentham, *c.* Hume, *d.* Spinoza) : DEDUCTION

Answer: (**d**). This analogy deals with methodologies used by major philosophers. Locke was an empiricist philosopher and hence his mode of reasoning was primarily inductive.

Spinoza, a rationalist philosopher, relied primarily on deductive reasoning in order to draw conclusions.

7. RELIGION

ADAM : (*a.* Eve, *b.* Eden, *c.* Heaven, *d.* Israel) :: OEDIPUS : THEBES

Answer: (**b**). This analogy concerns places from which people were expelled. Adam was expelled from Eden. Oedipus was expelled from Thebes.

8. ART

RENOIR : IMPRESSIONIST :: (*a.* Monet, *b.* Bosch, *c.* Van Gogh, *d.* Munch) : EXPRESSIONIST

Answer: (**d**). This analogy involves schools of famous painters. Renoir was an impressionist painter. Munch was an expressionist painter.

9. MUSIC

(*a.* coda, *b.* aria, *c.* overture, *d.* coloratura) : OPERA :: PREFACE : BOOK

Answer: (**c**). This analogy is about introductions to works of art. An overture introduces an opera. A preface introduces a book.

10. SOCIAL SCIENCES

FREUD : OEDIPUS COMPLEX :: (*a.* Jung, *b.* Horney, *c.* Adler, *d.* Allport) : INFERIORITY COMPLEX

Answer: (**c**). This analogy requires recognition of originators of terms describing psychological complexes. Freud coined the expression *Oedipus complex*; Adler coined the expression *inferiority complex*.

11. BIOLOGY

(*a.* stomach, *b.* throat, *c.* lung, *d.* gullet) : PHARYNX :: WINDPIPE : TRACHEA

Answer: (**b**). This analogy deals with organs in the body. The pharynx is the throat. The trachea is the windpipe.

12. PHYSICS

MECHANICAL ADVANTAGE : RESISTANCE :: (*a.* distance, *b.* rate, *c.* effort, *d.* seconds) : TIME

Answer: (**a**). This analogy concerns variation between physical concepts. Mechanical advantage varies directly with resistance (when effort is held constant). Distance varies directly with time (when rate is held constant).

13. CHEMISTRY

HCl : hydrochloric :: H_2SO_4 : (*a.* hydrofluoric, *b.* hydrocyanic, *c.* sulfuric, *d.* nitric)

Answer: (**c**). This analogy involves chemical symbols for acids. HCl is the chemical formula for hydrochloric acid. H_2SO_4 is the chemical formula for sulfuric acid.

14. MATHEMATICS

$2^1 : 2^3 :: 1^2 :$ (*a.* 0, *b.* 1, *c.* 2, *d.* 4)

Answer: (**d**). This analogy is about equivalent ratios. 2 is to 8 as 1 is to 4.

15. NONSEMANTIC

DEER : DEER :: OX : (*a.* oxen, *b.* oxes, *c.* oxae, *d.* oxena)

Answer: (**a**). This analogy requires recognition of plurals of words. The plural of deer is deer. The plural of ox is oxen.

> ## NOTE
>
> One thing to keep in mind while solving analogies is that the two relationships that comprise the analogy need not come from the same content domain. In the analogy presented as an example of literary content, NAPOLEON : FRENCH ARMY :: MAJOR BARBARA : SALVATION ARMY, the left side of the analogy is taken from the content domain of history, while the right side, the one requiring selection of a correct answer, comes from the content category of literature.

Directions: The following practice quiz consists of 30 pairs of words. Your task is to write next to each pair of words the relationship between the words and then to classify the pair of words in terms of the 15 content categories just described. The purpose of the quiz is to get you thinking actively about the different content areas from which *MAT* items are drawn. There are two examples of each content area. Answer Explanations are given at the end of the quiz.

Word Pair	*Relationship*	*Content Area*
1. PIAGET : STAGE THEORY	_____	_____
2. NEON : INERT	_____	_____
3. MARS : WAR	_____	_____
4. DESCARTES : RATIONALIST	_____	_____
5. ANDES : SOUTH AMERICA	_____	_____
6. RESISTANCE : OHMS	_____	_____
7. SKIN : ORGAN	_____	_____
8. MITIGATE : ASSUAGE	_____	_____
9. EROICA : BEETHOVEN	_____	_____
10. SAWYER : FINN	_____	_____
11. PETER : THE GREAT	_____	_____
12. KORAN : ISLAM	_____	_____
13. IMAGINARY : COMPLEX	_____	_____
14. PERSONA : PERSONAE	_____	_____
15. MUNCH : EXPRESSIONIST	_____	_____
16. LINCOLN : REPUBLICAN	_____	_____
17. STEP : PETS	_____	_____
18. PATON : SOUTH AFRICA	_____	_____

19. DURKHEIM : SUICIDE _____ _____

20. TRENCHANT : INCISIVE _____ _____

21. AORTA : ARTERY _____ _____

22. MICHELANGELO : DAVID _____ _____

23. TREBLE : BASS _____ _____

24. BASE : EXPONENT _____ _____

25. HOLLANDAISE : CREAM _____ _____

26. MONK : MONASTERY _____ _____

27. CAMUS : EXISTENTIALIST _____ _____

28. FORCE : MASS × ACCELERATION _____ _____

29. PLUTO : HADES _____ _____

30. WATER : HYDROGEN _____ _____

Answer Explanations

Relationship	*Content Area*
1. Piaget's theory of intellectual development is a stage theory.	SOCIAL SCIENCES (10)
2. Neon is an inert gas.	CHEMISTRY (13)
3. Mars was the god of war in Roman mythology.	MYTHOLOGY (5)
4. Descartes was a rationalist philosopher.	PHILOSOPHY (6)
5. The Andes Mountains are in South America.	GENERAL INFORMATION (2)
6. Resistance is measured in ohms.	PHYSICS (12)
7. The skin is an organ.	BIOLOGY (11)
8. *Mitigate* and *assuage* are synonyms (meaning "to make less severe or to improve").	VOCABULARY (1)
9. Beethoven wrote the Eroica Symphony.	MUSIC (9)
10. Tom Sawyer and Huck Finn are characters in novels by Mark Twain (named after these characters).	LITERATURE (4)
11. Peter the Great was a Russian czar.	HISTORY (3)
12. The Koran is the holy book of Islam.	RELIGION (7)
13. *Imaginary* and *complex* are two kinds of numbers.	MATHEMATICS (14)
14. *Personae* is the plural form of *persona*.	NONSEMANTIC (15)
15. Munch was an expressionist painter.	ART (8)
16. President Lincoln was a member of the Republican Party.	HISTORY (3)
17. *Pets* is *Step* spelled backwards.	NONSEMANTIC (15)
18. Paton is a famous South African author.	LITERATURE (4)

Relationship	Content Area
19. Durkheim is the author of *Suicide*.	SOCIAL SCIENCES (10)
20. *Trenchant* and *incisive*, both of which mean "penetrating," are synonyms.	VOCABULARY (1)
21. The aorta is an artery in the body.	BIOLOGY (11)
22. Michelangelo was the sculptor of *David*. (Alternatively, David was an artist, as was Michelangelo.)	ART (8)
23. Treble and bass are musical clefs.	MUSIC (9)
24. In the numerical expression x^y, x is the base and y the exponent.	MATHEMATICS (14)
25. Hollandaise is a cream sauce.	GENERAL INFORMATION (2)
26. A monk lives in a monastery.	RELIGION (7)
27. Camus was an existentialist philosopher.	PHILOSOPHY (6)
28. In physics, force = mass × acceleration.	PHYSICS (12)
29. Pluto (the Roman name) and Hades (the Greek name) were the gods of the underworld.	MYTHOLOGY (5)
30. Water is composed in part of hydrogen gas.	CHEMISTRY (13)

NOTE

In some cases, more than one content area could be justified. For example, Camus was also an existentialist writer, and hence item 27 could have been classified under LITERATURE. Also, multiple relationships are sometimes possible, meaning that you may have discovered a relationship other than or in addition to the one mentioned in each item.

RELATIONSHIPS USED IN *MAT* ANALOGIES

Analogical reasoning requires you to recognize many possible relationships between pairs of concepts. Unfortunately, classification of relationships is not nearly so straightforward as classification of content areas. There have been numerous attempts to classify the possible ways in which words can be related, but none of the systems is completely successful. To quote George Miller, "Words are related to one another in an amazing number of ways."

The classification system outlined on the following pages, similar to one proposed by George Miller, comprises 14 specific categories, which are organized into 7 general groups. Such a scheme, which makes use of a relatively small number of categories, strikes a balance between being too general and being too particular in describing a relationship.

Pearson recently reclassified their preferred nomenclature for content and relationships with the current denominations outlined in the Item Classification Chart below. It is important to note, however, that focusing on content and relationships can be a time-consuming exercise bordering on futility. We will cover the types of analogies contained within so that you might have passing familiarity with the concepts. The taxonomy is an often arbitrary concept used by Pearson to provide some semblance of repetition in structure. Unless your goal is to write your own practice tests, it is not an economically prudent use of your time to learn how to properly classify each analogy. Your task is simply to get the questions right; there are no bonus points for recognizing that the analogy is a "humanities classification" question, for instance. This is why you will see only the classifications of the analogies being tested on the Pretest pages.

Table 1. Relationship Types and Content Areas

Relationship	Description
Semantic	Meaning, definition, synonym, antonym, contrast, degree, intensity, word parts, expressions
Classification	Hierarchy, classification, category, membership, whole/part
Association	Object/characteristic, order, sequence, transformation, agent/object, creator/creation, function, purpose
Logical/Mathematical	Mathematical equivalence, letter or sound patterns
Content Area	**Description**
General	Culture, work, business, life experience
Humanities	History, fine art, literature, philosophy, religion, music
Mathematics	Numerical, quantitative, computation
Language	Vocabulary, word meanings, grammar, usage
Natural Sciences	Biology, chemistry, physics, ecology, astronomy
Social Sciences	Psychology, sociology, economics, political science, anthropology

I Similarity/Contrast

1. Similarity
2. Contrast

II Description

3. Predication

III Class

4. Subordination

5. Coordination

6. Superordination

IV Completion

7. Completion

V Part/Whole

8. Part–Whole

9. Whole–Part

VI Equality/Negation

10. Equality (equivalence)

11. Negation

VII Nonsemantic

12. Sound Relationships

13. Letter Relationships

14. Word Relationships

The following examples will give you an idea of what each relationship means.

1. SIMILARITY

Relationships are between synonyms or words that are nearly the same in meaning.

HAPPY : GLAD :: DULL : (*a.* razor, *b.* blunt, *c.* sharp, *d.* bright)
Answer: (**b**). This analogy deals with similarities in meaning. *Happy* and *glad* are synonyms, as are *dull* and *blunt*.

2. CONTRAST

Relationships are between antonyms or words that are nearly the opposite in meaning.

WET : (*a.* dry, *b.* moist, *c.* towel, *d.* water) :: STOP : GO
Answer: (**a**). This analogy concerns contrasts in meaning. *Wet* and *dry* are opposites, as are *stop* and *go*.

3. PREDICATION

Terms of the analogy are related by a verb or verb relationship. One term *describes* something about the other term. Most analogies fall in this category. Some of the variations are as follows: A is caused by B; A makes B; A rides on B; A eats B; A is a source of B; A induces B; A studies B; A is made of B; A uses B.

AUTOMOBILE : ROAD :: TRAIN : (*a.* conductor, *b.* track, *c.* engine, *d.* ticket)
Answer (**b**). This analogy involves surfaces on which vehicles travel. An automobile travels on a road, and a train travels on a track. The implicit verb is *travels*.

DOG : BARK :: (*a.* cat, *b.* giraffe, *c.* frog, *d.* rabbit) : MEOW
Answer: (**a**). This analogy involves sounds made by animals. A dog barks. A cat meows.

4. SUBORDINATION

Relationships are those in which an object A is a type of B.

(*a.* lizard, *b.* toad, *c.* sponge, *d.* trout) : FISH :: FROG : AMPHIBIAN
Answer: (**d**). This analogy is about types of animals. A trout is a type of fish and a frog is a type of amphibian.

5. COORDINATION

The first two terms are one type of thing and the last two are another.

LETTUCE : CABBAGE :: PEAR : (*a.* fruit, *b.* peach, *c.* radish, *d.* carrot)
Answer: (**b**). This analogy requires recognition of members of classes. Lettuce and cabbage are both types of vegetables, while a pear and a peach are both types of fruit.

6. SUPERORDINATION

Relationships are those in which A is a category into which B falls.

BIRD : ROBIN :: MOLLUSK : (*a.* fish, *b.* water, *c.* sponge, *d.* snail)
Answer: (**d**). This analogy deals with category membership. Bird is a category that includes the robin; mollusk is a category that includes the snail.

7. COMPLETION

Each term of this kind of analogy is part of a complete expression.

SAN : FRANCISCO :: (*a.* San, *b.* Santa, *c.* La, *d.* Los) : ANGELES
Answer: (**d**). This analogy concerns full names of cites. *San* and *Los* complete the names of two cities, San Francisco and Los Angeles, respectively.

8. PART-WHOLE

Relationships are those in which A is a part of B.

DAY : WEEK :: MONTH : (*a.* hour, *b.* minute, *c.* year, *d.* time)
Answer: (**c**). This analogy involves parts of larger amounts of time. A day is part of a week, and a month is part of a year.

9. WHOLE-PART

Relationships are those in which B is a part of A.

(*a.* hour, *b.* minute, *c.* year, *d.* time) : MONTH :: WEEK : DAY
Answer: (**c**). This analogy is about parts of the calendar. A month is part of a year. A day is part of a week.

10. EQUALITY

Relationships involve mathematical or logical equivalence.

$^1/_2 : ^1/_4 :: 0.26 : (a.\ 0.52,\ b.\ 0.18,\ c.\ 0.13,\ d.\ 0.11)$
Answer: (c). This analogy requires recognition of mathematical equalities. Whereas $^1/_4$ is equal to one-half of $^1/_2$, 0.13 is equal to one-half of 0.26.

11. NEGATION

Relationships involve logical or mathematical negation.

EQUAL : UNEQUAL :: GREATER THAN : (a. less than, b. equal to, c. greater than or equal to, d. less than or equal to)
Answer: (d). This analogy deals with possible relationships between pairs of numbers. Any number is either *equal* to or *unequal* to another number. Any number is either *greater than* or *less than or equal* to another number.

12. SOUND RELATIONSHIPS

Two words are related because they sound similar in some way. The relationship is nonsemantic in that it has nothing to do with the meanings of the words.

TOE : ROW :: LO : (a. now, b. crow, c. boy, d. you)
Answer: (b). This analogy concerns vowel sounds in words. All the terms have a long ō vowel sound.

13. LETTER RELATIONSHIPS

The letters of one term are permuted or in some other way transformed to form the letters of another term.

PAT : TAP :: RAT : (a. trap, b. skunk, c. tar, d. eat)
Answer: (c). This analogy involves backward spelling of words. *Tap* is obtained by spelling *pat* backward; *tar*, by spelling *rat* backward.

14. WORD RELATIONSHIPS

These usually express grammatical relationships between words.

EAT : ATE :: MEET : (a. meat, b. meet, c. met, d. meets)
Answer: (c). This analogy involves past tenses of verbs. *Ate* is the past tense of *eat* and *met* is the past tense of *meet*.

THE FINAL WORD ON CLASSIFICATION

Though we have taken a cursory glance at the types of content and relationships included on the *MAT*, it should again be emphasized that learning to classify analogies should not be a significant priority during your studying. Rather, when reviewing your incorrect answers during practice tests, attempt to diagnose your own patterns: perhaps you consistently miss questions pertaining to Shakespeare's plays, or perhaps you struggle with numerical patterns. In those particular instances, the Shakespeare questions might be classified as "Humanities Association" problems, but that is a category that can encompass an infinite number of things. It would not be sensible to study every single humanities question, where you will encounter history, religion, music, philosophy, and fine art (among others). Perhaps you are an expert at religion, music, and philosophy; reviewing the humanities questions of those topics would be a poor allocation of your time if your goal is to improve your Shakespearean knowledge. The best approach in this example would be to review the encyclopedic section of this book for Shakespearean information. It also might behoove you to review quick plot summaries of his plays or at minimum, familiarize yourself with his most prominent works. If mathematical patterns are a weakness, attempt to diagnose where your faulty reasoning lies. Do you struggle with geometric sequences involving multiplication and division? If so, it might be wise to review your times tables. Have you missed multiple questions where knowledge of a certain mathematical formula was a prerequisite? If so, then review the most common math formulas (volume of a cube, circumference of a circle, and area of a quadrilateral, to name a few).

As mentioned in the Introduction, this book is not a one-size-fits-all magic bullet. The fact that you are sitting for the *MAT* is a wonderful indication that you are not a one-size-fits-all student; you possess both the intelligence and self-reliance to help yourself, and I am certain that you are well equipped to recognize your own strengths and weaknesses. After all, if you needed constant hand-holding, you never would have made it this far.

References

Kuncel, N. R., S. A. Hezlett, and D. S. Ones. (2004). Academic performance, career potential, creativity, and job performance: Can one construct predict them all? *Journal of Personality and Social Psychology*, Vol. 86(1), 148–161.

Meagher, D., and C. Perez. *An introduction to the MAT*. Presentation at the Annual Meeting of the National Association of Graduate Admissions Professionals, May 2, 2008.

The *Miller Analogies Test* 4

- Validity
- Stability of *MAT* scores
- What *MAT* scores mean
- A word of caution
- A note to be reread when you get your score

SUCCESS OF THE *MAT* AS A MEASURING INSTRUMENT

Many studies have looked at how well the *MAT* predicts graduate school performance. A much smaller number have looked at the test as a predictor of success in occupational settings. Since the number of such studies is limited, we shall be concerned only with research of the former kind.

A review of the literature on the validity of the *MAT* (how well it measures what it is supposed to measure) safely permits one uninformative generalization about the usefulness of the *MAT* in various types of situations: About the only way to find out how valid the *MAT* will be in a given situation is to try it and find out. There are no stunning and clear-cut patterns in the results, perhaps in part because what one school calls basket weaving another calls textile engineering. While situational generalizations are not possible, more global statements can nonetheless be made.

Validity

On the average, the *MAT* accounts for slightly more than 5% of the variance in various types of graduate school performance. In the large majority of studies, it accounts for more than 1%, but less than 15%, of this variance. This means that the *MAT* generally affords a low level of predictive accuracy to those who use it.

The best predictive scholastic aptitude tests account for up to 20% (or perhaps even 25%) of the variance in school performance, so on this basis the *MAT* does not rank with the best tests as a predictor. However, these "best tests" tend to be predictors of high school and sometimes undergraduate grades. At this level, straightforward verbal ability tends to be as good a predictor as anything else. In graduate school, however, professors look for such exotic traits as creativity in designing experiments (in science) and level of rapport achieved with patients (in medicine). Even straightforward course work requires more complex combinations of abilities than are usually needed in high school and undergraduate programs. As a result, graduate school performance is harder to predict in part because all students who go on to graduate school tend to be high in ability, so there is not so much range in performance to predict!

It may surprise you to learn that, on the whole, the *MAT* is about as good a predictor of graduate school performance as any other test around, and that even undergraduate grades usually provide only a little better prediction. The simple fact is that *nothing* provides consistently good prediction of performance in graduate-level programs, and educators resort to the *MAT* and similar tests on the assumption that some prediction is better than none at all. This is true as long as the test results are not misused. If the test scores are considered in conjunction with various other sources of information, if they are interpreted as indicating a range rather than a specific level of ability, and if the limitations on their validity are fully appreciated, then they can be somewhat helpful in spite of their usually low predictive power. If the scores are misused, usually by being overinterpreted, then they certainly illustrate an application of the maxim that "A little knowledge is a dangerous thing." Fortunately, gross misinterpretation is becoming increasingly rare as educators become more sophisticated in the use of standardized tests.

Now that you have become aware of some limitations surrounding *MAT* and other test scores, you won't feel it necessary to hide in a dark corner if your test score isn't what you'd hoped for, and you won't sell autographs (not quite yet, anyway) if your score is much better than you'd imagined possible. Your score can give you and others who properly interpret it some guidance as to how you might perform in graduate work or employment. Many other factors—motivation, study habits, intellectual curiosity, personal sense of well-being, and the like, as well as abilities not tapped by the *MAT*—will also enter into your future success in whatever program you enter.

Meagher and Perez (2008) have reported relatively recent validity data for the *MAT*. The validity data are reported on a scale of 0 to 1, where 0 indicates no relationship between two variables and 1 indicates a perfect relationship. In 2005–2006, across studies, the average correlation between *MAT* scores and graduate school GPA was 0.27, compared with 0.21 for the Graduate Record Examination (*GRE*) verbal, 0.27 for the *GRE* quantitative, and 0.11 for the *GRE* analytical-writing scores. The correlation for previous graduate GPA was 0.30. These correlations indicate somewhat modest but statistically significant relationships between the test scores and graduate GPA. Available data suggest that the *MAT* and the *GRE* verbal section measure very similar but not identical psychological constructs. The *MAT* puts more emphasis on general knowledge, the *GRE* verbal on in-depth reading skills.

A detailed study on the validity of the *MAT* was conducted by Kuncel, Hezlett, and Ones (2004). They found a correlation of 0.70 between the *MAT* and the *GRE* verbal test, which is a relatively strong relationship. When they corrected for various statistical factors, the correlation increased to 0.88, suggesting that the two tests measure almost the same construct. The *MAT* also correlates moderately to highly with other tests of verbal ability. The correlation with the *GRE* quantitative test was 0.42, which is moderate and indicates some (but far from complete) overlap. Correlations with measures of graduate school performance were generally in the high 0.20s. The *MAT* also showed modest but significant correlations with work performance, ranging from 0.15 to 0.33. A curious finding of this study was that higher *MAT* scores were associated with *longer* times to degree completion (with a correlation of 0.35). It is unclear what this means, other than that people who scored higher took longer to finish their degrees!

Stability of *MAT* Scores

As the preceding section states, scores on a given form of the *MAT* usually account for only 1% to 15% of the variance in diverse criteria of performance in graduate school. However, there is something for which such scores usually account for 85% to 90% of the variance, and that is scores on another form of the *MAT*. There you have it. Scores on one form of the *MAT* are excellent predictors of scores when retaking the *MAT*. But you should realize just what this tidbit means. It means that, when a group of people take the test twice (a different form each time), their ranks within the group will probably not change much. However, even if their *ranks* in relation to each other remain stable, their scores may not. Most people gain around 5 points on a second administration. Does this mean you should take the test twice? Probably not. First, you will have capitalized on much of this *practice effect* by reading this book and working at the practice tests it contains. Second, educators and administrators using the test realize that people tend to gain in score from one testing to the next, and they are therefore likely to discount small gains. Large gains, however, are another story and often indicate that for one reason or another, one of the scores is not representative of the candidate's true ability. In such cases, the higher score almost always counts as much as or more than the lower score. For this reason, if you feel reasonably confident that you were at some sort of disadvantage during the first administration, you may want to consider taking the test again. However, such retesting will be a waste of time and money unless the disadvantage was genuine. You should remember that, even if your score was not quite what you'd hoped for, it is only one of many factors considered in making most admissions, financial aid, and employment decisions.

What *MAT* Scores Mean

Your score on the *MAT* will be reported to you as a *raw score*—you are informed of the number of questions you answered correctly, which may range anywhere from zero to one hundred. Before learning what the score means, you should learn what it does *not* mean.

The first thing for you to do is to rid yourself of any preconceptions you may have about percentage scores. A frequent one is that 90–100% = A, 80–89% = B, 70–79% = C, 60–69% = D, and anything below that is failing. Unfortunately, some *MAT* preparation books foster rather than dispel such erroneous notions. For example, one such book provides five practice tests, and suggests that a score of 475 (95%) is excellent, 425 (85%) is good, 350 (70%) is passing, and anything less is failing. Forget it! These standards may or may not be appropriate for the practice tests in that particular book, but they have no conceivable relation to the *MAT*.

In the first place, there is no such thing as a failing score on the *MAT*. Although very few institutions may establish cut-off scores (a practice of dubious merit), almost none rely on the *MAT* to the exclusion of other sources of information. Such total reliance would be irresponsible and counterproductive. Second, what is an excellent score in one program may be just average in another, and quite low in a third. *MAT* scores simply cannot be interpreted in absolute terms. They can be interpreted only in relation to those of other individuals applying to programs similar or identical to your own.

Because raw scores are virtually uninterpretable taken by themselves, the test publisher provides percentile equivalents for various groups of individuals who have taken the *MAT*. What is a percentile equivalent? It is the number of people out of 100 whose scores your own score exceeds. Thus, if your score places you in the 56th percentile, this means that your score was higher than those of 56% of the people who were in the particular reference group for which the percentiles were computed. In general terms, the middle score in a group is the 50th percentile, and the highest score is the 100th percentile.

A Word of Caution

A final word of caution is in order with regard to the prediction of your *MAT* score. Obviously, one way to make this prediction is to average your scores on the practice tests in this book, but such a procedure is risky. Items on actual editions of the *MAT* are pretested by giving them as experimental items to large numbers of individuals who take the *MAT*. Only experimental items that precisely match older items are used on new forms of the test. The various forms of the *MAT* are thus referred to as *equated*.

Since the *MAT* is a restricted test, it was of course not possible to equate the practice tests in this book to actual *MAT* forms, and hence estimates of *MAT* scores attained by averaging scores on these practice tests will be imprecise. Experience indicates that scores on the practice tests tend to run slightly lower than actual *MAT* scores. You might therefore look at your scores on these tests as conservative estimates of what you can expect your *MAT* score to be. Of course, in some cases, individuals may do worse on the actual test; the prediction game, as you know by now, is a very uncertain one. The important thing, however, is not that you go into the test knowing what your score will be, but that you go in knowing that you will get a score that reflects your intellectual ability and not an inability to take tests. After working through this book, you can be confident that you will do your very best on the actual test.

A Note to Be Reread After Taking the Exam

If you did well, congratulations. You have good reason to be proud of yourself. The *MAT* is one of the most difficult standardized tests around, and a high score is a genuine accomplishment.

If you didn't do as well as you'd hoped, don't despair. Follow the simple steps below:

STEP 1 Look back and observe how well the *MAT* predicts (or, rather, doesn't predict) graduate school performance. It's not that the *MAT* is worse than other similar tests. It's just that none of these tests predicts that well. You should be feeling a little better already.

STEP 2 Ask your friendly local librarian for a copy of the January 1973 issue of *The American Psychologist*, and check out the article by David McClelland, "Testing for Competence Rather Than for 'Intelligence.'" McClelland's main point is simple. While aptitude tests provide some (but not much) prediction of performance in school, their ability to predict success in life (as measured by virtually any criterion except test scores and grades) is practically zero. So keep your test score in perspective. In the long run, it isn't that important.

Review for the *Miller Analogies Test*

5

- What this review contains
- Vocabulary
- Special collective nouns
- *-ology* words
- Word demons
- Selected foreign words and phrases used in English
- Alphabets and their characteristics
- Geography
- History
- Social sciences
- Art and architecture
- Literary forms and figures
- Music
- Science
- Mythology

WHAT THIS REVIEW CONTAINS

As stated earlier in this book, the *MAT* is a test of vocabulary and general information as well as specific information in diverse areas. It is not possible to review the content of all the subjects that may be included in an *MAT* exam. The reviews provided in this chapter are intended as brief refreshers. They may help you recall important names, events, and terms in different areas of study. Use this review in conjunction with the practice tests in this book and online. If you encounter unfamiliar words, learn them as well.

VOCABULARY

The vocabulary list below consists of words often used in graduate tests. For some entries, synonyms, antonyms, or other related words are provided as added help in handling analogy questions.

abdicate   to denounce; to discard; to abandon

aberration   something not typical; a deviation

abhorrence   repugnance; detestation

abjure   to renounce upon oath

abnegation   self-denial

abrogate   to break, as a treaty or law

abscond   to depart secretly; to hide (oneself)

absolve   to set free from an obligation or the consequences of guilt

abstain   to refrain deliberately from an action or practice, usu. as a form of self-denial

abstemious   sparing or moderate, especially in eating or drinking (antonym: **gluttonous**)

abstruse   hard to understand or grasp; esoteric

abut   to border; to terminate at the boundary or point of contact

abysmal   immeasurable; bottomless

accolade   an award or honor; high praise

acquiesce   to agree silently; to accept tacitly

acrid   unpleasantly pungent in odor or taste

acrimonious   caustic; biting in feeling or manner

acrophobia   the fear of heights

acumen   keenness

adamant   unyielding; stubborn

addle   to throw into confusion; to confound

adduce   to offer as example or proof

adjure   to command solemnly; to advise earnestly; to beg

admonition   warning against oversight

adroit   showing skill, cleverness, or resourcefulness

adulation   excessive praise

adumbrate   to intimate or foreshadow; to obscure

aestivate (estivate)   to spend the summer in an inactive state

affable   being pleasant and friendly with others

agglomeration   a collection in a mass, heap, or cluster; aggrandizement

agoraphobia   the fear of open spaces

alacrity   liveliness or eagerness; readiness (antonym: **lassitude**)

allegory   a symbolic expression or description

allusion   an indirect reference to something else; a hint

alms   charity; something given to the poor (usu. refers to small change)

alpinism   mountain climbing

altruistic   unselfish; concerned with the welfare of others

ambergris   a product of sperm whales used in the manufacture of perfume

amphora   an ancient two-handled Greek jar

anathema   a ban or curse; a denunciation accompanied by excommunication

andiron   a metal support used for holding logs in a hearth

androphobia   the fear of men

anneal   to toughen or to strengthen

anodyne   a pain reliever

anomaly   an aberration; a deviation; an irregularity

antipathy   firm dislike; hatred (antonym: **sympathy**)

antiseptic   free from germs; exceptionally clean

antithesis   the direct opposite

aphelion   the point in a planet's orbit that is farthest from the sun

apocalyptic   of, or relating to, a revelation or discovery

apocryphal   of doubtful authenticity; spurious

apogee   the point in a satellite's orbit that is farthest from the center of the earth
  (antonym: **perigree**)

apothegm   a short, instructive pithy saying

aquiline   hooked; like an eagle

arachnophobia   the fear of spiders

archon   the chief magistrate in ancient Athens; any ruler

arid   dull; unimaginative; extremely dry

arrogate   to claim or seize without justification; to usurp

artifice   cleverness; ingenuity

assiduous   diligent

assuage   to ease the intensity of; to appease; to pacify (antonym: **exacerbate**)

astraphobia   the fear of lightning

atrophy   a wasting away; degeneration

attenuate   to lessen in amount, force, or value; to weaken

audacity   daring spirit

austral   southern (antonym: **boreal**)

axiom   a self-evident rule or truth; a widely accepted saying

ayatollah   a high-ranking Islamic leader

azure   sky blue

baleful   menacing; harmful

balmy   soothing; mild

banal   trite; commonplace

bellicose   inclined to start wars or fights (antonym: **pacific**)

beneficent   beneficial (antonym: **deleterious**)

benign   gracious; favorable; not threatening to health (antonym: **malignant**)

benison   spoken blessing

bibliophile   one who loves books

biennial   occurring every two years; not to be confused with **biannual**, which is occurring twice
   every year

bifurcate   divide in two branches; fork

biped   having two feet

blighted   withered or rotten; destroyed; frustrated

blithe   happy; merry; cheerful

bombastic   pompous; overblown; turgid

boreal   northern (antonym: **austral**)

boycott   to engage in a concerted refusal to have dealings with (a person, store, organization) as
   a sign of disapproval [derived from Charles C. Boycott, an English land agent who was ostra-
   cized in Ireland because of his refusal to lower rents]

broach   to make known for the first time; to open up (a subject) for discussion

bromidic   lacking originality; trite (antonym: **visionary**)

brontophobia   the fear of thunder

brook   to bear or tolerate; to put up with

brusque   abrupt or short in manner or speech

buccal   pertaining to the cheeks or side of the mouth

bucolic   pastoral; relating to rural life

buffoon   a clown or ludicrous figure; someone who amuses with jokes or tricks

bulbous   rotund; round like a bulb

bumptious   aggressive and assertive in an offensive way (antonym: **shy; self-effacing**)

buoyant   (1) having the ability to float; (2) cheerful; gay

burgeon   to grow and flourish

burnish   to make shiny or lustrous; to polish

burnoose   a hooded Arabic cloak

   cassock   a loose robe worn by priests

cabal   group united to plot, esp. the overthrow of authority

cache   (1) a hiding place; (2) something hidden in a secure place

cacophony   a harsh-sounding mixture of words, voices, or sounds

caduceus   the emblem of the medical profession (a staff with intertwined snakes and wings
   at the top)

cajole   to persuade a reluctant person to do something; to coax

caliber   the diameter of the bore of a gun

> **gauge**   the size of a shotgun; measure of the interior diameter of the barrel

calumny   a lie told to damage another's reputation; slander

candid   frank

canonical   orthodox; authoritative

capitulate   to cease resisting; to surrender (often after negotiations)

capricious   unpredictable; governed by a whim

captious   critical; fault-finding

carp   to complain

cashmere   a fine wool from a cashmere goat [derived from Kashmir, India]

catharsis   purification of emotions, esp. through art

> **bathos**   sentimentalism; overdone pathos; triteness; anticlimax

> **pathos**   something that evokes pity, compassion, or sorrow

catholic   universal (antonym: **provincial; parochial**)

caustic   acrid; biting

cavil   to raise trivial objections; to nitpick

cerulean   resembling the blue of the sky

chaff   waste material from the threshing of wheat

> **dross**   waste material from molten metal

> **slag**   scoria; refuse from the melting of metals or reduction of ore

> **tailings**   waste material from the preparation of ores or grains

chalice   a bowl-shaped drinking cup

chartreuse   yellow-green

chastise   to criticize harshly; to castigate

chauvinism   excessive or blind patriotism [derived from Nicholas Chauvin, a character in a French play]

chicanery   trickery; artful deception

chimerical   fantastically visionary; wildly fanciful

choleric   easily angered or irritated

Cimmerian   (1) *adj.* shrouded in gloom and darkness; (2) *n.* a mythical people described by Homer as dwelling in gloom

> **stygian**   (1) dark and gloomy; (2) relating to the Styx (in Greek mythology, the river of the underworld)

circumlocution   an indirect expression; wordy or evasive language

circumspect   considering all options; cautious

clandestine   surreptitious; secret

claustrophobia   the fear of closed places

clemency   an act of leniency; mercy

cloy   to satiate

> **glut**   to oversupply; to satiate

coalesce   to grow together; to unite into a whole

coda   a passage that concludes a musical or literary work

cogent   pertinent; compelling; convincing

cognizant   perceptive; observant

colloquial   of or relating to conversation; characteristic of informal speech

collusion   a secret agreement, esp. for an illegal purpose

compulsion   an impulse to perform an irrational act

   phobia   an inexplicable fear of something

conjoin   to join or act together

contentious   argumentative; quarrelsome

contumacious   rebellious; stubbornly disobedient; renegade

conundrum   a puzzle; a riddle

cooper   a maker of casks or barrels

corroborate   to confirm; to back up with evidence

cowl   (1) a hood; (2) a cover for an engine

croupier   a collector and payer of bets at a casino

culinary   having to do with the kitchen or cooking

cynophobia   the fear of dogs

cynosure   the center of interest

dauntless   fearless

dearth   severe shortage

debacle   a violent breakdown; a sudden overthrow

debauchery   wild living; corruption by sensuality

debilitate   to weaken (antonym: **invigorate**)

debonair   suave; courteous; sophisticated

deciduous   falling off or shedding at a certain season; ephemeral; not permanent

declaim   to make a bombastic speech

decorous   proper; in good taste; correct

defalcate   to embezzle; to abscond with money

deleterious   harmful (antonym: **beneficial; salubrious; salutary**)

delineate   to describe; to portray; to sketch

deliquesce   to melt away or dissolve; to become soft, esp. with age

delusion   a deception; a false psychotic belief regarding oneself or others

demur   to object; to take exception

denim   a durable, twilled, usually cotton fabric woven with white filling thread [derived from
   serge de Nime (Nîmes, France)]

denouement   the unfolding or outcome of a series of events

denounce   to express strong disapproval, esp. publicly

depraved   morally corrupt or evil

deprecate   to play down; to belittle

depredate   to lay waste; to plunder

desiccate   to dry out

despot   a ruler with absolute power

desultory   lacking plan, regularity, or purpose; random

dexterous   mentally skillful; artful; clever

dialectic   logical argumentation

diametric   completely opposed; at opposite extremes

diaphanous   sheer; extremely delicate

diatribe   a bitter denunciation (antonym: **panegyric**)

dichotomy   division, esp. into two contradictory groups

didactic   intended to teach, moralize, or preach

diffident   shy; lacking in self-confidence

dilatory   tending to cause delay (antonym: **expeditious**)

dilettante   one who is involved in a variety of things, none of them seriously; dabbler

diminution   a decrease; a lessening

dint   a force; a power

disavow   to deny

discomfit   to confuse, to deject; to frustrate; to deceive

discourse   to converse; to discuss formally

disingenuous   lacking in candor

disinterested   unbiased

dissemble   to feign or pretend

dissenter   one who goes against an opinion; nonconformist

dissuade   to persuade someone not to do something

djellabah   a loose-fitting gown worn in North Africa (see also **burnoose**)

doctrinaire   dogmatic

doggerel   comic, loose verse

dolt   a stupid person

doughty   fearless; valiant

dour   stubbornly unyielding; uninviting

draconian   severe (as a code of laws); cruel

dray   a vehicle used to haul goods

   teamster   a person who drives a truck as an occupation; a blue-collar union member

ductile   malleable

dunce   a dull-witted or stupid person [derived from John Duns Scotus, whose writings were ridiculed in the 16th century]

duplicity   concealment of one's true intentions by misleading words or actions; deception

ebullient   lively; enthusiastic; boiling up

eclectic   selecting from many sources what seems to be the best; catholic

ecumenical   (1) having to do with a body of churches; (2) worldwide or general in extent or application

edification   instruction; improvement; enlightenment

efface   to make indistinct by wearing away; to erase or remove

effervescent   lively; bubbly (antonym: **effete**)

effete   exhausted; worn-out (antonym: **effervescent**)

effluvium   a disagreeable or noxious vapor; escaping gas

effusive   overflowing; very demonstrative

egregious   conspicuously bad; flagrant

egress   (1) *n.* exit; (2) *v.* to go out from

elan   dash; vigorous spirit

elegy   a lament for the dead

elucidate   to shed light upon; to make clear

emanate   to send out; to emit

eminent   prominent; famous; standing above others in some quality or position

encomium   formal expression of praise

endue   to provide; to endow

enervate   to exhaust, weaken, or unnerve (antonym: **invigorate**)

engender   to bring into being; to produce

enigma   a baffling situation; something that is hard to explain or solve

ennui   boredom

entreat   to request earnestly

ephemeral   lasting a short time; transient

epiphany   a sudden, and often divine, enlightenment or realization

epitome   a typical or ideal example

epoch   era

equivocal   ambiguous; deliberately confusing; able to be interpreted in more than one way

erratic   unpredictable; wandering; arbitrary (antonym: **static; stable**)

eschew   to avoid; to shun

ethereal   so exquisite as to seem unearthly

eulogy   formal expression of praise

euphemism   (1) the substitution of a positive expression for something that may be interpreted
   as negative or distasteful; (2) the expression that is substituted

evanescent   fleeting; hardly visible; ephemeral

exacerbate   to make more violent or more severe (antonym: **assuage; appease**)

excoriate   to wear off the skin

exculpate   to exonerate; to clear of guilt or blame

exegesis   an interpretation of a text

exigent   urgent; requiring prompt action; taxing

expedite   to speed up; to hasten

expiate   to make amends for

expletive   a syllable or word that fills a vacancy but does not add to the sense of what was said

explicate   to explain

expunge   to strike out; to obliterate or erase

extemporaneous   with little preparation

extirpate   to destroy completely

facetious   humorous; not serious

factitious   artificial; sham (antonym: **authentic**)

fagoting   a type of embroidery

fallacious   erroneous; deceiving; misleading

fallible   capable of making a mistake or error

fastidious   hard to please; fickle

fatuous   silly; inane

fealty   allegiance

feasible   practical; workable

feckless   worthless; feeble

fecund   fruitful; fertile

fervid   very hot; intense in feeling or emotion; impassioned

fetid   having an offensive odor

   vapid   flat; uninteresting; insipid

fetish   (1) a charm; a talisman; an amulet; an object thought to deflect evil or bring luck;
   (2) a fixation; an object of obsessive desire; a preoccupation

fiduciary   a trustee

fitful   irregular; spasmodic

flaccid   limp; flabby (antonym: **resilient**)

flag   to weaken; to slow down

flagon   a flask with a handle and lid

   tureen   a casserole or bowl usually used to serve soup

flibbertigibbet   female fool

foible   a minor flaw or shortcoming in character; a weakness

foment   to instigate, incite, or arouse

foray   (1) *v.* to ravage for spoils; to pillage; (2) *n.* sudden, sometimes brief, invasion

forbear   an ancestor or forefather

fortuitous   happening by chance; unplanned

fractious   unruly; quarrelsome

franchise   the right to vote; a special privilege granted to a few; the right to market certain goods in a particular region

fraught   laden; charged

frenetic   frantic; frenzied

fricative   produced by forcing air through a constricted passage

froward   habitually disobedient; not willing to compromise

frugal   economical; thrifty; sparing

fuchsia   vivid reddish purple

fugacious   disappearing after a short time; short-lived; evanescent

fulminate   to denounce; to send forth invectives; to explode

fulsome   (1) abundant; copious; (2) morally offensive; disgusting

furtive   sly; shifty

gainsay   to deny; to contradict

galvanize   (1) to stimulate or excite; (2) to coat with zinc

gamut   the entire range

garner   to collect; to accumulate

garrison   to station troops in a small area so as to defend it

garrote   to strangle and rob

garrulous   wordy; extremely talkative; gabby (antonym: **taciturn**)

gauche   lacking social grace; crude; awkward

gaunt   excessively thin; lean

gelding   a castrated male horse

genre   an artistic category or type

genuflect   to go down on one's knee; to kneel, usu. in obedience or respect

germane   closely related; relevant; fitting

glabrous   smooth; referring to a surface without hair or projections

   hirsute   roughly hairy

goad   to urge, egg on, or incite to do something (antonym: **curb**)

gorgon   one of three snake-haired sisters whose glance turned the beholder into stone

gourmand   one who eats and drinks excessively; glutton

gratuitous   not required by the circumstances; unwarranted; unnecessary

gregarious   liking companionship; sociable

griffin   a mythical animal having the head and wings of an eagle and the body and legs of a lion

   chimera   (1) a fire-breathing monster with the head of a lion, the body of a goat, and the tail of a serpent; (2) illusion or mental fabrication.

   minotaur   a monster, half man and half bull, confined in a labyrinth

guffaw   a loud, boisterous burst of laughter

guile   deceitful cunning; cleverness

gulch   a deep pit; a ravine

hackneyed   overused; trite; commonplace

haiku   a type of unrhymed Japanese poem consisting of three lines

halcyon   peaceful; tranquil

harangue   a ranting speech without much real meaning

harbinger   someone or something that foreshadows what is to come

Hellene   a native or inhabitant of Greece

heretic   one who goes against an established religion or belief; nonconformist

hermeneutics   the study of principles of interpretation (e.g., of the Bible)

hermetic   sealed off from external influence; airtight; abstruse or occult

herpetophobia   the fear of snakes

hiatus   a gap or interruption in time or in a continuum

hibernate   to spend the winter in a dormant, inactive state

hierarchy   a graded or ranked classification determined on the basis of age, economic status, or class

hirsute   hairy (antonym: **glabrous**)

hoary   gray or white with age

homily   an inspirational discourse; a sermon

homogeneous   of uniform structure or composition

homophobia   the fear of homosexuals

homophones   words that sound alike but have different meanings

    homonyms   homophones; also, words that are spelled the same but have different meanings (e.g., *cleave, quail, bear*)

hone   to sharpen

husbandry   the care of animals and growing of crops

hyaline   transparent or almost so; glassy

hybrid   anything that is the product of at least two different sources

hydroponics   cultivation of plants in liquid nutrients

hyperbole   an exaggeration

hypertrophy   an exaggerated increase or complexity

hypocritical   pretending to have qualities or virtues that are not possessed; dissembling

hypothetical   based on conjecture; conditional

    empirical   based on expertise, observation, or experimental evidence

iconoclast   one who destroys religious images or attacks established beliefs

    vandal   one who destroys property

idyllic   carefree and lighthearted; peaceful

igneous   referring to rock formed from molten magma; volcanic

    metamorphic   referring to rock formed from sedimentary rock and changed through pressure or heat

ignoble   dishonorable; shameful

ignominious   infamous; despicable

imbue   to permeate or influence

imminent   about to happen (usu. referring to something threatening)

immiscible   incapable of being mixed

immutable   not susceptible to change

impassive   apathetic; expressionless

impecunious   having little or no money

impermeable   impervious; not permitting passage through

impetuous   impulsively violent or passionate

impolitic   unwise; injudicious

imprecate   to curse

improvident   not providing for the future; careless

   prescient   having foresight or foreknowledge of the future

impugn   to attack, esp. as false or lacking integrity

inanition   a loss of vitality from lack of food and water

incarnadine   blood red

inchoate   beginning; insipient; only imperfectly formed

incipient   just beginning; in the early stages; commencing

incisive   keen; direct; decisive

incommodious   troublesome; inconvenient

incongruous   not like the others in a group; out of place; incompatible

incontrovertible   unquestionable; indisputable

incorrigible   unruly; delinquent

inculcate   to teach and impress by repetition

indemnify   (1) to secure against loss; (2) to compensate for hurt or loss

indigenous   having originated naturally in a particular environment

indigent   impoverished

induction   (1) an initiation into military service; (2) reasoning from parts to whole

   ordination   an initiation into religious service

ineluctable   inescapable; inevitable

inimical   hostile; unfriendly (antonym: **amicable**)

iniquitous   vicious; wicked

innuendo   a veiled allusion; insinuation

insurgent   a person who revolts against established authority

intractable   hard to manage; unruly; obstinate

intransigent   stubborn; uncompromising

intrepid   fearless (antonym: **timorous**)

inure   to accustom to accept something undesirable; to habituate

invective   insulting or abusive language

invidious   offensive; envious; obnoxious

irascible   easily angered; choleric; malevolent

jalousie   a type of blind or shutter having adjustable slats or louvers and usu. made of glass

jargon   specialized terminology of a certain group; a lingo

jejune   immature; juvenile

jenny   a female donkey

jettison   to sacrifice cargo to lighten a ship or vehicle

jetty   a projection or structure extending into a body of water

jezebel   a shameless, brazen woman

jocose   humorous; witty

jocular   habitually happy or cheerful

jocund   gay; cheerful

judicious   wise; sagacious; prudent

junk   (1) trash; something that is not worth saving; (2) a type of Chinese ship

junta   a political group or committee, esp. after a revolution

juxtapose   to place right next to something

kaleidoscope   (1) a succession of changing patterns or scenes; (2) a changing pattern or scene

kindle   to activate or inspire; to arouse

kindred   (1) *n.* relatives; kinship; (2) *adj.* similar in nature; like

kinetic   related to motion

knave   a sly, deceitful man or boy

kudos   praise; compliments

labyrinth   a place full of intricate passageways; something extremely complex or intricate

laconic   concise (antonym: **verbose; redundant**)

lambent   flickering; softly bright or radiant, as a candle

lampoon   harsh, satirical writing, usu. attacking an individual

lascivious   lewd; lustful; wanton

lassitude   fatigue; weariness (antonym: **alacrity**)

laudable   worthy of praise

lave   to wash or bathe

lethargic   slow moving; sluggish

levity   lightness; lack of seriousness; frivolity

libel   a published false statement that is injurious to another

libertine   a person who is not restrained by convention or morality

licentious   lacking moral restraints, esp. sexual ones; lustful

ligneous   woodlike

limpid   clear and simple in style; transparent; serene and untroubled

   lucid   clear; sane; translucent; luminous

   pellucid   reflecting light evenly; easy to understand

litigate   to try in court; to contest in law

littoral   relating to the shore or coastal region

loggia   a roofed, open gallery, like a porch

loquacious   talkative

lucre   monetary gain; profit

ludicrous   laughable; ridiculous

lugubrious   gloomy; sorrowful

lurid   (1) gruesome; shocking; (2) ghastly pale

maelstrom   a whirlpool

magenta   deep purplish red

magnanimous   exceptionally generous

malefactor   an evil-doer; a criminal

malfeasance   wrongdoing; official misconduct

malignant   evil; injurious; tending to produce death; cancerous (antonym: **benign**)

mandatory   necessary; obligatory

marred   injured; blemished; damaged

martinet   a strict disciplinarian

masticate   to chew

maudlin   foolishly sentimental or morose

maverick   a rebel; a nonconformist

megalomaniac   one who exhibits delusions of omnipotence or grandeur

mercurial   quickly changing; inconstant

meretricious   attractive only on the surface; superficial; pretentious

meticulous   extremely concerned with details; well organized

miasma   a depleting or corrupting influence or atmosphere

millennium   a thousand years

miscreant   a heretic; a villain; one who commits illegal acts

misogynistic   characterized by hatred of women

mitigate   to soften; to lessen the severity of

moot   questionable; debatable

mordant   biting in manner or style; incisive

motility   movement

munificent   lavish; generous; liberal

nadir   (1) the lowest point; (2) a point in the sky opposite the zenith

naiad   a water nymph

napery   table linens

necromancy   magic; witchcraft

   chiromancy   palmistry

necrophobia   the fear of death

necropolis   a cemetery

nefarious   wicked; vile

neophyte   a novice

nexus   a connection or link

niggardly   stingy

noisome   offensive; harmful

nomenclature   a standardized system of symbols for a particular subject, usu. art or science

nonfeasance   failure to perform an act that should have been completed

notorious   widely and unfavorably known

nuance   a subtle distinction, variation, or quality

nugatory   inconsequential; trifling

nullify   to void legally; to make of no consequence

numismatist   one who studies and collects coins and tokens

nuncupative   not written; oral

nyctophobia   the fear of darkness

obdurate   persistent; unyielding

obfuscate   to confuse (antonym: **clarify**)

objurgate   to denounce harshly; to declaim; to castigate

obliterate   to destroy completely; to cause to disappear

obloquy   (1) abusive language; (2) bad repute

obscurant   tending to make obscure

obsequious   obedient; subservient

   sycophant   a servile, self-seeking flatterer

obtrude   to force, usu. oneself or one's ideas on another without request

obviate   to make unnecessary

ocher   earthy yellow or red

ochlophobia   the fear of crowds

odyssey   a long, eventful journey

officious   meddling; interfering

olfactory   relating to the sense of smell

oligarchy   form of government in which control is placed in the hands of a few, esp. associated with corruption

omnipotent   all-powerful

omnipresent   being all places at once

omniscient   knowing everything

omnivore   one who eats both animals and vegetables

onerous   burdensome; oppressive

onomatopoeia   the use of words whose sounds convey their meanings (e.g., *buzz, hiss*)

ontogeny   the development of an organism

onus   a burden; an obligation

ophidiophobia   the fear of snakes

opprobrium   disgrace due to a shameful act

opus   a major work, esp. a set of musical compositions

ornithophobia   the fear of birds

oscillate   to swing back and forth; to vary

osmosis   diffusion through a membrane

ossify   to become hard as a bone

ostentatious   showy; pretentious

oviparous   producing eggs that hatch outside the maternal body

palindrome   a word, sentence, or number that reads the same backward and forward (e.g., *mom*)

palliate   to cover up with excuses; to extenuate

panegyric   high praise; a tribute; an encomium (antonym: **diatribe**)

paradigm   an example; a pattern; an archetype

paradox   (1) something true that appears to be false; (2) something false that appears to be logical

pariah   an outcast

parry   (1) to ward off; (2) to escape by dodging

parsimony   the quality of being careful with money; thrift (synonym: **thrift**) (antonym: **extravagance**)

partisan   one who is committed to a particular person, cause, or idea

parvenu   one recently risen to an unaccustomed position and not yet possessing the requisite dignity or characteristics; upstart

paucity   a small amount; a scarcity

pecuniary   having to do with money

pedantic   characterized by an ostentatious display of learning

pedometer   an instrument used to measure the distance walked

penultimate   next to last

peremptory   precluding a right of action, delay, or debate; admitting of no contradiction

perfidious   faithless; disloyal; treacherous

peripatetic   wandering; itinerant

peruse   to read carefully; to study

pervade   to spread throughout

petulant   ill-tempered; irritable; fractious

philatelist   one who studies and collects stamps

   -phile   a love of or affinity for (e.g., *philogyny*: love of women)

   -phobe   a fear of or aversion to

philistine   (1) characterized by material rather than spiritual or artistic values; (2) narrow-minded or uninformed with respect to a specific topic area

piscatorial   of or relating to fish

platen   (1) a roller on a typewriter; (2) a flat plate

platitude   the state of being dull, banal, or trite

plethora   a superfluity; an excess

plumb   (1) *n.* a lead weight used to find the true vertical; (2) *v.* to measure the depth of; to fathom

polemic   strong argument in refutation of another; disputation; practice of engaging in controversy

poltroon   a coward

potlatch   (1) a ceremonial feast, with gifts, of northwest coast Indians; (2) a festival or celebration

precipitous   steep

precocious   exhibiting maturity at an early age

prescience   the anticipation of upcoming events; foresight

prevaricate   to deviate from the truth; to lie

probity   honesty; uprightness; rectitude

prodigal   recklessly wasteful; very generous

profusion   a great amount; an abundance

prognosticate   to forecast; to prophesy

propensity   a tendency or inclination

propinquity   closeness; proximity

proxy   a person authorized to act for another (e.g., to vote corporate stock)

pseudonym   a fictitious or pen name

surname   (1) a family name; (2) an added name or nickname

puce   dark red

puerile   childish; juvenile

pundit   an expert; an authority; a critic; a savant

purloin   to steal

purview   a range of authority, competence, or responsibility; scope

pusillanimous   cowardly; fearful

Pyrrhic   usu. referring to a victory won at excessively high cost

quaff   to drink heartily

quagmire   a bog; a difficult or entrapping situation; a predicament

qualm   (1) a sudden onset of illness, esp. of nausea; (2) a feeling of unease about a point of conscience

quandary   a state of confusion or doubt

quell   to suppress

querulous   complaining; whining

quintessence   the essence of something in its most concentrated form; the purest representative from a certain category

quisling   a traitor [derived from Vidkum Quisling, a Norwegian who collaborated with the Nazis during World War II]

quittance   a release from debt or obligation

quixotic   foolishly impractical and idealistic; capricious

quizzical   (1) eccentric; odd; (2) inquisitive; questioning

quondam   former; sometime

quorum   the minimum number of a group that must be present to conduct business legally

quotidian   daily

rancorous   with ill-will; with enmity (antonym: **benevolent**)

raze   to demolish completely; to destroy

recalcitrant   obstinately defiant of authority; resistant

recidivism   repeated relapse, as in tendency to repeat criminal activity

reciprocal   (1) mutual; shared; common; (2) inversely related

recondite   obscure; concealed; incomprehensible; esoteric

recumbent   lying down; leaning; resting

recusant   marked by refusal to obey authority

redolent   having a pleasing scent; fragrant

refurbish   to freshen or make new; to renovate

relegate   to assign to a place of insignificance; to banish

relume   to light or light again; to rekindle; to reestablish

remonstrate   to object; to protest

reprehend   to voice disapproval of

reprobate   a villain; an immoral person

repugnant   distasteful; abhorrent; obnoxious (antonym: **congenial**)

rescind   to take away; to remove

resilient   able to recover easily from hardship or misfortune; flexible

restive   tense

retrenchment   a reduction in expenses

revile   to use abusive speech; to rail; to scold

ribald   rude or offensive; indecent

risible   capable of laughing or provoking laughter

rookery   a breeding place among rocks for mammals (e.g., seals) or birds

roseate   overoptimistic; cheerful

rotund   round; plump; chubby

ruminate   to reflect on something; to ponder

saboteur   one who willfully hinders, through destruction or obstruction, industrial production or a nation's war effort

    fifth column   supporters of an enemy that engage in sabotage within defense lines or national boundaries

sagacious   wise; astute; perspicacious

salubrious   healthy; promoting well-being; salutary (antonym: **deleterious**)

sanctimonious   (1) devout; holy; (2) hypocritically devout or holy

sanction   to authorize or approve

sanguine   hopeful

sardonic   disdainful; sarcastic

sarsaparilla   a soft drink made from the *Smilax ornata* plant

satiric   using ridicule or sarcasm to convey criticism; lampooning

saturnine   gloomy; sullen; morose

savant   one with detailed knowledge in a specialized field

    prodigy   highly talented child

    virtuoso   one who is highly skilled in the practice of an art, esp. music

scintilla   a minute trace or jot; an iota

    tittle   a particle

sectarian   of or relating to a sect or a smaller group within a larger group that adopts only certain beliefs; narrow-minded

sequester   (1) to set apart from others; to segregate; (2) to confiscate

sidereal   related to the stars; astral

solicitous   careful; attentive

sophomoric (literally "wise fool") believing one's level of knowledge and maturity to be higher than it actually is

soporific marked by, or causing, sleepiness or lethargy; drowsy

sordid wretched; vile; foul

spelunker one who studies and explores caves as a hobby

splenetic hot-tempered; easily angered

spurious false; forged; counterfeit

staid sedate; serious; grave

sterile unimaginative; unfruitful; bare (antonym: **fecund; fertile**)

stolid dull; unemotional; immovable

stoma, stomata a minute opening in outside surface of a plant (e.g., a leaf) for the passage of gases

striated referring to muscle with alternate light and dark bands, as opposed to smooth muscle

strident loud; harsh; grating

stygian hellish

superfluous more than necessary; extra

surfeit overabundant supply; immoderate indulgence

surmise to imagine; to make inferences based on insufficient evidence

surreptitious secret; covert (antonym: **brazen; overt**)

susurration whispering

sybaritic voluptuous; sensual

sycophant servile flatterer; parasite

synthesis the combination of parts to form a whole, or of thesis and antithesis to form a higher truth

tacit unspoken; implied (antonym: **explicit**)

taciturn silent; having little inclination to talk (antonym: **garrulous**)

tactile perceptible by touch; tangible

tangential touching only the edge; marginally relevant

tangerine a deep orange to almost scarlet mandarin orange [derived from Tangiers, Morocco]

tawdry appearing gaudy or cheap

temerity audacity; effrontery; boldness (antonym: **caution**)

tempest storm

temporal referring to time, as opposed to eternity; secular

tenet a doctrine upheld by members of an organization

tepid moderately warm; lukewarm

termagant a shrew; a nagging woman, as Xanthippe (Socrates' wife); a virago; an ogress; a harpy

terrestrial having to do with the earth

terse (1) polished; refined; (2) short and to the point; concise

therapeutic used in the treatment of diseases or disorders; curative

timbre the quality of a sound or tone, distinctive of a particular voice or instrument

timorous fearful; timid (antonym: **intrepid**)

tirade a long, intemperate speech; diatribe

torpid dormant; lacking energy; lethargic; apathetic; dull

  vapid lacking vitality; flat; uninteresting

torque (1) *n.* a twisting or turning force; (2) *v.* to cause to rotate or twist

torrid oppressively hot

tort a civil wrong for which the injured party is entitled to compensation

tractable docile; malleable; obedient (antonym: **unruly**)

transient   lasting only a short time; changing; ephemeral; transitory

trenchant   (1) caustic; penetrating; (2) separate; distinct

triskaidekaphobia   the fear of the number 13

troglodyte   someone who lives in solitude

truculent   cruel; brutal; belligerent

turbid   muddy

turpitude   baseness; corruption; depravity

ultima   a word's final syllable

umbrage   (1) a feeling of offense or annoyance; (2) a shadow; a hint; a suspicion

unctuous   oily; smug; suave

undulate   to move in wavelike motions; to fluctuate

unduly   excessively

unequivocal   clear; obvious; certain

ungainly   hard to handle; unwieldy; clumsy

ungulate   hooflike; referring to hoofed animals

urbane   polished; polite or finished in manner

utopian   referring to paradise or an impossible ideal

uxoricide   the murder of one's wife

vacillate   to waver; to fluctuate; to oscillate

vacuous   stupid; lacking intelligence

vagrancy   the state of being homeless (legally, a misdemeanor)

vapid   insipid; spiritless

venal   corruptible

venerate   to honor

venial   forgivable

veracity   truth

verbose   wordy (antonym: **laconic**)

vernal   suggestive of youth

vertigo   sensation of dizziness or disorientation

viable   (1) capable of living; (2) able to stand or develop independently

vicarious   experienced through another medium; experienced through imaginary participation
  in the events of another's life

vilify   to slander; to verbally abuse; to defame

virago   a loud, overbearing woman; a termagant

viscous   thick; having a gummy consistency

vitriolic   caustic; biting

viviparous   producing living young, as most mammals, some reptiles, and a few fishes

volatile   easily aroused; explosive

volition   choice or decision; will

voracious   ravenous; gluttonous; insatiable

vulpine   foxlike; crafty

wan   pale; sickly

wanton   flirtatious; lascivious

whet   to stimulate; to incite; to make more intense, esp. an appetite

wizened   shrunken and wrinkled with age

wright   a worker, esp. in wood; used in combination with another word (e.g., *wheelwright,*
  playwright)

wroth intensely angry; incensed

xanthic yellowish

xenophobia the fear of strangers

yean to give birth, used of sheep or goats

yore time long past

yowl to cry out loudly; to wail

zealot one who is enthusiastic, sometimes fanatical, about a cause

zeitgeist the cultural climate of a specific time

zenith (1) the highest point; (2) the highest point reached by a celestial body (antonym: **nadir**)

SPECIAL COLLECTIVE NOUNS

bed of roses

bevy of beauties

cache of jewels

clew of worms

clutch of eggs

coven of witches

covey of quails

drift of swans

gaggle of geese

kindle of kittens

leap of leopards

litter of puppies

lock of hair

murder of crows

muster of peacocks

parade of elephants

parcel of penguins

pod or **gam** of whales

pride of lions

rafter of turkeys

shoal or **school** of fish

string of pearls

swarm of bees

walk of snails

-OLOGY WORDS

The suffix *-ology* means the study of or the science of. The root of the word gives you the key to the field of study. The suffix *-ist* added to the name of the field of study refers to someone who works in that area. For example, the root *herpe* means reptile. Herpetology is the study of reptiles, and a herpetologist is one who studies snakes.

   In the following definitions, "the study of" or "the science of" is understood.

alalogy algae

anthropology human beings—their distributions, origins, classifications, physical characteristics, environmental and social relations, and cultures

archaeology remains of past human life and activities

axiology values and value judgments (e.g., in ethics)

bacteriology bacteria

biology living organisms and vital processes

cosmology nature, origin, structure, and space-time relationships of the universe

cryptology codes and ciphers

cytology cell and its functions

deontology ethics

enology wines and wine making

entomology insects

epistemology the nature, grounds, and limits of knowledge

eschatology end of the world

ethology animal behavior under natural conditions

etiology   causes of phenomena

geology   earth and its history

gerontology   aging and the problems of the aged

hagiology   saints and other revered persons

herpetology   reptiles and amphibians

histology   living tissue

homology   similarity in structure (thought to be due to common origin)

horology   measurement of time

ichthyology   fishes

kinesiology   principles of mechanics and anatomy in relation to human movement

limnology   fresh waters

mammalogy   mammals

morphology   structures and forms of plants and animals; word formation in a language

mycology   fungi

numismatology   coins

oncology   tumors

ontology   nature and relations of being

ophthalmology   structure, function, and diseases of the eye

ornithology   birds

paleontology   fossils

parasitology   parasites and parasitism

pathology   diseases

philology   language, speech, linguistics, and literature

physiology   functions and activities of living organisms

primatology   primates, especially other than recent humans

radiology   use of radiant energy (X-rays, radium, etc.) in the diagnosis and treatment of disease

teleology   final causes or purpose in nature

thanatology   death and dying

toxicology   poisons, their effects, and the problems involved

urology   urinary system

virology   structure and function of viruses

zoology   animals

WORD DEMONS

Some words are frequently misused because they sound alike, are spelled almost the same, or are very close in meaning. The following is a list of such words. You should be familiar with the correct spelling, meaning, and use of each word.

adapt   to change or adjust

  When she moved to the foreign country, she had to adapt to new customs.

adept   skilled

  He was adept in all aspects of carpentry.

adopt   to accept or embrace, to accept formally

  The couple hopes to adopt several children.

  The council voted to adopt the new amendment.

adverse   unfavorable, unfriendly, opposing

  She overcame several adverse conditions to win the race.

averse   opposed

The councilwoman was averse to the new proposal.

advice   suggestion

The best advice I can give you is to read as much as you can.

advise   to counsel, to give suggestions

We advise you to start studying for the test as soon as possible.

affect   influence, be of importance to, produce an effect on

The rain will affect the picnic plans.

affect   to make a pretense of, to fake, to feign

She affects a British accent.

effect   result, consequence; to bring about, to produce

The farmers felt the effect of the drought.

The drought effected a major change in the farmers' life.

affront   insult, offense

His comment was an affront to the speaker.

confront   to face

He will confront the student with the evidence.

allusion   reference to

The author uses several allusions to Greek mythology in his story.

illusion   unreal image

She has the illusion that I like jazz; I don't.

apprise   to let know, to inform

The judge will apprise the jury of the pertinent statutes.

appraise   to estimate the value of

The painting was appraised at two million dollars.

chronic   constant, long-lasting

Parking is a chronic problem in the inner city.

acute   short-lived, perhaps severe

He had acute appendicitis.

coherent   intelligible, meaningful, logical

The newscaster gave a coherent report of the accident.

inherent   innate, essential, intrinsic

Freedom of speech is an inherent part of the Bill of Rights.

complacent   contented

The students were complacent about their grades.

complaisant   willing, obliging

All day long the complaisant horse pulled the vegetable cart.

complement   to complete, to go well with

Two angles complement each other when they add up to 180 degrees.

Cranberries complement a turkey dinner.

compliment   a remark of courtesy or respect, praise

I'd like to compliment you on the excellent job that you did.

continual   repeated, happening often

His continual absence from classes resulted in his suspension.

continuous   uninterrupted, ceaseless

The continuous hum of the machine gave her a headache.

credible   believable, plausible

The child's story simply was not credible.

creditable   worthy of credit or praise, commendable

The teacher did a creditable job in preparing the students for the test.

credulous   ready to believe, gullible, easily convinced

The credulous woman accepted the neighbor's story without question.

denote   to refer to explicitly

The word *black* denotes the characteristic of an object that reflects no color.

connote   to suggest

The word *black* has been taken to connote wickedness or evil.

depredation   sack, plunder, robbing

The effects of the Huns' depredation of the villages were obvious.

deprecation   disapproval, disparagement

The deprecation of the new exhibit hall by all of the townspeople was disheartening to the architect.

detract   to take away from, to diminish

The cracked sidewalks detract from the appearance of the house.

distract   to divert, to turn away from

The student was unable to concentrate because the loud noises from the street distracted him.

discreet   prudent, careful, tactful

The attorney was discreet in his questioning of the young girl.

discrete   separate, distinct, separate

The party was composed of two discrete groups—the progressives and the conservatives.

disinterested   impartial, having nothing to gain

The chairperson was completely disinterested in the outcome of the committee vote.

uninterested   not interested in, unconcerned, incurious

The boy was completely uninterested in the subjects he had to study.

elicit   to draw out

She questioned him for an hour but was unable to elicit any information.

illicit   unlawful, illegal

The police will crack down on all illicit parking.

eminent   prominent, illustrious, preeminent

Gandhi was an eminent statesman.

imminent   close at hand, impending

　　The jury's verdict is imminent.

immanent   inherent, innate, intrinsic

　　Psychologists are studying behavior patterns to determine which are immanent and which are acquired.

farther   to a greater distance

　　The runway was only one-half mile farther than the site of the plane crash.

further   more, additionally (in time or degree)

　　The council will discuss the budget further in the next meeting.

fewer   smaller in number

　　There are fewer students in school now than 10 years ago.

less   more limited in amount

　　Inflation is less now than in the late 1970s.

flammable   combustible, able to burn

inflammable   combustible, able to burn

　　You must be careful when storing flammable material.

　　(The antonym of *flammable* and *inflammable* is *unflammable*.)

flout   to scorn, to treat with disdain

　　Her unconventional dress flouted the guests' sensibilities.

flaunt   to show off, to exhibit

　　The boy flaunted his new scout badge.

homogeneous   of the same kind, uniform, unmixed, similar in structure

　　It was a homogeneous class, all the students having basically the same socioeconomic and educational background.

　　The classes were homogeneously grouped according to abilities.

heterogeneous   mixed or varied in composition

　　The class was heterogeneous, with students from different economic and educational backgrounds.

　　The crowd outside the theater was a heterogeneous group of students and townspeople.

imply   to hint, to suggest, to indicate

　　The teacher's frown implied that the girl's answer was wrong.

infer   to conclude from known facts or premises

　　From the evidence presented, the judge inferred that the defendant was guilty.

ingenious   clever

　　The ingenious monkey figured out how to reach the bananas by constructing a platform.

ingenuous   frank, artless, naive

　　The ingenuous child told his grandmother that he didn't like her dress.

ludicrous   ridiculous

　　Italian western movies may seem ludicrous to an American.

lugubrious   gloomy

The music was lugubrious, suitable for a funeral.

perquisite   privilege that comes with a job

Members of Congress receive mailing privileges as a perquisite.

prerequisite   necessity, something required beforehand

Mathematics is a prerequisite for most physics courses.

precipitate   to bring on, to hasten, to quicken

The Great Depression precipitated the rise of fascism in Germany.

precipitous   steep

Prices during the inflation period rose precipitously.

persecute   to harass, to badger, to victimize

The Puritans came to America after they were persecuted for their religious beliefs.

prosecute   to put on trial, to indict, to bring legal action against

The state will prosecute him for drug trafficking.

perspective   viewpoint

From the perspective of the Native American, land is sacred.

prospective   future, expected

The prospective merger of the two companies caused a flurry of activity on the stock market.

precede   to go in front of

An incubation period usually precedes the onset of the disease.

proceed   to go ahead

After you reach the center of town, proceed three more blocks to the hotel.

prescribe   to order or advise (as in medicine)

The physician will prescribe a drug to combat the infection.

proscribe   to condemn, to disapprove, to outlaw

During the Middle Ages, the Catholic Church proscribed certain books by scientists.

supplement   to add to something

He will supplement his regular school work with night and summer courses.

supplant   to replace, to usurp the place of

Robots will supplant workers in some factories.

venal   capable of being bribed, corrupt

The judge was accused of being venal and accepting large sums of money.

venial   forgivable

His continual tardiness was often annoying but venial.

SELECTED FOREIGN WORDS AND PHRASES USED IN ENGLISH

addenda   a list of additions (Latin)

ad hoc   for a particular purpose (Latin)

aficionado   an ardent devotee (Spanish)

agent provocateur   one who incites another person or an organization (French)

alfresco   outdoors (Italian)

alter ego   a second self; a trusted friend (Latin)

amour-propre   self-esteem (French)

angst   dread, anxiety (German)

a priori   based on theory rather than observation (Latin)

au courant   informed of the latest (French)

baksheesh   tip, gratuity (Persian)

bête noire   a strongly detested person or thing (French)

bildungsroman   personal development novel (German)

bona fide   in good faith (Latin)

bon vivant   an epicure; a lover of good living (French)

bravura   a display of spirit and dash (Italian)

casus belli   a pretext or reason that justifies or allegedly justifies an attack of war (Latin)

caveat emptor   let the buyer beware (Latin)

chef d'oeuvre   chief work; masterpiece (French)

chutzpah   gall, arrogance, audacity (Yiddish)

comme il faut   as it ought to be; proper (French)

contretemps   an inopportune or embarrassing situation (French)

corpus delicti   the evidence necessary to prove that a crime has been committed (Latin)

coup de grâce   a final, decisive blow or event (French)

cul-de-sac   a dead end (French)

de facto   actual (Latin)

déjà vu   illusion of having experienced something already (French)

de jure   technically (Latin)

de rigueur   necessary, obligatory (French)

dernier cri   the last word; the newest fashion (French)

déshabillé   undressed or partially undressed (French)

doppelgänger   a counterpart of a living person (German)

enfant terrible   a bad child; one whose behavior is embarrassing (French)

errata   a list of errors (Latin)

ex cathedra   by virtue of one's position or office (Latin)

faux pas   a social blunder (French)

fiasco   disaster (Italian)

habeas corpus   a writ to report an unlawful detention so that the detained may have due process (Latin)

idée fixe   an idea that dominates one's mind, especially for a long time (French)

in extenso   at full length (Latin)

in extremis   near death (Latin)

ingenue   the stage role of an ingenuous girl; a naive girl (French)

in loco parentis   in the place of a parent; acting as a guardian (Latin)

in medias res   in the middle of things (Latin)

in re   in reference to (Latin)

insouciance   indifference; lack of concern (French)

in vacuo   in a vacuum (Latin)

jefe   boss (Spanish)

junta   group (usually military) that assumes leadership after a coup or overthrow of a government (Spanish)

laissez-faire   a policy of free trade or noninterference (French)

leitmotif   recurring theme (German)

mélange   a mixture or medley, often of incongruous elements (French)

ménage   a household (French)

mirabilis dictu   wonderful to relate (Latin)

modus operandi   a method of procedure, working, or operating (Latin)

ne plus ultra   the highest point that can be attained; the acme (Latin)

noblesse oblige   nobility obligates; the behavior and graciousness of the nobility (French)

nolo contendere   no contest; legally, not contesting a charge against one, but without pleading guilty (Latin)

nom de guerre   a pseudonym used during war (French)

nom de plume   a pen name (French)

non sequitur   something that does not logically follow (Latin)

nuance   a subtle distinction (French)

pax vobiscum   peace be with you; peace (Latin)

persona non grata   an unacceptable or unwelcome person (Latin)

pièce de resistance   the main course or dish; the most valuable object (French)

presto   rapidly, quickly (Italian)

prima facie   on the face of; at first view (Latin)

pro bono publico   for the public good (Latin)

pro forma   done as a matter of form (Latin)

pro rata   proportionally according to a factor (Latin)

pro tempore (pro tem)   for the time being; temporarily (Latin)

punctilio   a fine point; a minute detail of conduct (Italian)

quid pro quo   something given or received for something else; substitute (Latin)

raison d'être   reason for being (French)

rapprochement   establishing a cordial relationship; developing mutual understanding (French)

rara avis   an unusual specimen (Latin)

rendezvous   an appointment for two or more people to meet at a particular place (French)

rigor mortis   stiffening that sets in following death (Latin)

riposte   a retort; a retaliatory verbal sally (French)

safari   a trip or journey (Swahili)

salaam   peace (as a salutation) (Arabic)

sanctum sanctorum   the holy of holies; the office of an awesome person (Latin)

sang froid   cold blood; self-possession, composure (French)

schadenfreude   pleasure at someone else's misfortunes (German)

sine qua non   indispensable (Latin)

soupçon   suspicion; a little bit or trace, as in a recipe (French)

sui genera   one of a kind (Latin)

tour de force   a feat of strength, skill, or ingenuity (French)

vendetta   a blood feud (Italian)

vis-à-vis   face to face with; in relation to; as compared with (French)

weltschmerz   sorrow over the evils of the world (German)

zeitgeist   the spirit of the times (German)

ALPHABETS AND THEIR CHARACTERISTICS

Alphabet	Characteristics/Comments
Cyrillic	Slavic and Russian languages
Cuneiform	Ancient Sumerian iconographic writing
Hieroglyphic	Ancient Egyptian ideographic writing
Devanagari	Indian writing with syllabic features
Greek	Ancient or modern; Greek alphabet
Hebrew	written right to left, no vowels
Arabic	written right to left, no vowels
Roman	used in Romance languages and English
ogham	Old Irish, 5th and 6th century, notches
rune	Germanic, from 3rd to 13th centuries

GEOGRAPHY

It is not possible to provide a review of basic geography here. Since questions involving name changes of countries and cities have appeared on some *MAT* exams, a table of such changes is given below.

Current Name	Previous Names
Angola	Portuguese West Africa
Bangladesh	East Pakistan
Belize	British Honduras
Cambodia	French Indochina
Chad	French Equatorial Africa
Ethiopia	Abyssinia
Ghana	Gold Coast
Guyana	British Guiana
Ho Chi Minh City	Saigon
Indonesia	Netherlands East Indies
Iran	Persia
Iraq	Mesopotamia, Babylon, Assyria
Istanbul	Constantinople
Laos	French Indochina
Madagascar	Malagasy
Myanmar	Burma
Namibia	South West Africa
Niger	French West Africa
Saint Petersburg	Leningrad, Petrograd

Current Name	Previous Names
Santo Domingo	Trujillo
Sri Lanka	Ceylon
Surinam	Dutch Guiana
Thailand	Siam
Vietnam	French Indochina
Volgograd	Stalingrad; Tsaritsyn
Zaire	Congo
Zambia	Northern Rhodesia
Zimbabwe	Rhodesia

HISTORY

MAT analogies may include the names of people, events, wars, treaties, conferences, and documents important in U.S. and world history. The following may serve as a quick review.

Explorers

Amundsen, Roald (1872–1928)   (Norwegian) was first to reach the South Pole and to fly over the North Pole

Balboa, Vasco Núñez de (1475–1517)   (Spanish) Pacific Ocean

Cabot, John (1450–1498)   (English) explored North America

Cartier, Jacques (1491–1557)   (French) St. Lawrence river region

Columbus, Christopher (1451–1506)   (Italian/Spanish) discovery of the New World

Coronado, Francisco Vásquez de (1510–1554)   (Spanish) mythical city of Cibola, SW region of the U.S.

Cortes, Hernando (1485–1547)   (Spanish) Mexico, Aztec nation

de Soto, Hernando (1500–1542)   (Spanish) Cuba, Florida, SE region of the U.S.

Diaz, Bartolomeu (1450–1500)   (Portuguese) Cape of Good Hope

Drake, Sir Francis (1540–1596)   (British) circumnavigated the globe; helped defeat Spanish Armada

Hudson, Henry (d. 1611)   (British) Hudson River, Hudson Bay area

Magellan, Ferdinand (1480–1521)   (Portuguese) the first to sail around the world

Marquette, Jacques (1637–1675)   (French) discovered the Mississippi

Peary, Robert E. (1856–1920)   (American) North Pole (disputed claim; prior claim of Fred Cook)

Pizarro, Francisco (1470–1541)   (Spanish) Peru, Inca empire

Polo, Marco (1254–1324)   (Italian) explored China and Asia

Ponce de Leon, Juan (1460–1521)   (Spanish) first European explorer in Florida

Raleigh, Sir Walter (1552–1618)   (British) eastern coast of the U.S.

Scott, Robert (1868–1912)   (British) Antarctica, South Pole (prior claim of Amundsen)

Vasquez de Coronado, Francisco (1510–1554)   (Spanish) first European to explore Arizona and New Mexico

Vespucci, Amerigo (1454–1521)   (Italian) America was named after him; first to realize that the Americas were a different continent than Asia

Inventors

Beaufort, Francis (1774–1854)   (French) Beaufort Scale: wind force scale named after him
Bell, Alexander Graham (1847–1922)   (American) telephone
Benz, Karl (1844–1929)   (German) the petrol-powered automobile
Berners-Lee, Tim   (b. 1955)   (English) with Robert Cailliau, the World Wide Web
Braille, Louis (1809–1852)   (French) the Braille writing system
Daimler, Gottlieb (1834–1900)   (German) first high-speed internal-combustion engine
Da Vinci, Leonardo (1452–1519)   (Italian) conceptualized a helicopter, painted the Mona Lisa, advanced anatomy, etc.
Diesel, Rudolf (1853–1913)   (German) first internal-combustion engine using fuel oil instead of gasoline
Drais, Karl (1785–1851)   (German) bicycle (Draisine)
Edison, Thomas Alva (1847–1931)   (American) lightbulb, phonograph
Einstein, Albert (1879–1955)   (German) theory of relativity
Engelbart, Douglas (b. 1925)   (American) the computer mouse
Fermi, Enrico (1901–1954)   (Italian) one of the first developers of the nuclear reactor
Fleming, Alexander (1881–1955)   (English) penicillin
Ford, Henry (1863–1947)   (American) developed modern assembly lines for mass production
Franklin, Benjamin (1706–1790)   (American) lightning rod
Galilei, Galileo (1564–1642)   (Italian) improved the telescope, physicist
Gutenberg, Johannes (1400–1468)   (German) movable type, printing press
Marconi, Guglielmo (1874–1937)   (Italian) wireless radio
Montgolfier, Joseph-Michel (1740–1810)   (French) hot-air balloon
Newton, Isaac (1642–1727)   (English) reflecting telescope (reduces chromatic aberration)
Nobel, Alfred (1833–1896)   (Swedish) dynamite
Roentgen, Wilhelm Conrad (1845–1923)   (German) the X-ray machine
Stephenson, George (1781–1848)   (English) first steam locomotive
Whitney, Eli (1765–1825)   (American) interchangeable parts, cotton gin

Liberators or Unifiers

Bismarck, Otto von (1815–1898)   Germany
Bolívar, Simón (1783–1830)   Venezuela, Peru, Bolivia
Garibaldi, Giuseppe (1807–1882)   Italy
O'Higgins, Bernardo (1778–1842)   Chile
San Martin, José de (1778–1850)   Peru, Chile (march across the Andes)

Major Wars

Knowledge of the most important events and treaties associated with major wars will help in taking the *MAT*. Below is a list of some major items that may be found in analogies.

THE AMERICAN REVOLUTION

first battles—Lexington and Concord (1775)
major battles—Bunker Hill (1775), Fort Ticonderoga (1775), Saratoga (1777), Valley Forge (1777)
Declaration of Independence—declared that colonies were free from England, 1776

Continental Congress—federal legislature of the 13 colonies under the Articles of Confederation
   (1774, 1775)
Constitution—replaced Articles of Confederation in 1789
end of war—surrender of British General Cornwallis to George Washington at Yorktown (1781);
   treaty recognizing the United States as a separate nation signed in Paris (1782)

AMERICAN CIVIL WAR

start of war—Harper's Ferry (1859)
first battles—Fort Sumter (1861) and Bull Run (1861) (both Confederate victories)
major battles—Antietam (1862), Fredericksburg (1862), Gettysburg (1863), Shiloh (1862) (the
   Union named battles after towns; the Confederates named battles after streams), Sherman's
   March to the Sea (1864), Vicksburg (1863) (great victory for Grant)
end of war—surrender of General Lee to General Grant at Appomatox Court House (1865)

FRENCH REVOLUTION

start of war—storming of the Bastille (1789)
important events/documents—Declaration of the Rights of Man and Citizen (Preamble to
   the Constitution), 1791; Reign of Terror, which ended. Thermidor (July 27, 1794) with the
   execution of Robespierre; coup d'etat of 18 Brumaire (November 9–10, 1799) whereby
   Napoleon I becomes consul
end of war—treaty of Amiens, France (1802)

RUSSIAN CIVIL WAR

conflicting sides—Bolsheviks (majority) vs. Mensheviks (minority)
leaders of opposing sides—Lenin and Trotsky (Reds) vs. Kerensky and Plekanov (Whites)

WORLD WAR I

start of war—assassination of Archduke Ferdinand (1914); sinking of *Lusitania* (1915) (British
   ship with American passengers) by the Germans led to U.S. entry into the war (1917)
major battles—Ypres (1917), Marne (1914), Verdun (1916), Somme (1916) offensive
   characteristics—trench warfare, use of poison gas
end of war—Treaty of Versailles (1918); attempt to divide nations on basis
   of national self-determination; establishment of the League of Nations; strict penalties
   imposed against Germany

WORLD WAR II

major events—Munich Pact (1938), policy of appeasement, associated with British Prime
   Minister Chamberlain
start of war—blitzkrieg over Poland (1939); sinking of *Arizona* and other ships at Pearl Harbor
   attack in Honolulu led to U.S. declaration of war against Japan and Germany (1941)
major battles—Dunkirk (1940), Ardennes (1944), Alamein (North Africa 1942), Stalingrad (1942–1943)
characteristics—tank warfare, blitzkrieg, use of massive bombing by air force; development of
   atomic weapons
end of war—Japan surrenders unconditionally at Potsdam Conference (1945)

OTHER CONFERENCES AND PEACE TREATIES

Ghent, Belgium—end of War of 1812

Vienna, Congress of—end of Napoleonic Wars (1814–1815)

Yalta Conference—meeting of Roosevelt, Churchill, and Stalin during World War II (1945)

Potsdam (German) Conference—meeting of Truman, Churchill (replaced by Atlee), and Stalin during World War II (1945)

Geneva Convention—outlined appropriate conduct during war (1949)

Panmunjon, Korea—end of Korean War (1953)

Reykjavik Conference—Reagan-Gorbachev summit meeting (1986)

Kyoto Protocol—International framework on climate change (1997)

SOCIAL SCIENCES

The following brief list of people and movements in the social sciences is intended as a quick review only.

Adler, Alfred (1870–1937)   Austrian psychiatrist; inferiority complex

Allison, Graham (b. 1940)   American political scientist, has worked in decision-making and is an important analyst of national security

Barzun, Jacques (b. 1907)   American historian specializing in expressions of culture like music, literature, and education

Behaviorism (Psychology)   School of thought in psychology since the early 1900s. Suggests that behavior can be explained by means of environmental causes. Proponents were John B. Watson, Ivan Pavlov, and B. F. Skinner, for example. Focus on classical and operant conditioning.

Benedict, Ruth (1887–1948)   American anthropologist; author of *Patterns of Culture*

Binet, Alfred (1851–1911) and **Simon, Théodore** (1873–1961)   French psychologists; development of IQ tests

Boas, Franz (1858–1942)   German American anthropologist; known for being the "father" of modern anthropology as he applied the scientific method to his anthropological studies

Cognitive psychology   Focuses on mental processes including how people think, perceive, remember, and learn. One of the most influential theories was the stages of cognitive development theory proposed by Jean Piaget. Other cognitive psychologists include Albert Bandura, Daniel Kahneman, Steven Pinker, Daniel Schacter, and Robert Sternberg.

Coleman, James (1926–1995)   American sociologist; one of the early users of the term "social capital"

Cultural materialism (Anthropology)   Attaches special importance to technology and economic factors in the development of a society.

Dewey, John (1859–1952)   American educator/philosopher; pragmatism

DuBois, W. E. B. (1868–1963)   American sociologist and historian; active in the area of racism

Durkheim, Emile (1859–1917)   French sociologist; considered one of the fathers of modern sociology

Erikson, Erik (1902–1994)   American psychologist; stage theory of development

Ferguson, Niall (b. 1964)   Scottish historian specializing in financial and economic history

Freud, Sigmund (1856–1939)   Austrian psychiatrist; sexual drive, Oedipus complex

Friedman, Milton (1912–2006)   American economist, recipient of the Nobel Prize in economics; opposed government regulation

Functionalism (Anthropology, Sociology)   Applies the scientific method to the examination of the social world (e.g., social surveys, interviews) and uses analogies between individual organisms and society. Emphasis is on use. Proponents include Emile Durkheim and Talcott Parsons.

Gall, Franz Joseph (1758–1828)   German anatomist/physiologist; study of nervous system and brain, founded pseudoscience of phrenology

Galton, Sir Francis (1822–1911)   English scientist; belief in heredity as predeterminant force, IQ tests

Geertz, Clifford (1926–2006)   American anthropologist; worked in the field of symbolic anthropology, which attributes special importance to thoughts (symbols)

Gestalt psychology   Developed in Germany and Austria in the late 19th century. Gestalt psychologists believe that the conscious experience must be considered as a whole, rather than broken down into small elements. The whole is greater than just the sum of its parts. Prononents include Max Wertheimer, Kurt Koffka, Wolfgang Koehler, and Fritz Perls.

Gibbon, Edward (1737–1794)   English historian who wrote *The History of the Decline and Fall of the Roman Empire*

Goffman, Erving (1922–1982)   American sociologist who studied social interaction

Goodall, Jane (b. 1934)   American anthropologist and primatologist; known for her chimpanzee studies in Tanzania

Greenspan, Alan (b. 1926)   American economist; former chairman of the Federal Reserve

Harlow, Harry (1905–1981)   American psychologist; importance of attachment for baby monkeys

Heterodox economics   Economic schools of thought that are outside of mainstream economics. They include the Austrian School, ecological economics, and Post-Keynesian economics.

Horney, Karen (1885–1952)   American psychiatrist; importance of social and cultural influences on behavior

Huizinga, Johan (1872–1945)   Dutch historian, one of the founders of modern cultural history

Humanistic psychology   Developed in the 1950s in response to both behaviorism and psychoanalysis. Focused on individual free will, personal growth, and self-actualization. Major proponents include Abraham Maslow and Carl Rogers.

Hume, David (1711–1776)   Scottish philosopher; use of induction

Huntington, Samuel (1927–2008)   American political scientist, famous for his theory of the "Clash of Civilizations"

James, William (1842–1910)   American philosopher; pragmatism, functionalism

Jung, Carl (1875–1961)   Swiss psychiatrist; self-realization

Kant, Immanuel (1724–1804)   German philosopher; proposed categorical imperative

Keynes, John Maynard (1883–1946)   British developer of Keynesian economics, founder of modern theoretical macroeconomics

Kohlberg, Lawrence (1927–1987)   American psychologist; moral stages of development

Köhler, Wolfgang (1887–1967)   German-American psychologist; Gestaltist, worked with chimps

Krugman, Paul (b. 1953)   American economist; won the Nobel Memorial Prize in Economic Sciences in 2008 for his work on New Trade Theory

Leibnitz, Gottfried (1646–1716)   German philosopher/mathematician; use of deduction

Malinowski, Bronislaw (1884–1942)   Polish anthropologist, pioneer in ethnographic fieldwork

Malthus, Thomas (1766–1834)   English demographer and political economist; noted the potential for populations to increase rapidly, and more rapidly than the food supply

Mansfield, Harvey (b. 1932)   American political scientist; conservative; author of *Manliness*

Marx, Karl (1818–1883)   German economist; founder of communism

Mill, John Stuart (1806–1873)   English philosopher; used principle of utility

Nye, Joseph (b. 1937)   American political scientist; developed the concepts of asymmetrical and complex interdependence with Robert Keohane

Parsons, Talcott (1902–1979)   American sociologist; developed structural functionalism as a means of analyzing society

Patterson, Orlando (b. 1940)   American sociologist known for his work on race

Pavlov, Ivan (1849–1936)   Russian physiologist/psychologist; conditioning of reflexes, worked with dogs

Peirce, Charles Sanders (1839–1914)   American philosopher; pragmatist

Piaget, Jean (1896–1980)   Swiss psychologist; stage theory of intellectual development

Psychoanalysis (Psychology)   Founded by Sigmund Freud. States that the human mind is composed of three elements: the id, the ego, and the superego. The unconscious plays an important role in the explanation of behavior. Other psychoanalysts include Anna Freud, Carl Jung, and Erik Erikson.

Sachs, Jeffrey (b. 1954)   American economist; author of *The End of Poverty*; Special Advisor to United Nations Secretary-General Ban Ki-Moon

Skinner, B[urrhus] F[rederic] (1904–1990)   American psychologist; behaviorist; studied effects of reinforcement on behavior; worked with rats, pigeons (Skinner box)

Smith, Adam (1723–1790)   English; one of the founders of modern economics, author of *The Wealth of Nations*

Strauss, Claude Levi (1908–2008)   French anthropologist; author of *Structural Anthropology*; viewed culture as a system of symbolic communication

Structuralism (Anthropology, Sociology)   Suggests that meaning is produced through practices and activities. The mind uses binary opposites (like day and night) that differ from culture to culture. Proponents include Claude Levi-Strauss.

Symbolic interactionism (Sociology)   People interact with each other by interpreting each other's actions. Their interactions are therefore based on the meaning they attach to the actions. Proponents include George H. Mead, Herbert Blumer, and Erving Goffman.

Thorndike, Edward (1874–1949)   American educator/psychologist; intelligence, I.Q. tests, worked with cats

Titchener, Edward (1867–1927)   American psychologist; structuralist

von Ranke, Leopold (1795–1886)   German historian considered one of the founders of modern source-based history

Walzer, Michael (b. 1935)   American political philosopher; known for his work on just and unjust wars, economic justice, and ethnicity

Watson, John (1878–1958)   American psychologist; behaviorist

Weber, Max (1864–1920)   German sociologist; argued in *The Protestant Ethic and the Spirit of Capitalism* that Protestantism influenced the development of capitalism

ART AND ARCHITECTURE

Use the following list of the most important artists and architects and schools and movements in art history as a quick review. The names of artists associated with the movement or school and the works of particular artists are given in parentheses.

Important Artists, Architects, and Schools/Movements

abstract art   art form that assumes that artistic values reside in form and color and are independent of the subject of the art or painting

abstract expressionism   1940s-to-1950s American art movement stressing spontaneous, nonrepresentational creation with emphasis on the paint itself; first truly American school of art (Pollock)

art deco   1920s-to-1930s art movement stressing highly decorative art, utilizing geometric, streamlined forms inspired by industrial design (Chrysler Building in New York City)

art nouveau   1895-to-1905 "new art" movement characterized by motifs of highly stylized flowing plants, curving lines, and fluent forms

ashcan school   early 20th century school of American realist painters who abandoned idealized subjects for more sordid aspects of urban life

Audubon, John James (1785–1851)   early 19th century American artist and illustrator known for his color engravings of birds (*Birds in America*)

Barbizon school   mid-19th century group of landscape artists who rejected the classical and romantic to portray nature as they perceived it; forerunner of impressionism (Rousseau)

baroque   late 16th-to-early 18th century movement, developed in Italy, that stressed grand theatrical effects and elaborate ornamentation (Palace of Versailles)

Bauhaus   most famous school of architecture and design of modern times; founded in Germany in 1919; austere, geometric style (founder: Gropius; teachers: Klee and Kandinsky)

beaux arts   architectural style, popular from 1890 to 1920, using formal and classical techniques

Bosch, Hieronymus (1450–1516)   early 16th century painter considered perhaps the greatest master of fantasy ever (*Garden of Earthly Delights*)

Botticelli, Sandro (1444–1510)   15th century Italian Renaissance artist (*The Birth of Venus, St. Sebastian*)

Brancusi, Constantin (1876–1957)   19th-to-20th century Romanian sculptor known for highly simplified archetypical human and animal forms (*The Kiss, Bird in Space*)

Brueghel, Pieter (the Elder) (1525–1569)   16th century Flemish painter known for peasant scenes and large landscapes; sometimes known as "Peasant Bruegel" (*Hunters in the Snow, The Harvesters*)

Byzantine art   Eastern (Greek) art of the 5th to 15th centuries, characterized by Oriental motifs, formal design, and free use of gilding

Caldecott, Randolph (1864–1886)   19th century English illustrator known for his illustrations of children's books; the prestigious Caldecott Award is given annually for excellence in children's book illustration

Calder, Alexander (1898–1976)   20th century American sculptor and abstract painter best known for mobiles and stabiles (nonmoving sculptures) (*Lobster Trap and Fish Tail, Spiral*)

Cellini, Benvenuto (1500–1571)   16th century Florentine sculptor, goldsmith, and designer of coins and medals (*Perseus* bronze, gold saltcellar)

Cézanne, Paul (1839–1906)   19th century French painter, often considered the forerunner of many 20th century art movements; romantic, impressionist, classical, and naturalistic influences are all condensed in his work (*Grande Baigneuses, Self Portrait, The Black Clock, Card Players*)

Chagall, Marc (1889–1985)   20th century French painter of Russian-Jewish origin, forerunner of surrealism (*The Juggler, The Green Violinist*)

chiaroscuro   the balance of light and shadow in a picture; used to describe works that are predominantly dark, like those of Rembrandt

classicism   art attributed to ancient Greece and Rome, characterized by discipline, harmony, objectivity, and reason

cloisonné   a process of enameling in which a design is displayed in strips of metal on a china or metal background, making channels, or cloisons, to hold the enamel colors

Cole, Thomas (1801–1848)   19th century American landscape painter; member of the Hudson River school of painting

collage a picture built up wholly or partly from pieces of paper, cloth, or other material stuck on canvas or other surface (early cubists, dadaists, Matisse)

Constable, John (1776–1837) 19th century English landscape painter (*The Holy Wain*)

constructivism movement, since the 1920s, principally in Russia, involving the creation of three-dimensional art, using iron, glass, plastic, and other materials to express technological society (Calder's mobiles)

Copley, John Singleton (1738–1815) 18th century American protrait painter

cubism 1907-to-1915 art movement, mainly French, characterized by fragmentation of reality; used geometric forms in nature as a departure from representational art; a reaction to impressionism (Picasso)

Currier, Nathaniel T. (1813–1888) and **Ives, James Merrit** (1824–1895) 19th century American lithographers known for prints depicting American life

dada 1915-to-1923 international anti-art movement reflecting cynicism by producing bizarre works that represented the absurd (*Mona Lisa with a Mustache*)

Dali, Salvador (1904–1989) 20th century Spanish painter, considered one of the foremost surrealists (*Premonition of the Civil War, Christ of St. John of the Cross, Persistence of Memory*)

Daumier, Honoré (1808–1879) 19th century French lithographer, cartoonist, and social satirist (*The Print Collector, The People of Justice*)

Degas, Edgar (1834–1917) late 19th–early 20th century French painter (*Study of a Dancer, Woman on Horseback*)

de Kooning, Willem (1904–1997) 20th century Dutch abstract painter known for distorted shapes and tragic expressions (*Woman, I*)

Delacroix, Eugène (1798–1863) 19th century French painter of the Romantic period (*Liberty at the Barricades*)

Donatello (1386–1466) 15th century Florentine sculptor; one of the founders of Italian Renaissance sculpture (*David, St. George Slaying the Dragon*)

Dürer, Albrecht (1471–1528) late 15th–early 16th century German artist known for his woodcuts and engravings (*His Mother*, a charcoal drawing; *Adam and Eve*, an engraving; and *The Apocalypse*, a series of woodcuts)

engraving a method of multiplying prints. See also **relief**, **intaglio**, and **lithography**

Ernst, Max (1891–1976) 20th century German-born French artist, a leading surrealist and one of the founders of dada; known for his "reveries" (*Europe After the Rain, Mundus est Fabula*)

expressionism 20th century art in which the expression of the artist takes precedence over rational and faithful rendering of the subject matter; stress on emotions and inner visions (van Gogh, El Greco)

fauvism work of early 20th-century impressionists, characterized by strident color and distortion; first artistic revolution of the 20th century (Matisse, Roualt)

Fayum portrait realistic form of portraiture found on shrouds and mummy cases from the 1st to 4th centuries

fresco wall painting; painting on wet plaster

frieze middle section of a building, where relief sculpture was often executed

Fuller, Buckminster (1895–1983) 20th century American avant-garde architect famous for his geodesic domes

futurism 1910 Italian art movement that stressed motion and sought to glorify the machine by painting and sculpting multitudes of moving parts

Gainsborough, Thomas (1727–1788) 18th century English painter of landscapes and portraits (*Blue Boy*)

gargoyle   in Gothic architecture, a bizarre creature whose open mouth was used as a gutter to carry water away from the walls

Gauguin, Paul (1848–1903)   19th century French painter best known for his depiction of simple life in Tahiti (*Indian Ocean Maiden*)

glazing   a process of applying a transparent layer of oil paint over a solid one so that the color of the first layer is greatly modified

Gothic   12th-to-16th century style of architecture typical of northern Europe (cathedrals with elaborate architecture and stained glass panels)

Goya, Francisco José de (1746–1828)   late 18th–early 19th century Spanish painter and printmaker (*Majas on a Balcony*)

Greco, El (1541–1614)   16th century Greek painter who lived and worked in Spain (*The Annunciation, The Burial of the Count of Orgaz*)

Hogarth, William (1697–1764)   18th century English artist (*Signing the Marriage Contract*)

Holbein, Hans (the Younger) (1497–1543)   16th century German Renaissance painter (*Dance of Death, Dead Christ*)

holograph   an image in three dimensions created by a laser passing through a photographic film or plate without a camera

Homer, Winslow (1836–1910)   late 19th century American painter and illustrator; Civil War illustrations

Hopper, Edward (1882–1967)   20th century American artist known for bleak, surreal scenes depicting city life and the ennui of workers

Hudson River school   mid-19th century American school of landscape painting known for its romantic scenes glorifying nature

impasto   thick application of pigment to canvas

impressionism   late 19th century French school that stressed visual impression; first of the modern art movements (Monet, Renoir, Degas)

intaglio   engraving on stone to achieve a concave effect; opposite of cameo

Johns, Jasper (b. 1930)   20th century American pop artist known for blown-up images (*Flags, Targets*)

Kandinsky, Wassily (1866–1944)   late 19th–early 20th century Russian-born German artist, one of the founders of the abstract movement; known for kinetic lines

Kinetic art   art that moves through magnets, motorized parts, etc.

Klee, Paul (1879–1940)   late 19th–early 20th century Swiss painter and etcher known for his whimsical works that sought to portray reality through its inner nature (*Inventions, Senecio*)

Leonardo da Vinci (1452–1519)   late 15th–early 16th century Italian artist and scientist; most versatile genius of the Renaissance (fresco: *The Last Supper*, painting: *Mona Lisa*; notebook drawings of human anatomy)

lithography   method of printing that uses wax and ink on hard plates

luminism   American art movement associated with impressionism, concerned with the effect of light

Maillol, Aristide (1861–1944)   late 19th–early 20th century French painter and sculptor (*The Three Graces, Seated Woman*)

Manet, Edouard (1832–1883)   19th century French painter who contributed much to the development of impressionism, although he himself was not a member of the group (*The Fifer, Guitarist*)

mannerism   1520s-to-1590s school of art and architecture characterized by the exotic and confusing and the distortion of the human form (El Greco, Vassari)

Matisse, Henri (1869–1954)   late 19th–early 20th century French artist known for his still-life subjects; a member of the fauve group and influenced by impressionism (*Jazz: Icarus, Fruits and Flowers*)

Michelangelo, Bounarotti (1475–1564)   late 15th–early 16th century Italian sculptor, painter, architect, and poet who embodied the Renaissance (*Pietà, David, Madonna and Child*, ceiling of the Sistine Chapel)

Mies van der Rohe, Ludwig (1886–1969)   20th century German-American architect known for clean-line skyscrapers of glass and metal and for steel-framed furniture (Barcelona chair)

minimal art   contemporary art movement that rejects emotional expression and stresses restraint, understatement, and precision

Miró, Joan (1893–1983)   20th century Spanish surrealist painter known for depicting fantasies (*Dutch Interior, Woman and Bird in the Moonlight*)

mobile   a kinetic sculpture consisting of shapes cut from different materials and hung at different levels (Calder)

modern art   art, since the 1850s, that has extricated itself from subject matter and stresses form

Modigliani, Amedeo (1884–1920)   late 19th–early 20th century Italian sculptor and painter known for his sad, elongated faces (*Seated Nude, The Brown Haired Girl*)

Mondrian, Piet (1872–1944)   late 19th–early 20th century Dutch abstract painter known for his geometric shapes (*Composition with Red, Yellow and Blue*)

Monet, Claude (1840–1926)   late 19th–early 20th century French painter, a leader of impressionism; known for seeing nature with an "objective eye" (*Water Lily paintings*)

montage   sticking one layer over another, especially photographs applied to an unusual background; associated with cubists

Moore, Henry (1898–1986)   20th century British sculptor known for large-scale abstract works and "truth to materials" doctrine (*Family Group*)

Moses, Anna Mary (Grandma) (1860–1961)   late 19th–early 20th century American painter known for her simple depictions of New England life and landscapes

Murillo, Bartolomé Estebon (1617–1682)   17th century Spanish painter (*Immaculate Conception, Beggar Boy*)

Nast, Thomas (1840–1902)   19th century American illustrator and cartoonist known for his depictions of Tweed ring and Tammany Hall

naturalism   late 19th century art movement that tried to depict humans and society true to life and in precise detail

neoclassicism   1790s-to-1830s rejection of rococo and a return to classical style; characterized by restraint and balance

O'Keeffe, Georgia (1887–1986)   20th century American painter known for her large New Mexican landscapes

pop art   1960s American art movement derived from popular culture and commercial art, with art culled from everyday life (Warhol)

pastiche   piece of art created in the style of a particular artist or movement but not faked, as in forgery

Picasso, Pablo (1881–1973)   20th century Spanish painter, sculptor, and printmaker considered one of the foremost artists of the 20th century. After his "Blue period" paintings of despairing people and his "Rose period" circus paintings, he turned to cubism and still later to surrealism and collage (*Guernica, Three Musicians, Artists*)

pointillism   1880s art form in which tiny dots of paint, when viewed from a distance, take on the shape of objects (Seurat)

Pollock, Jackson (1912–1956)   20th century American painter of the abstract expressionist school known for his large canvases (later cut up) that aim to create subconscious reality

Raphael (1483–1520)   early 16th century Italian painter who, along with Leonardo da Vinci and Michelangelo, is considered a creator of the Renaissance (*Transfiguration, St. Michael, Saint George and the Dragon*)

realism   art form that attempts to search for the squalid and depressing with a style of strict attention to detail

relief   sculpture that is not free standing; in having a background, the sculpture resembles a painting

Rembrandt, Harmensz (1606–1669)   17th century Dutch painter who is best known for his portraits but who also did landscapes, Biblical subjects, and etchings (*Self Portrait with Sprouting Beard, Night Watch, The Anatomy Lesson of Dr. Nicolaes Tulp*)

Remington, Frederic (1861–1909)   19th century American painter, illustrator, and sculptor known for his romantic scenes of the American Old West

Renoir, Pierre-Auguste (1841–1919)   late 19th–early 20th century French painter; a founder of impressionism (*Moulin de la Galette, Les Grandes Baigneuses*)

Reynolds, Sir Joshua (1723–1792)   18th century British portrait painter

rococo   1730s-to-1780s style of European art that glorified asymmetrical ornamentation on paneling, porcelain, and jewelry to display a love of gaiety and elegance

Rockwell, Norman (1894–1978)   20th century painter known for his paintings of idyllic American life

Rodin, Auguste (1840–1917)   late 19th–early 20th century French sculptor, the most famous sculptor of the late 19th century (*The Thinker, The Kiss*)

romanticism   a current throughout art history that stresses the importance of fantasy and the imagination over reason and order

Rothko, Mark (1903–1970)   20th century Russian-born American abstract expressionist painter known for his canvases of irregular shapes and bands of color

Rouault, Georges (1871–1958)   late 19th–early 20th century French expressionist painter (*The Apprentice, Christian Nocturne, The Holy Face*)

Rousseau, Henri (1844–1910)   19th century French painter, one of the foremost primitive artists of the modern age (*The Sleeping Gypsy, The Dream*)

Rubens, Peter Paul (1577–1640)   late 16th–early 17th century Flemish baroque painter, the most famous artist of northern Europe in his day (*The Judgment of Paris, Portrait of Helene Fourment, The Descent from the Cross*)

Sargent, John Singer (1856–1925)   late 19th–early 20th century American portrait painter (*Lady Hamilton*)

serial art   the repetition, possibly with slight variation, of a particular image in a work of art (Warhol)

serigraphy   a type of silk screen painting

Seurat, Georges (1859–1891)   19th century French artist who introduced pointillism (*Sunday Afternoon on the Island of La Grande Jatte*)

sfumato   painting technique in which one tone is blended into another without an abrupt outline

still life   the depiction of inanimate objects

surrealism   art form, since 1924, that seeks to reveal psychological reality behind appearances; subject matter stresses dreams, fantasies, and the subconscious (Magritte, Dali, Miró)

symbolism   1885 movement in art that sought to depict the world through the visionary eye of dreams and illusions

Titian (1488–1576)   16th century Italian artist, one of the greatest masters of the Renaissance (*Assumption, Venus of Urbino, Venus and Adonis*)

Toulouse-Lautrec, Henri de (1864–1901)   19th century French artist influenced by the impressionists (*Jane Avril, The Moulin Rouge*)

triptych   three panels, usually arranged or joined by hinges so that the two wings can be folded over to cover the larger central panel

Turner, Joseph Mallord William (1775–1851)   late 18th–early 19th century British landscape artist (*Fighting Téméraire*)

Utrillo, Maurice (1883–1955)   late 19th–early 20th century French painter (*Sacré Coeur*)

van Dyck, Sir Anthony (1599–1641)   17th century Flemish painter (*Charles I of England in Hunting Dress, Portrait of Charles V*)

van Eyck, Jan (1390–1440)   15th century Flemish painter known for his perfection of the oil medium

van Gogh, Vincent (1853–1890)   19th century Dutch postimpressionist painter (*The Sunflowers, Starry Night, Self-Portrait*)

Velázquez, Diego (1599–1660)   17th century Spanish painter (*The Maids of Honor, Pope Innocent X*)

Vermeer, Jan (1632–1675)   17th century Dutch painter known for his domestic scenes (*Woman With a Water Jug, The Lacemaker*)

vignette   decoration, often of leaves, adorning the first letter of a chapter of book section

Vuillard, Edouard (1868–1940)   late 19th–early 20th century French post-impressionist painter (*Under the Trees*)

Warhol, Andy (1928–1987)   20th century American pop artist (*Ten-Foot Flowers*)

Whistler, James Abbott McNeill (1834–1903)   19th century American painter and etcher (*Whistler's Mother*)

Wood, Grant (1892–1942)   20th century American regionalist painter famous for midwestern American themes (*American Gothic*)

Wren, Sir Christopher (1632–1723)   late 17th–early 18th century English architect known for his reconstruction of St. Paul's Cathedral and other parts of London

Wright, Frank Lloyd (1867–1959)   20th century American architect known for "organic architecture" (Taliesin West, Guggenheim Museum in New York City)

Wyeth, Andrew (1917–2009)   20th century American painter known for his depictions of Chadds Ford, Pennsylvania, and Maine fishing village subjects (*Ground Hog Day*)

Famous Art Museums in the World

Getty	Los Angeles
Guggenheim	New York
Hagia Sophia	Istanbul
Hermitage	Leningrad
Louvre	Paris
Metropolitan	New York
Pergamon	Berlin
Prado	Madrid
Rijks	Amsterdam
Tate	London
Tretyakov	Moscow
Uffizi	Florence

LITERARY FORMS AND FIGURES

The following is a list of many important writers and literary terms. The works of particular authors are given in parentheses.

Aeschylus (525–456 B.C.)   earliest Greek dramatist (*Prometheus Bound, The Oresteia*)

allegory   a narrative poem or prose work in which persons, events, and objects represent or stand for something else, frequently abstract ideas

alliteration   the repetition of consonant sounds in two or more neighboring words or syllables

assonance   the close repetition of similar vowel sounds

Aristophanes (445–380 B.C.)   Greek playwright, master of Old Comedy (*Lysistrata, The Frogs*)

Austen, Jane (1775–1817)   English novelist (*Pride and Prejudice, Emma*)

Baldwin, James (1924–1987)   American author (*Go Tell It on the Mountain*)

Balzac, Honoré de (1799–1850)   French novelist (*The Human Comedy, Cousin Bette, Pere Goriot*)

Baudelaire, Charles-Pierre (1821–1867)   French symbolist writer (*The Flowers of Evil*)

Beat Movement   American writers of the 1950s who expressed their feelings of alienation from society (*Kerouac, Ginsberg, Ferlinghetti*)

Beckett, Samuel (1906–1989)   Irish-born novelist, dramatist, and poet; lived in France (*Waiting for Godot, Molloy*)

Bellow, Saul (1915–2005)   American novelist (*Seize the Day, Herzog*)

Beyle, Marie-Henri (pseudonym **Stendhal**) (1783–1842)   one of the leading 19th century French novelists, famous for the psychological and political insight of his works (*The Red and the Black, The Charterhouse of Parma*)

bildungsroman   a novel, usually autobiographical, that covers the principal subject's life from adolescence to maturity

Blair, Eric (pseudonym **George Orwell**) (1903–1950)   British novelist (*Animal Farm, 1984*)

Blake, William (1757–1827)   visionary English poet, engraver, and artist; early Romantic (*Songs of Innocence, Songs of Experience, The Marriage of Heaven and Hell*)

blank verse   poetry in which each line must have 10 syllables and a specific rhythm (iambic pentameter); the lines are unrhymed

free verse   a verse form without regular meter (Whitman's Leaves of Grass is written in free verse)

Boswell, James (1740–1795)   wrote famous biography of Samuel Johnson

Brontë, Charlotte (1816–1855) and **Emily** (1818–1848)   English authors (*Charlotte, Jane Eyre; Emily, Wuthering Heights*)

Browning, Elizabeth Barrett (1806–1861)   English poet, married to Robert Browning (*Sonnets from the Portuguese*)

Browning, Robert (1812–1889)   English poet, married to Elizabeth Barrett Browning, known for dramatic monologues (*My Last Duchess*)

Bryant, William Cullen (1794–1878)   American nature poet ("Thanatopsis")

Bunyan, John (1628–1688)   17th century English writer of religious allegories (*Pilgrim's Progress*)

Byron, Lord George Gordon (1788–1824)   English Romantic poet (*Childe Harold's Pilgrimage, Don Juan*)

Camus, Albert (1913–1960)   French existentialist writer (*The Stranger*)

canto   a major division of a long poem

Cather, Willa Sibert (1873–1947)   American author, wrote about 1880s pioneering life in the Midwest (*O Pioneers!, My Antonia*)

Cervantes, Miguel de (1547-1616)   Spanish writer (*Don Quixote de la Mancha*)

Chaucer, Geoffrey (1343-1400)   14th century English author, often called the Father of English Poetry (*The Canterbury Tales*)

Chekhov, Anton Pavlovich (1860-1904)   Russian writer, best known for his plays (*The Cherry Orchard, The Three Sisters*)

Christie, Agatha (1890-1976)   English mystery writer; created the famous detective Hercule Poirot

classicism   literature characterized by balance, restraint, unity, and proportion; epitomized by Virgil, Pope, Homer

Clemens, Samuel (pseudonym **Mark Twain**) (1835-1910)   American author (*Tom Sawyer, Huckleberry Finn, A Connecticut Yankee in King Arthur's Court*)

Coleridge, Samuel Taylor (1772-1834)   English Romantic poet; with Wordsworth, published *Lyrical Ballads*, which inaugurated the romantic movement in England (*The Rime of the Ancient Mariner*, "Kubla Khan," "Christabel")

Conrad, Joseph (1857-1924)   English novelist born in Poland (*Heart of Darkness, Lord Jim*)

Cooper, James Fenimore (1789-1851)   18th century American novelist who wrote about the American frontier (*Leather-Stocking Tales*, which includes *The Last of the Mohicans* and *The Deerslayer*)

couplet   two successive rhyming lines of poetry, usually having the same meter

Dante (1265-1321)   (13th-early 14th century) considered the greatest Italian poet (*The Divine Comedy*, an allegory in verse consisting of 100 cantos)

deconstructionism   contemporary literary criticism

Defoe, Daniel (1660-1731)   early English novelist (*Robinson Crusoe, Moll Flanders*)

Dickens, Charles (1812-1870)   English novelist (*David Copperfield, A Tale of Two Cities, Oliver Twist, Nicholas Nickleby, A Christmas Carol*)

Dickinson, Emily (1830-1886)   one of the great American poets of the 19th century ("Because I Could Not Stop for Death")

Donne, John (1572-1631)   considered the greatest English metaphysical poet ("The Flea," "Death Be Not Proud")

Dos Passos, John (1896-1970)   American author, best known for his trilogy *U.S.A.* about the first 30 years of 20th century America

Dostoyevsky, Fyodor Mikhaylovich (1821-1881)   Russian novelist (*Crime and Punishment, The Brothers Karamazov, The Idiot*)

Doyle, Sir Arthur Conan (1859-1930)   English author, creator of Sherlock Holmes and his aide, Watson

Dreiser, Theodore (1871-1945)   American novelist associated with naturalist movement (*Sister Carrie, An American Tragedy*)

Dumas, Alexandre (1802-1870)   French novelist and dramatist (*The Three Musketeers, The Count of Monte Cristo*)

Eliot, T[homas] S[tearns] (1888-1965)   20th century English (American born) poet, dramatist, and critic (*Prufrock and Other Observations, The Waste Land, Murder in the Cathedral*)

Emerson, Ralph Waldo (1803-1882)   American poet and essayist; central figure in American transcendentalism

epistolary novel   a novel in which the story is carried forward entirely through letters from one or more persons (Richardson's *Pamela*)

epithalamion or epithalamium   a song or poem written to celebrate marriage

Euripides (480-406 B.C.)   Greek tragic dramatist (*Medea*)

Evans, Mary Anne (pseudonym **George Eliot**) (1819–1880)   English novelist (*Middlemarch, The Mill on the Floss, Silas Marner*)

existentialism   school of thought based on belief that people have free will and are therefore completely responsible for their actions (Sartre, Camus)

Faulkner, William (1897–1962)   20th century American novelist; wrote about the South; known for his use of stream of consciousness (*The Sound and the Fury, As I Lay Dying, Absalom, Absalom!*)

Fielding, Henry (1707–1754)   early English novelist (*Tom Jones, Joseph Andrews*)

Fitzgerald, F[rancis] Scott (1896–1940)   considered the literary spokesperson for America's "Jazz Age" [the "Lost Generation"] (*This Side of Paradise, The Great Gatsby*)

Flaubert, Gustave (1821–1880)   French novelist (*Madame Bovary*)

Frost, Robert (1874–1963)   most popular 20th century American poet ("Stopping by Woods on a Snowy Evening," "Mending Wall," "After Apple-Picking")

García Márquez, Gabriel (1927–2014)   Colombian author who popularized Spanish literature in the Anglophone world; father of magic realism (*One Hundred Years of Solitude, Love in the Time of Cholera*)

Gardner, Erle Stanley (1889–1970)   American writer, author of Perry Mason mysteries

genre   a type or classification of literary work (e.g., tragedy, comedy, epic, satire, lyric, novel, essay, biography)

Goethe, Johann Wolfgang von (1749–1832)   German poet, playwright, and novelist (*Faust*, a verse play in which the character Mephistopheles is the devil; *The Sorrows of Young Werther*, an epistolary novel)

Golding, William (1911–1993)   20th century English author (*Lord of the Flies*)

Gray, Thomas (1716–1771)   early English Romantic poet ("Elegy Written in a Country Churchyard")

haiku   form of verse or poetry made up of 3 unrhymed lines containing 5, 7, and 5 syllables, respectively

   sonnet   14-line poem with rigidly prescribed rhyme scheme

Hardy, Thomas (1840–1928)   the last of England's great Victorian novelists (*Mayor of Casterbridge, Tess of the D'Urbervilles, Jude the Obscure, Far from the Madding Crowd, The Return of the Native*)

Hawthorne, Nathaniel (1804–1864)   19th century American author who set many of his stories against the somber background of Puritan New England (*The Scarlet Letter*, in which Hester Pryne is the adulteress, Arthur Dimmesdale the adulterer, and Roger Chillingworth the husband; *The House of the Seven Gables*)

Hemingway, Ernest (1899–1961)   American author, noted for his crisp, economical, highly charged prose style and his ideals of courage, endurance, and honor (*A Farewell to Arms, For Whom the Bell Tolls, The Old Man and the Sea*)

Hersey, John (1914–1993)   American novelist, known for his works about World War II (*A Bell for Adano*)

Hesse, Hermann (1877–1962)   German author (*Siddhartha, Steppenwolf, Narcissus and Goldmund, Magister Ludi*)

Homer (9th–8th century B.C.)   the earliest Greek writer whose works have survived; his two major epics, *The Iliad* and *The Odyssey*, are both about events connected with the Trojan War

hubris   excessive pride leading to the downfall of the hero in a tragic drama

Hugo, Victor (1802–1885)   French novelist (*The Hunchback of Notre Dame, Les Misérables*)

Huxley, Aldous (1894–1963)   English novelist and critic (*Brave New World*)

hyperbole   bold overstatement or extravagant exaggeration of fact, used for either serious or comic effect

Ibsen, Henrik (1828-1906)   Norwegian playwright; considered the father of modern realistic drama (*A Doll's House, Hedda Gabler*)

irony   a literary device in which the meaning stated is contrary to the one intended

James, Henry (1843-1916)   American author, known for his subtle psychological character studies (T*he Turn of the Screw, The Ambassadors, Daisy Miller, Washington Square, The Portrait of a Lady*)

Johnson, Samuel (1709-1784)   18th century English writer, noted for Boswell's famous biography of him, as well as for his *Dictionary of the English Language, The Lives of the English Poets*, and *Rasselas*

Joyce, James (1882-1941)   Irish author, noted for use of interior monologue and stream of consciousness (*Ulysses, Portrait of the Artist as a Young Man, The Dubliners, Finnegan's Wake*)

Keats, John (1795-1821)   English Romantic poet ("Endymion," "Ode to a Nightingale," "Ode on a Grecian Urn," "La Belle Dame sans Merci")

Kipling, Rudyard (1865-1936)   Nobel prize-winning British author (*The Jungle Book*) and poet ("If")

kitsch   a German word that literally means "trash" and frequently is applied to a work of poor quality that appeals to low-brow tastes

Lamb, Charles (1775-1834)   English essayist

lampoon   in prose or poetry, a vicious character sketch or satire of a person

Lawrence, D[avid] H[erbert] (1885-1930)   English novelist, poet, and short-story writer (*Sons and Lovers, Lady Chatterley's Lover*)

Lewis, Sinclair (1885-1951)   early 20th century American novelist and social critic (*Main Street, Babbitt, Arrowsmith, Elmer Gantry*)

London, Jack (1876-1916)   American novelist and short-story writer, whose works deal romantically with elemental struggles for survival (*Call of the Wild*)

Longfellow, Henry Wadsworth (1807-1882)   most popular American poet of the 19th century (*Evangeline, Hiawatha*)

lost generation   term coined by Gertrude Stein, originally referring to the many young American writers who gathered in Paris after World War I (Hemingway, Fitzgerald)

Mailer, Norman (1923-2007)   contemporary American novelist, essayist, and journalist (*The Naked and the Dead*)

Mann, Thomas (1875-1955)   American (German-born) author (*Death in Venice, The Magic Mountain*)

Marlowe, Christopher (1564-1593)   16th century English poet and dramatist; he was the first to use blank verse on the stage, influenced Shakespeare (*Dr. Faustus, The Jew of Malta*)

Melville, Herman (1819-1891)   19th century American novelist (*Moby Dick*, in which Ismael narrates the story of Captain Ahab's search for a white whale; *Billy Budd; Typee*)

Mencken, H[enry] L[ouis] (1880-1956)   the most influential American critic of the 1920s and early 1930s

Miller, Arthur (1915-2005)   contemporary American dramatist (*Death of a Salesman, The Crucible, The Misfits*)

Miller, Henry (1891-1980)   20th century American author (*Tropic of Cancer, Tropic of Capricorn*)

Milne, A[lan] A[lexander] (1882-1956)   English author, creator of *Winnie-the-Pooh*

Milton, John (1608-1674)   17th century English poet (*Paradise Lost, Paradise Regained, Samson Agonistes*, all three written when he was blind)

Molière (1622-1673)   (stage name of **Jean Baptiste Poquelin**) the greatest French writer of comedy (*Tartuffe, The Misanthrope*)

motif the recurrence of a theme, word pattern, or character in a literary work

Nabokov, Vladimir (1899–1977) Russian-American author (*Lolita, Invitation to a Beheading*)

naturalism a type of realistic fiction that developed in France, America, and England in the late 19th and early 20th centuries. It presupposes that human beings are like puppets, controlled completely by external and internal forces

  realism the idea that people have a measure of free will

octave a poetic stanza with eight lines

  sestet a poetic stanza with six lines

ode a sustained lyric poem with a noble theme and intellectual tone

O'Neill, Eugene (1888–1953) one of the greatest American playwrights (*The Emperor Jones, Desire Under the Elms, Ah! Wilderness, The Iceman Cometh, Long Day's Journey Into Night*)

onomatopoeia a word whose sound is descriptive of its sense of meaning

Orwell see Eric Blair

Ovid (43 B.C.–17 A.D.) Roman poet (*Metamorphoses, The Art of Love*)

oxymoron an expression that employs two opposing terms; for example, "benign neglect"

parable a story told to illustrate a moral truth or lesson

parody a humorous literary work that ridicules a serious work by imitating and exaggerating its style

personification a figure of speech that gives human forms and characteristics to abstractions, objects, animals, etc.

Petrarch (1304–1374) 14th century Italian poet and scholar, known for his love poems and his discovery of classical authors (*Canzoniere* [*Book of Songs*], a collection of 400 of his poems, most of them about a woman named Laura)

Poe, Edgar Allan (1809–1849) 19th century American poet, critic, and short-story writer; the father of modern mystery and detective fiction ("The Murders in the Rue Morgue," "The Fall of the House of Usher," "The Raven")

Pope, Alexander (1688–1744) the greatest English poet of the early 1700s, brilliant satirist (*The Rape of the Lock, An Essay on Criticism, An Essay on Man*)

potboiler an inferior literary work written solely to provide the author with money

Pound, Ezra (1885–1972) American poet and critic, one of the most influential poets and controversial figures of the 20th century (*Cantos*)

Proust, Marcel (1871–1922) French author (*The Remembrance of Things Past*, the story of his life told as an allegorical search for truth)

Pushkin, Aleksandr Sergeyvich (1799–1837) Russia's most celebrated poet; also wrote plays and other prose (*Eugene Onegin, The Bronze Horseman*)

Racine, Jean (1639–1699) 17th century French classicist writer of tragic drama (*Phaedra, Andromache*)

roman à clef a novel based on real persons and events

romantic movement 19th century literary movement that began in England; contrasts with classicism; emphasizes passion rather than reason, and imagination and inspiration rather than logic (Blake, Wordsworth, Coleridge, Shelley, Keats, Byron)

Sandburg, Carl (1878–1967) major 20th century American poet, also an historian and a biographer (*Abraham Lincoln*, "The Fog," "Chicago")

satire a type of literary work that uses sarcasm, wit, and irony to ridicule and expose the follies of mankind (*The Rape of the Lock, Gulliver's Travels*)

Scott, Sir Walter (1771–1832) later 18th–early 19th century Scottish novelist and poet; inventor of the historical novel (*The Lady of the Lake, Waverly, Ivanhoe*)

Shakespeare, William (1564–1616)   the towering figure in English literature, considered both the greatest dramatist and the greatest poet

Shaw, George Bernard (1856–1950)   English (Irish-born) author of satirical plays (*Pygmalion*, used as basis for *My Fair Lady*; *Man and Superman*; *Saint Joan*)

Shelley, Percy Bysshe (1792–1822)   early 19th century English Romantic poet (*Prometheus Unbound, Adonais, Ode to the West Wind*)

simile   figure of speech in which a comparison between two distinctly different things is indicated by the word *like* or *as* ("O my love is like a red, red rose")

   metaphor   figure of speech in which a statement of identity instead of comparison is made ("O my love is a red, red rose")

sonnet   a poem of 14 iambic pentameter lines and a rigidly prescribed rhyme scheme; two types: Italian or Petrarchan, and English or Shakespearean

Sophocles (496–406 B.C.)   Greek dramatist (*Oedipus the King, Antigone*)

Spenser, Edmund (1552–1599)   great Elizabethan poet (*The Faerie Queene*)

Stein, Gertrude (1874–1946)   American author, central figure in a circle of outstanding artist and writer expatriates in Paris (*The Autobiography of Alice B. Toklas*)

Steinbeck, John (1902–1968)   20th century American author, known for his powerful novels about agricultural workers (*The Grapes of Wrath, Of Mice and Men, East of Eden*)

Stendhal   see **Beyle, Marie-Henri**

Stevenson, Robert Louis (1850–1894)   19th century Scottish novelist, essayist, and poet; known for his adventure stories (*Treasure Island, Kidnapped, A Child's Garden of Verses*)

stream of consciousness   literary style, employed especially by Joyce and Faulkner, that presents the inner thoughts of a character in an uneven, endless stream that simulates the character's consciousness

Swift, Jonathan (1667–1745)   late 17th–18th century English author, great satirist (*Gulliver's Travels*, "A Modest Proposal")

Thoreau, Henry David (1817–1862)   American philosopher and writer; renowned for having lived the doctrines of transcendentalism ("Civil Disobedience," *Walden*)

Tolkien, J. R. R. (1892–1973)   English author (*The Hobbit, The Lord of the Rings*)

Tolstoy, Count Leo (1828–1910)   19th century Russian author, one of the world's greatest novelists (*War and Peace, Anna Karenina*)

transcendentalism   school of thought based on belief in the essential unity of all creation, the innate goodness of human beings, and the supremacy of insight over logic and experience for the revelation of the deepest truths (Thoreau, Emerson)

Twain   see **Clemens, Samuel**

Updike, John (1932–2009)   contemporary American author (*Rabbit series*)

Vergil or Virgil (70–19 B.C.)   greatest Roman poet; wrote the *Aeneid*, the epic that tells of the founding of Rome and describes the adventures of Aeneas, the legendary Trojan hero who founded the city

Victorian Age   refers to 19th century England; typified by optimism and conservative ideals

Voltaire (1694–1778)   18th century French author (*Candide*)

Walker, Alice (b. 1944)   20th century American author (*The Color Purple*)

Whitman, Walt (1819–1892)   one of the great American poets; his poems sing the praise of America and democracy (*Leaves of Grass*, "O Captain! My Captain!" a poem on Lincoln's death)

Wilde, Oscar (1854–1900)   late 19th century Irish playwright, poet, and novelist; attacked Victorian narrow-mindedness and complacency (*The Picture of Dorian Gray, The Importance of Being Earnest*)

Wilder, Thornton (1897–1975)   American novelist and playwright (*The Bridge of San Luis Rey, Our Town, Matchmaker*, which was the basis for the Broadway musical *Hello, Dolly*)

Williams, Tennessee (1911–1983)   considered the greatest American playwright (*The Glass Menagerie, A Streetcar Named Desire, Cat on a Hot Tin Roof*)

Wolfe, Thomas (1900–1938)   American author, known for his autobiographical novels (*Look Homeward, Angel; You Can't Go Home Again*)

Woolf, Virginia (1882–1941)   English novelist and critic; with her husband Leonard, provided a center for the Bloomsbury Group, an informal group of famous intellectuals (*Mrs. Dalloway, To the Lighthouse*)

Wordsworth, William (1770–1850)   English romantic poet (*Lyrical Ballads, The Prelude*)

Wright, Richard (1908–1960)   20th century American author, known for his description of black life in America (*Native Son, Black Boy*, his autobiography)

Yeats, William Butler (1865–1939)   Irish poet and dramatist, considered by many the greatest poet of his time; led the Irish Literary Revival; his love for Maud Gonne, a beautiful Irish nationalist leader, influenced many of his plays and love lyrics

Zola, Émile (1840–1902)   leader of the French naturalistic school, which de-emphasized the role of free will in human life (*Nana; J'accuse*, which helped win a new trail for Alfred Dreyfus)

MUSIC

Use the following list of the most important composers and music terms as a quick review. The works of particular composers are given in parentheses.

adagio   slow; a slow movement; slower than andante, faster than largo

allegro   lively; rather fast, but not as fast as presto

alto   a high adult male voice, employing falsetto; a lower female voice

andante   at moderate speed, between allegro and adagio

Argerich, Martha (b. 1941)   Argentinean pianist

aria   air; song, especially a complex one in an opera or oratorio ("Batti, Batti" from Mozart's opera *Don Giovanni*)

arpeggio   chord (e.g., on a piano) performed spread out

Bach, Johann Sebastian (1685–1750)   late 17th–early 18th century German composer of baroque style; organ music and cantatas (*Brandenburg Concertos; St. Matthew Passion*)

bagatelle   short, light piece, often for piano (Beethoven)

ballad   old song, often a folk song, that tells a story, with the music repeated for each verse (Wagner's *The Flying Dutchman*)

ballet   form of dancing, of Italian origin, that usually uses orchestra music, full stage decoration (*The Sleeping Beauty, Giselle, The Nutcracker*)

Barenboim, Daniel (b. 1942)   Israeli conductor and pianist

baroque   1600-to-1750 style of music (Monteverdi, Bach)

Bartók, Béla (1881–1945)   20th century Hungarian composer who developed Hungarian national musical style; known for dissonant, atonal sounds (*Bluebeard's Castle*)

bass   lowest male voice; the lower regions of musical pitch

Beecham, Sir Thomas (1879–1961)   English conductor

Beethoven, Ludwig van (1770–1827)   late 18th–early 19th century German composer, considered one of the greatest composers of all time (9 symphonies, including *Eroica, Pastoral*, the *Ninth* or *Choral*; piano concerto *Emperor*; opera *Fidelio*)

Bell, Joshua (b. 1967)   American violinist

Berlioz, Hector (1803–1869)   19th century French composer (*Fantastic Symphony*)

Bernstein, Leonard (1918–1990)   20th century American conductor and composer (*The Age of Anxiety* symphony; *West Side Story* musical)

bolero   Spanish dance

Borodin, Aleksandr Porfiryevich (1833–1887)   19th century Russian composer (opera *Prince Igor*)

Brahms, Johannes (1833–1897)   19th century German composer and pianist known for his symphonies, piano concertos, and chamber music (*First, Second, Third, Fourth symphonies*; song *Lullaby*)

Brandenburg Concertos   six works by J. S. Bach for varying instrumental combinations

Britten, Benjamin (1913–1976)   English conductor and composer (*The Young Person's Guide to the Orchestra*)

Bruch, Max (1838–1920)   German composer and conductor (*Kol Nidrei*)

Bruckner, Anton (1824–1896)   19th century Austrian composer and organist known for his symphonies

buffo (buffa)   comic bass, as in an opera

cadence   a progression of chords giving an effect of closing a sentence

cantata   an extended choral work, with or without solo voices, and usually with orchestral accompaniment

Casals, Pablo (1876–1973)   20th century Spanish cellist

chamber music   music intended for a room as distinct from a large hall or theater

chanson   type of song popular in 14th-to-16th century France

Chopin, Frédéric (1810–1849)   19th century Polish composer known for his piano works

chorale   a type of traditional German hymn-tune for congregational use; an instrumental piece based on a chorale

chord   a blending of two or more notes

classicism   1770s-to-1830s period; opposed to romanticism and folk or popular music (Haydn, Mozart, and Beethoven)

coda   section of movement added as a rounding off rather than a structural necessity

coloratura   agile, florid style of vocal music

concerto   work making contrasted use of solo instruments and orchestra, generally in 3 movements (Beethoven, Mozart)

contralto   lowest female singing range

Copland, Aaron (1900–1990)   20th century American composer and pianist (opera *The Tender Land, Music for the Theater*, many film scores)

counterpart   simultaneous combination of 2 or more melodies to make musical sense

crescendo   music that gradually becomes louder

Debussy, Claude (1862–1918)   late 19th–early 20th century French impressionist-style composer (opera *Pelleas and Melisande, The Afternoon of a Faun, La Mer*)

diminuendo   music that slowly becomes softer

Du Pre, Jacqueline (1945–1987)   English cellist

Dvořák, Antonin (1841–1904)   19th century Czech (Bohemian) composer known for his symphonies (*From the New World*)

étude   an instrumental piece written to demonstrate the facility of the performer

fortissimo   music played very loudly

fugue   a musical composition in which one or two themes are repeated by different interweaving voices (Bach)

Gershwin, George (1898–1937)   20th century American pianist and composer of popular music (*Rhapsody in Blue, An American in Paris*)

Gould, Glenn (1932–1982)   Canadian pianist

Grieg, Edvard (1843–1907)   19th century Norwegian composer and pianist (music for *Peer Gynt*)

Hahn, Hilary (b. 1979)   American violinist

Handel, George Frideric (1685–1759)   late 17th–early 18th century German baroque composer (oratorio *Messiah*, opera *Rinaldo*)

Haydn, Franz Joseph (1732–1809)   18th century Austrian composer (symphonies *The Surprise* and *The Clock*, oratorios *The Creation* and *The Seasons*)

Heifetz, Jascha (1901–1967)   Lithuanian violinist

Horowitz, Vladimir (b. 1937)   Russian pianist and conductor

interval   distance between 2 notes insofar as one is higher or lower than the other

Kodaly, Zoltán (1882–1967)   late 19th–20th century Hungarian composer; edited Hungarian folk songs (with Bartók) (*Psalmas Hungaricus*, opera *Háry Janos*)

largo   slow

lento   slow

libretto   text of an opera or oratorio

liederkranz   song-cycle (Schumann's *Liederkreis*)

Liszt, Franz (1811–1886)   19th century Hungarian romantic-style pianist and composer (*Dante Sonata, The Preludes*)

Ma, Yo-Yo (b. 1955)   Chinese-American cellist

madrigal   16th–17th century composition for several voices

Mahler, Gustav (1860–1911)   late 19th–early 20th century Austrian composer and conductor (*Symphony of a Thousand*)

Mehta, Zubin (b. 1936)   Indian conductor

Mendelssohn, Felix (1809–1847)   19th century German composer and conductor (operetta *Son and Stranger*, *Scottish* symphony, *Elijah*, overture to *Midsummer Night's Dream*)

Menotti, Gian Carlo (1911–2007)   20th century Italian-American composer of opera (*Amahl and the Night Visitors*)

Menuhin, Yehudi (1916–1999)   American-born British violinist, violist, and conductor

Milhaud, Darius (1892–1974)   20th century French composer (operas *David* and *Christopher Columbus*, ballets *Jeux de printemps* and *Creation of the World*)

Monteverdi, Claudio (1567–1643)   late 16th–early 17th century Italian composer (opera *La favola d'Orfeo*)

Mozart, Wolfgang Amadeus (1756–1791)   18th century Austrian composer, mainly of operas and piano concertos (*Don Giovanni, The Marriage of Figaro, The Magic Flute, Cosi Fan Tutte*)

Mussorgsky, Modest Petrovich (1839–1881)   19th century Russian composer (operas *Boris Godunov, Pictures at an Exhibition, Night on Bald Mountain*)

Mutter, Anne-Sofie (b. 1963)   German violinist

nocturne   melancholy composition for one or more instruments

opera   drama in which all or most characters sing and music constitutes a principal element

opera buffa   comic opera

oratorio   religious compositions for orchestra, chorus, and soloists

Orff, Carl (1895–1982)   20th century German composer and conductor (operas: *Oedipus the Tyrant*, incidental music and choral works, *Songs of Catullus, Carmina Burana*)

Pachelbel, Johann (1653–1706)   17th century German organist and composer of keyboard music

Paganini, Nicolò (1782–1840)   late 18th–early 19th century Italian violinist and composer (*Bell Rondo, The Carnival of Venice*)

presto   fast

Prokofiev, Sergey Sergeyevich (1891–1953)   20th century Russian composer and pianist (*Peter and the Wolf*)

Puccini, Giacomo (1858–1924)   late 19th–early 20th century Italian composer (operas *Madame Butterfly, La Bohème, Tosca*)

quartet   four musical instruments played together

Rachmaninoff, Sergey Vasilyevich (1873–1943)   late 19th–early 20th century Russian composer and pianist (*Rhapsody on a Theme of Paganini, The Isle of the Dead*)

Rameau, Jean-Philippe (1683–1764)   18th century French composer and organist (*Castor et Pollux*)

Ravel, Maurice Joseph (1875–1937)   late 19th–early 20th century French composer (*Bolero, Gaspard de la Nuit, Spanish Rhapsody*)

Rodgers, Richard (1902–1979)   20th century American composer of light music; worked with writers Hart and Hammerstein (*The Sound of Music, A Connecticut Yankee, Oklahoma!*)

rondo   form of composition in which one section recurs intermittently

Rossini, Gioacchino Antonio (1792–1868)   19th century Italian composer (operas *The Barber of Seville, Othello, William Tell*)

Rubinstein, Anton (1829–1894)   20th century Polish-born American pianist

Scarlatti, Domenico (1685–1757)   late 17th–early 18th century Italian composer, chiefly of opera

Schoenberg, Arnold (1874–1951)   20th century Austrian-American composer (*Ode to Napoleon*, opera *Moses and Aaron*)

Schubert, Franz (1797–1828)   19th century Austrian composer (*Impromptus, Moments Musicaux*)

Schumann, Robert (1810–1856)   19th century German composer and pianist

Scriabin, Aleksandr Nikoloyevich (1872–1915)   late 19th–early 20th century Russian composer and pianist (*Divine Poem*)

Segovia, Andrés (1893–1987)   20th century Spanish classical guitarist

Shostakovich, Dmitry Dmitriyevich (1906–1975)   20th century Russian composer (*Leningrad* symphony, opera *The Golden Age*, ballet *Songs of the Forests*)

Sibelius, Jean (1865–1957)   late 19th–early 20th century Finnish composer (*Finlandia*)

Smetana, Bedřich (1824–1884)   19th century Czech composer and pianist (opera *The Bartered Bride*)

sonata   instrumental musical composition usually of 3 or 4 movements (sonatina–short sonata)

soprano   highest female voice

Sousa, John Philip (1854–1932)   late 19th–early 20th century American band conductor and composer of marches (*Stars and Stripes Forever*)

Stern, Isaac (1920–2001)   20th century Russian-born American violinist

Stradivari   family of renowned violin makers

Strauss, Johann (1825–1899)   19th century Austrian violinist, conductor, and composer of waltzes (*The Blue Danube, Tales from the Vienna Woods*)

Strauss, Richard (1864–1949)   late 19th–early 20th century German composer and conductor (*Symphonic Poem*, operas *Salome, Elektra*)

Stravinsky, Igor (1882–1971)   20th century Russian-born composer, pianist, and conductor (ballets *The Firebird, Petrushka,* and *The Rite of Spring*, opera *The Rake's Progress*)

symphony   grand orchestral work in 4 movements

Tchaikovsky, Pyotr Ilich (1840–1893)   19th century Russian composer (*Pathéthique* symphony, ballets *Swan Lake, The Sleeping Beauty, The Nutcracker*)

tenor   highest normal male voice (apart from alto, which uses falsetto)

Toscanini, Arturo (1867–1957)   Italian conductor

Verdi, Giuseppe (1813–1901)   19th century Italian composer (operas *Rigoletto, il Trovatore, Don Carlos, Falstaff, Aïda, Requiem*)

Vivaldi, Antonio (1678–1741)   late 17th–early 18th century Italian violinist and composer (*The Four Seasons*)

von Karajan, Herbert (1908–1989)   Austrian-born German conductor

Wagner, Richard (1813–1883)   19th century German composer and conductor known for cycles of opera and use of leitmotif (operas *The Flying Dutchman, Tristan and Isolde, Der Ring*)

Weber, Carl Maria von (1786–1826)   late 18th–early 19th century German composer, conductor, and pianist (operas *Der Freischütz, Oberon*)

Weil, Kurt (1900–1950)   20th century German-born American composer (opera *The Threepenny Opera*)

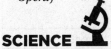

SCIENCE

Detailed knowledge of the sciences is not required for the *MAT*. What is necessary is a general familiarity with the major people, theories, and terms of science. It is impossible to review biology, physics, chemistry, geology and the other sciences here. Below are a list of major scientists, a table of animal names that include vocabulary that may appear in an analogy, a brief explanation of classification terms, and a geologic time scale chart.

Important Scientists

Becquerel, Antoine (1788–1878)   (French) discovered radioactivity

Copernicus, Nicolaus (1473–1543)   (Polish) founded modern astronomy, declared that sun is center of solar system

Curie, Marie (1867–1934) and **Pierre** (1859–1906)   (French) discovered radium, polonium

Darwin, Charles (1809–1882)   (English) natural selection, theory of evolution

Einstein, Albert (1879–1955)   (German) theory of relativity

Fermi, Enrico (1901–1954)   (Italian-American) radioactivity, chain reactions, H-bomb

Fleming, Sir Alexander (1881–1955)   (British) discovered penicillin

Galen (129–199 A.D.)   (ancient Greek) physician, studied personality

Galileo (1564–1642)   (Italian) astronomer and physicist, laws of gravity

Gauss, Carl Friedrich (1777–1855)   (German) mathematician and astronomer, invented electric telegraph

Herschel, Sir John Frederick William (1738–1822)   (British) astronomer

Hippocrates (460–377 B.C.)   (ancient Greek) physician, father of medicine (oath)

Jenner, Edward (1749–1823)   (British) physician, cowpox vaccine

Lamarck, Chevalier de (1744–1829)   (French) naturalist, theory of inheritance of acquired characteristics

Linnaeus, Carolus (1707–1778)   (Swedish) devised system of classifying living organisms

Lister, Joseph (1827–1912)   (British) surgeon, promoted antiseptic methods

Lysenko, Trofim Denisovich (1898–1976)   (Soviet) geneticist, follower of Lamarck, led to demise of Soviet biology

Mendel, Gregor (1822–1884)   (Austrian) botanist, transmission of characteristics in plants (genetics)

Pasteur, Louis (1822–1895)   (French) chemist, germ theory, use of heat to destroy bacteria

Ptolemy (90–168 A.D.)   (Egyptian) astronomer, geocentric theory of solar system

Rutherford, Ernest (1871–1937)   (British) physicist, radioactivity

Sabin, Albert (1906–1993)   (American) developed oral vaccine against polio

Salk, Jonas (1914–1995)   (American) developed first vaccine against polio

Watson, James (b. 1928)   (American) and **Crick, Francis** (b. 1916–2004) (British) biophysicists, discovered structure of DNA molecule (double helix)

ANIMAL NAMES

Animal	Male	Female	Offspring	Adjective Form
bear	boar	sow	cub	ursine
cattle	bull steer (castrated)	cow	calf	bovine
chicken	rooster capon (castrated)	hen	chick	
deer	buck	doe	fawn	cervine
fox	fox	vixen	cub/kit	vulpine
goat	billy	nanny	kid	
hog	boar	sow	shoat	
horse	stallion gelding (castrated)	mare	foal, colt (m.) filly (f.)	equine
lion	lion	lioness	cub	leonine
pig	boar	sow	piglet	porcine
sheep	ram	ewe	lamb	ovine
swan	cob	pen	cygnet	

Taxonomy

Taxonomy is the science of classifying living organisms. Each living organism is given a scientific name—for example, *Homo sapiens* for human beings—that consists of a genus name—in our example, *Homo*—and a species name—*sapiens*. Organisms are also grouped into larger taxa (singular, taxon) based on similarities in structure and evolutionary relationships. The following table lists the major taxonomic groups, briefly describes each, and provides an example.

Classification Group	Definition	Example
kingdom	largest classification unit; most scientists agree on a basic 5-kingdom system	Animalia
phylum	major division of a kingdom	Chordata
class	division of a phylum	Vertebrata
order	division of a class; contains one or more related families	Primates
family	division of an order; contains one or more related genera; members often show obvious similarities	Hominidae
genus	division of a family; contains one or more closely related species; part of scientific name (written with initial capital letter and italicized)	*Homo*
species	basic unit of classification; a group of organisms that can mate and produce offspring; second word of scientific name; always lowercase and italicized	*sapiens*

Geologic Time Scale

Era	Periods	Life Forms
Azoic era	(earliest period after formation of the earth)	

Precambrian time:
    Archeozoic era (3800–2500 mya)
    Proterozoic era (2500–543 mya)
    Paleozoic era
    (543–249 mya)
		spores, marine algae

	Cambrian period (543–490 mya)	
	Ordovician (490–443 mya)	fishes
	Silurian (443–417 mya)	
	Devonian (417–354 mya)	amphibians
	Carboniferous (354–290 mya)	insects, reptiles, gymnosperm
	Permian (290–248 mya)	ferns
Mesozoic (248–65 mya)	Triassic (248–206 mya)	first dinosaurs
	Jurassic (206–144 mya)	reptiles dominant, first birds, mammals
	Cretacious (144–65 mya)	dinosaurs climax, disappear; flowering plants
Cenozoic (65 mya–today)	Tertiary Paleocene (65–54.8 mya)	earliest placental mammals
	Eocene (54.8–33.7 mya)	modern mammals
	Oligocene (33.7–23.8 mya)	
	Miocene (23.8–5.3 mya)	
	Pliocene Epochs (5.3–1.8 mya)	
	Quaternary Pleistocene epoch (1.8 mya–10,000 years ago)	humankind (glacial)
	Holocene epoch (10,000 years–today)	

Note: mya = million years ago

MYTHOLOGY

Adonis   Greek god of male beauty

Aphrodite   Greek goddess of love, beauty, and fertility. Roman counterpart: Venus; Norse counterpart: Freyja

Apollo   one of the twin children of Zeus (the other twin is Artemis); Greek god of prophecy, medicine, and music. Norse counterpart: Frey

Ares   Greek god of war; son of Zeus and Hera. Roman counterpart: Mars

Artemis   one of the twin children of Zeus (the other twin is Apollo); Greek goddess of the moon, woods, forest, animals, and the hunt. Roman counterpart: Diana

Asgard   home of the Norse gods

Athena   Greek goddess of wisdom, cities, and handicrafts; "sprung full-blown from the head of Zeus." Roman counterpart: Minerva

Balder   Norse god of the sun. Greek counterpart: Helios

Ceres   Roman god of grain. Greek counterpart: Demeter

Cronus and Rhea   Greek gods; parents of the gods. Roman counterparts: Saturn and Ops

Demeter   Greek goddess of harvest and fertility. Roman counterpart: Ceres

Diana   Roman goddess of the moon, forest, animals, and the hunt. Greek counterpart: Artemis

Dionysus   Greek god of wine and joy, son of Zeus. Roman counterpart: Bacchus

Frey   Norse god; twin brother of Freyja. Greek counterpart: Apollo

Freyja   Norse goddess; twin of Frey; goddess of love and fertility. Greek counterpart: Aphrodite

Frigga   Norse goddess of heavens, love, and household; wife of Odin

Hades   Greek ruler of the dead and god of the underworld. Roman counterpart: Pluto

Helios   Greek sun god. Roman counterpart: Sol; Norse counterpart: Balder

Hera   Greek goddess; sister and wife of Zeus and queen of the gods. Roman counterpart: Juno; Norse counterpart: Frigga

Hermes   Greek messenger of the gods; symbol is caduceus. Roman counterpart: Mercury

Ishtar   Babylonian goddess of love and war. Greek counterpart: Aphrodite

Juno   Roman goddess; wife and sister of Jupiter. Greek counterpart: Hera; Norse counterpart: Frigga

Jupiter   Roman king of the gods. Greek counterpart: Zeus; Norse counterpart: Odin

Mercury   Roman messenger and god of commerce. Greek counterpart: Hermes

Minerva   Roman goddess of wisdom, cities, and handicrafts; like Greek Athena, said to have sprung fullblown from king of the gods. Greek counterpart: Athena

Neptune   Roman sea god. Greek counterpart: Poseidon; Norse counterpart: Njord

Njord   Norse god of the sea. Greek counterpart: Poseidon; Roman counterpart: Neptune

Odin   Norse king of the gods. Greek counterpart: Zeus; Roman counterpart: Jupiter

Olympus   Home of the Greek gods

Pluto   Roman ruler of the underworld. Greek counterpart: Hades

Poseidon   Greek god of the sea; symbol is a trident. Roman counterpart: Neptune; Norse counterpart: Njord

Saturn and **Ops**   Roman gods; parents of the gods. Greek counterparts: Cronus and Rhea

Thor   Norse god of thunder

Valhalla   Norse hall of heroes

Venus   Roman goddess of love, good fortune, and vegetation. Greek counter-part: Aphrodite; Norse counterpart: Freyja

Zeus   Greek king of the gods. Roman counterpart: Jupiter; Norse counterpart: Odin

MAT Practice Tests

6

In this part, you will find 11 complete Practice Tests. Each is preceded by an answer sheet that you can use to mark all of your responses. Each test consists of 120 items that need to be completed within 60 minutes. At the end of each test you will find an answer key for scoring as well as answer explanations. Good luck!

Don't forget about the online tests! You can take two additional full-length practice tests with answers explained via online. Visit *barronsbooks.com/TP/MAT*

ANSWER SHEET
Practice Test 1

1. Ⓐ Ⓑ Ⓒ Ⓓ	31. Ⓐ Ⓑ Ⓒ Ⓓ	61. Ⓐ Ⓑ Ⓒ Ⓓ	91. Ⓐ Ⓑ Ⓒ Ⓓ
2. Ⓐ Ⓑ Ⓒ Ⓓ	32. Ⓐ Ⓑ Ⓒ Ⓓ	62. Ⓐ Ⓑ Ⓒ Ⓓ	92. Ⓐ Ⓑ Ⓒ Ⓓ
3. Ⓐ Ⓑ Ⓒ Ⓓ	33. Ⓐ Ⓑ Ⓒ Ⓓ	63. Ⓐ Ⓑ Ⓒ Ⓓ	93. Ⓐ Ⓑ Ⓒ Ⓓ
4. Ⓐ Ⓑ Ⓒ Ⓓ	34. Ⓐ Ⓑ Ⓒ Ⓓ	64. Ⓐ Ⓑ Ⓒ Ⓓ	94. Ⓐ Ⓑ Ⓒ Ⓓ
5. Ⓐ Ⓑ Ⓒ Ⓓ	35. Ⓐ Ⓑ Ⓒ Ⓓ	65. Ⓐ Ⓑ Ⓒ Ⓓ	95. Ⓐ Ⓑ Ⓒ Ⓓ
6. Ⓐ Ⓑ Ⓒ Ⓓ	36. Ⓐ Ⓑ Ⓒ Ⓓ	66. Ⓐ Ⓑ Ⓒ Ⓓ	96. Ⓐ Ⓑ Ⓒ Ⓓ
7. Ⓐ Ⓑ Ⓒ Ⓓ	37. Ⓐ Ⓑ Ⓒ Ⓓ	67. Ⓐ Ⓑ Ⓒ Ⓓ	97. Ⓐ Ⓑ Ⓒ Ⓓ
8. Ⓐ Ⓑ Ⓒ Ⓓ	38. Ⓐ Ⓑ Ⓒ Ⓓ	68. Ⓐ Ⓑ Ⓒ Ⓓ	98. Ⓐ Ⓑ Ⓒ Ⓓ
9. Ⓐ Ⓑ Ⓒ Ⓓ	39. Ⓐ Ⓑ Ⓒ Ⓓ	69. Ⓐ Ⓑ Ⓒ Ⓓ	99. Ⓐ Ⓑ Ⓒ Ⓓ
10. Ⓐ Ⓑ Ⓒ Ⓓ	40. Ⓐ Ⓑ Ⓒ Ⓓ	70. Ⓐ Ⓑ Ⓒ Ⓓ	100. Ⓐ Ⓑ Ⓒ Ⓓ
11. Ⓐ Ⓑ Ⓒ Ⓓ	41. Ⓐ Ⓑ Ⓒ Ⓓ	71. Ⓐ Ⓑ Ⓒ Ⓓ	101. Ⓐ Ⓑ Ⓒ Ⓓ
12. Ⓐ Ⓑ Ⓒ Ⓓ	42. Ⓐ Ⓑ Ⓒ Ⓓ	72. Ⓐ Ⓑ Ⓒ Ⓓ	102. Ⓐ Ⓑ Ⓒ Ⓓ
13. Ⓐ Ⓑ Ⓒ Ⓓ	43. Ⓐ Ⓑ Ⓒ Ⓓ	73. Ⓐ Ⓑ Ⓒ Ⓓ	103. Ⓐ Ⓑ Ⓒ Ⓓ
14. Ⓐ Ⓑ Ⓒ Ⓓ	44. Ⓐ Ⓑ Ⓒ Ⓓ	74. Ⓐ Ⓑ Ⓒ Ⓓ	104. Ⓐ Ⓑ Ⓒ Ⓓ
15. Ⓐ Ⓑ Ⓒ Ⓓ	45. Ⓐ Ⓑ Ⓒ Ⓓ	75. Ⓐ Ⓑ Ⓒ Ⓓ	105. Ⓐ Ⓑ Ⓒ Ⓓ
16. Ⓐ Ⓑ Ⓒ Ⓓ	46. Ⓐ Ⓑ Ⓒ Ⓓ	76. Ⓐ Ⓑ Ⓒ Ⓓ	106. Ⓐ Ⓑ Ⓒ Ⓓ
17. Ⓐ Ⓑ Ⓒ Ⓓ	47. Ⓐ Ⓑ Ⓒ Ⓓ	77. Ⓐ Ⓑ Ⓒ Ⓓ	107. Ⓐ Ⓑ Ⓒ Ⓓ
18. Ⓐ Ⓑ Ⓒ Ⓓ	48. Ⓐ Ⓑ Ⓒ Ⓓ	78. Ⓐ Ⓑ Ⓒ Ⓓ	108. Ⓐ Ⓑ Ⓒ Ⓓ
19. Ⓐ Ⓑ Ⓒ Ⓓ	49. Ⓐ Ⓑ Ⓒ Ⓓ	79. Ⓐ Ⓑ Ⓒ Ⓓ	109. Ⓐ Ⓑ Ⓒ Ⓓ
20. Ⓐ Ⓑ Ⓒ Ⓓ	50. Ⓐ Ⓑ Ⓒ Ⓓ	80. Ⓐ Ⓑ Ⓒ Ⓓ	110. Ⓐ Ⓑ Ⓒ Ⓓ
21. Ⓐ Ⓑ Ⓒ Ⓓ	51. Ⓐ Ⓑ Ⓒ Ⓓ	81. Ⓐ Ⓑ Ⓒ Ⓓ	111. Ⓐ Ⓑ Ⓒ Ⓓ
22. Ⓐ Ⓑ Ⓒ Ⓓ	52. Ⓐ Ⓑ Ⓒ Ⓓ	82. Ⓐ Ⓑ Ⓒ Ⓓ	112. Ⓐ Ⓑ Ⓒ Ⓓ
23. Ⓐ Ⓑ Ⓒ Ⓓ	53. Ⓐ Ⓑ Ⓒ Ⓓ	83. Ⓐ Ⓑ Ⓒ Ⓓ	113. Ⓐ Ⓑ Ⓒ Ⓓ
24. Ⓐ Ⓑ Ⓒ Ⓓ	54. Ⓐ Ⓑ Ⓒ Ⓓ	84. Ⓐ Ⓑ Ⓒ Ⓓ	114. Ⓐ Ⓑ Ⓒ Ⓓ
25. Ⓐ Ⓑ Ⓒ Ⓓ	55. Ⓐ Ⓑ Ⓒ Ⓓ	85. Ⓐ Ⓑ Ⓒ Ⓓ	115. Ⓐ Ⓑ Ⓒ Ⓓ
26. Ⓐ Ⓑ Ⓒ Ⓓ	56. Ⓐ Ⓑ Ⓒ Ⓓ	86. Ⓐ Ⓑ Ⓒ Ⓓ	116. Ⓐ Ⓑ Ⓒ Ⓓ
27. Ⓐ Ⓑ Ⓒ Ⓓ	57. Ⓐ Ⓑ Ⓒ Ⓓ	87. Ⓐ Ⓑ Ⓒ Ⓓ	117. Ⓐ Ⓑ Ⓒ Ⓓ
28. Ⓐ Ⓑ Ⓒ Ⓓ	58. Ⓐ Ⓑ Ⓒ Ⓓ	88. Ⓐ Ⓑ Ⓒ Ⓓ	118. Ⓐ Ⓑ Ⓒ Ⓓ
29. Ⓐ Ⓑ Ⓒ Ⓓ	59. Ⓐ Ⓑ Ⓒ Ⓓ	89. Ⓐ Ⓑ Ⓒ Ⓓ	119. Ⓐ Ⓑ Ⓒ Ⓓ
30. Ⓐ Ⓑ Ⓒ Ⓓ	60. Ⓐ Ⓑ Ⓒ Ⓓ	90. Ⓐ Ⓑ Ⓒ Ⓓ	120. Ⓐ Ⓑ Ⓒ Ⓓ

Time: 60 MINUTES

> **Directions:** In each of the following questions, you will find three initial terms and, in parentheses, four answer options designated *a, b, c,* and *d.* You are to select from the four answer options the one that *best* completes the analogy with the three initial terms. To record your answers, use the answer sheet provided.

1. MACHIAVELLIAN: (*a.* isolationist, *b.* quixotic, *c.* cunning, *d.* Pavlovian) :: ORWELLIAN : DRACONIAN

2. ROE : WADE :: (*a.* Miranda, *b.* McCulloch, *c.* McCain, *d.* McMurray) : ARIZONA

3. TUESDAY : MARCH :: WEEK : (*a.* day, *b.* month, *c.* April, *d.* year)

4. ALKALI : (*a.* copper, *b.* caesium, *c.* zinc, *d.* tin) :: NOBLE : ARGON

5. COHO : SOCKEYE :: ALBACORE : (*a.* walleye, *b.* yellowfin, *c.* smallmouth, *d.* salmon)

6. NOBEL : SWEDEN :: (*a.* Man Booker, *b.* Pulitzer, *c.* Kafka, *d.* Caldecott) : UNITED KINGDOM

7. MARS : REMUS :: JUPITER : (*a.* Zeus, *b.* Aeneas, *c.* Romulus, *d.* Hercules)

8. KINDLING : KIND :: TINDER : (*a.* noble, *b.* courteous, *c.* tender, *d.* nigh)

9. ROTGUT : (*a.* moonshine, *b.* nausea, *c.* regular, *d.* bottom shelf) :: BRANDY : PREMIUM

10. LEVER : PULLEY :: FULCRUM : (*a.* lift, *b.* wheel, *c.* pivot, *d.* seesaw)

11. (*a.* expel, *b.* abrupt, *c.* stop, *d.* pause) : CANCEL :: HALT : SUSPEND

12. .4 : 8 :: 160 : (*a.* 320, *b.* 6400, *c.* 3200, *d.* 4800)

13. ULULATION : (*a.* sing, *b.* alliteration, *c.* hum, *d.* hoot) :: SUSURRATION : WHISPER

14. (*a.* verdigris, *b.* weathering, *c.* deterioration, *d.* nickel) : COPPER :: EROSION : SOIL

15. (*a.* flaunt, *b.* hang, *c.* carnival, *d.* rise) : LEVITATE :: PARADE : FLOAT

16. RUBOR : (*a.* calor, *b.* malignancy, *c.* ardor, *d.* growth) :: DOLOR : TUMOR

17. CEO : VICE PRESIDENT :: (*a.* chairman, *b.* employee, *c.* board, *d.* director) : MANAGER

18. (*a.* Jordan, *b.* Unitas, *c.* Ruth, *d.* Ovechkin) : FOOTBALL :: ORR : HOCKEY

19. XII : (*a.* XIII, *b.* XIV, *c.* XVII, *d.* XVI) :: XXXVI : XLVIII

20. MERCURY : (*a.* Jupiter, *b.* Saturn, *c.* Venus, *d.* Neptune) :: EARTH : MARS

21. (*a.* aerobics, *b.* cavity, *c.* stroke, *d.* antibiotic) : INFRACTION :: FLOSS : GINGIVITIS

22. FLUTE : (*a.* champagne, *b.* piccolo, *c.* woodwind, *d.* orchestra) :: STEIN : BEER

23. TINTINNABULATION : (*a.* Poe, *b.* illumination, *c.* fly, *d.* bell) :: DRONE : WASP

24. LANGE : LIEBOVITZ :: ADAMS : (*a.* Rockwell, *b.* Karsh, *c.* Burns, *d.* Dreiser)

25. 78 : 13 :: (*a.* 42, *b.* 70, *c.* 56, *d.* 49) : 7

26. PHALANX : DIGIT :: STAPES : (*a.* nose, *b.* ear, *c.* ankle, *d.* wrist)

27. PROSE : POETRY :: EMERSON : (*a.* Cather, *b.* Crichton, *c.* Neruda, *d.* Martin)

28. (*a.* colossal, *b.* zebra, *c.* mollusk, *d.* Australian) : MUSSEL :: ASIAN : CARP

29. LACONIC : (*a.* sentimental, *b.* sad, *c.* brief, *d.* maritime) :: PICARESQUE : ROGUISH

30. PROPOSAL : ULTIMATUM :: OFFER : (*a.* demand, *b.* acceptance, *c.* rejection, *d.* final)

31. TEAR : LCL :: (*a.* tendon, *b.* rip, *c.* fracture, *d.* sprain) : TARSAL

32. DUCHAMP : (*a.* Voltaire, *b.* Romanticism, *c.* Michelangelo, *d.* Picasso) :: DADA : CUBISM

33. (*a.* Caucasian, *b.* Creek, *c.* Tenderfoot, *d.* Sunni) : CHOCTAW :: BLACKFEET : PUEBLO

34. MASTERS : (*a.* orthopedics, *b.* pulmonology, *c.* nephrology, *d.* gynecology) :: SPOCK : PEDIATRICS

35. (*a.* Herod, *b.* Samaritan, *c.* Lazarus, *d.* Judas) : BETHANY :: JESUS : NAZARETH

36. FERRIC : CUPROUS :: (*a.* steel, *b.* aluminum, *c.* sliver, *d.* iron) : COPPER

37. STARBUCK : SODAPOP :: (*a.* Moby-Dick, *b.* Pilgrim's Progress, *c.* Portnoy's Complaint, *d.* Emma) : OUTSIDERS

38. MORGAN : MERRILL :: (*a.* Stanley, *b.* J.P., *c.* Lehigh, *d.* Lafayette) : LYNCH

39. KELVIN : (*a.* 100, *b.* 273, *c.* 0, *d.* 212) :: CELSIUS : 0

40. NOVEL : (*a.* fiction, *b.* encyclopedia, *c.* novella, *d.* author) :: LONG : SHORT

41. (*a.* port, *b.* starboard, *c.* aft, *d.* spinnaker) : RIGHT :: BOW : FRONT

42. TUTORIAL : INSTRUCTION :: (*a.* sartorial, *b.* piscatorial, *c.* urticarial, *d.* fashion) : CLOTHING

43. TIBER : ITALY :: YELLOW : (*a.* France, *b.* Canada, *c.* India, *d.* China)

44. REAL : MANCHESTER :: MADRID : (*a.* Barcelona, *b.* United, *c.* Spain, *d.* Arsenal)

45. THORN : ROSE :: MATTERHORN : (*a.* mountain, *b.* elbows, *c.* Everest, *d.* Pyrenees)

46. HOPKINS : LECTER :: (*a.* Brosnan, *b.* Anthony, *c.* Cruise, *d.* Ford) : BOND

47. ENTOMOLOGY : GRASSHOPPER :: ICHTHYOLOGY : (*a.* bluejay, *b.* fish, *c.* trout, *d.* bird)

48. GAGGLE : ARSENAL :: (*a.* goose, *b.* marksmanship, *c.* weaponry, *d.* rifle) : PISTOL

49. RADIUS : ULNA :: (*a.* tibia, *b.* femur, *c.* tarsus, *d.* humerus) : FIBULA

50. THE REPUBLIC : PLATO :: MEDITATIONS : (*a.* Caesar, *b.* Aurelius, *c.* Socrates, *d.* Sophocles)

51. ORNATE : HIBERNATION :: THREADBARE : (*a.* insomnia, *b.* nap, *c.* repose, *d.* homeostasis)

52. (*a.* apple, *b.* pepper, *c.* vegetable, *d.* spicy) : JALAPENO :: FRUIT : GRANNY SMITH

53. GRASS : (*a.* seed, *b.* equine, *c.* dark, *d.* Clydesdale) :: ROOTS : HORSE

54. (*a.* delta, *b.* six, *c.* product, *d.* alpha) : QUALITY :: SIGMA : CONTROL

55. (*a.* Sting, *b.* Lennon, *c.* Wonder, *d.* Jagger) : CLAPTON :: PIANO : GUITAR

56. MASQUERADE : DISSIMULATION :: MAUSOLEUM : (*a.* sepulcher, *b.* dystopia, *c.* reality, *d.* simulation)

57. (*a.* pillow, *b.* soot, *c.* formal, *d.* court) : SUIT :: CASE : CASE

58. ARCHBISHOP : POPE :: (*a.* priest, *b.* Catholic, *c.* deacon, *d.* bishop) :: CARDINAL

59. ONCE : (*a.* one, *b.* twice, *c.* two, *d.* three) :: THRICE : FOUR

60. FLORA : (*a.* chrysanthemum, *b.* flower, *c.* garden, *d.* moose) :: FAUNA : ELK

61. UNDERWATER : SCUBA :: (*a.* detection, *b.* sky, *c.* radio, *d.* ranging) : RADAR

62. TEPID : IRREGULAR :: (*a.* commonplace, *b.* rapid, *c.* scorching, *d.* warm) : UNPRECEDENTED

63. LEGUME : PEANUT :: TUBER : (*a.* melon, *b.* maize, *c.* yam, *d.* pear)

64. TINNITUS : GLAUCOMA :: AURICULAR : (*a.* astigmatism, *b.* ear, *c.* visual, *d.* ocular)

65. (*a.* eastern, *b.* occidental, *c.* China, *d.* Asia) : ORIENT :: EASTERN : CALIFORNIA

66. BLACK JACK : DESERT FOX :: PERSHING : (*a.* Sheridan, *b.* Rommel, *c.* Bradley, *d.* Sherman)

67. FISH : SCHOOL :: (*a.* assassination, *b.* zebra, *c.* bear, *d.* crow) : MURDER

68. (*a.* variability, *b.* mode, *c.* cruel, *d.* middle) : FREQUENCY :: MEAN : CENTER

69. KINESIOLOGY : MOVEMENT :: HISTOLOGY : (*a.* uterus, *b.* past, *c.* tissue, *d.* inertia)

70. AVUNCULAR : (*a.* uncle, *b.* aunt, *c.* matronly, *d.* familial) :: PATERNAL : MOTHER

71. N'Djamena : (*a.* Niger, *b.* Chad, *c.* Egypt, *d.* South Sudan) :: MOGADISHU : SOMALIA

72. JAY : TAFT :: WARREN : (*a.* Holmes, *b.* Harding, *c.* Kennedy, *d.* Burger)

73. (*a.* Aaron, *b.* Moses, *c.* Jacob, *d.* Noah) : ABRAHAM :: RACHEL : SARAH

74. ORPHAN : PARENT :: PAUPER : (*a.* father, *b.* poverty, *c.* hobo, *d.* wealth)

75. CONFLICT : BLOOD :: MINERAL : (*a.* zinc, *b.* rock, *c.* calcium, *d.* diamond)

76. CURTAIN : (*a.* prism, *b.* reflect, *c.* shade, *d.* cover) :: HINDER : REFRACT

77. AXIOM : (*a.* postulate, *b.* conclusion, *c.* requiem, *d.* ultimatum) :: PROPOSITION : HYPOTHESIS

78. 16 : (*a.* 61, *b.* 64, *c.* 121, *d.* 81) :: 256 : 625

79. CELERITOUS : (*a.* thrifty, *b.* dour, *c.* swift, *d.* verbose) :: MAGNANIMOUS : GENEROUS

80. LAUREN : ROCKEFELLER :: POLO : (*a.* pony, *b.* Standard Oil, *c.* Exxon, *d.* John)

81. QUADRICEPS: TRICEPS :: PUSH : (*a.* over, *b.* push, *c.* three, *d.* pull)

82. (*a.* southern, *b.* student, *c.* court, *d.* supreme) : SNCC :: SUPREME : SCOTUS

83. DEAD : (*a.* picture, *b.* grave, *c.* splitting, *d.* mortal) :: RINGER : IMAGE

84. CHLOROFLUOROCARBONS : OZONE :: PESTICIDES : (*a.* weed-killer, *b.* food, *c.* oxygen, *d.* solar deflection)

85. AMENITIES : (*a.* ornate, *b.* cumbersome, *c.* Utopian, *d.* Spartan) :: BACKBONE : INVERTEBRATE

86. PEEVED : LIVID :: STRANGE : (*a.* odd, *b.* unbelievable, *c.* incensed, *d.* awkward)

87. ALEXANDRINE : PETRARCHAN :: COUPLET : (*a.* sonnet, *b.* triplet, *c.* stanza, *d.* ballad)

88. CLINTON : BUSH :: GORE : (*a.* Quayle, *b.* Rice, *c.* Dole, *d.* Trump)

89.ˈ TICK : CLICK :: TOCK : (*a.* clicks, *b.* clack, *c.* clock, *d.* tack)

90. GRANT : (*a.* permission, *b.* legislation, *c.* distribution, *d.* entitlement) :: TAXATION : COLLECTION

91. BUSH : AUSTIN :: REAGAN : (*a.* Sacramento, *b.* Hollywood, *c.* Big Sur, *d.* Arkansas)

92. SYMBIOTIC : INDEPENDENT :: SOPORIFIC : (*a.* invigorating, *b.* dependent, *c.* somniferous, *d.* authoritarian)

93. TACIT : (*a.* tangible, *b.* urchin, *c.* child, *d.* tactful) :: IMPLIED : IMP

94. (*a.* through, *b.* walk, *c.* near, *d.* side) : BY :: STEP : PASS

95. 27 : 125 :: 64 : (*a.* 256, *b.* 216, *c.* 320, *d.* 160)

96. (*a.* defeat, *b.* napkin, *c.* cheerleader, *d.* stain) : BIB :: VICTORY : CLEANLINESS

97. (*a.* Les Miserables, *b.* Cats, *c.* Chicago, *d.* Picasso) : LLOYD WEBBER :: A CHORUS LINE : HAMLISCH

98. 16 : .0625 :: 32 : (*a.* 1.25, *b.* 64, *c.* .03125, *d.* .015625)

99. WONDERLAND : CARROLL :: (*a.* Macondo, *b.* Bogotá, *c.* Mariposa, *d.* Santa Teresa) : GARCIA MARQUEZ

100. GEOFFREY : (*a.* William, *b.* poet, *c.* English, *d.* sonnet) :: CHAUCER : SHAKESPEARE

101. SNEAKER : FOOT :: MITTEN : (*a.* glove, *b.* toe, *c.* shoe, *d.* hand)

102. 8 : 13 :: 21 : (*a.* 26, *b.* 29, *c.* 32, *d.* 34)

103. PORCINE : (*a.* dog, *b.* porcupine, *c.* pigeon, *d.* pig) :: AQUILINE : EAGLE

104. CEDAR : PINE :: MAHOGANY : (*a.* redwood, *b.* hickory, *c.* juniper *d.* spruce)

105. TAXONOMY : LINNAEUS :: (*a.* ornithology, *b.* primatology, *c.* cetology, *d.* geology) : AUDUBON

106. COGNATE : (*a.* etymology, *b.* appearance, *c.* thought, *d.* background) :: HOMOPHONE : SOUND

107. FECUND : FECKLESS :: (*a.* useless, *b.* fertile, *c.* fecal, *d.* potent) : INEFFECTIVE

108. MISCHIEVOUS : (*a.* upstanding, *b.* injurious, *c.* horrific, *d.* homogenous) ::
     MISCELLANEOUS : HETEROGENEOUS

109. CHILE : BEAN :: (*a.* state, *b.* pepper, *c.* soup, *d.* kidney) : LEGUME

110. COLORADO : SQUARE :: (*a.* Italy, *b.* England, *c.* Australia, *d.* Madagascar) : BOOT

111. CHICAGO : WRIGLEY :: (*a.* Boston, *b.* New York, *c.* Los Angeles, *d.* Detroit) : FENWAY

112. DISEASE : LEPER :: (*a.* seaside, *b.* oppose, *c.* repulsion, *d.* sickness) : REPEL

113. POPCORN : FRANK :: BUTTER : (*a.* salt, *b.* mustard, *c.* bun, *d.* oil)

114. CEDARS : (*a.* McKinley, *b.* Zion, *c.* Horeb, *d.* Sinai) :: SLOAN : KETTERING

115. BANDICOOTS : (*a.* monotremes, *b.* platypuses, *c.* crocodiles, *d.* koalas) :: BILBIES :
     TASMANIAN DEVILS

116. STETHOSCOPE : OTOSCOPE :: (*a.* baromater, *b.* electrocardiogram, *c.* ultrasound,
     d. chest) : HYGROMETER

117. BEVERAGE : (*a.* Neufchatel, *b.* sarsaparilla, *c.* pimento, *d.* rhubarb) :: FOOD : SWEETBREAD

118. (*a.* Guterres, *b.* Kofi, *c.* Ki-moon, *d.* Hammarskjold) : ANNAN :: BOUTROS-GHALI : PEREZ
     DE CUELLAR

119. (*a.* Roosevelt, *b.* Geronimo, *c.* Custer, *d.* Lee) : NAPOLEON :: LITTLE BIG HORN :
     WATERLOO

120. SILVERWARE : BATHROOM :: CUTLERY : (*a.* kitchen, *b.* washroom, *c.* plumbing, *d.* toilet)

1.	C	31.	C	61.	A	91.	A
2.	A	32.	D	62.	C	92.	A
3.	D	33.	B	63.	C	93.	B
4.	B	34.	D	64.	D	94.	D
5.	B	35.	C	65.	B	95.	B
6.	A	36.	D	66.	B	96.	C
7.	D	37.	A	67.	D	97.	B
8.	B	38.	A	68.	B	98.	C
9.	D	39.	B	69.	C	99.	A
10.	B	40.	C	70.	B	100.	A
11.	C	41.	B	71.	B	101.	D
12.	C	42.	A	72.	D	102.	D
13.	D	43.	D	73.	C	103.	D
14.	A	44.	B	74.	D	104.	B
15.	A	45.	B	75.	D	105.	A
16.	A	46.	A	76.	A	106.	A
17.	D	47.	C	77.	A	107.	B
18.	B	48.	A	78.	D	108.	B
19.	D	49.	A	79.	C	109.	A
20.	C	50.	B	80.	B	110.	A
21.	A	51.	A	81.	B	111.	A
22.	A	52.	C	82.	B	112.	A
23.	D	53.	C	83.	C	113.	B
24.	B	54.	B	84.	B	114.	D
25.	A	55.	C	85.	D	115.	D
26.	B	56.	A	86.	B	116.	A
27.	C	57.	A	87.	A	117.	B
28.	B	58.	D	88.	A	118.	C
29.	C	59.	C	89.	C	119.	C
30.	A	60.	A	90.	C	120.	B

ANSWER EXPLANATIONS FOR PRACTICE TEST 1

In the following, explanations concerning the correct responses are in roman font. Explanations regarding distracters (incorrect responses) that are not self-explaining or could be misinterpreted are in italics in order to highlight the explanations of the answers that are correct.

1. MACHIAVELLIAN : (*a.* isolationist, *b.* quixotic, ***c.* cunning**, *d.* pavlovian) :: ORWELLIAN : DRACONIAN

   (c) Machiavelli was known for being very *cunning*, as evidenced by his work in *The Prince*. George Orwell, particularly in *1984*, wrote of a world characterized by cruelty and subjugation: *Draconian* is that adjective (the word comes interestingly from Draco, a politician in Ancient Athens who adopted a notoriously strict set of laws).

2. ROE : WADE :: (***a.* Miranda**, *b.* McCulloch, *c.* McCain, *d.* McMurray) : ARIZONA

   (a) This analogy revolves around landmark Supreme Court decisions: Roe v. Wade involving abortion, and Miranda v. Arizona that established a suspect's rights during interrogation when detained. **"You have the right to remain silent . . ."**

3. TUESDAY : MARCH :: WEEK :(*a.* day, *b.* month, *c.* April, ***d.* year**)

   (d) Tuesday is one of the 7 days that make up a week, and March is one of the 12 months that make up a year.

4. ALKALI : (*a.* copper, ***b.* caesium**, *c.* Zinc, *d.* tin) :: NOBLE : ARGON

   (b) This is a periodic table analogy. Caesium is an alkali metal, and argon is a noble gas. *Copper is a coinage metal. Zinc is a transition metal. Tin is a post-transition metal.*

5. COHO : SOCKEYE :: ALBACORE : (*a.* walleye, ***b.* yellowfin**, *c.* smallmouth, *d.* salmon)

   (b) Coho and sockeye are varieties of salmon. Albacore and yellowfin are varieties of tuna.

6. NOBEL : SWEDEN :: (***a.* Man Booker**, *b.* Pulitzer, *c.* Kafka, *d.* Caldecott) : UNITED KINGDOM

   (a) The Nobel Prize is a Swedish award of various categories, while the Man Booker Prize is a British award for excellence in literature.

7. MARS : REMUS :: JUPITER : (*a.* Zeus, *b.* Aeneas, *c.* Romulus, ***d.* Hercules**)

   (d) In Roman mythology, Mars is the father of twins Romulus and Remus, so term one is to term two. Jupiter is the father of Hercules.

8. KINDLING : KIND :: TINDER : (*a.* noble, ***b.* courteous**, *c.* tender, *d.* nigh)

   (b) Kindling and tinder are both small pieces of firewood. One who is kind is also courteous.

9. ROTGUT : (*a.* moonshine, *b.* nausea, *c.* regular, ***d.* bottom shelf**) :: BRANDY : PREMIUM

   (d) Rotgut is slang for very cheap alcohol; cheap alcohol is found on the bottom shelf of a liquor store, while brandy is typically a premium, expensive potable.

10. LEVER : PULLEY :: FULCRUM : (*a.* lift, ***b.* wheel**, *c.* pivot, *d.* seesaw)

    (b) A fulcrum is the point on which a lever pivots. The focal point of a pulley is a wheel.

11. (*a.* expel, *b.* abrupt, *c.* **stop**, *d.* pause) : CANCEL :: HALT : SUSPEND

(c) These four terms all are quite similar. The principal difference is that cancel and stop both have a connotation of being a permanent cessation, while halt and suspend both have the implication that it's merely a momentary pause that will resume at a later time. *Choice d is a common incorrect choice.*

12. .4 : 8 :: 160 : (*a.* 320, *b.* 6400, *c.* **3200**, *d.* 4800)

(c) 8 is .4 × 20, and 3200 is 160 × 20.

13. ULULATION : (*a.* sing, *b.* alliteration, *c.* hum, *d.* **hoot**) :: SUSURRATION : WHISPER

(d) An ululation is a form of hoot (or *yell*). Susurration is a beautiful word for a whisper.

14. (*a.* **verdigris**, *b.* weathering, *c.* deterioration, *d.* nickel) : COPPER :: EROSION : SOIL

(a) As soil is exposed to weathering, it erodes. As copper is exposed to weathering, it forms a greenish patina called *verdigris*.

15. (*a.* **flaunt**, *b.* hang, *c.* carnival, *d.* rise) : LEVITATE :: PARADE : FLOAT

(a) *Terms two and four are synonyms. Term three can be both a noun for a celebration, or a verb with various meanings.* The most logical selection is choice a as a synonym.

16. RUBOR : (*a.* **calor**, *b.* malignancy, *c.* ardor, *d.* growth) :: DOLOR : TUMOR

(a) Rubor, calor, dolor, and tumor (or redness, fever, pain, or swelling) were the four symptoms indicative of infection, as recorded by Ancient Roman encyclopedist Celsus.

17. CEO : VICE PRESIDENT :: (*a.* chairman, *b.* employee, *c.* board, *d.* **director**) : MANAGER

(d) In a corporate hierarchy, a CEO ranks directly above a vice president, and a director ranks directly above a manager.

18. (*a.* Jordan, *b.* **Unitas**, *c.* Ruth, *d.* Ovechkin) : FOOTBALL :: ORR : HOCKEY

(b) Bobby Orr is considered by some to be the greatest hockey player of all time. Johnny Unitas is considered one of the greatest football players of all time. *There is no mention of basketball or baseball where Jordan and Ruth would be correct.*

19. XII : (*a.* XIII, *b.* XIV, *c.* XVII, *d.* **XVI**) :: XXXVI : XLVIII

(d) When dealing with Roman numerals, convert the terms to base 10 for familiarity purposes (unless you are from a very antiquated community). When converted, the analogy becomes 12 : ? :: 36 : 48. The relationship between 12 and 36 is that the latter is 3 times the former. In order for that analogy to continue, 48 must be 3 times the second term. 48/3=16. 16 is expressed as XVI. Thus, choice d is correct.

20. MERCURY : (*a.* Jupiter, *b.* Saturn, *c.* **Venus**, *d.* Neptune) :: EARTH : MARS

(c) In order of distance from the sun (from least to greatest), the planets are Mercury, Venus, Earth, then Mars. Recall the mnemonic "My very entertaining mother just served us nine pancakes". Discount the "pancakes," however, as Pluto is no longer considered a planet.

21. (*a.* **aerobics**, *b.* cavity, *c.* stroke, *d.* antibiotic) : INFARCTION :: FLOSS : GINGIVITIS

(a) Aerobic exercise (commonly, *aerobics*) is a form of preventative medicine against heart disease. An infarction is a heart attack. Similarly, floss is designed to prevent gingivitis.

22. FLUTE : (*a.* **champagne**, *b.* piccolo, *c.* woodwind, *d.* orchestra) :: STEIN : BEER

(a) Beer is often served in a stein, and champagne in a flute. Recall that some words have multiple meanings; *this was not a musical flute, although one's first impression most likely was that it was.* Be flexible in your thought processes.

23. TINTINNABULATION : (*a.* Poe, *b.* illumination, *c.* fly, ***d.* bell**) :: DRONE : WASP

(d) A wasp makes a droning sound. Tintinnabulation is a sound derived from a bell. It was coined by Poe, but notice the relationship: the sound of one thing compared to another.

24. LANGE : LIEBOVITZ :: ADAMS : (*a.* Rockwell, ***b.* Karsh**, *c.* Burns, *d.* Dreiser)

(b) Lange and Liebovitz are both female photographers. Adams and Karsh are male photographers. *The incorrect three options are all male, but not photographers.*

25. 78 : 13 :: (***a.* 42**, *b.* 70, *c.* 56, *d.* 49) : 7

(a) 78 is 6×13. 42 is 6×7.

26. PHALANX : DIGIT :: STAPES : (*a.* nose, ***b.* ear**, *c.* ankle, *d.* wrist)

(b) The phalanx is a bone in a finger, or *digit*. The stapes is a bone in the ear.

27. PROSE : POETRY :: EMERSON : (*a.* Cather, *b.* Crichton, ***c.* Neruda**, *d.* Martin)

(c) Ralph Waldo Emerson is renowned for his prose. Pablo Neruda wrote in a variety of styles, but is primarily known for his poetry.

28. (*a.* colossal, ***b.* zebra**, *c.* mollusk, *d.* Australian) : MUSSEL :: ASIAN : CARP

(b) The zebra mussel and Asian carp are especially problematic examples of invasive species.

29. LACONIC : (*a.* sentimental, *b.* sad, ***c.* brief**, *d.* maritime) :: PICARESQUE : ROGUISH

(c) Laconic and brief are similar in meaning, as are picaresque and roguish.

30. PROPOSAL : ULTIMATUM :: OFFER : (***a.* demand**, *b.* acceptance, *c.* rejection, *d.* final)

(a) A proposal is an offer, ostensibly leaving room for negotiation. An ultimatum, however, is stronger: it is a demand.

31. TEAR : LCL :: (*a.* tendon, *b.* rip, ***c.* fracture**, *d.* sprain) : TARSAL

(c) One tears the LCL, or lateral collateral ligament, located in the knee. One fractures a tarsal, which is a bone. *One cannot sprain or rip a bone. Tendon fails to recognize the need for a verb.*

32. DUCHAMP : (*a.* Voltaire, *b.* Romanticism, *c.* Michelangelo, ***d.* Picasso**) :: DADA : CUBISM

(d) Marcel Duchamp was famous for his works in the Dada art movement. Pablo Picasso popularized art in the cubism movement.

33. (*a.* Caucasian, ***b.* Creek**, *c.* Tenderfoot, *d.* Sunni) : CHOCTAW :: BLACKFEET : PUEBLO

(b) Choctaw and Pueblo are Native American tribes, as are Creek and Blackfeet.

34. MASTERS : (*a.* orthopedics, *b.* pulmonology, *c.* nephrology, ***d.* gynecology**) :: SPOCK : PEDIATRICS

(d) William Masters was a physician in the field of gynecology who was a pioneer in the study of human sexuality. Benjamin Spock was a pediatrician who wrote a seminal piece on parental advice for handling young children. *Pulmonology deals with the respiratory system and nephrology is medicine that studies the kidneys.*

35. (*a.* Herod, *b.* Samaritan, ***c.* Lazarus**, *d.* Judas) : BETHANY :: JESUS : NAZARETH

(c) In the Bible, Lazarus of Bethany was raised from the dead in the Gospel of John. Jesus of Nazareth requires little introduction.

36. FERRIC : CUPROUS :: (*a.* steel, *b.* aluminum, *c.* silver, ***d.* iron**) : COPPER

(d) *Ferric* is of or relating to iron (note iron's periodic table symbol of *Fe*). *Cuprous* is a term referring to copper (note copper's symbol of *Cu*).

37. STARBUCK : SODAPOP :: (***a.* Moby-Dick**, *b.* Pilgrim's Progress, *c.* Portnoy's Complaint, *d.* Emma) : OUTSIDERS

(a) Starbuck is a character in Melville's *Moby Dick*. Sodapop is a character in S.E. Hilton's *The Outsiders*, which she wrote while still attending high school.

38. MORGAN : MERRILL :: (**a. Stanley**, *b.* J.P., *c.* Lehigh, *d.* Lafayette) : LYNCH

   (a) Morgan Stanley and Merrill Lynch are both financial conglomerates.

39. KELVIN: (*a.* 100, **b. 273**, *c.* 0, *d.* 212) :: CELSIUS : 0

   (b) This analogy deals with freezing points of temperature scales. Water freezes at 273 degrees Kelvin and 0 degrees Celsius.

40. NOVEL : (*a.* fiction, b. encyclopedia, **c. novella**, d. author) :: LONG : SHORT

   (c) In comparing lengths of pieces of fiction, a novel is long and a novella is shorter.

41. (*a.* port, **b. starboard**, *c.* aft, *d.* spinnaker) : RIGHT :: BOW : FRONT

   (b) On a ship, the bow is the front of the boat, the stern is the back, starboard is to the right, and port is to the left. The next time you are on a yatch party, you'll now be right at home.

42. TUTORIAL : INSTRUCTION :: (**a. sartorial**, *b.* piscatorial, *c.* urticarial, *d.* fashion) : CLOTHING

   (a) Tutorial is an adjective referring to instruction. Sartorial is a wonderful word referring to clothing. *If you chose choice d, you missed the adjective : noun component.*

43. TIBER : ITALY :: YELLOW :(*a.* France, *b.* Canada, *c.* India, **d. China**)

   (d) The Tiber is a river in Italy, and the Yellow is a river in China.

44. REAL : MANCHESTER :: MADRID : (*a.* Barcelona, **b. United**, *c.* Spain, *d.* Arsenal)

   (b) Real Madrid (Spain) and Manchester United (Britain) are two of the most accomplished association football clubs in the world.

45. THORN : ROSE :: MATTERHORN : (*a.* mountain, **b. elbows**, *c.* Everest, *d.* Pyrenees)

   (b) This is a rhyming analogy. Thorn and matterhorn have identical ending sounds, just like rose and elbows (though spelled differently) end with the same sound. *The Pyrenees are a mountain range.*

46. HOPKINS : LECTER :: (**a. Brosnan**, *b.* Anthony, *c.* Cruise, *d.* Ford) : BOND

   (a) Anthony Hopkins reprised the role of Hannibal Lecter in *The Silence of the Lambs*. Pierce Brosnan played James Bond before Daniel Craig assumed the role.

47. ENTOMOLOGY : GRASSHOPPER :: ICHTHYOLOGY : (*a.* bluejay, *b.* fish, **c. trout**, *d.* bird)

   (c) Entomology is the study of insects. A grasshopper is a type of insect. Note the specifics of that relationship: *term two is a* type *of term one, which makes choice b incorrect.* Ichthyology is the study of fish, and a trout is a *type* of fish.

48. GAGGLE : ARSENAL :: (**a. goose**, *b.* marksmanship, *c.* weaponry, *d.* rifle) : PISTOL

   (a) A pistol is a possible component of an arsenal (a collection of weaponry). A gaggle is a group of geese.

49. RADIUS : ULNA :: (**a. tibia**, *b.* femur, *c.* tarsus, *d.* humerus) : FIBULA

   (a) The radius and ulna are bones in the forearm, while the tibia and fibula are bones in the lower leg. *The femur is incorrect because it is in the upper leg.*

50. THE REPUBLIC : PLATO :: MEDITATIONS : (*a.* Caesar, **b. Aurelius**, *c.* Socrates, *d.* Sophocles)

   (b) Plato wrote *The Republic*. Marcus Aurelius penned the stoic masterpiece *Meditations*.

51. ORNATE : HIBERNATION :: THREADBARE : (**a. insomnia**, *b.* nap, *c.* repose, *d.* homeostasis)

   (a) Ornate and hibernation have little to do with one another. Examine the third term as it relates to the first, instead; terms one and three are antonyms. Terms two and four therefore must be antonyms, and they are: hibernation is a deep sleep. Insomnia is the inability to fall asleep.

52. (*a.* apple, *b.* pepper, ***c.* vegetable**, *d.* spicy) : JALAPENO :: FRUIT : GRANNY SMITH

    (c) The Granny Smith apple is a type of fruit. The jalapeno is a pepper, but that is too specific; vegetable is more analogous to fruit.

53. GRASS : (*a.* seed, *b.* equine, ***c.* dark**, *d.* Clydesdale) :: ROOTS : HORSE

    (c) Grassroots and darkhorse are common political phrases.

54. (*a.* delta, ***b.* six**, *c.* product, *d.* alpha) : QUALITY :: SIGMA : CONTROL

    (b) Six Sigma is a quality control method popularized by business maven Jack Welch during his tenure at General Electric.

55. (*a.* Sting, *b.* Lennon, ***c.* Wonder**, *d.* Jagger) : CLAPTON :: PIANO :: GUITAR

    (c) Eric Clapton is a Hall of Fame musician known as "Slowhand" for his guitar mastery. Stevie Wonder is best known for his piano prowess.

56. MASQUERADE : DISSIMULATION :: MAUSOLEUM : (***a.* sepulcher**, *b.* dystopia, *c.* reality, *d.* simulation)

    (a) Mausoleum and sepulcher are both burial places. A masquerade can be a form of concealment, just as dissimulation can mean the same.

57. (***a.* pillow**, *b.* soot, *c.* formal, *d.* court) : SUIT :: CASE : CASE

    (a) *Pillowcase* and *suitcase* are common compound words.

58. ARCHBISHOP : POPE :: (*a.* priest, *b.* Catholic, *c.* deacon, ***d.* bishop**) :: CARDINAL

    (d) In the hierarchy of the Catholic Church, a cardinal is immediately beneath the pope, and a bishop is immediately beneath an archbishop.

59. ONCE: (*a.* one, *b.* twice, ***c.* two**, *d.* three) :: THRICE : FOUR

    (c) If you missed this question, you most likely were working too quickly. The second and fourth terms are integers, while once and thrice describe the number of times something occurred. The terms also proceed in numerical order.

60. FLORA : (***a.* chrysanthemum**, *b.* flower, *c.* garden, *d.* moose) :: FAUNA : ELK

    (a) *Flora* is a word for the types of flowers indigenous in an area. *Fauna* is the word for the collection of indigenous animals. Elk is a type of fauna. Similarly, chrysanthemum is a type of flower. *The word flower improperly completes the analogy, which requires a type of flower.*

61. UNDERWATER : SCUBA :: (***a.* detection**, *b.* sky, *c.* radio, *d.* ranging) : RADAR

    (a) SCUBA and RADAR are acronyms, which is a little known fact. *Underwater* is the third word in the acronym SCUBA, and *detection* is the third word in the acronym RADAR.

62. TEPID : IRREGULAR :: (*a.* commonplace, *b.* rapid, ***c.* scorching**, *d.* warm) : UNPRECEDENTED

    (c) Tepid means lukewarm, or somewhat warm. Scorching is much more intense. Similarly, unprecedented is more intense than irregular.

63. LEGUME : PEANUT :: TUBER : (*a.* melon, *b.* maize, ***c.* yam**, *d.* pear)

    (c) A peanut is a type of legume, and a yam is a type of tuber.

64. TINNITUS : GLAUCOMA :: AURICULAR : (*a.* astigmatism, b.ear, *c.* visual, ***d.* ocular**)

    (d) Tinnitus is an ailment of the ear. Auricular is an adjective pertaining to the ear. Glaucoma affects the eye, making it an ocular disease.

65. (*a.* eastern, ***b.* occidental**, *c.* China, *d.* Asia) : ORIENT :: EASTERN : CALIFORNIA

(b) Occidental means western, which is the opposite of eastern. There is no true antonym for a proper noun like Orient, but it refers to Asia; California and The Orient are on separate sides of the world, which is as antonymic as proper nouns can be.

66. BLACK JACK : DESERT FOX :: PERSHING : (*a.* Sheridan, ***b.* Rommel**, *c.* Bradley, *d.* Sherman)

(b) These are military nicknames. Black Jack Pershing was a U.S. general during World War One. Erwin Rommel, the *desert fox*, was a high-ranking Nazi general during The Third Reich.

67. FISH : SCHOOL :: (*a.* assassination, *b.* zebra, *c.* bear, ***d.* crow**) : MURDER

(d) A group of fish is known as a *school*. That was probably apparent. Less known, however, is the term for a group of crows: it is a *murder*.

68. (*a.* variability, ***b.* mode**, *c.* cruel, *d.* middle) : FREQUENCY :: MEAN : CENTER

(b) Mode is a mathematical term for the value that occurs most frequently, and mean is the average, or the calculated *center* of all data points.

69. KINESIOLOGY : MOVEMENT :: HISTOLOGY : (a.uterus, *b.* past, ***c.* tissue**, *d.* inertia)

(c) The first and third terms are the studies of the second and fourth terms, respectively. Vocabulary knowledge on the MAT is paramount.

70. AVUNCULAR : (*a.* uncle, ***b.* aunt**, *c.* matronly, *d.* familial) :: PATERNAL : MOTHER

(b) It is readily apparent that paternal refers to the father, and not the mother; the mother is the wife of the father. Avuncular pertains to an uncle, whose wife would be one's aunt. *Choice a is relevant, but it neglects to account for the given relationship.*

71. N'Djamena : (*a.* Niger. ***b.* Chad**, *c.* Egypt, *d.* South Sudan) :: MOGADISHU : SOMALIA

(b) Mogadishu is the capital city of Somalia. N'Djamena is the capital city of Chad.

72. JAY : TAFT :: WARREN : (*a.* Holmes, *b.* Harding, *c.* Kennedy, ***d.* Burger**)

(d) John Jay, William Howard Taft, Earl Warren, and Warren Burger were all Supreme Court Chief Justices.

73. (*a.* Aaron, *b.* Moses, ***c.* Jacob**, *d.* Noah) : ABRAHAM :: RACHEL : SARAH

(c) In the Bible, Jacob wed Rachel, and Abraham wed Sarah.

74. ORPHAN : PARENT :: PAUPER : (*a.* father, *b.* poverty, *c.* hobo, ***d.* wealth**)

(d) An orphan is one without parents, just as a pauper (or *poor person*) lacks wealth.

75. CONFLICT : BLOOD :: MINERAL : (*a.* zinc, *b.* rock, *c.* calcium, ***d.* diamond**)

(d) *Blood diamond* is a common phrase, perhaps most popularized by the Leonardo DiCaprio film of the same name. A *conflict mineral* can be many different minerals, but it has a similar connotation of a premium product obtained by exploiting the third world and its governmental volatility.

76. CURTAIN : (***a.* prism**, *b.* reflect, *c.* shade, *d.* cover) :: HINDER : REFRACT

(a) A curtain hinders the passage of light. A prism reflects light.

77. AXIOM : (***a.* postulate**, *b.* conclusion, *c.* requiem, *d.* ultimatum) :: PROPOSITION : THEOREM

(a) This was a question of supreme difficulty. Axiom and postulate are interchangeable, albeit esoteric, words in the field of philosophy referring to concepts that are indisputable. Theorem and postulate refer to speculative, unproven concepts.

78. 16 : (*a.* 61, *b.* 64, *c.* 121, *d.* **81**) :: 256 : 625

   (d) This analogy involves numbers raised to the 4th power. It is most likely more difficult than what you will encounter, but is nonetheless good practice, at any rate (and an excellent reminder to remain flexible in mathematical analogies). 16, 81, 256, and 625 are 2, 3, 4, and 5 to the 4th power, respectively.

79. CELERITOUS : (*a.* thrifty, *b.* dour, *c.* **swift**, *d.* verbose) :: MAGNANIMOUS : GENEROUS

   (c) Celeritous and swift are synonymous, while magnanimous and generous mean roughly the same thing.

80. LAUREN : ROCKEFELLER :: POLO : (*a.* pony, *b.* **Standard Oil**, *c.* Exxon, *d.* John)

   (b) Ralph Lauren is a clothing designer whose signature brand is Polo Ralph Lauren. John Rockefeller, once the world's richest man, was the proprietor of Standard Oil, a petroleum conglomerate of immense profitability and influence.

81. QUADRICEPS : TRICEPS :: PUSH : (*a.* over, *b.* **push**, *c.* three, *d.* pull)

   (b) The quadriceps is a muscle on the top of the thigh that is used to push against something (the hamstrings and glutes pull). The triceps is a muscle in the back of the upper arm that similarly is used to push (the biceps pulls).

82. (*a.* southern, *b.* **student**, *c.* court, *d.* supreme) : SNCC :: SUPREME : SCOTUS

   (b) This analogy deals with acronyms, where the second and fourth terms are the acronyms, and the first and third terms are the first word of each acronym. SCOTUS you are probably familiar with: the Supreme Court of the United States. SNCC is less widely-known: it stood for "Student Nonviolent Coordinating Committee" and was a group instrumental during the 1960s during the Civil Rights Era.

83. DEAD : (*a.* picture, *b.* grave, *c.* **spitting**, *d.* mortal) :: RINGER : IMAGE

   (c) Dead ringer and spitting image are both idiomatic expressions used to express similarity in appearance.

84. CHLOROFLUOROCARBONS : OZONE :: PESTICIDES : (*a.* weed-killer, *b.* **food**, *c.* oxygen, *d.* solar deflection)

   (b) Chlorofluorocarbons (commonly, CFCs) are deleterious to the ozone layer and were banned decades ago. Pesticides, though designed to help plant growth by eliminating insects, are often harmful when ingested on plants via food.

85. AMENITIES: (*a.* ornate, *b.* cumbersome, *c.* Utopian, *d.* **Spartan**) :: BACKBONE : INVERTEBRATE

   (d) The operative principle here is that invertebrates lack backbones. A *Spartan* lifestyle is one devoid of (or *lacking*) amenities.

86. PEEVED : LIVID :: STRANGE : (*a.* odd, *b.* **unbelievable**, *c.* incensed, *d.* awkward)

   (b) To be livid is to be significantly more upset than to be merely peeved. Similarly, unbelievable is significantly stronger in its incredulity than simply strange.

87. ALEXANDRINE : PETRARCHAN :: COUPLET : (*a.* **sonnet**, *b.* triplet, *c.* stanza, *d.* ballad)

   (a) The Alexandrine couplet and the Petrarchan sonnet are famous devices in poetry.

88. CLINTON : BUSH :: GORE : (*a.* **Quayle**, *b.* Rice, *c.* Dole, *d.* Trump)

   (a) This is an analogy that is initially difficult because the first three names are interrelated in so many ways. Moreover, it is unclear to which Bush the analogy refers. In this case, it is George H. W. Bush, and not his son, George W. Bush. Al Gore was Bill Clinton's Vice President, while Dan Quayle was the elder Bush's running mate.

89. TICK : CLICK :: TOCK : (*a.* clicks, *b.* clack, ***c.* clock**, *d.* tack)

(c) Tick rhymes with click, and tock rhymes with clock.

90. GRANT : (*a.* permission, *b.* legislation, ***c.* distribution**, *d.* entitlement) :: TAXATION : COLLECTION

(c) Taxation is a form of monetary collection by the government. A grant is monetary distribution (generally also by the government).

91. BUSH : AUSTIN :: REAGAN : (***a.* Sacramento**, *b.* Hollywood, *c.* Big Sur, *d.* Arkansas)

(a) George W. Bush was the governor of Texas. Its state capital is Austin. Ronald Reagan was governor of California. Its capital is Sacramento.

92. SYMBIOTIC : INDEPENDENT :: SOPORIFIC : (***a.* invigorating**, *b.* dependent, *c.* somniferous, *d.* authoritarian)

(a) Symbiotic and independent are words with an antonymic relationship. Of the four choices, the best antonym for soporific is invigorating.

93. TACIT : (*a.* tangible, ***b.* urchin**, *c.* child, *d.* tactful) :: IMPLIED : IMP

(b) Tacit and implied are similar in denotation, as are urchin and imp.

94. (*a.* through, *b.* walk, *c.* near, ***d.* side**) : BY :: STEP : PASS

(d) Bypass and sidestep are common compound words.

95. 27 : 125 :: 64 : (*a.* 256, ***b.* 216**, *c.* 320, *d.* 160)

(b) This analogy requires knowledge of cubes. 27 is the cube of 3. 125 is the cube of 5. 64 is the cube of 4. Logically, then, our correct answer should the cube of 6. Hopefully, you remember your times tables: $6 \times 6 = 36$. From there, solve by hand. $6 \times 30 = 180$; $6 \times 6 = 36$; $180 + 36 = 216$.

96. (*a.* defeat, *b.* napkin, ***c.* cheerleader**, *d.* stain) : BIB :: VICTORY : CLEANLINESS

(c) The purpose of a cheerleader is to inspire a team to victory. The purpose of a bib is to maintain cleanliness during the eating process.

97. (*a.* Les Miserables, ***b.* Cats**, *c.* Chicago, *d.* Picasso) : LLOYD WEBBER :: A CHORUS LINE : HAMLISCH

(b) Andrew Lloyd Webber is an accomplished Broadway writer; one of his seminal works is "Cats." "A Chorus Line" was written by Marvin Hamlisch.

98. 16 : .0625 :: 32 : (*a.* 1.25, *b.* 64, ***c.* .03125**, *d.* .015625)

(c) $16 \times .0625 = 1$. Similarly, $32 \times .0325 = 1$.

99. WONDERLAND : CARROLL :: (***a.* Macondo**, *b.* Bogotá, *c.* Mariposa, *d.* Santa Teresa) : GARCIA MARQUEZ

(a) Wonderland is the fictional locale of Lewis Carroll's *Alice in Wonderland*. Gabriel Garcia Marquez's poignant *100 Years of Solitude* takes place in the fictional Colombian town of Macondo.

100. GEOFFREY : (***a.* William**, *b.* poet, *c.* English, *d.* sonnet) :: CHAUCER : SHAKESPEARE

(a) Geoffrey Chaucer and William Shakespeare are renowned British writers from the 14th and 16th/17th centuries, respectively.

101. SNEAKER : FOOT :: MITTEN : (*a.* glove, *b.* toe, *c.* shoe, ***d.* hand**)

(d) A sneaker is worn on the foot. A mitten is worn on the hand.

102. 8 : 13 :: 21 : (*a.* 26, *b.* 29, *c.* 32, ***d.* 34**)

(d) 8 and 13 are consecutive terms in the Fibonacci sequence, where each subsequent term is the sum of the previous two terms. $8 + 13 = 21$, and $21 + 13 = 34$.

PRACTICE TEST 1

PRACTICE TEST 1   145

103. PORCINE : (*a.* dog, *b.* porcupine, *c.* pigeon, ***d.* pig**) :: AQUILINE : EAGLE

(d) The first and third terms are adjective terms relating to the nouns of two and four, respectively.

104. CEDAR : PINE :: MAHOGANY : (*a.* redwood, ***b.* hickory**, *c.* juniper, *d.* spruce)

(b) Cedar and pine are both softwoods that burn very easily due to their low densities. Mahogany and hickory are both hardwoods. *The other three choices are simply other softwood trees.*

105. TAXONOMY : LINNAEUS :: (***a.* ornithology**, *b.* primatology, *c.* cetology, *d.* geology) : AUDUBON

(a) Carolus Linnaeus was instrumental in taxology, establishing the common binomial nomenclature still used today for species classification. John James Audubon dedicated his life to ornithology. In fact, you probably have heard of "The Audubon Society," an organization dedicated to habitat preservation for birds.

106. COGNATE : (***a.* etymology**, *b.* appearance, *c.* thought, *d.* background) :: HOMOPHONE : SOUND

(a) Cognates are words in different languages that are derived from the same root and are similar enough to be easily recognizable as pairs. Homophones are words that sound the same.

107. FECUND : FECKLESS :: (*a.* useless, ***b.* fertile**, *c.* fecal, *d.* potent) : INEFFECTIVE

(b) Fecund means fertile. Feckless is ineffective.

108. MISCHIEVOUS : (*a.* upstanding, ***b.* injurious**, *c.* horrific, *d.* homogenous) :: MISCELLANEOUS : HETEROGENEOUS

(b) Miscellaneous and heterogeneous both mean a random assortment. Injurious is the closest synonym for mischievous.

109. CHILE : BEAN :: (***a.* state**, *b.* pepper, *c.* soup, *d.* kidney) : LEGUME

(a) Note the spelling of the first term. It is *Chile* a country, rather than *chili* the bean. Thus one is to three because Chile is a country, or *state* in international terminology. Beans are a type of legume.

110. COLORADO : SQUARE :: (***a.* Italy**, *b.* England, *c.* Australia, *d.* Madagascar) : BOOT

(a) When viewed on a map, the shape of Colorado is remarkably square, just as the shape of Italy is remarkably like that of a boot.

111. CHICAGO : WRIGLEY :: (***a.* Boston**, *b.* New York, *c.* Los Angeles, *d.* Detroit) : FENWAY

(a) Wrigley Field is an iconic baseball park in Chicago. Fenway Park is an equally iconic stadium in Boston.

112. DISEASE : LEPER :: (***a.* seaside**, *b.* oppose, *c.* repulsion, *d.* sickness) : REPEL

(a) Leper and repel are anagrams. Disease and seaside are as well. *At first, it may have seemed as if a leper were one suffering from a disease, but that relationship did not fit the whole analogy.*

113. POPCORN : FRANK :: BUTTER : (*a.* salt, ***b.* mustard**, *c.* bun, *d.* oil)

(b) Butter, of course, is a condiment commonly added to popcorn. *Frank* is another term for hot dog. Mustard is the most common condiment added to that ballpark culinary staple.

114. CEDARS : (*a.* McKinley, *b.* Zion, *c.* Horeb, ***d.* Sinai**) :: SLOAN : KETTERING

(d) Cedars-Sinai is a hospital in Los Angeles perhaps most famous for its celebrity patients. Memorial Sloan Kettering Cancer Center is a reputable hospital in New York City.

115. BANDICOOTS : (*a.* monotremes, *b.* platypuses, *c.* crocodiles, ***d.* koalas**) :: BILBIES : TASMANIAN DEVILS

(d) Bilbies and Tasmanian devils are marsupials, just as bandicoots and koalas are marsupials. Notice that the relationship is more in-depth than simply animals found in Australia.

116. STETHOSCOPE : OTOSCOPE :: (***a.* barometer**, *b.* electrocardiogram, *c.* ultrasound, *d.* chest) : HYGROMETER

(a) A stethoscope is used to listen to the chest, and an otoscope to the ear. Thus, they are both instruments for monitoring biological processes. A barometer and hygrometer are used to measure atmospheric pressure and moisture content, respectively.

117. BEVERAGE : (*a.* Neufchatel, ***b.* sarsaparilla**, *c.* pimento, *d.* rhubarb) :: FOOD : SWEETBREAD

(b) Sarsaparilla is a beverage. Sweetbread is a food.

118. (*a.* Rodriguez, *b.* Ki-moon, ***c.* Guterres**, *d.* Hammarskjold) : ANNAN :: BOUTROS-GHALI : PEREZ DE CUELLAR

(c) Guterres is the current United Nations Secretary General (as of this printing). He was preceded by Ki-moon. Similarly, Boutros Boutros-Ghali was preceded by Javier Perez de Cuellar in the same office.

119. (*a.* Roosevelt, *b.* Geronimo, ***c.* Custer**, *d.* Lee) : NAPOLEON :: LITTLE BIG HORN : WATERLOO

(c) General George Custer and General Napoleon Bonaparte (commonly, "Napoléon") are two of the most illustrious military minds in Western History. Custer's downfall (and his death) occurred in a battle against Native Americans at Little Big Horn in Montana (commonly known as "Custer's Last Stand"). Napoleon lost at Waterloo, and then abdicated four days later.

120. SILVERWARE : BATHROOM :: CUTLERY : (*a.* kitchen, ***b.* washroom**, *c.* plumbing, *d.* toilet)

(b) Silverware and bathroom are United States terms. Cutlery and washroom are the Canadian verbal preferences for the same items, but the latter two terms are also used (albeit, less frequently) across the Anglo-speaking world.

ANSWER SHEET
Practice Test 2

1. Ⓐ Ⓑ Ⓒ Ⓓ	31. Ⓐ Ⓑ Ⓒ Ⓓ	61. Ⓐ Ⓑ Ⓒ Ⓓ	91. Ⓐ Ⓑ Ⓒ Ⓓ
2. Ⓐ Ⓑ Ⓒ Ⓓ	32. Ⓐ Ⓑ Ⓒ Ⓓ	62. Ⓐ Ⓑ Ⓒ Ⓓ	92. Ⓐ Ⓑ Ⓒ Ⓓ
3. Ⓐ Ⓑ Ⓒ Ⓓ	33. Ⓐ Ⓑ Ⓒ Ⓓ	63. Ⓐ Ⓑ Ⓒ Ⓓ	93. Ⓐ Ⓑ Ⓒ Ⓓ
4. Ⓐ Ⓑ Ⓒ Ⓓ	34. Ⓐ Ⓑ Ⓒ Ⓓ	64. Ⓐ Ⓑ Ⓒ Ⓓ	94. Ⓐ Ⓑ Ⓒ Ⓓ
5. Ⓐ Ⓑ Ⓒ Ⓓ	35. Ⓐ Ⓑ Ⓒ Ⓓ	65. Ⓐ Ⓑ Ⓒ Ⓓ	95. Ⓐ Ⓑ Ⓒ Ⓓ
6. Ⓐ Ⓑ Ⓒ Ⓓ	36. Ⓐ Ⓑ Ⓒ Ⓓ	66. Ⓐ Ⓑ Ⓒ Ⓓ	96. Ⓐ Ⓑ Ⓒ Ⓓ
7. Ⓐ Ⓑ Ⓒ Ⓓ	37. Ⓐ Ⓑ Ⓒ Ⓓ	67. Ⓐ Ⓑ Ⓒ Ⓓ	97. Ⓐ Ⓑ Ⓒ Ⓓ
8. Ⓐ Ⓑ Ⓒ Ⓓ	38. Ⓐ Ⓑ Ⓒ Ⓓ	68. Ⓐ Ⓑ Ⓒ Ⓓ	98. Ⓐ Ⓑ Ⓒ Ⓓ
9. Ⓐ Ⓑ Ⓒ Ⓓ	39. Ⓐ Ⓑ Ⓒ Ⓓ	69. Ⓐ Ⓑ Ⓒ Ⓓ	99. Ⓐ Ⓑ Ⓒ Ⓓ
10. Ⓐ Ⓑ Ⓒ Ⓓ	40. Ⓐ Ⓑ Ⓒ Ⓓ	70. Ⓐ Ⓑ Ⓒ Ⓓ	100. Ⓐ Ⓑ Ⓒ Ⓓ
11. Ⓐ Ⓑ Ⓒ Ⓓ	41. Ⓐ Ⓑ Ⓒ Ⓓ	71. Ⓐ Ⓑ Ⓒ Ⓓ	101. Ⓐ Ⓑ Ⓒ Ⓓ
12. Ⓐ Ⓑ Ⓒ Ⓓ	42. Ⓐ Ⓑ Ⓒ Ⓓ	72. Ⓐ Ⓑ Ⓒ Ⓓ	102. Ⓐ Ⓑ Ⓒ Ⓓ
13. Ⓐ Ⓑ Ⓒ Ⓓ	43. Ⓐ Ⓑ Ⓒ Ⓓ	73. Ⓐ Ⓑ Ⓒ Ⓓ	103. Ⓐ Ⓑ Ⓒ Ⓓ
14. Ⓐ Ⓑ Ⓒ Ⓓ	44. Ⓐ Ⓑ Ⓒ Ⓓ	74. Ⓐ Ⓑ Ⓒ Ⓓ	104. Ⓐ Ⓑ Ⓒ Ⓓ
15. Ⓐ Ⓑ Ⓒ Ⓓ	45. Ⓐ Ⓑ Ⓒ Ⓓ	75. Ⓐ Ⓑ Ⓒ Ⓓ	105. Ⓐ Ⓑ Ⓒ Ⓓ
16. Ⓐ Ⓑ Ⓒ Ⓓ	46. Ⓐ Ⓑ Ⓒ Ⓓ	76. Ⓐ Ⓑ Ⓒ Ⓓ	106. Ⓐ Ⓑ Ⓒ Ⓓ
17. Ⓐ Ⓑ Ⓒ Ⓓ	47. Ⓐ Ⓑ Ⓒ Ⓓ	77. Ⓐ Ⓑ Ⓒ Ⓓ	107. Ⓐ Ⓑ Ⓒ Ⓓ
18. Ⓐ Ⓑ Ⓒ Ⓓ	48. Ⓐ Ⓑ Ⓒ Ⓓ	78. Ⓐ Ⓑ Ⓒ Ⓓ	108. Ⓐ Ⓑ Ⓒ Ⓓ
19. Ⓐ Ⓑ Ⓒ Ⓓ	49. Ⓐ Ⓑ Ⓒ Ⓓ	79. Ⓐ Ⓑ Ⓒ Ⓓ	109. Ⓐ Ⓑ Ⓒ Ⓓ
20. Ⓐ Ⓑ Ⓒ Ⓓ	50. Ⓐ Ⓑ Ⓒ Ⓓ	80. Ⓐ Ⓑ Ⓒ Ⓓ	110. Ⓐ Ⓑ Ⓒ Ⓓ
21. Ⓐ Ⓑ Ⓒ Ⓓ	51. Ⓐ Ⓑ Ⓒ Ⓓ	81. Ⓐ Ⓑ Ⓒ Ⓓ	111. Ⓐ Ⓑ Ⓒ Ⓓ
22. Ⓐ Ⓑ Ⓒ Ⓓ	52. Ⓐ Ⓑ Ⓒ Ⓓ	82. Ⓐ Ⓑ Ⓒ Ⓓ	112. Ⓐ Ⓑ Ⓒ Ⓓ
23. Ⓐ Ⓑ Ⓒ Ⓓ	53. Ⓐ Ⓑ Ⓒ Ⓓ	83. Ⓐ Ⓑ Ⓒ Ⓓ	113. Ⓐ Ⓑ Ⓒ Ⓓ
24. Ⓐ Ⓑ Ⓒ Ⓓ	54. Ⓐ Ⓑ Ⓒ Ⓓ	84. Ⓐ Ⓑ Ⓒ Ⓓ	114. Ⓐ Ⓑ Ⓒ Ⓓ
25. Ⓐ Ⓑ Ⓒ Ⓓ	55. Ⓐ Ⓑ Ⓒ Ⓓ	85. Ⓐ Ⓑ Ⓒ Ⓓ	115. Ⓐ Ⓑ Ⓒ Ⓓ
26. Ⓐ Ⓑ Ⓒ Ⓓ	56. Ⓐ Ⓑ Ⓒ Ⓓ	86. Ⓐ Ⓑ Ⓒ Ⓓ	116. Ⓐ Ⓑ Ⓒ Ⓓ
27. Ⓐ Ⓑ Ⓒ Ⓓ	57. Ⓐ Ⓑ Ⓒ Ⓓ	87. Ⓐ Ⓑ Ⓒ Ⓓ	117. Ⓐ Ⓑ Ⓒ Ⓓ
28. Ⓐ Ⓑ Ⓒ Ⓓ	58. Ⓐ Ⓑ Ⓒ Ⓓ	88. Ⓐ Ⓑ Ⓒ Ⓓ	118. Ⓐ Ⓑ Ⓒ Ⓓ
29. Ⓐ Ⓑ Ⓒ Ⓓ	59. Ⓐ Ⓑ Ⓒ Ⓓ	89. Ⓐ Ⓑ Ⓒ Ⓓ	119. Ⓐ Ⓑ Ⓒ Ⓓ
30. Ⓐ Ⓑ Ⓒ Ⓓ	60. Ⓐ Ⓑ Ⓒ Ⓓ	90. Ⓐ Ⓑ Ⓒ Ⓓ	120. Ⓐ Ⓑ Ⓒ Ⓓ

Time: 60 MINUTES

> **Directions:** In each of the following questions, you will find three initial terms and, in parentheses, four answer options designated *a*, *b*, *c*, and *d*. You are to select from the four answer options the one that *best* completes the analogy with the three initial terms. To record your answers, use the answer sheet provided.

1. CANDLE : TALLOW :: TIRE : (*a*. automobile, *b*. round, *c*. rubber, *d*. hollow)

2. TERRESTRIAL : (*a*. palatial, *b*. partial, *c*. martial, *d*. celestial) :: EARTH : HEAVEN

3. (*a*. father, *b*. uncle, *c*. brother, *d*. son) : SIBLING :: HUSBAND : SPOUSE

4. 3.6% : (*a*. 0.0036, *b*. 0.036, *c*. 0.36, *d*. 3.6) :: 480% : 4.8

5. PERIODIC : INTERMITTENT :: CONSTANT : (*a*. incessant, *b*. occasional, *c*. infrequent, *d*. never)

6. DARWIN : (*a*. gravity, *b*. planetary orbits, *c*. evolution, *d*. magnetism) :: EINSTEIN : RELATIVITY

7. COMPOSER : SONATA :: (*a*. physicist, *b*. artist, *c*. sculptor, *d*. author) : LITHOGRAPH

8. HUNGRY : LION :: BUSY : (*a*. squirrel, *b*. beaver, *c*. hare, *d*. chipmunk)

9. MATRICIDE : MOTHER :: FRATRICIDE : (*a*. uncle, *b*. father, *c*. brother, *d*. son)

10. (*a*. United, *b*. League, *c*. National, *d*. NFL) : METS :: AMERICAN : YANKEES

11. KNOCK : PIGEON :: KNEED : (*a*. toed, *b*. waisted, *c*. armed, *d*. headed)

12. (*a*. Memorial Day, *b*. Thanksgiving, *c*. Christmas, *d*. Labor Day) : DECORATION DAY :: VETERANS' DAY : ARMISTICE DAY

13. HANG : NOOSE :: BEHEAD : (*a*. guillotine, *b*. Savonarola, *c*. Robespierre, *d*. ablation)

14. APPROPRIATE : INAPPROPRIATE :: APROPOS : (*a*. inapropos, *b*. misapropos, *c*. anapropos, *d*. malapropos)

15. (*a*. gases, *b*. good eating, *c*. intestinal tract, *d*. gasoline) : GASTRONOMY :: HEAVENLY BODIES : ASTRONOMY

16. CONGRESS : UNITED STATES :: (*a*. UNICEF, *b*. Secretary-General, *c*. Security Council, *d*. General Assembly) : UNITED NATIONS

17. EXECUTOR : (*a.* executriss, *b.* executress, *c.* executrex, *d.* executrix) :: ACTOR : ACTRESS

18. CANCEROUS : NONCANCEROUS :: MALIGNANT : (*a.* benign, *b.* benevolent, *c.* beneficent, *d.* latent)

19. (*a.* syllogism, *b.* intellect, *c.* troop movements, *d.* weapons) : LOGISTICS :: LANGUAGE : LINGUISTICS

20. SUBWAY : NEW YORK :: (*a.* Metro, *b.* monorail, *c.* cable car, *d.* airplane) : D.C.

21. (*a.* velocity, *b.* humidity, *c.* pressure, *d.* THI) : BAROMETER :: MILEAGE : ODOMETER

22. KANSAS : WHEAT :: (*a.* Nebraska, *b.* Arkansas, *c.* Wisconsin, *d.* Idaho) : POTATO

23. HYPO : DERMIC :: UNDER : (*a.* skin, *b.* medicine, *c.* blood, *d.* syringe)

24. PECCADILLO : (*a.* stutter, *b.* pretense, *c.* amnesia, *d.* sin) :: MISDEMEANOR : CRIME

25. MISANTHROPE : (*a.* life, *b.* religion, *c.* women, *d.* people) :: MISOGAMIST : MARRIAGE

26. OSTENTATIOUS : (*a.* showy, *b.* proud, *c.* modest, *d.* fickle) :: ONEROUS : BURDENSOME

27. NATURE : NURTURE :: HEREDITY : (*a.* gene, *b.* progenitor, *c.* evolution, *d.* environment)

28. HURRY : SCURRY :: HURLY : (*a.* burly, *b.* curly, *c.* gurly, *d.* wurly)

29. STEM : METS :: (*a.* tab, *b.* ball, *c.* team, *d.* root) : BAT

30. SATAN : BEELZEBUB :: DEVIL : (*a.* Charon, *b.* Pandemonium, *c.* Lucifer, *d.* Hades)

31. FORT SUMTER : CIVIL WAR :: (*a.* Valley Forge, *b.* Princeton, *c.* Lexington, *d.* Trenton) : AMERICAN REVOLUTION

32. (*a.* chameleon, *b.* salamander, *c.* tadpole, *d.* chamois) : FICKLE :: MULE : STUBBORN

33. NEW AMSTERDAM : NEW YORK :: CONSTANTINOPLE : (*a.* Budapest, *b.* Istanbul, *c.* Cairo, *d.* Baghdad)

34. ANESTHESIA : FEEL :: (*a.* eyeball, *b.* eyes, *c.* glasses, *d.* blindness) : SEE

35. CORPORAL : BEAT :: CAPITAL : (*a.* stun, *b.* spend, *c.* kill, *d.* shock)

36. (*a.* neutron, *b.* electron, *c.* nucleon, *d.* positron) : PROTON :: NEGATIVE : POSITIVE

37. CARPE : DIEM :: CAVEAT : (*a.* corpus, *b.* emptor, *c.* deum, *d.* mandamus)

38. RAIN : (*a.* tempest, *b.* frost, *c.* hail, *d.* dry ice) :: WATER : ICE

39. FEINT : (*a*. fall, *b*. remove, *c*. pretend, *d*. authenticate) :: SEVER : SEPARATE

40. 10 : COMMANDMENTS :: (*a*. 5, *b*. 7, *c*. 10, *d*. 12) : DEADLY SINS

41. DOUBLE ENTENDRE : (*a*. ambiguity, *b*. treachery, *c*. meaninglessness, *d*. misperception) :: DOUBLE TAKE : DELAYED REACTION

42. (*a*. nominalism, *b*. phenomenalism, *c*. determinism, *d*. rationalism) : FATALISM :: EXISTENTIALISM : FREE WILL

43. (*a*. carmine, *b*. yellow, *c*. brown, *d*. orange) : RED :: AZURE : BLUE

44. FRAME : PICTURE :: (*a*. cell wall, *b*. endoplasmic reticulum, *c*. cytoplasm, *d*. nuclear envelope) : CELL

45. (*a*. keno, *b*. kalaha, *c*. wari, *d*. soma) : CRAPS :: ROULETTE : TWENTY-ONE

46. HECTOR : (*a*. Rome, *b*. Carthage, *c*. Sicily, *d*. Troy) :: ACHILLES : GREECE

47. KUNG FU : JUDO :: (*a*. Korean, *b*. Chinese, *c*. Vietnamese, *d*. Japanese) : JAPANESE

48. SWARM : BEES :: (*a*. colony, *b*. covey, *c*. pack, *d*. pride) : QUAIL

49. BITUMINOUS : ANTHRACITE :: (*a*. wood, *b*. lead, *c*. lignite, *d*. oil) : STEEL

50. CARRIE NATION : (*a*. women's suffrage, *b*. low-income housing, *c*. temperance, *d*. abolition of child labor) :: MARTIN LUTHER KING, JR. : CIVIL RIGHTS

51. STENCIL : LETTERS :: COMPASS : (*a*. time, *b*. direction, *c*. northwest, *d*. circle)

52. (*a*. proposal, *b*. talk, *c*. dissertation, *d*. dialogue) : ORATION :: QUIZ : EXAMINATION

53. ANTERIOR : POSTERIOR :: (*a*. ventral, *b*. lateral, *c*. external, *d*. internal) : DORSAL

54. IMMIGRATION : EMIGRATION :: ENTRY : (*a*. expulsion, *b*. migration, *c*. egress, *d*. estuary)

55. SATRAP : (*a*. ruler, *b*. bush, *c*. miser, *d*. loner) :: TRAP : AMBUSH

56. ELEGY : LAMENTING :: EPIGRAM : (*a*. inane, *b*. abstruse, *c*. witty, *d*. obtuse)

57. REFORMATION : PROTESTANTS :: COUNTER-REFORMATION : (*a*. Catholics, *b*. Protestants, *c*. Anglicans, *d*. Jews)

58. (*a*. beriberi, *b*. rickets, *c*. anemia, *d*. pellagra) : D :: SCURVY : C

59. GO DUTCH : PAY YOUR OWN EXPENSES :: IN DUTCH : (*a*. in luck, *b*. in trouble, *c*. rich, *d*. poor)

60. FOOL'S GOLD : (*a.* ore, *b.* pyrite, *c.* bauxite, *d.* manganese) :: PENCIL LEAD : GRAPHITE

61. MILL : (*a.* franc, *b.* centime, *c.* shilling, *d.* cent) :: PENNY : DIME

62. (*a.* Spain, *b.* Italy, *c.* Israel, *d.* Lebanon) : RUSSIA :: EL AL : AEROFLOT

63. GAUGUIN : (*a.* England, *b.* U.S.A., *c.* Tahiti, *d.* Madagascar) :: GOYA : SPAIN

64. (*a.* bifteck, *b.* legume, *c.* glace, *d.* poulet) : STEAK :: ESCARGOTS : SNAILS

65. TEMERITY : AUDACITY :: (*a.* softness, *b.* boldness, *c.* shyness, *d.* depravity) : BRAVERY

66. CALORIE : (*a.* weight, *b.* basal metabolism, *c.* fat, *d.* energy) :: DECADE : TIME

67. PETROLOGY : (*a.* sandstone, *b.* brontosaurus, *c.* moth, *d.* nylon) :: BOTANY : ROSE

68. HANSEL : GRETEL :: ORESTES : (*a.* Jocasta, *b.* Electra, *c.* Ophelia, *d.* Alicia)

69. (*a.* rude, *b.* talkative, *c.* immodest, *d.* brash) : GARRULOUS :: PETULANT : PEEVISH

70. PONCE DE LEON : (*a.* Atlantic Ocean, *b.* Mexico, *c.* Georgia, *d.* Florida) ::
BALBOA : PACIFIC OCEAN

71. ATTENUATE : (*a.* disprove, *b.* weaken, *c.* prove, *d.* strengthen) :: ATTRACT : REPEL

72. CEREBRUM : THINKING :: CEREBELLUM : (*a.* olfaction, *b.* muscular coordination,
c. glandular secretion, *d.* audition)

73. BEHAVIORISM : U.S.A. :: GESTALT : (*a.* France, *b.* England, *c.* Switzerland, *d.* Germany)

74. MONROE : (*a.* Treatise, *b.* Edict, *c.* Decree, *d.* Code) :: DOCTRINE : NAPOLEON

75. LXII : CLXXXVI :: D : (*a.* M, *b.* MC, *c.* MD, *d.* MM)

76. (*a.* loudness, *b.* compression, *c.* brightness, *d.* hardness) : MOHS :: TEMPERATURE :
KELVIN

77. FOX : OWL :: (*a.* Saul, *b.* David, *c.* Iago, *d.* Lear) : SOLOMON

78. 1 : LINE :: 2 : (*a.* length, *b.* ellipse, *c.* point, *d.* sphere)

79. EXOSKELETON : LOBSTER :: ENDOSKELETON : (*a.* oyster, *b.* tiger, *c.* barnacle, *d.* worm)

80. FEZ : SOMBRERO :: BERET : (*a.* phylactery, *b.* millinery, *c.* muffler, *d.* fedora)

81. (*a.* angry, *b.* sanguine, *c.* dejected, *d.* pale) : PESSIMISTIC :: HOPEFUL : DISPIRITED

82. $4^{1/2} : 9^{1/2} :: 36^{1/2}$: (*a.* 6, *b.* 9, *c.* 12, *d.* 81)

83. INCUBUS : (*a.* faccubus, *b.* excubus, *c.* succubus, *d.* maccubus) :: WOMEN : MEN

84. HEAD MONEY : (*a.* warn, *b.* punish, *c.* capture, *d.* bribe) :: HUSH MONEY : SILENCE

85. SUSTAIN : OVERRULE :: IN CAMERA : (*a.* in trouble, *b.* in public, *c.* in court, *d.* out of court)

86. CRONUS : SATURN :: (*a.* Poseidon, *b.* Ares, *c.* Zeus, *d.* Hermes) : MARS

87. D MINOR : F MAJOR :: (*a.* E minor, *b.* F minor, *c.* F# minor, *d.* G# minor) : A MAJOR

88. TAME : MATE :: LAME : (*a.* female, *b.* injured, *c.* male, *d.* excuse)

89. (*a.* spinal, *b.* neutral, *c.* temporal, *d.* spatial) : PARIETAL :: OCCIPITAL : FRONTAL

90. PARADISE : LOST :: JERUSALEM : (*a.* Sanctified, *b.* Discovered, *c.* Delivered, *d.* Vanquished)

91. PENN : PENNSYLVANIA :: CALVERT : (*a.* South Carolina, *b.* Vermont, *c.* Maryland, *d.* Rhode Island)

92. ETEOCLES : (*a.* Theseus, *b.* Laius, *c.* Oedipus, *d.* Polynices) :: ANTIGONE : ISMENE

93. DECIMAL : 10 :: DUODECIMAL : (*a.* 2, *b.* 8, *c.* 12, *d.* 16)

94. RATIONALIST : EMPIRICIST :: (*a.* Berkeley, *b.* Hume, *c.* Mill, *d.* Leibniz) : LOCKE

95. (*a.* Ivan Karamazov, *b.* Anna Karenina, *c.* Nicolai Gogol, *d.* Grigory Smirnov) : DOSTOYEVSKY :: THÉRÈSE : MAURIAC

96. PALESTRINA : 16th :: (*a.* Beethoven, *b.* Bach, *c.* Tchaikovsky, *d.* Stravinsky) : 20th

97. NICHOLAS II : RUSSIAN REVOLUTION :: (*a.* Louis XIV, *b.* Louis XV, *c.* Louis XVI, *d.* Louis XVII) : FRENCH REVOLUTION

98. GLENN GOULD : PIANO :: YO-YO MA : (*a.* piano, *b.* violin, *c.* cello, *d.* clarinet)

99. (*a.* Versailles, *b.* Xanadu, *c.* St. Malo, *d.* Rouen) : LOUIS XIV :: AMBOISE : FRANCIS II

100. ISHMAEL : (*a.* Hagar, *b.* Rebecca, *c.* Esther, *d.* Sophia) :: ISAAC : SARAH

101. COLITIS : COLON :: ENCEPHALITIS : (*a.* brain, *b.* duodenum, *c.* pancreas, *d.* liver)

102. GOLDA MEIR : (*a.* Poland, *b.* Israel, *c.* United States, *d.* Czech Republic) :: MARGARET THATCHER : GREAT BRITAIN

103. PICCOLO : FLUTE :: EUPHONIUM : (*a.* phonograph, *b.* tuba, *c.* organ, *d.* homonym)

104. FORCE : DISTANCE :: (*a.* mass × acceleration, *b.* friction × momentum, *c.* volume / temperature, *d.* mass / energy) : RATE × TIME

105. (*a.* spear, *b.* cupid, *c.* arrow, *d.* wing) : LOVE :: SCYTHE : DEATH

106. CEILING : GLASS :: (*a.* heart, *b.* wall, *c.* side, *d.* curtain) : IRON

107. LEGS : EGGS :: FROG : (*a.* chicken, *b.* dolphin, *c.* sturgeon, *d.* goose)

108. GOAT : (*a.* pan, *b.* faun, *c.* pegasus, *d.* minotaur) :: HORSE : CENTAUR

109. ORCZY : PIMPERNEL :: HAWTHORNE : (*a.* letter, *b.* rose, *c.* wind, *d.* tide)

110. GUSTAV : (*a.* Wolfgang, *b.* Friedrich, *c.* Johann, *d.* Ludwig) :: MAHLER : BEETHOVEN

111. RESTIVE : TRANQUIL :: VERBOSE : (*a.* loquacious, *b.* timorous, *c.* talkative, *d.* taciturn)

112. HOLY SEE : (*a.* Rome, *b.* Hungary, *c.* Italy, *d.* Chad) :: LESOTHO : SOUTH AFRICA

113. LEAGUE OF NATIONS : UNITED NATIONS :: THE ARTICLES OF CONFEDERATION : (*a.* U.S. Constitution, *b.* The Bill of Rights, *c.* Human Rights Treaty, *d.* The Constitution of the Confederate States)

114. AM : AMPLITUDE :: FM : (*a.* force, *b.* frequency, *c.* Fahrenheit, *d.* friction)

115. (*a.* England, *b.* Waterloo, *c.* Russia, *d.* Elba) : NAPOLEON :: LITTLE BIG HORN RIVER : CUSTER

116. ROMEO : JULIET :: PYRAMUS : (*a.* Thisbe, *b.* Titania, *c.* Helen, *d.* Athena)

117. GOAT : WORM :: (*a.* wool, *b.* felt, *c.* cashmere, *d.* chinchilla) : SILK

118. XXIX : 29 :: MDVI : (*a.* 1551, *b.* 1056, *c.* 1061, *d.* 1506)

119. GUANINE : (*a.* cytosine, *b.* purine, *c.* uracil, *d.* pyrimidine) :: ADENINE : THYMINE

120. ESOPHAGUS : SARCOPHAGUS :: GULLET : (*a.* trachea, *b.* monument, *c.* stone coffin, *d.* crystal chandelier)

ANSWER KEY
Practice Test 2

1.	**C**	31.	**C**	61.	**D**	91.	**C**
2.	**D**	32.	**A**	62.	**C**	92.	**D**
3.	**C**	33.	**B**	63.	**C**	93.	**C**
4.	**B**	34.	**D**	64.	**A**	94.	**D**
5.	**A**	35.	**C**	65.	**B**	95.	**A**
6.	**C**	36.	**B**	66.	**D**	96.	**D**
7.	**B**	37.	**B**	67.	**A**	97.	**C**
8.	**B**	38.	**C**	68.	**B**	98.	**C**
9.	**C**	39.	**C**	69.	**B**	99.	**A**
10.	**C**	40.	**B**	70.	**D**	100.	**A**
11.	**A**	41.	**A**	71.	**D**	101.	**A**
12.	**A**	42.	**C**	72.	**B**	102.	**B**
13.	**A**	43.	**A**	73.	**D**	103.	**B**
14.	**D**	44.	**A**	74.	**D**	104.	**A**
15.	**B**	45.	**A**	75.	**C**	105.	**C**
16.	**D**	46.	**D**	76.	**D**	106.	**D**
17.	**D**	47.	**B**	77.	**C**	107.	**C**
18.	**A**	48.	**B**	78.	**B**	108.	**B**
19.	**C**	49.	**B**	79.	**B**	109.	**A**
20.	**A**	50.	**C**	80.	**D**	110.	**D**
21.	**C**	51.	**D**	81.	**B**	111.	**D**
22.	**D**	52.	**B**	82.	**B**	112.	**C**
23.	**A**	53.	**A**	83.	**C**	113.	**A**
24.	**D**	54.	**C**	84.	**C**	114.	**B**
25.	**D**	55.	**A**	85.	**B**	115.	**B**
26.	**A**	56.	**C**	86.	**B**	116.	**A**
27.	**D**	57.	**A**	87.	**C**	117.	**C**
28.	**A**	58.	**B**	88.	**C**	118.	**D**
29.	**A**	59.	**B**	89.	**C**	119.	**A**
30.	**C**	60.	**B**	90.	**C**	120.	**C**

ANSWER EXPLANATIONS FOR PRACTICE TEST 2

> In the following, explanations concerning the correct responses are in roman font. Explanations regarding distracters (incorrect responses) that are not self-explaining or could be misinterpreted are in italics in order to highlight the explanations of the answers that are correct.

1. CANDLE : TALLOW :: TIRE : (*a.* automobile, *b.* round, **c. rubber**, *d.* hollow)
   (c) A candle is frequently made of tallow. A tire is frequently made of rubber.

2. TERRESTRIAL : (*a.* palatial, *b.* partial, *c.* martial, **d. celestial**) :: EARTH : HEAVEN
   (d) Something that is terrestrial is of the earth. Something that is celestial is of heaven.

3. (*a.* father, *b.* uncle, **c. brother**, *d.* son) : SIBLING :: HUSBAND : SPOUSE
   (c) A brother is a sibling. A husband is a spouse.

4. 3.6% : (*a.* 0.0036, **b. 0.036**, *c.* 0.36, *d.* 3.6) :: 480% : 4.8
   (b) 3.6% is equal to 0.036. 480% is equal to 4.8.

5. PERIODIC : INTERMITTENT :: CONSTANT : (**a. incessant**, *b.* occasional, *c.* infrequent, *d.* never)
   (a) Periodic and intermittent are synonyms, as are constant and incessant.

6. DARWIN : (*a.* gravity, *b.* planetary orbits, **c. evolution**, *d.* magnetism) :: EINSTEIN : RELATIVITY
   (c) Charles Darwin is primarily responsible for the theory of evolution, while Albert Einstein is primarily responsible for relativity theory.

7. COMPOSER : SONATA :: (*a.* physicist, **b. artist**, *c.* sculptor, *d.* author) : LITHOGRAPH
   (b) A sonata is the creation of a composer. A lithograph is the creation of an artist.

8. HUNGRY : LION :: BUSY : (*a.* squirrel, **b. beaver**, *c.* hare, *d.* chipmunk)
   (b) "Hungry as a lion" and "busy as a beaver" are both common similes used in everyday speech.

9. MATRICIDE : MOTHER :: FRATRICIDE : (*a.* uncle, *b.* father, **c. brother**, *d.* son)
   (c) The act of killing one's mother is called *matricide. The act of killing one's brother is called fratricide. The act of killing one's uncle is called avunculicide; the act of killing one's father is called patricide; the act of killing one's son is called filicide.*

10. (*a.* United, *b.* League, **c. National**, *d.* NFL) : METS :: AMERICAN : YANKEES
    (c) The Mets are a National League baseball team, while the Yankees are an American League team. Both teams are from New York and famously met in the 2000 World Series (dubbed "The Subway Series").

11. KNOCK : PIGEON :: KNEED : (**a. toed**, *b.* waisted, *c.* armed, *d.* headed)
    (a) A person may be referred to as knock-kneed or pigeon-toed. *Knock-kneed* means that a person's knees touch each other when he or she is standing straight. *Pigeon-toed* means that a person's toes point inward when he or she walks.

12. (**a. Memorial Day**, *b.* Thanksgiving, *c.* Christmas, *d.* Labor Day) : DECORATION DAY :: VETERANS' DAY : ARMISTICE DAY
    (a) Memorial Day and Decoration Day are two names for the same holiday. Veterans' Day and Armistice Day are also two names for the same holiday.

13. HANG : NOOSE :: BEHEAD : (***a. guillotine***, *b.* Savonarola, *c.* Robespierre, *d.* ablation)

(a) A person is hanged with a noose, but beheaded with a guillotine. *Girolamo Savonarola was a religious and political reformer, known for his book burnings and opposition to Pope Alexander VI. Maximilien Robespierre was one of the most famous personalities of the French Revolution and played an important role during what is known as the* Reign of Terror. Ablation *refers to the surgical removal of tissue.*

14. APPROPRIATE : INAPPROPRIATE :: APROPOS : (*a.* inapropos, *b.* misapropos, *c.* anapropos, ***d.* malapropos**)

(d) Something that is not appropriate is inappropriate. Something that is not apropos is malapropos.

15. (*a.* gases, ***b.* good eating**, *c.* intestinal tract, *d.* gasoline) : GASTRONOMY :: HEAVENLY BODIES : ASTRONOMY

(b) Gastronomy is the study of good eating. Astronomy is the study of heavenly bodies.

16. CONGRESS : UNITED STATES :: (*a.* UNICEF, *b.* Secretary-General, *c.* Security Council, ***d.* General Assembly**) : UNITED NATIONS

(d) The Congress is the main legislative body of the United States. The General Assembly is the main legislative body of the United Nations.

17. EXECUTOR : (*a.* executriss, *b.* executress, *c.* executrex, ***d.* executrix**) :: ACTOR : ACTRESS

(d) The feminine form of executor is executrix. The feminine form of actor is actress.

18. CANCEROUS : NONCANCEROUS :: MALIGNANT : (***a.* benign**, *b.* benevolent, *c.* beneficent, *d.* latent)

(a) A cancerous tumor is called malignant. A noncancerous tumor is called benign.

19. (*a.* syllogism, *b.* intellect, ***c.* troop movements**, *d.* weapons) : LOGISTICS :: LANGUAGE : LINGUISTICS

(c) Logistics is the study of troop movements. Linguistics is the study of language.

20. SUBWAY : NEW YORK :: (***a.* Metro**, *b.* monorail, *c.* cable car, *d.* airplane) : D.C.

(a) What is called a subway in New York is called the Metro in Washington, D.C.

21. (*a.* velocity, *b.* humidity, ***c.* pressure**, *d.* THI) : BAROMETER :: MILEAGE : ODOMETER

(c) A barometer measures pressure. An odometer measures mileage.

22. KANSAS : WHEAT :: (*a.* Nebraska, *b.* Arkansas, *c.* Wisconsin, ***d.* Idaho**) : POTATO

(d) Kansas is known for its wheat fields, Idaho for its potato fields.

23. HYPO : DERMIC :: UNDER : (***a.* skin**, *b.* medicine, *c.* blood, *d.* syringe)

(a) A hypodermic needle goes under (hypo) the skin (dermis).

24. PECCADILLO : (*a.* stutter, *b.* pretense, *c.* amnesia, ***d.* sin**) :: MISDEMEANOR : CRIME

(d) A peccadillo is a minor sin. A misdemeanor is a minor crime.

25. MISANTHROPE : (*a.* life, *b.* religion, *c.* women, ***d.* people**) :: MISOGAMIST : MARRIAGE

(d) A misanthrope detests people. A misogamist detests marriage.

26. OSTENTATIOUS : (***a.* showy**, *b.* proud, *c.* modest, *d.* fickle) :: ONEROUS : BURDENSOME

(a) Ostentatious means showy. Onerous means burdensome.

27. NATURE : NURTURE :: HEREDITY : (*a.* gene, *b.* progenitor, *c.* evolution, ***d.* environment**)

(d) A "nature–nurture" controversy is one between the effects of heredity and environment.

28. HURRY : SCURRY :: HURLY : (***a. burly***, *b.* curly, *c.* gurly, *d.* wurly)

 (a) Hurry-scurry and hurly-burly both refer to disorder and confusion.

29. STEM : METS :: (***a. tab***, *b.* ball, *c.* team, *d.* root) : BAT

 (a) *Stem* spelled backward is *mets. Tab* spelled backward is *bat.*

30. SATAN : BEELZEBUB :: DEVIL : (*a.* Charon, *b.* Pandemonium, ***c. Lucifer***, *d.* Hades)

 (c) Satan, Beelzebub, the Devil, and Lucifer are all different names for the same entity. *Charon is a figure from Greek mythology. He was a ferryman and carried the dead across the river Styx into the underworld, Hades. Pandemonium commonly refers to a state of wild confusion and is derived from its Greek mythological meaning of "the entirety of all Demons."*

31. FORT SUMTER : CIVIL WAR :: (*a.* Valley Forge, *b.* Princeton, ***c. Lexington***, *d.* Trenton) : AMERICAN REVOLUTION

 (c) Fort Sumter was the scene of the first battle of the Civil War. Lexington was the scene of the first battle of the American Revolution. *The Continental Army had its campsite over the winter of 1777–1778 in Valley Forge during the American Revolutionary War. The forces of General Washington defeated the British in the Battle of Princeton in 1777. The Battle of Trenton took place in 1776 after General Washington's crossing of the Delaware.*

32. (***a. chameleon***, *b.* salamander, *c.* tadpole, *d.* chamois) : FICKLE :: MULE : STUBBORN

 (a) A chameleon is fickle or quick to change; a mule, stubborn.

33. NEW AMSTERDAM : NEW YORK :: CONSTANTINOPLE : (*a.* Budapest, ***b. Istanbul***, *c.* Cairo, *d.* Baghdad)

 (b) New Amsterdam is a former name of New York City. Constantinople is a former name of Istanbul.

34. ANESTHESIA : FEEL :: (*a.* eyeball, *b.* eyes, *c.* glasses, ***d. blindness***) : SEE

 (d) Anesthesia is a state in which one does not feel. Blindness is a state in which one does not see.

35. CORPORAL : BEAT :: CAPITAL : (*a.* stun, *b.* spend, ***c. kill***, *d.* shock)

 (c) In corporal punishment, a person is beaten. In capital punishment, a person is killed.

36. (*a.* neutron, ***b. electron***, *c.* nucleon, *d.* positron) : PROTON :: NEGATIVE : POSITIVE

 (b) An electron has a negative electrical charge. A proton has a positive electrical charge.

37. CARPE : DIEM :: CAVEAT : (*a.* corpus, ***b. emptor***, *c.* deum, *d.* mandamus)

 (b) *Carpe diem* (seize the opportunity—literally, the day) and *caveat emptor* (let the buyer beware) are both Latinisms used in English. Corpus *means "body";* deum *is the accusative of the Latin word* deus *(God);* mandamus *means "we command."*

38. RAIN : (*a.* tempest, *b.* frost, ***c. hail***, *d.* dry ice) :: WATER : ICE

 (c) Hail is frozen rain; ice is frozen water.

39. FEINT : (*a.* fall, *b.* remove, ***c. pretend***, *d.* authenticate) :: SEVER : SEPARATE

 (c) To feint is to pretend. To sever is to separate.

40. 10 : COMMANDMENTS :: (*a.* 5, ***b. 7***, *c.* 10, *d.* 12) : DEADLY SINS

 (b) There are 10 Commandments and 7 deadly sins. The 10 Commandments are found in the Old Testament of the Bible; the 7 deadly sins originated in early Christian doctrine.

41. DOUBLE ENTENDRE : (***a. ambiguity***, *b.* treachery, *c.* meaninglessness, *d.* misperception) :: DOUBLE TAKE : DELAYED REACTION

(a) A double entendre is characterized by ambiguity. A double take is characterized by a delayed reaction.

42. (*a.* nominalism, *b.* phenomenalism, ***c. determinism***, *d.* rationalism) : FATALISM :: EXISTENTIALISM : FREE WILL

(c) The philosophical doctrine of determinism argues for fatalism. The doctrine of existentialism argues for free will. *Nominalism refers to a doctrine stating that various objects that have the same name have nothing in common but that name. Phenomenalism refers to a theory that limits knowledge to phenomena only. Rationalism is a theory stating that reason is a source of knowledge superior to the perceptions of senses.*

43. (***a. carmine***, *b.* yellow, *c.* brown, *d.* orange) : RED :: AZURE : BLUE

(a) Carmine is a shade of red. Azure is a shade of blue.

44. FRAME : PICTURE :: (***a. cell wall***, *b.* endoplasmic reticulum, *c.* cytoplasm, *d.* nuclear envelope) : CELL

(a) A frame surrounds a picture. A cell wall surrounds a cell. *The endoplasmic reticulum is a system of interconnected cytoplasmic membranes that functions especially in the transport of materials within the cell. Cytoplasm is the organized complex of inorganic and organic substances external to the nuclear membrane of a cell. The nuclear envelope is a membrane system that surrounds the nucleus of eukaryotic cells.*

45. (***a. keno***, *b.* kalaha, *c.* wari, *d.* soma) : CRAPS :: ROULETTE : TWENTY-ONE

(a) Keno, craps, roulette, and twenty-one are all gambling games. *Kalaha is a game in the mancala family (board games mainly played in Africa that have a role similar to chess in Western culture). Wari is the Malinese name of an adult game often called Oware, which is played in Africa and the Caribbean. Soma is an intoxicating, ritual drink used in Ancient India.*

46. HECTOR : (*a.* Rome, *b.* Carthage, *c.* Sicily, ***d. Troy***) :: ACHILLES : GREECE

(d) In the Trojan War, Hector fought for Troy and Achilles fought for Greece.

47. KUNG FU : JUDO :: (*a.* Korean, ***b. Chinese***, *c.* Vietnamese, *d.* Japanese) : JAPANESE

(b) Kung Fu is a Chinese form of martial arts; Judo is a Japanese form of martial arts.

48. SWARM : BEES :: (*a.* colony, ***b. covey***, *c.* pack, *d.* pride) : QUAIL

(b) A group of bees is referred to as a swarm. A group of quail is referred to as a covey.

49. BITUMINOUS : ANTHRACITE :: (*a.* wood, ***b. lead***, *c.* lignite, *d.* oil) : STEEL

(b) Bituminous coal is soft, and anthracite coal is hard. Lead is a soft metal, and steel a hard metal.

50. CARRIE NATION : (*a.* women's suffrage, *b.* low-income housing, ***c. temperance***, *d.* abolition of child labor) :: MARTIN LUTHER KING, JR. : CIVIL RIGHTS

(c) Carrie Nation fought for temperance, while Martin Luther King, Jr. fought for civil rights.

51. STENCIL : LETTERS :: COMPASS : (*a.* time, *b.* direction, *c.* northwest, ***d. circle***)

(d) A stencil is used to draw letters. A compass is used to draw a circle.

52. (*a*. proposal, **b. talk**, *c*. dissertation, *d*. dialogue) : ORATION :: QUIZ : EXAMINATION

(b) An oration is a large-scale talk. An examination is a large-scale quiz.

53. ANTERIOR : POSTERIOR :: (***a*. ventral**, *b*. lateral, *c*. external, *d*. internal) : DORSAL

(a) In humans, the anterior and ventral sides are the front. The posterior and dorsal sides are the rear.

54. IMMIGRATION : EMIGRATION :: ENTRY : (*a*. expulsion, *b*. migration, **c. egress**, *d*. estuary)

(c) Immigration is entry into a country, while emigration is egress from a country.

55. SATRAP : (***a*. ruler**, *b*. bush, *c*. miser, *d*. loner) :: TRAP : AMBUSH

(a) A satrap is one kind of ruler (a governor of provinces in Ancient Persia). A trap is a kind of ambush.

56. ELEGY : LAMENTING :: EPIGRAM : (*a*. inane, *b*. abstruse, **c. witty**, *d*. obtuse)

(c) An elegy is lamenting. An epigram is witty.

57. REFORMATION : PROTESTANTS :: COUNTER-REFORMATION : (***a*. Catholics**, *b*. Protestants, *c*. Anglicans, *d*. Jews)

(a) The Reformation was staged by Protestants, while the Counter-Reformation was staged by Catholics.

58. (*a*. beriberi, ***b*. rickets**, *c*. anemia, *d*. pellagra) : D :: SCURVY : C

(b) Rickets is caused by a deficiency of vitamin D. Scurvy is caused by a deficiency of vitamin C. *Beriberi is caused by a lack of thiamine. Anemia can be caused through a decreased production of red blood cells in the bone marrow or heavy blood loss, among other causes. Pellagra is caused by lack of niacin.*

59. GO DUTCH : PAY YOUR OWN EXPENSES :: IN DUTCH : (*a*. in luck, ***b*. in trouble**, *c*. rich, *d*. poor)

(b) To go Dutch is to pay your own expenses. To be in Dutch is to be in trouble.

60. FOOL'S GOLD : (*a*. ore, ***b*. pyrite**, *c*. bauxite, *d*. manganese) :: PENCIL LEAD : GRAPHITE

(b) Fool's gold is pyrite. Pencil lead is graphite.

61. MILL : (*a*. franc, *b*. centime, *c*. shilling, ***d*. cent**) :: PENNY : DIME

(d) A mill is a tenth of a cent. A penny is a tenth of a dime.

62. (*a*. Spain, *b*. Italy, ***c*. Israel**, *d*. Lebanon) : RUSSIA :: EL AL : AEROFLOT

(c) El Al is an Israeli airline, while Aeroflot is an airline of Russia. *An airline in Spain is Iberia, an airline in Italy is Alitalia, and an airline in Lebanon is Airliban.*

63. GAUGUIN : (*a*. England, *b*. U.S.A., ***c*. Tahiti**, *d*. Madagascar) :: GOYA : SPAIN

(c) Gauguin is famous for his paintings relating to Tahiti. Goya is famous for his paintings relating to Spain.

64. (***a*. bifteck**, *b*. legume, *c*. glace, *d*. poulet) : STEAK :: ESCARGOTS : SNAILS

(a) In France, steak is called bifteck, while snails are called escargots.

65. TEMERITY : AUDACITY :: (*a*. softness, ***b*. boldness**, *c*. shyness, *d*. depravity) : BRAVERY

(b) Temerity, audacity, boldness, and bravery are synonyms.

66. CALORIE : (*a*. weight, *b*. basal metabolism, *c*. fat, ***d*. energy**) :: DECADE : TIME

(d) A calorie is a measure of energy. A decade is a measure of time.

67. PETROLOGY : (*a.* **sandstone**, *b.* Brontosaurus, *c.* moth, *d.* nylon) :: BOTANY : ROSE

(a) Petrology is the study of rocks, among which is sandstone. Botany is the study of plants, among which is a rose.

68. HANSEL : GRETEL :: ORESTES : (*a.* Jocasta, *b.* **Electra**, *c.* Ophelia, *d.* Alicia)

(b) Hansel and Gretel were brother and sister, as were Orestes and Electra. Hansel and Gretel are characters in one of the Brother Grimm's fairytales. Orestes and Electra were son and daughter of Agamemnon. *Jocasta was the wife of Laius, mother and wife of Oedipus, and the mother of Antigone. Ophelia is Hamlet's love in Shakespeare's play* Hamlet. *Alicia is a distracter term that has no particular meaning in this context.*

69. (*a.* rude, *b.* **talkative**, *c.* immodest, *d.* brash) : GARRULOUS :: PETULANT : PEEVISH

(b) A garrulous person is talkative; a petulant person is peevish.

70. PONCE DE LEON : (*a.* Atlantic Ocean, *b.* Mexico, *c.* Georgia, *d.* **Florida**) :: BALBOA : PACIFIC OCEAN

(d) Ponce de Leon discovered Florida; Balboa discovered the Pacific Ocean.

71. ATTENUATE : (*a.* disprove, *b.* weaken, *c.* prove, *d.* **strengthen**) :: ATTRACT : REPEL

(d) Attenuate and strengthen are antonyms, as are attract and repel.

72. CEREBRUM : THINKING :: CEREBELLUM : (*a.* olfaction, *b.* **muscular coordination**, *c.* glandular secretion, *d.* audition)

(b) In the brain, the cerebrum controls thinking, while the cerebellum controls muscular coordination.

73. BEHAVIORISM : U.S.A. :: GESTALT : (*a.* France, *b.* England, *c.* Switzerland, *d.* **Germany**)

(d) In psychology, behaviorism originated in the United States, while the Gestalt movement originated in Germany.

74. MONROE : (*a.* Treatise, *b.* Edict, *c.* Decree, *d.* **Code**) :: DOCTRINE : NAPOLEON

(d) The Monroe Doctrine and the Code Napoleon were both policy statements. The Monroe Doctrine (1823) states that the European powers were no longer to regard the countries of the western hemisphere as "subjects for future colonization." The Code Napoleon is a set of civil laws that Napoleon instituted.

75. LXII : CLXXXVI :: D : (*a.* M, *b.* MC, *c.* **MD**, *d.* MM)

(c) 62 is to 186 as 500 is to 1,500. The second and fourth terms are triple the first and third terms, respectively. *In Roman numerals, I = 1, V = 5, X = 10, L = 50, C = 100, D = 500, M = 1,000.*

76. (*a.* loudness, *b.* compression, *c.* brightness, *d.* **hardness**) : MOHS :: TEMPERATURE : KELVIN

(d) The Mohs scale measures hardness, while the Kelvin scale measures temperature.

77. FOX : OWL :: (*a.* Saul, *b.* David, *c.* **Iago**, *d.* Lear) : SOLOMON

(c) Iago was cunning, as a fox is supposed to be. Solomon was wise, as an owl is supposed to be. Iago tricked Othello into murdering his wife in Shakespeare's tragedy *Othello.* Solomon was the son of David and also became a king of the Israelites. *Saul was the first king of the Israelites. David was the second king of the Israelites and fought the giant Goliath. Lear was betrayed by two of his daughters in Shakespeare's King Lear.*

78. 1 : LINE :: 2 : (*a.* length, *b.* **ellipse**, *c.* point, *d.* sphere)

(b) A line is one-dimensional, while an ellipse is two-dimensional.

79. EXOSKELETON : LOBSTER :: ENDOSKELETON : (*a.* oyster, ***b.* tiger**, *c.* barnacle, *d.* worm)

(b) A lobster has an exoskeleton; a tiger has an endoskeleton. An exoskeleton is an external supportive covering of an animal. An endoskeleton is an internal skeleton.

80. FEZ : SOMBRERO :: BERET : (*a.* phylactery, *b.* millinery, *c.* muffler, ***d.* fedora**)

(d) A fez, a sombrero, a beret, and a fedora are all forms of headgear. *A phylactery is an amulet worn by observant Jewish men. Millinery refers to hats for women or the shop that sells them. A muffler is a noise-reducing device in the exhaust system of a car as well as a thick scarf.*

81. (*a.* angry, ***b.* sanguine**, *c.* dejected, *d.* pale) : PESSIMISTIC :: HOPEFUL : DISPIRITED

(b) Sanguine means hopeful; pessimistic means dispirited.

82. $4^{1/2} : 9^{1/2} :: 36^{1/2} :$ (*a.* 6, ***b.* 9**, *c.* 12, *d.* 81)

(b) 2 is to 3 as 6 is to 9. An integer to the $\frac{1}{2}$ power is the square root of that integer.

83. INCUBUS : (*a.* faccubus, *b.* excubus, ***c.* succubus**, *d.* maccubus) :: WOMEN : MEN

(c) An incubus was once thought to be a demon that sought to have intercourse with sleeping women. A succubus sought to have intercourse with sleeping men.

84. HEAD MONEY : (*a.* warn, *b.* punish, ***c.* capture**, *d.* bribe) :: HUSH MONEY : SILENCE

(c) Head money is used as payment for capture. Hush money is used as payment for silence.

85. SUSTAIN : OVERRULE :: IN CAMERA : (*a.* in trouble, ***b.* in public**, *c.* in court, *d.* out of court)

(b) Sustain and overrule are opposites, as are in camera and in public.

86. CRONUS : SATURN :: (*a.* Poseidon, ***b.* Ares**, *c.* Zeus, *d.* Hermes) : MARS

(b) Cronus was the Greek name, and Saturn the Roman name, of the Titan who overthrew his father to become ruler of the universe, only to be overthrown by his own son (named Zeus by the Greeks, Jupiter by the Romans). Ares is the Greek name and Mars is the Roman name for the god of war.

87. D MINOR : F MAJOR :: (*a.* E minor, *b.* F minor, ***c.* F# minor**, *d.* G# minor) : A MAJOR

(c) The musical keys of D minor and F major both have one flat, while the keys of F# minor and A major both have three sharps.

88. TAME : MATE :: LAME : (*a.* female, *b.* injured, ***c.* male**, *d.* excuse)

(c) Mate can be obtained from tame by reversing the initial three letters. Male can be obtained from lame, also by reversing the initial three letters.

89. (*a.* spinal, *b.* neutral, ***c.* temporal**, *d.* spatial) : PARIETAL :: OCCIPITAL : FRONTAL

(c) The four lobes of the brain are the temporal, parietal, occipital, and frontal.

90. PARADISE : LOST :: JERUSALEM : (*a.* Sanctified, *b.* Discovered, ***c.* Delivered**, *d.* Vanquished)

(c) *Paradise Lost* and *Jerusalem Delivered* are both epics, the former by Milton and the latter by Tasso.

91. PENN : PENNSYLVANIA :: CALVERT : (*a.* South Carolina, *b.* Vermont, ***c.* Maryland**, *d.* Rhode Island)

(c) Penn founded Pennsylvania, while Calvert founded Maryland. *South Carolina was named by King Charles II of England. Vermont was created by Ethan Allen and his brothers as well as Seth Warner whom they recruited for an informal militia, the Green Mountain Boys. Roger Williams was the founder of Rhode Island.*

92. ETEOCLES : (*a.* Theseus, *b.* Laius, *c.* Oedipus, **d. Polynices**) :: ANTIGONE : ISMENE

(d) Eteocles and Polynices were siblings, as were Antigone and Ismene. *Theseus was a king of Athens and son of either Aegeus and Aethra or of Poseidon and Aethra. Laius was a king of Thebes who was killed by his son Oedipus.*

93. DECIMAL : 10 :: DUODECIMAL : (*a.* 2, *b.* 8, **c. 12**, *d.* 16)

(c) The decimal system has 10 as its base. The duodecimal system has 12 as its base.

94. RATIONALIST : EMPIRICIST :: (*a.* Berkeley, *b.* Hume, *c.* Mill, **d. Leibniz**) : LOCKE

(d) Leibniz was a famous rationalist philosopher. Locke was a famous empiricist. *Hume and Berkeley were empiricists. John Stuart Mill was a utilitarianist.*

95. (**a. Ivan Karamazov**, *b.* Anna Karenina, *c.* Nicolai Gogol, *d.* Grigory Smirnov) : DOSTOYEVSKY :: THÉRÈSE : MAURIAC

(a) Ivan Karamazov is a literary character created by Dostoyevsky. Thérèse is a literary character created by Mauriac. *Anna Karenina is a novel by Leo Tolstoy. Nicolai Gogol was a Russian writer. Grigory Smirnov is a figure skater.*

96. PALESTRINA : 16th :: (*a.* Beethoven, *b.* Bach, *c.* Tchaikovsky, **d. Stravinsky**) : 20th

(d) Palestrina (ca. 1525–1594) was a 16th century composer; Stravinsky (1882–1971) was a 20th century composer. *Beethoven lived from 1770 to 1827. Johann Sebastian Bach lived from 1685 to 1750. Tchaikovsky lived from 1840 to 1893.*

97. NICHOLAS II : RUSSIAN REVOLUTION :: (*a.* Louis XIV, *b.* Louis XV, **c. Louis XVI**, *d.* Louis XVII) : FRENCH REVOLUTION

(c) The Russian Revolution overthrew Nicholas II in 1905. The French Revolution (1789–1799) overthrew Louis XVI.

98. GLENN GOULD : PIANO :: YO-YO MA : (*a.* piano, *b.* violin, **c. cello**, *d.* clarinet)

(c) Glenn Gould was a famous pianist; Yo-Yo Ma is a famous cellist.

99. (**a. Versailles**, *b.* Xanadu, *c.* St. Malo, *d.* Rouen) : LOUIS XIV :: AMBOISE : FRANCIS II

(a) Amboise is the location of the palace of Francis II. Versailles is the location of the palace of Louis XIV.

100. ISHMAEL : (**a. Hagar**, *b.* Rebecca, *c.* Esther, *d.* Sophia) :: ISAAC : SARAH

(a) According to the Bible, Ishmael was the son of Hagar and Abraham, while Isaac was the son of Sarah and Abraham. *Rebecca was the wife of Isaac. Esther was a queen of Persia; a book in the Old Testament is named after her. Sophia is a Greek name meaning "wisdom."*

101. COLITIS : COLON :: ENCEPHALITIS : (**a. brain**, *b.* duodenum, *c.* pancreas, *d.* liver)

(a) Colitis refers to a swelling of the colon and encephalitis describes a swelling of the brain.

102. GOLDA MEIR : (*a.* Poland, **b. Israel**, *c.* United States, *d.* Czech Republic) :: MARGARET THATCHER : GREAT BRITAIN

(b) Golda Meir was the first female prime minister of Israel (1969–1973). Margaret Thatcher was the first female prime minister of Great Britain (1979–1990).

103. PICCOLO : FLUTE :: EUPHONIUM : (*a.* phonograph, **b. tuba**, *c.* organ, *d.* homonym)

(b) A piccolo is an instrument much like a flute, but smaller. A euphonium is an instrument much like a tuba, but smaller.

104. FORCE:DISTANCE::(***a*. mass×acceleration**, *b*. friction×momentum, *c*. volume/temperature, *d*. mass / energy) : RATE × TIME

  (a) Force is equal to mass times acceleration just as distance is equal to rate times time.

105. (*a*. spear, *b*. cupid, ***c*. arrow**, *d*. wing) : LOVE :: SCYTHE : DEATH

  (c) An arrow is the classical symbol of impending love, and the scythe is the classical symbol of impending death.

106. CEILING : GLASS :: (*a*. heart, *b*. wall, *c*. side, ***d*. curtain**) : IRON

  (d) One metaphorical barrier is a glass ceiling. Another is the iron curtain.

107. LEGS : EGGS :: FROG : (*a*. chicken, *b*. dolphin, ***c*. sturgeon**, *d*. goose)

  (c) Frog legs are considered a delicacy, while eggs from a sturgeon, also known as caviar, are also a delicacy.

108. GOAT : (*a*. pan, ***b*. faun**, *c*. pegasus, *d*. minotaur) :: HORSE : CENTAUR

  (b) The mythical creature of a man combined with a goat is called a faun. A man combined with a horse is called a centaur. *Minotaur is a creature with the head of a bull and the body of a man. Pegasus was a winged horse that sprang from Medusa's body when she was killed. Pan is the Greek god of sheperds, woods, and mountains.*

109. ORCZY : PIMPERNEL :: HAWTHORNE : (***a*. letter**, *b*. rose, *c*. wind, *d*. tide)

  (a) Orczy wrote the novel *The Scarlet Pimpernel*. Hawthorne wrote the novel *The Scarlet Letter*.

110. GUSTAV : (*a*. Wolfgang, *b*. Friedrich, *c*. Johann, ***d*. Ludwig**) :: MAHLER : BEETHOVEN

  (d) Gustav is the first name of composer Mahler. Ludwig is the first name of composer Beethoven.

111. RESTIVE : TRANQUIL :: VERBOSE : (*a*. loquacious, *b*. timorous, *c*. talkative, ***d*. taciturn**)

  (d) Restive, which describes someone who is active or restless, means the opposite of tranquil. Verbose, which describes someone who is very talkative, means the opposite of taciturn.

112. HOLY SEE : (*a*. Rome, *b*. Hungary, ***c*. Italy**, *d*. Chad) :: LESOTHO : SOUTH AFRICA

  (c) Holy See is a jurisdiction completely landlocked within Italy. Lesotho is a country completely landlocked within South Africa.

113. LEAGUE OF NATIONS : UNITED NATIONS :: THE ARTICLES OF CONFEDERATION : (***a*. U.S. Constitution**, *b*. The Bill of Rights, *c*. Human Rights Treaty, *d*. The Constitution of the Confederate States)

  (a) The League of Nations was the failed predecessor of the United Nations, just as The Articles of Confederation were the failed predecessor of the U.S. Constitution.

114. AM : AMPLITUDE :: FM : (*a*. force, ***b*. frequency**, *c*. Fahrenheit, *d*. friction)

  (b) The radio term AM stands for Amplitude Modulation just as the term FM stands for Frequency Modulation.

115. (*a*. England, ***b*. Waterloo**, *c*. Russia, *d*. Elba) : NAPOLEON :: LITTLE BIG HORN RIVER : CUSTER

  (b) Waterloo was where Napoleon was defeated. The Little Big Horn River was where Custer was defeated.

116. ROMEO : JULIET :: PYRAMUS : (*a. **Thisbe***, *b.* Titania, *c.* Helen, *d.* Athena)

(a) Romeo died while in love with Juliet just as Pyramus died while in love with Thisbe. *Romeo and Juliet* was written by Shakespeare. The story of Pyramus and Thisbe was told by Ovid. *Titania is the name of a character in Shakespeare's* A Midsummer Night's Dream. *Helen was the daughter of Zeus and Leda and was abducted by Paris, which led to the Trojan War. Athena was the goddess of wisdom, useful arts, and prudent warfare.*

117. GOAT : WORM :: (*a.* wool, *b.* felt, ***c. cashmere***, *d.* chinchilla) : SILK

(c) The goat produces the hair that is used to make the fabric cashmere. A worm produces the thread used to make the fabric silk.

118. XXIX : 29 :: MDVI : (*a.* 1551, *b.* 1056, *c.* 1061, ***d. 1506***)

(d) XXIX is the Roman numeral expression of the value 29. MDVI is the Roman numeral expression of the value 1,506. *In Roman numerals, I = 1, V = 5, X = 10, L = 50, C = 100, D = 500, M = 1,000.*

119. GUANINE : (***a. cytosine***, *b.* purine, *c.* uracil, *d.* pyrimidine) :: ADENINE : THYMINE

(a) In human DNA, guanine is the purine that pairs with the pyrimidine cytosine. Likewise, adenine is the purine that pairs with the pyrimidine thymine. *Pyrimidine is a base that is a component of DNA.*

120. ESOPHAGUS : SARCOPHAGUS :: GULLET : (*a.* trachea, *b.* monument, ***c. stone coffin***, *d.* crystal chandelier)

(c) Esophagus is another name for the gullet. Sarcophagus is the name for a stone coffin.

ANSWER SHEET
Practice Test 3

1. Ⓐ Ⓑ Ⓒ Ⓓ	31. Ⓐ Ⓑ Ⓒ Ⓓ	61. Ⓐ Ⓑ Ⓒ Ⓓ	91. Ⓐ Ⓑ Ⓒ Ⓓ
2. Ⓐ Ⓑ Ⓒ Ⓓ	32. Ⓐ Ⓑ Ⓒ Ⓓ	62. Ⓐ Ⓑ Ⓒ Ⓓ	92. Ⓐ Ⓑ Ⓒ Ⓓ
3. Ⓐ Ⓑ Ⓒ Ⓓ	33. Ⓐ Ⓑ Ⓒ Ⓓ	63. Ⓐ Ⓑ Ⓒ Ⓓ	93. Ⓐ Ⓑ Ⓒ Ⓓ
4. Ⓐ Ⓑ Ⓒ Ⓓ	34. Ⓐ Ⓑ Ⓒ Ⓓ	64. Ⓐ Ⓑ Ⓒ Ⓓ	94. Ⓐ Ⓑ Ⓒ Ⓓ
5. Ⓐ Ⓑ Ⓒ Ⓓ	35. Ⓐ Ⓑ Ⓒ Ⓓ	65. Ⓐ Ⓑ Ⓒ Ⓓ	95. Ⓐ Ⓑ Ⓒ Ⓓ
6. Ⓐ Ⓑ Ⓒ Ⓓ	36. Ⓐ Ⓑ Ⓒ Ⓓ	66. Ⓐ Ⓑ Ⓒ Ⓓ	96. Ⓐ Ⓑ Ⓒ Ⓓ
7. Ⓐ Ⓑ Ⓒ Ⓓ	37. Ⓐ Ⓑ Ⓒ Ⓓ	67. Ⓐ Ⓑ Ⓒ Ⓓ	97. Ⓐ Ⓑ Ⓒ Ⓓ
8. Ⓐ Ⓑ Ⓒ Ⓓ	38. Ⓐ Ⓑ Ⓒ Ⓓ	68. Ⓐ Ⓑ Ⓒ Ⓓ	98. Ⓐ Ⓑ Ⓒ Ⓓ
9. Ⓐ Ⓑ Ⓒ Ⓓ	39. Ⓐ Ⓑ Ⓒ Ⓓ	69. Ⓐ Ⓑ Ⓒ Ⓓ	99. Ⓐ Ⓑ Ⓒ Ⓓ
10. Ⓐ Ⓑ Ⓒ Ⓓ	40. Ⓐ Ⓑ Ⓒ Ⓓ	70. Ⓐ Ⓑ Ⓒ Ⓓ	100. Ⓐ Ⓑ Ⓒ Ⓓ
11. Ⓐ Ⓑ Ⓒ Ⓓ	41. Ⓐ Ⓑ Ⓒ Ⓓ	71. Ⓐ Ⓑ Ⓒ Ⓓ	101. Ⓐ Ⓑ Ⓒ Ⓓ
12. Ⓐ Ⓑ Ⓒ Ⓓ	42. Ⓐ Ⓑ Ⓒ Ⓓ	72. Ⓐ Ⓑ Ⓒ Ⓓ	102. Ⓐ Ⓑ Ⓒ Ⓓ
13. Ⓐ Ⓑ Ⓒ Ⓓ	43. Ⓐ Ⓑ Ⓒ Ⓓ	73. Ⓐ Ⓑ Ⓒ Ⓓ	103. Ⓐ Ⓑ Ⓒ Ⓓ
14. Ⓐ Ⓑ Ⓒ Ⓓ	44. Ⓐ Ⓑ Ⓒ Ⓓ	74. Ⓐ Ⓑ Ⓒ Ⓓ	104. Ⓐ Ⓑ Ⓒ Ⓓ
15. Ⓐ Ⓑ Ⓒ Ⓓ	45. Ⓐ Ⓑ Ⓒ Ⓓ	75. Ⓐ Ⓑ Ⓒ Ⓓ	105. Ⓐ Ⓑ Ⓒ Ⓓ
16. Ⓐ Ⓑ Ⓒ Ⓓ	46. Ⓐ Ⓑ Ⓒ Ⓓ	76. Ⓐ Ⓑ Ⓒ Ⓓ	106. Ⓐ Ⓑ Ⓒ Ⓓ
17. Ⓐ Ⓑ Ⓒ Ⓓ	47. Ⓐ Ⓑ Ⓒ Ⓓ	77. Ⓐ Ⓑ Ⓒ Ⓓ	107. Ⓐ Ⓑ Ⓒ Ⓓ
18. Ⓐ Ⓑ Ⓒ Ⓓ	48. Ⓐ Ⓑ Ⓒ Ⓓ	78. Ⓐ Ⓑ Ⓒ Ⓓ	108. Ⓐ Ⓑ Ⓒ Ⓓ
19. Ⓐ Ⓑ Ⓒ Ⓓ	49. Ⓐ Ⓑ Ⓒ Ⓓ	79. Ⓐ Ⓑ Ⓒ Ⓓ	109. Ⓐ Ⓑ Ⓒ Ⓓ
20. Ⓐ Ⓑ Ⓒ Ⓓ	50. Ⓐ Ⓑ Ⓒ Ⓓ	80. Ⓐ Ⓑ Ⓒ Ⓓ	110. Ⓐ Ⓑ Ⓒ Ⓓ
21. Ⓐ Ⓑ Ⓒ Ⓓ	51. Ⓐ Ⓑ Ⓒ Ⓓ	81. Ⓐ Ⓑ Ⓒ Ⓓ	111. Ⓐ Ⓑ Ⓒ Ⓓ
22. Ⓐ Ⓑ Ⓒ Ⓓ	52. Ⓐ Ⓑ Ⓒ Ⓓ	82. Ⓐ Ⓑ Ⓒ Ⓓ	112. Ⓐ Ⓑ Ⓒ Ⓓ
23. Ⓐ Ⓑ Ⓒ Ⓓ	53. Ⓐ Ⓑ Ⓒ Ⓓ	83. Ⓐ Ⓑ Ⓒ Ⓓ	113. Ⓐ Ⓑ Ⓒ Ⓓ
24. Ⓐ Ⓑ Ⓒ Ⓓ	54. Ⓐ Ⓑ Ⓒ Ⓓ	84. Ⓐ Ⓑ Ⓒ Ⓓ	114. Ⓐ Ⓑ Ⓒ Ⓓ
25. Ⓐ Ⓑ Ⓒ Ⓓ	55. Ⓐ Ⓑ Ⓒ Ⓓ	85. Ⓐ Ⓑ Ⓒ Ⓓ	115. Ⓐ Ⓑ Ⓒ Ⓓ
26. Ⓐ Ⓑ Ⓒ Ⓓ	56. Ⓐ Ⓑ Ⓒ Ⓓ	86. Ⓐ Ⓑ Ⓒ Ⓓ	116. Ⓐ Ⓑ Ⓒ Ⓓ
27. Ⓐ Ⓑ Ⓒ Ⓓ	57. Ⓐ Ⓑ Ⓒ Ⓓ	87. Ⓐ Ⓑ Ⓒ Ⓓ	117. Ⓐ Ⓑ Ⓒ Ⓓ
28. Ⓐ Ⓑ Ⓒ Ⓓ	58. Ⓐ Ⓑ Ⓒ Ⓓ	88. Ⓐ Ⓑ Ⓒ Ⓓ	118. Ⓐ Ⓑ Ⓒ Ⓓ
29. Ⓐ Ⓑ Ⓒ Ⓓ	59. Ⓐ Ⓑ Ⓒ Ⓓ	89. Ⓐ Ⓑ Ⓒ Ⓓ	119. Ⓐ Ⓑ Ⓒ Ⓓ
30. Ⓐ Ⓑ Ⓒ Ⓓ	60. Ⓐ Ⓑ Ⓒ Ⓓ	90. Ⓐ Ⓑ Ⓒ Ⓓ	120. Ⓐ Ⓑ Ⓒ Ⓓ

Time: 60 MINUTES

> **Directions:** In each of the following questions, you will find three initial terms and, in parentheses, four answer options designated *a*, *b*, *c*, and *d*. You are to select from the four answer options the one that *best* completes the analogy with the three initial terms. To record your answers, use the answer sheet provided.

1. LAMB : (*a.* goat, *b.* sheep, *c.* mule, *d.* cow) :: COLT : HORSE

2. DOCTOR : ACCOUNTANT :: PATIENT : (*a.* judge, *b.* client, *c.* jury, *d.* district attorney)

3. IRELAND : EIRE :: (*a.* Holland, *b.* Switzerland, *c.* Denmark, *d.* Germany) : DEUTSCHLAND

4. DEFICIT : RED :: SURPLUS : (*a.* black, *b.* green, *c.* brown, *d.* white)

5. LEMON : SOUR :: HOREHOUND : (*a.* tasty, *b.* sour, *c.* bitter, *d.* salty)

6. YELLOW : (*a.* blue, *b.* white, *c.* green, *d.* red) :: COWARDLY : GLOOMY

7. HOUDINI : (*a.* magician, *b.* surgeon, *c.* lawyer, *d.* detective) :: FRANKLIN : STATESMAN

8. CURRIER : (*a.* Loewe, *b.* Ives, *c.* Cowe, *d.* Best) :: GILBERT : SULLIVAN

9. DE FACTO : IN FACT :: (*a.* de jure, *b.* de legibus, *c.* ex facto, *d.* ex legato) : IN LAW

10. SQUARE : CUBE :: CIRCLE : (*a.* rectangle, *b.* solid, *c.* ellipse, *d.* sphere)

11. FIDDLER : PRAYING :: (*a.* bow, *b.* bear, *c.* violinist, *d.* crab) : MANTIS

12. WINCHESTER : SHOOT :: CAT-O'-NINE-TAILS : (*a.* stab, *b.* whip, *c.* poison, *d.* drown)

13. FULTON : (*a.* locomotive, *b.* steamboat, *c.* incandescent lamp, *d.* crystal radio) :: WHITNEY : COTTON GIN

14. (*a.* jugular, *b.* carotid, *c.* thorax, *d.* sclerotic) : VEIN :: AORTA : ARTERY

15. HISTRIONICS : (*a.* geriatrics, *b.* hysterics, *c.* theatrics, *d.* pediatrics) :: PATRONYMICS : SURNAMES

16. NUN : HABIT :: (*a.* postal carrier, *b.* surgeon, *c.* knight, *d.* solicitor) : COAT OF MAIL

17. (*a.* people, *b.* automobiles, *c.* horses, *d.* bicycles) : INDIANAPOLIS 500 :: HORSES : KENTUCKY DERBY

18. LOBBYIST : LEGISLATOR :: (*a.* lawyer, *b.* judge, *c.* court stenographer, *d.* foreman) : JURY

19. CONGRESSIONAL MEDAL OF HONOR : SOLDIER :: PULITZER PRIZE : (*a.* lawyer, *b.* journalist, *c.* chemist, *d.* doctor)

20. PART : TRAP :: (*a.* good-bye, *b.* whole, *c.* bait, *d.* tar) : RAT

21. BARTON : (*a.* Candy, *b.* Helen, *c.* Clara, *d.* Elsa) :: NIGHTINGALE : FLORENCE

22. EMERALD : MINE :: PEARL : (*a.* oyster, *b.* clam, *c.* mine, *d.* river)

23. BIOGRAPHY : AUTOBIOGRAPHY :: (*a.* first, *b.* third, *c.* fourth, *d.* fifth) : FIRST

24. DUET : PAIR :: DIALOGUE : (*a.* monologue, *b.* quandary, *c.* bipolar, *d.* quartet)

25. (*a.* foot, *b.* ball, *c.* skate, *d.* stick) : HOCKEY :: BAT : BASEBALL

26. (*a.* chroma, *b.* violet, *c.* rainbow, *d.* black) : COLOR :: VACUUM : AIR

27. FLORIDA : PENINSULA :: CUBA : (*a.* state, *b.* gulf, *c.* nation, *d.* island)

28. URBAN : RURAL :: URBANE : (*a.* lazy, *b.* suburban, *c.* boorish, *d.* effete)

29. (*a.* air, *b.* earth, *c.* fire, *d.* plastic) : PYRO :: WATER : HYDRO

30. (*a.* sailor, *b.* mountebank, *c.* salesman, *d.* villain) : CHARLATAN :: FRAUD : QUACK

31. RULER : LINE SEGMENT :: PROTRACTOR : (*a.* distance, *b.* angle, *c.* perimeter, *d.* velocity)

32. WILLIAMS : (*a.* Massachusetts, *b.* Vermont, *c.* New Hampshire, *d.* Rhode Island) :: PENN : PENNSYLVANIA

33. OLD : (*a.* Two, *b.* Twenty, *c.* Forty, *d.* Sixty) :: MAID : ONE

34. (*a.* princess, *b.* worker, *c.* drone, *d.* servant) : QUEEN :: GANDER : GOOSE

35. XL : LX :: CC : (*a.* CCC, *b.* CD, *c.* DC, *d.* CM)

36. CASTOR : (*a.* Pisces, *b.* Orion, *c.* Pollux, *d.* Andromeda) :: JACOB : ESAU

37. KEYNES : (*a.* psychology, *b.* economics, *c.* anthropology, *d.* ecology) :: EINSTEIN : PHYSICS

38. (*a.* New Jersey, *b.* Missouri, *c.* Indian, *d.* Byrd) : ANTARCTIC :: HUDSON : MISSISSIPPI

39. SPRINGS : PALM :: (*a.* Old, *b.* Mineral, *c.* York, *d.* Tree) : NEW

40. MEGAPHONE : CONE :: (*a.* funnel, *b.* cloud, *c.* hurricane, *d.* dictaphone) : TORNADO

41. HARVARD : CAMBRIDGE :: CAMBRIDGE : (*a.* Oxford, *b.* Yale, *c.* Cambridge, *d.* Gloucester)

42. ACTUAL : VIRTUAL :: IN FACT : (*a.* in cause, *b.* in time, *c.* in truth, *d.* in effect)

43. BRAVE NEW WORLD : (*a.* Winston, *b.* Huxley, *c.* O'Brian, *d.* Wells) :: 1984 : ORWELL

44. CANINE : DOG :: EQUINE : (*a.* cow, *b.* goat, *c.* horse, *d.* pig)

45. CENSURE : (*a.* expurgate, *b.* condemn, *c.* praise, *d.* oppose) :: OBTUSE : DULL

46. USHER : POE :: (*a.* ill Repute, *b.* Seven Gables, *c.* Tara, *d.* No Return) : HAWTHORNE

47. NUMISMATIST : PHILATELIST :: (*a.* coins, *b.* numbers, *c.* rocks, *d.* trinkets) : STAMPS

48. CASTLE : BISHOP :: HORIZONTAL : (*a.* vertical, *b.* diagonal, *c.* cathedral, *d.* abbey)

49. (*a.* endemic, *b.* mercurial, *c.* unabating, *d.* retrogressive) : CONSTANT ::
    CHANGEABLE : IMMUTABLE

50. TRAGEDY : MELODRAMA :: PATHOS : (*a.* bathos, *b.* ethos, *c.* comedy, *d.* catharsis)

51. PERVADE : PERMEATE :: (*a.* trusting, *b.* mistrustful, *c.* favorable, *d.* unfavorable) : AUSPICIOUS

52. GOOSE : GEESE :: MOOSE : (*a.* moosen, *b.* meese, *c.* mooses, *d.* moose)

53. (*a.* passenger pigeon, *b.* sphinx, *c.* phoenix, *d.* hummingbird) : DODO :: RAVEN : SPARROW

54. EASTERN STANDARD : 8 A.M. :: PACIFIC STANDARD : (*a.* 5 A.M., *b.* 6 A.M., *c.* 10 A.M.,
    d. 11 A.M.)

55. CENTIGRADE : 100 :: CELSIUS : (*a.* −173, *b.* 0, *c.* 100, *d.* 212)

56. SURFEIT : EXCESS :: EVANESCENT : (*a.* silent, *b.* eternal, *c.* ephemeral, *d.* celestial)

57. PLUTARCH : (*a.* drama, *b.* biography, *c.* epic, *d.* oration) :: AESOP : FABLE

58. HYDRO : AQUA :: (*a.* air, *b.* gas, *c.* liquid, *d.* water) : WATER

59. REMISS : (*a.* negligent, *b.* careful, *c.* auspicious, *d.* remote) :: DARK : LIGHT

60. FUSTIAN : GALATEA :: MUSLIN : (*a.* grandam, *b.* lydgate, *c.* gabardine, *d.* rhodium)

61. BLUE : STRAW :: RASP : (*a.* yellow, *b.* hay, *c.* black, *d.* shriek)

62. BUFFALO BILL : (*a.* Cody, *b.* James, *c.* Bowman, *d.* Broderick) :: WILD BILL : HICKOK

63. MOURNER : TEARS :: (*a.* hypochondriac, *b.* lover, *c.* troglodyte, *d.* hypocrite) : CROCODILE TEARS

64. CEDE : SEED :: (*a.* run, *b.* win, *c.* yield, *d.* go) : PLANT

65. INGENUOUS : (*a.* clever, *b.* innocent, *c.* pastoral, *d.* hopeful) :: INFRACTION : VIOLATION

66. SECULAR : (*a.* sacred, *b.* ecclesiastical, *c.* lay, *d.* regular) :: BISHOP : MONK

67. EXTIRPATE : (*a.* evade, *b.* examine, *c.* exude, *d.* eradicate) :: BUOY : ENCOURAGE

68. THREE : (*a.* Two, *b.* Three, *c.* Seven, *d.* Ten) :: MUSKETEERS : LITTLE PIGS

69. WEND : END :: (*a.* food, *b.* wait, *c.* tend, *d.* beginning) : ATE

70. VOLT : POTENTIAL DIFFERENCE :: WATT : (*a.* resistance, *b.* brightness, *c.* power, *d.* actual difference)

71. POINT : 0 :: HEXAGON : (*a.* 1, *b.* 2, *c.* 3, *d.* 4)

72. (*a.* Troy, *b.* Athens, *c.* Carthage, *d.* Milan) : PUNIC :: SPARTA : PELOPONNESIAN

73. WINDY CITY : CHICAGO :: GOTHAM : (*a.* San Francisco, *b.* Paris, *c.* New York City, *d.* London)

74. INCANDESCENT : FILAMENT :: FLUORESCENT : (*a.* air, *b.* vacuum, *c.* energy, *d.* phosphor)

75. CABAL : (*a.* trivia, *b.* plot, *c.* wire, *d.* quibble) :: CAPABLE : COMPETENT

76. ORDER : (*a.* human, *b.* primates, *c.* erectus, *d.* mammalia) :: SPECIES : SAPIENS

77. GRENDEL : BEOWULF :: HYDRA : (*a.* Achilles, *b.* Vulcan, *c.* Atlas, *d.* Hercules)

78. 2^{-2} : 2^{-1} :: 2^2 : (*a.* 2^0, *b.* 2^1, *c.* 2^2, *d.* 2^3)

79. DEARTH : SHORTAGE :: PLETHORA : (*a.* abundance, *b.* scarcity, *c.* excess, *d.* necessity)

80. WANDERING JEW : EARTH :: FLYING DUTCHMAN : (*a.* seas, *b.* stars, *c.* heaven, *d.* hell)

81. ASTROLABE : SEXTANT :: SUNDIAL : (*a.* time, *b.* electric clock, *c.* ruler, *d.* light rays)

82. VENAL : (*a.* rigid, *b.* cold, *c.* humorless, *d.* mercenary) :: VENIAL : EXCUSABLE

83. E# : F♭ :: B : (*a.* C♭, *b.* B♭, *c.* C, *d.* B)

84. MELIORATE : AMELIORATE :: HASTEN : (*a.* speed up, *b.* slow down, *c.* better, *d.* worsen)

85. MACHIAVELLI : PRINCE :: CASTIGLIONE : (*a.* Knight, *b.* Courtier, *c.* King, *d.* Yeoman)

86. NOSTRUM : (*a.* pedestal, *b.* disease, *c.* panacea, *d.* pabulum) :: VERACIOUS : HONEST

87. DWARF : PITUITARY :: CRETIN : (*a.* endocrine, *b.* thyroid, *c.* thalamus, *d.* hypothalamus)

88. (*a.* barometer, *b.* tachometer, *c.* hydrometer, *d.* voltmeter) : THERMOMETER :: SPEED : TEMPERATURE

89. FROWARD : BACKWARD :: (*a.* dilatory, *b.* upside down, *c.* refractory, *d.* right side up) : REVERSED

90. LEWIN : (*a.* attribution theory, *b.* dissonance theory, *c.* field theory, *d.* psychoanalytic theory) :: JUNG : ANALYTIC THEORY

91. BUNSEN BURNER : GAS :: AUTOCLAVE : (*a.* oil, *b.* electricity, *c.* steam, *d.* solar energy)

92. BACH : (*a.* invention, *b.* symphony, *c.* waltz, *d.* polyphony) :: CHOPIN : MAZURKA

93. BANISHMENT : COUNTRY :: DEFENESTRATION : (*a.* ceiling, *b.* floor, *c.* city, *d.* window)

94. CADMEAN : (*a.* Caesarian, *b.* Augustan, *c.* Napoleonic, *d.* Pyrrhic) :: EXPENSIVE : COSTLY

95. MOSES : (*a.* Abraham, *b.* Joseph, *c.* Joshua, *d.* Gideon) :: ROOSEVELT : TRUMAN

96. PARASYMPATHETIC : (*a.* sympathetic, *b.* protosympathetic, *c.* asympathetic, *d.* prosympathetic) :: SLOW DOWN : SPEED UP

97. (*a.* Galileo, *b.* Newton, *c.* Galen, *d.* Ptolemy) : COPERNICUS :: GEOCENTRIC : HELIOCENTRIC

98. TOSCANINI : (*a.* Fournier, *b.* Ormandy, *c.* Goodman, *d.* Heifetz) :: VAN CLIBURN : RUBENSTEIN

99. RICHELIEU : CARDINAL :: (*a.* Henry IV, *b.* Louis XIII, *c.* Francis I, *d.* Napoleon III) : KING

100. JAMES : FUNCTIONALISM :: (*a.* Dewey, *b.* Levi-Strauss, *c.* Watson, *d.* Klineberg) : STRUCTURALISM

101. FAUST : DR. FAUSTUS :: (*a.* Goethe, *b.* Mr. Marlowe, *c.* Hyde, *d.* Kafka) : MARLOWE

102. RHODESIA : (*a.* Indonesia, *b.* Zimbabwe, *c.* Namibia, *d.* Israel) :: BURMA : MYANMAR

103. SALT : WATER :: (*a.* desalinate, *b.* desaltify, *c.* purify, *d.* reduce) : DEHYDRATE

104. BUCK : DEER :: COLT : (*a*. stallion, *b*. horse, *c*. filly, *d*. foal)

105. (*a*. liver, *b*. brain, *c*. ear, *d*. pancreas) : HEART :: LOBE : CHAMBER

106. NADIR : (*a*. penultimate, *b*. depth, *c*. zenith, *d*. low) :: STYGIAN : BRIGHT

107. 32 : FAHRENHEIT :: (*a*. -32, *b*. 100, *c*. 10, *d*. 0) : CELSIUS

108. GRAPE : RAISIN :: PLUM : (*a*. date, *b*. fig, *c*. prune, *d*. currant)

109. NORTH : CANCER :: SOUTH : (*a*. Virgo, *b*. Capricorn, *c*. Sagittarius, *d*. Equator)

110. EVELYN : DACTYL :: (*a*. Michelle, *b*. Holly, *c*. Erica, *d*. Emily) : IAMB

111. MOZART : (*a*. Violin, *b*. Flute, *c*. Viola, *d*. Cello) :: BACH : ORGAN

112. (*a*. pizzicato, *b*. staccato, *c*. diminuendo, *d*. piano) : FORTE :: SOFT : LOUD

113. INDIA : HINDUISM :: INDONESIA : (*a*. Buddhism, *b*. Confucianism, *c*. Christianity, *d*. Islam)

114. OBOE : REED :: (*a*. viola, *b*. bassoon, *c*. timpani, *d*. french horn) : STRING

115. MORE : (*a*. Utopia, *b*. Paradise Lost, *c*. 1984, *d*. On the Beach) :: HUXLEY : BRAVE NEW WORLD

116. BASEBALL : BAT :: TABLE TENNIS : (*a*. mallet, *b*. paddle, *c*. stick, *d*. racquet)

117. ETYMOLOGY : ENTOMOLOGY :: (*a*. letters, *b*. arachnids, *c*. disease, *d*. words) : INSECTS

118. ADAM : (*a*. Eden, *b*. Israel, *c*. heaven, *d*. hell) :: ROMEO : VERONA

119. $8^{1/3} : 25^{1/2}$ :: (*a*. 25^2, *b*. $100^{1/3}$, *c*. $100^{1/2}$, *d*. $16^{1/2}$) : $625^{1/2}$

120. AUGMENTED THIRD : DIMINISHED THIRD :: FOUR : (*a*. two and a half, *b*. three, *c*. two, *d*. three and a half)

ANSWER KEY
Practice Test 3

1.	B	31.	B	61.	C	91.	C
2.	B	32.	D	62.	A	92.	A
3.	D	33.	B	63.	D	93.	D
4.	A	34.	C	64.	C	94.	D
5.	C	35.	A	65.	B	95.	C
6.	A	36.	C	66.	D	96.	A
7.	A	37.	B	67.	D	97.	D
8.	B	38.	C	68.	B	98.	B
9.	A	39.	C	69.	B	99.	B
10.	D	40.	A	70.	C	100.	B
11.	D	41.	C	71.	B	101.	A
12.	B	42.	D	72.	C	102.	B
13.	B	43.	B	73.	C	103.	A
14.	A	44.	C	74.	D	104.	D
15.	C	45.	B	75.	B	105.	B
16.	C	46.	B	76.	B	106.	C
17.	B	47.	A	77.	D	107.	D
18.	A	48.	B	78.	D	108.	C
19.	B	49.	B	79.	C	109.	B
20.	D	50.	A	80.	A	110.	A
21.	C	51.	C	81.	B	111.	A
22.	A	52.	D	82.	D	112.	D
23.	B	53.	A	83.	B	113.	D
24.	C	54.	A	84.	A	114.	A
25.	D	55.	C	85.	B	115.	A
26.	D	56.	C	86.	C	116.	B
27.	D	57.	B	87.	B	117.	D
28.	C	58.	D	88.	B	118.	A
29.	C	59.	B	89.	C	119.	C
30.	B	60.	C	90.	C	120.	A

ANSWER EXPLANATIONS FOR PRACTICE TEST 3

In the following, explanations concerning the correct responses are in roman font. Explanations regarding distracters (incorrect responses) that are not self-explaining or could be misinterpreted are in italics in order to highlight the explanations of the answers that are correct.

1. LAMB : (*a.* goat, ***b.* sheep**, *c.* mule, *d.* cow) :: COLT : HORSE
   (b) A lamb is a young sheep; a colt is a young horse.

2. DOCTOR : ACCOUNTANT :: PATIENT : (*a.* judge, ***b.* client**, *c.* jury, *d.* district attorney)
   (b) A doctor serves patients; an accountant serves clients.

3. IRELAND : EIRE :: (*a.* Holland, *b.* Switzerland, *c.* Denmark, ***d.* Germany**) : DEUTSCHLAND
   (d) Ireland and Eire are the same country, as are Germany and Deutschland (in the native language of each country).

4. DEFICIT : RED :: SURPLUS : (***a.* black**, *b.* green, *c.* brown, *d.* white)
   (a) To be in the red is to show a deficit, while to be in the black is to show a surplus.

5. LEMON : SOUR :: HOREHOUND : (*a.* tasty, *b.* sour, ***c.* bitter**, *d.* salty)
   (c) A lemon is sour; a horehound is bitter.

6. YELLOW : (***a.* blue**, *b.* white, *c.* green, *d.* red) :: COWARDLY : GLOOMY
   (a) A cowardly person is sometimes referred to as "yellow." A gloomy person is sometimes referred to as feeling "blue."

7. HOUDINI : (***a.* magician**, *b.* surgeon, *c.* lawyer, *d.* detective) :: FRANKLIN : STATESMAN
   (a) Harry Houdini was a magician; Benjamin Franklin, a statesman.

8. CURRIER : (*a.* Loewe, ***b.* Ives**, *c.* Cowe, *d.* Best) :: GILBERT : SULLIVAN
   (b) Currier and Ives were a team of artists, while Gilbert and Sullivan were a team who wrote operettas, including "The Mikado." Currier and Ives had a printmaking firm that produced some of the most popular art of the 19th century.

9. DE FACTO : IN FACT :: (***a.* de jure**, *b.* de legibus, *c.* ex facto, *d.* ex legato) : IN LAW
   (a) *De facto* means "in fact." *De jure* means "in law." De legibus *is a dialogue written by Cicero.* Ex facto *means "after the fact." All have Latin etymologies.*

10. SQUARE : CUBE :: CIRCLE : (*a.* rectangle, *b.* solid, *c.* ellipse, ***d.* sphere**)
    (d) A two-dimensional "slice" through a cube yields a square. A two-dimensional "slice" through a sphere yields a circle.

11. FIDDLER : PRAYING :: (*a.* bow, *b.* bear, *c.* violinist, ***d.* crab**) : MANTIS
    (d) The fiddler crab and praying mantis are both types of animal.

12. WINCHESTER : SHOOT :: CAT-O'-NINE-TAILS : (*a.* stab, ***b.* whip**, *c.* poison, *d.* drown)
    (b) A Winchester can be used to shoot someone. A cat-o'-nine-tails can be used to whip someone. A Winchester is a shoulder rifle. A cat-o'-nine-tails is a whip with nine separate woven tails.

13. FULTON : (*a.* locomotive, ***b.* steamboat**, *c.* incandescent lamp, *d.* crystal radio) :: WHITNEY : COTTON GIN

    (b) Robert Fulton invented the steamboat. Eli Whitney invented the cotton gin.

14. (***a.* jugular**, *b.* carotid, *c.* thorax, *d.* sclerotic) : VEIN :: AORTA : ARTERY

    (a) The jugular is a vein; the aorta is an artery. Carotid *relates to the chief arteries that pass up the neck. The thorax is the part of the body between the neck and abdomen.* Sclerotic *relates to the dense fibrous outer coat of the eyeball.*

15. HISTRIONICS : (*a.* geriatrics,   *b.* hysterics,   ***c.* theatrics**,   *d.* pediatrics) :: PATRONYMICS : SURNAMES

    (c) Histrionics are theatrics; patronymics are surnames.

16. NUN : HABIT :: (*a.* postal carrier, *b.* surgeon, ***c.* knight**, *d.* solicitor) : COAT OF MAIL

    (c) A nun sometimes wears a habit. A knight wore a coat of mail.

17. (*a.* people, ***b.* automobiles**, *c.* horses, *d.* bicycles) : INDIANAPOLIS 500 :: HORSES : KENTUCKY DERBY

    (b) The Indianapolis 500 is an automobile race. The Kentucky Derby is a horse race.

18. LOBBYIST : LEGISLATOR :: (***a.* lawyer**, *b.* judge, *c.* court stenographer, *d.* foreman) : JURY

    (a) The job of a lobbyist is to persuade a legislator. The job of a lawyer is to persuade a jury.

19. CONGRESSIONAL MEDAL OF HONOR : SOLDIER :: PULITZER PRIZE : (*a.* lawyer, ***b.* journalist**, *c.* chemist, *d.* doctor)

    (b) The Congressional Medal of Honor is given to outstanding soldiers. The Pulitzer Prize is given to outstanding journalists.

20. PART : TRAP :: (*a.* good-bye, *b.* whole, *c.* bait, ***d.* tar**) : RAT

    (d) Part is trap spelled backward. Tar is rat spelled backward.

21. BARTON : (*a.* Candy, *b.* Helen, ***c.* Clara**, *d.* Elsa) :: NIGHTINGALE : FLORENCE

    (c) Clara Barton (1821–1912) and Florence Nightingale (1821–1910) are both famous for their work in nursing.

22. EMERALD : MINE :: PEARL : (***a.* oyster**, *b.* clam, *c.* mine, *d.* river)

    (a) Emeralds are found in mines. Pearls are found in oysters.

23. BIOGRAPHY : AUTOBIOGRAPHY :: (*a.* first, ***b.* third**, *c.* fourth, *d.* fifth) : FIRST

    (b) A biography is written in third person. An autobiography is written in first person.

24. DUET : PAIR :: DIALOGUE : (*a.* monologue, *b.* quandary, ***c.* bipolar**, *d.* quartet)

    (c) Duet, pair, dialogue, and bipolar all refer to two of something. *A monologue refers to one; a quartet refers to four; a quandary refers to a state of perplexity or doubt.*

25. (*a.* foot, *b.* ball, *c.* skate, ***d.* stick**) : HOCKEY :: BAT : BASEBALL

    (d) In hockey, players hit a puck with a stick. In baseball, players hit a ball with a bat.

26. (*a.* chroma, *b.* violet, *c.* rainbow, ***d.* black**) : COLOR :: VACUUM : AIR

    (d) Black is an absence of color. A vacuum is an absence of air.

27. FLORIDA : PENINSULA :: CUBA : (*a.* state, *b.* gulf, *c.* nation, ***d.* island**)

    (d) Florida is a peninsula. Cuba is an island.

28. URBAN : RURAL :: URBANE : (*a.* lazy, *b.* suburban, ***c.* boorish**, *d.* effete)

(c) Urban and rural are antonyms, as are urbane and boorish.

29. (*a.* air, *b.* earth, ***c.* fire**, *d.* plastic) : PYRO :: WATER : HYDRO

(c) Pyro- is a prefix meaning fire, while hydro- is a prefix meaning water.

30. (*a.* sailor, ***b.* mountebank**, *c.* salesman, *d.* villain) : CHARLATAN :: FRAUD : QUACK

(b) A mountebank is a charlatan, and a fraud is a quack.

31. RULER : LINE SEGMENT :: PROTRACTOR : (*a.* distance, ***b.* angle**, *c.* perimeter, *d.* velocity)

(b) A ruler is used to measure a line segment, while a protractor is used to measure an angle.

32. WILLIAMS : (*a.* Massachusetts, *b.* Vermont, *c.* New Hampshire, ***d.* Rhode Island**) :: PENN : PENNSYLVANIA

(d) Roger Williams founded the state of Rhode Island; William Penn founded the state of Pennsylvania. *The colony of Massachusetts Bay was founded by John Winthrop. Vermont was founded by Ethan Allen and his brothers as well as Seth Warner, whom they recruited for an informal militia, the Green Mountain Boys. John Mason was the founder of New Hampshire.*

33. OLD : (*a.* Two, ***b.* Twenty**, *c.* Forty, *d.* Sixty) :: MAID : ONE

(b) Old Maid and Twenty-One are both card games.

34. (*a.* princess, *b.* worker, ***c.* drone**, *d.* servant) : QUEEN :: GANDER : GOOSE

(c) A drone bee is male, and a queen bee is female. A gander is a male, and a goose is a female.

35. XL : LX :: CC : (***a.* CCC**, *b.* CD, *c.* DC, *d.* CM)

(a) 40 is to 60 as 200 is to 300. The first and third terms are $\frac{2}{3}$ of the second and fourth terms respectively. *In Roman numerals, I = 1, V = 5, X = 10, L = 50, C = 100, D = 500, M = 1,000.*

36. CASTOR : (*a.* Pisces, *b.* Orion, ***c.* Pollux**, *d.* Andromeda) :: JACOB : ESAU

(c) Castor and Pollux were twins, as were Jacob and Esau. *Pisces, Orion, and Andromeda are all constellations. Orion was a hunter in Greek mythology. Andromeda was the wife of Perseus.*

37. KEYNES : (*a.* psychology, ***b.* economics**, *c.* anthropology, *d.* ecology) :: EINSTEIN : PHYSICS

(b) John Maynard Keynes revolutionized economic theory, while Albert Einstein revolutionized theory in physics.

38. (*a.* New Jersey, *b.* Missouri, ***c.* Indian**, *d.* Byrd) : ANTARCTIC :: HUDSON : MISSISSIPPI

(c) The Indian and the Antarctic are both oceans. The Hudson and the Mississippi are both rivers.

39. SPRINGS : PALM :: (*a.* Old, *b.* Mineral, ***c.* York**, *d.* Tree) : NEW

(c) Palm Springs and New York are both major cities.

40. MEGAPHONE : CONE :: (***a.* funnel**, *b.* cloud, *c.* hurricane, *d.* dictaphone) : TORNADO

(a) A megaphone, a funnel, a cone, and a tornado all have approximately the same shape.

41. HARVARD : CAMBRIDGE :: CAMBRIDGE : (*a.* Oxford, *b.* Yale, ***c.* Cambridge**, *d.* Gloucester)

(c) Harvard University is in Cambridge, Massachusetts, and Cambridge University is in Cambridge, England.

42. ACTUAL : VIRTUAL :: IN FACT : (*a.* in cause, *b.* in time, *c.* in truth, ***d.* in effect**)

(d) Actual means in fact. Virtual means in effect.

43. BRAVE NEW WORLD : (*a.* Winston, ***b.* Huxley**, *c.* O'Brian, *d.* Wells) :: 1984 : ORWELL

(b) *Brave New World* is a novel by Huxley; *1984* is a novel by Orwell. (Both describe Dystopian societies of the future.)

44. CANINE : DOG :: EQUINE : (*a.* cow, *b.* goat, ***c.* horse**, *d.* pig)

(c) Canine means doglike. Equine means horselike. *Cowlike is bovine, goatlike is hircine, and piglike is porcine.*

45. CENSURE : (*a.* expurgate, ***b.* condemn**, *c.* praise, *d.* oppose) :: OBTUSE : DULL

(b) To censure is to condemn. To be obtuse is to be dull.

46. USHER : POE :: (*a.* ill Repute, ***b.* Seven Gables**, *c.* Tara, *d.* No Return) : HAWTHORNE

(b) Poe wrote about the House of Usher; Hawthorne wrote about the House of the Seven Gables.

47. NUMISMATIST : PHILATELIST :: (***a.* coins**, *b.* numbers, *c.* rocks, *d.* trinkets) : STAMPS

(a) A numismatist collects coins; a philatelist collects stamps.

48. CASTLE : BISHOP :: HORIZONTAL : (*a.* vertical, ***b.* diagonal**, *c.* cathedral, *d.* abbey)

(b) In the game of chess, a castle is capable of horizontal movement, while a bishop is capable of diagonal movement.

49. (*a.* endemic, ***b.* mercurial**, *c.* unabating, *d.* retrogressive) : CONSTANT :: CHANGEABLE : IMMUTABLE

(b) Mercurial and constant are antonyms, as are changeable and immutable.

50. TRAGEDY : MELODRAMA :: PATHOS : (***a.* bathos**, *b.* ethos, *c.* comedy, *d.* catharsis)

(a) Tragedy expresses pathos, while melodrama expresses bathos. (See the vocabulary section for more on these terms.)

51. PERVADE : PERMEATE :: (*a.* trusting, *b.* mistrustful, ***c.* favorable**, *d.* unfavorable) : AUSPICIOUS

(c) Pervade and permeate are synonyms, as are favorable and auspicious.

52. GOOSE : GEESE :: MOOSE : (*a.* moosen, *b.* meese, *c.* mooses, ***d.* moose**)

(d) The plural of goose is geese. The plural of moose is moose.

53. (***a.* passenger pigeon**, *b.* sphinx, *c.* phoenix, *d.* hummingbird) : DODO :: RAVEN : SPARROW

(a) The passenger pigeon and the dodo are both extinct species of birds. The raven and the sparrow are not extinct. *The hummingbird is also not extinct; a phoenix is a mythical bird that burns itself and rises from the ashes to live again; the sphinx is a mythical Egyptian creature that has the body of a lion and the head of a man.*

54. EASTERN STANDARD : 8 A.M. :: PACIFIC STANDARD : (***a.* 5 A.M.**, *b.* 6 A.M., *c.* 10 A.M., *d.* 11 A.M.)

(a) When it is 8 A.M. Eastern Standard Time, it is 5 A.M. Pacific Standard Time.

55. CENTIGRADE : 100 :: CELSIUS : (*a.* -173, *b.* 0, ***c.* 100**, *d.* 212)

(c) The centigrade and Celsius temperature scales are identical, so 100 degrees centigrade equals 100 degrees Celsius.

56. SURFEIT : EXCESS :: EVANESCENT : (*a.* silent, *b.* eternal, ***c.* ephemeral**, *d.* celestial)

(c) Surfeit and excess are synonyms, as are evanescent and ephemeral.

57. PLUTARCH : (*a.* drama, ***b.* biography**, *c.* epic, *d.* oration) :: AESOP : FABLE

(b) Plutarch is famous as a writer of biography. Aesop is famous as a writer of fables. Plutarch wrote *Parallel Lives*; famous fables of Aesop are, for example, *The Fox and the Grapes* and *The Tortoise and the Hare*.

58. HYDRO : AQUA :: (*a.* air, *b.* gas, *c.* liquid, ***d.* water**) : WATER

(d) Hydro- and aqua- are both prefixes meaning water.

59. REMISS : (*a.* negligent, ***b.* careful**, *c.* auspicious, *d.* remote) :: DARK : LIGHT

(b) Remiss is the opposite of careful; dark is the opposite of light.

60. FUSTIAN : GALATEA :: MUSLIN : (*a.* grandam, *b.* lydgate, ***c.* gabardine**, *d.* rhodium)

(c) Fustian, galatea, muslin, and gabardine are all types of cloth. *Grandam refers to an old woman. John Lydgate was an English poet (ca. 1370–1450). Rhodium is a rare metallic element.*

61. BLUE : STRAW :: RASP : (*a.* yellow, *b.* hay, ***c.* black**, *d.* shriek)

(c) A blueberry, a strawberry, a raspberry, and a blackberry are all types of berries.

62. BUFFALO BILL : (***a.* Cody**, *b.* James, *c.* Bowman, *d.* Broderick) :: WILD BILL : HICKOK

(a) Buffalo Bill Cody and Wild Bill Hickok were both famous cowboys.

63. MOURNER : TEARS :: (*a.* hypochondriac, *b.* lover, *c.* troglodyte, ***d.* hypocrite**) : CROCODILE TEARS

(d) A mourner sheds tears. A hypocrite sheds crocodile, or fake, tears.

64. CEDE : SEED :: (*a.* run, *b.* win, ***c.* yield**, *d.* go) : PLANT

(c) To cede is to yield. To seed is to plant.

65. INGENUOUS : (*a.* clever, ***b.* innocent**, *c.* pastoral, *d.* hopeful) :: INFRACTION : VIOLATION

(b) Ingenuous and innocent are synonyms, as are infraction and violation.

66. SECULAR : (*a.* sacred, *b.* ecclesiastical, *c.* lay, ***d.* regular**) :: BISHOP : MONK

(d) A bishop is a member of the secular clergy. A monk is a member of the regular clergy. Secular and regular clergy are terms from the Catholic Church. Secular clergy are priests and deacons, for example, who are not bound by the vows of a monastic order. Regular clergy, to the contrary, take vows of a monastic order, such as poverty and obedience.

67. EXTIRPATE : (*a.* evade, *b.* examine, *c.* exude, ***d.* eradicate**) :: BUOY : ENCOURAGE

(d) To extirpate is to eradicate. To buoy is to encourage.

68. THREE : (*a.* Two, ***b.* Three**, *c.* Seven, *d.* Ten) :: MUSKETEERS : LITTLE PIGS

(b) There were, so the stories go, Three Musketeers and three little pigs.

69. WEND : END :: (*a.* food, ***b.* wait**, *c.* tend, *d.* beginning) : ATE

(b) Wend is pronounced like end, except for the added initial *w* consonant sound. Wait is pronounced like ate, also except for the initial *w* consonant sound.

70. VOLT : POTENTIAL DIFFERENCE :: WATT : (*a.* resistance, *b.* brightness, ***c.* power**, *d.* actual difference)

(c) The volt is a measure of potential difference. The watt is a measure of power.

71. POINT : 0 :: HEXAGON : (*a.* 1, ***b.* 2**, *c.* 3, *d.* 4)

(b) A point occupies 0 dimension, while a hexagon occupies 2 dimensions.

72. (*a.* Troy, *b.* Athens, *c.* **Carthage**, *d.* Milan) : PUNIC :: SPARTA : PELOPONNESIAN

(c) Carthage was one of the opposing sides in the Punic Wars (264–241 B.C., 218–201 B.C., 149–146 B.C.); the other side was Rome. Sparta was one of the opposing sides in the Peloponnesian Wars (431–404 B.C.); the other side was Athens and its allies. Rome and Sparta eventually won their respective wars.

73. WINDY CITY : CHICAGO :: GOTHAM : (*a.* San Francisco, *b.* Paris, *c.* **New York City**, *d.* London)

(c) Windy City is another name for Chicago. Gotham is another name for New York City.

74. INCANDESCENT : FILAMENT :: FLUORESCENT : (*a.* air, *b.* vacuum, *c.* energy, *d.* **phosphor**)

(d) The filament glows in an incandescent lamp. The phosphor glows in a fluorescent lamp.

75. CABAL : (*a.* trivia, *b.* **plot**, *c.* wire, *d.* quibble) :: CAPABLE : COMPETENT

(b) Cabal and plot are synonyms, as are capable and competent.

76. ORDER : (*a.* human, *b.* **primates**, *c.* erectus, *d.* mammalia) :: SPECIES : SAPIENS

(b) Human beings are of order Primates and species sapiens.

77. GRENDEL : BEOWULF :: HYDRA : (*a.* Achilles, *b.* Vulcan, *c.* Atlas, *d.* **Hercules**)

(d) Beowulf slew Grendel; Hercules slew Hydra. *Achilles was the greatest warrior of the Greeks in the Trojan War. Vulcan was the god of fire and metalworking in Roman mythology. Atlas was a titan who was forced by Zeus to carry the heavens on his shoulders.*

78. $2^{-2} : 2^{-1} :: 2^2 : (a.\ 2^0,\ b.\ 2^1,\ c.\ 2^2,\ d.\ \mathbf{2^3})$

(d) $\frac{1}{4}$ is to $\frac{1}{2}$ as 4 is to 8. When dealing with negative exponents, invert the fraction.

79. DEARTH : SHORTAGE :: PLETHORA : (*a.* abundance, *b.* scarcity, *c.* **excess**, *d.* necessity)

(c) A dearth is a shortage. A plethora is an excess.

80. WANDERING JEW : EARTH :: FLYING DUTCHMAN : (*a.* **seas**, *b.* stars, *c.* heaven, *d.* hell)

(a) The Wandering Jew was doomed to wander the earth. The Flying Dutchman was doomed to wander the seas.

81. ASTROLABE : SEXTANT :: SUNDIAL : (*a.* time, *b.* **electric clock**, *c.* ruler, *d.* light rays)

(b) The sextant replaced the astrolabe in navigation; the electric clock replaced the sundial in timekeeping.

82. VENAL : (*a.* rigid, *b.* cold, *c.* humorless, *d.* **mercenary**) :: VENIAL : EXCUSABLE

(d) Venal and mercenary are synonyms, as are venial and excusable.

83. E# : F♭ :: B : (*a.* C♭, *b.* **B♭**, *c.* C, *d.* B)

(b) E# is a half-tone higher than F♭. B is a half-tone higher than B♭.

84. MELIORATE : AMELIORATE :: HASTEN : (*a.* **speed up**, *b.* slow down, *c.* better, *d.* worsen)

(a) Meliorate and ameliorate mean the same thing, as do hasten and speed up.

85. MACHIAVELLI : PRINCE :: CASTIGLIONE : (*a.* Knight, *b.* **Courtier**, *c.* King, *d.* Yeoman)

(b) Machiavelli is the author of *The Prince*. Castiglione is the author of *The Courtier*.

86. NOSTRUM : (*a.* pedestal, *b.* disease, *c.* **panacea**, *d.* pabulum) :: VERACIOUS : HONEST

(c) A nostrum is a panacea (remedy for all ills). A veracious person is an honest person.

87. DWARF : PITUITARY :: CRETIN : (*a.* endocrine, *b.* **thyroid**, *c.* thalamus, *d.* hypothalamus)

(b) A dwarf has a malfunctioning pituitary gland. A cretin has a malfunctioning thyroid gland.

88. (*a.* barometer, ***b.* tachometer**, *c.* hydrometer, *d.* voltmeter) : THERMOMETER :: SPEED : TEMPERATURE

(b) A tachometer measures speed. A thermometer measures temperature.

89. FROWARD : BACKWARD :: (*a.* dilatory, *b.* upside down, ***c.* refractory**, *d.* right side up) : REVERSED

(c) Froward means refractory. Backward means reversed.

90. LEWIN : (*a.* attribution theory, *b.* dissonance theory, ***c.* field theory**, *d.* psychoanalytic theory) :: JUNG : ANALYTIC THEORY

(c) Lewin's theory of personality is classified as a field theory. Jung's theory of personality is called analytic theory.

91. BUNSEN BURNER : GAS :: AUTOCLAVE : (*a.* oil, *b.* electricity, ***c.* steam**, *d.* solar energy)

(c) A Bunsen burner produces heat through gas. An autoclave produces heat through steam.

92. BACH : (***a.* invention**, *b.* symphony, *c.* waltz, *d.* polyphony) :: CHOPIN : MAZURKA

(a) Bach was a composer of inventions. Chopin was a composer of mazurkas. Mazurkas are Polish folk dances; inventions are short pieces developing a single theme contrapuntally.

93. BANISHMENT : COUNTRY :: DEFENESTRATION : (*a.* ceiling, *b.* floor, *c.* city, ***d.* window**)

(d) Banishment occurs when someone is thrown out of a country. Defenestration occurs when someone is thrown out of a window.

94. CADMEAN : (*a.* Caesarian, *b.* Augustan, *c.* Napoleonic, ***d.* Pyrrhic**) :: EXPENSIVE : COSTLY

(d) Both a Cadmean and a Pyrrhic victory are excessively (costly) types of victory. The armed men who sprang from the teeth of the dragon sown by Cadmus killed each other. A Pyrrhic victory is so called because the army of King Pyrrhus of Epirus suffered enormous losses during the Pyrrhic War in which the Romans were eventually defeated at Heraclea (280 B.C.) and Asculum (279 B.C.).

95. MOSES : (*a.* Abraham, *b.* Joseph, ***c.* Joshua**, *d.* Gideon) :: ROOSEVELT : TRUMAN

(c) Joshua succeeded Moses as leader of the Israelites. Truman succeeded Roosevelt as president of the United States. *Abraham is regarded by Jews as the founder of the Hebrew people (via his son Isaac) and by Muslims as the founder of the Muslim people (via his son Ishmael). Joseph was one of Jacob's sons who was sold into slavery by his brothers; Joseph was also the name of Mary's husband. Gideon appears in the Book of Judges and defeated the Midianites.*

96. PARASYMPATHETIC : (***a.* sympathetic**, *b.* protosympathetic, *c.* asympathetic, *d.* prosympathetic) :: SLOW DOWN : SPEED UP

(a) The parasympathetic nervous system slows down the heartbeat, while the sympathetic nervous system speeds it up.

97. (*a.* Galileo, *b.* Newton, *c.* Galen, ***d.* Ptolemy**) : COPERNICUS :: GEOCENTRIC : HELIOCENTRIC

(d) Ptolemy is known for his geocentric theory of the solar system, while Copernicus is known for his heliocentric theory. *Newton is known for describing universal gravitation; Galen was a Greek physician and one of the first experimental physiologists. Galileo was an Italian physicist and astronomer who improved the telescope and is called the "father of modern observational astronomy." He was a supporter of Copernicanism.*

98. TOSCANINI : (*a.* Fournier, ***b.* Ormandy**, *c.* Goodman, *d.* Heifetz) :: VAN CLIBURN : RUBENSTEIN

    (b) Toscanini and Ormandy attained fame as conductors; Van Cliburn and Rubenstein became famous as pianists.

99. RICHELIEU : CARDINAL :: (*a.* Henry IV, ***b.* Louis XIII**, *c.* Francis I, *d.* Napoleon III) : KING

    (b) Richelieu (1585–1642) was cardinal when Louis XIII (1601–1643) was king.

100. JAMES : FUNCTIONALISM :: (*a.* Dewey, ***b.*Levi-Strauss**, *c.* Watson, *d.* Klineberg) : STRUCTURALISM

    (b) James was a functionalist; Levi-Strauss, a structuralist. *Dewey was a pragmatist and functionalist. John B. Watson was a behaviorist. Klineberg was an anthropologist.*

101. FAUST : DR. FAUSTUS :: (***a.* Goethe**, *b.* Mr. Marlowe, *c.* Hyde, *d.* Kafka) : MARLOWE

    (a) *Faust* was written by Goethe just as *Dr. Faustus* was written by Marlowe.

102. RHODESIA : (*a.* Indonesia, ***b.* Zimbabwe**, *c.* Namibia, *d.* Israel) :: BURMA : MYANMAR

    (b) Rhodesia is the former name of the country today known as Zimbabwe. Burma is the former name of present-day Myanmar. *Indonesia was previously known as Dutch East Indies. Namibia was formerly known as German Southwest Africa.*

103. SALT : WATER :: (***a.* desalinate**, *b.* desaltify, *c.* purify, *d.* reduce) : DEHYDRATE

    (a) To reduce salt content is to desalinate. To reduce water content is to dehydrate.

104. BUCK : DEER :: COLT : (*a.* stallion, *b.* horse, *c.* filly, ***d.* foal**)

    (d) A buck is a male deer, and a colt is a male foal.

105. (*a.* liver, ***b.* brain**, *c.* ear, *d.* pancreas) : HEART :: LOBE : CHAMBER

    (b) The brain is made up of separate lobes, while the heart is made up of separate chambers.

106. NADIR : (*a.* penultimate, *b.* depth, ***c.* zenith**, *d.* low) :: STYGIAN : BRIGHT

    (c) The nadir, or lowest point, is the opposite of the zenith. Likewise, stygian, meaning dark and dismal, is the opposite of bright.

107. 32 : FAHRENHEIT :: (*a.* –32, *b.* 100, *c.* 10, ***d.* 0**) : CELSIUS

    (d) 32 degrees Fahrenheit is the point at which water freezes, just as 0 degrees Celsius is the point at which water freezes.

108. GRAPE : RAISIN :: PLUM : (*a.* date, *b.* fig, ***c.* prune**, *d.* currant)

    (c) A dried grape is called a raisin and a dried plum is called a prune.

109. NORTH : CANCER :: SOUTH : (*a.* Virgo, ***b.* Capricorn**, *c.* Sagittarius, *d.* Equator)

    (b) North of the equator lies the Tropic of Cancer and south of it lies the Tropic of Capricorn (lines of altitude about 23° north and south of the equator).

110. EVELYN : DACTYL :: (***a.* Michelle**, *b.* Holly, *c.* Erica, *d.* Emily) : IAMB

    (a) Evelyn is a name whose metric foot is a dactyl. Michelle is a name whose metric foot is an iamb. A dactyl is a metrical foot consisting of one stressed and two unstressed syllables. An iamb is a metrical foot that consists of one unstressed and one stressed syllable.

111. MOZART : (***a.* Violin**, *b.* Flute, *c.* Viola, *d.* Cello) :: BACH : ORGAN

    (a) Mozart was most accomplished instrumentally on the violin. Bach was most accomplished on the organ.

112. (*a.* pizzicato, *b.* staccato, *c.* diminuendo, ***d.* piano**) : FORTE :: SOFT : LOUD

(d) The musical term piano indicates that one should play softly, whereas forte directs one to play loudly. *A pizzicato is a passage played by plucking strings. Staccato means that notes are being played in a detached manner that separates them from each other. Diminuendo means decreasing the volume of a played passage.*

113. INDIA : HINDUISM :: INDONESIA : (*a.* Buddhism, *b.* Confucianism, *c.* Christianity, ***d.* Islam**)

(d) India is the country with the greatest population of people practicing Hinduism, whereas Indonesia is the country with the greatest population of people practicing Islam.

114. OBOE : REED :: (***a.* viola**, *b.* bassoon, *c.* timpani, *d.* french horn) : STRING

(a) The vibration of a reed produces the sound of an oboe, just as the vibration of a string produces the sound of a viola.

115. MORE : (***a.* Utopia**, *b.* Paradise Lost, *c.* 1984, *d.* On the Beach) :: HUXLEY : BRAVE NEW WORLD

(a) Aldous Huxley wrote a futuristic novel entitled *Brave New World*. Thomas More wrote about a fictitious island in a book entitled *Utopia*.

116. BASEBALL : BAT :: TABLE TENNIS : (*a.* mallet, ***b.* paddle**, *c.* stick, *d.* racquet)

(b) In baseball, the ball is hit with a bat. In table tennis, the ball is hit with a paddle.

117. ETYMOLOGY : ENTOMOLOGY :: (*a.* letters, *b.* arachnids, *c.* disease, ***d.* words**) : INSECTS

(d) Etymology is the study of the origin of words just as entomology is the study of insects.

118. ADAM : (***a.* Eden**, *b.* Israel, *c.* heaven, *d.* hell) :: ROMEO : VERONA

(a) Adam was banished from Eden and Romeo was banished from Verona.

119. $8^{1/3} : 25^{1/2} ::$ (*a.* 25^2, *b.* $100^{1/3}$, ***c.* $100^{1/2}$**, *d.* $16^{1/2}$) : $625^{1/2}$

(c) The cube root of eight is 2, and the square root of 25 is 5, creating a ratio of 2 to 5. Similarly, the square root of 100 is 10 and the square root of 625 is 25, creating a ratio of 2 to 5.

120. AUGMENTED THIRD : DIMINISHED THIRD :: FOUR : (***a.* two-and-a-half**, *b.* three, *c.* two, *d.* three-and-a-half)

(a) An augmented third and a diminished third are one-and-a-half units apart, as are the numbers four and two-and-a-half.

ANSWER SHEET
Practice Test 4

1. Ⓐ Ⓑ Ⓒ Ⓓ
2. Ⓐ Ⓑ Ⓒ Ⓓ
3. Ⓐ Ⓑ Ⓒ Ⓓ
4. Ⓐ Ⓑ Ⓒ Ⓓ
5. Ⓐ Ⓑ Ⓒ Ⓓ
6. Ⓐ Ⓑ Ⓒ Ⓓ
7. Ⓐ Ⓑ Ⓒ Ⓓ
8. Ⓐ Ⓑ Ⓒ Ⓓ
9. Ⓐ Ⓑ Ⓒ Ⓓ
10. Ⓐ Ⓑ Ⓒ Ⓓ
11. Ⓐ Ⓑ Ⓒ Ⓓ
12. Ⓐ Ⓑ Ⓒ Ⓓ
13. Ⓐ Ⓑ Ⓒ Ⓓ
14. Ⓐ Ⓑ Ⓒ Ⓓ
15. Ⓐ Ⓑ Ⓒ Ⓓ
16. Ⓐ Ⓑ Ⓒ Ⓓ
17. Ⓐ Ⓑ Ⓒ Ⓓ
18. Ⓐ Ⓑ Ⓒ Ⓓ
19. Ⓐ Ⓑ Ⓒ Ⓓ
20. Ⓐ Ⓑ Ⓒ Ⓓ
21. Ⓐ Ⓑ Ⓒ Ⓓ
22. Ⓐ Ⓑ Ⓒ Ⓓ
23. Ⓐ Ⓑ Ⓒ Ⓓ
24. Ⓐ Ⓑ Ⓒ Ⓓ
25. Ⓐ Ⓑ Ⓒ Ⓓ
26. Ⓐ Ⓑ Ⓒ Ⓓ
27. Ⓐ Ⓑ Ⓒ Ⓓ
28. Ⓐ Ⓑ Ⓒ Ⓓ
29. Ⓐ Ⓑ Ⓒ Ⓓ
30. Ⓐ Ⓑ Ⓒ Ⓓ

31. Ⓐ Ⓑ Ⓒ Ⓓ
32. Ⓐ Ⓑ Ⓒ Ⓓ
33. Ⓐ Ⓑ Ⓒ Ⓓ
34. Ⓐ Ⓑ Ⓒ Ⓓ
35. Ⓐ Ⓑ Ⓒ Ⓓ
36. Ⓐ Ⓑ Ⓒ Ⓓ
37. Ⓐ Ⓑ Ⓒ Ⓓ
38. Ⓐ Ⓑ Ⓒ Ⓓ
39. Ⓐ Ⓑ Ⓒ Ⓓ
40. Ⓐ Ⓑ Ⓒ Ⓓ
41. Ⓐ Ⓑ Ⓒ Ⓓ
42. Ⓐ Ⓑ Ⓒ Ⓓ
43. Ⓐ Ⓑ Ⓒ Ⓓ
44. Ⓐ Ⓑ Ⓒ Ⓓ
45. Ⓐ Ⓑ Ⓒ Ⓓ
46. Ⓐ Ⓑ Ⓒ Ⓓ
47. Ⓐ Ⓑ Ⓒ Ⓓ
48. Ⓐ Ⓑ Ⓒ Ⓓ
49. Ⓐ Ⓑ Ⓒ Ⓓ
50. Ⓐ Ⓑ Ⓒ Ⓓ
51. Ⓐ Ⓑ Ⓒ Ⓓ
52. Ⓐ Ⓑ Ⓒ Ⓓ
53. Ⓐ Ⓑ Ⓒ Ⓓ
54. Ⓐ Ⓑ Ⓒ Ⓓ
55. Ⓐ Ⓑ Ⓒ Ⓓ
56. Ⓐ Ⓑ Ⓒ Ⓓ
57. Ⓐ Ⓑ Ⓒ Ⓓ
58. Ⓐ Ⓑ Ⓒ Ⓓ
59. Ⓐ Ⓑ Ⓒ Ⓓ
60. Ⓐ Ⓑ Ⓒ Ⓓ

61. Ⓐ Ⓑ Ⓒ Ⓓ
62. Ⓐ Ⓑ Ⓒ Ⓓ
63. Ⓐ Ⓑ Ⓒ Ⓓ
64. Ⓐ Ⓑ Ⓒ Ⓓ
65. Ⓐ Ⓑ Ⓒ Ⓓ
66. Ⓐ Ⓑ Ⓒ Ⓓ
67. Ⓐ Ⓑ Ⓒ Ⓓ
68. Ⓐ Ⓑ Ⓒ Ⓓ
69. Ⓐ Ⓑ Ⓒ Ⓓ
70. Ⓐ Ⓑ Ⓒ Ⓓ
71. Ⓐ Ⓑ Ⓒ Ⓓ
72. Ⓐ Ⓑ Ⓒ Ⓓ
73. Ⓐ Ⓑ Ⓒ Ⓓ
74. Ⓐ Ⓑ Ⓒ Ⓓ
75. Ⓐ Ⓑ Ⓒ Ⓓ
76. Ⓐ Ⓑ Ⓒ Ⓓ
77. Ⓐ Ⓑ Ⓒ Ⓓ
78. Ⓐ Ⓑ Ⓒ Ⓓ
79. Ⓐ Ⓑ Ⓒ Ⓓ
80. Ⓐ Ⓑ Ⓒ Ⓓ
81. Ⓐ Ⓑ Ⓒ Ⓓ
82. Ⓐ Ⓑ Ⓒ Ⓓ
83. Ⓐ Ⓑ Ⓒ Ⓓ
84. Ⓐ Ⓑ Ⓒ Ⓓ
85. Ⓐ Ⓑ Ⓒ Ⓓ
86. Ⓐ Ⓑ Ⓒ Ⓓ
87. Ⓐ Ⓑ Ⓒ Ⓓ
88. Ⓐ Ⓑ Ⓒ Ⓓ
89. Ⓐ Ⓑ Ⓒ Ⓓ
90. Ⓐ Ⓑ Ⓒ Ⓓ

91. Ⓐ Ⓑ Ⓒ Ⓓ
92. Ⓐ Ⓑ Ⓒ Ⓓ
93. Ⓐ Ⓑ Ⓒ Ⓓ
94. Ⓐ Ⓑ Ⓒ Ⓓ
95. Ⓐ Ⓑ Ⓒ Ⓓ
96. Ⓐ Ⓑ Ⓒ Ⓓ
97. Ⓐ Ⓑ Ⓒ Ⓓ
98. Ⓐ Ⓑ Ⓒ Ⓓ
99. Ⓐ Ⓑ Ⓒ Ⓓ
100. Ⓐ Ⓑ Ⓒ Ⓓ
101. Ⓐ Ⓑ Ⓒ Ⓓ
102. Ⓐ Ⓑ Ⓒ Ⓓ
103. Ⓐ Ⓑ Ⓒ Ⓓ
104. Ⓐ Ⓑ Ⓒ Ⓓ
105. Ⓐ Ⓑ Ⓒ Ⓓ
106. Ⓐ Ⓑ Ⓒ Ⓓ
107. Ⓐ Ⓑ Ⓒ Ⓓ
108. Ⓐ Ⓑ Ⓒ Ⓓ
109. Ⓐ Ⓑ Ⓒ Ⓓ
110. Ⓐ Ⓑ Ⓒ Ⓓ
111. Ⓐ Ⓑ Ⓒ Ⓓ
112. Ⓐ Ⓑ Ⓒ Ⓓ
113. Ⓐ Ⓑ Ⓒ Ⓓ
114. Ⓐ Ⓑ Ⓒ Ⓓ
115. Ⓐ Ⓑ Ⓒ Ⓓ
116. Ⓐ Ⓑ Ⓒ Ⓓ
117. Ⓐ Ⓑ Ⓒ Ⓓ
118. Ⓐ Ⓑ Ⓒ Ⓓ
119. Ⓐ Ⓑ Ⓒ Ⓓ
120. Ⓐ Ⓑ Ⓒ Ⓓ

Time: 60 MINUTES

Directions: In each of the following questions, you will find three initial terms and, in parentheses, four answer options designated *a*, *b*, *c*, and *d*. You are to select from the four answer options the one that *best* completes the analogy with the three initial terms. To record your answers, use the answer sheet provided.

1. POLAND : POLISH :: (*a.* Holland, *b.* Dublin, *c.* Denmark, *d.* Dansk) : DANISH

2. UNION : (*a.* green, *b.* brown, *c.* blue, *d.* white) :: CONFEDERACY : GRAY

3. ARTICLE : (*a.* preposition, *b.* conjunction, *c.* adjective, *d.* verb) :: THE : AND

4. SAFETY : 2 :: TOUCHDOWN : (*a.* 2, *b.* 4, *c.* 6, *d.* 8)

5. CIRCLE : ELLIPSE :: SQUARE : (*a.* triangle, *b.* rectangle, *c.* pentagon, *d.* hexagon)

6. BIRD : (*a.* nest, *b.* worm, *c.* wings, *d.* fly) :: GENIE : MAGIC CARPET

7. FOXHOLE : (*a.* foxes, *b.* mortar, *c.* discovery, *d.* earthquakes) :: RAINCOAT : RAIN

8. FOOLISH : OWL :: (*a.* timid, *b.* large, *c.* wise, *d.* temperamental) : LION

9. SINBAD : (*a.* sailor, *b.* squire, *c.* sinner, *d.* poet) :: ARTHUR : KING

10. SOLOMON : WISE :: NERO : (*a.* stupid, *b.* bold, *c.* just, *d.* cruel)

11. GRAPE : VINE :: RUBBER : (*a.* tree, *b.* conifer, *c.* root, *d.* leaf)

12. (*a.* Georgia, *b.* Massachusetts, *c.* New Jersey, *d.* Ohio) : MIDDLE ATLANTIC :: VERMONT : NEW ENGLAND

13. BALD : HAIR :: ALBINO : (*a.* height, *b.* pain, *c.* sight, *d.* pigment)

14. BOW : (*a.* arrow, *b.* curtsey, *c.* stern, *d.* fore) :: FRONT : REAR

15. MONOGYNY : POLYGYNY :: ONE : (*a.* none, *b.* two, *c.* eight, *d.* many)

16. BEAMER : BINGHAM :: BURNETT : (*a.* Banks, *b.* Tibbets, *c.* Glick, *d.* Sullivan)

17. (*a.* secret codes, *b.* inscriptions on church vaults, *c.* science fiction, *d.* religious rituals) : CRYPTOGRAPHY :: DICTIONARIES : LEXICOGRAPHY

18. $E = mc^2$: EINSTEIN :: $C^2 = A^2 + B^2$: (*a.* Bernoulli, *b.* Cauchy, *c.* Descartes, *d.* Pythagoras)

19. GREEK : GREEK :: ROMAN : (*a.* Indo-European, *b.* Latin, *c.* Mediterranean, *d.* Romanish)

20. (*a.* Jesus, *b.* hell, *c.* heaven, *d.* Satan) : CHRISTIANITY :: NIRVANA : BUDDHISM

21. U.S. CALENDAR : U.S. FISCAL CALENDAR :: JANUARY : (*a.* December, *b.* March, *c.* October, *d.* September)

22. PHOTOMETER : (*a.* light, *b.* distance, *c.* magnetism, *d.* velocity) :: AUDIOMETER : SOUND

23. (*a.* believable, *b.* wrong, *c.* fanciful, *d.* humorous) : INCREDIBLE :: AUGMENT : DIMINISH

24. INFINITIVE : (*a.* having eaten, *b.* to sleep, *c.* has tried, *d.* to the store) :: PARTICIPLE : WALKING

25. MARX : COMMUNISM :: (*a.* Hamilton, *b.* Lenin, *c.* Smith, *d.* Davis) : CAPITALISM

26. (*a.* Iambic, *b.* Doric, *c.* Spartan, *d.* Grecian) : CORINTHIAN :: SONATA : CONCERTO

27. SOCCER : BALL :: (*a.* cricket, *b.* rugby, *c.* hockey, *d.* lacrosse) : PUCK

28. (*a.* sheep, *b.* plasma, *c.* vulture, *d.* harass) : BLOOD :: DOG : HOUND

29. (*a.* hawk, *b.* owl, *c.* bluejay, *d.* ostrich) : NOCTURNAL :: ROBIN : DIURNAL

30. PHLEGM : PHLEGMATIC :: BILE : (*a.* bilious, *b.* billiard, *c.* binding, *d.* bilabial)

31. HEAVY-HANDED : (*a.* uncoordinated, *b.* tactless, *c.* strong, *d.* coordinated) :: HEAVY-FOOTED : PLODDING

32. PALEFACE : WHITE :: BLUENOSE : (*a.* frigid, *b.* tough, *c.* unkind, *d.* puritanical)

33. PROTON : NEUTRON :: POSITIVE : (*a.* negative, *b.* uncharged, *c.* positive, *d.* nucleonic)

34. SPHINX : (*a.* pterodactyl, *b.* dodo, *c.* vulture, *d.* phoenix) :: LION : EAGLE

35. ANDAMAN : ACEH :: SRI LANKA : (*a.* Bali, *b.* Phuket, *c.* Fiji, *d.* Guam)

36. RADIUS : 4 :: DIAMETER : (*a.* 16, *b.* 8, *c.* 87π, *d.* 167π)

37. PIKE : (*a.* sturgeon, *b.* lion, *c.* whale, *d.* buffalo) :: COW : PIG

38. WASSERMANN : (*a.* heart disease, *b.* diabetes, *c.* syphilis, *d.* lung cancer) :: PAPANICOLAOU : CERVICAL CANCER

39. COMPLEMENTARY : SUPPLEMENTARY :: (*a.* 0, *b.* 45, *c.* 90, *d.* 360) : 180

40. E.G. : FOR EXAMPLE :: VIZ. : (*a.* namely, *b.* except for, *c.* according to, *d.* generally)

41. GRAPE : WINE :: (*a.* apple, *b.* potato, *c.* pomegranate, *d.* malt) : VODKA

42. RISING : FALLING :: (*a.* bull, *b.* bird, *c.* sparrow, *d.* antelope) : BEAR

43. XX : FEMALE :: (*a.* XY, *b.* YY, *c.* XZ, *d.* ZZ) : MALE

44. RESPECT : (*a.* love, *b.* protect, *c.* revere, *d.* obey) :: DISLIKE : HATE

45. PARLIAMENT : LORDS :: (*a.* House of Representatives, *b.* Congress, *c.* White House, *d.* Supreme Court) : SENATE

46. (*a.* parsing, *b.* gender, *c.* case, *d.* declension) : NOUN :: CONJUGATION : VERB

47. MC : MD :: MMCC : (*a.* MCM, *b.* MGM, *c.* MDM, *d.* MMM)

48. (*a.* dour, *b.* caustic, *c.* sweet, *d.* mild) : ACRID :: BITTER : ACRIMONIOUS

49. PORCINE : (*a.* porcupine, *b.* goat, *c.* dog, *d.* pig) :: FELINE : CAT

50. TIPPECANOE : AND TYLER TOO :: FIFTY-FOUR FORTY : (*a.* forever, *b.* or fight, *c.* and forward, *d.* to fortune)

51. IMPEACH : (*a.* prove the guilt of, *b.* overturn, *c.* acquit, *d.* accuse) :: CONVICT : FIND GUILTY

52. CITY OF SEVEN HILLS : ROME :: CITY OF GOD : (*a.* heaven, *b.* Jerusalem, *c.* Bethlehem, *d.* Jericho)

53. WOOD : PAPER :: LATEX : (*a.* cotton, *b.* plastic, *c.* rayon, *d.* rubber)

54. TEXTILE : RAYON :: GEM : (*a.* sapphire, *b.* diamond, *c.* spinel, *d.* quartz)

55. SIAM : (*a.* Mongolia, *b.* China, *c.* Thailand, *d.* Nepal) :: PERSIA : IRAN

56. HABEAS CORPUS : LAW :: EXEUNT OMNES : (*a.* medicine, *b.* drama, *c.* law, *d.* political theory)

57. PENTHOUSE APARTMENT : TOP FLOOR :: DUPLEX APARTMENT : (*a.* two rooms, *b.* two floors, *c.* two bedrooms, *d.* two persons)

58. XENOPHOBIA : (*a.* foreigners, *b.* death, *c.* insanity, *d.* live burial) :: CLAUSTROPHOBIA : CONFINED PLACES

59. LOCKJAW : TETANUS :: HYDROPHOBIA : (*a.* encephalitis, *b.* malaria, *c.* syphilis, *d.* rabies)

60. ENGLISH : CANADA :: (*a.* Italian, *b.* Portuguese, *c.* Brazilian, *d.* French) : BRAZIL

61. MITIGATE : ASSUAGE :: MODERATE : (*a.* lessen, *b.* make worse, *c.* disprove, *d.* approve)

62. $1^0 : 1^{10} :: 10^0 :$ (*a.* 10^0, *b.* 10^1, *c.* 10^2, *d.* 10^{10})

63. PUSILLANIMOUS : AUDACIOUS :: (*a.* brave, *b.* purposive, *c.* cowardly,
    d. evanescent) : BOLD

64. HANNIBAL : (*a.* Theseus, *b.* Scipio, *c.* Cicero, *d.* Marcion) :: NAPOLEON : WELLINGTON

65. EPITOME : (*a.* monologue, *b.* prevarication, *c.* summary, *d.* diatribe) :: PREFACE : PROLOGUE

66. (*a.* wave, *b.* radian, *c.* alpha, *d.* roentgen) : RADIATION :: MINUTE : TIME

67. VERACIOUS : (*a.* repeated, *b.* horizontal, *c.* diagonal, *d.* truthful) :: CONTINUAL : INCESSANT

68. SOLAR : SUN :: (*a.* lunar, *b.* diurnal, *c.* stellar, *d.* nocturnal) : MOON

69. LINCOLN STEFFENS : POLITICAL MACHINES :: UPTON SINCLAIR : (*a.* meat-packing
    industry, *b.* financial speculators, *c.* railroad magnates, *d.* patent medicine quacks)

70. FAMILY : HOMINIDAE :: (*a.* sapiens, *b.* species, *c.* genus, *d.* class) : HOMO

71. OVERWEENING : (*a.* conceited, *b.* modest, *c.* spoiled, *d.* underprotected) :: BLUNT : SHARP

72. HEARSAY : GOSSIP :: GAINSAY : (*a.* oppose, *b.* protect, *c.* lose, *d.* take)

73. (*a.* thin, *b.* analogy, *c.* happy, *d.* fat) : FIAT :: SMILE : SIMILE

74. ROUNDHEAD : SHORT HAIR :: (*a.* Tory, *b.* Whig, *c.* Royalist, *d.* Cavalier) : LONG HAIR

75. EUGENICS : HEREDITY :: (*a.* euthanasia, *b.* euthenics, *c.* mnemonics,
    d. dialectics) : ENVIRONMENT

76. THERMO : (*a.* cryo, *b.* iso, *c.* crypto, *d.* paleo) :: HOT : COLD

77. (*a.* North Carolina, *b.* South Carolina, *c.* Georgia, *d.* Florida) : OGLETHORPE ::
    PENNSYLVANIA : PENN

78. BANEFUL : (*a.* baleful, *b.* salutary, *c.* promiscuous, *d.* remorseful) :: PERSONABLE :
    HANDSOME

79. WERTHEIMER : GESTALT :: (*a.* Watson, *b.* Köhler, *c.* Koffka, *d.* Piaget) : BEHAVIORIST

80. (*a.* depilate, *b.* dampen, *c.* derogate, *d.* desiccate) : DRY :: MOISTEN : WET

81. GLUCOSE : (*a.* comatose, *b.* malactose, *c.* lactose, *d.* adipose) :: SUCROSE : FRUCTOSE

82. ABLE : MELBA :: (*a.* colt, *b.* peach, *c.* era, *d.* willing) : MARE

83. (*a.* Mars, *b.* Jupiter, *c.* Venus, *d.* Pluto) : PROSERPINA :: ZEUS : HERA

84. FLEET STREET : (*a.* press, *b.* police, *c.* amusement, *d.* high fashion) :: DOWNING
    STREET : GOVERNMENT

85. ARTUR RUBINSTEIN : PIANO :: ISAAC STERN : (*a.* piano, *b.* violin, *c.* trumpet, *d.* oboe)

86. DURKHEIM : (*a.* Homocide, *b.* Matricide, *c.* Suicide, *d.* Genocide) :: BECKER : OUTSIDERS

87. JOHN WESLEY : METHODIST :: MARY BAKER EDDY : (*a.* Presbyterian, *b.* Baha'i,
    c. Jehovah's Witness, *d.* Christian Science)

88. BACH : BAROQUE :: GRIEG : (*a.* classical, *b.* modern, *c.* romantic, *d.* medieval)

89. (*a.* Husserl, *b.* Heidegger, *c.* Comte, *d.* Camus) : POSITIVISM :: SARTRE : EXISTENTIALISM

90. F# : Gb :: B : (*a.* C_b, *b.* A_b, *c.* G#, *d.* G_b)

91. SECOND : THIRD :: (*a.* clergy, *b.* king, *c.* commoners, *d.* nobility) : BOURGEOISIE

92. ALEXANDER : GREAT :: JULIAN : (*a.* Ingenious, *b.* Meek, *c.* Bold, *d.* Apostate)

93. (*a.* Helen, *b.* Jezebel, *c.* Una, *d.* Archimago) : DUESSA :: GOOD : EVIL

94. D : R × T :: (*a.* A, *b.* C, *c.* F, *d.* H) : M × A

95. PURLOINED : (*a.* Melville, *b.* Doyle, *c.* Poe, *d.* Conrad) :: SCARLET : HAWTHORNE

96. PROPHASE : METAPHASE :: ANAPHASE : (*a.* meiophase, *b.* telophase, *c.* mitophase,
    d. protophase)

97. NEWBERY : (*a.* Wohlenberg, *b.* Caldecott, *c.* Pulitzer, *d.* Thompsen) :: STORY : ARTWORK

98. COUNTESS AURELIA : THE MADWOMAN OF CHAILLOT :: (*a.* Lear, *b.* Othello, *c.* Antonio,
    d. Iago) : THE MERCHANT OF VENICE

99. PICASSO : GUERNICA :: (*a.* Manet, *b.* Raphael, *c.* David, *d.* Leger) : LUNCHEON ON
    THE GRASS

100. RACINE : MOLIÈRE :: SOPHOCLES : (*a.* Zeno, *b.* Aristophanes, *c.* Plato, *d.* Aristotle)

101. (*a.* Queen Victoria, *b.* Queen Virginia, *c.* Queen Elizabeth, *d.* Queen Mary) : VIRGINIA ::
     KING GEORGE : GEORGIA

102. MITOSIS : MEIOSIS :: (*a.* 1, *b.* 2, *c.* 4, *d.* 8) : 4

103. DAGGER : STAR :: (*a.* rune, *b.* allograph, *c.* knife, *d.* obelisk) : ASTERISK

104. MISER : (*a.* chary, *b.* mercurial, *c.* acquisitive, *d.* munificent) :: GLUTTON : ABSTEMIOUS

105. (*a.* pork, *b.* sweet, *c.* appetizer, *d.* vegetable) : SWEETMEAT :: FRUIT : BREADFRUIT

106. $2\pi r^2 : \pi(2r)^2$ :: LW : (*a.* (1/2)LW, *b.* LW, *c.* 2LW, *d.* 4LW)

107. (*a.* hatred, *b.* naiveté, *c.* envy, *d.* sickness) : SORROW :: GREEN : BLUE

108. MOHS : HARDNESS :: RICHTER : (*a.* magnitude, *b.* earthquake, *c.* quality, *d.* extremity)

109. FROGS : SEAGULL :: (*a.* Shakespeare, *b.* Marlowe, *c.* Wilde, *d.* Aristophanes) : CHEKHOV

110. INDIA : PAKISTAN :: PAKISTAN : (*a.* Kashmir, *b.* Bangladesh, *c.* Nepal, *d.* Sri Lanka)

111. ORGAN : ORGANELLE :: LIVER : (*a.* vacuole, *b.* pancreas, *c.* kidney, *d.* cell)

112. MASS AND ENERGY : (*a.* Bernoulli, *b.* Newton, *c.* Gauss, *d.* Einstein) :: VOLUME AND DISPLACEMENT : ARCHIMEDES

113. DOGS : PEAS :: PAVLOV : (*a.* Darwin, *b.* Gauss, *c.* Curie, *d.* Mendel)

114. (*a.* King, *b.* Martha, *c.* Reverend, *d.* Priest) : CARVER :: MARTIN LUTHER : GEORGE WASHINGTON

115. SESAME SEEDS : TAHINI :: PEANUTS : (*a.* roots, *b.* shell, *c.* peanut butter, *d.* oil)

116. BASS : (*a.* clarinet, *b.* viola, *c.* cello, *d.* trumpet) :: TREBLE : FLUTE

117. MAL : BEN :: ANTI : (*a.* un, *b.* inter, *c.* pro, *d.* pre)

118. (*a.* meat packing, *b.* clear cutting, *c.* poaching, *d.* iron mining) : PESTICIDES :: THE JUNGLE : SILENT SPRING

119. HANUKKAH : DIVALI :: JUDAISM : (*a.* Buddhism, *b.* Hinduism, *c.* Zoroastrianism, *d.* Islam)

120. SQUARE ROOT : SQUARE :: (*a.* dividend, *b.* root, *c.* log, *d.* integral) : DERIVATIVE

ANSWER KEY
Practice Test 4

1.	C	31.	B	61.	A	91.	D
2.	C	32.	D	62.	A	92.	D
3.	B	33.	B	63.	C	93.	C
4.	C	34.	D	64.	B	94.	C
5.	B	35.	B	65.	C	95.	C
6.	C	36.	B	66.	D	96.	B
7.	B	37.	A	67.	D	97.	B
8.	A	38.	C	68.	A	98.	C
9.	A	39.	C	69.	A	99.	A
10.	D	40.	A	70.	C	100.	B
11.	A	41.	B	71.	B	101.	C
12.	C	42.	A	72.	A	102.	B
13.	D	43.	A	73.	D	103.	D
14.	C	44.	C	74.	D	104.	D
15.	D	45.	B	75.	B	105.	B
16.	C	46.	D	76.	A	106.	C
17.	A	47.	D	77.	C	107.	C
18.	D	48.	B	78.	A	108.	A
19.	B	49.	D	79.	A	109.	D
20.	C	50.	B	80.	D	110.	B
21.	C	51.	D	81.	C	111.	A
22.	A	52.	A	82.	C	112.	D
23.	A	53.	D	83.	D	113.	D
24.	B	54.	C	84.	A	114.	A
25.	C	55.	C	85.	B	115.	C
26.	B	56.	B	86.	C	116.	C
27.	C	57.	B	87.	D	117.	C
28.	A	58.	A	88.	C	118.	A
29.	B	59.	D	89.	C	119.	B
30.	A	60.	B	90.	A	120.	D

ANSWER EXPLANATIONS FOR PRACTICE TEST 4

> In the following, explanations concerning the correct responses are in roman font. Explanations regarding distracters (incorrect responses) that are not self-explaining or could be misinterpreted are in italics in order to highlight the explanations of the answers that are correct.

1. POLAND : POLISH :: (*a.* Holland, *b.* Dublin, ***c.* Denmark**, *d.* Dansk) : DANISH

   (c) A Polish person is from Poland; a Danish person is from Denmark.

2. UNION : (*a.* green, *b.* brown, ***c.* blue**, *d.* white) :: CONFEDERACY : GRAY

   (c) During the Civil War, Union soldiers wore blue uniforms and soldiers of the Confederacy wore gray uniforms.

3. ARTICLE : (*a.* preposition, ***b.* conjunction**, *c.* adjective, *d.* verb) :: THE : AND

   (b) The is an article; and is a conjunction. A conjunction is a linguistic form that connects two complete clauses.

4. SAFETY : 2 :: TOUCHDOWN : (*a.* 2, *b.* 4, ***c.* 6**, *d.* 8)

   (c) In football, a safety is worth 2 points and a touchdown is worth 6 points.

5. CIRCLE : ELLIPSE :: SQUARE : (*a.* triangle, ***b.* rectangle**, *c.* pentagon, *d.* hexagon)

   (b) Both a circle and an ellipse are closed curves. Both a square and a rectangle are polygons with four sides.

6. BIRD : (*a.* nest, *b.* worm, ***c.* wings**, *d.* fly) :: GENIE : MAGIC CARPET

   (c) A bird flies by means of its wings. A genie flies by means of a magic carpet.

7. FOXHOLE : (*a.* foxes, ***b.* mortar**, *c.* discovery, *d.* earthquakes) :: RAINCOAT : RAIN

   (b) A foxhole provides protection from mortar rounds. A raincoat provides protection from rain.

8. FOOLISH : OWL :: (***a.* timid**, *b.* large, *c.* wise, *d.* temperamental) : LION

   (a) An owl is reputed to be wise, which is the opposite of foolish. A lion is reputed to be bold, which is the opposite of timid.

9. SINBAD : (***a.* sailor**, *b.* squire, *c.* sinner, *d.* poet) :: ARTHUR : KING

   (a) Sinbad was a sailor, Arthur a king. Sinbad was a sailor whose stories are told in *The Book of One Thousand and One Nights*; King Arthur was a legendary king of the Britons.

10. SOLOMON : WISE :: NERO : (*a.* stupid, *b.* bold, *c.* just, ***d.* cruel**)

    (d) Solomon was wise; Nero was cruel.

11. GRAPE : VINE :: RUBBER : (***a.* tree**, *b.* conifer, *c.* root, *d.* leaf)

    (a) Grapes come from a vine; rubber comes from a tree.

12. (*a.* Georgia, *b.* Massachusetts, ***c.* New Jersey**, *d.* Ohio) : MIDDLE ATLANTIC :: VERMONT : NEW ENGLAND

    (c) New Jersey is a Middle Atlantic state. Vermont is a New England state. *Massachusetts is a New England state, Georgia a Southern state, and Ohio a Midwestern state.*

13. BALD : HAIR :: ALBINO : (*a.* height, *b.* pain, *c.* sight, ***d.* pigment**)

(d) A bald person lacks hair. An albino lacks pigment.

14. BOW : (*a.* arrow, *b.* curtsey, ***c.* stern**, *d.* fore) :: FRONT : REAR

(c) The bow is the front of a ship; the stern is the rear.

15. MONOGYNY : POLYGYNY :: ONE : (*a.* none, *b.* two, *c.* eight, ***d.* many**)

(d) Monogyny is marriage to one spouse. Polygyny is marriage to many spouses.

16. BEAMER : BINGHAM :: BURNETT : (*a.* Banks, *b.* Tibbets, ***c.* Glick**, *d.* Sullivan)

(c) Todd Beamer, Mark Bingham, Thomas Burnett, and Jeremy Glick were the four heroes who regained control of United Flight 93 on September 11th, giving their own lives to save those of others.

17. (***a.* secret codes**, *b.* inscriptions on church vaults, *c.* science fiction, *d.* religious rituals) : CRYPTOGRAPHY :: DICTIONARIES : LEXICOGRAPHY

(a) Cryptography is the art of writing secret codes. Lexicography is the art of writing dictionaries.

18. $E = mc^2$: EINSTEIN :: $C^2 = A^2 + B^2$: (*a.* Bernoulli, *b.* Cauchy, *c.* Descartes, ***d.* Pythagoras**)

(d) The equation $E = mc^2$ is attributable to Einstein. The equation $C^2 = A^2 + B^2$ is attributable to Pythagoras. *Bernoulli applied mathematics to mechanics and is especially known for the Bernoulli principle. Descartes introduced the use of coordinates to locate a point in one or two dimensions (Cartesian coordinate system). Cauchy (a French mathematician) was a pioneer in analysis and the theory of substitution of groups.*

19. GREEK : GREEK :: ROMAN : (*a.* Indo-European, ***b.* Latin**, *c.* Mediterranean, *d.* Romansh)

(b) The ancient Greeks spoke Greek. The ancient Romans spoke Latin.

20. (*a.* Jesus, *b.* Hell, ***c.* Heaven**, *d.* Satan) : CHRISTIANITY :: NIRVANA : BUDDHISM

(c) The concept of heaven in Christianity serves a function similar to that of nirvana in Buddhism.

21. U.S. CALENDAR : U.S. FISCAL CALENDAR :: JANUARY : (*a.* December, *b.* March, ***c.* October**, *d.* September)

(c) The first month of the U.S. calendar is January. The first month of the U.S. fiscal calendar is October.

22. PHOTOMETER : (***a.* light**, *b.* distance, *c.* magnetism, *d.* velocity) :: AUDIOMETER : SOUND

(a) A photometer is used to measure light; an audiometer is used to measure sound.

23. (***a.* believable**, *b.* wrong, *c.* fanciful, *d.* humorous) : INCREDIBLE :: AUGMENT : DIMINISH

(a) Incredible and believable are antonyms, as are augment and diminish.

24. INFINITIVE : (*a.* having eaten, ***b.* to sleep**, *c.* has tried, *d.* to the store) :: PARTICIPLE : WALKING

(b) To sleep is an infinitive. Walking is a participle.

25. MARX : COMMUNISM :: (*a.* Hamilton, *b.* Lenin, ***c.* Smith**, *d.* Davis) : CAPITALISM

(c) Karl Marx is famous for his writing on communism. Adam Smith is famous for his writing on capitalism. *Hamilton was the first Secretary of Treasury in the United States as well as an economist and philosopher. Lenin was the first head of the Soviet Socialist Republic. Davis is a distracter term.*

26. (*a.* Iambic, ***b.* Doric**, *c.* Spartan, *d.* Grecian) : CORINTHIAN :: SONATA : CONCERTO

(b) Doric and Corinthian are both types of columns. A sonata and a concerto are both types of musical compositions. Doric refers to the Ancient Greeks of Doris or to a dialect of Ancient Greek that is spoken in the Peloponnesus. Corinthian refers to somebody from the city of Corinth or to somebody who likes to seek pleasure. A sonata is a composition for one or two instruments that typically has three or four movements. A concerto is a composition for an entire orchestra and one or more soloists. *Iamb is a metrical foot that consists of one unstressed and one stressed syllable. Grecian refers to something from Greece. Spartan refers to something from the Greek city of Sparta.*

27. SOCCER : BALL :: (*a.* cricket, *b.* rugby, ***c.* hockey**, *d.* lacrosse) : PUCK

(c) Soccer is played with a ball, hockey with a puck.

28. (***a.* sheep**, *b.* plasma, *c.* vulture, *d.* harass) : BLOOD :: DOG : HOUND

(a) A sheep dog and a bloodhound are both types of dogs.

29. (*a.* hawk, ***b.* owl**, *c.* bluejay, *d.* ostrich) : NOCTURNAL :: ROBIN : DIURNAL

(b) An owl is a nocturnal bird; a robin is a diurnal bird.

30. PHLEGM : PHLEGMATIC :: BILE : (***a.* bilious**, *b.* billiard, *c.* binding, *d.* bilabial)

(a) The word phlegmatic derives from phlegm. The word bilious derives from bile.

31. HEAVY-HANDED : (*a.* uncoordinated, ***b.* tactless**, *c.* strong, *d.* coordinated) :: HEAVY-FOOTED : PLODDING

(b) Someone who is heavy-handed is tactless. Someone who is heavy-footed is plodding.

32. PALEFACE : WHITE :: BLUENOSE : (*a.* frigid, *b.* tough, *c.* unkind, ***d.* puritanical**)

(d) A paleface is a white person. A bluenose is puritanical.

33. PROTON : NEUTRON :: POSITIVE : (*a.* negative, ***b.* uncharged**, *c.* positive, *d.* nucleonic)

(b) A proton has a positive electrical charge. A neutron is uncharged.

34. SPHINX : (*a.* pterodactyl, *b.* dodo, *c.* vulture, ***d.* phoenix**) :: LION : EAGLE

(d) A sphinx and a phoenix are both mythological animals. A lion and an eagle are both real animals. The sphinx is a mythical Egyptian creature that has a lion's body and a man's head. A phoenix is a mythical bird that burned itself and arose from the ashes to live again. *A pterodactyl is a winged flying reptile that is extinct. A dodo is an extinct flightless bird from Mauritius.*

35. ANDAMAN : ACEH :: SRI LANKA : (*a.* Bali, ***b.* Phuket**, *c.* Fiji, *d.* Guam)

(b) The Andaman Islands, Aceh, Sri Lanka, and Phuket were regions that were affected by the Indian Ocean Tsunami on December 26, 2004.

36. RADIUS : 4 :: DIAMETER : (*a.* 16, ***b.* 8**, *c.* 87π, *d.* 167π)

(b) If the radius of a circle is 4, the circle's diameter is 8.

37. PIKE : (***a.* sturgeon**, *b.* lion, *c.* whale, *d.* buffalo) :: COW : PIG

(a) A pike and a sturgeon are both fish. A cow and a pig are both mammals.

38. WASSERMANN : (*a.* heart disease, *b.* diabetes, ***c.* syphilis**, *d.* lung cancer) :: PAPANICOLAOU : CERVICAL CANCER

(c) The Wassermann test is for syphilis. The Papanicolaou test (commonly, Pap smear) is for cervical cancer.

39. COMPLEMENTARY : SUPPLEMENTARY :: (*a.* 0, *b.* 45, ***c.* 90**, *d.* 360) : 180

   (c) Complementary angles sum to 90 degrees. Supplementary angles sum to 180 degrees.

40. E.G. : FOR EXAMPLE :: VIZ. : (***a.* namely**, *b.* except for, *c.* according to, *d.* generally)

   (a) The abbreviation *e.g.* means "for example"; viz. means "namely." *e.g.* is the abbreviation for *exempli gratia* (for example); viz. is the abbreviation for *videlicet* (namely).

41. GRAPE : WINE :: (*a.* apple, ***b.* potato**, *c.* pomegranate, *d.* malt) : VODKA

   (b) Grapes are used to make wine, potatoes to make vodka.

42. RISING : FALLING :: (***a.* bull**, *b.* bird, *c.* sparrow, *d.* antelope) : BEAR

   (a) A rising market is a bull market. A falling market is a bear market.

43. XX : FEMALE :: (***a.* XY**, *b.* YY, *c.* XZ, *d.* ZZ) : MALE

   (a) A female is distinguished by an XX chromosome. A male is distinguished by an XY chromosome.

44. RESPECT : (*a.* love, *b.* protect, ***c.* revere**, *d.* obey) :: DISLIKE : HATE

   (c) To revere is to respect a great deal. To hate is to dislike a great deal.

45. PARLIAMENT : LORDS :: (*a.* House of Representatives, ***b.* Congress**, *c.* White House, *d.* Supreme Court) : SENATE

   (b) The House of Lords is the upper chamber of the British Parliament. The Senate is the upper chamber of the U.S. Congress.

46. (*a.* parsing, *b.* gender, *c.* case, ***d.* declension**) : NOUN :: CONJUGATION : VERB

   (d) Nouns may belong to a declension, verbs to a conjugation.

47. MC : MD :: MMCC : (*a.* MCM, *b.* MGM, *c.* MDM, ***d.* MMM**)

   (d) 1,100 is to 1,500 as 2,200 is to 3,000. In Roman numerals, I = 1, V = 5, X = 10, L = 50, C = 100, D = 500, M = 1,000.

48. (*a.* dour, ***b.* caustic**, *c.* sweet, *d.* mild) : ACRID :: BITTER : ACRIMONIOUS

   (b) Caustic, acrid, bitter, and acrimonious all mean the same thing.

49. PORCINE : (*a.* porcupine, *b.* goat, *c.* dog, ***d.* pig**) :: FELINE : CAT

   (d) Porcine means piglike. Feline means catlike. Goatlike is hircine. Doglike is canine. A porcupine is a rodent.

50. TIPPECANOE : AND TYLER TOO :: FIFTY-FOUR FORTY : (*a.* forever, ***b.* or fight**, *c.* and forward, *d.* to fortune)

   (b) "Tippecanoe and Tyler too" and "Fifty-four forty or fight" were both slogans in the American past. The former was the Whig presidential campaign slogan in 1840. The latter relates to the Oregon boundary dispute.

51. IMPEACH : (*a.* prove the guilt of, *b.* overturn, *c.* acquit, ***d.* accuse**) :: CONVICT : FIND GUILTY

   (d) To impeach is to accuse. To convict is to find guilty. In the United States, the House of Representatives can impeach a person; the Senate tries the accused.

52. CITY OF SEVEN HILLS : ROME :: CITY OF GOD : (***a.* heaven**, *b.* Jerusalem, *c.* Bethlehem, *d.* Jericho)

   (a) Rome is the City of Seven Hills. Heaven is the City of God. The seven hills of Rome are called Palatine, Capitoline, Quirinal, Viminal, Esquiline, Caelian, and Aventine.

53. WOOD : PAPER :: LATEX : (*a.* cotton, *b.* plastic, *c.* rayon, ***d.* rubber**)

(d) Wood is used to make paper. Latex is used to make rubber.

54. TEXTILE : RAYON :: GEM : (*a.* sapphire, *b.* diamond, ***c.* spinel**, *d.* quartz)

(c) Rayon is a synthetic textile. Spinel is a synthetic gem.

55. SIAM : (*a.* Mongolia, *b.* China, ***c.* Thailand**, *d.* Nepal) :: PERSIA : IRAN

(c) Siam is the former name of Thailand. Persia is the former name of Iran. Nepal was once the Kingdom of Mustang.

56. HABEAS CORPUS : LAW :: EXEUNT OMNES : (*a.* medicine, ***b.* drama**, *c.* law, *d.* political theory)

(b) *Habeas corpus* is an expression used in law. *Exeunt omnes* is an expression used in drama. *Habeas corpus* refers to a writ needed to bring a party before court. *Exeunt omnes* means that all characters exit the stage.

57. PENTHOUSE APARTMENT : TOP FLOOR :: DUPLEX APARTMENT : (*a.* two rooms, ***b.* two floors**, *c.* two bedrooms, *d.* two persons)

(b) A penthouse apartment is on the top floor. A duplex apartment has two floors.

58. XENOPHOBIA : (***a.* foreigners**, *b.* death, *c.* insanity, *d.* live burial) :: CLAUSTROPHOBIA : CONFINED PLACES

(a) Xenophobia is a fear of foreigners. Claustrophobia is a fear of confined places.

59. LOCKJAW : TETANUS :: HYDROPHOBIA : (*a.* encephalitis, *b.* malaria, *c.* syphilis, ***d.* rabies**)

(d) Tetanus is sometimes called lockjaw. Rabies is sometimes called hydrophobia.

60. ENGLISH : CANADA :: (*a.* Italian, ***b.* Portuguese**, *c.* Brazilian, *d.* French) : BRAZIL

(b) English is the most widely spoken language in Canada. Portuguese is the most widely spoken language in Brazil.

61. MITIGATE : ASSUAGE :: MODERATE : (***a.* lessen**, *b.* make worse, *c.* disprove, *d.* approve)

(a) Mitigate, assuage, moderate, and lessen can all be used interchangeably.

62. $1^0 : 1^{10} :: 10^0 :$ (***a.* 10^0**, *b.* 10^1, *c.* 10^2, *d.* 10^{10})

(a) 1 is to 1 as 1 is to 1. Any positive number to the 0 power = 1.

63. PUSILLANIMOUS : AUDACIOUS :: (*a.* brave, *b.* purposive, ***c.* cowardly**, *d.* evanescent) : BOLD

(c) Pusillanimous and cowardly are synonyms, as are audacious and bold.

64. HANNIBAL : (*a.* Theseus, ***b.* Scipio**, *c.* Cicero, *d.* Marcion) :: NAPOLEON : WELLINGTON

(b) Hannibal was defeated by Scipio in the Punic Wars. Napoleon was defeated by Wellington at the Battle of Waterloo. *Theseus was a king of Athens. Cicero was a Roman statesman and philosopher. Marcion was an early Christian theologian who was excommunicated by the Church at Rome.*

65. EPITOME : (*a.* monologue, *b.* prevarication, ***c.* summary**, *d.* diatribe) :: PREFACE : PROLOGUE

(c) An epitome is a summary. A preface is a prologue. *To prevaricate means to deviate from the truth. A monologue is a long speech by one person. A diatribe is a sharp denunciation.*

66. (*a.* wave, *b.* radian, *c.* alpha, ***d.* roentgen**) : RADIATION :: MINUTE : TIME

(d) A roentgen is a unit of radiation. A minute is a unit of time.

67. VERACIOUS : (*a.* repeated, *b.* horizontal, *c.* diagonal, ***d.* truthful**) :: CONTINUAL : INCESSANT

(d) Veracious means truthful. Continual means incessant.

68. SOLAR : SUN :: (***a. lunar***, *b.* diurnal, *c.* stellar, *d.* nocturnal) : MOON

(**a**) The word solar derives from Sol, the Roman god of the sun. The word lunar derives from Luna, the Roman goddess of the moon.

69. LINCOLN STEFFENS : POLITICAL MACHINES :: UPTON SINCLAIR : (***a.* meat-packing industry**, *b.* financial speculators, *c.* railroad magnates, *d.* patent medicine quacks)

(**a**) Lincoln Steffens was a muckraker who exposed political machines. Upton Sinclair was a muckraker who exposed the sordid conditions in the meat-packing industry in his novel *The Jungle*.

70. FAMILY : HOMINIDAE :: (*a.* sapiens, *b.* species, ***c. genus***, *d.* class) : HOMO

(**c**) Human beings are of family Hominidae and genus *Homo*.

71. OVERWEENING : (*a.* conceited, ***b. modest***, *c.* spoiled, *d.* underprotected) :: BLUNT : SHARP

(**b**) Overweening is the opposite of modest. Blunt is the opposite of sharp.

72. HEARSAY : GOSSIP :: GAINSAY : (***a. oppose***, *b.* protect, *c.* lose, *d.* take)

(**a**) Hearsay is gossip. To gainsay is to oppose.

73. (*a.* thin, *b.* analogy, *c.* happy, ***d. fat***) : FIAT :: SMILE : SIMILE

(**d**) Simile is smile with an *i* added to the interior of the word. Fiat is fat with an *i* added to the interior of the word.

74. ROUNDHEAD : SHORT HAIR :: (*a.* Tory, *b.* Whig, *c.* Royalist, ***d. Cavalier***) : LONG HAIR

(**d**) The Roundheads were known for their short hair. The Cavaliers were known for their long hair. Roundheads was a nickname for the supporters of the English Parliament during the English Civil War. Cavaliers were Royalist supporters during that war.

75. EUGENICS : HEREDITY :: (*a.* euthanasia, ***b. euthenics***, *c.* mnemonics, *d.* dialectics) : ENVIRONMENT

(**b**) Eugenics studies how to "improve" the human "race" through the manipulation of heredity. Euthenics studies how to do the same through the manipulation of the environment. *Euthanasia means "to kill someone painlessly." Mnemonics are techniques to improve memory. Dialectics involve reasoning by dialogue.*

76. THERMO : (***a. cryo***, *b.* iso, *c.* crypto, *d.* paleo) :: HOT : COLD

(**a**) Thermo- is a prefix meaning heat. Cryo- is a prefix meaning cold.

77. (*a.* North Carolina, *b.* South Carolina, ***c. Georgia***, *d.* Florida) : OGLETHORPE :: PENNSYLVANIA : PENN

(**c**) Oglethorpe founded Georgia. Penn founded Pennsylvania. *Ponce de Leon discovered Florida and gave it its name. South Carolina was named by King Charles II of England. North Carolina is not associated with a single founder.*

78. BANEFUL : (***a. baleful***, *b.* salutary, *c.* promiscuous, *d.* remorseful) :: PERSONABLE : HANDSOME

(**a**) *Baneful* means *baleful*. *Personable* means *handsome*.

79. WERTHEIMER : GESTALT :: (***a. Watson***, *b.* Köhler, *c.* Koffka, *d.* Piaget) : BEHAVIORIST

(**a**) Wertheimer was a leading psychologist in the Gestalt movement. Watson was a leading psychologist in the behaviorist movement. *Kurt Koffka was a Gestalt psychologist, as was Wolfgang Köhler. Jean Piaget was a famous developmental psychologist and genetic epistemologist.*

80. (*a*. depilate, *b*. dampen, *c*. derogate, ***d*. desiccate**) : DRY :: MOISTEN : WET

(d) To desiccate is to dry. To moisten is to wet.

81. GLUCOSE : (*a*. comatose, *b*. malactose, ***c*. lactose**, *d*. adipose) :: SUCROSE : FRUCTOSE

(c) Glucose, lactose, sucrose, and fructose are all sugars.

82. ABLE : MELBA :: (*a*. colt, *b*. peach, ***c*. era**, *d*. willing) : MARE

(c) Melba is able spelled backward, with an added initial *m*. Mare is era spelled backward, with an added initial *m*.

83. (*a*. Mars, *b*. Jupiter, *c*. Venus, ***d*. Pluto**) : PROSERPINA :: ZEUS : HERA

(d) In Roman mythology, Proserpina was the wife of Pluto. In Greek mythology, Hera was the wife of Zeus. *Mars was the god of war in Roman mythology. Jupiter was the god of sky and thunder. Venus was the Roman goddess of love and beauty.*

84. FLEET STREET : (***a*. press**, *b*. police, *c*. amusement, *d*. high fashion) :: DOWNING STREET : GOVERNMENT

(a) In London, Fleet Street has many of the offices of the press, while Downing Street has many of the offices of the government.

85. ARTUR RUBINSTEIN : PIANO :: ISAAC STERN : (*a*. piano, ***b*. violin**, *c*. trumpet, *d*. oboe)

(b) Artur Rubenstein was a pianist. Isaac Stern is a violinist.

86. DURKHEIM : (*a*. Homocide, *b*. Matricide, ***c*. Suicide**, *d*. Genocide) :: BECKER : OUTSIDERS

(c) Durkheim is the author of the sociological work *Suicide*. Becker is the author of the sociological study *Outsiders*.

87. JOHN WESLEY : METHODIST :: MARY BAKER EDDY : (*a*. Presbyterian, *b*. Baha'i, *c*. Jehovah's Witness, ***d*. Christian Science**)

(d) John Wesley was the founder of the Methodist church. Mary Baker Eddy was the founder of the Christian Science church. *The founder of the Presbyterian church was John Calvin; the founder of the Baha'i faith was the Baha'u'llah; the founder of Jehovah's Witnesses was Charles Russell.*

88. BACH : BAROQUE :: GRIEG : (*a*. classical, *b*. modern, ***c*. romantic**, *d*. medieval)

(c) Bach was a composer in the baroque period of music. Grieg was a romantic composer.

89. (*a*. Husserl, *b*. Heidegger, ***c*. Comte**, *d*. Camus) : POSITIVISM :: SARTRE : EXISTENTIALISM

(c) Comte helped shape the movement in philosophy now known as positivism. Sartre was a major shaper of existentialism. *Edmund Husserl was the founder of phenomenology. Martin Heidegger was a philosopher; his most popular book is* Being and Time. *Albert Camus was a French writer who wrote* The Plague *and* The Stranger.

90. F# : G$_b$ :: B : (***a*. C$_b$**, *b*. A$_b$, *c*. G#, *d*. G$_b$)

(a) F# is the same as G$_b$. B is the same as C$_b$.

91. SECOND : THIRD :: (*a*. clergy, *b*. king, *c*. commoners, ***d*. nobility**) : BOURGEOISIE

(d) The nobility comprised the Second Estate of the French Estates-General. The bourgeoisie comprised the Third Estate.

92. ALEXANDER : GREAT :: JULIAN : (*a*. Ingenious, *b*. Meek, *c*. Bold, ***d*. Apostate**)

(d) Alexander was called the Great and was an ancient Greek king of Macedon. Julian was called the Apostate and was a Roman Emperor.

93. (*a.* Helen, *b.* Jezebel, *c.* **Una**, *d.* Archimago) : DUESSA :: GOOD : EVIL

(c) In Spenser's poem, *The Faerie Queene*, Una represents the forces of good and Duessa the forces of evil. *Archimago is a sorcerer in Spenser's* Faerie Queene. *Helen was the daughter of Zeus and Leda, and was abducted by Paris, which led to the Trojan War. Jezebel was a queen of Ancient Israel, married to King Ahab.*

94. D : R × T :: (*a.* A, *b.* C, *c.* **F**, *d.* H) : M × A

(c) In physics, Distance = Rate × Time and Force = Mass × Acceleration.

95. PURLOINED : (*a.* Melville, *b.* Doyle, *c.* **Poe**, *d.* Conrad) :: SCARLET : HAWTHORNE

(c) *The Purloined Letter* is a story by Poe. *The Scarlet Letter* is a story by Hawthorne.

96. PROPHASE : METAPHASE :: ANAPHASE : (*a.* meiophase, *b.* **telophase**, *c.* mitophase, *d.* protophase)

(b) Prophase, metaphase, anaphase, and telophase are all stages in mitosis (a form of cell division).

97. NEWBERY : (*a.* Wohlenberg, *b.* **Caldecott**, *c.* Pulitzer, *d.* Thompsen) :: STORY : ARTWORK

(b) The Newbery Medal is awarded annually to a distinguished children's story book. The Caldecott Medal is also awarded annually for distinguished artwork in a children's book. *The Wohlenberg Prize is a prize for seniors of the physical sciences or engineering at Berkeley College of Yale. The Pulitzer Prize is a prize in journalism and literature. Thompsen is a distracter term.*

98. COUNTESS AURELIA : THE MADWOMAN OF CHAILLOT :: (*a.* Lear, *b.* Othello, *c.* **Antonio**, *d.* Iago) : THE MERCHANT OF VENICE

(c) Countess Aurelia is the Madwoman of Chaillot in the play by the same name. Antonio is the Merchant of Venice in the play by the same name. *Iago tricked Othello into murdering his wife in Shakespeare's tragedy* Othello. King Lear *is another tragedy written by Shakespeare.*

99. PICASSO : GUERNICA :: (*a.* **Manet**, *b.* Raphael, *c.* David, *d.* Leger) : LUNCHEON ON THE GRASS

(a) Picasso is the artist who painted *Guernica*. Manet is the artist who painted *Luncheon on the Grass*. *A famous work of Raphael is the* Sistine Madonna. *A famous painting of Fernand Leger is* Nudes in the Forest. *A well-known painting of Jacques-Louis David is the* Oath of the Horatii.

100. RACINE : MOLIÈRE :: SOPHOCLES : (*a.* Zeno, *b.* **Aristophanes**, *c.* Plato, *d.* Aristotle)

(b) Racine was a French playwright who wrote tragedies, while Molière was a French playwright who wrote comedies. Sophocles was a Greek playwright who wrote tragedies, while Aristophanes was a Greek playwright who wrote comedies. *Zeno, Plato, and Aristotle were ancient Greek philosophers.*

101. (*a.* Queen Victoria, *b.* Queen Virginia, *c.* **Queen Elizabeth**, *d.* Queen Mary) : VIRGINIA :: KING GEORGE : GEORGIA

(c) Queen Elizabeth, known as "the virgin queen," had the state of Virginia named for her. King George inspired the naming of the state of Georgia.

102. MITOSIS : MEIOSIS :: (*a.* 1, *b.* **2**, *c.* 4, *d.* 8) : 4

(b) Mitosis is the process of cell division that results in two discrete cells. Meiosis results in four.

103. DAGGER : STAR :: (*a.* rune, *b.* allograph, *c.* knife, ***d.* obelisk**) : ASTERISK

(d) The name of the written symbol that looks like a dagger is an obelisk just as the star-shaped symbol is called an asterisk. *Rune is the name for any letter belonging to the ancient Germanic alphabet. An allograph is a signature that is made by one person for another.*

104. MISER : (*a.* chary, *b.* mercurial, *c.* acquisitive, ***d.* munificent**) :: GLUTTON : ABSTEMIOUS

(d) A miser is the opposite of munificent, meaning giving, and a glutton is the opposite of abstemious, meaning abstaining from excess food and drink.

105. (*a.* pork, ***b.* sweet**, *c.* appetizer, *d.* vegetable) : SWEETMEAT :: FRUIT : BREADFRUIT

(b) A sweetmeat is a type of sweet food, and a breadfruit is a type of fruit.

106. $2\pi r^2$: $\pi(2r)^2$ :: LW : (*a.* (1/2)LW, *b.* LW, ***c.* 2LW**, *d.* 4LW)

(c) $2\pi r^2$ is half of $\pi(2r)^2$, which is to say the area of two circles of the same radius is half the size of the area of one circle with twice that radius. Similarly, LW, the area of a rectangle, is half of 2LW.

107. (*a.* hatred, *b.* naiveté, ***c.* envy**, *d.* sickness) : SORROW :: GREEN : BLUE

(c) Envy is the emotion that is represented by the color green just as sorrow is the emotion symbolized by the color blue.

108. MOHS : HARDNESS :: RICHTER : (***a.* magnitude**, *b.* earthquake, *c.* quality, *d.* extremity)

(a) The Mohs Scale measures hardness (of solid objects). The Richter Scale measures magnitude (of earthquakes).

109. FROGS : SEAGULL :: (*a.* Shakespeare, *b.* Marlowe, *c.* Wilde, ***d.* Aristophanes**) : CHEKHOV

(d) *The Frogs* was a play written by Aristophanes, and *The Seagull* was a play written by Chekhov. *Shakespeare is known for, among others, his tragedies* Hamlet, King Lear, *and* Macbeth. *Marlowe is known for his plays which include* Doctor Faustus *and* The Massacre at Paris. *Oscar Wilde is known, for example, for his play* The Importance of Being Earnest.

110. INDIA : PAKISTAN :: PAKISTAN : (*a.* Kashmir, ***b.* Bangladesh**, *c.* Nepal, *d.* Sri Lanka)

(b) Pakistan was part of India until it seceded and became sovereign. Bangladesh was part of Pakistan until it seceded and became sovereign.

111. ORGAN : ORGANELLE :: LIVER : (***a.* vacuole**, *b.* pancreas, *c.* kidney, *d.* cell)

(a) The liver is an example of an organ, and a vacuole is an example of an organelle, or intra-cellular structure.

112. MASS AND ENERGY : (*a.* Bernoulli, *b.* Newton, *c.* Gauss, ***d.* Einstein**) :: VOLUME AND DISPLACEMENT : ARCHIMEDES

(d) Einstein was the first to directly relate mass and energy and Archimedes was the first to relate volume and displacement. *Bernoulli applied mathematics to mechanics and is especially known for the Bernoulli principle. Newton is known for describing universal gravitation. Gauss is associated with the normal distribution, also called Gaussian distribution.*

113. DOGS : PEAS :: PAVLOV : (*a.* Darwin, *b.* Gauss, *c.* Curie, ***d.* Mendel**)

(d) Pavlov is famous for his groundbreaking scientific work with dogs in classical conditioning. Mendel is famous for his scientific discoveries made with peas in the area of genetics and inheritance. *Darwin developed the Theory of Evolution. Gauss is associated with the normal distribution, also called Gaussian distribution. Curie won the Nobel Prize in chemistry in 1911 for her discovery of the elements radium and polonium.*

114. (**a. King**, b. Martha, c. Reverend, d. Priest) : CARVER :: MARTIN LUTHER : GEORGE WASHINGTON

(a) Both Martin Luther King (Jr.) and George Washington Carver went on to become famous, as were those men for whom they were named at birth.

115. SESAME SEEDS : TAHINI :: PEANUTS : (a. roots, b. shell, **c. peanut butter**, d. oil)

(c) Sesame seeds are ground to make the spread known as tahini just as peanuts are ground to make peanut butter.

116. BASS : (a. clarinet, b. viola, **c. cello**, d. trumpet) :: TREBLE : FLUTE

(c) Most written music for the cello is presented in the bass clef. Most flute music is written in the treble clef.

117. MAL : BEN :: ANTI : (a. un, b. inter, **c. pro**, d. pre)

(c) *Mal-* and *ben-* are prefixes with opposite connotations (negative and positive, respectively). Likewise, *anti-* and *pro-* are prefixes with opposite meanings (negating and supporting, respectively). *The prefix* un- *means "not, or lack of";* inter- *means "in between";* pre- *means "before."*

118. (**a. meat packing**, b. clear cutting, c. poaching, d. iron mining) : PESTICIDES :: THE JUNGLE : SILENT SPRING

(a) Upton Sinclair's book *The Jungle* exposed abuses in the meat-packing industry just as Rachel Carson's *Silent Spring* exposed abuses of pesticides.

119. HANUKKAH : DIVALI :: JUDAISM : (a. Buddhism, **b. Hinduism**, c. Zoroastrianism, d. Islam)

(b) The holidays Hanukkah and Divali are also known in their respective religions, Judaism and Hinduism, as the Festival of Lights.

120. SQUARE ROOT : SQUARE :: (a. dividend, b. root, c. log, **d. integral**) : DERIVATIVE

(d) Finding the square root requires the opposite action as finding the square of a number. Likewise, finding the integral is the opposite of finding the derivative of a number.

ANSWER SHEET
Practice Test 5

1. Ⓐ Ⓑ Ⓒ Ⓓ
2. Ⓐ Ⓑ Ⓒ Ⓓ
3. Ⓐ Ⓑ Ⓒ Ⓓ
4. Ⓐ Ⓑ Ⓒ Ⓓ
5. Ⓐ Ⓑ Ⓒ Ⓓ
6. Ⓐ Ⓑ Ⓒ Ⓓ
7. Ⓐ Ⓑ Ⓒ Ⓓ
8. Ⓐ Ⓑ Ⓒ Ⓓ
9. Ⓐ Ⓑ Ⓒ Ⓓ
10. Ⓐ Ⓑ Ⓒ Ⓓ
11. Ⓐ Ⓑ Ⓒ Ⓓ
12. Ⓐ Ⓑ Ⓒ Ⓓ
13. Ⓐ Ⓑ Ⓒ Ⓓ
14. Ⓐ Ⓑ Ⓒ Ⓓ
15. Ⓐ Ⓑ Ⓒ Ⓓ
16. Ⓐ Ⓑ Ⓒ Ⓓ
17. Ⓐ Ⓑ Ⓒ Ⓓ
18. Ⓐ Ⓑ Ⓒ Ⓓ
19. Ⓐ Ⓑ Ⓒ Ⓓ
20. Ⓐ Ⓑ Ⓒ Ⓓ
21. Ⓐ Ⓑ Ⓒ Ⓓ
22. Ⓐ Ⓑ Ⓒ Ⓓ
23. Ⓐ Ⓑ Ⓒ Ⓓ
24. Ⓐ Ⓑ Ⓒ Ⓓ
25. Ⓐ Ⓑ Ⓒ Ⓓ
26. Ⓐ Ⓑ Ⓒ Ⓓ
27. Ⓐ Ⓑ Ⓒ Ⓓ
28. Ⓐ Ⓑ Ⓒ Ⓓ
29. Ⓐ Ⓑ Ⓒ Ⓓ
30. Ⓐ Ⓑ Ⓒ Ⓓ

31. Ⓐ Ⓑ Ⓒ Ⓓ
32. Ⓐ Ⓑ Ⓒ Ⓓ
33. Ⓐ Ⓑ Ⓒ Ⓓ
34. Ⓐ Ⓑ Ⓒ Ⓓ
35. Ⓐ Ⓑ Ⓒ Ⓓ
36. Ⓐ Ⓑ Ⓒ Ⓓ
37. Ⓐ Ⓑ Ⓒ Ⓓ
38. Ⓐ Ⓑ Ⓒ Ⓓ
39. Ⓐ Ⓑ Ⓒ Ⓓ
40. Ⓐ Ⓑ Ⓒ Ⓓ
41. Ⓐ Ⓑ Ⓒ Ⓓ
42. Ⓐ Ⓑ Ⓒ Ⓓ
43. Ⓐ Ⓑ Ⓒ Ⓓ
44. Ⓐ Ⓑ Ⓒ Ⓓ
45. Ⓐ Ⓑ Ⓒ Ⓓ
46. Ⓐ Ⓑ Ⓒ Ⓓ
47. Ⓐ Ⓑ Ⓒ Ⓓ
48. Ⓐ Ⓑ Ⓒ Ⓓ
49. Ⓐ Ⓑ Ⓒ Ⓓ
50. Ⓐ Ⓑ Ⓒ Ⓓ
51. Ⓐ Ⓑ Ⓒ Ⓓ
52. Ⓐ Ⓑ Ⓒ Ⓓ
53. Ⓐ Ⓑ Ⓒ Ⓓ
54. Ⓐ Ⓑ Ⓒ Ⓓ
55. Ⓐ Ⓑ Ⓒ Ⓓ
56. Ⓐ Ⓑ Ⓒ Ⓓ
57. Ⓐ Ⓑ Ⓒ Ⓓ
58. Ⓐ Ⓑ Ⓒ Ⓓ
59. Ⓐ Ⓑ Ⓒ Ⓓ
60. Ⓐ Ⓑ Ⓒ Ⓓ

61. Ⓐ Ⓑ Ⓒ Ⓓ
62. Ⓐ Ⓑ Ⓒ Ⓓ
63. Ⓐ Ⓑ Ⓒ Ⓓ
64. Ⓐ Ⓑ Ⓒ Ⓓ
65. Ⓐ Ⓑ Ⓒ Ⓓ
66. Ⓐ Ⓑ Ⓒ Ⓓ
67. Ⓐ Ⓑ Ⓒ Ⓓ
68. Ⓐ Ⓑ Ⓒ Ⓓ
69. Ⓐ Ⓑ Ⓒ Ⓓ
70. Ⓐ Ⓑ Ⓒ Ⓓ
71. Ⓐ Ⓑ Ⓒ Ⓓ
72. Ⓐ Ⓑ Ⓒ Ⓓ
73. Ⓐ Ⓑ Ⓒ Ⓓ
74. Ⓐ Ⓑ Ⓒ Ⓓ
75. Ⓐ Ⓑ Ⓒ Ⓓ
76. Ⓐ Ⓑ Ⓒ Ⓓ
77. Ⓐ Ⓑ Ⓒ Ⓓ
78. Ⓐ Ⓑ Ⓒ Ⓓ
79. Ⓐ Ⓑ Ⓒ Ⓓ
80. Ⓐ Ⓑ Ⓒ Ⓓ
81. Ⓐ Ⓑ Ⓒ Ⓓ
82. Ⓐ Ⓑ Ⓒ Ⓓ
83. Ⓐ Ⓑ Ⓒ Ⓓ
84. Ⓐ Ⓑ Ⓒ Ⓓ
85. Ⓐ Ⓑ Ⓒ Ⓓ
86. Ⓐ Ⓑ Ⓒ Ⓓ
87. Ⓐ Ⓑ Ⓒ Ⓓ
88. Ⓐ Ⓑ Ⓒ Ⓓ
89. Ⓐ Ⓑ Ⓒ Ⓓ
90. Ⓐ Ⓑ Ⓒ Ⓓ

91. Ⓐ Ⓑ Ⓒ Ⓓ
92. Ⓐ Ⓑ Ⓒ Ⓓ
93. Ⓐ Ⓑ Ⓒ Ⓓ
94. Ⓐ Ⓑ Ⓒ Ⓓ
95. Ⓐ Ⓑ Ⓒ Ⓓ
96. Ⓐ Ⓑ Ⓒ Ⓓ
97. Ⓐ Ⓑ Ⓒ Ⓓ
98. Ⓐ Ⓑ Ⓒ Ⓓ
99. Ⓐ Ⓑ Ⓒ Ⓓ
100. Ⓐ Ⓑ Ⓒ Ⓓ
101. Ⓐ Ⓑ Ⓒ Ⓓ
102. Ⓐ Ⓑ Ⓒ Ⓓ
103. Ⓐ Ⓑ Ⓒ Ⓓ
104. Ⓐ Ⓑ Ⓒ Ⓓ
105. Ⓐ Ⓑ Ⓒ Ⓓ
106. Ⓐ Ⓑ Ⓒ Ⓓ
107. Ⓐ Ⓑ Ⓒ Ⓓ
108. Ⓐ Ⓑ Ⓒ Ⓓ
109. Ⓐ Ⓑ Ⓒ Ⓓ
110. Ⓐ Ⓑ Ⓒ Ⓓ
111. Ⓐ Ⓑ Ⓒ Ⓓ
112. Ⓐ Ⓑ Ⓒ Ⓓ
113. Ⓐ Ⓑ Ⓒ Ⓓ
114. Ⓐ Ⓑ Ⓒ Ⓓ
115. Ⓐ Ⓑ Ⓒ Ⓓ
116. Ⓐ Ⓑ Ⓒ Ⓓ
117. Ⓐ Ⓑ Ⓒ Ⓓ
118. Ⓐ Ⓑ Ⓒ Ⓓ
119. Ⓐ Ⓑ Ⓒ Ⓓ
120. Ⓐ Ⓑ Ⓒ Ⓓ

Time: 60 MINUTES

> **Directions:** In each of the following questions, you will find three initial terms and, in parentheses, four answer options designated *a*, *b*, *c*, and *d*. You are to select from the four answer options the one that *best* completes the analogy with the three initial terms. To record your answers, use the answer sheet provided.

1. BOW : (*a.* arrow, *b.* grenade, *c.* quiver, *d.* target) :: RIFLE : BULLET

2. MARK TWAIN : HANNIBAL :: (*a.* Ernest Hemingway, *b.* Stephen Crane, *c.* William Shakespeare, *d.* Victor Hugo) : STRATFORD-UPON-AVON

3. UNITED : STAND :: DIVIDED : (*a.* fall, *b.* sit, *c.* lie, *d.* rise)

4. (*a.* Asia, *b.* South America, *c.* Africa, *d.* North America) : SAHARA :: NORTH AMERICA : PAINTED

5. TARANTULA : (*a.* spider, *b.* rabbit, *c.* cat, *d.* cockroach) :: COBRA : SNAKE

6. (*a.* 6, *b.* 9, *c.* 12, *d.* 15) : BASEBALL :: 5 : BASKETBALL

7. SEINE : (*a.* Canada, *b.* Holland, *c.* Germany, *d.* France) :: THAMES : ENGLAND

8. PLIABLE : BEND :: (*a.* brittle, *b.* transparent, *c.* opaque, *d.* flexible) : BREAK

9. ADVERB : HAPPILY :: PREPOSITION : (*a.* the, *b.* or, *c.* on, *d.* none)

10. RIGHT ANGLE : (*a.* 0, *b.* 45, *c.* 90, *d.* 360) :: STRAIGHT ANGLE : 180

11. AUTHOR : PEN :: PAINTER : (*a.* brush, *b.* paint, *c.* canvas, *d.* picture)

12. ASTRONAUT : ROCKET SHIP :: WITCH : (*a.* cauldron, *b.* vulture, *c.* black cat, *d.* broomstick)

13. (*a.* achievement, *b.* permission, *c.* month, *d.* desire) : ABILITY :: MAY : CAN

14. IBM : (*a.* Industrial Business Machines, *b.* Innovative Business Machines, *c.* International Business Machines, *d.* Intelligent Business Machines) :: GOP : REPUBLICAN PARTY

15. (*a.* earthling, *b.* earthian, *c.* earthing, *d.* earthan) : EARTH :: MARTIAN : MARS

16. ASBESTOS : FIRE :: (*a.* vinyl, *b.* air, *c.* cotton, *d.* faucet) : WATER

17. DAVY JONES'S LOCKER : (*a.* Great Britain, *b.* Planet Earth, *c.* the sun, *d.* the sea) :: LAND OF THE RISING SUN : JAPAN

18. PAIR : PARE :: COUPLE : (*a.* several, *b.* one, *c.* pear, *d.* prune)

19. ASCETIC : (*a.* businessman, *b.* monk, *c.* carpenter, *d.* policeman) :: CRAFTY : CONFIDENCE MAN

20. GUILLOTINE : ROBESPIERRE :: (*a.* noose, *b.* poison, *c.* knife, *d.* illness) : SOCRATES

21. GIN : BLACK :: (*a.* apple, *b.* whiskey, *c.* cotton, *d.* rummy) : JACK

22. PESO : MEXICO :: (*a.* ounce, *b.* pound, *c.* ruble, *d.* mark) : ENGLAND

23. SILVER : GOLD :: (*a.* Si, *b.* Sl, *c.* Ag, *d.* Hg) : Au

24. VALEDICTORIAN : SALUTATORIAN :: PRIME : (*a.* excellent, *b.* good, *c.* choice, *d.* alternative)

25. CHEROKEE : (*a.* Indian, *b.* aborigine, *c.* Seminole, *d.* pariah) :: APACHE : NAVAHO

26. (*a.* musical instruments, *b.* books, *c.* weather systems, *d.* diseases) : DEWEY :: LIVING THINGS : LINNAEUS

27. IVAN : TERRIBLE :: PETER : (*a.* Hairy, *b.* Reformer, *c.* Great, *d.* Awful)

28. SQUARE : 360 :: RECTANGLE : (*a.* 90, *b.* 180, *c.* 270, *d.* 360)

29. WHALE : (*a.* mammal, *b.* reptile, *c.* amphibian, *d.* fish) :: LIZARD : REPTILE

30. LINCOLN : (*a.* 1, *b.* 5, *c.* 10, *d.* 16) :: JACKSON : 20

31. CONJUNCTION : DISJUNCTION :: AND : (*a.* but, *b.* if . . . then, *c.* or, *d.* because)

32. AENEAS : (*a.* Virgil, *b.* Plutarch, *c.* Caesar, *d.* Demosthenes) :: ODYSSEUS: HOMER

33. AGORAPHOBIA : ARACHNOPHOBIA :: OPEN SPACES : (*a.* lizards, *b.* snakes, *c.* spiders, *d.* dragons)

34. GRIMM : (*a.* Donne, *b.* Petrarch, *c.* Nash, *d.* Andersen) :: CHAUCER : BOCCACCIO

35. CYCLONE : TORNADO :: HURRICANE : (*a.* storm, *b.* typhoon, *c.* rain, *d.* miasma)

36. GREENHOUSE : PLANTS :: AVIARY : (*a.* birds, *b.* bees, *c.* rodents, *d.* fish)

37. (*a.* $A \cap B$, *b.* $B \cap A$, *c.* $A \cup B$, *d.* $B \cup A$) : $B \cup A$ :: $X \wedge Y$: $Y \vee X$

38. OFFER : JOB :: TENDER : (*a.* resignation, *b.* retirement, *c.* delicate, *d.* rough)

39. HICCUP : HICCOUGH :: EYE : (*a.* light, *b.* ice, *c.* I, *d.* iris)

40. (*a.* black, *b.* white, *c.* orange, *d.* brown) : BLUE :: RED : GREEN

41. ASPIRIN : (*a.* anaphoric, *b.* mycin, *c.* antibiotic, *d.* analgesic) :: PENICILLIN : ANTIBIOTIC

42. (*a.* Istanbul, *b.* Dar es Salaam, *c.* Jerusalem, *d.* Mecca) : MOHAMMED :: BETHLEHEM : JESUS

43. CETANE : DIESEL FUEL OIL :: (*a.* octane, *b.* heptane, *c.* methane, *d.* propane) : GASOLINE

44. DEAD DUCK : GONER :: LAME DUCK : (*a.* one who finishes a term after failing re-election, *b.* one who gives up easily, *c.* one who invests cautiously, *d.* one who complains incessantly)

45. ARGONAUTS : (*a.* Francis Marion, *b.* Jason, *c.* Achilles, *d.* George Washington) :: GREEN MOUNTAIN BOYS : ETHAN ALLEN

46. LYNX : CAT :: BOAR : (*a.* hog, *b.* dog, *c.* goat, *d.* ram)

47. LENIN : BOLSHEVIK :: (*a.* Stalin, *b.* Kerensky, *c.* Trotsky, *d.* Marx) : MENSHEVIK

48. (*a.* oak, *b.* walnut, *c.* balsa, *d.* corundum) : HICKORY :: TIN : STEEL

49. ROCK : ROCKET :: (*a.* coat, *b.* cloth, *c.* jack, *d.* wasp) : JACKET

50. MALARIA : CHILLS :: GOITER : (*a.* pockmarks, *b.* swelling, *c.* fever, *d.* hypertension)

51. PIZARRO : INCA :: (*a.* Ponce de Leon, *b.* Hudson, *c.* Velásquez, *d.* Cortez) : AZTEC

52. ASTROLOGY : (*a.* astronomy, *b.* physics, *c.* pharmacology, *d.* phrenology) :: ASTRONOMY : ANATOMY

53. DUET : SEXTET :: SOLO : (*a.* quartet, *b.* quintet, *c.* chorus, *d.* trio)

54. ANDES : (*a.* Asia, *b.* Africa, *c.* South America, *d.* Europe) :: ALPS : EUROPE

55. MYOPIA : (*a.* hyperopia, *b.* scotopia, *c.* photopia, *d.* metropia) :: NEARSIGHTED : FARSIGHTED

56. PASTORAL : (*a.* religious, *b.* rustic, *c.* metropolitan, *d.* worldly) :: URBAN : CITIFIED

57. SEA : TIGER :: LION : (*a.* land, *b.* fauna, *c.* lily, *d.* heart)

58. ASTRONAUT : SPACESUIT :: (*a.* judge, *b.* baker, *c.* ballerina, *d.* monk) : HABIT

59. MONOGAMY : BIGAMY :: BIPED : (*a.* unipod, *b.* pedate, *c.* millipede, *d.* quadruped)

60. POPE : ROMAN :: (*a.* Metropolitan, *b.* Patriarch, *c.* Cardinal, *d.* Bishop) : GREEK ORTHODOX

61. SEXTANT : (*a.* navigator, *b.* architect, *c.* archeologist, *d.* priest) :: SCALPEL : SURGEON

62. PRIDE : PREJUDICE :: SENSE : (*a.* Folly, *b.* Prentense, *c.* Sensibility, *d.* Sanity)

63. PACIFIST : PEACE :: (*a.* revolutionary, *b.* diplomat, *c.* charlatan, *d.* traitor) : CHANGE

64. (*a.* brown, *b.* gray, *c.* purple, *d.* blue) : UMBER :: GREEN : CHARTREUSE

65. INCREASE : LESSEN :: (*a.* fair, *b.* final, *c.* incipient, *d.* unfair) : INCHOATE

66. EXCALIBUR : (*a.* sword, *b.* pony, *c.* lioness, *d.* cannon) :: LASSIE : DOG

67. (*a.* Bern, *b.* Geneva, *c.* Zurich, *d.* Lucerne) : SWITZERLAND :: NEW DELHI : INDIA

68. SILVER-TONGUED : ELOQUENT :: JANUS-FACED : (*a.* duplicitous, *b.* versatile, *c.* incredibly ugly, *d.* honest)

69. PRESENT : FUTURE PERFECT :: GO : (*a.* would go, *b.* will go, *c.* will have gone, *d.* would have gone)

70. AMPLITUDE : FREQUENCY :: RATE : (*a.* distance, *b.* velocity, *c.* acceleration, *d.* time)

71. GREENHORN : NOVICE :: NEOPHYTE : (*a.* expert, *b.* priest, *c.* beginner, *d.* novelist)

72. PANEGYRIC : (*a.* prayer, *b.* joke, *c.* threat, *d.* eulogy) :: TEMPEST : STORM

73. CARMEN : (*a.* Verdi, *b.* Bizet, *c.* Gounod, *d.* Wagner) :: BARBER OF SEVILLE : ROSSINI

74. PALPITATE : QUIVER :: MASTICATE : (*a.* abuse, *b.* remove, *c.* stomp, *d.* chew)

75. BOLÍVAR : (*a.* Venezuela, *b.* Spain, *c.* United States, *d.* Mexico) :: WASHINGTON : ENGLAND

76. CORNUCOPIA : (*a.* horn of plenty, *b.* horn of Roland, *c.* hornpipe, *d.* hornstone) :: TENET : PRECEPT

77. SHRIMP : CRUSTACEAN :: (*a.* snail, *b.* lobster, *c.* goldfish, *d.* brine) : MOLLUSK

78. NEW AMSTERDAM : NEW YORK :: SIAM : (*a.* Thailand, *b.* Cambodia, *c.* Laos, *d.* China)

79. HIRSUTE : (*a.* pleasantly plump, *b.* well-dressed, *c.* handsome, *d.* hairy) :: EXTROVERTED : OUTGOING

80. EYE : LIP :: ELBOW : (*a.* forehead, *b.* nose, *c.* foot, *d.* chest)

81. (*a.* feldspar, *b.* talc, *c.* quartz, *d.* topaz) : 1 :: DIAMOND : 10

82. TORTUOUS : (*a.* painless, *b.* painful, *c.* straight, *d.* winding) :: SOBER : INEBRIATED

83. NONPLUS : (*a.* perplexity, *b.* disappointment, *c.* deletion, *d.* elation) :: NONPAREIL : UNEQUALED

84. CROCKETT : ALAMO :: BONAPARTE : (*a.* Madrid, *b.* St. Helena, *c.* Rome, *d.* London)

85. EL GRECO : (*a.* impressionist, *b.* mannerist, *c.* expressionist, *d.* realist) :: DAVID : NEOCLASSICIST

86. GRAY : COUNTRY CHURCHYARD :: (*a.* Keats, *b.* Poe, *c.* Byron, *d.* Longfellow) : GRECIAN URN

87. MITER : (*a.* dancer, *b.* cartoonist, *c.* queen, *d.* bishop) :: CROWN : KING

88. $2^0 : 2^{-2} :: 2^2 : (a.\ 2^{1/4}, b.\ 2^0, c.\ 2^1, d.\ 2^{-1})$

89. FLOWER : GARDEN :: (*a.* pinnacle, *b.* stalagmite, *c.* cavern, *d.* explorer) : CAVE

90. LEVITICUS : OLD :: (*a.* Deuteronomy, *b.* Isaiah, *c.* Numbers, *d.* Ephesians) : NEW

91. LOUVRE : PARIS :: PRADO : (*a.* Madrid, *b.* Seville, *c.* Florence, *d.* Chartres)

92. CUL-DE-SAC : BLIND ALLEY :: SANGFROID : (*a.* carelessness, *b.* timidity, *c.* courage, *d.* imperturbability)

93. ENCOMIUM : TRIBUTE :: (*a.* admonition, *b.* excoriation, *c.* benison, *d.* exegesis) : CRITICAL ANALYSIS

94. CARPETBAGGER : NORTH :: (*a.* Granger, *b.* Scalawag, *c.* Bull Moose, *d.* Tweety Pie) : SOUTH

95. MERCURIAL : (*a.* pretty, *b.* plutonic, *c.* hateful, *d.* hermetic) :: MARTIAL : AREOLOGY

96. LEGATO : BOW :: PIZZICATO : (*a.* fingers, *b.* bow, *c.* reed, *d.* feet)

97. NICK ADAMS : (*a.* Fitzgerald, *b.* Faulkner, *c.* Hemingway, *d.* Joyce) :: ARROWSMITH : LEWIS

98. (*a.* Burgundian, *b.* Prussian, *c.* Turkish, *d.* Bulgarian) : OTTOMAN :: FRENCH : BOURBON

99. ORPHEUS : EURYDICE :: DAPHNIS : (*a.* Pyramus, *b.* Thisbe, *c.* Chloe, *d.* Helen)

100. (*a.* darling, *b.* wench, *c.* harridan, *d.* myrmidon) : SHREW :: MOLLYCODDLE : SISSY

101. PULLEY : (*a.* screw, *b.* saw, *c.* pliers, *d.* nail) :: WEDGE : INCLINED PLANE

102. LIVE WIRE : LOOSE CANNON :: ENERGETIC : (*a.* powerful, *b.* threatening, *c.* reckless, *d.* peaceable)

103. ARM : LEG :: (*a.* radius, *b.* ulna, *c.* humerus, *d.* scapula) : FEMUR

104. VENUSIAN : (*a.* Venus, *b.* Earth, *c.* Moon, *d.* Mercury) :: MARTIAN : JUPITER

105. (*a.* oil, *b.* air, *c.* nitrates, *d.* blood) : TOURNIQUET :: WATER : DAM

106. OBJURGATE : (*a.* vituperate, *b.* venerate, *c.* abrogate, *d.* enervate) :: RECANT : RETRACT

107. PERFIDIOUS : BENEFICENT :: (*a.* obvious, *b.* capricious, *c.* intractable, *d.* renitent) : STEADFAST

108. MAN : LAZARUS :: BIRD : (*a.* dragon, *b.* albatross, *c.* phoenix, *d.* dodo)

109. FIREWORKS : (*a.* Japan, *b.* Korea, *c.* Indonesia, *d.* China) :: LIGHTBULB : THE UNITED STATES

110. GI TRACT : GI JOE :: GASTROINTESTINAL : (*a.* General Infantry, *b.* Galvanized Iron, *c.* Government Issue, *d.* General Information)

111. WET SUIT : (*a.* spandex, *b.* neoprene, *c.* nylon, *d.* Lycra) :: BULLETPROOF VEST : KEVLAR

112. (*a.* yellow, *b.* pink, *c.* white, *d.* green) : BLUE :: JAUNDICED : CYANOTIC

113. MONET : WATER LILIES :: DEGAS : (*a.* windmills, *b.* sailboats, *c.* polo players, *d.* ballet dancers)

114. WAR : (*a.* birth, *b.* flood, *c.* death, *d.* fall) :: ANTEBELLUM : ANTEDILUVIAN

115. DILETTANTE : DEBUTANTE :: (*a.* amateur, *b.* professional, *c.* actor, *d.* student) : YOUNG WOMAN

116. DOG : CAT :: (*a.* loud, *b.* skinny, *c.* under, *d.* hound) : FAT

117. RIDE : (*a.* U.S. senator, *b.* doctor, *c.* pilot, *d.* astronaut) :: O'CONNOR : SUPREME COURT JUSTICE

118. (*a.* panda, *b.* opossum, *c.* mouse, *d.* anteater) : WALLABY :: KANGAROO : WOMBAT

119. ANDREW : ABRAHAM :: LYNDON : (*a.* John, *b.* Robert, *c.* Joseph, *d.* Edward)

120. MYOPIA : CONCAVE :: (*a.* mytopia, *b.* astigmatism, *c.* hyperopia, *d.* diopia) : CONVEX

1. **A**	31. **C**	61. **A**	91. **A**
2. **C**	32. **A**	62. **C**	92. **D**
3. **A**	33. **C**	63. **A**	93. **D**
4. **C**	34. **D**	64. **A**	94. **B**
5. **A**	35. **B**	65. **B**	95. **D**
6. **B**	36. **A**	66. **A**	96. **A**
7. **D**	37. **A**	67. **A**	97. **C**
8. **A**	38. **A**	68. **A**	98. **C**
9. **C**	39. **C**	69. **C**	99. **C**
10. **C**	40. **C**	70. **D**	100. **C**
11. **A**	41. **D**	71. **C**	101. **A**
12. **D**	42. **D**	72. **D**	102. **C**
13. **B**	43. **A**	73. **B**	103. **C**
14. **C**	44. **A**	74. **D**	104. **B**
15. **A**	45. **B**	75. **B**	105. **D**
16. **A**	46. **A**	76. **A**	106. **A**
17. **D**	47. **B**	77. **A**	107. **B**
18. **D**	48. **C**	78. **A**	108. **C**
19. **B**	49. **C**	79. **D**	109. **D**
20. **B**	50. **B**	80. **C**	110. **C**
21. **D**	51. **D**	81. **B**	111. **B**
22. **B**	52. **D**	82. **C**	112. **A**
23. **C**	53. **D**	83. **A**	113. **D**
24. **C**	54. **C**	84. **B**	114. **B**
25. **C**	55. **A**	85. **B**	115. **A**
26. **B**	56. **B**	86. **A**	116. **C**
27. **C**	57. **C**	87. **D**	117. **D**
28. **D**	58. **D**	88. **B**	118. **B**
29. **A**	59. **D**	89. **B**	119. **A**
30. **B**	60. **B**	90. **D**	120. **C**

In the following, explanations concerning the correct responses are in roman font. Explanations regarding distracters (incorrect responses) that are not self-explaining or could be misinterpreted are in italics in order to highlight the explanations of the answers that are correct.

1. BOW : (***a*. arrow**, *b*. grenade, *c*. quiver, *d*. target) :: RIFLE : BULLET

    (a) An arrow is shot from a bow; a bullet is shot from a rifle.

2. MARK TWAIN : HANNIBAL :: (*a*. Ernest Hemingway, *b*. Stephen Crane, **c. William Shakespeare**, *d*. Victor Hugo) : STRATFORD-UPON-AVON

    (c) Mark Twain was born in Hannibal, Missouri. William Shakespeare was born in Stratford-upon-Avon, England. *Ernest Hemingway was born in Oak Park, Illinois; Stephen Crane was born in Newark, New Jersey; Victor Hugo was born in Besancon, France.*

3. UNITED : STAND :: DIVIDED : (***a*. fall**, *b*. sit, *c*. lie, *d*. rise)

    (a) "United we stand, divided we fall" is a familiar saying.

4. (*a*. Asia, *b*. South America, ***c*. Africa**, *d*. North America) : SAHARA :: NORTH AMERICA : PAINTED

    (c) The Sahara Desert is in Africa. The Painted Desert is in North America.

5. TARANTULA : (***a*. spider**, *b*. rabbit, *c*. cat, *d*. cockroach) :: COBRA : SNAKE

    (a) A tarantula is a type of spider; a cobra is a type of snake.

6. (*a*. 6, ***b*. 9**, *c*. 12, *d*. 15) : BASEBALL :: 5 : BASKETBALL

    (b) There are 9 players on a baseball team, and 5 on a basketball team.

7. SEINE : (*a*. Canada, *b*. Holland, *c*. Germany, ***d*. France**) :: THAMES : ENGLAND

    (d) The Seine River is in France, while the Thames River is in England.

8. PLIABLE : BEND :: (***a*. brittle**, *b*. transparent, *c*. opaque, *d*. flexible) : BREAK

    (a) A pliable object will easily bend, while a brittle substance will easily break.

9. ADVERB : HAPPILY :: PREPOSITION : (*a*. the, *b*. or, ***c*. on**, *d*. none)

    (c) Happily is an adverb. On is a preposition.

10. RIGHT ANGLE : (*a*. 0, *b*. 45, ***c*. 90**, *d*. 360) :: STRAIGHT ANGLE : 180

    (c) A right angle is 90 degrees; a straight angle is 180 degrees.

11. AUTHOR : PEN :: PAINTER : (***a*. brush**, *b*. paint, *c*. canvas, *d*. picture)

    (a) An author does his or her writing with a pen; a painter does his or her painting with a brush.

12. ASTRONAUT : ROCKET SHIP :: WITCH : (*a*. cauldron, *b*. vulture, *c*. black cat, ***d*. broomstick**)

    (d) An astronaut flies by rocket ship. A witch "flies" by broomstick.

13. (*a*. achievement, ***b*. permission**, *c*. month, *d*. desire) : ABILITY :: MAY : CAN

    (b) Someone who can do something is able to do it. Someone who may do something has permission to do it.

14. IBM : (*a*. Industrial Business Machines, *b*. Innovative Business Machines, ***c*. International Business Machines**, *d*. Intelligent Business Machines) :: GOP : Republican Party

(c) IBM is a common abbreviation for International Business Machines. GOP is an abbreviation for the Grand Old Party, which is the Republican Party.

15. (***a*. earthling**, *b*. earthian, *c*. earthing, *d*. earthan) : EARTH :: MARTIAN : MARS

(a) An earthling is an inhabitant of the Earth. A Martian is an inhabitant of Mars.

16. ASBESTOS : FIRE :: (***a*. vinyl**, *b*. air, *c*. cotton, *d*. faucet) : WATER

(a) Asbestos is fireproof. Vinyl is waterproof.

17. DAVY JONES'S LOCKER : (*a*. Great Britain, *b*. Planet Earth, *c*. the sun, ***d*. the sea**) :: LAND OF THE RISING SUN : JAPAN

(d) Davy Jones's Locker refers to the bottom of the sea; the origins of this term are unclear. The Land of the Rising Sun is Japan, as the sun rises in the east.

18. PAIR : PARE :: COUPLE : (*a*. several, *b*. one, *c*. pear, ***d*. prune**)

(d) A pair is a couple. To pare is to prune.

19. ASCETIC : (*a*. businessman, ***b*. monk**, *c*. carpenter, *d*. policeman) :: CRAFTY : CONFIDENCE MAN

(b) A monk is ascetic. A confidence man is crafty.

20. GUILLOTINE : ROBESPIERRE :: (*a*. noose, ***b*. poison**, *c*. knife, *d*. illness) : SOCRATES

(b) Robespierre was killed by the guillotine. Socrates was killed by poison.

21. GIN : BLACK :: (*a*. apple, *b*. whiskey, *c*. cotton, ***d*. rummy**) : JACK

(d) Gin rummy and blackjack are both card games.

22. PESO : MEXICO :: (*a*. ounce, ***b*. pound**, *c*. ruble, *d*. mark) : ENGLAND

(b) The peso is the unit of currency in Mexico. The pound is the unit of currency in England. *An ounce is a unit of weight. The ruble is the unit of currency in Russia. The mark was formerly the unit of currency in Germany.*

23. SILVER : GOLD :: (*a*. Si, *b*. Sl, ***c*. Ag**, *d*. Hg) : Au

(c) The chemical symbol for silver is Ag; that for gold is Au. *Si stands for silicon; Hg stands for mercury. Sl is not an element.*

24. VALEDICTORIAN : SALUTATORIAN :: PRIME : (*a*. excellent, *b*. good, ***c*. choice**, *d*. alternative)

(c) A valedictorian is the highest-ranking student in a class, while a salutatorian is the second highest. Prime meat is the highest-ranked type of meat, while choice meat is the second highest-ranked.

25. CHEROKEE : (*a*. Indian, *b*. aborigine, ***c*. Seminole**, *d*. pariah) :: APACHE : NAVAJO

(c) The Cherokee, Seminole, Apache, and Navajo are all tribes of American Indians. *Aborigines are members of the original population of a place, as opposed to the colonizing people. Pariahs are members of a traditionally low caste in India.*

26. (*a*. musical instruments, ***b*. books**, *c*. weather systems, *d*. diseases) : DEWEY :: LIVING THINGS : LINNAEUS

(b) Dewey devised a system for classifying books (Dewey Decimal Classification, DDC). Linnaeus devised a system for classifying living things (biological classification).

27. IVAN : TERRIBLE :: PETER : (*a.* Hairy, *b.* Reformer, ***c.* Great**, *d.* Awful)

(c) Ivan the Terrible (1530–1584) and Peter the Great (1672–1725) were both rulers of Russia.

28. SQUARE : 360 :: RECTANGLE : (*a.* 90, *b.* 180, *c.* 270, ***d.* 360**)

(d) Both a square and a rectangle have interior angles summing to 360 degrees.

29. WHALE : (***a.* mammal**, *b.* reptile, *c.* amphibian, *d.* fish) :: LIZARD : REPTILE

(a) A whale is a mammal; a lizard is a reptile.

30. LINCOLN : (*a.* 1, ***b.* 5**, *c.* 10, *d.* 16) :: JACKSON : 20

(b) President Lincoln's portrait appears on a $5 bill; President Jackson's portrait appears on a $20 bill. *George Washington appears on the $1 bill. Alexander Hamilton appears on the $10 bill. Ulysses Grant appears on the $50 bill. Benjamin Franklin appears on the $100 bill.*

31. CONJUNCTION : DISJUNCTION :: AND : (*a.* but, *b.* if . . . then, ***c.* or**, *d.* because)

(c) In logic, *and* expresses conjunction and *or* expresses disjunction.

32. AENEAS : (***a.* Virgil**, *b.* Plutarch, *c.* Caesar, *d.* Demosthenes) :: ODYSSEUS : HOMER

(a) Virgil wrote about the travels of Aeneas; Homer wrote about the travels of Odysseus. *Plutarch wrote* Parallel Lives; *famous fables of Aesop are, for example,* The Fox and the Grapes *and* The Tortoise and the Hare. *Caesar was a dictator of the Roman Republic and wrote* Commentarii de Bello Gallico, *among other works. Demosthenes was a Greek orator who published many of his orations.*

33. AGORAPHOBIA : ARACHNOPHOBIA :: OPEN SPACES : (*a.* lizards, *b.* snakes, ***c.* spiders**, *d.* dragons)

(c) Agoraphobia is a fear of open spaces. Arachnophobia is a fear of spiders.

34. GRIMM : (*a.* Donne, *b.* Petrarch, *c.* Nash, ***d.* Andersen**) :: CHAUCER : BOCCACCIO

(d) Grimm and Andersen both wrote fairy tales. Chaucer and Boccaccio both wrote collections of tales told by groups of people.

35. CYCLONE : TORNADO :: HURRICANE : (*a.* storm, ***b.* typhoon**, *c.* rain, *d.* miasma)

(b) Cyclone, tornado, hurricane, and typhoon are all types of major storms. Cyclones are storms that rotate around a center and often come with rain. Hurricanes are tropical cyclones that are faster than 73 miles per hour; they mostly appear in the western Atlantic. Typhoons are a kind of hurricane that mostly appears in the China Sea or the Philippines. Tornadoes occur over land.

36. GREENHOUSE : PLANTS :: AVIARY : (***a.* birds**, *b.* bees, *c.* rodents, *d.* fish)

(a) A greenhouse houses plants. An aviary houses birds.

37. (***a.* $A \cap B$**, *b.* $B \cap A$, *c.* $A \cup B$, *d.* $B \cup A$) : $B \cup A$ :: $X \wedge Y$: $Y \vee X$

(a) $A \cap B$ and $X \wedge Y$ are equivalent, as are $B \cup A$ and $Y \vee X$.

38. OFFER : JOB :: TENDER : (***a.* resignation**, *b.* retirement, *c.* delicate, *d.* rough)

(a) One offers a job, but tenders a resignation.

39. HICCUP : HICCOUGH :: EYE : (*a.* light, *b.* ice, ***c.* I**, *d.* iris)

(c) Hiccup and hiccough are pronounced identically, as are eye and I.

40. (*a.* black, *b.* white, ***c.* orange**, *d.* brown) : BLUE :: RED : GREEN

(c) Orange and blue are complementary colors, as are red and green. Complementary colors are colors that produce white light when combined.

41. ASPIRIN : (*a.* anaphoric, *b.* mycin, *c.* antibiotic, ***d.* analgesic**) :: PENICILLIN : ANTIBIOTIC

   (d) Aspirin is an analgesic, while penicillin is an antibiotic. Analgesic medication alleviates pain. An antibiotic kills or inhibits the growth of microorganisms. *Anaphoric refers to the repetition of a word or phrase at the beginning of a clause; mycin is a suffix that refers to a substance gained from a fungus-like bacterium.*

42. (*a.* Istanbul, *b.* Dar es Salaam, *c.* Jerusalem, ***d.* Mecca**) : MOHAMMED :: BETHLEHEM : JESUS

   (d) Mecca was the birthplace of Mohammed, while Bethlehem was the birthplace of Jesus.

43. CETANE : DIESEL FUEL OIL :: (***a.* octane**, *b.* heptane, *c.* methane, *d.* propane) : GASOLINE

   (a) Diesel fuel oil is given a cetane rating as an index of quality, while gasoline is given an octane rating for the same purpose.

44. DEAD DUCK : GONER :: LAME DUCK : (***a.* one who finishes a term after failing re-election**, *b.* one who gives up easily, *c.* one who invests cautiously, *d.* one who complains incessantly)

   (a) A dead duck is a goner; a lame duck is an elected official who finishes his or her term after failing re-election, or whose term is about to expire due to term limits.

45. ARGONAUTS : (*a.* Francis Marion, ***b.* Jason**, *c.* Achilles, *d.* George Washington) :: GREEN MOUNTAIN BOYS : ETHAN ALLEN

   (b) The Argonauts accompanied Jason in his exploits; the Green Mountain Boys accompanied Ethan Allen in his exploits. *Argonautica* is an Ancient Greek poem. The Green Mountain Boys were an informal militia of the Vermont Republic.

46. LYNX : CAT :: BOAR : (***a.* hog**, *b.* dog, *c.* goat, *d.* ram)

   (a) A lynx is a type of wild cat. A boar is a type of wild hog.

47. LENIN : BOLSHEVIK :: (*a.* Stalin, ***b.* Kerensky**, *c.* Trotsky, *d.* Marx) : MENSHEVIK

   (b) After the Russian Revolution, Lenin led the Bolsheviks and Kerensky led the Mensheviks.

48. (*a.* oak, *b.* walnut, ***c.* balsa**, *d.* corundum) : HICKORY :: TIN : STEEL

   (c) Balsa is a soft wood; hickory a hard wood. Tin is a soft metal; steel a hard metal. *Oak is a hard wood, as is walnut. Corundum is a very hard mineral.*

49. ROCK : ROCKET :: (*a.* coat, *b.* cloth, ***c.* jack**, *d.* wasp) : JACKET

   (c) Rocket is rock with *-et* at the end. Jacket is jack with *-et* at the end.

50. MALARIA : CHILLS :: GOITER : (*a.* pockmarks, ***b.* swelling**, *c.* fever, *d.* hypertension)

   (b) Malaria results in chills. Goiter results in swelling.

51. PIZARRO : INCA :: (*a.* Ponce de Leon, *b.* Hudson, *c.* Velásquez, ***d.* Cortez**) : AZTEC

   (d) Pizarro (ca. 1475–1541) conquered the Inca. Cortez (1485–1547) conquered the Aztec.

52. ASTROLOGY : (*a.* astronomy, *b.* physics, *c.* pharmacology, ***d.* phrenology**) :: ASTRONOMY : ANATOMY

   (d) Astrology and phrenology (drawing conclusions from the shape of skull to character traits) are commonly considered pseudosciences, while astronomy and anatomy are accepted as natural sciences.

53. DUET : SEXTET :: SOLO : (*a.* quartet, *b.* quintet, *c.* chorus, ***d.* trio**)

   (d) Two is to six as one is to three.

54. ANDES : (*a.* Asia, *b.* Africa, ***c.* South America**, *d.* Europe) :: ALPS : EUROPE

(c) The Andes mountain range is in South America; the Alps are in Europe.

55. MYOPIA : (***a.* hyperopia**, *b.* scotopia, *c.* photopia, *d.* metropia) :: NEARSIGHTED : FARSIGHTED

(a) A nearsighted person has myopia, while a farsighted person has hyperopia. *Scotopia is the ability to see in darkness. Photopia is vision in bright light.*

56. PASTORAL : (*a.* religious, ***b.* rustic**, *c.* metropolitan, *d.* worldly) :: URBAN : CITIFIED

(b) Pastoral and rustic are synonyms, as are urban and citified.

57. SEA : TIGER :: LION : (*a.* land, *b.* fauna, ***c.* lily**, *d.* heart)

(c) A sea lion and a tiger lily are both living things.

58. ASTRONAUT : SPACESUIT :: (*a.* judge, *b.* baker, *c.* ballerina, ***d.* monk**) : HABIT

(d) An astronaut wears a spacesuit; a monk wears a habit.

59. MONOGAMY : BIGAMY :: BIPED : (*a.* unipod, *b.* pedate, *c.* millipede, ***d.* quadruped**)

(d) One is to two as two is to four. A biped is a two-footed animal. *A millipede is an invertebrate with many legs.* Pedate *means "having or resembling a foot." A unipod is a pole to support cameras (similar to a tripod).*

60. POPE : ROMAN :: (*a.* Metropolitan, ***b.* Patriarch**, *c.* Cardinal, *d.* Bishop) : GREEK ORTHODOX

(b) The Pope is the spiritual leader of the Roman Catholic Church, while the Patriarch is the spiritual leader of the Greek Orthodox Catholic Church. *A cardinal is a member of the Sacred College in the Roman Catholic Church. Cardinals elect the Pope and serve as his advisors. A bishop is a clergyman overseeing a diocese.*

61. SEXTANT : (***a.* navigator**, *b.* architect, *c.* archeologist, *d.* priest) :: SCALPEL : SURGEON

(a) A sextant is used by a navigator, while a scalpel is used by a surgeon.

62. PRIDE : PREJUDICE :: SENSE : (*a.* Folly, *b.* Pretense, ***c.* Sensibility**, *d.* Sanity)

(c) *Pride and Prejudice* and *Sense and Sensibility* are both novels by Jane Austen.

63. PACIFIST : PEACE :: (***a.* revolutionary**, *b.* diplomat, *c.* charlatan, *d.* traitor) : CHANGE

(a) A pacifist seeks peace; a revolutionary seeks radical change, often at the expense of bloodshed.

64. (***a.* brown**, *b.* gray, *c.* purple, *d.* blue) : UMBER :: GREEN : CHARTREUSE

(a) Umber is a shade of brown; chartreuse is a shade of green.

65. INCREASE : LESSEN :: (*a.* fair, ***b.* final**, *c.* incipient, *d.* unfair) : INCHOATE

(b) Increase and lessen are antonyms, as are final and inchoate.

66. EXCALIBUR : (***a.* sword**, *b.* pony, *c.* lioness, *d.* cannon) :: LASSIE : DOG

(a) Excalibur was the name of a sword (King Arthur's). Lassie was the name of a dog (Jeff Miller's).

67. (***a.* Bern**, *b.* Geneva, *c.* Zurich, *d.* Lucerne) : SWITZERLAND :: NEW DELHI : INDIA

(a) Bern is the capital of Switzerland; New Delhi is the capital of India.

68. SILVER-TONGUED : ELOQUENT :: JANUS-FACED : (***a.* duplicitous**, *b.* versatile, *c.* incredibly ugly, *d.* honest)

(a) A silver-tongued person is eloquent. A Janus-faced person is duplicitous—literally, two-faced.

69. PRESENT : FUTURE PERFECT :: GO : (*a.* would go, *b.* will go, *c.* **will have gone**, *d.* would have gone)

   (c) Go is the present tense, and will have gone the future perfect tense, of the same verb.

70. AMPLITUDE : FREQUENCY :: RATE : (*a.* distance, *b.* velocity, *c.* acceleration, *d.* **time**)

   (d) Amplitude and frequency of a wave are inversely related, as are rate and time traveled by an object.

71. GREENHORN : NOVICE :: NEOPHYTE : (*a.* expert, *b.* priest, *c.* **beginner**, *d.* novelist)

   (c) Greenhorn, novice, neophyte, and beginner are all synonymous.

72. PANEGYRIC : (*a.* prayer, *b.* joke, *c.* threat, *d.* **eulogy**) :: TEMPEST : STORM

   (d) A panegyric is a eulogy. A tempest is a storm.

73. CARMEN : (*a.* Verdi, *b.* **Bizet**, *c.* Gounod, *d.* Wagner) :: BARBER OF SEVILLE : ROSSINI

   (b) *Carmen* is an opera by Bizet. *The Barber of Seville* is an opera by Rossini. *Rigoletto and* Nabucco *were composed by Verdi. The opera* Faust *is by Gounod. Wagner wrote* The Ring of the Nibelung.

74. PALPITATE : QUIVER :: MASTICATE : (*a.* abuse, *b.* remove, *c.* stomp, *d.* **chew**)

   (d) To palpitate is to quiver. To masticate is to chew.

75. BOLÍVAR : (*a.* Venezuela, *b.* **Spain**, *c.* United States, *d.* Mexico) :: WASHINGTON : ENGLAND

   (b) Simon Bolívar fought against Spain for the liberation of South American countries. George Washington fought against England for the liberation of the newly formed United States.

76. CORNUCOPIA : (*a.* **horn of plenty**, *b.* horn of Roland, *c.* hornpipe, *d.* hornstone) :: TENET : PRECEPT

   (a) A cornucopia is a horn of plenty. A tenet is a precept.

77. SHRIMP : CRUSTACEAN :: (*a.* **snail**, *b.* lobster, *c.* goldfish, *d.* brine) : MOLLUSK

   (a) A shrimp is a form of crustacean. A snail is a form of mollusk. *A lobster is a crustacean; a goldfish is a freshwater fish; brine is water containing salts.*

78. NEW AMSTERDAM : NEW YORK :: SIAM : (*a.* **Thailand**, *b.* Cambodia, *c.* Laos, *d.* China)

   (a) New York was formerly called New Amsterdam. Thailand was formerly called Siam. *Cambodia was formerly named the Khmer Republic and Kampuchea.*

79. HIRSUTE : (*a.* pleasantly plump, *b.* well-dressed, *c.* handsome, *d.* **hairy**) :: EXTROVERTED : OUTGOING

   (d) A hirsute person is hairy. An extroverted person is outgoing.

80. EYE : LIP :: ELBOW : (*a.* forehead, *b.* nose, *c.* **foot**, *d.* chest)

   (c) A normal human being has two eyes, lips, elbows, and feet.

81. (*a.* feldspar, *b.* **talc**, *c.* quartz, *d.* topaz) : 1 :: DIAMOND : 10

   (b) On the Mohs scale of hardness, talc is rated 1 (softest) and diamond is rated 10 (hardest). Quartz is rated 7; feldspar is rated 6; topaz is rated 8.

82. TORTUOUS : (*a.* painless, *b.* painful, *c.* **straight**, *d.* winding) :: SOBER : INEBRIATED

   (c) Tortuous and straight are opposites, as are sober and inebriated.

83. NONPLUS : (**a. perplexity**, *b.* disappointment, *c.* deletion, *d.* elation) :: NONPAREIL : UNEQUALED

(a) Nonplus is perplexity. Something that is nonpareil is unequaled.

84. CROCKETT : ALAMO :: BONAPARTE : (*a.* Madrid, **b. St. Helena**, *c.* Rome, *d.* London)

(b) Davy Crockett died at the Alamo. Napoleon Bonaparte died on St. Helena.

85. EL GRECO : (*a.* impressionist, **b. mannerist**, *c.* expressionist, *d.* realist) :: DAVID : NEOCLASSICIST

(b) El Greco was a mannerist painter. David was a neoclassicist painter.

86. GRAY : COUNTRY CHURCHYARD :: (**a. Keats**, *b.* Poe, *c.* Byron, *d.* Longfellow) : GRECIAN URN

(a) Thomas Gray is famous for his "Elegy in a Country Churchyard," while John Keats is famous for his "Ode on a Grecian Urn." *Edgar Allan Poe is famous as a macabre writer; one of his works is* The Pit and the Pendulum. *Henry Wadsworth Longfellow was an American poet whose works include* Paul Revere's Ride. *George Byron was a British poet and wrote* When We Two Parted.

87. MITER : (*a.* dancer, *b.* cartoonist, *c.* queen, **d. bishop**) :: CROWN : KING

(d) A miter is a headpiece worn by a bishop. A crown is a headpiece worn by a king.

88. $2^0 : 2^{-2} :: 2^2 : (a.\ 2^{1/4}, \textbf{b.}\ \textbf{2}^0, c.\ 2^1, d.\ 2^{-1})$

(b) 1 is to $^1/_4$ as 4 is to 1.

89. FLOWER : GARDEN :: (*a.* pinnacle, **b. stalagmite**, *c.* cavern, *d.* explorer) : CAVE

(b) Flowers grow up from a garden; stalagmites "grow" up from the floor of a cave.

90. LEVITICUS : OLD :: (*a.* Deuteronomy, *b.* Isaiah, *c.* Numbers, **d. Ephesians**) : NEW

(d) Leviticus is a book in the Old Testament, while Ephesians is a book in the New Testament. *Deuteronomy, Numbers, and Isaiah are books in the Old Testament of the Bible.*

91. LOUVRE : PARIS :: PRADO : (**a. Madrid**, *b.* Seville, *c.* Florence, *d.* Chartres)

(a) The Louvre is an art museum in Paris; the Prado is an art museum in Madrid.

92. CUL-DE-SAC : BLIND ALLEY :: SANGFROID : (*a.* carelessness, *b.* timidity, *c.* courage, **d. imperturbability**)

(d) A cul-de-sac is a blind alley. Sangfroid is imperturbability.

93. ENCOMIUM : TRIBUTE :: (*a.* admonition, *b.* excoriation, *c.* benison, **d. exegesis**) : CRITICAL ANALYSIS

(d) An encomium is a tribute. An exegesis is a critical analysis.

94. CARPETBAGGER : NORTH :: (*a.* Granger, **b. Scalawag**, *c.* Bull Moose, *d.* Tweety Pie) : SOUTH

(b) After the Civil War, intruders from the North were called carpetbaggers, and Northern sympathizers (usually Republicans) from the South were called scalawags. *The Bull Moose Party is a former political party in the United States founded by Theodore Roosevelt. Tweety Pie is a cartoon character. A granger is a farmer.*

95. MERCURIAL : (*a.* pretty, *b.* plutonic, *c.* hateful, **d. hermetic**) :: MARTIAL : AREOLOGY

(d) The word mercurial is derived from the Roman name and the word hermetic from the Greek name, for the messenger of the gods (Mercury or Hermes, respectively). The word martial is derived from the Roman name, and the word *areology* from the Greek name, for the god of war (Mars or Ares, respectively).

96. LEGATO : BOW :: PIZZICATO : (*a. fingers*, *b.* bow, *c.* reed, *d.* feet)
   (a) On a string instrument, legato notes are played with a bow, while pizzicato notes are played with the fingers.

97. NICK ADAMS : (*a.* Fitzgerald, *b.* Faulkner, *c. Hemingway*, *d.* Joyce) :: ARROWSMITH : LEWIS
   (c) Nick Adams was a character in stories by Ernest Hemingway. Arrowsmith was a character in a novel (entitled *Arrowsmith*) by Sinclair Lewis.

98. (*a.* Burgundian, *b.* Prussian, *c. Turkish*, *d.* Bulgarian) : OTTOMAN :: FRENCH : BOURBON
   (c) The Ottomans were Turkish; the Bourbons were French. *The Burgundians were French; the Prussians were German.*

99. ORPHEUS : EURYDICE :: DAPHNIS : (*a.* Pyramus, *b.* Thisbe, *c. Chloe*, *d.* Helen)
   (c) Orpheus and Eurydice were lovers, as were Daphnis and Chloe. *The story of Pyramus and Thisbe was told by Ovid; they were lovers as well. Helen was the daughter of Zeus and Leda and was abducted by Paris, which led to the Trojan War.*

100. (*a.* darling, *b.* wench, *c. harridan*, *d.* myrmidon) : SHREW :: MOLLYCODDLE : SISSY
   (c) A harridan is a shrew. A mollycoddle is a sissy.

101. PULLEY : (*a. screw*, *b.* saw, *c.* pliers, *d.* nail) :: WEDGE : INCLINED PLANE
   (a) Among the six basic simple machines are a pulley, screw, wedge, and inclined plane (as well as the lever and the wheel and axle).

102. LIVE WIRE : LOOSE CANNON :: ENERGETIC : (*a.* powerful, *b.* threatening, *c. reckless*, *d.* peaceable)
   (c) A person who is very energetic can be described as a live wire, whereas a reckless person can be described as a loose cannon.

103. ARM : LEG :: (*a.* radius, *b.* ulna, *c. humerus*, *d.* scapula) : FEMUR
   (c) The humerus is the upper armbone just as the femur is the upper legbone. *The ulna is the elbow bone. The radius is the bone on the side of the thumb of a forearm. The scapulae are a pair of large triangular bones that form the posterior part of the shoulder.*

104. VENUSIAN : (*a.* Venus, *b. Earth*, *c.* Moon, *d.* Mercury) :: MARTIAN : JUPITER
   (b) A Venusian is a hypothetical inhabitant of the planet whose orbit around the Sun is just inside that of the planet Earth. A Martian is a hypothetical inhabitant of the planet whose orbit is just inside that of Jupiter. The order of the planets orbiting the Sun is (in order from the Sun): Mercury, Venus, Earth, Mars, Jupiter, Saturn, Uranus, Neptune.

105. (*a.* oil, *b.* air, *c.* nitrates, *d. blood*) : TOURNIQUET :: WATER : DAM
   (d) The function of a tourniquet is to stop the flow of blood beyond a certain point just as the function of a dam is to stop the flow of water beyond a certain point.

106. OBJURGATE : (*a. vituperate*, *b.* venerate, *c.* abrogate, *d.* enervate) :: RECANT : RETRACT
   (a) To objurgate is to harshly criticize, as is to vituperate. Likewise, recant and retract share the same meaning, to withdraw in a way.

107. PERFIDIOUS : BENEFICENT :: (*a.* obvious, *b. capricious*, *c.* intractable, *d.* renitent) : STEADFAST
   (b) Perfidious and beneficent are antonyms, as are capricious, meaning changing quickly, and steadfast, meaning dependable and constant.

108. MAN : LAZARUS :: BIRD : (*a.* dragon, *b.* albatross, *c.* **phoenix**, *d.* dodo)

(**c**) Lazarus was a man said to rise from the dead. The phoenix was a bird said to rise from the dead.

109. FIREWORKS : (*a.* Japan, *b.* Korea, *c.* Indonesia, *d.* **China**) :: LIGHTBULB : THE UNITED STATES

(**d**) Fireworks were first invented in China just as the lightbulb was first known in the United States.

110. GI TRACT : GI JOE :: GASTROINTESTINAL : (*a.* General Infantry, *b.* Galvanized Iron, *c.* **Government Issue**, *d.* General Information)

(**c**) GI Tract is short for Gastrointestinal Tract. GI Joe is short for Government Issue Joe (which is also an action figure).

111. WET SUIT : (*a.* spandex, *b.* **neoprene**, *c.* nylon, *d.* Lycra) :: BULLETPROOF VEST : KEVLAR

(**b**) The artificial material used to make wet suits is neoprene just as the artificial material used to make bulletproof vests is Kevlar. *Spandex is an elastic synthetic fiber; the most famous brand name associated with Spandex is Lycra. Nylon is a strong elastic polyamide material.*

112. (*a.* **yellow**, *b.* pink, *c.* white, *d.* green) : BLUE :: JAUNDICED : CYANOTIC

(**a**) Someone who is jaundiced has a skin color that is tinted yellow. Likewise, a cyanotic person has blue-tinted skin.

113. MONET : WATER LILIES :: DEGAS : (*a.* windmills, *b.* sailboats, *c.* polo players, *d.* **ballet dancers**)

(**d**) Just as Monet had water lilies as a favorite subject for his art, so did Degas often feature ballet dancers in his paintings and sculptures.

114. WAR : (*a.* birth, *b.* **flood**, *c.* death, *d.* fall) :: ANTEBELLUM : ANTEDILUVIAN

(**b**) Antebellum refers to a time before a war and antediluvian refers to a time before the flood. Prenatal means "before birth"; antemortem refers to the time before death.

115. DILETTANTE : DEBUTANTE :: (*a.* **amateur**, *b.* professional, *c.* actor, *d.* student) : YOUNG WOMAN

(**a**) Dilettantes are amateurs and debutantes are young women.

116. DOG : CAT :: (*a.* loud, *b.* skinny, *c.* **under**, *d.* hound) : FAT

(**c**) "Underdog" and "fat cat" are both terms used to describe types of people.

117. RIDE : (*a.* U.S. senator, *b.* doctor, *c.* pilot, *d.* **astronaut**) :: O'CONNOR : SUPREME COURT JUSTICE

(**d**) Sally Ride was the first female astronaut. Sandra Day O'Connor was the first female Supreme Court Justice.

118. (*a.* panda, *b.* **opossum**, *c.* mouse, *d.* anteater) : WALLABY :: KANGAROO : WOMBAT

(**b**) Opossums, wallabies, kangaroos, and wombats are all marsupial mammals.

119. ANDREW : ABRAHAM :: LYNDON : (*a.* **John**, *b.* Robert, *c.* Joseph, *d.* Edward)

(**a**) Andrew Johnson succeeded Abraham Lincoln as president. Lyndon Johnson succeeded John Kennedy as president.

120. MYOPIA : CONCAVE :: (*a.* mytopia, *b.* astigmatism, *c.* **hyperopia**, *d.* diopia) : CONVEX

(**c**) A concave lens is typically used to correct for myopia, or nearsightedness. A convex lens corrects for hyperopia (farsightedness).

ANSWER SHEET
Practice Test 6

1. Ⓐ Ⓑ Ⓒ Ⓓ	31. Ⓐ Ⓑ Ⓒ Ⓓ	61. Ⓐ Ⓑ Ⓒ Ⓓ	91. Ⓐ Ⓑ Ⓒ Ⓓ
2. Ⓐ Ⓑ Ⓒ Ⓓ	32. Ⓐ Ⓑ Ⓒ Ⓓ	62. Ⓐ Ⓑ Ⓒ Ⓓ	92. Ⓐ Ⓑ Ⓒ Ⓓ
3. Ⓐ Ⓑ Ⓒ Ⓓ	33. Ⓐ Ⓑ Ⓒ Ⓓ	63. Ⓐ Ⓑ Ⓒ Ⓓ	93. Ⓐ Ⓑ Ⓒ Ⓓ
4. Ⓐ Ⓑ Ⓒ Ⓓ	34. Ⓐ Ⓑ Ⓒ Ⓓ	64. Ⓐ Ⓑ Ⓒ Ⓓ	94. Ⓐ Ⓑ Ⓒ Ⓓ
5. Ⓐ Ⓑ Ⓒ Ⓓ	35. Ⓐ Ⓑ Ⓒ Ⓓ	65. Ⓐ Ⓑ Ⓒ Ⓓ	95. Ⓐ Ⓑ Ⓒ Ⓓ
6. Ⓐ Ⓑ Ⓒ Ⓓ	36. Ⓐ Ⓑ Ⓒ Ⓓ	66. Ⓐ Ⓑ Ⓒ Ⓓ	96. Ⓐ Ⓑ Ⓒ Ⓓ
7. Ⓐ Ⓑ Ⓒ Ⓓ	37. Ⓐ Ⓑ Ⓒ Ⓓ	67. Ⓐ Ⓑ Ⓒ Ⓓ	97. Ⓐ Ⓑ Ⓒ Ⓓ
8. Ⓐ Ⓑ Ⓒ Ⓓ	38. Ⓐ Ⓑ Ⓒ Ⓓ	68. Ⓐ Ⓑ Ⓒ Ⓓ	98. Ⓐ Ⓑ Ⓒ Ⓓ
9. Ⓐ Ⓑ Ⓒ Ⓓ	39. Ⓐ Ⓑ Ⓒ Ⓓ	69. Ⓐ Ⓑ Ⓒ Ⓓ	99. Ⓐ Ⓑ Ⓒ Ⓓ
10. Ⓐ Ⓑ Ⓒ Ⓓ	40. Ⓐ Ⓑ Ⓒ Ⓓ	70. Ⓐ Ⓑ Ⓒ Ⓓ	100. Ⓐ Ⓑ Ⓒ Ⓓ
11. Ⓐ Ⓑ Ⓒ Ⓓ	41. Ⓐ Ⓑ Ⓒ Ⓓ	71. Ⓐ Ⓑ Ⓒ Ⓓ	101. Ⓐ Ⓑ Ⓒ Ⓓ
12. Ⓐ Ⓑ Ⓒ Ⓓ	42. Ⓐ Ⓑ Ⓒ Ⓓ	72. Ⓐ Ⓑ Ⓒ Ⓓ	102. Ⓐ Ⓑ Ⓒ Ⓓ
13. Ⓐ Ⓑ Ⓒ Ⓓ	43. Ⓐ Ⓑ Ⓒ Ⓓ	73. Ⓐ Ⓑ Ⓒ Ⓓ	103. Ⓐ Ⓑ Ⓒ Ⓓ
14. Ⓐ Ⓑ Ⓒ Ⓓ	44. Ⓐ Ⓑ Ⓒ Ⓓ	74. Ⓐ Ⓑ Ⓒ Ⓓ	104. Ⓐ Ⓑ Ⓒ Ⓓ
15. Ⓐ Ⓑ Ⓒ Ⓓ	45. Ⓐ Ⓑ Ⓒ Ⓓ	75. Ⓐ Ⓑ Ⓒ Ⓓ	105. Ⓐ Ⓑ Ⓒ Ⓓ
16. Ⓐ Ⓑ Ⓒ Ⓓ	46. Ⓐ Ⓑ Ⓒ Ⓓ	76. Ⓐ Ⓑ Ⓒ Ⓓ	106. Ⓐ Ⓑ Ⓒ Ⓓ
17. Ⓐ Ⓑ Ⓒ Ⓓ	47. Ⓐ Ⓑ Ⓒ Ⓓ	77. Ⓐ Ⓑ Ⓒ Ⓓ	107. Ⓐ Ⓑ Ⓒ Ⓓ
18. Ⓐ Ⓑ Ⓒ Ⓓ	48. Ⓐ Ⓑ Ⓒ Ⓓ	78. Ⓐ Ⓑ Ⓒ Ⓓ	108. Ⓐ Ⓑ Ⓒ Ⓓ
19. Ⓐ Ⓑ Ⓒ Ⓓ	49. Ⓐ Ⓑ Ⓒ Ⓓ	79. Ⓐ Ⓑ Ⓒ Ⓓ	109. Ⓐ Ⓑ Ⓒ Ⓓ
20. Ⓐ Ⓑ Ⓒ Ⓓ	50. Ⓐ Ⓑ Ⓒ Ⓓ	80. Ⓐ Ⓑ Ⓒ Ⓓ	110. Ⓐ Ⓑ Ⓒ Ⓓ
21. Ⓐ Ⓑ Ⓒ Ⓓ	51. Ⓐ Ⓑ Ⓒ Ⓓ	81. Ⓐ Ⓑ Ⓒ Ⓓ	111. Ⓐ Ⓑ Ⓒ Ⓓ
22. Ⓐ Ⓑ Ⓒ Ⓓ	52. Ⓐ Ⓑ Ⓒ Ⓓ	82. Ⓐ Ⓑ Ⓒ Ⓓ	112. Ⓐ Ⓑ Ⓒ Ⓓ
23. Ⓐ Ⓑ Ⓒ Ⓓ	53. Ⓐ Ⓑ Ⓒ Ⓓ	83. Ⓐ Ⓑ Ⓒ Ⓓ	113. Ⓐ Ⓑ Ⓒ Ⓓ
24. Ⓐ Ⓑ Ⓒ Ⓓ	54. Ⓐ Ⓑ Ⓒ Ⓓ	84. Ⓐ Ⓑ Ⓒ Ⓓ	114. Ⓐ Ⓑ Ⓒ Ⓓ
25. Ⓐ Ⓑ Ⓒ Ⓓ	55. Ⓐ Ⓑ Ⓒ Ⓓ	85. Ⓐ Ⓑ Ⓒ Ⓓ	115. Ⓐ Ⓑ Ⓒ Ⓓ
26. Ⓐ Ⓑ Ⓒ Ⓓ	56. Ⓐ Ⓑ Ⓒ Ⓓ	86. Ⓐ Ⓑ Ⓒ Ⓓ	116. Ⓐ Ⓑ Ⓒ Ⓓ
27. Ⓐ Ⓑ Ⓒ Ⓓ	57. Ⓐ Ⓑ Ⓒ Ⓓ	87. Ⓐ Ⓑ Ⓒ Ⓓ	117. Ⓐ Ⓑ Ⓒ Ⓓ
28. Ⓐ Ⓑ Ⓒ Ⓓ	58. Ⓐ Ⓑ Ⓒ Ⓓ	88. Ⓐ Ⓑ Ⓒ Ⓓ	118. Ⓐ Ⓑ Ⓒ Ⓓ
29. Ⓐ Ⓑ Ⓒ Ⓓ	59. Ⓐ Ⓑ Ⓒ Ⓓ	89. Ⓐ Ⓑ Ⓒ Ⓓ	119. Ⓐ Ⓑ Ⓒ Ⓓ
30. Ⓐ Ⓑ Ⓒ Ⓓ	60. Ⓐ Ⓑ Ⓒ Ⓓ	90. Ⓐ Ⓑ Ⓒ Ⓓ	120. Ⓐ Ⓑ Ⓒ Ⓓ

Time: 60 MINUTES

> **Directions:** In each of the following questions, you will find three initial terms and, in parentheses, four answer options designated *a*, *b*, *c*, and *d*. You are to select from the four answer options the one that *best* completes the analogy with the three initial terms. To record your answers, use the answer sheet provided.

1. LETTER : WORD :: (*a.* paragraph, *b.* word, *c.* period, *d.* meaning) : SENTENCE

2. GIVEN NAME : FIRST :: (*a.* Christian name, *b.* real name, *c.* nickname, *d.* surname) : LAST

3. JUDICIARY : (*a.* Circuit Court, *b.* Supreme Court, *c.* District Court, *d.* Court of Appeals) :: LEGISLATIVE : CONGRESS

4. (*a.* magna cum laude, *b.* optima cum laude, *c.* puella cum laude, *d.* summa cum laude) : HIGHEST HONOR :: CUM LAUDE : HONOR

5. WILLIAM JAMES : PHILOSOPHER :: HENRY JAMES : (*a.* chemist, *b.* novelist, *c.* lawyer, *d.* politician)

6. OUNCE : PREVENTION :: POUND : (*a.* remedy, *b.* prophylaxis, *c.* medicine, *d.* cure)

7. (*a.* decline, *b.* recline, *c.* acclaim, *d.* reclaim) : ASCEND :: INCLINE : DESCEND

8. CARNIVORE : ANIMALS :: (*a.* omnivore, *b.* herbivore, *c.* carnivore, *d.* vegetivore) : VEGETABLES

9. COLD : (*a.* caress, *b.* shiver, *c.* legs, *d.* shoulder) :: OPEN : ARMS

10. DROUGHT : (*a.* desert, *b.* thirst, *c.* rain, *d.* crops) :: FAMINE : FOOD

11. WESTMINSTER ABBEY : ENGLAND :: TAJ MAHAL : (*a.* Iran, *b.* India, *c.* Pakistan, *d.* China)

12. LEGISLATOR : MAKES :: POLICE OFFICER : (*a.* interprets, *b.* enforces, *c.* breaks, *d.* enacts)

13. DIRECT : INDIRECT :: HIM : (*a.* him, *b.* his, *c.* he, *d.* he'd)

14. ZIP : LETTER :: AREA : (*a.* volume, *b.* πr^2, *c.* post box, *d.* telephone call)

15. COURSE : COARSE :: (*a.* ruffle, *b.* direction, *c.* jagged, *d.* golf) : ROUGH

16. DIRIGIBLE : (*a.* air, *b.* sea, *c.* land, *d.* underground) :: AUTOMOBILE : LAND

17. MENDEL : (*a.* inequality, *b.* dominance, *c.* depression, *d.* orbits) :: MENDELEEV : PERIODICITY

18. LIVID : ASHEN :: JAUNDICED : (*a.* white, *b.* black, *c.* red, *d.* yellow)

19. AMIABLE : UNFRIENDLY :: AFFABLE : (*a.* unpleasant, *b.* ugly, *c.* beautiful, *d.* kindly)

20. JUNEAU : ALASKA :: (*a.* Waikiki, *b.* Honolulu, *c.* Oahu, *d.* Hawaii) : HAWAII

21. EAT : DRINK :: EDIBLE : (*a.* palpable, *b.* potable, *c.* lacteal, *d.* labile)

22. WHITE LIE : LIE :: (*a.* hurricane, *b.* drizzle, *c.* storm, *d.* humidity) : RAINFALL

23. (*a.* net, *b.* ten, *c.* met, *d.* end) : TEND :: MEN : MEND

24. FLAPJACK : (*a.* pumpkin pie, *b.* pancake, *c.* sponge cake, *d.* paddycake) :: GRIDDLECAKE : HOTCAKE

25. BINOMIAL : POLYNOMIAL :: TWO : (*a.* four, *b.* eight, *c.* all, *d.* many)

26. SAUDI ARABIA : OIL :: (*a.* Iran, *b.* Ethiopia, *c.* Hungary, *d.* Panama) : COFFEE

27. MONARCHY : ONE :: OLIGARCHY : (*a.* two, *b.* three, *c.* several, *d.* multitudes)

28. PASADENA : FOOTBALL :: WIMBLEDON : (*a.* tennis, *b.* boxing, *c.* golf, *d.* basketball)

29. MOLEHILL : EARTH :: DUNE : (*a.* rock, *b.* desert, *c.* mud, *d.* sand)

30. (*a.* plankton, *b.* gizzard, *c.* oyster, *d.* dinosaur) : REPTILE :: FROG : AMPHIBIAN

31. (*a.* Andersen, *b.* Grimm, *c.* Milne, *d.* Alcott) : WINNIE :: DISNEY : MICKEY

32. PATRICIAN : PLEBEIAN :: NOBILITY : (*a.* clergy, *b.* lordship, *c.* proletariat, *d.* bourgeoisie)

33. (*a.* fungi, *b.* water, *c.* gases, *d.* algae) : HYDROLOGY :: LIFE : BIOLOGY

34. GOTHIC : POINTED :: ROMANESQUE : (*a.* rounded, *b.* scalloped, *c.* squared, *d.* buttressed)

35. (*a.* 7, *b.* 9, *c.* 10, *d.* 12) : PLAGUES :: 7 : DEADLY SINS

36. STEP : PETS :: REEL : (*a.* fishes, *b.* rod, *c.* leer, *d.* real)

37. HAWK : PREY :: SWINDLER : (*a.* dupe, *b.* dodge, *c.* doll, *d.* dolt)

38. SOPORIFIC : (*a.* pain, *b.* sleepiness, *c.* hunger, *d.* thirst) :: APHRODISIAC : SEXUAL DESIRE

39. PASTEURIZE : (*a.* chemically treat, *b.* strain, *c.* chill, *d.* partially sterilize) :: HOMOGENIZE : MAKE UNIFORM

40. DECLARATIVE : . :: INTERROGATIVE : (*a.* !, *b.* :, *c.* -, *d.* ?)

41. ALLEGRO : (*a.* largo, *b.* presto, *c.* crescendo, *d.* cantabile) :: FAST : SLOW

42. PENCE : POUND :: CENTS : (*a.* nickel, *b.* dime, *c.* quarter, *d.* dollar)

43. CLANDESTINE : (*a.* surreptitious, *b.* tacit, *c.* sanguine, *d.* outgoing) :: SHY : DIFFIDENT

44. INCOGNITO : (*a.* ignorant, *b.* uninterested, *c.* unofficial, *d.* disguised) :: SATISFACTORY : ADEQUATE

45. ANTIDOTE : POISON :: (*a.* mycin, *b.* antibiotic, *c.* analgesic, *d.* antigen) : INFECTION

46. DIRTY : LINEN :: FILTHY : (*a.* flax, *b.* burlap, *c.* lummox, *d.* lucre)

47. POLAR : (*a.* equatorial, *b.* mammoth, *c.* coordinate, *d.* grizzly) :: FORD : CHEVROLET

48. ONTOLOGY : BEING :: EPISTEMOLOGY : (*a.* spirit, *b.* knowledge, *c.* metaphysics, *d.* causality)

49. RECORDER : (*a.* flute, *b.* magnetic tape, *c.* player piano, *d.* trombone) :: LUTE : GUITAR

50. MILLIMETER : METER :: METER : (*a.* centimeter, *b.* decimeter, *c.* decameter, *d.* kilometer)

51. GENDARMES : FRANCE :: CARABINIERI : (*a.* Spain, *b.* Italy, *c.* Switzerland, *d.* Turkey)

52. RENOIR : IMPRESSIONIST :: (*a.* Braque, *b.* Matisse, *c.* Monet, *d.* Stella) : CUBIST

53. SCOTLAND YARD : CRIME :: EXCHEQUER : (*a.* agriculture, *b.* industry, *c.* defense, *d.* money)

54. (*a.* magician, *b.* tycoon, *c.* adventurer, *d.* usurer) : GENTLEMAN OF FORTUNE :: ATTENDANT : GENTLEMAN IN WAITING

55. HALCYON : (*a.* tranquil, *b.* agitated, *c.* bounteous, *d.* impoverished) :: FORTUITOUS : PLANNED

56. UTOPIA : (*a.* More, *b.* Plato, *c.* Becket, *d.* Aquinas) :: LILLIPUT : SWIFT

57. MERIDIAN : LONGITUDE :: (*a.* meridian, *b.* prime, *c.* parallel, *d.* perpendicular) : LATITUDE

58. CENTURY : HUNDRED :: MILLENNIUM : (*a.* A.D. 1, *b.* eternity, *c.* thousand, *d.* million)

59. COLD-BLOODED : HARD-HEARTED :: HOT-BLOODED : (*a.* cruel, *b.* listless, *c.* cold-hearted, *d.* excitable)

60. ASSIDUOUS : (*a.* ambitious, *b.* favorable, *c.* diligent, *d.* evergreen) :: ASSIMILATE : ABSORB

61. NETREBKO : SOPRANO :: DOMINGO : (*a.* soprano, *b.* contralto, *c.* tenor, *d.* bass)

62. CARDINAL : ORDINAL :: 8 : (*a.* −2, *b.* 60%, *c.* 5th, *d.* 9)

63. VALJEAN : (*a.* Mauriac, *b.* Balzac, *c.* Hugo, *d.* Molière) :: GORIOT : BALZAC

64. MAUVE : (*a.* brown, *b.* red, *c.* purple, *d.* green) :: TAN : BROWN

65. RANGERS : (*a.* basketball, *b.* polo, *c.* football, *d.* hockey) :: CARDINALS : BASEBALL

66. CARTIER : (*a.* Hudson, *b.* Missouri, *c.* St. Lawrence, *d.* Cartesian) :: MARQUETTE : MISSISSIPPI

67. BUCOLIC : (*a.* rural, *b.* urban, *c.* spicy, *d.* mild) :: TIMID : SHY

68. MERSEAULT : (*a.* Linda, *b.* Suzanne, *c.* Jacqueline, *d.* Marie) :: TOM : BECKY

69. (*a.* scrupulous, *b.* shrewd, *c.* ingenuous, *d.* indigenous) : WILY :: NAIVE : SOPHISTICATED

70. MAXIM : (*a.* chisel, *b.* saw, *c.* palindrome, *d.* deed) :: ADAGE : PROVERB

71. BUCKINGHAM PALACE : MONARCH OF ENGLAND :: PANDEMONIUM : (*a.* Neptune, *b.* Genghis Khan, *c.* Satan, *d.* Citizen Kane)

72. TAXONOMY : LIFE FORMS :: NOSOLOGY : (*a.* noses, *b.* laws, *c.* coins, *d.* diseases)

73. PENOLOGY : OENOLOGY :: PEAL : (*a.* wine, *b.* oil, *c.* poll, *d.* eel)

74. FATHERS : SONS :: SONS (*a.* Daughters, *b.* Lovers, *c.* Strangers, *d.* Mothers)

75. CATATONIC : HEBEPHRENIC :: ANAL : (*a.* genital, *b.* phallic, *c.* oral, *d.* Oedipal)

76. (*a.* Joyce, *b.* Wilde, *c.* James, *d.* O'Henry) : DORIAN GRAY :: JOYCE : ARTIST AS A YOUNG MAN

77. EISENHOWER : REPUBLICAN :: (*a.* T. Roosevelt, *b.* Harrison, *c.* Fillmore, *d.* Wilson) : BULL MOOSE

78. TANGENT X : COTANGENT X :: X : (*a.* X^2, *b.* $1/X$, *c.* $X-1$, *d.* $\tan X - \sin X$)

79. (*a.* mammals, *b.* life, *c.* fish, *d.* humans) : PALEOZOIC :: DINOSAURS : MESOZOIC

80. CITY OF SEVEN HILLS : ROME :: CITY OF LIGHT : (*a.* New York, *b.* Paris, *c.* London, *d.* Venice)

81. SLEEP : SOMNAMBULIST :: (*a.* pimp, *b.* crime, *c.* street, *d.* bed) : GANG

82. CELSIUS : 0 :: KELVIN : (*a.* 32, *b.* 0, *c.* −100, *d.* 273)

83. DIONYSUS : DAMOCLES :: (*a.* Zeus, *b.* Pandora, *c.* Ares, *d.* Cronus) : PROMETHEUS

84. PENCIL LEAD : GRAPHITE :: CHALK : (*a.* limestone, *b.* sandstone, *c.* talc, *d.* gypsum)

85. MAUDLIN : (*a.* immature, *b.* humorous, *c.* munificent, *d.* mawkish) :: MODERATE : TEMPERATE

86. RHEOSTAT : ELECTRICITY :: (*a.* automobile, *b.* traffic light, *c.* car-counter, *d.* bottleneck) : TRAFFIC

87. CHAUCER : SWEET SHOWERS :: ELIOT : (*a.* stinging rain, *b.* sweet breath, *c.* swich licour, *d.* cruellest month)

88. $8^{-1} : 8^1 :: -1 : (a. -64, b. -8, c. 8, d. 64)$

89. BIGOT : ZEALOT :: TROGLODYTE : (*a.* cave dweller, *b.* hero, *c.* traitor, *d.* reformer)

90. TEMPER : (*a.* piano, *b.* moisture, *c.* docility, *d.* tape recorder) :: FOCUS : CAMERA

91. ZEUS : HERA :: (*a.* Ulysses, *b.* Orestes, *c.* Agamemnon, *d.* Paris) : CLYTEMNESTRA

92. TRITIUM : HYDROGEN :: OZONE : (*a.* oxygen, *b.* nitrogen, *c.* carbon dioxide, *d.* cesium)

93. METROPOLITAN MUSEUM : NEW YORK :: RIJKSMUSEUM : (*a.* Utrecht, *b.* Munich, *c.* Paris, *d.* Amsterdam)

94. POSEIDON : (*a.* Uranus, *b.* Mars, *c.* Saturn, *d.* Neptune) :: ZEUS : JUPITER

95. (*a.* zz, *b.* Zuider, *c.* zero, *d.* zee) : ZED :: BAR : PUB

96. (*a.* hot, *b.* bacterium, *c.* virus, *d.* lungs) : TUBERCULOSIS :: VIRUS : COLD

97. MOLLY : (*a.* Madison, *b.* Monroe, *c.* Maguire, *d.* Malone) :: KNOW : NOTHING

98. ANEMOMETER : WIND SPEED :: MANOMETER : (*a.* blood pressure, *b.* heart rate, *c.* visual acuity, *d.* auditory acuity)

99. HERODOTUS : (*a.* history, *b.* medicine, *c.* his city, *d.* Greece) :: WASHINGTON : HIS COUNTRY

100. (*a.* Washington, *b.* Jackson, *c.* Eisenhower, *d.* Polk) : CORNWALLIS :: GRANT : LEE

101. $Y = X^2$: PARABOLA :: $Y = X + 1$: (*a.* cube, *b.* slope, *c.* circle, *d.* line)

102. NOM DE PLUME : (*a.* maiden name, *b.* middle name, *c.* pen name, *d.* married name) :: JE NE SAIS QUOI : INDEFINABLE QUALITY

103. (*a.* sheep, *b.* mutton, *c.* offal, *d.* venison) : LAMB :: BEEF : VEAL

104. RADIOACTIVE FALLOUT : CHERNOBYL :: (*a.* oil, *b.* propane, *c.* carbon monoxide, *d.* benzene) : PRINCE WILLIAM SOUND

105. HELIUM : NEON :: ARGON : (*a.* cryon, *b.* iodine, *c.* xenon, *d.* hydrogen)

106. BATHYSPHERE : (*a.* rain forest, *b.* ice field, *c.* ocean, *d.* cave) :: SHUTTLE : SPACE

107. DEBUT : GURU :: FRENCH : (*a.* Greek, *b.* Spanish, *c.* Zulu, *d.* Hindi)

108. SHEPHERD : (*a.* sheep, *b.* human, *c.* goat, *d.* dog) :: MAHOUT : ELEPHANT

109. HMS : GREAT BRITAIN :: (*a.* SSS, *b.* SOS, *c.* USAS, *d.* USS) : UNITED STATES

110. (*a.* Ethiopia, *b.* Somalia, *c.* Djibouti, *d.* Eritrea) : MOGADISHU :: KENYA : NAIROBI

111. ALLUSION : ALLEGORY :: REFERENCE : (*a.* summary, *b.* parable, *c.* idiom, *d.* anecdote)

112. HORUS : (*a.* horse, *b.* dog, *c.* hawk, *d.* hare) :: ANUBIS : JACKAL

113. GOERING : NUREMBERG :: (*a.* Hitler, *b.* Hussein, *c.* Mussolini, *d.* Milosevic) : THE HAGUE

114. FOUR SCORE : (*a.* 40, *b.* 4, *c.* 28, *d.* 80) :: BAKER'S DOZEN : 13

115. KHOI SAN : SOUTH AFRICA :: MAORI : (*a.* New Zealand, *b.* Papua New Guinea, *c.* Fiji, *d.* Australia)

116. BEMUSE : AMUSE :: (*a.* humor, *b.* confuse, *c.* irritate, *d.* inspire) : ENTERTAIN

117. PLESSY : FERGUSON :: BROWN : (*a.* The State, *b.* Topeka, *c.* Board of Education, *d.* Wade)

118. HONG KONG : (*a.* Hang Seng, *b.* NASDAQ, *c.* HKSE, *d.* Nikkei) :: UNITED STATES : DOW JONES

119. LAKERS : DODGERS :: (*a.* Orlando, *b.* Minneapolis, *c.* Albany, *d.* New Orleans) : BROOKLYN

120. (*a.* juniper, *b.* hickory, *c.* aspen, *d.* beech) : CEDAR :: TAMARAC : PINE

1.	B	31.	C	61.	C	91.	C
2.	D	32.	C	62.	C	92.	A
3.	B	33.	B	63.	C	93.	D
4.	D	34.	A	64.	C	94.	D
5.	B	35.	C	65.	D	95.	D
6.	D	36.	C	66.	C	96.	B
7.	A	37.	A	67.	A	97.	C
8.	B	38.	B	68.	D	98.	A
9.	D	39.	D	69.	C	99.	A
10.	C	40.	D	70.	B	100.	A
11.	B	41.	A	71.	C	101.	D
12.	A	42.	D	72.	D	102.	C
13.	A	43.	A	73.	D	103.	B
14.	D	44.	D	74.	B	104.	A
15.	B	45.	B	75.	C	105.	C
16.	A	46.	D	76.	B	106.	C
17.	B	47.	D	77.	A	107.	D
18.	D	48.	B	78.	B	108.	A
19.	A	49.	A	79.	C	109.	D
20.	B	50.	D	80.	B	110.	B
21.	B	51.	B	81.	C	111.	B
22.	B	52.	A	82.	D	112.	C
23.	B	53.	D	83.	A	113.	C
24.	B	54.	C	84.	A	114.	D
25.	D	55.	B	85.	D	115.	A
26.	B	56.	A	86.	B	116.	B
27.	C	57.	C	87.	D	117.	C
28.	A	58.	C	88.	A	118.	A
29.	D	59.	D	89.	A	119.	B
30.	D	60.	C	90.	A	120.	A

ANSWER EXPLANATIONS FOR PRACTICE TEST 6

> In the following, explanations concerning the correct responses are in roman font. Explanations regarding distracters (incorrect responses) that are not self-explaining or could be misinterpreted are in italics in order to highlight the explanations of the answers that are correct.

1. LETTER : WORD :: (*a.* paragraph, ***b.* word**, *c.* period, *d.* meaning) : SENTENCE
   (b) A word is composed of letters. A sentence is composed of words.

2. GIVEN NAME : FIRST :: (*a.* Christian name, *b.* real name, *c.* nickname, ***d.* surname**) : LAST
   (d) A given name is a first name. A surname is a last name.

3. JUDICIARY : (*a.* Circuit Court, ***b.* Supreme Court**, *c.* District Court, *d.* Court of Appeals) :: LEGISLATIVE : CONGRESS
   (b) The Supreme Court is the highest judiciary body in the United States. The Congress is the highest legislative body in the United States.

4. (*a.* magna cum laude, *b.* optima cum laude, *c.* puella cum laude, ***d.* summa cum laude**) : HIGHEST HONOR :: CUM LAUDE : HONOR
   (d) *Summa cum laude* denotes highest honor; *cum laude*, honor. *Magna cum laude* means "with great honor." The terms all have Latin roots.

5. WILLIAM JAMES : PHILOSOPHER :: HENRY JAMES : (*a.* chemist, ***b.* novelist**, *c.* lawyer, *d.* politician)
   (b) William James was a philosopher; his brother Henry was a novelist.

6. OUNCE : PREVENTION :: POUND : (*a.* remedy, *b.* prophylaxis, *c.* medicine, ***d.* cure**)
   (d) "An ounce of prevention is worth a pound of cure," or so the saying goes.

7. (***a.* decline**, *b.* recline, *c.* acclaim, *d.* reclaim) : ASCEND :: INCLINE : DESCEND
   (a) Decline and incline are antonyms, as are ascend and descend.

8. CARNIVORE : ANIMALS :: (*a.* omnivore, ***b.* herbivore**, *c.* carnivore, *d.* vegetivore) : VEGETABLES
   (b) A carnivore eats (the flesh of) animals; an herbivore eats vegetables. An omnivore eats both plants and animals.

9. COLD : (*a.* caress, *b.* shiver, *c.* legs, ***d.* shoulder**) :: OPEN : ARMS
   (d) A person may be greeted either with a cold shoulder or with open arms.

10. DROUGHT : (*a.* desert, *b.* thirst, ***c.* rain**, *d.* crops) :: FAMINE : FOOD
    (c) A drought is caused by lack of rain; a famine is caused by lack of food.

11. WESTMINSTER ABBEY : ENGLAND :: TAJ MAHAL : (*a.* Iran, ***b.* India**, *c.* Pakistan, *d.* China)
    (b) Westminster Abbey is in England. The Taj Mahal is in India.

12. LEGISLATOR : MAKES :: POLICE OFFICER : (*a.* interprets, ***b.* enforces**, *c.* breaks, *d.* enacts)
    (b) A legislator makes laws; a police officer enforces them.

13. DIRECT : INDIRECT :: HIM : (***a.* him**, *b.* his, *c.* he, *d.* he'd)
    (a) "Him" is the correct form of the personal pronoun for use as either a direct or an indirect object.

14. ZIP : LETTER :: AREA : (*a.* volume, *b.* πr^2, *c.* post box, ***d.* telephone call**)

   (d) A zip code is used for mailing a letter, while an area code is used for making a telephone call.

15. COURSE : COARSE :: (*a.* ruffle, ***b.* direction**, *c.* jagged, *d.* golf) : ROUGH

   (b) Course and direction are synonyms, as are coarse and rough.

16. DIRIGIBLE : (***a.* air**, *b.* sea, *c.* land, *d.* underground) :: AUTOMOBILE : LAND

   (a) A dirigible travels by air, while an automobile travels by land.

17. MENDEL : (*a.* inequality, ***b.* dominance**, *c.* depression, *d.* orbits) :: MENDELEEV : PERIODICITY

   (b) Mendel formulated the law of dominance (in the field of inheritance); Mendeleev formulated the law of periodicity (in the field of chemistry).

18. LIVID : ASHEN :: JAUNDICED : (*a.* white, *b.* black, *c.* red, ***d.* yellow**)

   (d) Something that is livid is ashen. Something that is jaundiced is yellow.

19. AMIABLE : UNFRIENDLY :: AFFABLE : (***a.* unpleasant**, *b.* ugly, *c.* beautiful, *d.* kindly)

   (a) Amiable and unfriendly are opposites, as are affable and unpleasant.

20. JUNEAU : ALASKA :: (*a.* Waikiki, ***b.* Honolulu**, *c.* Oahu, *d.* Hawaii) : HAWAII

   (b) Juneau is the capital of Alaska; Honolulu is the capital of Hawaii. *Hawaii and Oahu are islands that are part of Hawaii. Waikiki is a neighborhood of Honolulu.*

21. EAT : DRINK :: EDIBLE : (*a.* palpable, ***b.* potable**, *c.* lacteal, *d.* labile)

   (b) One can eat what is edible and drink what is potable.

22. WHITE LIE : LIE :: (*a.* hurricane, ***b.* drizzle**, *c.* storm, *d.* humidity) : RAINFALL

   (b) A white lie is a minor lie; a drizzle is a minor rainfall.

23. (*a.* net, ***b.* ten**, *c.* met, *d.* end) : TEND :: MEN : MEND

   (b) Tend is pronounced as ten, but with an added *d* consonant sound at the end. Mend is pronounced as men, but again with an added *d* consonant sound at the end.

24. FLAPJACK : (*a.* pumpkin pie, ***b.* pancake**, *c.* sponge cake, *d.* paddycake) :: GRIDDLECAKE : HOTCAKE

   (b) Flapjack, pancake, griddlecake, and hotcake are all names for the same food.

25. BINOMIAL : POLYNOMIAL :: TWO : (*a.* four, *b.* eight, *c.* all, ***d.* many**)

   (d) A binomial is an equation with two terms. A polynomial is an equation with many terms.

26. SAUDI ARABIA : OIL :: (*a.* Iran, ***b.* Ethiopia**, *c.* Hungary, *d.* Panama) : COFFEE

   (b) Saudi Arabia is a major source of oil. Ethiopia is a major source of coffee. Though Panama has a tropical climate, its coffee production is surprisingly insignificant.

27. MONARCHY : ONE :: OLIGARCHY : (*a.* two, *b.* three, ***c.* several**, *d.* multitudes)

   (c) A monarchy is a government of one ruler; an oligarchy is a government several individuals rule jointly.

28. PASADENA : FOOTBALL :: WIMBLEDON : (***a.* tennis**, *b.* boxing, *c.* golf, *d.* basketball)

   (a) Pasadena, outside of L.A., is the location of a major football game (the Rose Bowl). Wimbledon is the location of a major tennis tournament in London.

29. MOLEHILL : EARTH :: DUNE : (*a.* rock, *b.* desert, *c.* mud, ***d.* sand**)

   (d) A molehill is composed of earth. A dune is composed of sand.

30. (*a.* plankton, *b.* gizzard, *c.* oyster, ***d.* dinosaur**) : REPTILE :: FROG : AMPHIBIAN

(d) A dinosaur is a form of reptile. A frog is a form of amphibian. Amphibians are cold-blooded vertebrates that have gilled aquatic larvae and air-breathing adults. Reptiles are cold-blooded vertebrates that are different from amphibians in that they have scales and lay hard-shelled amniotic eggs.

31. (*a.* Andersen, *b.* Grimm, ***c.* Milne**, *d.* Alcott) : WINNIE :: DISNEY : MICKEY

(c) A. A. Milne created the character Winnie (the Pooh). Walt Disney created the character Mickey (Mouse). *Anderson wrote* The Princess and the Pea. *The Brothers Grimm wrote* Hansel and Gretel, *among other fairy tales. Alcott wrote* Little Women.

32. PATRICIAN : PLEBEIAN :: NOBILITY : (*a.* clergy, *b.* lordship, ***c.* proletariat**, *d.* bourgeoisie)

(c) In ancient Rome, the patricians were members of the nobility and the plebeians were members of the proletariat.

33. (*a.* fungi, ***b.* water**, *c.* gases, *d.* algae) : HYDROLOGY :: LIFE : BIOLOGY

(b) Hydrology is the study of water; biology is the study of life.

34. GOTHIC : POINTED :: ROMANESQUE : (***a.* rounded**, *b.* scalloped, *c.* squared, *d.* buttressed)

(a) Gothic arches are pointed, while Romanesque arches are rounded.

35. (*a.* 7, *b.* 9, ***c.* 10**, *d.* 12) : PLAGUES :: 7 : DEADLY SINS

(c) There were 10 plagues in Egypt, and there are 7 deadly sins. The 7 deadly sins are pride, avarice, envy, wrath, lust, gluttony, and sloth. The 10 plagues were water to blood, frogs, lice, flies, livestock disease, boils, thunder and hail, locusts, darkness, and the death of the firstborns.

36. STEP : PETS :: REEL : (*a.* fishes, *b.* rod, ***c.* leer**, *d.* real)

(c) *Pets* is *step* spelled backwards. *Leer* is *reel* spelled backwards.

37. HAWK : PREY :: SWINDLER : (***a.* dupe**, *b.* dodge, *c.* doll, *d.* dolt)

(a) A hawk victimizes prey. A swindler victimizes dupes.

38. SOPORIFIC : (*a.* pain, ***b.* sleepiness**, *c.* hunger, *d.* thirst) :: APHRODISIAC : SEXUAL DESIRE

(b) A soporific induces sleepiness. An aphrodisiac induces sexual desire.

39. PASTEURIZE : (*a.* chemically treat, *b.* strain, *c.* chill, ***d.* partially sterilize**) :: HOMOGENIZE : MAKE UNIFORM

(d) To pasteurize milk is to partially sterilize it. To homogenize milk is to make it uniform.

40. DECLARATIVE : . :: INTERROGATIVE : (*a.* !, *b.* :, *c.* -, ***d.* ?**)

(d) A declarative sentence ends with a period (.). An interrogative sentence ends with a question mark (?).

41. ALLEGRO : (***a.* largo**, *b.* presto, *c.* crescendo, *d.* cantabile) :: FAST : SLOW

(a) In music, an allegro tempo is a fast one, while a largo tempo is a slow one. *Presto* means "fast," *crescendo* means "increasing loudness," and *cantabile* means "singing."

42. PENCE : POUND :: CENTS : (*a.* nickel, *b.* dime, *c.* quarter, ***d.* dollar**)

(d) There are 100 pence in a pound (in English currency) and 100 cents in a dollar (in American currency).

43. CLANDESTINE : (***a.* surreptitious**, *b.* tacit, *c.* sanguine, *d.* outgoing) :: SHY : DIFFIDENT

(a) Clandestine means surreptitious. Shy means diffident.

44. INCOGNITO : (*a.* ignorant, *b.* uninterested, *c.* unofficial, ***d.* disguised**) :: SATISFACTORY : ADEQUATE

(d) Incognito means disguised. Satisfactory means adequate.

45. ANTIDOTE : POISON :: (*a.* mycin, ***b.* antibiotic**, *c.* analgesic, *d.* antigen) : INFECTION

(b) An antidote is a cure for the effects of poison; an antibiotic is a remedy for the effects of infection. *Mycin is a suffix that refers to a substance gained from a fungus-like bacterium. Analgesic medication alleviates pain. An antigen is a substance capable of triggering a response from the immune system.*

46. DIRTY : LINEN :: FILTHY : (*a.* flax, *b.* burlap, *c.* lummox, ***d.* lucre**)

(d) Dirty linen and filthy lucre are two common English expressions.

47. POLAR : (*a.* equatorial, *b.* mammoth, *c.* coordinate, ***d.* grizzly**) :: FORD : CHEVROLET

(d) A polar bear and a grizzly bear are two types of bears. A Ford and a Chevrolet are two types of cars.

48. ONTOLOGY : BEING :: EPISTEMOLOGY : (*a.* spirit, ***b.* knowledge**, *c.* metaphysics, *d.* causality)

(b) Ontology is the study of being; epistemology, the study of knowledge.

49. RECORDER : (***a.* flute**, *b.* magnetic tape, *c.* player piano, *d.* trombone) :: LUTE : GUITAR

(a) A recorder is an early form of flute; a lute is an early form of guitar.

50. MILLIMETER : METER :: METER : (*a.* centimeter, *b.* decimeter, *c.* decameter, ***d.* kilometer**)

(d) There are 1000 millimeters in a meter, and 1000 meters in a kilometer.

51. GENDARMES : FRANCE :: CARABINIERI : (*a.* Spain, ***b.* Italy**, *c.* Switzerland, *d.* Turkey)

(b) Police officers in France are called gendarmes; in Italy, they are called carabinieri.

52. RENOIR : IMPRESSIONIST :: (***a.* Braque**, *b.* Matisse, *c.* Monet, *d.* Stella) : CUBIST

(a) Renoir was an impressionist painter; Braque was a cubist. *Matisse was a leading figure in modern art. Monet was an impressionist. Stella was a minimalist.*

53. SCOTLAND YARD : CRIME :: EXCHEQUER : (*a.* agriculture, *b.* industry, *c.* defense, ***d.* money**)

(d) In England, Scotland Yard is charged with the control of crime, the Exchequer with the control of money.

54. (*a.* magician, *b.* tycoon, ***c.* adventurer**, *d.* usurer) : GENTLEMAN OF FORTUNE :: ATTENDANT : GENTLEMAN IN WAITING

(c) A gentleman of fortune is an adventurer. A gentleman in waiting is an attendant.

55. HALCYON : (*a.* tranquil, ***b.* agitated**, *c.* bounteous, *d.* impoverished) :: FORTUITOUS : PLANNED

(b) Halcyon in an antonym of agitated. Fortuitous is an antonym of planned.

56. UTOPIA : (***a.* Moore**, *b.* Plato, *c.* Becket, *d.* Aquinas) :: LILLIPUT : SWIFT

(a) Utopia is a land invented by More; Lilliput is a land invented by Swift in *Gulliver's Travels. Plato wrote the* Socratic Dialogues. *Becket was Archbishop of Canterbury from 1162 to 1170. Aquinas wrote* Summa Theologica *and the* Summa Contra Gentiles.

57. MERIDIAN : LONGITUDE :: (*a.* meridian, *b.* prime, ***c.* parallel**, *d.* perpendicular) : LATITUDE

(c) A meridian is a line of longitude; a parallel is a line of latitude.

58. CENTURY : HUNDRED :: MILLENNIUM : (*a.* A.D. 1, *b.* eternity, ***c.* thousand**, *d.* million)

(c) A century is one hundred years; a millennium is one thousand years.

59. COLD-BLOODED : HARD-HEARTED :: HOT-BLOODED : (*a.* cruel, *b.* listless, *c.* cold-hearted, ***d.* excitable**)

(d) Cold-blooded means hard-hearted. Hot-blooded means excitable.

60. ASSIDUOUS : (*a.* ambitious, *b.* favorable, ***c.* diligent**, *d.* evergreen) :: ASSIMILATE : ABSORB

(c) Assiduous is a synonym of diligent. Assimilate is a synonym of absorb.

61. NETREBKO : SOPRANO :: DOMINGO : (*a.* soprano, *b.* contralto, ***c.* tenor**, *d.* bass)

(c) Anna Netrebko is a renowned soprano; Placido Domingo is a renowned tenor.

62. CARDINAL : ORDINAL :: 8 : (*a.* −2, *b.* 60%, ***c.* 5th**, *d.* 9)

(c) 8 is a cardinal number, and 5th is an ordinal number.

63. VALJEAN : (*a.* Mauriac, *b.* Balzac, ***c.* Hugo**, *d.* Molière) :: GORIOT : BALZAC

(c) Jean Valjean is a character created by the French novelist Victor Hugo. Père Goriot is a character created by the French novelist Honoré de Balzac. *Francois Mauriac wrote* Le Desert de l'Amour. *Honore de Balzac wrote* La Comedie Humaine, *which contains about 100 novels and plays that describe French life after the fall of Napoleon. Moliere (Jean-Baptiste Poquelin) is known for the drama* Le Misanthrope, *among other plays.*

64. MAUVE : (*a.* brown, *b.* red, ***c.* purple**, *d.* green) :: TAN : BROWN

(c) Mauve is a shade of purple; tan is a shade of brown.

65. RANGERS : (*a.* basketball, *b.* polo, *c.* football, ***d.* hockey**) :: CARDINALS : BASEBALL

(d) The Rangers are both a hockey team in NewYork, and a baseball team in Arlington, TX. Here, however, hockey fits best. The Cardinals are a baseball team.

66. CARTIER : (*a.* Hudson, *b.* Missouri, ***c.* St. Lawrence**, *d.* Cartesian) :: MARQUETTE : MISSISSIPPI

(c) Cartier explored the St. Lawrence River; Marquette explored the Mississippi River. *Henry Hudson was the first European who sailed up the Hudson River. The Missouri was first explored by the French: Louis Jolliet and Jacques Marquette. Cartesian means that something is related to the French philosopher Rene Descartes.*

67. BUCOLIC : (***a.* rural**, *b.* urban, *c.* spicy, *d.* mild) :: TIMID : SHY

(a) Bucolic means rural; timid means shy.

68. MERSEAULT : (*a.* Linda, *b.* Suzanne, *c.* Jacqueline, ***d.* Marie**) :: TOM : BECKY

(d) In *The Stranger* (by Albert Camus), Marie is the girlfriend of Merseault. In *Tom Sawyer* (by Mark Twain), Becky is the girlfriend to Tom.

69. (*a.* scrupulous, *b.* shrewd, ***c.* ingenuous**, *d.* indigenous) : WILY :: NAIVE : SOPHISTICATED

(c) Ingenuous and wily are opposites, as are naive and sophisticated.

70. MAXIM : (*a.* chisel, ***b.* saw**, *c.* palindrome, *d.* deed) :: ADAGE : PROVERB

(b) Maxim, saw, adage, and proverb are all synonymous. *A palindrome is a word or number that can be read the same way in any direction (e.g., "mom" or "101").*

71. BUCKINGHAM PALACE : MONARCH OF ENGLAND :: PANDEMONIUM : (*a.* Neptune, *b.* Genghis Khan, ***c.* Satan**, *d.* Citizen Kane)

(c) Buckingham Palace is the palace of the monarch of England. Pandemonium, in *Paradise Lost* (by John Milton), is the palace of Satan.

72. TAXONOMY : LIFE FORMS :: NOSOLOGY : (*a.* noses, *b.* laws, *c.* coins, ***d.* diseases**)

(d) Taxonomy is classification of life forms. Nosology is classification of diseases.

73. PENOLOGY : OENOLOGY :: PEAL : (*a*. wine, *b*. oil, *c*. poll, ***d*. eel**)

    (d) Penology and oenology have the same initial vowel sound, as do peal and eel.

74. FATHERS : SONS :: SONS (*a*. Daughters, ***b*. Lovers**, *c*. Strangers, *d*. Mothers)

    (b) *Fathers and Sons* is a novel by Ivan Turgenev. *Sons and Lovers* is a novel by D. H. Lawrence.

75. CATATONIC : HEBEPHRENIC :: ANAL : (*a*. genital, *b*. phallic, ***c*. oral**, *d*. Oedipal)

    (c) A catatonic shows anal symptomatology. A hebephrenic shows oral symptomatology.

76. (*a*. Joyce, ***b*. Wilde**, *c*. James, *d*. O'Henry) : DORIAN GRAY :: JOYCE : ARTIST AS A YOUNG MAN

    (b) Oscar Wilde wrote *The Picture of Dorian Gray*. James Joyce wrote *A Portrait of the Artist as a Young Man*.

77. EISENHOWER : REPUBLICAN :: (***a*. T. Roosevelt**, *b*. Harrison, *c*. Fillmore, *d*. Wilson) : BULL MOOSE

    (a) President Eisenhower was a member of the Republican Party. President T. (Theodore) Roosevelt was a member of the Bull Moose Party. *Harrison was a Republican; Fillmore was a member of the Whig Party; Wilson was a Democrat.*

78. TANGENT X : COTANGENT X :: X : (*a*. X^2, ***b*. 1/X**, *c*. $X - 1$, *d*. $\tan X - \sin X$)

    (b) The cotangent of X is equal to 1 divided by the tangent of X.

79. (*a*. mammals, *b*. life, ***c*. fish**, *d*. humans) : PALEOZOIC :: DINOSAURS : MESOZOIC

    (c) Fish first appeared in the Paleozoic Era (542–751 million years ago). Dinosaurs first appeared in the Mesozoic Era (251–65 million years ago).

80. CITY OF SEVEN HILLS : ROME :: CITY OF LIGHT : (*a*. New York, ***b*. Paris**, *c*. London, *d*. Venice)

    (b) Rome is the City of Seven Hills; Paris is the City of Light. The seven hills of Rome are called Palatine, Capitoline, Quirinal, Viminal, Esquiline, Caelian, and Aventine.

81. SLEEP : SOMNAMBULIST :: (*a*. pimp, *b*. crime, ***c*. street**, *d*. bed) : GANG

    (c) A somnambulist walks in his or her sleep. A gang may hang out or walk around on the streets.

82. CELSIUS : 0 :: KELVIN : (*a*. 32, *b*. 0, *c*. –100, ***d*. 273**)

    (d) Zero degrees Celsius is equal to 273 Kelvin (to the nearest unit).

83. DIONYSUS : DAMOCLES :: (***a*. Zeus**, *b*. Pandora, *c*. Ares, *d*. Cronus) : PROMETHEUS

    (a) Dionysus punished Damocles (by hanging a sword over his head). Zeus punished Prometheus (by chaining him to a rock). *Pandora was the first woman in Greek mythology. Ares was the Greek god of war. Cronus was the Greek god of agriculture and harvest.*

84. PENCIL LEAD : GRAPHITE :: CHALK : (***a*. limestone**, *b*. sandstone, *c*. talc, *d*. gypsum)

    (a) Pencil lead is made of graphite. Chalk is made of limestone.

85. MAUDLIN : (*a*. immature, *b*. humorous, *c*. munificent, ***d*. mawkish**) :: MODERATE : TEMPERATE

    (d) Maudlin means mawkish. Moderate means temperate.

86. RHEOSTAT : ELECTRICITY :: (*a*. automobile, ***b*. traffic light**, *c*. car-counter, *d*. bottleneck) : TRAFFIC

    (b) A rheostat regulates the flow of electricity. A traffic light regulates the flow of traffic.

87. CHAUCER : SWEET SHOWERS :: ELIOT : (*a.* stinging rain, *b.* sweet breath, *c.* swich licour, **d. cruellest month**)

(d) In the opening line of *The Canterbury Tales*, Chaucer mentions April in the context of its sweet showers. In the opening line of *The Wasteland*, Eliot alludes to Chaucer, but changes things by mentioning April as the cruellest month.

88. $8^{-1} : 8^{1} :: -1 :$ (**a. −64**, *b.* −8, *c.* 8, *d.* 64)

(a) $^1/_8$ is to 8 as −1 is to −64.

89. BIGOT : ZEALOT :: TROGLODYTE : (**a. cave dweller**, *b.* hero, *c.* traitor, *d.* reformer)

(a) A bigot is a zealot; a troglodyte was a cave dweller.

90. TEMPER : (**a. piano**, *b.* moisture, *c.* docility, *d.* tape recorder) :: FOCUS : CAMERA

(a) One tempers a piano; one focuses a camera.

91. ZEUS : HERA :: (*a.* Ulysses, *b.* Orestes, **c. Agamemnon**, *d.* Paris) : CLYTEMNESTRA

(c) In Greek mythology, Zeus was the husband of Hera. In Greek literature, Agamemnon was the husband of Clytemnestra. *Ulysses is the Latin name for Odysseus. Orestes and Electra were the son and daughter of Agamemnon. Paris was the son of Priam, who in turn was the youngest son of Laomedon and king of Troy during the Trojan War.*

92. TRITIUM : HYDROGEN :: OZONE : (**a. oxygen**, *b.* nitrogen, *c.* carbon dioxide, *d.* cesium)

(a) Tritium is an isotope of hydrogen, H_3. Ozone is an isotope of oxygen, O_3. *Nitrogen is a chemical element (N). Cesium is a chemical element as well (Cs). Carbon dioxide (CO_2) is a chemical compound comprising two atoms of oxygen and one atom of carbon.*

93. METROPOLITAN MUSEUM : NEW YORK :: RIJKSMUSEUM : (*a.* Utrecht, *b.* Munich, *c.* Paris, **d. Amsterdam**)

(d) The Metropolitan Museum of Modern Art (or *MOMA*) is in New York. The Rijksmuseum is in Amsterdam.

94. POSEIDON : (*a.* Uranus, *b.* Mars, *c.* Saturn, **d. Neptune**) :: ZEUS : JUPITER

(d) Poseidon was the Greek name, and Neptune the Roman name, for the god of the sea. Zeus was the Greek name, and Jupiter the Roman name, for the king of the gods. *Uranus was the god of the sky and had the same name in Greek and Latin. Mars was the god of war, his Greek name was Ares. Saturn is the Latin name of the Greek god Cronus (god of agriculture and harvest).*

95. (*a.* zz, *b.* Zuider, *c.* zero, **d. zee**) : ZED :: BAR : PUB

(d) The British call zed what Americans call zee (the letter Z). The British call a pub what Americans call a bar.

96. (*a.* hot, **b. bacterium**, *c.* virus, *d.* lungs) : TUBERCULOSIS :: VIRUS : COLD

(b) Tuberculosis is caused by a bacterium; a cold is caused by a virus.

97. MOLLY : (*a.* Madison, *b.* Monroe, **c. Maguire**, *d.* Malone) :: KNOW : NOTHING

(c) The Molly Maguires and the Know-Nothings were both secret political action groups. The Molly Maguires were an Irish rebel group who fought for better working conditions in the coal mines of Pennsylvania (ca. 1860s–1870s). The Know-Nothings were a nativistic movement to combat foreign influences in the United States (ca. 1850s).

98. ANEMOMETER : WIND SPEED :: MANOMETER : (**a. blood pressure**, *b.* heart rate, *c.* visual acuity, *d.* auditory acuity)

(a) An anemometer measures wind speed; a manometer measures blood pressure.

99. HERODOTUS : (**a. history**, *b.* medicine, *c.* his city, *d.* Greece) :: WASHINGTON : HIS COUNTRY

(a) Herodotus is sometimes called the Father of History (and was the first to have a scientific approach to history). George Washington is sometimes called the Father of His Country.

100. (***a.* Washington**, *b.* Jackson, *c.* Eisenhower, *d.* Polk) : CORNWALLIS :: GRANT : LEE

(a) General Cornwallis surrendered to George Washington. General Lee surrendered to Ulysses S. Grant.

101. $Y = X^2$: PARABOLA :: $Y = X + 1$: (*a.* cube, *b.* slope, *c.* circle, **d. line**)

(d) When graphed, the equation $y = x^2$ produces a parabola just as when graphed, the equation $y = x + 1$ produces a line.

102. NOM DE PLUME : (*a.* maiden name, *b.* middle name, **c. pen name**, *d.* married name) :: JE NE SAIS QUOI : INDEFINABLE QUALITY

(c) A *nom de plume* is the commonly used French term for a pen name, just as *je ne sais quoi* is the commonly used French term for an indefinable quality.

103. (*a.* sheep, **b. mutton**, *c.* offal, *d.* venison) : LAMB :: BEEF : VEAL

(b) Meat eaten from a full-grown sheep is called mutton, whereas meat from a young sheep is called lamb. Likewise, meat from full-grown cattle is called beef and from young cattle is called veal.

104. RADIOACTIVE FALLOUT : CHERNOBYL :: (**a. oil**, *b.* propane, *c.* carbon monoxide, *d.* benzene) : PRINCE WILLIAM SOUND

(a) Just as the Ukrainian city of Chernobyl was poisoned by radioactive fallout from a nuclear plant (1986), Prince William Sound was polluted by a massive oil spill (1989) from the *Exxon Valdez*.

105. HELIUM : NEON :: ARGON : (*a.* cryon, *b.* iodine, **c. xenon**, *d.* hydrogen)

(c) Helium, neon, argon, and xenon are all noble gasses.

106. BATHYSPHERE : (*a.* rain forest, *b.* ice field, **c. ocean**, *d.* cave) :: SHUTTLE : SPACE

(c) A bathysphere transports people into the ocean just as a shuttle transports people into space.

107. DEBUT : GURU :: FRENCH : (*a.* Greek, *b.* Spanish, *c.* Zulu, **d. Hindi**)

(d) Just as the English language has borrowed the word debut from French, so has it also borrowed the word guru from Hindi.

108. SHEPHERD : (***a.* sheep**, *b.* human, *c.* goat, *d.* dog) :: MAHOUT : ELEPHANT

(a) A mahout cares for and leads elephants just as a shepherd cares for and leads sheep.

109. HMS : GREAT BRITAIN :: (*a.* SSS, *b.* SOS, *c.* USAS, **d. USS**) : UNITED STATES

(d) In Great Britain, state ships are prefixed with "HMS," for "Her Majesty's ship" and in the United States, state ships are prefixed with "USS," for "United States ship." *SSS may refer to Server Side Scripting, among other things; SOS stands for Save Our Ship/Souls; USAS stands for the United States Antarctic Service, among other things.*

110. (*a.* Ethiopia, **b. Somalia**, *c.* Djibouti, *d.* Eritrea) : MOGADISHU :: KENYA : NAIROBI

(b) Somalia's capital city is Mogadishu just as Kenya's is Nairobi. *The capital of Ethiopia is Addis Ababa. The capital of Djibouti is Djibouti. The capital of Eritrea is Asmara.*

111. ALLUSION : ALLEGORY :: REFERENCE : (*a.* summary, **b. parable**, *c.* idiom, *d.* anecdote)

(b) Allusion is reference (either direct or indirect) to something. Allegory is a sort of parable.

112. HORUS : (*a*. horse, *b*. dog, ***c*. hawk**, *d*. hare) :: ANUBIS : JACKAL

(c) Horus and Anubis, the sons of Egyptian god Osiris, had the heads of a hawk and a jackal, respectively.

113. GOERING : NUREMBERG :: (*a*. Hitler, *b*. Hussein, *c*. Mussolini, ***d*. Milosevic**) : THE HAGUE

(d) Goering was prosecuted at an international war crimes tribunal in Nuremberg, Germany. Milosevic was prosecuted in The Hague, Netherlands.

114. FOUR SCORE : (*a*. 40, *b*. 4, *c*. 28, ***d*. 80**) :: BAKER'S DOZEN : 13

(d) Four score is the equivalent of 80 (a score is 20), just as a baker's dozen is 13. The expression of a baker's dozen comes from 13th century England where bakers could be severely punished if found to cheat their customers. Therefore, they preferred to bake more items to make sure they would not betray their customers.

115. KHOI SAN : SOUTH AFRICA :: MAORI : (***a*. New Zealand**, *b*. Papua New Guinea, *c*. Fiji, *d*. Australia)

(a) The Khoi San are native peoples of South Africa and the Maori are native peoples of New Zealand.

116. BEMUSE : AMUSE :: (*a*. humor, ***b*. confuse**, *c*. irritate, *d*. inspire) : ENTERTAIN

(b) To bemuse is to confuse, whereas to amuse is to entertain.

117. PLESSY : FERGUSON :: BROWN : (*a*. The State, *b*. Topeka, ***c*. Board of Education**, *d*. Wade)

(c) *Plessy vs. Ferguson* was a historic Supreme Court Case (1886; it upheld the constitutionality of racial segregation) as was *Brown vs. Board of Education* (1954; it overturned rulings from the *Plessy vs. Ferguson* case).

118. HONG KONG : (***a*. Hang Seng**, *b*. NASDAQ, *c*. HKSE, *d*. Nikkei) :: UNITED STATES : DOW JONES

(a) Hong Kong's primary stock index is the Hang Seng. The primary stock index of the United States is the Dow Jones. *The Nikkei is the primary stock index of Japan. HKSE stands for Hong Kong Stock Exchange. NASDAQ (National Association of Securities Dealers Automated Quotations) is an electronic securities market in the United States.*

119. LAKERS : DODGERS :: (*a*. Orlando, ***b*. Minneapolis**, *c*. Albany, *d*. New Orleans) : BROOKLYN

(b) The Los Angeles Lakers were originally called the Minneapolis Lakers just as the Los Angeles Dodgers were originally called the Brooklyn Dodgers.

120. (***a*. juniper**, *b*. hickory, *c*. aspen, *d*. beech) : CEDAR :: TAMARAC : PINE

(a) Juniper, cedar, tamarac, and pine trees are all coniferous evergreen trees.

1. Ⓐ Ⓑ Ⓒ Ⓓ
2. Ⓐ Ⓑ Ⓒ Ⓓ
3. Ⓐ Ⓑ Ⓒ Ⓓ
4. Ⓐ Ⓑ Ⓒ Ⓓ
5. Ⓐ Ⓑ Ⓒ Ⓓ
6. Ⓐ Ⓑ Ⓒ Ⓓ
7. Ⓐ Ⓑ Ⓒ Ⓓ
8. Ⓐ Ⓑ Ⓒ Ⓓ
9. Ⓐ Ⓑ Ⓒ Ⓓ
10. Ⓐ Ⓑ Ⓒ Ⓓ
11. Ⓐ Ⓑ Ⓒ Ⓓ
12. Ⓐ Ⓑ Ⓒ Ⓓ
13. Ⓐ Ⓑ Ⓒ Ⓓ
14. Ⓐ Ⓑ Ⓒ Ⓓ
15. Ⓐ Ⓑ Ⓒ Ⓓ
16. Ⓐ Ⓑ Ⓒ Ⓓ
17. Ⓐ Ⓑ Ⓒ Ⓓ
18. Ⓐ Ⓑ Ⓒ Ⓓ
19. Ⓐ Ⓑ Ⓒ Ⓓ
20. Ⓐ Ⓑ Ⓒ Ⓓ
21. Ⓐ Ⓑ Ⓒ Ⓓ
22. Ⓐ Ⓑ Ⓒ Ⓓ
23. Ⓐ Ⓑ Ⓒ Ⓓ
24. Ⓐ Ⓑ Ⓒ Ⓓ
25. Ⓐ Ⓑ Ⓒ Ⓓ
26. Ⓐ Ⓑ Ⓒ Ⓓ
27. Ⓐ Ⓑ Ⓒ Ⓓ
28. Ⓐ Ⓑ Ⓒ Ⓓ
29. Ⓐ Ⓑ Ⓒ Ⓓ
30. Ⓐ Ⓑ Ⓒ Ⓓ

31. Ⓐ Ⓑ Ⓒ Ⓓ
32. Ⓐ Ⓑ Ⓒ Ⓓ
33. Ⓐ Ⓑ Ⓒ Ⓓ
34. Ⓐ Ⓑ Ⓒ Ⓓ
35. Ⓐ Ⓑ Ⓒ Ⓓ
36. Ⓐ Ⓑ Ⓒ Ⓓ
37. Ⓐ Ⓑ Ⓒ Ⓓ
38. Ⓐ Ⓑ Ⓒ Ⓓ
39. Ⓐ Ⓑ Ⓒ Ⓓ
40. Ⓐ Ⓑ Ⓒ Ⓓ
41. Ⓐ Ⓑ Ⓒ Ⓓ
42. Ⓐ Ⓑ Ⓒ Ⓓ
43. Ⓐ Ⓑ Ⓒ Ⓓ
44. Ⓐ Ⓑ Ⓒ Ⓓ
45. Ⓐ Ⓑ Ⓒ Ⓓ
46. Ⓐ Ⓑ Ⓒ Ⓓ
47. Ⓐ Ⓑ Ⓒ Ⓓ
48. Ⓐ Ⓑ Ⓒ Ⓓ
49. Ⓐ Ⓑ Ⓒ Ⓓ
50. Ⓐ Ⓑ Ⓒ Ⓓ
51. Ⓐ Ⓑ Ⓒ Ⓓ
52. Ⓐ Ⓑ Ⓒ Ⓓ
53. Ⓐ Ⓑ Ⓒ Ⓓ
54. Ⓐ Ⓑ Ⓒ Ⓓ
55. Ⓐ Ⓑ Ⓒ Ⓓ
56. Ⓐ Ⓑ Ⓒ Ⓓ
57. Ⓐ Ⓑ Ⓒ Ⓓ
58. Ⓐ Ⓑ Ⓒ Ⓓ
59. Ⓐ Ⓑ Ⓒ Ⓓ
60. Ⓐ Ⓑ Ⓒ Ⓓ

61. Ⓐ Ⓑ Ⓒ Ⓓ
62. Ⓐ Ⓑ Ⓒ Ⓓ
63. Ⓐ Ⓑ Ⓒ Ⓓ
64. Ⓐ Ⓑ Ⓒ Ⓓ
65. Ⓐ Ⓑ Ⓒ Ⓓ
66. Ⓐ Ⓑ Ⓒ Ⓓ
67. Ⓐ Ⓑ Ⓒ Ⓓ
68. Ⓐ Ⓑ Ⓒ Ⓓ
69. Ⓐ Ⓑ Ⓒ Ⓓ
70. Ⓐ Ⓑ Ⓒ Ⓓ
71. Ⓐ Ⓑ Ⓒ Ⓓ
72. Ⓐ Ⓑ Ⓒ Ⓓ
73. Ⓐ Ⓑ Ⓒ Ⓓ
74. Ⓐ Ⓑ Ⓒ Ⓓ
75. Ⓐ Ⓑ Ⓒ Ⓓ
76. Ⓐ Ⓑ Ⓒ Ⓓ
77. Ⓐ Ⓑ Ⓒ Ⓓ
78. Ⓐ Ⓑ Ⓒ Ⓓ
79. Ⓐ Ⓑ Ⓒ Ⓓ
80. Ⓐ Ⓑ Ⓒ Ⓓ
81. Ⓐ Ⓑ Ⓒ Ⓓ
82. Ⓐ Ⓑ Ⓒ Ⓓ
83. Ⓐ Ⓑ Ⓒ Ⓓ
84. Ⓐ Ⓑ Ⓒ Ⓓ
85. Ⓐ Ⓑ Ⓒ Ⓓ
86. Ⓐ Ⓑ Ⓒ Ⓓ
87. Ⓐ Ⓑ Ⓒ Ⓓ
88. Ⓐ Ⓑ Ⓒ Ⓓ
89. Ⓐ Ⓑ Ⓒ Ⓓ
90. Ⓐ Ⓑ Ⓒ Ⓓ

91. Ⓐ Ⓑ Ⓒ Ⓓ
92. Ⓐ Ⓑ Ⓒ Ⓓ
93. Ⓐ Ⓑ Ⓒ Ⓓ
94. Ⓐ Ⓑ Ⓒ Ⓓ
95. Ⓐ Ⓑ Ⓒ Ⓓ
96. Ⓐ Ⓑ Ⓒ Ⓓ
97. Ⓐ Ⓑ Ⓒ Ⓓ
98. Ⓐ Ⓑ Ⓒ Ⓓ
99. Ⓐ Ⓑ Ⓒ Ⓓ
100. Ⓐ Ⓑ Ⓒ Ⓓ
101. Ⓐ Ⓑ Ⓒ Ⓓ
102. Ⓐ Ⓑ Ⓒ Ⓓ
103. Ⓐ Ⓑ Ⓒ Ⓓ
104. Ⓐ Ⓑ Ⓒ Ⓓ
105. Ⓐ Ⓑ Ⓒ Ⓓ
106. Ⓐ Ⓑ Ⓒ Ⓓ
107. Ⓐ Ⓑ Ⓒ Ⓓ
108. Ⓐ Ⓑ Ⓒ Ⓓ
109. Ⓐ Ⓑ Ⓒ Ⓓ
110. Ⓐ Ⓑ Ⓒ Ⓓ
111. Ⓐ Ⓑ Ⓒ Ⓓ
112. Ⓐ Ⓑ Ⓒ Ⓓ
113. Ⓐ Ⓑ Ⓒ Ⓓ
114. Ⓐ Ⓑ Ⓒ Ⓓ
115. Ⓐ Ⓑ Ⓒ Ⓓ
116. Ⓐ Ⓑ Ⓒ Ⓓ
117. Ⓐ Ⓑ Ⓒ Ⓓ
118. Ⓐ Ⓑ Ⓒ Ⓓ
119. Ⓐ Ⓑ Ⓒ Ⓓ
120. Ⓐ Ⓑ Ⓒ Ⓓ

Time: 60 MINUTES

Directions: In each of the following questions, you will find three initial terms and, in parentheses, four answer options designated *a*, *b*, *c*, and *d*. You are to select from the four answer options the one that *best* completes the analogy with the three initial terms. To record your answers, use the answer sheet provided.

1. SUFFOCATION : AIR :: DEHYDRATION : (*a.* food, *b.* shelter, *c.* water, *d.* sunlight)

2. RISE : (*a.* set, *b.* raise, *c.* sit, *d.* decrease) :: EAST : WEST

3. (*a.* greedy, *b.* pleasure-seeking, *c.* lazy, *d.* warlike) : SPARTA :: CULTURED : ATHENS

4. CUBE : SQUARE :: (*a.* ellipsis, *b.* ellipsoid, *c.* oblong, *d.* tetrahedron) : ELLIPSE

5. INFRARED : BELOW :: (*a.* maroon, *b.* aquamarine, *c.* chartreuse, *d.* ultraviolet) : ABOVE

6. (*a.* NW, *b.* SW, *c.* NE, *d.* SE) : SE :: S : N

7. DIASTOLIC : DILATATION :: (*a.* anatolic, *b.* controlic, *c.* catatolic, *d.* systolic) : CONTRACTION

8. CAVALRY : HORSE :: INFANTRY : (*a.* platoon, *b.* stallion, *c.* tank, *d.* foot)

9. MADISON : (*a.* American Revolution, *b.* French-Indian War, *c.* War of 1812, *d.* Spanish-American War) :: LINCOLN : CIVIL WAR

10. SHEEP : (*a.* sheeps, *b.* sheep, *c.* sheepes, *d.* sheepses) :: LIFE : LIVES

11. MICKEY : MOUSE :: POLYPHEMOUS : (*a.* Scylla, *b.* Cyclops, *c.* daemon, *d.* satyr)

12. LABOUR : (*a.* Conservative, *b.* Federalist, *c.* Socialist, *d.* Progressive) :: DEMOCRAT : REPUBLICAN

13. A.M. : (*a.* ab, *b.* ante, *c.* amon, *d.* annuo) :: P.M. : post

14. JUDAISM : TORAH :: (*a.* Hinduism, *b.* Buddhism, *c.* Islam, *d.* Confucianism) : KORAN

15. (*a.* gin, *b.* rummy, *c.* check, *d.* mate) : GIN RUMMY :: CHECKMATE : CHESS

16. SAWYER : THATCHER :: TOM : (*a.* Susie, *b.* Becky, *c.* Janey, *d.* Judy)

17. PRAIRIE SCHOONER : (*a.* covered wagon, *b.* horse, *c.* mule, *d.* railroad train) :: PRAIRIE WOLF : COYOTE

18. YEN : JAPAN :: MARK : (*a.* Germany, *b.* Sweden, *c.* Holland, *d.* France)

19. GENOTYPE : PHENOTYPE :: (*a.* expected, *b.* ontogeny, *c.* philogeny, *d.* environmental) : OBSERVED

20. HOLLAND : NETHERLANDS :: FORMOSA : (*a.* Kemoy, *b.* Matsu, *c.* Taiwan, *d.* Oahu)

21. TABLE : ABLE :: TRACK : (*a.* field, *b.* willing, *c.* rack, *d.* truck)

22. MIDWIFE : (*a.* marriage, *b.* birth, *c.* disease, *d.* death) :: SHERIFF : LAW ENFORCEMENT

23. PRISONER : RELEASE :: SOLDIER : (*a.* draft, *b.* fight, *c.* enlist, *d.* discharge)

24. YELLOW : (*a.* coat, *b.* chicken, *c.* hornet, *d.* jacket) :: BUMBLE : BEE

25. AMERICAN : (*a.* British, *b.* Swiss, *c.* Colombian, *d.* Belgian) :: PARMESAN : CAMEMBERT

26. (*a.* hawk, *b.* dove, *c.* eagle, *d.* robin) : U.S.A. :: MAPLE LEAF : CANADA

27. CIRCE : SWINE :: MEDUSA : (*a.* jackal, *b.* stone, *c.* gold, *d.* snake)

28. (*a.* bones, *b.* skin, *c.* muscles, *d.* blood) : DERMATOLOGY :: IMMUNITY : IMMUNOLOGY

29. TWIDDLE : TWADDLE :: (*a.* jambo, *b.* jimbo, *c.* mumbo, *d.* rumbo) : JUMBO

30. OLFACTORY : (*a.* mouth, *b.* ears, *c.* nose, *d.* fingers) :: VISUAL : EYES

31. ECUADOR : SOUTH AMERICA :: EGYPT : (*a.* Africa, *b.* Asia, *c.* Europe, *d.* India)

32. RED CROSS : RELIEF FROM DISASTERS :: BLUE CROSS : (*a.* health insurance, *b.* relief from tyranny, *c.* relief from mental illness, *d.* medical supplies)

33. EEG : BRAIN :: EKG : (*a.* heart, *b.* brain, *c.* gall bladder, *d.* vagus nerve)

34. ABRAHAM : SARAH :: PUNCH : (*a.* Judy, *b.* Paula, *c.* Pat, *d.* Joanie)

35. MPH : RPM :: MILES : (*a.* rotations, *b.* revolutions, *c.* minutes, *d.* hours)

36. ORDAIN : MINISTER :: (*a.* approve, *b.* obey, *c.* admit, *d.* certify) : TEACHER

37. WATER : HYDROGEN :: TABLE SALT : (*a.* chlorine, *b.* potassium, *c.* nitrogen, *d.* oxygen)

38. ELBOW : ARM :: (*a.* shin, *b.* thigh, *c.* calf, *d.* knee) : LEG

39. NUMBER : GENDER :: SINGULAR : (*a.* plural, *b.* feminine, *c.* nominative, *d.* present)

40. PATRICIDE : FATHER :: GENOCIDE : (*a.* enemy, *b.* group, *c.* mother, *d.* brother)

41. INCA : (*a.* Mexico, *b.* Panama, *c.* Honduras, *d.* Peru) :: AZTEC : MEXICO

42. ODIOUS : (*a.* burdensome, *b.* easy, *c.* pleasing, *d.* disgusting) :: HONORABLE : DISGRACEFUL

43. SITTING BULL : CUSTER :: (*a.* Eddington, *b.* Howe, *c.* Sheridan, *d.* Wellington) : NAPOLEON BONAPARTE

44. LOG 10 : 1 :: LOG 100 : (*a.* 2, *b.* 5, *c.* 10, *d.* 90)

45. HOMING PIGEON : CARRIER PIGEON :: STOOL PIGEON : (*a.* fool, *b.* informer, *c.* loser, *d.* passenger pigeon)

46. STOP : POTS :: NOON : (*a.* morning, *b.* noon, *c.* night, *d.* never)

47. EBENEEZER SCROOGE : MISERLY :: SIMON LEGREE : (*a.* humane, *b.* generous, *c.* stingy, *d.* cruel)

48. PALEONTOLOGIST : (*a.* vertebrates, *b.* rocks, *c.* earthquakes, *d.* fossils) :: ZOOLOGIST : ANIMALS

49. (*a.* emperor, *b.* pharaoh, *c.* shah, *d.* diet) : CONGRESS :: PRIME MINISTER : PRESIDENT

50. B$_1$: THIAMINE :: (*a.* B$_2$, *b.* B$_6$, *c.* C, *d.* D) : RIBOFLAVIN

51. GUERNSEY : (*a.* York, *b.* Jersey, *c.* British, *d.* French) :: CHESHIRE : SIAMESE

52. TOURNEY : TOURNAMENT :: TEMPORARY : (*a.* permanent, *b.* sudden, *c.* transitory, *d.* temptation)

53. STOMACH : DIGESTION :: ANATOMY : (*a.* cartography, *b.* biology, *c.* physiology, *d.* proctology)

54. PRE : PRIOR :: PRETER : (*a.* beyond, *b.* as if, *c.* therefore, *d.* only)

55. LINCOLN : KENNEDY :: (*a.* Tyler, *b.* Johnson, *c.* Eisenhower, *d.* Garfield) : McKINLEY

56. FORTE : LOUD :: (*a.* largo, *b.* rubato, *c.* violin, *d.* piano) : SOFT

57. LATIN ALPHABET : FRENCH :: CYRILLIC ALPHABET : (*a.* Russian, *b.* Sanskrit, *c.* Greek, *d.* Chinese)

58. CENTRIFUGAL : (*a.* centripetal, *b.* centrigonal, *c.* centrobaric, *d.* centrosomal) :: AWAY FROM : TOWARD

59. ICHTHYOLOGY : (*a.* insects, *b.* reptiles, *c.* arthropods, *d.* fish) :: ORNITHOLOGY : BIRDS

60. (*a.* wool, *b.* synthetic, *c.* dinosaur, *d.* gasoline) : PETROL :: U.S.A. : BRITAIN

61. (*a.* overindulge, *b.* persevere, *c.* quit, *d.* deprive) : SURFEIT :: CLOY : SATIATE

62. (*a.* Hesse, *b.* Joyce, *c.* Mann, *d.* Proust) : DEATH IN VENICE :: SHAKESPEARE : MERCHANT OF VENICE

63. ROOK : CASTLE :: HORSE : (*a.* knight, *b.* track, *c.* chess, *d.* winner)

64. (*a.* Greuze, *b.* Utrillo, *c.* Seurat, *d.* Manet) : POINTILLISM :: DAVID : NEOCLASSICISM

65. BILL : BEAK :: (*a.* finger, *b.* leg, *c.* hand, *d.* kneecap) : DIGIT

66. GEWGAW : (*a.* trinket, *b.* bottle, *c.* rhinestone, *d.* candy) :: TACITURN : QUIET

67. (*a.* fortunate, *b.* entreat, *c.* unfortunate, *d.* order) : IMPORTUNE :: IMPREGNABLE : UNSHAKABLE

68. CULPABLE : GUILTY :: (*a.* preculpable, *b.* exculpable, *c.* multiculpable, *d.* malculpable) : ACQUITTED

69. FOX : (*a.* bovine, *b.* vulpine, *c.* porcine, *d.* equine) :: CAT : FELINE

70. AGONY : ECSTASY :: SOUND : (*a.* Light, *b.* Trumpet, *c.* Signpost, *d.* Fury)

71. LANG SYNE : (*a.* bygone days, *b.* future days, *c.* here and now, *d.* nonexistent times) :: IMMEDIATELY : AT ONCE

72. (*a.* India, *b.* Brazil, *c.* Mexico, *d.* Spain) : GUANAJUATO :: CANADA : MANITOBA

73. VERDI : AIDA :: (*a.* Bach, *b.* Mozart, *c.* Beethoven, *d.* Brahms) : FIDELIO

74. TORTUOUS : (*a.* winding, *b.* barbaric, *c.* long, *d.* incomprehensible) :: HAPPY : FELICITOUS

75. (*a.* present, *b.* past, *c.* recent, *d.* never) : CURRENT :: ERSTWHILE : FORMER

76. DAVID : GOLIATH :: HOLMES : (*a.* Moriarty, *b.* Watson, *c.* Doyle, *d.* Devlin)

77. LUGUBRIOUS : (*a.* shallow, *b.* cheerful, *c.* expensive, *d.* fatuous) :: PONDEROUS : LIGHT

78. EXPLETIVE : (*a.* interrogative, *b.* factotum, *c.* oath, *d.* lie) :: EXPOSÉ : DISCLOSURE

79. 11 : BINARY :: (*a.* 2, *b.* 3, *c.* 4, *d.* 10) : DECIMAL

80. CHALICE : GOBLET :: LEAF : (*a.* plant, *b.* tree, *c.* sheet, *d.* gold)

81. (*a.* nut, *b.* fruit, *c.* root, *d.* berry) : TURNIP :: STEM : CELERY

82. ABRAM : ABRAHAM :: (*a.* Sarabelle, *b.* Sarai, *c.* Salome, *d.* Sharon) : SARAH

83. VELÁSQUEZ : MAIDS OF HONOR :: (*a.* Botticelli, *b.* Bellini, *c.* Bosch, *d.* Uccello) : THE BIRTH OF VENUS

84. CIVIL : (*a.* misdemeanor, *b.* larceny, *c.* tort, *d.* perjury) :: CRIMINAL : FELONY

85. GREGORIAN : NOVEMBER :: FRENCH REVOLUTIONARY : (*a.* Novembre, *b.* February, *c.* Julian, *d.* Thermidor)

86. GOLDEN RULE : LUKE :: CATEGORICAL IMPERATIVE : (*a.* Hegel, *b.* Kant, *c.* Ardrey, *d.* Lorenz)

87. EQUIVOCATION : (*a.* perversity, *b.* exultation, *c.* veracity, *d.* perjury) :: UNCERTAINTY : CERTAINTY

88. TIMBREL : (*a.* cymbals, *b.* zither, *c.* flute, *d.* tambourine) :: LUTE : GUITAR

89. (*a.* Apollo, *b.* Phaeton, *c.* Furies, *d.* Sirens) : EUMENIDES :: PLUTO : HADES

90. JOSEPH K. : TRIAL :: GREGOR SAMSA : (*a.* Hunger Artist, *b.* Death in Venice, *c.* The Flies, *d.* Metamorphosis)

91. $\sqrt{2} : \sqrt{18}$ :: 1 : (*a.* 2, *b.* 3, *c.* 6, *d.* 9)

92. TRANSUBSTANTIATION : ACTUAL :: (*a.* insubstantiation, *b.* absubstantiation, *c.* consubstantiation, *d.* desubstantiation) : COEXISTING

93. ABACUS : COMPUTER :: DAGUERROTYPE : (*a.* stereo, *b.* photograph, *c.* tape recorder, *d.* telephone)

94. DECLARATION OF INDEPENDENCE : PHILADELPHIA :: MAGNA CARTA : (*a.* Gloucester, *b.* Runnymede, *c.* Canterbury, *d.* Norwalk)

95. MINTON : ROYAL DOULTON :: MIKASA (*a.* Sony, *b.* Rosenthal, *c.* Lenox, *d.* Noritake)

96. SHYLOCK : SCROOGE :: DON JUAN : (*a.* Antonio, *b.* Don Giovanni, *c.* Lothario, *d.* Don Quixote)

97. SKINNER : EMPIRICIST :: (*a.* Watson, *b.* Aristotle, *c.* Chomsky, *d.* Locke) : RATIONALIST

98. MOHAWK : IROQUOIS :: (*a.* Apache, *b.* Zuni, *c.* Seminole, *d.* Creek) : PUEBLO

99. (*a.* half-life, *b.* radioactivity, *c.* atomic mass, *d.* atomic number) : ISOTOPE :: ATOMIC WEIGHT : ISOBAR

100. SARACEN : (*a.* Hindu, *b.* Muslim, *c.* Shintoist, *d.* Taoist) :: EPISCOPALIAN : ANGLICAN

101. WATERGATE : NIXON :: IRAN CONTRA : (*a.* Ford, *b.* Carter, *c.* Reagan, *d.* Bush)

102. GALAPAGOS : SAMOA :: (*a.* Linnaeus, *b.* Magellan, *c.* Rhodes, *d.* Darwin) : MEAD

103. BIGGER THOMAS : (*a.* New York, *b.* Chicago, *c.* St. Louis, *d.* Montgomery) :: RODION RASKOLNIKOV : ST. PETERSBURG

104. TAXONOMY : CLASSIFY :: NOMENCLATURE : (*a.* order, *b.* color, *c.* name, *d.* number)

105. PHYSIOGNOMY : (*a.* face, *b.* stature, *c.* physiology, *d.* gate) :: CHIROMANCY : PALM

106. MUTINY : SHIP CAPTAIN :: COUP D'ÉTAT : (*a.* college dean, *b.* military commander, *c.* government, *d.* CEO)

107. (*a.* exaggerated, *b.* understated, *c.* metaphorical, *d.* literal) : HYPERBOLIC :: DRAMATIC : HISTRIONIC

108. APPLE : EVE :: (*a.* pear, *b.* pomegranate, *c.* peach, *d.* papaya) : PERSEPHONE

109. CEMENTUM : ROOT :: (*a.* bone, *b.* fluoride, *c.* keratin, *d.* enamel) : CROWN

110. (*a.* acorn, *b.* cornmeal, *c.* millet, *d.* filbert) : BULGUR :: QUINOA : BARLEY

111. MOBY DICK : LEVIATHAN :: MELVILLE : (*a.* Rousseau, *b.* Hobbes, *c.* Kant, *d.* Smith)

112. (*a.* Locke, *b.* Galileo, *c.* Bacon, *d.* Calvin) : ENLIGHTENMENT :: DESCARTES : RENAISSANCE

113. STEINWAY : (*a.* piano, *b.* cello, *c.* flute, *d.* organ) :: STRADIVARIUS : VIOLIN

114. TERKEL : (*a.* manuscripts, *b.* photographs, *c.* oral histories, *d.* maps) :: LOMAX : FOLK MUSIC

115. 6×10^{23} : (*a.* e, *b.* Avogadro's number, *c.* i, *d.* Planck's constant) :: 3.14 : PI

116. CIRRUS : NIMBUS :: CUMULUS : (*a.* bilious, *b.* birrus, *c.* mobius, *d.* stratus)

117. SOCIALISM : (*a.* state, *b.* family, *c.* town, *d.* universal) :: CAPITALISM : PRIVATE

118. (*a.* Pikes Peak, *b.* Mt. Kilimanjaro, *c.* Mt. Vesuvius, *d.* K2) : MT. ST. HELENS :: EXTINCT : ACTIVE

119. IMPERIOUS : IMPERVIOUS :: (*a.* grandiose, *b.* disbelieving, *c.* judgmental, *d.* domineering) : IMMUNE

120. NEUTRAL : NEUTRON :: NEGATIVE : (*a.* atom, *b.* electron, *c.* positron, *d.* negatron)

ANSWER KEY
Practice Test 7

P R A C T I C E   T E S T   7

1.	C	31.	A	61.	A	91.	B
2.	A	32.	A	62.	C	92.	C
3.	D	33.	A	63.	A	93.	B
4.	B	34.	A	64.	C	94.	B
5.	D	35.	B	65.	A	95.	D
6.	A	36.	D	66.	A	96.	C
7.	D	37.	A	67.	B	97.	C
8.	D	38.	D	68.	B	98.	B
9.	C	39.	B	69.	B	99.	D
10.	B	40.	B	70.	D	100.	B
11.	B	41.	D	71.	A	101.	C
12.	A	42.	C	72.	C	102.	D
13.	B	43.	D	73.	C	103.	B
14.	C	44.	A	74.	A	104.	C
15.	A	45.	B	75.	A	105.	A
16.	B	46.	B	76.	A	106.	C
17.	A	47.	D	77.	B	107.	A
18.	A	48.	D	78.	C	108.	B
19.	A	49.	D	79.	B	109.	D
20.	C	50.	A	80.	C	110.	C
21.	C	51.	B	81.	C	111.	B
22.	B	52.	C	82.	B	112.	A
23.	D	53.	C	83.	A	113.	A
24.	D	54.	A	84.	C	114.	C
25.	B	55.	D	85.	D	115.	B
26.	C	56.	D	86.	B	116.	D
27.	B	57.	A	87.	C	117.	A
28.	B	58.	A	88.	D	118.	B
29.	C	59.	D	89.	C	119.	D
30.	C	60.	D	90.	D	120.	B

PRACTICE TEST 7   253

ANSWER EXPLANATIONS FOR PRACTICE TEST 7

In the following, explanations concerning the correct responses are in roman font. Explanations regarding distracters (incorrect responses) that are not self-explaining or could be misinterpreted are in italics in order to highlight the explanations of the answers that are correct.

1. SUFFOCATION : AIR :: DEHYDRATION : (*a.* food, *b.* shelter, **c. water,** *d.* sunlight)

   (c) Suffocation is caused by lack of air. Dehydration is caused by lack of water.

2. RISE : (***a.* set,** *b.* raise, *c.* sit, *d.* decrease) :: EAST : WEST

   (a) The sun rises in the east and sets in the west.

3. (*a.* greedy, *b.* pleasure-seeking, *c.* lazy, ***d.* warlike**) : SPARTA :: CULTURED : ATHENS

   (d) In ancient Greece, the people of Sparta were known to be warlike, while the people of Athens were known to be cultured.

4. CUBE : SQUARE :: (*a.* ellipsis, ***b.* ellipsoid,** *c.* oblong, *d.* tetrahedron) : ELLIPSE

   (b) When a plane is passed through a cube at a right angle, the intersection is a square. When a plane is passed through an ellipsoid at a right angle, the intersection is an ellipse.

5. INFRARED : BELOW :: (*a.* maroon, *b.* aquamarine, *c.* chartreuse, ***d.* ultraviolet**) : ABOVE

   (d) Infrared light is below the visible spectrum for human beings; ultraviolet light is above the visible spectrum. The human eye can perceive wavelengths between 380 and 750 nm.

6. (**a. NW,** *b.* SW, *c.* NE, *d.* SE) : SE :: S : N

   (a) NW (northwest) and SE (southeast) are opposing directions, as are S (south) and N (north).

7. DIASTOLIC : DILATATION :: (*a.* anatolic, *b.* controlic, *c.* catatolic, ***d.* systolic**) : CONTRACTION

   (d) Diastolic blood pressure refers to the dilatation of the heart, while systolic blood pressure refers to the contraction of the heart.

8. CAVALRY : HORSE :: INFANTRY : (*a.* platoon, *b.* stallion, *c.* tank, ***d.* foot**)

   (d) In an army, the cavalry travels by horse, the infantry by foot.

9. MADISON : (*a.* American Revolution, *b.* French-Indian War, **c. War of 1812,** *d.* Spanish-American War) :: LINCOLN : CIVIL WAR

   (c) Madison (1751–1836) was president during the War of 1812; Lincoln (1809–1865) was president during the Civil War.

10. SHEEP : (*a.* sheeps, ***b.* sheep,** *c.* sheepes, *d.* sheepses) :: LIFE : LIVES

    (b) The plural of sheep is sheep. The plural of life is lives.

11. MICKEY : MOUSE :: POLYPHEMOUS : (*a.* Scylla, ***b.* Cyclops,** *c.* daemon, *d.* satyr)

    (b) Mickey is the name of a fictional mouse; Polyphemous is the name of a fictional Cyclops (in Homer's *Odyssey*). *In Greek mythology, Scylla was one of two monsters that lived on either side of a very narrow river. Daemons are supernatural beings between humans and gods in ancient Greek religion. They could be bad or good. Satyrs are woodland deities.*

254 MILLER ANALOGIES TEST

12. LABOUR : (**a. Conservative**, b. Federalist, c. Socialist, d. Progressive) :: DEMOCRAT : REPUBLICAN

(a) In British politics, the Labour party has generally been a left of center political party opposing the right of center Conservative party. In U.S. politics, the more left-leaning Democrats have traditionally opposed the more right-leaning Republicans.

13. A.M. : (a. ab, **b. ante**, c. amon, d. annuo) :: P.M. : post

(b) the *A* in A.M. is an abbreviation for ante; the *P* in P.M. is an abbreviation for post. The *m* stands for meridiem.

14. JUDAISM : TORAH :: (a. Hinduism, b. Buddhism, **c. Islam**, d. Confucianism) : KORAN

(c) The Torah is a holy book of Judaism, while the Koran is a holy book of Islam. *The holy scriptures of Hinduism are the Vedas. A holy text in Confucianism is the Analects. A holy text in Buddhism is the Tipitaka.*

15. (**a. gin**, b. rummy, c. check, d. mate) : GIN RUMMY :: CHECKMATE : CHESS

(a) The state of gin ends a gin rummy game, just as the state of checkmate ends a chess game.

16. SAWYER : THATCHER :: TOM : (a. Susie, **b. Becky**, c. Janey, d. Judy)

(b) Tom Sawyer and Becky Thatcher are both characters in Mark Twain's novel *Tom Sawyer.*

17. PRAIRIE SCHOONER : (**a. covered wagon**, b. horse, c. mule, d. railroad train) :: PRAIRIE WOLF : COYOTE

(a) A prairie schooner is a covered wagon; a prairie wolf is a coyote.

18. YEN : JAPAN :: MARK : (**a. Germany**, b. Sweden, c. Holland, d. France)

(a) The yen is the unit of currency in Japan, while the mark was the unit of currency in Germany. *The crown is the unit of currency in Sweden; in Holland it was the guilder; and in France, the franc. It is now the euro in Holland, France, and Germany.*

19. GENOTYPE : PHENOTYPE :: (**a. expected**, b. ontogeny, c. philogeny, d. environmental) : OBSERVED

(a) A genotype is what is expected on the basis of heredity, while a phenotype is what is observed on the basis of heredity, environment, and the interaction between them. *Ontogeny is the process of an organism growing organically.*

20. HOLLAND : NETHERLANDS :: FORMOSA : (a. Kemoy, b. Matsu, **c. Taiwan**, d. Oahu)

(c) Holland and Netherlands refer to the same country, as do Formosa and Taiwan.

21. TABLE : ABLE :: TRACK : (a. field, b. willing, **c. rack**, d. truck)

(c) Able is table without the initial *t*; rack is track without the initial *t*.

22. MIDWIFE : (a. marriage, **b. birth**, c. disease, d. death) :: SHERIFF : LAW ENFORCEMENT

(b) The job of a midwife is to help in birth; the job of a sheriff is to help in law enforcement.

23. PRISONER : RELEASE :: SOLDIER : (a. draft, b. fight, c. enlist, **d. discharge**)

(d) A prisoner receives a release from prison; a soldier receives a discharge from the army.

24. YELLOW : (a. coat, b. chicken, c. hornet, **d. jacket**) :: BUMBLE : BEE

(d) A yellow jacket and a bumblebee are both types of insect.

25. AMERICAN : (*a.* British, ***b.* Swiss**, *c.* Colombian, *d.* Belgian) :: PARMESAN : CAMEMBERT

    (b) American, Swiss, Parmesan, and Camembert are all types of cheese.

26. (*a.* hawk, *b.* dove, ***c.* eagle**, *d.* robin) : U.S.A. :: MAPLE LEAF : CANADA

    (c) The eagle is an emblem of the United States, while the maple leaf is an emblem of Canada.

27. CIRCE : SWINE :: MEDUSA : (*a.* jackal, ***b.* stone**, *c.* gold, *d.* snake)

    (b) Circe transformed men into swine; Medusa transformed them into stone.

28. (*a.* bones, ***b.* skin**, *c.* muscles, *d.* blood) : DERMATOLOGY :: IMMUNITY : IMMUNOLOGY

    (b) Dermatology is the branch of medicine dealing with the skin; immunology is the branch of medicine dealing with immunity.

29. TWIDDLE : TWADDLE :: (*a.* jambo, *b.* jimbo, ***c.* mumbo**, *d.* rumbo) : JUMBO

    (c) Twiddle twaddle and mumbo jumbo both refer to gibberish.

30. OLFACTORY : (*a.* mouth, *b.* ears, ***c.* nose**, *d.* fingers) :: VISUAL : EYES

    (c) The olfactory sense (smell) receives sensation through the nose; the visual sense (seeing) receives sensation through the eyes.

31. ECUADOR : SOUTH AMERICA :: EGYPT : (***a.* Africa**, *b.* Asia, *c.* Europe, *d.* India)

    (a) Ecuador is a country in South America. Egypt is a country in Africa.

32. RED CROSS : RELIEF FROM DISASTERS :: BLUE CROSS : (***a.* health insurance**, *b.* relief from tyranny, *c.* relief from mental illness, *d.* medical supplies)

    (a) The Red Cross organization provides relief from disasters; the Blue Cross organization provides health insurance.

33. EEG : BRAIN :: EKG : (***a.* heart**, *b.* brain, *c.* gall bladder, *d.* vagus nerve)

    (a) An EEG is a tracing of the changes in electric potential produced by the brain, while an EKG is a tracing of the changes in electric potential produced by the heart. EEG stands for "electroencephalogram." EKG stands for "electrocardiogram."

34. ABRAHAM : SARAH :: PUNCH : (***a.* Judy**, *b.* Paula, *c.* Pat, *d.* Joanie)

    (a) In the Bible, Abraham was the husband of Sarah. In a Punch-and-Judy puppet show, Punch is the husband of Judy.

35. MPH : RPM :: MILES : (*a.* rotations, ***b.* revolutions**, *c.* minutes, *d.* hours)

    (b) The *m* in mph is an abbreviation for miles (per hour). The *r* in rpm is an abbreviation for revolutions (per minute).

36. ORDAIN : MINISTER :: (*a.* approve, *b.* obey, *c.* admit, ***d.* certify**) : TEACHER

    (d) A minister is ordained before beginning to preach. A teacher is certified before beginning to teach.

37. WATER : HYDROGEN :: TABLE SALT : (***a.* chlorine**, *b.* potassium, *c.* nitrogen, *d.* oxygen)

    (a) Water is a chemical compound containing hydrogen, while table salt is a chemical compound containing chlorine. *Potassium, nitrogen, and oxygen are chemical elements.*

38. ELBOW : ARM :: (*a.* shin, *b.* thigh, *c.* calf, ***d.* knee**) : LEG

    (d) The elbow is the joint separating the upper and lower arms. The knee is the joint separating the upper and lower legs.

39. NUMBER : GENDER :: SINGULAR : (*a.* plural, ***b.* feminine**, *c.* nominative, *d.* present)

   (b) In grammar, singular is an example of number, and feminine is an example of gender.

40. PATRICIDE : FATHER :: GENOCIDE : (*a.* enemy, ***b.* group**, *c.* mother, *d.* brother)

   (b) Patricide is the murder of a father; genocide is the murder of a group. Matricide is the murder of a mother; fratricide is the murder of a brother.

41. INCA : (*a.* Mexico, *b.* Panama, *c.* Honduras, ***d.* Peru**) :: AZTEC : MEXICO

   (d) The Inca Indians resided in Peru; the Aztecs resided in Mexico.

42. ODIOUS : (*a.* burdensome, *b.* easy, ***c.* pleasing**, *d.* disgusting) :: HONORABLE : DISGRACEFUL

   (c) Odious and pleasing are antonyms, as are honorable and disgraceful.

43. SITTING BULL : CUSTER :: (*a.* Eddington, *b.* Howe, *c.* Sheridan, ***d.* Wellington**) : NAPOLEON BONAPARTE

   (d) Sitting Bull defeated General Custer at Little Big Horn in 1876. Wellington defeated Napoleon Bonaparte at the Battle of Waterloo in 1815.

44. LOG 10 : 1 :: LOG 100 : (***a.* 2**, *b.* 5, *c.* 10, *d.* 90)

   (a) Log 10 is equal to 1. Log 100 is equal to 2.

45. HOMING PIGEON : CARRIER PIGEON :: STOOL PIGEON : (*a.* fool, ***b.* informer**, *c.* loser, *d.* passenger pigeon)

   (b) A homing pigeon is a carrier pigeon. A stool pigeon is an informer.

46. STOP : POTS :: NOON : (*a.* morning, ***b.* noon**, *c.* night, *d.* never)

   (b) Stop spelled backward is pots. Noon spelled backward is noon.

47. EBENEEZER SCROOGE : MISERLY :: SIMON LEGREE : (*a.* humane, *b.* generous, *c.* stingy, ***d.* cruel**)

   (d) The literary character Ebeneezer Scrooge was miserly (*A Christmas Carol*), while the character Simon Legree was cruel in *Uncle Tom's Cabin*.

48. PALEONTOLOGIST : (*a.* vertebrates, *b.* rocks, *c.* earthquakes, ***d.* fossils**) :: ZOOLOGIST : ANIMALS

   (d) A paleontologist studies fossils; a zoologist studies animals.

49. (*a.* emperor, *b.* pharaoh, *c.* shah, ***d.* diet**) : CONGRESS :: PRIME MINISTER : PRESIDENT

   (d) A diet and a congress are both legislative bodies of government. A prime minister and a president are both executive officers of government.

50. B_1 : THIAMINE :: (***a.* B_2**, *b.* B_6, *c.* C, *d.* D) : RIBOFLAVIN

   (a) Thiamine is vitamin B_1. Riboflavin is vitamin B_2. *Vitamin C is also called L-ascorbate. Vitamin B_6 can consist of different compounds: pyridoxine, pyridoxal, and pyridoxamine. Vitamin D comes in several different forms like D_2 (or ergocalciferol) and vitamin D_3 (or cholecalciferol).*

51. GUERNSEY : (*a.* York, ***b.* Jersey**, *c.* British, *d.* French) :: CHESHIRE : SIAMESE

   (b) Guernsey and Jersey are both types of cow. Cheshire and Siamese are both types of cat.

52. TOURNEY : TOURNAMENT :: TEMPORARY : (*a.* permanent, *b.* sudden, ***c.* transitory**, *d.* temptation)

   (c) Tourney and tournament are synonyms, as are temporary and transitory.

53. STOMACH : DIGESTION :: ANATOMY : (*a.* cartography, *b.* biology, *c.* **physiology**, *d.* proctology)

(c) Anatomy is the study of body structures, such as the stomach. Physiology is the study of body functions, such as digestion.

54. PRE : PRIOR :: PRETER : (***a.* beyond**, *b.* as if, *c.* therefore, *d.* only)

(a) *Pre-* is a prefix meaning prior. *Preter-* is a prefix meaning beyond.

55. LINCOLN : KENNEDY :: (*a.* Tyler, *b.* Johnson, *c.* Eisenhower, ***d.* Garfield**) : McKINLEY

(d) Presidents Lincoln (1865), Garfield (1881), McKinley (1901), and Kennedy (1963) were all assassinated while in office.

56. FORTE : LOUD :: (*a.* largo, *b.* rubato, *c.* violin, ***d.* piano**) : SOFT

(d) In musical contexts, *forte* means loud and *piano* means soft. *Largo* means slow; *rubato* means that the tempo can slightly be varied at the discretion of the player.

57. LATIN ALPHABET : FRENCH :: CYRILLIC ALPHABET : (***a.* Russian**, *b.* Sanskrit, *c.* Greek, *d.* Chinese)

(a) The Latin alphabet is used for writing French, while the Cyrillic alphabet is used for writing Russian.

58. CENTRIFUGAL : (***a.* centripetal**, *b.* centrigonal, *c.* centrobaric, *d.* centrosomal) :: AWAY FROM : TOWARD

(a) Centrifugal means "away from center," while centripetal means "toward center." Centrobaric refers to a center of gravity.

59. ICHTHYOLOGY : (*a.* insects, *b.* reptiles, *c.* arthropods, ***d.* fish**) :: ORNITHOLOGY : BIRDS

(d) Ichthyology is the study of fish; ornithology is the study of birds.

60. (*a.* wool, *b.* synthetic, *c.* dinosaur, ***d.* gasoline**) : PETROL :: U.S.A. : BRITAIN

(d) The fuel called gasoline in the United States is called petrol in Britain.

61. (***a.* overindulge**, *b.* persevere, *c.* quit, *d.* deprive) : SURFEIT :: CLOY : SATIATE

(a) Overindulge, surfeit, cloy, and satiate are synonyms.

62. (*a.* Hesse, *b.* Joyce, ***c.* Mann**, *d.* Proust) : DEATH IN VENICE :: SHAKESPEARE : MERCHANT OF VENICE

(c) Mann is the author of *Death in Venice*; Shakespeare is the author of *The Merchant of Venice. Hesse is the author of* Steppenwolf. *Joyce is the author of* Ulysses. *Proust is the author of* Remembrances of Times Past.

63. ROOK : CASTLE :: HORSE : (***a.* knight**, *b.* track, *c.* chess, *d.* winner)

(a) In the game of chess, rook and castle refer to the same piece, as do knight and horse.

64. (*a.* Greuze, *b.* Utrillo, ***c.* Seurat**, *d.* Manet) : POINTILLISM :: DAVID : NEOCLASSICISM

(c) Seurat was a leading member in the French school of pointillism. David was a leading member in the French school of neoclassicism. *Greuze was a Rococo era painter. Utrillo specialized in painting cityscapes. Manet was a realist/impressionist painter.*

65. BILL : BEAK :: (***a.* finger**, *b.* leg, *c.* hand, *d.* kneecap) : DIGIT

(a) A bill is a beak. A finger is a digit.

66. GEWGAW : (***a.* trinket**, *b.* bottle, *c.* rhinestone, *d.* candy) :: TACITURN : QUIET

(a) A gewgaw is a trinket. A taciturn person is quiet.

67. (*a.* fortunate, *b.* **entreat**, *c.* unfortunate, *d.* order) : IMPORTUNE :: IMPREGNABLE : UNSHAKABLE

(b) Entreat and importune are synonyms, as are impregnable and unshakable.

68. CULPABLE : GUILTY :: (*a.* preculpable, *b.* **exculpable**, *c.* multiculpable, *d.* malculpable) : ACQUITTED

(b) Someone who is culpable is guilty; someone who is exculpable is acquitted.

69. FOX : (*a.* bovine, *b.* **vulpine**, *c.* porcine, *d.* equine) :: CAT : FELINE

(b) Vulpine means foxlike, while feline means catlike. Bovine means cowlike; porcine means piglike; equine means horselike.

70. AGONY : ECSTASY :: SOUND : (*a.* Light, *b.* Trumpet, *c.* Signpost, *d.* **Fury**)

(d) *The Agony and the Ecstasy* (by Irving Stone) and *The Sound and the Fury* (by William Faulkner) are both book titles.

71. LANG SYNE : (*a.* **bygone days**, *b.* future days, *c.* here and now, *d.* nonexistent times) :: IMMEDIATELY : AT ONCE

(a) Lang syne means bygone days; immediately means at once.

72. (*a.* India, *b.* Brazil, *c.* **Mexico**, *d.* Spain) : GUANAJUATO :: CANADA : MANITOBA

(c) Guanajuato is a political subdivision of Mexico. Manitoba is a political subdivision of Canada.

73. VERDI : AIDA :: (*a.* Bach, *b.* Mozart, *c.* **Beethoven**, *d.* Brahms) : FIDELIO

(c) Verdi composed the opera *Aida*. Beethoven composed the opera *Fidelio. Bach composed* The Well-Tempered Clavier; *Mozart composed* The Magic Flute; *Brahms composed* A German Requiem.

74. TORTUOUS : (*a.* **winding**, *b.* barbaric, *c.* long, *d.* incomprehensible) :: HAPPY : FELICITOUS

(a) Tortuous and winding are synonyms, as are happy and felicitous.

75. (*a.* **present**, *b.* past, *c.* recent, *d.* never) : CURRENT :: ERSTWHILE : FORMER

(a) A present event is current; a former event is erstwhile.

76. DAVID : GOLIATH :: HOLMES : (*a.* **Moriarty**, *b.* Watson, *c.* Doyle, *d.* Devlin)

(a) Goliath was the mortal enemy of David; Moriarty was the mortal enemy of Holmes. *Arthur Conan Doyle was the author of Sherlock Holmes. Watson was Sherlock Holmes's assistant. Devlin is a distracter term.*

77. LUGUBRIOUS : (*a.* shallow, *b.* **cheerful**, *c.* expensive, *d.* fatuous) :: PONDEROUS : LIGHT

(b) Lugubrious and cheerful are antonyms, as are ponderous and light.

78. EXPLETIVE : (*a.* interrogative, *b.* factotum, *c.* **oath**, *d.* lie) :: EXPOSÉ : DISCLOSURE

(c) An expletive is an oath. An exposé is a disclosure.

79. 11 : BINARY :: (*a.* 2, *b.* **3**, *c.* 4, *d.* 10) : DECIMAL

(b) The number 11 in binary notation is equal to the number 3 in decimal notation.

80. CHALICE : GOBLET :: LEAF : (*a.* plant, *b.* tree, *c.* **sheet**, *d.* gold)

(c) A chalice is a goblet. A leaf is a sheet (of paper).

81. (*a.* nut, *b.* fruit, *c.* **root**, *d.* berry) : TURNIP :: STEM : CELERY

(c) The stem of celery is edible, as is the root of turnip.

82. ABRAM : ABRAHAM :: (*a.* Sarabelle, ***b.* Sarai**, *c.* Salome, *d.* Sharon) : SARAH

(b) After the Covenant with God, Abram's name was changed to Abraham, and Sarai's name was changed to Sarah.

83. VELÁSQUEZ : MAIDS OF HONOR :: (***a.* Botticelli**, *b.* Bellini, *c.* Bosch, *d.* Uccello) : THE BIRTH OF VENUS

(a) *Maids of Honor* is a famous painting by Velásquez; *The Birth of Venus* is a famous painting by Botticelli. *Bellini painted many Christian scenes, like* St. Francis in Ecstasy. The Garden of Earthly Delights *is one of Bosch's famous paintings. Uccello painted the* Battle of San Romano *in a series of three paintings.*

84. CIVIL : (*a.* misdemeanor, *b.* larceny, ***c.* tort**, *d.* perjury) :: CRIMINAL : FELONY

(c) A tort is a civil offense, while a felony is a criminal offense.

85. GREGORIAN : NOVEMBER :: FRENCH REVOLUTIONARY : (*a.* Novembre, *b.* February, *c.* Julian, ***d.* Thermidor**)

(d) Thermidor in the French Revolutionary calendar corresponded to November in the conventional Gregorian calendar in their both being the 11th month. The months of the French Revolutionary calendar (starting in September) were Vendémiaire, Brumaire, Frimaire, Nivôse, Pluviôse, Ventôse, Germinal, Floréal, Prairial, Messidor, Thermidor, Fructidor.

86. GOLDEN RULE : LUKE :: CATEGORICAL IMPERATIVE : (*a.* Hegel, ***b.* Kant**, *c.* Ardrey, *d.* Lorenz)

(b) The golden rule—"Do unto others as you would have them do unto you"—is found in the Gospel of Luke. The categorical imperative—"One's behavior should be governed by the same principles that one would have govern other people's behavior"—is found in the philosophy of Kant.

87. EQUIVOCATION : (*a.* perversity, *b.* exultation, ***c.* veracity**, *d.* perjury) :: UNCERTAINTY : CERTAINTY

(c) Equivocation is the opposite of veracity. Uncertainty is the opposite of certainty.

88. TIMBREL : (*a.* cymbals, *b.* zither, *c.* flute, ***d.* tambourine**) :: LUTE : GUITAR

(d) A timbrel is an early form of tambourine; a lute is an early form of guitar.

89. (*a.* Apollo, *b.* Phaeton, ***c.* Furies**, *d.* Sirens) : EUMENIDES :: PLUTO : HADES

(c) The Furies and the Eumenides were one and the same; similarly, Pluto and Hades were one and the same. *Apollo was the legendary son of Zeus and Leto; he is the Greek and Roman god of light, prophesy, poetry, and music. Phaeton was the son of Helios; he tried to drive his father's chariot and was killed when he came too close to Earth. A siren is a sea nymph that lures sailors into their demise.*

90. JOSEPH K. : TRIAL :: GREGOR SAMSA : (*a.* Hunger Artist, *b.* Death in Venice, *c.* The Flies, ***d.* Metamorphosis**)

(d) Joseph K. is the main character in Kafka's *The Trial*. Gregor Samsa is the main character in Kafka's *The Metamorphosis*. Death in Venice *is by Thomas Mann;* The Flies *is by Jean-Paul Sartre;* A Hunger Artist *is by Franz Kafka.*

91. $\sqrt{2}$: $\sqrt{18}$ :: 1 : (*a.* 2, ***b.* 3**, *c.* 6, *d.* 9)

(b) The ratio of $\sqrt{2}$ to $\sqrt{18}$ is equal to the ratio of 1 to 3.

92. TRANSUBSTANTIATION : ACTUAL :: (*a.* insubstantiation, *b.* absubstantiation, *c.* **consubstantiation**, *d.* desubstantiation) : COEXISTING

(c) According to the doctrine of transubstantiation, the actual substances of the bread and of the wine in the Eucharist are changed into the body and blood of Christ; according to the doctrine of consubstantiation, the bread and wine are merely coexisting.

93. ABACUS : COMPUTER :: DAGUERROTYPE : (*a.* stereo, *b.* **photograph**, *c.* tape recorder, *d.* telephone)

(b) The abacus is a primitive computer; the daguerrotype is a primitive photograph.

94. DECLARATION OF INDEPENDENCE : PHILADELPHIA :: MAGNA CARTA : (*a.* Gloucester, *b.* **Runnymede**, *c.* Canterbury, *d.* Norwalk)

(b) The Declaration of Independence (1776) was signed in Philadelphia; the Magna Carta was signed at Runnymede (1215). *The Magna Carta was a charter given to the English barons by King John to recognize their rights and privileges.*

95. MINTON : ROYAL DOULTON :: MIKASA (*a.* Sony, *b.* Rosenthal, *c.* Lenox, *d.* **Noritake**)

(d) Minton and Royal Doulton are both English makers of fine china, while Mikasa and Noritake are both Japanese makers of fine china. *Rosenthal is a German brand of china. Lenox is an American brand of china.*

96. SHYLOCK : SCROOGE :: DON JUAN : (*a.* Antonio, *b.* Don Giovanni, *c.* **Lothario**, *d.* Don Quixote)

(c) In literature, Shylock (of *The Merchant of Venice* by Shakespeare) and Scrooge (of *A Christmas Carol* by Charles Dickens) are both miserly characters, while Don Juan (many authors, e.g., Moliere and Byron) and Lothario (of *The Fair Penitent* by Nicholas Rowe) are both great lovers.

97. SKINNER : EMPIRICIST :: (*a.* Watson, *b.* Aristotle, *c.* **Chomsky**, *d.* Locke) : RATIONALIST

(c) Skinner was a philosophical empiricist, while Chomsky is a philosophical rationalist. *Watson was a behaviorist; Locke was an empiricist; Aristotle was a Greek empiricist philosopher.*

98. MOHAWK : IROQUOIS :: (*a.* Apache, *b.* **Zuni**, *c.* Seminole, *d.* Creek) : PUEBLO

(b) The Mohawks were one of the Iroquois Indian tribes; the Zuni were one of the Pueblo Indian tribes. *The Seminoles are a Native American people from the American southeast who now reside primarily in Florida. The Creek are closely related to the Seminoles and call themselves Muscogee today. Apache is a term that refers to several groups of Native Americans who lived in the Great Plains and the southwest of the United States.*

99. (*a.* half-life, *b.* radioactivity, *c.* atomic mass, *d.* **atomic number**) : ISOTOPE :: ATOMIC WEIGHT : ISOBAR

(d) Chemical isotopes have the same atomic number; chemical isobars have the same atomic weight.

100. SARACEN : (*a.* Hindu, *b.* **Muslim**, *c.* Shintoist, *d.* Taoist) :: EPISCOPALIAN : ANGLICAN

(b) A Saracen is a Muslim. An Episcopalian is an Anglican.

101. WATERGATE : NIXON :: IRAN CONTRA : (*a.* Ford, *b.* Carter, *c.* **Reagan**, *d.* Bush)

(c) The Watergate and Iran Contra scandals respectively marred the presidential administrations of Nixon and Reagan. Watergate is a term for a series of scandals that resulted in President Nixon's resignation in 1974. The Iran Contra affair was a series of scandals under Ronald Reagan that involved arms sales to Iran and funding of Contra militants in Nicaragua.

102. GALAPAGOS : SAMOA :: (*a.* Linnaeus, *b.* Magellan, *c.* Rhodes, ***d.* Darwin**) : MEAD

(d) Charles Darwin began some of his most prominent scientific work in the South Pacific Galapagos Islands. Likewise, Margaret Mead began some of her most prominent scientific work in the South Pacific, in Samoa.

103. BIGGER THOMAS : (*a.* New York, ***b.* Chicago**, *c.* St. Louis, *d.* Montgomery) :: RODION RASKOLNIKOV : ST. PETERSBURG

(b) Fictional characters Bigger Thomas (in *Native Son* by Richard Wright) and Rodion Raskolnikov (in *Crime and Punishment* by Fyodor Dostoyevsky) despair after committing murders in their respective homes of Chicago and St. Petersburg.

104. TAXONOMY : CLASSIFY :: NOMENCLATURE : (*a.* order, *b.* color, ***c.* name**, *d.* number)

(c) A taxonomy is the principled system by which things are classified. Nomenclature is the principled system by which things are named.

105. PHYSIOGNOMY : (***a.* face**, *b.* stature, *c.* physiology, *d.* gate) :: CHIROMANCY : PALM

(a) Physiognomy is the art of determining something about a person from his/her face. Chiromancy is the art of determining something about a person from his/her palm.

106. MUTINY : SHIP CAPTAIN :: COUP D'ÉTAT : (*a.* college dean, *b.* military commander, ***c.* government**, *d.* CEO)

(c) Just as a mutiny typically refers to the overthrow of a ship's captain, so a *coup d'état* (literally, *stroke of the state*) traditionally refers to the overthrow of a government.

107. (***a.* exaggerated**, *b.* understated, *c.* metaphorical, *d.* literal) : HYPERBOLIC :: DRAMATIC : HISTRIONIC

(a) An exaggerated statement may be described as hyperbolic just as a dramatic display may be described as histrionic.

108. APPLE : EVE :: (*a.* pear, ***b.* pomegranate**, *c.* peach, *d.* papaya) : PERSEPHONE

(b) Eve was punished for eating the forbidden fruit that tradition in the Bible holds was an apple, and Persephone was punished in Greek mythology for eating the forbidden fruit pomegranate.

109. CEMENTUM : ROOT :: (*a.* bone, *b.* fluoride, *c.* keratin, ***d.* enamel**) : CROWN

(d) Cementum makes up the outer surface of a tooth's root just as enamel makes up the outer surface of a tooth's crown.

110. (*a.* acorn, *b.* cornmeal, ***c.* millet**, *d.* filbert) : BULGUR :: QUINOA : BARLEY

(c) Millet, bulgur, quinoa, and barley are all whole grains.

111. MOBY DICK : LEVIATHAN :: MELVILLE : (*a.* Rousseau, ***b.* Hobbes**, *c.* Kant, *d.* Smith)

(b) Melville is famous for his book *Moby Dick*, and Hobbes is famous for his book *Leviathan. Rousseau is known for* Pygmalion *and the* Confessions of a Solitary Walker. *Kant is famous for his* Critique of Pure Reason. *Smith is the author of* The Theory of Moral Sentiments.

112. (***a*. Locke**, *b*. Galileo, *c*. Bacon, *d*. Calvin) : ENLIGHTENMENT :: DESCARTES : RENAISSANCE

(a) Locke was a philosopher of the Enlightenment, as Descartes was a philosopher of the Renaissance. *Galileo was an Italian physicist and astronomer who improved the telescope and is called the "father of modern observational astronomy." He was a supporter of Copernicanism. Bacon was an English philosopher and statesman. Calvin was the founder of the Presbyterian church.*

113. STEINWAY : (***a*. piano**, *b*. cello, *c*. flute, *d*. organ) :: STRADIVARIUS : VIOLIN

(a) Steinway is a maker of highly prized pianos, as Stradivarius is a maker of highly prized violins.

114. TERKEL : (*a*. manuscripts, *b*. photographs, ***c*. oral histories**, *d*. maps) :: LOMAX : FOLK MUSIC

(c) Terkel was a pioneering anthologist of oral histories and Lomax was a pioneering anthologist of folk music.

115. 6×10^{23} : (*a*. e, ***b*. Avogadro's number**, *c*. i, *d*. Planck's constant) :: 3.14 : PI

(b) 6×10^{23} (rounded) is also known as Avogadro's number. Likewise, 3.14 (rounded) is known as pi, or the symbol π.

116. CIRRUS : NIMBUS :: CUMULUS : (*a*. bilious, *b*. birrus, *c*. mobius, ***d*. stratus**)

(d) Cirrus, nimbus, cumulus, and stratus are all types of clouds. *Bilious refers to the bile; a birrus is a coarse kind of cloth worn by poor people in the Middle Ages. Mobius was a German mathematician who developed the Mobius strip.*

117. SOCIALISM : (***a*. state**, *b*. family, *c*. town, *d*. universal) :: CAPITALISM : PRIVATE

(a) Socialism is an economic system based on state ownership of capital. Capitalism is an economic system based on private ownership of capital.

118. (*a*. Pikes Peak, ***b*. Mt. Kilimanjaro**, *c*. Mt. Vesuvius, *d*. K2) : MT. ST. HELENS :: EXTINCT : ACTIVE

(b) Mt. Kilimanjaro is an extinct volcano whereas Mt. St. Helens is an active volcano. *Mt. Vesuvius is also an active volcano. Pikes Peak and K2 are mountain summits.*

119. IMPERIOUS : IMPERVIOUS :: (*a*. grandiose, *b*. disbelieving, *c*. judgmental, ***d*. domineering**) : IMMUNE

(d) Imperious means domineering just as impervious means immune.

120. NEUTRAL : NEUTRON :: NEGATIVE : (*a*. atom, ***b*. electron**, *c*. positron, *d*. negatron)

(b) Neutrons are subatomic particles with a neutral charge. Electrons are subatomic particles with a negative charge.

ANSWER SHEET
Practice Test 8

1. Ⓐ Ⓑ Ⓒ Ⓓ
2. Ⓐ Ⓑ Ⓒ Ⓓ
3. Ⓐ Ⓑ Ⓒ Ⓓ
4. Ⓐ Ⓑ Ⓒ Ⓓ
5. Ⓐ Ⓑ Ⓒ Ⓓ
6. Ⓐ Ⓑ Ⓒ Ⓓ
7. Ⓐ Ⓑ Ⓒ Ⓓ
8. Ⓐ Ⓑ Ⓒ Ⓓ
9. Ⓐ Ⓑ Ⓒ Ⓓ
10. Ⓐ Ⓑ Ⓒ Ⓓ
11. Ⓐ Ⓑ Ⓒ Ⓓ
12. Ⓐ Ⓑ Ⓒ Ⓓ
13. Ⓐ Ⓑ Ⓒ Ⓓ
14. Ⓐ Ⓑ Ⓒ Ⓓ
15. Ⓐ Ⓑ Ⓒ Ⓓ
16. Ⓐ Ⓑ Ⓒ Ⓓ
17. Ⓐ Ⓑ Ⓒ Ⓓ
18. Ⓐ Ⓑ Ⓒ Ⓓ
19. Ⓐ Ⓑ Ⓒ Ⓓ
20. Ⓐ Ⓑ Ⓒ Ⓓ
21. Ⓐ Ⓑ Ⓒ Ⓓ
22. Ⓐ Ⓑ Ⓒ Ⓓ
23. Ⓐ Ⓑ Ⓒ Ⓓ
24. Ⓐ Ⓑ Ⓒ Ⓓ
25. Ⓐ Ⓑ Ⓒ Ⓓ
26. Ⓐ Ⓑ Ⓒ Ⓓ
27. Ⓐ Ⓑ Ⓒ Ⓓ
28. Ⓐ Ⓑ Ⓒ Ⓓ
29. Ⓐ Ⓑ Ⓒ Ⓓ
30. Ⓐ Ⓑ Ⓒ Ⓓ

31. Ⓐ Ⓑ Ⓒ Ⓓ
32. Ⓐ Ⓑ Ⓒ Ⓓ
33. Ⓐ Ⓑ Ⓒ Ⓓ
34. Ⓐ Ⓑ Ⓒ Ⓓ
35. Ⓐ Ⓑ Ⓒ Ⓓ
36. Ⓐ Ⓑ Ⓒ Ⓓ
37. Ⓐ Ⓑ Ⓒ Ⓓ
38. Ⓐ Ⓑ Ⓒ Ⓓ
39. Ⓐ Ⓑ Ⓒ Ⓓ
40. Ⓐ Ⓑ Ⓒ Ⓓ
41. Ⓐ Ⓑ Ⓒ Ⓓ
42. Ⓐ Ⓑ Ⓒ Ⓓ
43. Ⓐ Ⓑ Ⓒ Ⓓ
44. Ⓐ Ⓑ Ⓒ Ⓓ
45. Ⓐ Ⓑ Ⓒ Ⓓ
46. Ⓐ Ⓑ Ⓒ Ⓓ
47. Ⓐ Ⓑ Ⓒ Ⓓ
48. Ⓐ Ⓑ Ⓒ Ⓓ
49. Ⓐ Ⓑ Ⓒ Ⓓ
50. Ⓐ Ⓑ Ⓒ Ⓓ
51. Ⓐ Ⓑ Ⓒ Ⓓ
52. Ⓐ Ⓑ Ⓒ Ⓓ
53. Ⓐ Ⓑ Ⓒ Ⓓ
54. Ⓐ Ⓑ Ⓒ Ⓓ
55. Ⓐ Ⓑ Ⓒ Ⓓ
56. Ⓐ Ⓑ Ⓒ Ⓓ
57. Ⓐ Ⓑ Ⓒ Ⓓ
58. Ⓐ Ⓑ Ⓒ Ⓓ
59. Ⓐ Ⓑ Ⓒ Ⓓ
60. Ⓐ Ⓑ Ⓒ Ⓓ

61. Ⓐ Ⓑ Ⓒ Ⓓ
62. Ⓐ Ⓑ Ⓒ Ⓓ
63. Ⓐ Ⓑ Ⓒ Ⓓ
64. Ⓐ Ⓑ Ⓒ Ⓓ
65. Ⓐ Ⓑ Ⓒ Ⓓ
66. Ⓐ Ⓑ Ⓒ Ⓓ
67. Ⓐ Ⓑ Ⓒ Ⓓ
68. Ⓐ Ⓑ Ⓒ Ⓓ
69. Ⓐ Ⓑ Ⓒ Ⓓ
70. Ⓐ Ⓑ Ⓒ Ⓓ
71. Ⓐ Ⓑ Ⓒ Ⓓ
72. Ⓐ Ⓑ Ⓒ Ⓓ
73. Ⓐ Ⓑ Ⓒ Ⓓ
74. Ⓐ Ⓑ Ⓒ Ⓓ
75. Ⓐ Ⓑ Ⓒ Ⓓ
76. Ⓐ Ⓑ Ⓒ Ⓓ
77. Ⓐ Ⓑ Ⓒ Ⓓ
78. Ⓐ Ⓑ Ⓒ Ⓓ
79. Ⓐ Ⓑ Ⓒ Ⓓ
80. Ⓐ Ⓑ Ⓒ Ⓓ
81. Ⓐ Ⓑ Ⓒ Ⓓ
82. Ⓐ Ⓑ Ⓒ Ⓓ
83. Ⓐ Ⓑ Ⓒ Ⓓ
84. Ⓐ Ⓑ Ⓒ Ⓓ
85. Ⓐ Ⓑ Ⓒ Ⓓ
86. Ⓐ Ⓑ Ⓒ Ⓓ
87. Ⓐ Ⓑ Ⓒ Ⓓ
88. Ⓐ Ⓑ Ⓒ Ⓓ
89. Ⓐ Ⓑ Ⓒ Ⓓ
90. Ⓐ Ⓑ Ⓒ Ⓓ

91. Ⓐ Ⓑ Ⓒ Ⓓ
92. Ⓐ Ⓑ Ⓒ Ⓓ
93. Ⓐ Ⓑ Ⓒ Ⓓ
94. Ⓐ Ⓑ Ⓒ Ⓓ
95. Ⓐ Ⓑ Ⓒ Ⓓ
96. Ⓐ Ⓑ Ⓒ Ⓓ
97. Ⓐ Ⓑ Ⓒ Ⓓ
98. Ⓐ Ⓑ Ⓒ Ⓓ
99. Ⓐ Ⓑ Ⓒ Ⓓ
100. Ⓐ Ⓑ Ⓒ Ⓓ
101. Ⓐ Ⓑ Ⓒ Ⓓ
102. Ⓐ Ⓑ Ⓒ Ⓓ
103. Ⓐ Ⓑ Ⓒ Ⓓ
104. Ⓐ Ⓑ Ⓒ Ⓓ
105. Ⓐ Ⓑ Ⓒ Ⓓ
106. Ⓐ Ⓑ Ⓒ Ⓓ
107. Ⓐ Ⓑ Ⓒ Ⓓ
108. Ⓐ Ⓑ Ⓒ Ⓓ
109. Ⓐ Ⓑ Ⓒ Ⓓ
110. Ⓐ Ⓑ Ⓒ Ⓓ
111. Ⓐ Ⓑ Ⓒ Ⓓ
112. Ⓐ Ⓑ Ⓒ Ⓓ
113. Ⓐ Ⓑ Ⓒ Ⓓ
114. Ⓐ Ⓑ Ⓒ Ⓓ
115. Ⓐ Ⓑ Ⓒ Ⓓ
116. Ⓐ Ⓑ Ⓒ Ⓓ
117. Ⓐ Ⓑ Ⓒ Ⓓ
118. Ⓐ Ⓑ Ⓒ Ⓓ
119. Ⓐ Ⓑ Ⓒ Ⓓ
120. Ⓐ Ⓑ Ⓒ Ⓓ

Time: 60 MINUTES

> **Directions:** In each of the following questions, you will find three initial terms and, in parentheses, four answer options designated *a*, *b*, *c*, and *d*. You are to select from the four answer options the one that *best* completes the analogy with the three initial terms. To record your answers, use the answer sheet provided.

1. STOCKHOLM : (*a.* Switzerland, *b.* Austria, *c.* Finland, *d.* Sweden) :: PARIS : FRANCE

2. ESCARGOTS : FRENCH :: SUKIYAKI : (*a.* Japanese, *b.* German, *c.* Hungarian, *d.* Mexican)

3. COBBLER : SHOES :: TAILOR : (*a.* needles, *b.* clothes, *c.* threads, *d.* thimbles)

4. (*a.* black, *b.* yellow, *c.* red, *d.* blue) : SULFUR :: WHITE : GYPSUM

5. TRANSITIVE : HIT :: (*a.* expletive, *b.* intransitive, *c.* nominative, *d.* subjunctive) : IS

6. COMPOSITE : 8 :: PRIME : (*a.* 4, *b.* 6, *c.* 7, *d.* 9)

7. FRESCO : PLASTER :: TAPESTRY : (*a.* stone, *b.* metal, *c.* cloth, *d.* wood)

8. VEGETARIAN : MEAT :: TEETOTALER : (*a.* fruit, *b.* alcoholic beverages, *c.* cooked food, *d.* tobacco)

9. TRAFALGAR SQUARE : (*a.* London, *b.* Florence, *c.* Moscow, *d.* Paris) :: TIMES SQUARE : NEW YORK

10. (*a.* appliance, *b.* food, *c.* explosive, *d.* automobile) : TNT :: COUNTRY : U.S.A.

11. YELLOW : COWARDLY :: (*a.* blue, *b.* black, *c.* red, *d.* green) : INEXPERIENCED

12. 2 : QUART :: (*a.* 1, *b.* 4, *c.* 8, *d.* 16) : GALLON

13. RED FLAG : REVOLUTION :: WHITE FLAG : (*a.* victory, *b.* surrender, *c.* established order, *d.* purity)

14. ZEBRA : STRIPES :: LEOPARD : (*a.* spots, *b.* stripes, *c.* diagonals, *d.* zigzags)

15. (*a.* tyrant, *b.* wealthy merchant, *c.* explorer, *d.* pirate) : BUCCANEER :: SETTLER : PIONEER

16. CENTIGRADE : 100 :: FAHRENHEIT : (*a.* 0, *b.* 32, *c.* 100, *d.* 212)

17. (*a.* 1, *b.* 5, *c.* 20, *d.* 25) : SILVER :: 50 : GOLD

18. BEEF : STEER :: MUTTON : (*a.* ox, *b.* sheep, *c.* deer, *d.* goat)

19. ATOM : (*a.* molecule, *b.* electron, *c.* nucleus, *d.* gamma ray) :: TREE : FOREST

20. IGNORANCE : (*a.* intelligence, *b.* knowledge, *c.* foresight, *d.* attention) :: STUPIDITY : INTELLIGENCE

21. NONAGENARIAN : 90 :: OCTOGENARIAN : (*a.* 60, *b.* 70, *c.* 80, *d.* 100)

22. LISBON : (*a.* Spain, *b.* Portugal, *c.* Hungary, *d.* Denmark) :: THE HAGUE : NETHERLANDS

23. WAMPUM : (*a.* Dutchman, *b.* Portuguese, *c.* Pakistani, *d.* American Indian) :: DOUBLOON : SPANIARD

24. GREEK ALPHABET : GREEK :: LATIN ALPHABET : (*a.* Russian, *b.* Cyrillic, *c.* Sanskrit, *d.* English)

25. (*a.* 90, *b.* 180, *c.* 270, *d.* 360) : TRIANGLE :: 360 : SQUARE

26. COLUMBIA : (*a.* South America, *b.* North America, *c.* United States, *d.* Brazil) :: BRITANNIA : BRITAIN

27. FINALE : MUSICAL COMPOSITION :: (*a.* check, *b.* checkmate, *c.* rook, *d.* jeopardy) : CHESS

28. YAHWEH : JUDAISM :: ALLAH : (*a.* Islam, *b.* Judaism, *c.* Taoism, *d.* Confucianism)

29. (*a.* nominative, *b.* dative, *c.* accusative, *d.* ablative) : OBJECTIVE :: SHE : HIM

30. RECTANGLE : OCTAGON :: (*a.* triangle, *b.* square, *c.* pentagon, *d.* rhombus) : HEXAGON

31. (*a.* prize, *b.* damn, *c.* reflect, *d.* complete) : PRAISE :: COMPLEMENT : COMPLIMENT

32. SUB : BUS :: TAR : (*a.* car, *b.* road, *c.* vehicle, *d.* rat)

33. MANDATORY : (*a.* laudatory, *b.* damning, *c.* optional, *d.* compulsory) :: DEFINITE : UNCERTAIN

34. ONE : LAND :: TWO : (*a.* air, *b.* sea, *c.* ground, *d.* island)

35. (*a.* eat, *b.* drink, *c.* sever, *d.* mend) : CHALICE :: DIG : SHOVEL

36. CONSONANT : (*a.* syncopated, *b.* rhythmic, *c.* euphemistic, *d.* euphonious) :: DISSONANT : DISCORDANT

37. (*a.* Montague, *b.* Scali, *c.* Dunlop, *d.* Mineo) : ROMEO :: CAPULET : JULIET

38. EMANCIPATE : (*a.* emaciate, *b.* free, *c.* enslave, *d.* deliver) :: EMPTY : FULL

39. PALMISTRY : PALM :: PHRENOLOGY : (*a.* handwriting, *b.* EEG, *c.* eyes, *d.* skull)

40. (*a.* Columbia Gem, *b.* Union Jack, *c.* Royal Ensign, *d.* Fleur-de-Lis) : GREAT BRITAIN :: STARS AND STRIPES : U.S.A.

41. COMMON LOG : 10 :: NATURAL LOG : (*a.* π, *b.* e, *c.* i, *d.* 1)

42. MAE WEST : LIFE JACKET :: MICKEY FINN : (*a.* blackjack, *b.* Molotov cocktail, *c.* drugged liquor, *d.* time bomb)

43. EARTH : AIR :: (*a.* bile, *b.* carbon, *c.* phlogiston, *d.* fire) : WATER

44. CAMUS : STRANGER :: (*a.* Sartre, *b.* Camus, *c.* Mauriac, *d.* Ionesco) : PLAGUE

45. DOG : PIE :: HOT : (*a.* cold, *b.* cat, *c.* pizza, *d.* cake)

46. PIETÀ : MICHELANGELO :: THE KISS : (*a.* Rodin, *b.* Pisano, *c.* Ghiberti, *d.* da Vinci)

47. (*a.* Congress of Vienna, *b.* League of Nations, *c.* Warsaw Pact, *d.* NATO) : UNITED NATIONS :: GASLIGHT : ELECTRIC LIGHT

48. CARAT : (*a.* size, *b.* weight, *c.* brilliance, *d.* value) :: ACRE : AREA

49. $a + b : b + a :: a(b + a)b : $ (*a.* $2a^2b^2$, *b.* $(a + b)^2$, *c.* $a^2b + ab^2$, *d.* $a^2b^2 + ab$)

50. FRANCIS CRICK : STRUCTURE OF DNA MOLECULE :: MARIE CURIE : (*a.* nobelium, *b.* uranium, *c.* radium, *d.* plutonium)

51. ANALOG : SLIDE RULE :: DIGITAL : (*a.* odometer, *b.* ruler, *c.* compass, *d.* protractor)

52. CHARLOTTE'S : PILGRIM'S :: WEB : (*a.* Follies, *b.* Progress, *c.* Pretense, *d.* Journey)

53. VOID : VACUUM :: FULL : (*a.* replete, *b.* deplete, *c.* compact, *d.* empty)

54. HIGH : DIE :: (*a.* gregarious, *b.* reticent, *c.* low, *d.* buy) : SHY

55. (*a.* retina, *b.* iris, *c.* lens, *d.* cone) : ROD :: CHROMATIC : ACHROMATIC

56. BOVINE : (*a.* jackal, *b.* monkey, *c.* ox, *d.* rabbit) :: URSINE : BEAR

57. (*a.* Plato, *b.* Aristotle, *c.* Leibniz, *d.* Locke) : REPUBLIC :: DESCARTES : MEDITATIONS

58. DEER : DEER :: CORPUS : (*a.* corpi, *b.* corpuses, *c.* corpora, *d.* corpes)

59. BUDAPEST : HANOI :: HUNGARY : (*a.* Cambodia, *b.* Laos, *c.* Thailand, *d.* Vietnam)

60. PROMISED LAND : CANAAN :: LAND OF NOD : (*a.* wakefulness, *b.* hell, *c.* sleep, *d.* heaven)

61. MISOGYNIST : WOMEN :: MISOGAMIST : (*a.* men, *b.* people, *c.* marriage, *d.* religion)

62. (*a.* Achilles, *b.* Hector, *c.* Paris, *d.* Troilus) : HELEN :: PLUTO : PROSERPINA

63. BENIGN : BENEVOLENT :: (*a.* beneficent, *b.* nefarious, *c.* tortuous, *d.* voracious) : MALEVOLENT

64. BLOCKHEAD : LUNKHEAD :: MUTTONHEAD : (*a.* fathead, *b.* sleepyhead, *c.* bighead, *d.* egghead)

65. UNCLE TOM : SERVILE :: DUTCH UNCLE : (*a.* hoary, *b.* kind, *c.* stern, *d.* stingy)

66. ALPHA : (*a.* gamma, *b.* zed, *c.* epsilon, *d.* omega) :: A : Z

67. THIAMINE : ASCORBIC ACID :: B_1 : (*a.* B_6, *b.* B_{12}, *c.* C, *d.* E)

68. BRAZIL : (*a.* Portuguese, *b.* Spanish, *c.* French, *d.* Brazilian) :: AUSTRIA : GERMAN

69. CENTURY : EON :: DOZEN : (*a.* one hundred, *b.* gross, *c.* zero, *d.* myriad)

70. SITTING BULL : SIOUX :: GERONIMO : (*a.* Apache, *b.* Pueblo, *c.* Mohawk, *d.* Seminole)

71. AUTOCRACY : AUTARCHY :: MONARCHY : (*a.* democracy, *b.* anarchy, *c.* oligarchy, *d.* kingdom)

72. GOGGLE-EYED : BULGING :: HOOK-NOSED : (*a.* opercular, *b.* oviparous, *c.* ovine, *d.* aquiline)

73. NEPTUNE : DIANA :: SEA : (*a.* hearth, *b.* sun, *c.* moon, *d.* home)

74. EXPEL : DRIVE AWAY :: EXPIATE : (*a.* atone for, *b.* talk at length, *c.* forgive, *d.* speak briefly)

75. LARGO : SLOW :: (*a.* moderato, *b.* allegro, *c.* piano, *d.* fortissimo) : FAST

76. (*a.* with faith, *b.* with truth, *c.* with passion, *d.* with authority) : EX CATHEDRA :: ON THE FACE : EX FACIE

77. FIFE : CLARINET :: TROMBONE : (*a.* lute, *b.* bagpipe, *c.* piano, *d.* violin)

78. PARASITE : LIVING :: (*a.* saprophyte, *b.* neophyte, *c.* pteridophyte, *d.* bryophyte) : DEAD

79. PRINCE : MACHIAVELLI :: PETIT PRINCE : (*a.* Saint-Exupéry, *b.* Mauriac, *c.* Camus, *d.* Lescaut)

80. INDIA : RUPEE :: (*a.* Mexico, *b.* Switzerland, *c.* Great Britain, *d.* Sweden) : FRANC

81. DEMOSTHENES : (*a.* Cicero, *b.* Socrates, *c.* Pericles, *d.* Ovid) :: HOMER : VIRGIL

82. (*a.* mg, *b.* gg, *c.* kg, *d.* cg) : g :: m : mm

83. CIPANGO : JAPAN :: CATHAY : (*a.* China, *b.* Tibet, *c.* Polynesia, *d.* Mongolia)

84. IMPROMPTU : EXTEMPORE :: PROBITY : (*a.* open-mindedness, *b.* dishonesty, *c.* narrow-mindedness, *d.* honesty)

85. FERMI : NUCLEAR PHYSICS :: JANE ADDAMS : (*a.* nursing, *b.* physics, *c.* social work, *d.* drama)

86. (*a.* Inferno, *b.* Decameron, *c.* The Wasteland, *d.* No Exit) : CANTERBURY TALES :: ANTHOLOGY : COLLECTION

87. RICHELIEU : (*a.* Cushing, *b.* Mazarin, *c.* Metternich, *d.* Marat) :: KENNEDY : JOHNSON

88. (*a.* uncertainty, *b.* luck, *c.* sample, *d.* variance) : POPULATION :: STATISTIC : PARAMETER

89. REGAN : GONERIL :: LEAH : (*a.* Jacob, *b.* Rebecca, *c.* Isaac, *d.* Rachel)

90. TEMPUS : CARPE :: FUGIT : (*a.* cibus, *b.* mater, *c.* diem, *d.* tempum)

91. ERSATZ : (*a.* genuine, *b.* superior, *c.* inferior, *d.* fake) :: FRESH : RANCID

92. EVE : DEED :: MADAM : (*a.* cuckoo, *b.* swoon, *c.* noon, *d.* pool)

93. SLEEPY : SOMNOLENT :: GROGGY : (*a.* asleep, *b.* unsteady, *c.* awake, *d.* dead)

94. AXON : DEPART :: (*a.* neuron, *b.* ganglion, *c.* dendrites, *d.* plasma) : APPROACH

95. BUDGE : TENNIS :: LOUIS : (*a.* hockey, *b.* football, *c.* baseball, *d.* boxing)

96. BLOOD : MELANCHOLY :: CHOLER : (*a.* plasma, *b.* lymph, *c.* phlegm, *d.* saliva)

97. MEXICO : YORK :: CAROLINA : (*a.* Virginia, *b.* Oregon, *c.* Washington, *d.* Dakota)

98. ARGON : NEON :: XENON : (*a.* helium, *b.* oxygen, *c.* mercury, *d.* carbon)

99. HORN : ROLAND :: HARP : (*a.* Gideon, *b.* David, *c.* Moses, *d.* Samuel)

100. GLUTTON : FOOD :: SATYR : (*a.* punishment, *b.* glory, *c.* alcoholic beverages, *d.* sex)

101. ACUTE : (*a.* small, *b.* obtuse, *c.* intense, *d.* right) :: APOGEE : PERIGEE

102. (*a.* berate, *b.* refine, *c.* attenuate, *d.* foreshadow) : ADUMBRATE :: INTIMATE : HINT

103. PNEUMONECTOMY : LUNG :: (*a.* tonsillectomy, *b.* meningectomy, *c.* lobotomy, *d.* encephalotomy) : BRAIN

104. EMPATHY : (*a.* lungs, *b.* soul, *c.* pancreas, *d.* heart) :: BRAVERY : LIVER

105. CIRCUMSPECT : CIRCUMSCRIBE :: (*a.* prudent, *b.* navigate, *c.* rounded, *d.* investigate) : ENCIRCLE

106. DEARTH : (*a.* poverty, *b.* abundance, *c.* warmth, *d.* nothing) :: PAUCITY : PLENTY

107. CAP : LID :: KNEE : (*a.* leg, *b.* patella, *c.* heel, *d.* eye)

108. (*a.* bitterness, *b.* wittiness, *c.* frivolity, *d.* accusation) : ACRIMONIOUS :: FRUGALITY : PARSIMONIOUS

109. CAESAR : DELIVERY :: ACHILLES : (*a.* surgery, *b.* ligament, *c.* tendon, *d.* bone)

110. PROMETHEUS : BOUND :: ATLAS : (*a.* carried, *b.* tied, *c.* shrugged, *d.* grew)

111. GENGHIS KHAN : (*a.* China, *b.* Mongolia, *c.* Persia, *d.* Prussia) :: SHAKA : SOUTH AFRICA

112. (*a.* right to bear arms, *b.* prohibition of alcohol, *c.* right to remain silent, *d.* freedom of religion) : 18th AMENDMENT :: WOMEN'S SUFFRAGE : 19th AMENDMENT

113. KID : (*a.* wolf, *b.* goat, *c.* moose, *d.* kangaroo) :: CALF : WHALE

114. HOPI : (*a.* southwest, *b.* southeast, *c.* northwest, *d.* great plains) :: TLINGIT : NORTHWEST

115. PTOLEMY : EARTH :: COPERNICUS : (*a.* Mars, *b.* Venus, *c.* Moon, *d.* Sun)

116. ADAM SMITH : 18th CENTURY :: JOHN MAYNARD KEYNES : (*a.* 20th century, *b.* 19th century, *c.* 17th century, *d.* 16th century)

117. (*a.* Laos, *b.* Japan, *c.* Taiwan, *d.* China) : JUDO :: KOREA : TAE KWON DO

118. KHMER ROUGE : POL POT :: COMMUNIST PARTY OF CHINA : (*a.* Kuomintang, *b.* Confucius, *c.* Mao Zedong, *d.* Chiang Kai-shek)

119. SUEZ CANAL : (*a.* Turkey, *b.* Morocco, *c.* Egypt, *d.* Israel) :: PANAMA CANAL : PANAMA

120. SOVIET UNION : (*a.* Portugal, *b.* Brazil, *c.* Cuba, *d.* Spain) :: CHAGALL : DALI

1.	**D**	31.	**D**	61.	**C**	91.	**A**
2.	**A**	32.	**D**	62.	**C**	92.	**C**
3.	**B**	33.	**C**	63.	**B**	93.	**B**
4.	**B**	34.	**B**	64.	**A**	94.	**C**
5.	**B**	35.	**B**	65.	**C**	95.	**D**
6.	**C**	36.	**D**	66.	**D**	96.	**C**
7.	**C**	37.	**A**	67.	**C**	97.	**D**
8.	**B**	38.	**C**	68.	**A**	98.	**A**
9.	**A**	39.	**D**	69.	**A**	99.	**B**
10.	**C**	40.	**B**	70.	**A**	100.	**D**
11.	**D**	41.	**B**	71.	**D**	101.	**B**
12.	**C**	42.	**C**	72.	**D**	102.	**D**
13.	**B**	43.	**D**	73.	**C**	103.	**C**
14.	**A**	44.	**B**	74.	**A**	104.	**D**
15.	**D**	45.	**C**	75.	**B**	105.	**A**
16.	**D**	46.	**A**	76.	**D**	106.	**B**
17.	**D**	47.	**B**	77.	**B**	107.	**D**
18.	**B**	48.	**B**	78.	**A**	108.	**A**
19.	**A**	49.	**C**	79.	**A**	109.	**C**
20.	**B**	50.	**C**	80.	**B**	110.	**C**
21.	**C**	51.	**A**	81.	**A**	111.	**B**
22.	**B**	52.	**B**	82.	**C**	112.	**B**
23.	**D**	53.	**A**	83.	**A**	113.	**B**
24.	**D**	54.	**D**	84.	**D**	114.	**A**
25.	**B**	55.	**D**	85.	**C**	115.	**D**
26.	**C**	56.	**C**	86.	**B**	116.	**A**
27.	**B**	57.	**A**	87.	**B**	117.	**B**
28.	**A**	58.	**C**	88.	**C**	118.	**C**
29.	**A**	59.	**D**	89.	**D**	119.	**C**
30.	**A**	60.	**C**	90.	**C**	120.	**D**

> In the following, explanations concerning the correct responses are in roman font. Explanations regarding distracters (incorrect responses) that are not self-explaining or could be misinterpreted are in italics in order to highlight the explanations of the answers that are correct.

1. STOCKHOLM : (*a.* Switzerland, *b.* Austria, *c.* Finland, ***d.* Sweden**) :: PARIS : FRANCE

   (d) Stockholm is the capital of Sweden. Paris is the capital of France. *The capital of Switzerland is Bern, the capital of Austria is Vienna, and the capital of Finland is Helsinki.*

2. ESCARGOTS : FRENCH :: SUKIYAKI : (***a.* Japanese**, *b.* German, *c.* Hungarian, *d.* Mexican)

   (a) Escargots are a French food (snails). Sukiyaki is a Japanese food dish (beef hot pot).

3. COBBLER : SHOES :: TAILOR : (*a.* needles, ***b.* clothes**, *c.* threads, *d.* thimbles)

   (b) A cobbler mends shoes; a tailor mends clothes.

4. (*a.* black, ***b.* yellow**, *c.* red, *d.* blue) : SULFUR :: WHITE : GYPSUM

   (b) Sulfur is usually yellow; gypsum is usually white.

5. TRANSITIVE : HIT :: (*a.* expletive, ***b.* intransitive**, *c.* nominative, *d.* subjunctive) : IS

   (b) Hit is a transitive verb. Is is an intransitive verb.

6. COMPOSITE : 8 :: PRIME : (*a.* 4, *b.* 6, ***c.* 7**, *d.* 9)

   (c) 8 is a composite number. 7 is a prime number. A composite number can be divided into two or more integers (whole numbers). A prime number is a number that is evenly divisible only by itself and 1.

7. FRESCO : PLASTER :: TAPESTRY : (*a.* stone, *b.* metal, ***c.* cloth**, *d.* wood)

   (c) A fresco is made of plaster. A tapestry is made of cloth.

8. VEGETARIAN : MEAT :: TEETOTALER : (*a.* fruit, ***b.* alcoholic beverages**, *c.* cooked food, *d.* tobacco)

   (b) A vegetarian will not eat meat. A teetotaler will not drink alcoholic beverages.

9. TRAFALGAR SQUARE : (***a.* London**, *b.* Florence, *c.* Moscow, *d.* Paris) :: TIMES SQUARE : NEW YORK

   (a) Trafalgar Square is in London. Times Square is in New York.

10. (*a.* appliance, *b.* food, ***c.* explosive**, *d.* automobile) : TNT :: COUNTRY : U.S.A.

    (c) TNT is an explosive. The United States is a country.

11. YELLOW : COWARDLY :: (*a.* blue, *b.* black, *c.* red, ***d.* green**) : INEXPERIENCED

    (d) A cowardly person is sometimes referred to as yellow. An inexperienced person is sometimes referred to as green. *The color blue stands for sadness. The color black stands for death. The color red stands for heat.*

12. 2 : QUART :: (*a.* 1, *b.* 4, ***c.* 8**, *d.* 16) : GALLON

    (c) There are 2 pints in a quart, and 8 pints in a gallon.

13. RED FLAG : REVOLUTION :: WHITE FLAG : (*a.* victory, ***b.* surrender**, *c.* established order, *d.* purity)

    (b) A red flag is often used to signify revolution, while a white flag is often used to signify surrender.

14. ZEBRA : STRIPES :: LEOPARD : (**a. spots**, b. stripes, c. diagonals, d. zigzags)

   (a) A zebra has stripes; a leopard spots.

15. (a. tyrant, b. wealthy merchant, c. explorer, **d. pirate**) : BUCCANEER :: SETTLER : PIONEER

   (d) A buccaneer is a pirate; a pioneer is a settler.

16. CENTIGRADE : 100 :: FAHRENHEIT : (a. 0, b. 32, c. 100, **d. 212**)

   (d) One hundred degrees centigrade (the boiling point of water) is equal to 212 degrees Fahrenheit. *Zero degree centigrade (the freezing point of water) is equal to 32 degrees Fahrenheit.*

17. (a. 1, b. 5, c. 20, **d. 25**) : SILVER :: 50 : GOLD

   (d) A 25th anniversary is often referred to as a silver anniversary, while a 50th anniversary is gold. *The 1st anniversary is often referred to as a paper anniversary; the 5th anniversary as a wood anniversary, and the 20th anniversary as a china anniversary.*

18. BEEF : STEER :: MUTTON : (a. ox, **b. sheep**, c. deer, d. goat)

   (b) Beef comes from a steer; mutton comes from a sheep.

19. ATOM : (**a. molecule**, b. electron, c. nucleus, d. gamma ray) :: TREE : FOREST

   (a) Atoms combine to form a molecule; trees combine to form a forest.

20. IGNORANCE : (a. intelligence, **b. knowledge**, c. foresight, d. attention) :: STUPIDITY : INTELLIGENCE

   (b) Ignorance is the absence of knowledge. Stupidity is the absence of intelligence.

21. NONAGENARIAN : 90 :: OCTOGENARIAN : (a. 60, b. 70, **c. 80**, d. 100)

   (c) A nonagenarian has lived to the age of 90; an octogenarian has lived to the age of 80. *Somebody who has lived to the age of 70 is a septuagenarian.*

22. LISBON : (a. Spain, **b. Portugal**, c. Hungary, d. Denmark) :: THE HAGUE : NETHERLANDS

   (b) Lisbon is the capital of Portugal; The Hague is the capital of the Netherlands. *Madrid is the capital of Spain; Budapest is the capital of Hungary; Copenhagen is the capital of Denmark.*

23. WAMPUM : (a. Dutchman, b. Portuguese, c. Pakistani, **d. American Indian**) :: DOUBLOON : SPANIARD

   (d) Wampum was used as a coin by certain American Indian tribes; the doubloon was formerly a Spanish coin.

24. GREEK ALPHABET : GREEK :: LATIN ALPHABET : (a. Russian, b. Cyrillic, c. Sanskrit, **d. English**)

   (d) The Greek language uses the Greek alphabet. The English language uses the Latin alphabet.

25. (a. 90, **b. 180**, c. 270, d. 360) : TRIANGLE :: 360 : SQUARE

   (b) A triangle has 180 degrees; a square has 360 degrees.

26. COLUMBIA : (a. South America, b. North America, **c. U.S.A.**, d. Brazil) :: BRITANNIA : BRITAIN

   (c) Columbia is a poetic name for the United States (from Columbus); Britannia is a poetic name for Britain.

27. FINALE : MUSICAL COMPOSITION :: (a. check, **b. checkmate**, c. rook, d. jeopardy) : CHESS

   (b) A finale ends a musical composition. Checkmate ends a game of chess.

28. YAHWEH : JUDAISM :: ALLAH : (**a. Islam**, b. Judaism, c. Taoism, d. Confucianism)

   (a) The concept of Yahweh in Judaism is analogous to the concept of Allah in Islam.

29. (**a. nominative**, *b.* dative, *c.* accusative, *d.* ablative) : OBJECTIVE :: SHE : HIM

    (a) The word she is in the nominative case; the word him is in the objective case.

30. RECTANGLE : OCTAGON :: (**a. triangle**, *b.* square, *c.* pentagon, *d.* rhombus) : HEXAGON

    (a) An octagon has twice as many sides as a rectangle; a hexagon has twice as many sides as a triangle.

31. (*a.* prize, *b.* damn, *c.* reflect, ***d.* complete**) : PRAISE :: COMPLEMENT : COMPLIMENT

    (d) A complement completes something; a compliment praises something.

32. SUB : BUS :: TAR : (*a.* car, *b.* road, *c.* vehicle, ***d.* rat**)

    (d) Bus is sub spelled backwards; rat is tar spelled backwards.

33. MANDATORY : (*a.* laudatory, *b.* damning, ***c.* optional**, *d.* compulsory) :: DEFINITE : UNCERTAIN

    (c) Mandatory and optional are antonyms; definite and uncertain are antonyms.

34. ONE : LAND :: TWO : (*a.* air, ***b.* sea**, *c.* ground, *d.* island)

    (b) Paul Revere was to be informed of the means by which British troops were coming through a system of shining lanterns. One lantern meant the British were coming by land; two meant they were coming by sea.

35. (*a.* eat, ***b.* drink**, *c.* sever, *d.* mend) : CHALICE :: DIG : SHOVEL

    (b) One uses a chalice to drink from and a shovel to dig with.

36. CONSONANT : (*a.* syncopated, *b.* rhythmic, *c.* euphemistic, ***d.* euphonious**) :: DISSONANT : DISCORDANT

    (d) Consonant sounds are euphonious; dissonant sounds are discordant. *Euphonious* means "pleasing to the ear." *Discordant* means "not harmonious, displeasing." Syncopated *means that a usually weak beat is stressed.* Rhythmic *means that something occurs with regularity.* Euphemistic *means that something is softened in expression.*

37. (***a.* Montague**, *b.* Scali, *c.* Dunlop, *d.* Mineo) : ROMEO :: CAPULET : JULIET

    (a) In Shakespeare's play, Montague is the surname of Romeo, Capulet the surname of Juliet.

38. EMANCIPATE : (*a.* emaciate, *b.* free, ***c.* enslave**, *d.* deliver) :: EMPTY : FULL

    (c) Emancipate and enslave are antonyms, as are empty and full.

39. PALMISTRY : PALM :: PHRENOLOGY : (*a.* handwriting, *b.* EEG, *c.* eyes, ***d.* skull**)

    (d) Palmistry makes use of the palm in telling about a person; phrenology makes use of the skull.

40. (*a.* Columbia Gem, ***b.* Union Jack**, *c.* Royal Ensign, *d.* Fleur-de-Lis) : GREAT BRITAIN :: STARS AND STRIPES : U.S.A.

    (b) The Union Jack is the flag of Great Britain; the Stars and Stripes is the flag of the United States. *The fleur-de-lis is associated with the Spanish monarchy and the Grand Duchy of Luxembourg. "Columbia, Gem of the Ocean" is a song.*

41. COMMON LOG : 10 :: NATURAL LOG : (*a.* π, ***b.* e**, *c.* i, *d.* 1)

    (b) Common logs are to base 10. Natural logs are to base *e*.

42. MAE WEST : LIFE JACKET :: MICKEY FINN : (*a.* blackjack, *b.* Molotov cocktail, ***c.* drugged liquor**, *d.* time bomb)

    (c) A Mae West is a type of life jacket. A Mickey Finn is a form of drugged liquor. *Blackjack is a popular Casino game, and a Molotov cocktail is a name for a variety of incendiary weapons.*

43. EARTH : AIR :: (*a.* bile, *b.* carbon, *c.* phlogiston, ***d.* fire**) : WATER

(d) Earth, air, fire, and water were once believed to be the four basic elements from which every other substance is composed.

44. CAMUS : STRANGER :: (*a.* Sartre, ***b.* Camus**, *c.* Mauriac, *d.* Ionesco) : PLAGUE

(b) Camus is the author of both *The Stranger* and *The Plague*. *Sartre wrote* No Exit *and* The Flies, *among other plays. Mauriac wrote* Le Desert de l'Amour. *Ionesco wrote the play* Rhinoceros.

45. DOG : PIE :: HOT : (*a.* cold, *b.* cat, ***c.* pizza**, *d.* cake)

(c) A hotdog and a pizza pie are both forms of food.

46. PIETÀ : MICHELANGELO :: THE KISS : (***a.* Rodin**, *b.* Pisano, *c.* Ghiberti, *d.* da Vinci)

(a) *The Pietà* is a sculpture by Michelangelo. *The Kiss* is a sculpture by Rodin. *Pisano was an Italian artist who was wrongly credited for the creation of the* Leaning Tower of Pisa. *Ghiberti is known for a set of metal panels called* Gates of Paradise. *Da Vinci painted the* Mona Lisa *and* The Last Supper, *among others.*

47. (*a.* Congress of Vienna, ***b.* League of Nations**, *c.* Warsaw Pact, *d.* NATO) : UNITED NATIONS :: GASLIGHT : ELECTRIC LIGHT

(b) The United Nations replaced the League of Nations. The electric light replaced the gaslight. The League of Nations was a supranational organization that was created in the aftermath of World War I; its goals were the prevention of war, settlement of disputes, etc. *The Congress of Vienna was a conference to reorganize Europe after the downfall of Napoleon I (1814–1815). The Warsaw Pact (1955) was an organization of Eastern European Communist states that was created in response to the creation of NATO.*

48. CARAT : (*a.* size, ***b.* weight**, *c.* brilliance, *d.* value) :: ACRE : AREA

(b) A carat is a measure of weight. An acre is a measure of area.

49. $a + b : b + a :: a(b + a)b : ($*a.* $2a^2b^2$, *b.* $(a + b)^2$, ***c.* $a^2b + ab^2$**, *d.* $a^2b^2 + ab)$

(c) $a + b$ is equal to $b + a$. $a(b + a)b$ is equal to $a^2b + ab^2$.

50. FRANCIS CRICK : STRUCTURE OF DNA MOLECULE :: MARIE CURIE : (*a.* nobelium, *b.* uranium, ***c.* radium**, *d.* plutonium)

(c) Francis Crick was a codiscoverer of the structure of the DNA molecule. Marie Curie was a codiscoverer of the element radium.

51. ANALOG : SLIDE RULE :: DIGITAL : (***a.* odometer**, *b.* ruler, *c.* compass, *d.* protractor)

(a) A slide rule is an analog device. An odometer is a digital device.

52. CHARLOTTE'S : PILGRIM'S :: WEB : (*a.* Follies, ***b.* Progress**, *c.* Pretense, *d.* Journey)

(b) *Charlotte's Web* (by E. B. White) and *Pilgrim's Progress* (by John Bunyan) are both titles of books.

53. VOID : VACUUM :: FULL : (***a.* replete**, *b.* deplete, *c.* compact, *d.* empty)

(a) Void and vacuum are synonyms, as are full and replete.

54. HIGH : DIE :: (*a.* gregarious, *b.* reticent, *c.* low, ***d.* buy**) : SHY

(d) High, die, buy, and shy all rhyme.

55. (*a.* retina, *b.* iris, *c.* lens, ***d.* cone**) : ROD :: CHROMATIC : ACHROMATIC

(d) In the visual system, the cones are responsible for chromatic vision, and the rods for achromatic vision.

56. BOVINE : (*a.* jackal, *b.* monkey, ***c.* ox**, *d.* rabbit) :: URSINE : BEAR

   (c) A bovine creature is oxlike. An ursine creature is bearlike.

57. (***a.* Plato**, *b.* Aristotle, *c.* Leibniz, *d.* Locke) : REPUBLIC :: DESCARTES : MEDITATIONS

   (a) Plato is the author of the *Republic*. Descartes is the author of *Meditations*. *Aristotle's works are collected in the* Corpus Aristotelicum. *Leibniz wrote the* Theodicee. *Locke is the author of* An Essay Concerning Human Understanding *and* Some Thoughts Concerning Education, *among others.*

58. DEER : DEER :: CORPUS : (*a.* corpi, *b.* corpuses, ***c.* corpora**, *d.* corpes)

   (c) Deer is the plural form of deer. Corpora is the plural form of corpus.

59. BUDAPEST : HANOI :: HUNGARY : (*a.* Cambodia, *b.* Laos, *c.* Thailand, ***d.* Vietnam**)

   (d) Budapest is the capital of Hungary. Hanoi is the capital of Vietnam. *The capital of Thailand is Bangkok. The capital of Cambodia is Phnom Penh. The capital of Laos is Vientiane.*

60. PROMISED LAND : CANAAN :: LAND OF NOD : (*a.* wakefulness, *b.* hell, ***c.* sleep**, *d.* heaven)

   (c) Canaan was the Promised Land for the Israelites. The Land of Nod is sleep. The Land of Nod has been mentioned in the Bible but has more recently been associated with sleep, as in Stevenson's poem "The Land of Nod."

61. MISOGYNIST : WOMEN :: MISOGAMIST : (*a.* men, *b.* people, ***c.* marriage**, *d.* religion)

   (c) A misogynist detests women. A misogamist detests marriage.

62. (*a.* Achilles, *b.* Hector, ***c.* Paris**, *d.* Troilus) : HELEN :: PLUTO : PROSERPINA

   (c) Paris abducted Helen. Pluto abducted Proserpina. *Achilles was the greatest warrior of the Greeks in the Trojan War. Hector was a Trojan prince and warrior in the Trojan War. Troilus was a Trojan prince murdered by Achilles.*

63. BENIGN : BENEVOLENT :: (*a.* beneficent, ***b.* nefarious**, *c.* tortuous, *d.* voracious) : MALEVOLENT

   (b) Benign and benevolent are synonyms, as are nefarious and malevolent.

64. BLOCKHEAD : LUNKHEAD :: MUTTONHEAD : (***a.* fathead**, *b.* sleepyhead, *c.* bighead, *d.* egghead)

   (a) A blockhead is a lunkhead is a muttonhead is a fathead.

65. UNCLE TOM : SERVILE :: DUTCH UNCLE : (*a.* hoary, *b.* kind, ***c.* stern**, *d.* stingy)

   (c) An Uncle Tom is servile. A Dutch uncle is stern.

66. ALPHA : (*a.* gamma, *b.* zed, *c.* epsilon, ***d.* omega**) :: A : Z

   (d) Alpha is the first letter of the Greek alphabet, and omega is the last. *A* is the first letter of the English alphabet, and *Z* is the last.

67. THIAMINE : ASCORBIC ACID :: B_1 : (*a.* B_6, *b.* B_{12}, ***c.* C**, *d.* E)

   (c) Thiamine is vitamin B_1. Ascorbic acid is vitamin C. *Vitamin B_6 can consist of different compounds: pyridoxine, pyridoxal, and pyridoxamine. B_{12} can be commonly found as cyanocobalamin. E refers to a group of tocopherols and tocotrienols.*

68. BRAZIL : (***a.* Portuguese**, *b.* Spanish, *c.* French, *d.* Brazilian) :: AUSTRIA : GERMAN

   (a) Portuguese is the principal language spoken in Brazil. German is the principal language spoken in Austria.

69. CENTURY : EON :: DOZEN : (*a.* one hundred, *b.* gross, *c.* zero, ***d.* myriad**)

   (d) A century is a specified period of time, and an eon is a long, unspecified period of time. A dozen is a specified amount, and a myriad is a large, unspecified amount.

70. SITTING BULL : SIOUX :: GERONIMO : (*a.* **Apache**, *b.* Pueblo, *c.* Mohawk, *d.* Seminole)

   (a) Sitting Bull was a Sioux Indian chief; Geronimo was an Apache Indian chief.

71. AUTOCRACY : AUTARCHY :: MONARCHY : (*a.* democracy, *b.* anarchy, *c.* oligarchy, *d.* **kingdom**)

   (d) An autocracy is an autarchy. A monarchy is a kingdom. *Anarchy is the absence of government. Oligarchy is a form of government where power is placed in the hands of a small group of people.*

72. GOGGLE-EYED : BULGING :: HOOK-NOSED : (*a.* opercular, *b.* oviparous, *c.* ovine, *d.* **aquiline**)

   (d) Someone who is goggle-eyed has bulging eyes. Someone who is hook-nosed has an aquiline nose.

73. NEPTUNE : DIANA :: SEA : (*a.* hearth, *b.* sun, *c.* **moon**, *d.* home)

   (c) In Roman mythology, Neptune was the god of the sea and Diana the goddess of the moon.

74. EXPEL : DRIVE AWAY :: EXPIATE : (*a.* **atone for**, *b.* talk at length, *c.* forgive, *d.* speak briefly)

   (a) To expel is to drive away. To expiate is to atone for.

75. LARGO : SLOW :: (*a.* moderato, *b.* **allegro**, *c.* piano, *d.* fortissimo) : FAST

   (b) In music, largo signifies a slow tempo; allegro, a fast tempo. *Moderato means "moderately fast." Piano means "soft." Fortissimo means "very loud."*

76. (*a.* with faith, *b.* with truth, *c.* with passion, *d.* **with authority**) : EX CATHEDRA :: ON THE FACE : EX FACIE

   (d) *Ex cathedra* means with authority. *Ex facie* means on the face.

77. FIFE : CLARINET :: TROMBONE : (*a.* lute, *b.* **bagpipe**, *c.* piano, *d.* violin)

   (b) A fife, a clarinet, a trombone, and a bagpipe are all wind instruments.

78. PARASITE : LIVING :: (*a.* **saprophyte**, *b.* neophyte, *c.* pteridophyte, *d.* bryophyte) : DEAD

   (a) A parasite lives off a living organism. A saprophyte lives off a dead organism.

79. PRINCE : MACHIAVELLI :: PETIT PRINCE : (*a.* **Saint-Exupéry**, *b.* Mauriac, *c.* Camus, *d.* Lescaut)

   (a) *The Prince* was written by Machiavelli. *Le Petit Prince* was written by Saint-Exupéry. *François Mauriac wrote* Le Desert de l'Amour, *for example. Albert Camus was a French writer who wrote* The Plague. Manon Lescaut *is an opera by Puccini.*

80. INDIA : RUPEE :: (*a.* Mexico, *b.* **Switzerland**, *c.* Great Britain, *d.* Sweden) : FRANC

   (b) The rupee is the currency of India. *The currency of Switzerland is the franc. The currency of Mexico is the peso. The currency of Great Britain is the pound and the currency of Sweden is the crown.*

81. DEMOSTHENES : (*a.* **Cicero**, *b.* Socrates, *c.* Pericles, *d.* Ovid) :: HOMER : VIRGIL

   (a) Demosthenes was a Greek orator, and Cicero a Roman orator. Homer was a Greek poet, and Virgil a Roman poet. *Socrates was a Greek philosopher. Ovid was a Roman poet. Pericles was a Greek statesman and orator.*

82. (*a.* mg, *b.* gg, *c.* **kg**, *d.* cg) : g :: m : mm

   (c) There are 1,000 grams (g) in a kilogram (kg). There are 1,000 millimeters (mm) in a meter (m). There are 1,000 milligrams (mg) in a gram (g).

83. CIPANGO : JAPAN :: CATHAY : (*a.* **China**, *b.* Tibet, *c.* Polynesia, *d.* Mongolia)

   (a) Cipango is a poetic name for Japan. Cathay is a poetic name for China.

84. IMPROMPTU : EXTEMPORE :: PROBITY : (*a.* open-mindedness, *b.* dishonesty, *c.* narrow-mindedness, ***d.* honesty**)

(d) Impromptu and extempore are synonyms, as are *probity* and *honesty.*

85. FERMI : NUCLEAR PHYSICS :: JANE ADDAMS : (*a.* nursing, *b.* physics, ***c.* social work**, *d.* drama)

(c) Fermi is famous for his work in nuclear physics. Jane Addams is famous for her social work.

86. (*a.* Inferno, ***b.* Decameron**, *c.* The Wasteland, *d.* No Exit) : CANTERBURY TALES :: ANTHOLOGY : COLLECTION

(b) *The Decameron* (by Giovanni Boccacio) and *The Canterbury Tales* (by Geoffrey Chaucer) are both anthologies (collections) of stories. Inferno *is the first canticle of Dante's* Divine Comedy. The Wasteland *is a poem by Eliot.* No Exit *is a play by Sartre.*

87. RICHELIEU : (*a.* Cushing, ***b.* Mazarin**, *c.* Metternich, *d.* Marat) :: KENNEDY : JOHNSON

(b) Cardinal Mazarin succeeded Cardinal Richelieu in his French diplomatic role. Johnson succeeded Kennedy as president of the United States.

88. (*a.* uncertainty, *b.* luck, ***c.* sample**, *d.* variance) : POPULATION :: STATISTIC : PARAMETER

(c) A statistic is a sample value, while a parameter is a population value.

89. REGAN : GONERIL :: LEAH : (*a.* Jacob, *b.* Rebecca, *c.* Isaac, ***d.* Rachel**)

(d) Regan and Goneril were sisters (in *King Lear*), as were Leah and Rachel (in the Bible). *Rebecca was the wife of Isaac. Jacob was their son.*

90. TEMPUS : CARPE :: FUGIT : (*a.* cibus, *b.* mater, ***c.* diem**, *d.* tempum)

(c) *Tempus fugit* and *carpe diem* are both Latinisms used in English. *Tempus fugit* means "time flies," while *carpe diem* means "seize the opportunity"—literally, the day.

91. ERSATZ : (***a.* genuine**, *b.* superior, *c.* inferior, *d.* fake) :: FRESH : RANCID

(a) Ersatz and genuine are antonyms, as are fresh and rancid.

92. EVE : DEED :: MADAM : (*a.* cuckoo, *b.* swoon, ***c.* noon**, *d.* pool)

(c) Eve, deed, madam, and noon are all palindromes—they read the same whether spelled forward or backward.

93. SLEEPY : SOMNOLENT :: GROGGY : (*a.* asleep, ***b.* unsteady**, *c.* awake, *d.* dead)

(b) A sleepy person is somnolent; a groggy person is unsteady.

94. AXON : DEPART :: (*a.* neuron, *b.* ganglion, ***c.* dendrites**, *d.* plasma) : APPROACH

(c) Nerve impulses depart from a cell body via the axon; they approach the cell body via the dendrites.

95. BUDGE : TENNIS :: LOUIS : (*a.* hockey, *b.* football, *c.* baseball, ***d.* boxing**)

(d) Joe Louis was a famous boxer. Don Budge was a famous tennis player.

96. BLOOD : MELANCHOLY :: CHOLER : (*a.* plasma, *b.* lymph, ***c.* phlegm**, *d.* saliva)

(c) Blood, phlegm, choler, and melancholy were once believed to be the four body humors (fluids). The idea of body humors is an old one dating back to ancient Egypt, but Hippocrates was the one who applied the concept to medicine.

97. MEXICO : YORK :: CAROLINA : (*a.* Virginia, *b.* Oregon, *c.* Washington, ***d.* Dakota**)

(d) Both (New) Mexico and (New) York are states. Both (North or South) Carolina and (North or South) Dakota are states.

98. ARGON : NEON :: XENON : (***a*. helium**, *b*. oxygen, *c*. mercury, *d*. carbon)

(a) Argon, neon, xenon, and helium are all inert (noble) gases. The six noble gases are helium, neon, argon, xenon, krypton, and radon.

99. HORN : ROLAND :: HARP : (*a*. Gideon, ***b*. David**, *c*. Moses, *d*. Samuel)

(b) Roland was famous for his horn; David, for his harp.

100. GLUTTON : FOOD :: SATYR : (*a*. punishment, *b*. glory, *c*. alcoholic beverages, ***d*. sex**)

(d) A glutton overindulges in food; a satyr, in sex.

101. ACUTE : (*a*. small, ***b*. obtuse**, *c*. intense, *d*. right) :: APOGEE : PERIGEE

(b) When speaking either of angles or the ability to comprehend something, acute means the opposite of obtuse, just as the apogee is the opposite of the perigee.

102. (*a*. berate, *b*. refine, *c*. attenuate, ***d*. foreshadow**) : ADUMBRATE :: INTIMATE : HINT

(d) To adumbrate is to foreshadow just as to intimate is to hint.

103. PNEUMONECTOMY : LUNG :: (*a*. tonsillectomy, *b*. meningectomy, ***c*. lobotomy**, *d*. encephalotomy) : BRAIN

(c) Pneumonectomy is the removal of part of the lung and lobotomy is the removal of part of the brain.

104. EMPATHY : (*a*. lungs, *b*. soul, *c*. pancreas, ***d*. heart**) :: BRAVERY : LIVER

(d) Tradition ascribes empathy and bravery to be seated in the organs of the heart and liver, respectively.

105. CIRCUMSPECT : CIRCUMSCRIBE :: (***a*. prudent**, *b*. navigate, *c*. rounded, *d*. investigate) : ENCIRCLE

(a) To be circumspect is to be prudent, and to circumscribe is to encircle.

106. DEARTH : (*a*. poverty, ***b*. abundance**, *c*. warmth, *d*. nothing) :: PAUCITY : PLENTY

(b) Dearth and paucity both describe an insufficiency, whereas abundance and plenty describe something bountiful.

107. CAP : LID :: KNEE : (*a*. leg, *b*. patella, *c*. heel, ***d*. eye**)

(d) The kneecap and eyelid are both parts of the body.

108. (***a*. bitterness**, *b*. wittiness, *c*. frivolity, *d*. accusation) : ACRIMONIOUS :: FRUGALITY : PARSIMONIOUS

(a) Acrimonious describes someone who acts with bitterness just as parsimonious describes someone who acts with frugality.

109. CAESAR : DELIVERY :: ACHILLES : (*a*. surgery, *b*. ligament, ***c*. tendon**, *d*. bone)

(c) The cesarean section, the name of a delivery, is named for Caesar. The Achilles tendon, the name of a tendon, is named for Achilles.

110. PROMETHEUS : BOUND :: ATLAS : (*a*. carried, *b*. tied, ***c*. shrugged**, *d*. grew)

(c) *Prometheus Bound* (by Aeschylus) and *Atlas Shrugged* (by Ayn Rand) are both prominent works of literature.

111. GENGHIS KHAN : (*a*. China, ***b*. Mongolia**, *c*. Persia, *d*. Prussia) :: SHAKA : SOUTH AFRICA

(b) Genghis Khan was a great conqueror born in present-day Mongolia. Shaka was a great conqueror born in present-day South Africa.

112. (*a.* right to bear arms, ***b.* prohibition of alcohol**, *c.* right to remain silent, *d.* freedom of religion) : 18th AMENDMENT :: WOMEN'S SUFFRAGE : 19th AMENDMENT

(b) The 18th Amendment prohibited the consumption of alcohol. The 19th Amendment granted women's suffrage.

113. KID : (*a.* wolf, ***b.* goat**, *c.* moose, *d.* kangaroo) :: CALF : WHALE

(b) A young goat is called a kid just as a young whale is called a calf.

114. HOPI : (***a.* Southwest**, *b.* Southeast, *c.* Northwest, *d.* Great Plains) :: TLINGIT : NORTHWEST

(a) The Hopi tribe is native to the Southwest of what is now the United States. The Tlingit tribe is native to the Northwest of what is now the United States.

115. PTOLEMY : EARTH :: COPERNICUS : (*a.* Mars, *b.* Venus, *c.* Moon, ***d.* Sun**)

(d) Ptolemy proposed a geocentric system in which the Earth was the center of the solar system. Copernicus proposed a heliocentric system, in which the sun was the center.

116. ADAM SMITH : 18th CENTURY :: JOHN MAYNARD KEYNES : (***a.* 20th century**, *b.* 19th century, *c.* 17th century, *d.* 16th century)

(a) Smith and Keynes were famous economists of the 18th and 20th centuries, respectively. Smith is well-known as the author of *The Wealth of Nations*. Keynes is the founder of Keynesian economics, which deals with total spending in the economy and its effects on output and inflation.

117. (*a.* Laos, ***b.* Japan**, *c.* Taiwan, *d.* China) : JUDO :: KOREA : TAE KWON DO

(b) The martial art of Judo originated in Japan just as the martial art Tae Kwon Do originated in Korea.

118. KHMER ROUGE : POL POT :: COMMUNIST PARTY OF CHINA : (*a.* Kuomintang, *b.* Confucius ***c.* Mao Zedong**, *d.* Chiang Kai-shek)

(c) Pol Pot was a leader of the Cambodian Communist Party, commonly known as the Khmer Rouge. Mao Zedong was a leader of the Communist Party of China. *Kuomintang is the founding party of Taiwan. Confucius was a Chinese thinker and philosopher in the 5th century B.C. Chiang Kai-shek was a Chinese political leader who served as head of state of the National Government of the Republic of China from 1928 to 1949.*

119. SUEZ CANAL : (*a.* Turkey, *b.* Morocco, ***c.* Egypt**, *d.* Israel) :: PANAMA CANAL : PANAMA

(c) The Suez Canal cuts through Egypt just as the Panama Canal cuts through Panama.

120. SOVIET UNION : (*a.* Portugal, *b.* Brazil, *c.* Cuba, ***d.* Spain**) :: CHAGALL : DALI

(d) Chagall and Dali were artists known for their surrealistic paintings; they were from the Soviet Union and Spain, respectively.

ANSWER SHEET
Practice Test 9

1. Ⓐ Ⓑ Ⓒ Ⓓ	31. Ⓐ Ⓑ Ⓒ Ⓓ	61. Ⓐ Ⓑ Ⓒ Ⓓ	91. Ⓐ Ⓑ Ⓒ Ⓓ
2. Ⓐ Ⓑ Ⓒ Ⓓ	32. Ⓐ Ⓑ Ⓒ Ⓓ	62. Ⓐ Ⓑ Ⓒ Ⓓ	92. Ⓐ Ⓑ Ⓒ Ⓓ
3. Ⓐ Ⓑ Ⓒ Ⓓ	33. Ⓐ Ⓑ Ⓒ Ⓓ	63. Ⓐ Ⓑ Ⓒ Ⓓ	93. Ⓐ Ⓑ Ⓒ Ⓓ
4. Ⓐ Ⓑ Ⓒ Ⓓ	34. Ⓐ Ⓑ Ⓒ Ⓓ	64. Ⓐ Ⓑ Ⓒ Ⓓ	94. Ⓐ Ⓑ Ⓒ Ⓓ
5. Ⓐ Ⓑ Ⓒ Ⓓ	35. Ⓐ Ⓑ Ⓒ Ⓓ	65. Ⓐ Ⓑ Ⓒ Ⓓ	95. Ⓐ Ⓑ Ⓒ Ⓓ
6. Ⓐ Ⓑ Ⓒ Ⓓ	36. Ⓐ Ⓑ Ⓒ Ⓓ	66. Ⓐ Ⓑ Ⓒ Ⓓ	96. Ⓐ Ⓑ Ⓒ Ⓓ
7. Ⓐ Ⓑ Ⓒ Ⓓ	37. Ⓐ Ⓑ Ⓒ Ⓓ	67. Ⓐ Ⓑ Ⓒ Ⓓ	97. Ⓐ Ⓑ Ⓒ Ⓓ
8. Ⓐ Ⓑ Ⓒ Ⓓ	38. Ⓐ Ⓑ Ⓒ Ⓓ	68. Ⓐ Ⓑ Ⓒ Ⓓ	98. Ⓐ Ⓑ Ⓒ Ⓓ
9. Ⓐ Ⓑ Ⓒ Ⓓ	39. Ⓐ Ⓑ Ⓒ Ⓓ	69. Ⓐ Ⓑ Ⓒ Ⓓ	99. Ⓐ Ⓑ Ⓒ Ⓓ
10. Ⓐ Ⓑ Ⓒ Ⓓ	40. Ⓐ Ⓑ Ⓒ Ⓓ	70. Ⓐ Ⓑ Ⓒ Ⓓ	100. Ⓐ Ⓑ Ⓒ Ⓓ
11. Ⓐ Ⓑ Ⓒ Ⓓ	41. Ⓐ Ⓑ Ⓒ Ⓓ	71. Ⓐ Ⓑ Ⓒ Ⓓ	101. Ⓐ Ⓑ Ⓒ Ⓓ
12. Ⓐ Ⓑ Ⓒ Ⓓ	42. Ⓐ Ⓑ Ⓒ Ⓓ	72. Ⓐ Ⓑ Ⓒ Ⓓ	102. Ⓐ Ⓑ Ⓒ Ⓓ
13. Ⓐ Ⓑ Ⓒ Ⓓ	43. Ⓐ Ⓑ Ⓒ Ⓓ	73. Ⓐ Ⓑ Ⓒ Ⓓ	103. Ⓐ Ⓑ Ⓒ Ⓓ
14. Ⓐ Ⓑ Ⓒ Ⓓ	44. Ⓐ Ⓑ Ⓒ Ⓓ	74. Ⓐ Ⓑ Ⓒ Ⓓ	104. Ⓐ Ⓑ Ⓒ Ⓓ
15. Ⓐ Ⓑ Ⓒ Ⓓ	45. Ⓐ Ⓑ Ⓒ Ⓓ	75. Ⓐ Ⓑ Ⓒ Ⓓ	105. Ⓐ Ⓑ Ⓒ Ⓓ
16. Ⓐ Ⓑ Ⓒ Ⓓ	46. Ⓐ Ⓑ Ⓒ Ⓓ	76. Ⓐ Ⓑ Ⓒ Ⓓ	106. Ⓐ Ⓑ Ⓒ Ⓓ
17. Ⓐ Ⓑ Ⓒ Ⓓ	47. Ⓐ Ⓑ Ⓒ Ⓓ	77. Ⓐ Ⓑ Ⓒ Ⓓ	107. Ⓐ Ⓑ Ⓒ Ⓓ
18. Ⓐ Ⓑ Ⓒ Ⓓ	48. Ⓐ Ⓑ Ⓒ Ⓓ	78. Ⓐ Ⓑ Ⓒ Ⓓ	108. Ⓐ Ⓑ Ⓒ Ⓓ
19. Ⓐ Ⓑ Ⓒ Ⓓ	49. Ⓐ Ⓑ Ⓒ Ⓓ	79. Ⓐ Ⓑ Ⓒ Ⓓ	109. Ⓐ Ⓑ Ⓒ Ⓓ
20. Ⓐ Ⓑ Ⓒ Ⓓ	50. Ⓐ Ⓑ Ⓒ Ⓓ	80. Ⓐ Ⓑ Ⓒ Ⓓ	110. Ⓐ Ⓑ Ⓒ Ⓓ
21. Ⓐ Ⓑ Ⓒ Ⓓ	51. Ⓐ Ⓑ Ⓒ Ⓓ	81. Ⓐ Ⓑ Ⓒ Ⓓ	111. Ⓐ Ⓑ Ⓒ Ⓓ
22. Ⓐ Ⓑ Ⓒ Ⓓ	52. Ⓐ Ⓑ Ⓒ Ⓓ	82. Ⓐ Ⓑ Ⓒ Ⓓ	112. Ⓐ Ⓑ Ⓒ Ⓓ
23. Ⓐ Ⓑ Ⓒ Ⓓ	53. Ⓐ Ⓑ Ⓒ Ⓓ	83. Ⓐ Ⓑ Ⓒ Ⓓ	113. Ⓐ Ⓑ Ⓒ Ⓓ
24. Ⓐ Ⓑ Ⓒ Ⓓ	54. Ⓐ Ⓑ Ⓒ Ⓓ	84. Ⓐ Ⓑ Ⓒ Ⓓ	114. Ⓐ Ⓑ Ⓒ Ⓓ
25. Ⓐ Ⓑ Ⓒ Ⓓ	55. Ⓐ Ⓑ Ⓒ Ⓓ	85. Ⓐ Ⓑ Ⓒ Ⓓ	115. Ⓐ Ⓑ Ⓒ Ⓓ
26. Ⓐ Ⓑ Ⓒ Ⓓ	56. Ⓐ Ⓑ Ⓒ Ⓓ	86. Ⓐ Ⓑ Ⓒ Ⓓ	116. Ⓐ Ⓑ Ⓒ Ⓓ
27. Ⓐ Ⓑ Ⓒ Ⓓ	57. Ⓐ Ⓑ Ⓒ Ⓓ	87. Ⓐ Ⓑ Ⓒ Ⓓ	117. Ⓐ Ⓑ Ⓒ Ⓓ
28. Ⓐ Ⓑ Ⓒ Ⓓ	58. Ⓐ Ⓑ Ⓒ Ⓓ	88. Ⓐ Ⓑ Ⓒ Ⓓ	118. Ⓐ Ⓑ Ⓒ Ⓓ
29. Ⓐ Ⓑ Ⓒ Ⓓ	59. Ⓐ Ⓑ Ⓒ Ⓓ	89. Ⓐ Ⓑ Ⓒ Ⓓ	119. Ⓐ Ⓑ Ⓒ Ⓓ
30. Ⓐ Ⓑ Ⓒ Ⓓ	60. Ⓐ Ⓑ Ⓒ Ⓓ	90. Ⓐ Ⓑ Ⓒ Ⓓ	120. Ⓐ Ⓑ Ⓒ Ⓓ

Time: 60 MINUTES

> **Directions:** In each of the following questions, you will find three initial terms and, in parentheses, four answer options designated *a*, *b*, *c*, and *d*. You are to select from the four answer options the one that *best* completes the analogy with the three initial terms. To record your answers, use the answer sheet provided.

1. POSTMAN : LETTER :: (*a.* surgeon, *b.* orthopedist, *c.* obstetrician, *d.* podiatrist) : BABY

2. CHLOROPHYLL : GREEN :: HEMOGLOBIN : (*a.* red, *b.* black, *c.* green, *d.* blue)

3. HAPPY : (*a.* sad, *b.* gay, *c.* indifferent, *d.* ecstatic) :: BRIGHT : BRILLIANT

4. PENCIL : PEN :: (*a.* wood, *b.* ballpoint, *c.* graphite, *d.* boron) : INK

5. ONE BIRD : HAND :: TWO BIRDS : (*a.* bush, *b.* foot, *c.* nest, *d.* head)

6. SILVER : TARNISH :: IRON : (*a.* oxidation, *b.* rust, *c.* magnet, *d.* tin)

7. BUTTERFLY : CATERPILLAR :: (*a.* amphibian, *b.* frog, *c.* salamander, *d.* larva) : TADPOLE

8. GREEN : (*a.* cowardice, *b.* viciousness, *c.* envy, *d.* delight) :: PURPLE : RAGE

9. JUDAS : JESUS :: (*a.* Augustus, *b.* Brutus, *c.* Lucius, *d.* Antony) : JULIUS CAESAR

10. JOLLY ROGER : (*a.* communists, *b.* fascists, *c.* pirates, *d.* anarchists) :: UNION JACK : UNITED KINGDOM

11. DIALECTIC : HEGEL :: DIALECTICAL MATERIALISM : (*a.* Marx, *b.* Fichte, *c.* Schelling, *d.* Kant)

12. (*a.* screen, *b.* camera, *c.* projector, *d.* frame) : MOVIE FILM :: LINK : CHAIN

13. PROLOGUE : (*a.* decalogue, *b.* epilogue, *c.* preface, *d.* forward) :: APPETIZER : DESSERT

14. HAMMERSTEIN : (*a.* Sondheim, *b.* Rodgers, *c.* Gilbert, *d.* Herman) :: LERNER : LOEWE

15. (*a.* dumb, *b.* stupid, *c.* loquacious, *d.* brilliant) : MUTE :: SMART : INTELLIGENT

16. ARCHIVES : (*a.* munitions, *b.* tombs, *c.* documents, *d.* animals) :: PANTRY : KITCHEN UTENSILS

17. DUNCAN : MACBETH :: MACBETH : (*a.* Lady Macbeth, *b.* Macduff, *c.* Polonius, *d.* Claudius)

18. V : X :: D : (*a.* I, *b.* M, *c.* D, *d.* C)

19. JACK SPRAT'S WIFE : LEAN :: VEGETARIAN : (*a.* meat, *b.* fat, *c.* vegetables, *d.* roots)

20. (*a.* politics, *b.* law, *c.* music, *d.* medicine) : HIPPOCRATES :: HISTORY : HERODOTUS

21. (*a.* Russia, *b.* China, *c.* Japan, *d.* Hungary) : BALALAIKA :: SCOTLAND : BAGPIPES

22. TAILPIPE : EXHAUST :: RADIUM : (*a.* beta rays, *b.* strontium, *c.* cosmic rays, *d.* lead)

23. ARGUS : 100 :: CYCLOPS : (*a.* 1000, *b.* 10, *c.* 5, *d.* 1)

24. CANNON : BIG BERTHA :: (*a.* battleship, *b.* bazooka, *c.* bell, *d.* church steeple) : BIG BEN

25. (*a.* pretty, *b.* pretentious, *c.* proud, *d.* portly) : PEACOCK :: SILLY : GOOSE

26. HYPOCRITICAL : INSINCERE :: HYPERCRITICAL : (*a.* overcritical, *b.* sincere, *c.* oversincere, *d.* critical)

27. (*a.* cross, *b.* aisle, *c.* refectory, *d.* nave) : TRANSEPT :: VERTICAL : HORIZONTAL

28. MNEMONIC : (*a.* nymph, *b.* elf, *c.* anger, *d.* knock) :: PNEUMATIC : GNOME

29. FAITH : JOB :: (*a.* wisdom, *b.* age, *c.* wickedness, *d.* courage) : METHUSELAH

30. MRS. GRUNDY : NARROW-MINDED :: POLLYANNA : (*a.* witty, *b.* dull, *c.* pessimistic, *d.* optimistic)

31. MIDNIGHT SUN : (*a.* Russia, *b.* Norway, *c.* China, *d.* South Pole) :: RISING SUN : JAPAN

32. RED-BLOODED : VIGOROUS :: BLUE-BLOODED : (*a.* cowardly, *b.* sickly, *c.* prudish, *d.* aristocratic)

33. (*a.* battle, *b.* artillery, *c.* ammunition, *d.* armory) : WEAPONS :: CLOSET : CLOTHING

34. CHARACTERISTIC : DEFINING :: USUALLY : (*a.* never, *b.* sometimes, *c.* rarely, *d.* always)

35. OBVIATE : (*a.* make unnecessary, *b.* make necessary, *c.* make obvious, *d.* make obscure) :: EXPUNGE : DELETE

36. BROBDINGNAGIAN : GIGANTIC :: (*a.* Lilliputian, *b.* Houyhnhnm, *c.* Vespasian, *d.* Yahoo) : TINY

37. RUSSIA : (*a.* tsar, *b.* king, *c.* emperor, *d.* autarch) :: FRANCE : KING

38. MINOTAUR : BULL :: CENTAUR : (*a.* cow, *b.* horse, *c.* pig, *d.* goat)

39. INTEGRAL : (*a.* acceleration, *b.* length, *c.* area, *d.* velocity) :: DERIVATIVE : SLOPE

40. GUSTATORY : (*a.* taste, *b.* touch, *c.* sight, *d.* smell) :: AUDITORY : HEARING

41. OCTOPI : OCTOPUSES :: (*a.* cannona, *b.* cannon, *c.* cannones, *d.* cannonade) : CANNONS

42. CRIME : WAR :: PUNISHMENT : (*a.* Destruction, *b.* Treaty, *c.* Peace, *d.* Retribution)

43. SUPPLY : DEMAND :: RATE : (*a.* distance, *b.* time, *c.* velocity, *d.* price)

44. ICONOCLAST : (*a.* religious images, *b.* autocracy, *c.* democratic ideals,
    d. anarchy) :: NIHILIST : SOCIAL ORDER

45. QUIXOTIC : CERVANTES :: FAUSTIAN : (*a.* Hegel, *b.* Faust, *c.* Schiller, *d.* Goethe)

46. EXPEL : STUDENT :: (*a.* expire, *b.* expunge, *c.* expropriate, *d.* exorcise) : SPIRIT

47. (*a.* Julian, *b.* Augustan, *c.* Caesarian, *d.* Publican) : GREGORIAN :: NEWTONIAN : EINSTEINIAN

48. (*a.* Koch, *b.* Pasteur, *c.* Lister, *d.* Sabin) : RABIES :: SALK : POLIO

49. MINNEAPOLIS : ST. PAUL :: (*a.* Uncle, *b.* Rabbit, *c.* Abelard, *d.* Romulus) : REMUS

50. POSSE : SHERIFF :: SQUIRE : (*a.* queen, *b.* bourgeoisie, *c.* knight, *d.* vassal)

51. UNTOUCHABLE : (*a.* Hindu, *b.* Vishnu, *c.* Brahman, *d.* Krishna) :: FLOOR : CEILING

52. PENTAGON : DECAGON :: RECTANGLE : (*a.* square, *b.* pentagon, *c.* heptagon, *d.* octagon)

53. TOWARD : IN THE DIRECTION OF :: UNTOWARD : (*a.* at the location of, *b.* away from,
    c. unseemly, *d.* unsafe)

54. EXOGAMY : OUTBREEDING :: (*a.* endogamy, *b.* inogamy, *c.* anogamy,
    d. onogamy) : INBREEDING

55. GRAND : (*a.* pauvre, *b.* petit, *c.* standard, *d.* legal) :: INDICT : CONVICT

56. CHROMATIC : PASTEL :: ACHROMATIC : (*a.* oil, *b.* tempera, *c.* chiasma, *d.* chiaroscuro)

57. EQUATOR : LATITUDE :: (*a.* North Pole, *b.* apogee, *c.* Greenwich, *d.* meridian) : LONGITUDE

58. ROMEO : JULIET :: PYRAMUS : (*a.* Chloe, *b.* Thisbe, *c.* Helen, *d.* Daphne)

59. PETROLEUM : GASOLINE :: BAUXITE : (*a.* aluminum, *b.* tin, *c.* lead, *d.* fool's gold)

60. 0 : ADDITION :: (*a.* 0, *b.* 1, *c.* –1, *d.* ∞) : MULTIPLICATION

61. GALAHAD : (*a.* Beatrice, *b.* Round Table, *c.* Holy Grail, *d.* True Cross) :: JASON :
     GOLDEN FLEECE

62. RED HERRING : (*a.* lie, *b.* peccadillo, *c.* diversion, *d.* secret plot) :: BLUE RIBBON :
     FIRST PRIZE

63. WATERMARK : EARMARK :: (*a.* crops, *b.* tide, *c.* silver, *d.* paper) : ANIMAL

64. ETHER : STARS :: PHLOGISTON : (*a.* earth, *b.* metal, *c.* fire, *d.* water)

65. PARTY : (*a.* revel, *b.* fight, *c.* meeting, *d.* dance) :: SWINE : BOAR

66. RHODE ISLAND : ALASKA :: MERCURY : (*a.* Earth, *b.* Jupiter, *c.* Saturn, *d.* Uranus)

67. MERETRICIOUS : (*a.* egregious, *b.* excellent, *c.* gaudy, *d.* plain) :: APEX : SUMMIT

68. ANTONY : CLEOPATRA :: (*a.* Lancelot, *b.* Arthur, *c.* Merlin, *d.* Gawain) : GUINEVERE

69. MERITOCRACY : MERIT :: PLUTOCRACY : (*a.* wisdom, *b.* money,
     c. power, *d.* physical prowess)

70. INTREPID : (*a.* cowardly, *b.* bold, *c.* voluble, *d.* taciturn) :: AGILE : CLUMSY

71. (*a.* Mars, *b.* Saturn, *c.* Jupiter, *d.* Mercury) : HERMES :: VENUS : APHRODITE

72. COMPLEMENTARY ANGLES : 90° :: COMPLEMENTARY COLORS :
     (*a.* white, *b.* black, *c.* violet, *d.* red)

73. (*a.* Jefferson, *b.* Adams, *c.* Hamilton, *d.* Madison) : BURR :: LINCOLN : BOOTH

74. PUFFIN : (*a.* bird, *b.* reptile, *c.* mammal, *d.* amphibian) :: STURGEON : FISH

75. BRONZE : (*a.* aluminum, *b.* tin, *c.* gold, *d.* silver) :: BRASS : ZINC

76. G MAJOR : (*a.* B minor, *b.* C minor, *c.* D minor, *d.* E minor) :: C MAJOR : A MINOR

77. (*a.* cow, *b.* jackal, *c.* wolf, *d.* rabbit) : LUPINE :: DOG : CANINE

78. (*a.* one, *b.* few, *c.* ten, *d.* all) : ISOCRACY :: ONE : AUTOCRACY

79. LOG 10 : LOG 100 :: LOG 100 : (*a.* log 1,000, *b.* log 10,000, *c.* log 100,000, *d.* log 1,000,000)

80. HAPPINESS : SHANGRI-LA :: (*a.* wealth, *b.* happiness, *c.* gods, *d.* freedom) : EL DORADO

81. DRACONIAN : (*a.* cowardly, *b.* bold, *c.* cruel, *d.* kindly) :: STENTORIAN : LOUD

82. MANSION : HOUSE :: TOME : (*a*. boat, *b*. book, *c*. desk, *d*. church)

83. NEUTRAL : 7 :: (*a*. alkaline, *b*. acidic, *c*. hydrated, *d*. oxidized) : 1

84. PERUSE : SKIM :: REPEL : (*a*. gloss, *b*. bowdlerize, *c*. drive back, *d*. attract)

85. NUCLEOLUS : NUCLEUS :: SET : (*a*. superset, *b*. set, *c*. subset, *d*. disjoint set)

86. HORSEBACK RIDING : EQUITATION :: (*a*. giving birth, *b*. skydiving, *c*. swimming, *d*. dancing) : NATATION

87. WHIGS : TORIES :: JACOBINS : (*a*. Fascists, *b*. Laborites, *c*. Roundheads, *d*. Girondists)

88. PRIME : (*a*. God, *b*. destiny, *c*. factum, *d*. mover) :: FIRST : CAUSE

89. FRANC : FRANCE :: (*a*. lira, *b*. mark, *c*. guilder, *d*. franc) : SWITZERLAND

90. (*a*. Jungfrau, *b*. Blanc, *c*. Matterhorn, *d*. Olympus) : ALPS :: EVEREST : HIMALAYAS

91. MELANCHOLY : (*a*. blue bile, *b*. green bile, *c*. red bile, *d*. black bile) :: CHOLER : YELLOW BILE

92. ORAL : ANAL :: DEPENDENCY : (*a*. lazy, *b*. thermometer, *c*. stinginess, *d*. independent)

93. (*a*. hit, *b*. die, *c*. invest, *d*. sprout) : BURGEON :: ENTREAT : IMPLORE

94. DEARTH : PAUCITY :: SCARCITY : (*a*. plethora, *b*. shortage, *c*. necessity, *d*. commodity)

95. DELFT : (*a*. glass, *b*. pottery, *c*. stoneware, *d*. silver) :: LIMOGES : CHINA

96. IAMB : RETURN :: TROCHEE : (*a*. stable, *b*. arrive, *c*. defend, *d*. eternal)

97. AUTOCHTHONOUS : (*a*. foreign, *b*. native, *c*. self-governing, *d*. dependent) :: LETTER : EPISTLE

98. (*a*. bells, *b*. horn, *c*. magpies, *d*. toads) : TINTINNABULATION :: GEESE : HONK

99. ELF : FLEE :: TON : (*a*. note, *b*. pound, *c*. dwarf, *d*. find)

100. CODA : (*a*. novel, *b*. musical composition, *c*. sculpture, *d*. ceramic jar) :: LANDING : FLIGHT

101. (*a*. months, *b*. tides, *c*. days, *d*. climates) : SEASONS :: MOON : SUN

102. TARANTELLA : ITALY :: CANCAN : (*a*. Argentina, *b*. Spain, *c*. Colombia, *d*. France)

103. AUDITORY : (*a*. olfactory, *b*. sensory, *c*. occipital, *d*. nasal) :: EAR : NOSE

104. TAILFEATHERS : PEACOCK :: (*a.* coat, *b.* tail, *c.* face, *d.* feet) : MANDRILL

105. BUFFALO : WHEAT :: NICKEL : (*a.* dollar, *b.* quarter, *c.* dime, *d.* penny)

106. ACIDIC : (*a.* 3, *b.* 7, *c.* 10, *d.* 14) :: ALKALINE : 12

107. (*a.* Romania, *b.* Croatia, *c.* Greece, *d.* Hungary) : YUGOSLAVIA :: CZECH REPUBLIC : CZECHOSLOVAKIA

108. ROCKY : SMOKY :: COLORADO : (*a.* West Virginia, *b.* New York, *c.* New Hampshire, *d.* Tennessee)

109. BADGER : DOG :: PESTER : (*a.* track, *b.* avoid, *c.* exhaust, *d.* behave)

110. ACCORDION : (*a.* bagpipe, *b.* flute, *c.* organ, *d.* clarinet) :: HARMONIUM : PIANO

111. RACECAR : RADAR :: (*a.* abbreviation, *b.* homonym, *c.* palindrome, *d.* gerund) : ACRONYM

112. (*a.* 82, *b.* 99, *c.* 22, *d.* 15) : 451 :: CATCH : FAHRENHEIT

113. A : Z :: Alpha : (*a.* Omega, *b.* Beta, *c.* Zed, *d.* Phi)

114. AMETHYST : (*a.* amber, *b.* purple, *c.* crimson, *d.* yellow) :: SAPPHIRE : BLUE

115. SYCOPHANT : TOADY :: MISCREANT : (*a.* artist, *b.* recluse, *c.* follower, *d.* criminal)

116. EKG : (*a.* heart, *b.* pancreas, *c.* bladder, *d.* lungs) :: EEG : brain

117. TONY : OSCAR :: (*a.* music, *b.* theater, *c.* literature, *d.* television) : FILM

118. (*a.* Colorado, *b.* Wyoming, *c.* Idaho, *d.* Alaska) : MCKINLEY :: NEPAL : EVEREST

119. I, CLAUDIUS : GRAVES :: (*a.* I, Julius, *b.* I, Criminal, *c.* I, Nixon, *d.* I, Robot) : ASIMOV

120. VIRGINIA : TENNESSEE :: WOOLF : (*a.* Faulkner, *b.* Percy, *c.* Williams, *d.* O'Connor)

ANSWER KEY
Practice Test 9

1.	C	31.	B	61.	C	91.	D
2.	A	32.	D	62.	C	92.	C
3.	D	33.	D	63.	D	93.	D
4.	C	34.	D	64.	C	94.	B
5.	A	35.	A	65.	A	95.	B
6.	B	36.	A	66.	B	96.	A
7.	B	37.	A	67.	C	97.	B
8.	C	38.	B	68.	A	98.	A
9.	B	39.	C	69.	B	99.	A
10.	C	40.	A	70.	A	100.	B
11.	A	41.	B	71.	D	101.	B
12.	D	42.	C	72.	A	102.	D
13.	B	43.	B	73.	C	103.	A
14.	B	44.	A	74.	A	104.	C
15.	A	45.	D	75.	B	105.	D
16.	C	46.	D	76.	D	106.	A
17.	B	47.	A	77.	C	107.	B
18.	B	48.	B	78.	D	108.	D
19.	A	49.	D	79.	B	109.	A
20.	D	50.	C	80.	A	110.	C
21.	A	51.	C	81.	C	111.	C
22.	A	52.	D	82.	B	112.	C
23.	D	53.	C	83.	B	113.	A
24.	C	54.	A	84.	D	114.	B
25.	C	55.	B	85.	A	115.	D
26.	A	56.	D	86.	C	116.	A
27.	D	57.	C	87.	D	117.	B
28.	D	58.	B	88.	D	118.	D
29.	B	59.	A	89.	D	119.	D
30.	D	60.	B	90.	B	120.	C

In the following, explanations concerning the correct responses are in roman font. Explanations regarding distracters (incorrect responses) that are not self-explaining or could be misinterpreted are in italics in order to highlight the explanations of the answers that are correct.

1. POSTMAN : LETTER :: (*a.* surgeon, *b.* orthopedist, ***c.* obstetrician**, *d.* podiatrist) : BABY

   (c) A postman delivers a letter; an obstetrician delivers a baby.

2. CHLOROPHYLL : GREEN :: HEMOGLOBIN : (***a.* red**, *b.* black, *c.* green, *d.* blue)

   (a) Chlorophyll is a green substance that gives leaves their green color; hemoglobin is a red substance that gives blood its red color.

3. HAPPY : (*a.* sad, *b.* gay, *c.* indifferent, ***d.* ecstatic**) :: BRIGHT : BRILLIANT

   (d) A person who is extremely happy is ecstatic; a person who is extremely bright is brilliant.

4. PENCIL : PEN :: (*a.* wood, *b.* ballpoint, ***c.* graphite**, *d.* boron) : INK

   (c) The writing substance in a pencil is usually graphite; the writing substance in a pen is usually ink.

5. ONE BIRD : HAND :: TWO BIRDS : (***a.* bush**, *b.* foot, *c.* nest, *d.* head)

   (a) A familiar proverb states, "A bird in the hand is worth two in the bush."

6. SILVER : TARNISH :: IRON : (*a.* oxidation, ***b.* rust**, *c.* magnet, *d.* tin)

   (b) When silver oxidizes, the result is called tarnish; when iron oxidizes, the result is called rust.

7. BUTTERFLY : CATERPILLAR :: (*a.* amphibian, ***b.* frog**, *c.* salamander, *d.* larva) : TADPOLE

   (b) A caterpillar is the larval form of a butterfly; a tadpole is the larval form of a frog.

8. GREEN : (*a.* cowardice, *b.* viciousness, ***c.* envy**, *d.* delight) :: PURPLE : RAGE

   (c) Green and purple are colors commonly used to denote emotional states. A person is said to be green with envy or purple with rage.

9. JUDAS : JESUS :: (*a.* Augustus, ***b.* Brutus**, *c.* Lucius, *d.* Antony) : JULIUS CAESAR

   (b) Judas betrayed Jesus; Brutus betrayed Julius Caesar.

10. JOLLY ROGER : (*a.* communists, *b.* fascists, ***c.* pirates**, *d.* anarchists) :: UNION JACK : UNITED KINGDOM

    (c) The Jolly Roger was the emblem of pirates, while the Union Jack is the emblem of the United Kingdom.

11. DIALECTIC : HEGEL :: DIALECTICAL MATERIALISM : (***a.* Marx**, *b.* Fichte, *c.* Schelling, *d.* Kant)

    (a) Hegel developed the philosophical notion of the dialectic, while Marx developed the philosophical notion of dialectical materialism. *Fichte was one of the founders of German Idealism, which developed on the basis of Kant's thoughts. He investigated self-consciousness. Schelling was involved in German Idealism and investigated conceptions of nature in his* Naturphilosophie. *Kant is famous for his* Critique of Pure Reason, *which investigates reason itself.*

12. (*a*. screen, *b*. camera, *c*. projector, *d*. **frame**) : MOVIE FILM :: LINK : CHAIN

(d) A movie film is composed of successive frames, while a chain is composed of successive links.

13. PROLOGUE : (*a*. decalogue, *b*. **epilogue**, *c*. preface, *d*. forward) :: APPETIZER : DESSERT

(b) A prologue introduces a book, and an epilogue closes it; an appetizer introduces a meal, and a dessert closes it.

14. HAMMERSTEIN : (*a*. Sondheim, *b*. **Rodgers**, *c*. Gilbert, *d*. Herman) :: LERNER : LOEWE

(b) Hammerstein and Rodgers created Broadway musicals, with Hammerstein writing the lyrics and Rodgers composing the music; Lerner and Loewe also created Broadway musicals, with Lerner writing the lyrics and Loewe composing the music.

15. (*a*. **dumb**, *b*. stupid, *c*. loquacious, *d*. brilliant) : MUTE :: SMART : INTELLIGENT

(a) Dumb and mute are synonyms, as are smart and intelligent.

16. ARCHIVES : (*a*. munitions, *b*. tombs, *c*. **documents**, *d*. animals) :: PANTRY : KITCHEN UTENSILS

(c) Documents are stored in archives, while kitchen utensils are stored in a pantry.

17. DUNCAN : MACBETH :: MACBETH : (*a*. Lady Macbeth, *b*. **Macduff**, *c*. Polonius, *d*. Claudius)

(b) In Shakespeare's play *Macbeth*, Macbeth kills Duncan and Macduff kills Macbeth. *Polonius was Chamberlain to King Claudius in Shakespeare's* Hamlet. *Lady Macbeth is the wife of Macbeth in Shakespeare's* Macbeth.

18. V : X :: D : (*a*. I, *b*. **M**, *c*. D, *d*. C)

(b) The terms of the analogy are Roman numerals; 10 is equal to twice 5, and 1,000 is equal to twice 500. In Roman numerals, I = 1, V = 5, X = 10, L = 50, C = 100, D = 500, M = 1,000.

19. JACK SPRAT'S WIFE : LEAN :: VEGETARIAN : (*a*. **meat**, *b*. fat, *c*. vegetables, *d*. roots)

(a) Jack Sprat's wife would eat no lean, according to the nursery rhyme; a vegetarian will eat no meat.

20. (*a*. politics, *b*. law, *c*. music, *d*. **medicine**) : HIPPOCRATES :: HISTORY : HERODOTUS

(d) Hippocrates is often referred to as the Father of Medicine, while Herodotus is known as the Father of History.

21. (*a*. **Russia**, *b*. China, *c*. Japan, *d*. Hungary) : BALALAIKA :: SCOTLAND : BAGPIPES

(a) The balalaika is a Russian musical instrument; the bagpipes are a Scottish musical instrument.

22. TAILPIPE : EXHAUST :: RADIUM : (*a*. **beta rays**, *b*. strontium, *c*. cosmic rays, *d*. lead)

(a) A tailpipe emits exhaust; radium emits beta rays.

23. ARGUS : 100 :: CYCLOPS : (*a*. 1000, *b*. 10, *c*. 5, *d*. **1**)

(d) According to legend, Argus had 100 eyes, while Cyclops had just 1.

24. CANNON : BIG BERTHA :: (*a*. battleship, *b*. bazooka, *c*. **bell**, *d*. church steeple) : BIG BEN

(c) Big Bertha is the name of a cannon; Big Ben is the name of a bell.

25. (*a*. pretty, *b*. pretentious, *c*. **proud**, *d*. portly) : PEACOCK :: SILLY : GOOSE

(c) People are often likened either to a peacock or to a goose. One may be proud as a peacock or silly as a goose.

26. HYPOCRITICAL : INSINCERE :: HYPERCRITICAL : (*a.* **overcritical**, *b.* sincere, *c.* oversincere, *d.* critical)

    (a) Hypocritical and insincere are synonyms, as are hypercritical and overcritical.

27. (*a.* cross, *b.* aisle, *c.* refectory, *d.* **nave**) : TRANSEPT :: VERTICAL : HORIZONTAL

    (d) In a cross-shaped church, the nave and the transept are perpendicular to each other, as are any objects that are vertical and horizontal with respect to each other.

28. MNEMONIC : (*a.* nymph, *b.* elf, *c.* anger, *d.* **knock**) :: PNEUMATIC : GNOME

    (d) Mnemonic, pneumatic, gnome, and knock each has a silent consonant preceding the initial voiced consonant, *n.*

29. FAITH : JOB :: (*a.* wisdom, *b.* **age**, *c.* wickedness, *d.* courage) : METHUSELAH

    (b) In the Bible, Job distinguished himself by his great faith in God, while Methuselah distinguished himself by the great age to which he lived (969 years).

30. MRS. GRUNDY : NARROW-MINDED :: POLLYANNA : (*a.* witty, *b.* dull, *c.* pessimistic, *d.* **optimistic**)

    (d) Mrs. Grundy is a literary character in Thomas Morton's play *Speed the Plow*, known for her narrow-mindedness. Pollyanna is a literary character in *Pollyanna* by Eleanor Porter, known for her optimism.

31. MIDNIGHT SUN : (*a.* Russia, *b.* **Norway**, *c.* China, *d.* South Pole) :: RISING SUN : JAPAN

    (b) Norway is the Land of the Midnight Sun, while Japan is the Land of the Rising Sun.

32. RED-BLOODED : VIGOROUS :: BLUE-BLOODED : (*a.* cowardly, *b.* sickly, *c.* prudish, *d.* **aristocratic**)

    (d) A vigorous person is sometimes referred to as red-blooded, while an aristocratic person is sometimes referred to as blue-blooded.

33. (*a.* battle, *b.* artillery, *c.* ammunition, *d.* **armory**) : WEAPONS :: CLOSET : CLOTHING

    (d) An armory is used to store weapons; a closet is used to store clothing.

34. CHARACTERISTIC : DEFINING :: USUALLY : (*a.* never, *b.* sometimes, *c.* rarely, *d.* **always**)

    (d) A characteristic feature is one usually possessed by an object, while a defining feature is one always possessed by an object.

35. OBVIATE : (*a.* **make unnecessary**, *b.* make necessary, *c.* make obvious, *d.* make obscure) :: EXPUNGE : DELETE

    (a) To obviate is to make unnecessary; to expunge is to delete.

36. BROBDINGNAGIAN : GIGANTIC :: (*a.* **Lilliputian**, *b.* Houyhnhnm, *c.* Vespasian, *d.* Yahoo) : TINY

    (a) In the novel *Gulliver's Travels* (by Jonathan Swift), the Brobdingnagians are gigantic people, while the Lilliputians are tiny ones.

37. RUSSIA : (*a.* **tsar**, *b.* king, *c.* emperor, *d.* autarch) :: FRANCE : KING

    (a) Russia was formerly ruled by a tsar, France by a king.

38. MINOTAUR : BULL :: CENTAUR : (*a.* cow, *b.* **horse**, *c.* pig, *d.* goat)

    (b) The minotaur, according to mythology, was part bull and part man; the centaur was part horse and part man.

39. INTEGRAL : (*a.* acceleration, *b.* length, ***c.* area**, *d.* velocity) :: DERIVATIVE : SLOPE

(c) In calculus, an integral can be computed to determine area, while a derivative can be calculated to determine slope.

40. GUSTATORY : (***a.* taste**, *b.* touch, *c.* sight, *d.* smell) :: AUDITORY : HEARING

(a) Gustatory refers to taste; auditory, to hearing. *Kinesthetic refers to touch, visual refers to sight, and olfactory refers to smell.*

41. OCTOPI : OCTOPUSES :: (*a.* cannona, ***b.* cannon**, *c.* cannones, *d.* cannonade) : CANNONS

(b) Octopi and octopuses are both plural forms of the word octopus; cannon and cannons are both plural forms of the word cannon.

42. CRIME : WAR :: PUNISHMENT : (*a.* Destruction, *b.* Treaty, ***c.* Peace**, *d.* Retribution)

(c) *Crime and Punishment* is a novel by the Russian author Dostoevski. *War and Peace* is a novel by the Russian author Tolstoy.

43. SUPPLY : DEMAND :: RATE : (*a.* distance, ***b.* time**, *c.* velocity, *d.* price)

(b) Supply and demand are inversely related, as are rate and time.

44. ICONOCLAST : (***a.* religious images**, *b.* autocracy, *c.* democratic ideals, *d.* anarchy) :: NIHILIST : SOCIAL ORDER

(a) The goal of an iconoclast is to destroy religious images; the goal of a nihilist is to destroy social order.

45. QUIXOTIC : CERVANTES :: FAUSTIAN : (*a.* Hegel, *b.* Faust, *c.* Schiller, ***d.* Goethe**)

(d) The word quixotic is derived from the name of a literary character, Don Quixote, who is the subject of a work by Cervantes; the word faustian is derived from the name of a character, Faust, who is the subject of a work by Goethe.

46. EXPEL : STUDENT :: (*a.* expire, *b.* expunge, *c.* expropriate, ***d.* exorcise**) : SPIRIT

(d) A student is expelled from school; a spirit is exorcised from the body.

47. (***a.* Julian**, *b.* Augustan, *c.* Caesarian, *d.* Publican) : GREGORIAN :: NEWTONIAN : EINSTEINIAN

(a) The Julian calendar was replaced by the Gregorian calendar; Newtonian physics was replaced by Einsteinian physics.

48. (*a.* Koch, ***b.* Pasteur**, *c.* Lister, *d.* Sabin) : RABIES :: SALK : POLIO

(b) Pasteur developed an antirabies vaccine; Salk developed an antipolio vaccine. *Lister promoted the idea of sterile surgery. Sabin developed the oral vaccine for polio. Koch is well known for isolating the tuberculosis bacillus,* Bacillus anthracis.

49. MINNEAPOLIS : ST. PAUL :: (*a.* Uncle, *b.* Rabbit, *c.* Abelard, ***d.* Romulus**) : REMUS

(d) Minneapolis and St. Paul are twin cities. Romulus and Remus, according to legend, were twin brothers.

50. POSSE : SHERIFF :: SQUIRE : (*a.* queen, *b.* bourgeoisie, ***c.* knight**, *d.* vassal)

(c) A posse assists a sheriff; a squire assisted a knight.

51. UNTOUCHABLE : (*a.* Hindu, *b.* Vishnu, ***c.* Brahman**, *d.* Krishna) :: FLOOR : CEILING

(c) In former times, an untouchable was a member of the lowest Indian caste, while a Brahman was a member of the highest one. A floor is the lowest part of a room, while a ceiling is the highest part.

52. PENTAGON : DECAGON :: RECTANGLE : (*a.* square, *b.* pentagon, *c.* heptagon, ***d.* octagon**)

   (d) A decagon has twice as many sides as a pentagon; an octagon has twice as many sides as a rectangle.

53. TOWARD : IN THE DIRECTION OF :: UNTOWARD : (*a.* at the location of, *b.* away from, ***c.* unseemly**, *d.* unsafe)

   (c) Toward means in the direction of. Untoward means unseemly.

54. EXOGAMY : OUTBREEDING :: (***a.* endogamy**, *b.* inogamy, *c.* anogamy, *d.* onogamy) : INBREEDING

   (a) Exogamy refers to outbreeding, while endogamy refers to inbreeding.

55. GRAND : (*a.* pauvre, ***b.* petit**, *c.* standard, *d.* legal) :: INDICT : CONVICT

   (b) A grand jury has the power to indict an individual for a crime, while a petit jury has the power to convict him or her of it.

56. CHROMATIC : PASTEL :: ACHROMATIC : (*a.* oil, *b.* tempera, *c.* chiasma, ***d.* chiaroscuro**)

   (d) Pastel is a chromatic form of artwork (with colors), while chiaroscuro is an achromatic form (black and white).

57. EQUATOR : LATITUDE :: (*a.* North Pole, *b.* apogee, ***c.* Greenwich**, *d.* meridian) : LONGITUDE

   (c) The equator is at 0° latitude; Greenwich is at 0° longitude.

58. ROMEO : JULIET :: PYRAMUS : (*a.* Chloe, ***b.* Thisbe**, *c.* Helen, *d.* Daphne)

   (b) Romeo and Juliet were lovers, as were Pyramus and Thisbe. *Chloe is another name for Demeter, who was the goddess of harvest and fertility in Greek mythology. Helen was the daughter of Zeus and Leda, wife of King Menelaus of Sparta, and was abducted by Paris, which led to the Trojan War. Daphne was a nymph in Greek mythology.*

59. PETROLEUM : GASOLINE :: BAUXITE : (***a.* aluminum**, *b.* tin, *c.* lead, *d.* fool's gold)

   (a) Petroleum is the raw material used to make gasoline, while bauxite is the raw material from which aluminum is obtained. Pewter is an alloy that contains tin. Lead is a heavy metal that may be added in smaller amounts to pewter as well.

60. 0 : ADDITION :: (*a.* 0, ***b.* 1**, *c.* –1, *d.* ∞) : MULTIPLICATION

   (b) Zero is the identity element for addition—any number plus 0 equals that number. One is the identity element for multiplication—any number times 1 equals that number.

61. GALAHAD : (*a.* Beatrice, *b.* Round Table, ***c.* Holy Grail**, *d.* True Cross) :: JASON : GOLDEN FLEECE

   (c) According to legend, Galahad succeeded in his quest for the Holy Grail, while Jason succeeded in his quest for the Golden Fleece.

62. RED HERRING : (*a.* lie, *b.* peccadillo, ***c.* diversion**, *d.* secret plot) :: BLUE RIBBON : FIRST PRIZE

   (c) A red herring is a diversion. A blue ribbon is a first prize.

63. WATERMARK : EARMARK :: (*a.* crops, *b.* tide, *c.* silver, ***d.* paper**) : ANIMAL

   (d) Paper is sometimes identified by a watermark; an animal is sometimes identified by an earmark.

64. ETHER : STARS :: PHLOGISTON : (*a.* earth, *b.* metal, *c.* **fire**, *d.* water)

(c) In medieval times, it was believed that the stars were composed of a substance called ether, and that fire was composed of a substance called phlogiston.

65. PARTY : (*a.* **revel**, *b.* fight, *c.* meeting, *d.* dance) :: SWINE : BOAR

(a) A revel is a wild party. A boar is a form of wild swine.

66. RHODE ISLAND : ALASKA :: MERCURY : (*a.* Earth, *b.* **Jupiter**, *c.* Saturn, *d.* Uranus)

(b) Rhode Island is the smallest state; Alaska, the largest. Mercury is the smallest planet (in our solar system); Jupiter, the largest. The size of the planets (starting with the smallest): Mercury, Mars, Venus, Earth, Neptune, Uranus, Saturn, Jupiter.

67. MERETRICIOUS : (*a.* egregious, *b.* excellent, *c.* **gaudy**, *d.* plain) :: APEX : SUMMIT

(c) Meretricious and gaudy are synonyms, as are apex and summit.

68. ANTONY : CLEOPATRA :: (*a.* **Lancelot**, *b.* Arthur, *c.* Merlin, *d.* Gawain) : GUINEVERE

(a) Cleopatra was the mistress of Antony; Guinevere was the mistress of Lancelot. *King Arthur was a British king in the 6th century who defended Britain against invaders from Saxony. Merlin was a wizard from the Arthurian legend. Gawain was King Arthur's nephew and a member of the Round Table.*

69. MERITOCRACY : MERIT :: PLUTOCRACY : (*a.* wisdom, *b.* **money**, *c.* power, *d.* physical prowess)

(b) A meritocracy is rule by those demonstrating merit; a plutocracy is rule by the wealthy.

70. INTREPID : (*a.* **cowardly**, *b.* bold, *c.* voluble, *d.* taciturn) :: AGILE : CLUMSY

(a) Intrepid and cowardly are antonyms, as are agile and clumsy.

71. (*a.* Mars, *b.* Saturn, *c.* Jupiter, *d.* **Mercury**) : HERMES :: VENUS : APHRODITE

(d) Mercury is the Roman name, and Hermes the Greek name, for the messenger of the gods. Venus is the Roman name, and Aphrodite the Greek name, for the goddess of beauty. *Mars was the god of war in Roman mythology. Jupiter was the god of sky and thunder. Saturn was the god of agriculture and harvest.*

72. COMPLEMENTARY ANGLES : 90° :: COMPLEMENTARY COLORS : (*a.* **white**, *b.* black, *c.* violet, *d.* red)

(a) Complementary angles sum to 90°; complementary colors sum to white.

73. (*a.* Jefferson, *b.* Adams, *c.* **Hamilton**, *d.* Madison) : BURR :: LINCOLN : BOOTH

(c) Aaron Burr killed Alexander Hamilton, while John Wilkes Booth killed Abraham Lincoln.

74. PUFFIN : (*a.* **bird**, *b.* reptile, *c.* mammal, *d.* amphibian) :: STURGEON : FISH

(a) A puffin is a kind of bird; a sturgeon is a kind of fish.

75. BRONZE : (*a.* aluminum, *b.* **tin**, *c.* gold, *d.* silver) :: BRASS : ZINC

(b) Bronze is a combination of copper and tin, while brass is a combination of copper and zinc.

76. G MAJOR : (*a.* B minor, *b.* C minor, *c.* D minor, *d.* **E minor**) :: C MAJOR : A MINOR

(d) The keys of G major and E minor both have one sharp, while the keys of C major and A minor have none.

77. (*a.* cow, *b.* jackal, *c.* **wolf**, *d.* rabbit) : LUPINE :: DOG : CANINE

(c) To be lupine is to be wolflike; to be canine is to be doglike.

78. (*a.* one, *b.* few, *c.* ten, *d.* **all**) : ISOCRACY :: ONE : AUTOCRACY

(d) An isocracy is rule by all; an autocracy is rule by one.

79. LOG 10 : LOG 100 :: LOG 100 : (*a.* log 1,000, ***b.* log 10,000**, *c.* log 100,000, *d.* log 1,000,000)

(b) Log 100 is twice as great as log 10 (2 : 1). Log 10,000 is twice as great as log 100 (4 : 2).

80. HAPPINESS : SHANGRI-LA :: (***a.* wealth**, *b.* happiness, *c.* gods, *d.* freedom) : EL DORADO

(a) Shangri-La is an imaginary land of great happiness; El Dorado is an imaginary land of great wealth.

81. DRACONIAN : (*a.* cowardly, *b.* bold, ***c.* cruel**, *d.* kindly) :: STENTORIAN : LOUD

(c) A draconian person is cruel; a stentorian person is loud.

82. MANSION : HOUSE :: TOME : (*a.* boat, ***b.* book**, *c.* desk, *d.* church)

(b) A mansion is a large house. A tome is a large book.

83. NEUTRAL : 7 :: (*a.* alkaline, ***b.* acidic**, *c.* hydrated, *d.* oxidized) : 1

(b) On the pH scale, 7 is neutral and 1 is acidic. Numbers greater than 7 indicate alkalinity.

84. PERUSE : SKIM :: REPEL : (*a.* gloss, *b.* bowdlerize, *c.* drive back, ***d.* attract**)

(d) Peruse and skim are antonyms, as are repel and attract.

85. NUCLEOLUS : NUCLEUS :: SET : (***a.* superset**, *b.* set, *c.* subset, *d.* disjoint set)

(a) In a cell, the nucleolus is contained in the nucleus. Similarly, a set is contained in a superset.

86. HORSEBACK RIDING : EQUITATION :: (*a.* giving birth, *b.* skydiving, ***c.* swimming**, *d.* dancing) : NATATION

(c) Equitation is the art of horseback riding; natation is the art of swimming.

87. WHIGS : TORIES :: JACOBINS : (*a.* Fascists, *b.* Laborites, *c.* Roundheads, ***d.* Girondists**)

(d) During the American Revolution, the Whigs represented a radical faction and the Tories a more conservative one. During the French Revolution, the Jacobins represented a radical faction and the Girondists a more conservative one.

88. PRIME : (*a.* God, *b.* destiny, *c.* factum, ***d.* mover**) :: FIRST : CAUSE

(d) In Aristotelian philosophy, the prime mover was a first cause (of all movement).

89. FRANC : FRANCE :: (*a.* lira, *b.* mark, *c.* guilder, ***d.* franc**) : SWITZERLAND

(d) The franc was the unit of currency in both France and Switzerland (although the two francs are not equivalent). *The lira was the currency of Italy, the mark was the currency of Germany, and the guilder was the currency of the Netherlands (before the euro).*

90. (*a.* Jungfrau, ***b.* Blanc**, *c.* Matterhorn, *d.* Olympus) : ALPS :: EVEREST : HIMALAYAS

(b) Mont Blanc is the highest peak in the Alps; Mount Everest is the highest peak in the Himalayas. *Jungfrau and Matterhorn are mountains of the Swiss Alps; Mount Olympus is the highest mountain of Greece.*

91. MELANCHOLY : (*a.* blue bile, *b.* green bile, *c.* red bile, ***d.* black bile**) :: CHOLER : YELLOW BILE

(d) According to the physiology of days gone by, melancholy is black bile, while choler is yellow bile.

92. ORAL : ANAL :: DEPENDENCY : (*a.* lazinesss, *b.* thermometer, ***c.* stinginess**, *d.* independence)

(c) In psychodynamic theory, dependency is an oral trait and stinginess an anal trait.

93. (*a.* hit, *b.* die, *c.* invest, ***d.* sprout**) : BURGEON :: ENTREAT : IMPLORE

(d) Sprout and burgeon are synonyms, as are entreat and implore.

94. DEARTH : PAUCITY :: SCARCITY : (*a.* plethora, ***b.* shortage**, *c.* necessity, *d.* commodity)

(b) Dearth and paucity are synonyms, as are scarcity and shortage. (All four words are synonymous.)

95. DELFT : (*a.* glass, ***b.* pottery**, *c.* stoneware, *d.* silver) :: LIMOGES : CHINA

(b) Delft is known for its beautiful painted pottery; Limoges is known for its beautiful painted china.

96. IAMB : RETURN :: TROCHEE : (***a.* stable**, *b.* arrive, *c.* defend, *d.* eternal)

(a) Return is pronounced as an iamb; stable is pronounced as a trochee. An iamb is a metrical foot that consists of one unstressed and one stressed syllable; a trochee consists of one long (stressed) syllable that is followed by a short (unstressed) one.

97. AUTOCHTHONOUS : (*a.* foreign, ***b.* native**, *c.* self-governing, *d.* dependent) :: LETTER : EPISTLE

(b) Autochthonous and native are synonyms, as are letter and epistle.

98. (***a.* bells**, *b.* horn, *c.* magpies, *d.* toads) : TINTINNABULATION :: GEESE : HONK

(a) Tintinnabulation is a sound made by bells; honk is a sound made by geese.

99. ELF : FLEE :: TON : (***a.* note**, *b.* pound, *c.* dwarf, *d.* find)

(a) Flee is elf spelled backward, but with an added *e* at the end. Note is ton spelled backward, also with an added *e* at the end.

100. CODA : (*a.* novel, ***b.* musical composition**, *c.* sculpture, *d.* ceramic jar) :: LANDING : FLIGHT

(b) A coda concludes a musical composition; a landing concludes a flight.

101. (*a.* months, ***b.* tides**, *c.* days, *d.* climates) : SEASONS :: MOON : SUN

(b) The tides change as the earth's positional relationship to the moon changes. The seasons change as the earth's positional relationship to the sun changes.

102. TARANTELLA : ITALY :: CANCAN : (*a.* Argentina, *b.* Spain, *c.* Colombia, ***d.* France**)

(d) The tarantella and cancan are dances that originated in Italy and France, respectively. Flamenco is a dance from Spain, tango is from Argentina, and bambuco is from Colombia.

103. AUDITORY : (***a.* olfactory**, *b.* sensory, *c.* occipital, *d.* nasal) :: EAR : NOSE

(a) The ear is responsible for auditory sensation, or hearing. The nose is responsible for olfactory sensation, or smelling.

104. TAILFEATHERS : PEACOCK :: (*a.* coat, *b.* tail, ***c.* face**, *d.* feet) : MANDRILL

(c) A peacock is known for its brightly colored tailfeathers just as a mandrill is known for its brightly colored face.

105. BUFFALO : WHEAT :: NICKEL : (*a.* dollar, *b.* quarter, *c.* dime, ***d.* penny**)

(d) A buffalo was formerly placed on one side of the nickel, and these coins were known as buffalo nickels. A shaft of wheat was formerly placed on one side of the penny, and these coins were known as wheat pennies.

106. ACIDIC : (***a.* 3**, *b.* 7, *c.* 10, *d.* 14) :: ALKALINE : 12

(a) A solution with a pH level of 3 is acidic, just as a solution with a pH level of 12 is alkaline.

107. (*a.* Romania, ***b.* Croatia**, *c.* Greece, *d.* Hungary) : YUGOSLAVIA :: CZECH REPUBLIC : CZECHOSLOVAKIA

(b) Croatia is part of the country once known as Yugoslavia. The Czech Republic is part of the country once known as Czechoslovakia.

108. ROCKY : SMOKY :: COLORADO : (*a.* West Virginia, *b.* New York, *c.* New Hampshire, ***d.* Tennessee**)

(d) The Rocky Mountains can be found in the state of Colorado just as the Smoky Mountains can be found in Tennessee.

109. BADGER : DOG :: PESTER : (***a.* track**, *b.* avoid, *c.* exhaust, *d.* behave)

(a) To badger is to pester someone persistently. To dog is to track someone or something persistently.

110. ACCORDION : (*a.* bagpipe, *b.* flute, ***c.* organ**, *d.* clarinet) :: HARMONIUM : PIANO

(c) The accordion, organ, harmonium, and piano are all instruments with black and white keyboards.

111. RACECAR : RADAR :: (*a.* abbreviation, *b.* homonym, ***c.* palindrome**, *d.* gerund) : ACRONYM

(c) The word racecar is a palindrome: it reads the same forward and backward. The word radar is an acronym: it stands for RAdio Detection And Ranging.

112. (*a.* 82, *b.* 99, ***c.* 22**, *d.* 15) : 451 :: CATCH : FAHRENHEIT

(c) *Catch 22* and *Fahrenheit 451* are both popular novels, by Joseph Heller and Ray Bradbury, respectively.

113. A : Z :: Alpha : (***a.* Omega**, *b.* Beta, *c.* Zed, *d.* Phi)

(a) A is the first and Z (Zed) the last letter of the English alphabet. Alpha is the first and Omega the last letter of the Greek alphabet.

114. AMETHYST : (*a.* amber, ***b.* purple**, *c.* crimson, *d.* yellow) :: SAPPHIRE : BLUE

(b) Amethyst is a gemstone that is typically purple in color. Sapphire is a gemstone that is typically blue in color.

115. SYCOPHANT : TOADY :: MISCREANT : (*a.* artist, *b.* recluse, *c.* follower, ***d.* criminal**)

(d) A sycophant is a toady, just as a miscreant is a criminal.

116. EKG : (***a.* heart**, *b.* pancreas, *c.* bladder, *d.* lungs) :: EEG : brain

(a) An EKG machine measures activity in the heart just as an EEG machine measures activity in the brain. EEG stands for electroencephalogram. EKG stands for electrocardiogram.

117. TONY : OSCAR :: (*a.* music, ***b.* theater**, *c.* literature, *d.* television) : FILM

(b) The Tony Award is given for accomplishments in theater just as the Oscar is given for accomplishments in film.

118. (*a.* Colorado, *b.* Wyoming, *c.* Idaho, ***d.* Alaska**) : MCKINLEY :: NEPAL : EVEREST

(d) Mount McKinley is in Alaska and Mount Everest is in Nepal.

119. I, CLAUDIUS : GRAVES :: (*a.* I, Julius, *b.* I, Criminal, *c.* I, Nixon, ***d.* I, Robot**) : ASIMOV

(d) Graves wrote the novel *I, Claudius* and Asimov wrote the novel *I, Robot*.

120. VIRGINIA : TENNESSEE :: WOOLF : (*a.* Faulkner, *b.* Percy, ***c.* Williams**, *d.* O'Connor)

(c) Virginia Woolf and Tennessee Williams were both writers. Woolf wrote *Mrs. Dalloway* and *Orlando*, for example. Williams' works include *Cat on a Hot Tin Roof* and *A Streetcar Named Desire*.

ANSWER SHEET
Practice Test 10

1. Ⓐ Ⓑ Ⓒ Ⓓ	31. Ⓐ Ⓑ Ⓒ Ⓓ	61. Ⓐ Ⓑ Ⓒ Ⓓ	91. Ⓐ Ⓑ Ⓒ Ⓓ
2. Ⓐ Ⓑ Ⓒ Ⓓ	32. Ⓐ Ⓑ Ⓒ Ⓓ	62. Ⓐ Ⓑ Ⓒ Ⓓ	92. Ⓐ Ⓑ Ⓒ Ⓓ
3. Ⓐ Ⓑ Ⓒ Ⓓ	33. Ⓐ Ⓑ Ⓒ Ⓓ	63. Ⓐ Ⓑ Ⓒ Ⓓ	93. Ⓐ Ⓑ Ⓒ Ⓓ
4. Ⓐ Ⓑ Ⓒ Ⓓ	34. Ⓐ Ⓑ Ⓒ Ⓓ	64. Ⓐ Ⓑ Ⓒ Ⓓ	94. Ⓐ Ⓑ Ⓒ Ⓓ
5. Ⓐ Ⓑ Ⓒ Ⓓ	35. Ⓐ Ⓑ Ⓒ Ⓓ	65. Ⓐ Ⓑ Ⓒ Ⓓ	95. Ⓐ Ⓑ Ⓒ Ⓓ
6. Ⓐ Ⓑ Ⓒ Ⓓ	36. Ⓐ Ⓑ Ⓒ Ⓓ	66. Ⓐ Ⓑ Ⓒ Ⓓ	96. Ⓐ Ⓑ Ⓒ Ⓓ
7. Ⓐ Ⓑ Ⓒ Ⓓ	37. Ⓐ Ⓑ Ⓒ Ⓓ	67. Ⓐ Ⓑ Ⓒ Ⓓ	97. Ⓐ Ⓑ Ⓒ Ⓓ
8. Ⓐ Ⓑ Ⓒ Ⓓ	38. Ⓐ Ⓑ Ⓒ Ⓓ	68. Ⓐ Ⓑ Ⓒ Ⓓ	98. Ⓐ Ⓑ Ⓒ Ⓓ
9. Ⓐ Ⓑ Ⓒ Ⓓ	39. Ⓐ Ⓑ Ⓒ Ⓓ	69. Ⓐ Ⓑ Ⓒ Ⓓ	99. Ⓐ Ⓑ Ⓒ Ⓓ
10. Ⓐ Ⓑ Ⓒ Ⓓ	40. Ⓐ Ⓑ Ⓒ Ⓓ	70. Ⓐ Ⓑ Ⓒ Ⓓ	100. Ⓐ Ⓑ Ⓒ Ⓓ
11. Ⓐ Ⓑ Ⓒ Ⓓ	41. Ⓐ Ⓑ Ⓒ Ⓓ	71. Ⓐ Ⓑ Ⓒ Ⓓ	101. Ⓐ Ⓑ Ⓒ Ⓓ
12. Ⓐ Ⓑ Ⓒ Ⓓ	42. Ⓐ Ⓑ Ⓒ Ⓓ	72. Ⓐ Ⓑ Ⓒ Ⓓ	102. Ⓐ Ⓑ Ⓒ Ⓓ
13. Ⓐ Ⓑ Ⓒ Ⓓ	43. Ⓐ Ⓑ Ⓒ Ⓓ	73. Ⓐ Ⓑ Ⓒ Ⓓ	103. Ⓐ Ⓑ Ⓒ Ⓓ
14. Ⓐ Ⓑ Ⓒ Ⓓ	44. Ⓐ Ⓑ Ⓒ Ⓓ	74. Ⓐ Ⓑ Ⓒ Ⓓ	104. Ⓐ Ⓑ Ⓒ Ⓓ
15. Ⓐ Ⓑ Ⓒ Ⓓ	45. Ⓐ Ⓑ Ⓒ Ⓓ	75. Ⓐ Ⓑ Ⓒ Ⓓ	105. Ⓐ Ⓑ Ⓒ Ⓓ
16. Ⓐ Ⓑ Ⓒ Ⓓ	46. Ⓐ Ⓑ Ⓒ Ⓓ	76. Ⓐ Ⓑ Ⓒ Ⓓ	106. Ⓐ Ⓑ Ⓒ Ⓓ
17. Ⓐ Ⓑ Ⓒ Ⓓ	47. Ⓐ Ⓑ Ⓒ Ⓓ	77. Ⓐ Ⓑ Ⓒ Ⓓ	107. Ⓐ Ⓑ Ⓒ Ⓓ
18. Ⓐ Ⓑ Ⓒ Ⓓ	48. Ⓐ Ⓑ Ⓒ Ⓓ	78. Ⓐ Ⓑ Ⓒ Ⓓ	108. Ⓐ Ⓑ Ⓒ Ⓓ
19. Ⓐ Ⓑ Ⓒ Ⓓ	49. Ⓐ Ⓑ Ⓒ Ⓓ	79. Ⓐ Ⓑ Ⓒ Ⓓ	109. Ⓐ Ⓑ Ⓒ Ⓓ
20. Ⓐ Ⓑ Ⓒ Ⓓ	50. Ⓐ Ⓑ Ⓒ Ⓓ	80. Ⓐ Ⓑ Ⓒ Ⓓ	110. Ⓐ Ⓑ Ⓒ Ⓓ
21. Ⓐ Ⓑ Ⓒ Ⓓ	51. Ⓐ Ⓑ Ⓒ Ⓓ	81. Ⓐ Ⓑ Ⓒ Ⓓ	111. Ⓐ Ⓑ Ⓒ Ⓓ
22. Ⓐ Ⓑ Ⓒ Ⓓ	52. Ⓐ Ⓑ Ⓒ Ⓓ	82. Ⓐ Ⓑ Ⓒ Ⓓ	112. Ⓐ Ⓑ Ⓒ Ⓓ
23. Ⓐ Ⓑ Ⓒ Ⓓ	53. Ⓐ Ⓑ Ⓒ Ⓓ	83. Ⓐ Ⓑ Ⓒ Ⓓ	113. Ⓐ Ⓑ Ⓒ Ⓓ
24. Ⓐ Ⓑ Ⓒ Ⓓ	54. Ⓐ Ⓑ Ⓒ Ⓓ	84. Ⓐ Ⓑ Ⓒ Ⓓ	114. Ⓐ Ⓑ Ⓒ Ⓓ
25. Ⓐ Ⓑ Ⓒ Ⓓ	55. Ⓐ Ⓑ Ⓒ Ⓓ	85. Ⓐ Ⓑ Ⓒ Ⓓ	115. Ⓐ Ⓑ Ⓒ Ⓓ
26. Ⓐ Ⓑ Ⓒ Ⓓ	56. Ⓐ Ⓑ Ⓒ Ⓓ	86. Ⓐ Ⓑ Ⓒ Ⓓ	116. Ⓐ Ⓑ Ⓒ Ⓓ
27. Ⓐ Ⓑ Ⓒ Ⓓ	57. Ⓐ Ⓑ Ⓒ Ⓓ	87. Ⓐ Ⓑ Ⓒ Ⓓ	117. Ⓐ Ⓑ Ⓒ Ⓓ
28. Ⓐ Ⓑ Ⓒ Ⓓ	58. Ⓐ Ⓑ Ⓒ Ⓓ	88. Ⓐ Ⓑ Ⓒ Ⓓ	118. Ⓐ Ⓑ Ⓒ Ⓓ
29. Ⓐ Ⓑ Ⓒ Ⓓ	59. Ⓐ Ⓑ Ⓒ Ⓓ	89. Ⓐ Ⓑ Ⓒ Ⓓ	119. Ⓐ Ⓑ Ⓒ Ⓓ
30. Ⓐ Ⓑ Ⓒ Ⓓ	60. Ⓐ Ⓑ Ⓒ Ⓓ	90. Ⓐ Ⓑ Ⓒ Ⓓ	120. Ⓐ Ⓑ Ⓒ Ⓓ

Time: 60 MINUTES

> **Directions:** In each of the following questions, you will find three initial terms and, in parentheses, four answer options designated *a, b, c,* and *d.* You are to select from the four answer options the one that *best* completes the analogy with the three initial terms. To record your answers, use the answer sheet provided.

1. CANARY : (*a.* red, *b.* blue, *c.* brown, *d.* yellow) :: POLAR BEAR : WHITE

2. SHIRT : WEAR :: BLOODY MARY : (*a.* kill, *b.* eat, *c.* dress, *d.* drink)

3. DAY : NIGHT :: DIURNAL : (*a.* nocturnal, *b.* eternal, *c.* vernal, *d.* external)

4. (*a.* Howard, *b.* Phineas, *c.* Ernest, *d.* Millard) : FILLMORE :: THOMAS : JEFFERSON

5. APRIL : 2 × 15 :: FEBRUARY : (*a.* 2 × 14, *b.* 2 × 15, *c.* 2 × 16, *d.* 2 × 17)

6. COMPARATIVE : (*a.* good, *b.* better, *c.* best, *d.* great) :: SUPERLATIVE : BEST

7. WINE : FRUIT :: BEER : (*a.* grape, *b.* hay, *c.* grain, *d.* lemon)

8. OTHELLO : JEALOUS :: HAMLET : (*a.* greedy, *b.* reflective, *c.* unintelligent, *d.* joyous)

9. (*a.* skirmish, *b.* war, *c.* disaster, *d.* truce) : BATTLE :: DRIZZLE : RAINFALL

10. SHETLAND : (*a.* monkey, *b.* lion, *c.* chicken, *d.* pony) :: HOLSTEIN : COW

11. (*a.* donkey, *b.* horse, *c.* bulldog, *d.* cougar) : DEMOCRAT :: ELEPHANT : REPUBLICAN

12. (*a.* green, *b.* red, *c.* blue, *d.* yellow) : CARDINAL :: ORANGE : ORIOLE

13. GERIATRICS : (*a.* old age, *b.* childhood, *c.* adolescence, *d.* adulthood) :: PEDIATRICS : CHILDHOOD

14. DOVE : PEACE :: (*a.* falcon, *b.* hawk, *c.* bluejay, *d.* vulture) : WAR

15. CHECK : (*a.* account, *b.* finesse, *c.* no trump, *d.* checkmate) :: TENTATIVE : FINAL

16. PHENOMENOLOGIST : HUSSERL :: EXISTENTIALIST : (*a.* Camus, *b.* Russell, *c.* Ryle, *d.* Quine)

17. GONDOLA : (*a.* canal, *b.* air, *c.* ocean, *d.* hangar) :: TRAIN : TRACK

18. (*a.* Babylonia, *b.* Phoenecia, *c.* Egypt, *d.* India) : PHARAOH :: ROMAN EMPIRE : EMPEROR

19. ACHILLES : TROJANS :: SAMSON : (*a.* Egyptians, *b.* Canaanites, *c.* Philistines, *d.* Moabites)

20. SPUMONI : TORTONI :: PARMESAN : (*a.* amontillado, *b.* mozzarella, *c.* manzanilla, *d.* maraschino)

21. HYPERBOLE : (*a.* geometric object, *b.* exaggeration, *c.* understatement, *d.* metaphysical object) :: HYPOCRITE : PRETENDER

22. MOOT COURT : HYPOTHETICAL CASES :: (*a.* kangaroo court, *b.* monkey court, *c.* cabbage court, *d.* dandelion court) : IRREGULAR PROCEDURES

23. ETHYL : METHYL :: GRAIN : (*a.* petrol, *b.* alcohol, *c.* sulfur, *d.* wood)

24. NEAPOLITAN : ITALY :: MUSCOVITE : (*a.* U.S.A., *b.* Hungary, *c.* Russia, *d.* Turkey)

25. APEX : SUMMIT :: ZENITH : (*a.* nadir, *b.* end, *c.* top, *d.* beginning)

26. (*a.* temporary, *b.* porous, *c.* impenetrable, *d.* permanent) : IMPERMEABLE :: COMMENCE : COMPLETE

27. PHILE : (*a.* love, *b.* hate, *c.* trust, *d.* distrust) :: PHOBE : FEAR

28. SOCRATES : (*a.* dagger, *b.* suffocation, *c.* noose, *d.* hemlock) :: GARFIELD : BULLET

29. OCHLOCRACY : MOB :: AUTOCRACY : (*a.* intellectual elite, *b.* rich, *c.* dictator, *d.* senate)

30. MOOR : PIN :: ROOM : (*a.* cue, *b.* nip, *c.* swim, *d.* thread)

31. FIREWATER : (*a.* acid, *b.* fire, *c.* liquor, *d.* lye) :: POTLATCH : FESTIVAL

32. (*a.* voluble, *b.* mum, *c.* lively, *d.* deaf) : MUTE :: SILENT : TACITURN

33. ATOM : MOLECULE :: CELL : (*a.* DNA, *b.* cytoplasm, *c.* tissue, *d.* ectoplasm)

34. AZURE : (*a.* blue, *b.* red, *c.* yellow, *d.* brown) :: MAGENTA : PURPLE

35. (*a.* quail, *b.* turkey, *c.* duck, *d.* pheasant) : DRAKE :: CHICKEN : ROOSTER

36. CIRRHOSIS : LIVER :: NEPHROSIS : (*a.* gallbladder, *b.* lung, *c.* pancreas, *d.* kidneys)

37. IMPEACH : HOUSE :: (*a.* protect, *b.* convict, *c.* rebut, *d.* remand) : SENATE

38. (*a.* metabolism, *b.* anabolism, *c.* menabolism, *d.* atabolism) : CONSTRUCTION :: CATABOLISM : DESTRUCTION

39. GALAHAD : (*a.* size, *b.* cowardice, *c.* nobility, *d.* lechery) :: GRISELDA : PATIENCE

40. INDUCTION : DEDUCTION :: (*a.* synthetic, *b.* inferential, *c.* a priori, *d.* a fortiori) : ANALYTIC

41. FLOOZY : DISREPUTABLE :: FLIBBERTIGIBBET : (*a.* immoral, *b.* unintelligent, *c.* mentally unbalanced, *d.* flighty)

42. RED : LONGEST :: (*a.* blue, *b.* yellow, *c.* violet, *d.* green) : SHORTEST

43. STABLE : TABLE :: START : (*a.* motion, *b.* horse, *c.* stop, *d.* tart)

44. IN VIVO : (*a.* in vitro, *b.* in moribus, *c.* in extremis, *d.* in vacuo) :: LIVING ORGANISM : TEST TUBE

45. f'' : f' :: (*a.* speed, *b.* distance, *c.* time, *d.* acceleration) : VELOCITY

46. UNICYCLE : BICYCLE :: BICYCLE : (*a.* locomotive, *b.* dirigible, *c.* motorcycle, *d.* automobile)

47. SPELUNKER : (*a.* deserts, *b.* caves, *c.* glaciers, *d.* forests) :: ALPINIST : MOUNTAINS

48. APOTHECARY : (*a.* doctor, *b.* pharmacist, *c.* drug addict, *d.* patient) :: LAWYER : ATTORNEY

49. (*a.* Daniel Boone, *b.* The Headless Horseman, *c.* Paul Bunyan, *d.* Tonto) : BABE :: LONE RANGER : SILVER

50. SCULPTOR : STATUE :: (*a.* composer, *b.* politician, *c.* psychiatrist, *d.* blacksmith) : FUGUE

51. JOURNEYMAN : APPRENTICE :: ASSOCIATE PROFESSOR : (*a.* professor, *b.* research associate, *c.* assistant professor, *d.* teacher)

52. HOLMES : (*a.* Baker, *b.* Bond, *c.* Watson, *d.* Moriarty) :: CRUSOE : FRIDAY

53. FILLY : MARE :: GIRL : (*a.* adult, *b.* human, *c.* mother, *d.* woman)

54. IMPECUNIOUS : (*a.* generous, *b.* poor, *c.* wealthy, *d.* greedy) :: OBESE : CORPULENT

55. WAR BETWEEN THE STATES : CIVIL WAR :: WAR TO END ALL WARS : (*a.* American Revolution, *b.* Hundred Years War, *c.* World War I, *d.* World War II)

56. HISTOLOGIST : TISSUE :: GRAPHOLOGIST : (*a.* maps, *b.* weather, *c.* handwriting, *d.* earthquakes)

57. (*a.* to play, *b.* will have played, *c.* playing, *d.* having played) : INFINITIVE :: WAITING : PARTICIPLE

58. PEDOMETER : (*a.* breaths, *b.* steps, *c.* heartbeats, *d.* salivations) :: PROTRACTOR : DEGREES

59. ANGLE OF INCIDENCE : 45° :: ANGLE OF REFLECTION : (*a.* 0°, *b.* 22.5°, *c.* 45°, *d.* 90°)

60. (*a.* professional, *b.* hireling, *c.* journeyman, *d.* tyro) : NOVICE :: AMATEUR : BEGINNER

61. (*a.* novella, *b.* trial, *c.* soliloquy, *d.* epic) : POETRY :: NOVEL : PROSE

62. CONGLOMERATION : AGGLOMERATION :: CLUSTER : (*a.* heap, *b.* dispersion, *c.* hierarchy, *d.* aggrandizement)

63. (*a.* Jackson, *b.* Jefferson, *c.* Howe, *d.* Taylor) : DAVIS :: SHERMAN : LINCOLN

64. UMBRAGE : (*a.* offense, *b.* defense, *c.* innocence, *d.* responsibility) :: GUILT : CULPABILITY

65. PERFECT : PREFECT :: FLAWLESS : (*a.* caretaker, *b.* government official, *c.* refectory, *d.* preface)

66. DOZEN : 12 :: BAKER'S DOZEN : (*a.* 8, *b.* 11, *c.* 13, *d.* 16)

67. (*a.* tawdry, *b.* dehiscent, *c.* seraphic, *d.* edacious) : GAUDY :: NADIR : BOTTOM

68. PLUTO : (*a.* Hades, *b.* Thanatos, *c.* heaven, *d.* purgatory) :: SATAN : HELL

69. DEMONSTRATE : SHOW :: FORSWEAR : (*a.* promise, *b.* curse, *c.* renounce, *d.* conceal)

70. SHEEP : SHEEP :: (*a.* rhinocerii, *b.* rhinoceres, *c.* rhinoceroses, *d.* rhinocerae) : RHINOCEROS

71. PRETEND : PORTEND :: FEIGN : (*a.* fain, *b.* act realistically, *c.* presage, *d.* look back on)

72. UNIVERSAL DONOR : (*a.* A, *b.* B, *c.* O, *d.* Rh⁻) :: UNIVERSAL RECIPIENT : AB

73. (*a.* landscape, *b.* portrait, *c.* madonna, *d.* still life) : CLAUDE LORRAIN :: CARICATURE : HONORÉ DAUMIER

74. BRUNET : DARK BROWN :: HOARY : (*a.* red, *b.* white, *c.* black, *d.* blonde)

75. POINT : LINE :: LINE : (*a.* solid, *b.* plane, *c.* hypersphere, *d.* polygon)

76. LA BOHEME : PUCCINI :: LA TRAVIATA : (*a.* Berlioz, *b.* Menotti, *c.* Verdi, *d.* Rossini)

77. PESETA : SPANIARDS :: SHEKEL : (*a.* Chinese, *b.* Israelis, *c.* French, *d.* Indians)

78. (*a.* Declaration of Independence, *b.* Articles of Confederation, *c.* Declaration of Rights and Grievances, *d.* Townshend Acts) : U.S. CONSTITUTION :: LEAGUE OF NATIONS : UNITED NATIONS

79. MILLIMETER : CENTIMETER :: CENTIMETER : (*a.* decimeter, *b.* meter, *c.* decameter, *d.* kilometer)

80. ENSIGN : NAVY :: (*a.* private, *b.* sergeant, *c.* second lieutenant, *d.* colonel) : ARMY

81. COLT : REVOLVER :: NOBEL : (*a.* A-bomb, *b.* tear gas, *c.* rifle, *d.* dynamite)

82. HYDRATED : WATER :: ORGANIC : (*a.* hydrogen, *b.* nitrogen, *c.* oxygen, *d.* carbon)

83. (*a.* doctors, *b.* officers, *c.* clergymen, *d.* saboteurs) : FIFTH COLUMN :: SPIES : INTELLIGENCE

84. PING-PONG : BADMINTON :: TENNIS : (*a.* lacrosse, *b.* football, *c.* handball, *d.* soccer)

85. (*a.* Aegisthus, *b.* Priam, *c.* Agamemnon, *d.* Theseus) : PARIS :: DAEDALUS : ICARUS

86. BLACKSTONE : (*a.* medicine, *b.* politics, *c.* law, *d.* teaching) :: ROBERTS : PARLIAMENTARY PROCEDURE

87. WIFE OF BATH : (*a.* Chaucer, *b.* Milton, *c.* Wordsworth, *d.* Spenser) :: BELINDA : POPE

88. SHAARA : CIVIL WAR :: (*a.* Plutarch, *b.* Thucydides, *c.* Herodotus, *d.* Pliny the Elder) : PELOPONNESIAN WAR

89. JEHOVAH'S WITNESSES : RUSSELL :: MORMONS : (*a.* Young, *b.* Smith, *c.* Thomas, *d.* Kirby)

90. 10 : OCTAL :: (*a.* 1, *b.* 1000, *c.* 111, *d.* 101) : BINARY

91. NEW JERSEY : THIRD :: (*a.* Virginia, *b.* New York, *c.* Delaware, *d.* New Hampshire) : FIRST

92. URIAH HEEP : HYPOCRITICALLY HUMBLE : WILKINS MICAWBER : (*a.* poor but optimistic, *b.* poor and pessimistic, *c.* rich and optimistic, *d.* rich but pessimistic)

93. ABBOTT : FLATLAND :: DANTE : (*a.* China, *b.* Purgatory, *c.* Never-Never Land, *d.* Moonland)

94. (*a.* catharsis, *b.* tragedy, *c.* bathos, *d.* ethos) UNIVERSAL :: PATHOS : PERSONAL

95. CANTOR : RABBI :: MUEZZIN : (*a.* minaret, *b.* guru, *c.* Brahmin, *d.* imam)

96. ORPHEUS : RETURN OF EURYDICE TO HADES :: WIFE OF LOT : (*a.* transformation into a star, *b.* return to Sodom, *c.* transformation into a pillar of salt, *d.* return to Canaan)

97. CENTIGRADE : 100 :: KELVIN : (*a.* 132, *b.* 100, *c.* 0, *d.* 373)

98. LA GIACONDA : (*a.* Mona Lisa, *b.* Pietà, *c.* Madonna, *d.* Venus de Milo) :: ARRANGEMENT IN BLACK AND GRAY : WHISTLER'S MOTHER

99. EMPIRICIST : UTILITARIAN :: HUME : (*a.* Spinoza, *b.* Leibnitz, *c.* Kant, *d.* Mill)

100. BLOOMFIELD : SURFACE STRUCTURE :: (*a.* Whorf, *b.* Sapir, *c.* Skinner, *d.* Chomsky) : DEEP STRUCTURE

101. GERMANIC : EUROPE :: (*a.* Swahili, *b.* Bantu, *c.* Zulu, *d.* Nigerian) : AFRICA

102. EVAPORATE : (*a.* freeze, *b.* melt, *c.* dehydrate, *d.* condense) :: VAPOR : SOLID

103. POSITION : VELOCITY :: VELOCITY : (*a.* speed, *b.* acceleration, *c.* torque, *d.* jerk)

104. TESTOSTERONE : HORMONE :: NEURON : (*a.* brain, *b.* dendrite, *c.* tissue, *d.* cell)

105. 1066 : BATTLE OF HASTINGS :: 1588 : (*a.* defeat of Napoleon, *b.* King Philip's War, *c.* defeat of the Spanish Armada, *d.* establishment of Jamestown)

106. PSYCHOSOCIAL STAGES : (*a.* Erickson, *b.* Freud, *c.* Chomsky, *d.* Lewin) :: DEVELOPMENTAL STAGES : PIAGET

107. HIP : PELVIS:: (*a.* shoulder blade, *b.* kneecap, *c.* jaw, *d.* cranium) : MANDIBLE

108. TANTALUS : SUSTENANCE :: SISYPHUS : (*a.* food, *b.* mobility, *c.* oxygen, *d.* rest)

109. (*a.* tsetse fly, *b.* snail, *c.* roundworm, *d.* housefly) : SLEEPING SICKNESS :: MOSQUITO : MALARIA

110. RICE : CHRISTOPHER :: (*a.* Kissinger, *b.* Christopher, *c.* Shultz, *d.* Baker III) : EAGLEBURG

111. (*a.* Mussolini, *b.* Carbonari, *c.* Ciampi, *d.* Virgil) : ITALY :: HIROHITO : JAPAN

112. VIRILE : FERAL :: ENERGETIC : (*a.* potent, *b.* tame, *c.* angry, *d.* wild)

113. EVA PERON : ARGENTINA :: IMELDA MARCOS : (*a.* Indonesia, *b.* Portugal, *c.* The Philippines, *d.* Spain)

114. (*a.* Rudyard Kipling, *b.* Salman Rushdie, *c.* Chinua Achebe, *d.* Graham Greene) : INDIA :: JOSEPH CONRAD : THE CONGO

115. MARY ANN CROSS : (*a.* Jane Eyre, *b.* Sense and Sensibility, *c.* Virginia Woolf, *d.* Middlemarch) :: SAMUEL CLEMENS : TOM SAWYER

116. TITANIC : ATLANTIC OCEAN :: EDMUND FITZGERALD : (*a.* Pacific Ocean, *b.* Lake Superior, *c.* Lake Michigan, *d.* Indian Ocean)

117. MURINE : RODENT :: (*a.* ursine, *b.* lupine, *c.* equine, *d.* vulpine) : FOX

118. (*a.* Sancho Panza, *b.* Tuesday, *c.* Don Quixote, *d.* Candide) : CERVANTES :: FRIDAY : DEFOE

119. SAILING: (*a.* trim, *b.* batten, *c.* jibe, *d.* turnbuckle) :: SKIING : SLALOM

120. NaCl : SALT :: NH_3 : (*a.* bleach, *b.* pepper, *c.* baking soda, *d.* ammonia)

1.	D	31.	C	61.	D	91.	C
2.	D	32.	B	62.	A	92.	A
3.	A	33.	C	63.	A	93.	B
4.	D	34.	A	64.	A	94.	D
5.	A	35.	C	65.	B	95.	D
6.	B	36.	D	66.	C	96.	C
7.	C	37.	B	67.	A	97.	D
8.	B	38.	B	68.	A	98.	A
9.	A	39.	C	69.	C	99.	D
10.	D	40.	A	70.	C	100.	D
11.	A	41.	D	71.	C	101.	B
12.	B	42.	C	72.	C	102.	A
13.	A	43.	D	73.	A	103.	B
14.	B	44.	A	74.	B	104.	D
15.	D	45.	D	75.	B	105.	C
16.	A	46.	D	76.	C	106.	A
17.	A	47.	B	77.	B	107.	C
18.	C	48.	B	78.	B	108.	D
19.	C	49.	C	79.	A	109.	A
20.	B	50.	A	80.	C	110.	A
21.	B	51.	C	81.	D	111.	A
22.	A	52.	C	82.	D	112.	D
23.	D	53.	D	83.	D	113.	C
24.	C	54.	B	84.	A	114.	A
25.	C	55.	C	85.	B	115.	D
26.	B	56.	C	86.	C	116.	B
27.	A	57.	A	87.	A	117.	D
28.	D	58.	B	88.	B	118.	A
29.	C	59.	C	89.	B	119.	C
30.	B	60.	D	90.	B	120.	D

ANSWER EXPLANATIONS FOR PRACTICE TEST 10

> In the following, explanations concerning the correct responses are in roman font. Explanations regarding distracters (incorrect responses) that are not self-explaining or could be misinterpreted are in italics in order to highlight the explanations of the answers that are correct.

1. CANARY : (*a.* red, *b.* blue, *c.* brown, ***d.* yellow**) :: POLAR BEAR : WHITE

    (d) A canary is usually yellow; a polar bear is generally white.

2. SHIRT : WEAR :: BLOODY MARY : (*a.* kill, *b.* eat, *c.* dress, ***d.* drink**)

    (d) One wears a shirt; one drinks a Bloody Mary.

3. DAY : NIGHT :: DIURNAL : (***a.* nocturnal**, *b.* eternal, *c.* vernal, *d.* external)

    (a) Diurnal refers to the daytime, while nocturnal refers to the nighttime. Eternal means "endless"; vernal means "youthful"; external means "outward."

4. (*a.* Howard, *b.* Phineas, *c.* Ernest, ***d.* Millard**) : FILLMORE :: THOMAS : JEFFERSON

    (d) Millard Fillmore and Thomas Jefferson were both presidents of the United States.

5. APRIL : 2×15 :: FEBRUARY : (***a.* 2×14**, *b.* 2×15, *c.* 2×16, *d.* 2×17)

    (a) April has 2×15, or 30 days; February outside of Leap Years has 2×14, or 28 days.

6. COMPARATIVE : (*a.* good, ***b.* better**, *c.* best, *d.* great) :: SUPERLATIVE : BEST

    (b) Better is the comparative form and best the superlative form of the adjective good.

7. WINE : FRUIT :: BEER : (*a.* grape, *b.* hay, ***c.* grain**, *d.* lemon)

    (c) Wine is fermented fruit; beer is fermented grain.

8. OTHELLO : JEALOUS :: HAMLET : (*a.* greedy, ***b.* reflective**, *c.* unintelligent, *d.* joyous)

    (b) In the respective Shakespearean plays in which they appear, Othello is a jealous character and Hamlet a reflective one.

9. (***a.* skirmish**, *b.* war, *c.* disaster, *d.* truce) : BATTLE :: DRIZZLE : RAINFALL

    (a) A skirmish is a minor battle; a drizzle is a minor rainfall.

10. SHETLAND : (*a.* monkey, *b.* lion, *c.* chicken, ***d.* pony**) :: HOLSTEIN : COW

    (d) A Shetland is a type of pony; a Holstein is a type of cow.

11. (***a.* donkey**, *b.* horse, *c.* bulldog, *d.* cougar) : DEMOCRAT :: ELEPHANT : REPUBLICAN

    (a) A donkey is the symbol of the Democratic Party, while an elephant is the symbol of the Republican Party.

12. (*a.* green, ***b.* red**, *c.* blue, *d.* yellow) : CARDINAL :: ORANGE : ORIOLE

    (b) A cardinal is red; an oriole is orange.

13. GERIATRICS : (***a.* old age**, *b.* childhood, *c.* adolescence, *d.* adulthood) :: PEDIATRICS : CHILDHOOD

    (a) Geriatrics is the branch of medicine dealing with old age; pediatrics is the branch of medicine dealing with childhood.

14. DOVE : PEACE :: (*a.* falcon, ***b.* hawk**, *c.* bluejay, *d.* vulture) : WAR

    (b) A dove is a symbol of peace; a hawk is a symbol of war.

15. CHECK : (*a.* account, *b.* finesse, *c.* no trump. ***d.* checkmate**) :: TENTATIVE : FINAL

    (d) In the game of chess, a king is in tentative danger when in check, and in final danger when in checkmate.

16. PHENOMENOLOGIST : HUSSERL :: EXISTENTIALIST : (***a.* Camus**, *b.* Russell, *c.* Ryle, *d.* Quine)

    (a) In modern philosophy, Husserl is identified with the phenomenologist movement, Camus with the existentialist movement. *Gilbert Ryle is primarily known for his critique of Cartesian Dualism; Bertrand Russell was a founder of Analytic Philosophy; Willard Van Orman Quine was an analytic philosopher.*

17. GONDOLA : (***a.* canal**, *b.* air, *c.* ocean, *d.* hangar) :: TRAIN : TRACK

    (a) A gondola moves along a canal; a train moves along a track.

18. (*a.* Babylonia, *b.* Phoenecia, ***c.* Egypt**, *d.* India) : PHARAOH :: ROMAN EMPIRE : EMPEROR

    (c) In ancient times, Egypt was ruled by a pharaoh and the Roman Empire was ruled by an emperor.

19. ACHILLES : TROJANS :: SAMSON : (*a.* Egyptians, *b.* Canaanites, ***c.* Philistines**, *d.* Moabites)

    (c) Achilles fought against the Trojans, Samson against the Philistines. Samson is a biblical figure; Achilles is a figure from Greek mythology.

20. SPUMONI : TORTONI :: PARMESAN : (*a.* amontillado, ***b.* mozzarella**, *c.* manzanilla, *d.* maraschino)

    (b) Spumoni and tortoni are both Italian ice-cream desserts; Parmesan and mozzarella are both Italian cheeses.

21. HYPERBOLE : (*a.* geometric object, ***b.* exaggeration**, *c.* understatement, *d.* metaphysical object) :: HYPOCRITE : PRETENDER

    (b) A hyperbole is an exaggeration; a hypocrite is a pretender.

22. MOOT COURT : HYPOTHETICAL CASES :: (***a.* kangaroo court**, *b.* monkey court, *c.* cabbage court, *d.* dandelion court) : IRREGULAR PROCEDURES

    (a) A moot court tries hypothetical cases; a kangaroo court exhibits irregular procedures.

23. ETHYL : METHYL :: GRAIN : (*a.* petrol, *b.* alcohol, *c.* sulfur, ***d.* wood**)

    (d) Ethyl alcohol is grain alcohol; methyl alcohol is wood alcohol.

24. NEAPOLITAN : ITALY :: MUSCOVITE : (*a.* U.S.A., *b.* Hungary, ***c.* Russia**, *d.* Turkey)

    (c) A Neapolitan is a resident of Naples, and thus lives in Italy. A Muscovite is a resident of Moscow, and therefore lives in Russia.

25. APEX : SUMMIT :: ZENITH : (*a.* nadir, *b.* end, ***c.* top**, *d.* beginning)

    (c) Apex, summit, zenith, and top are all synonyms. The nadir is the point directly below the observer directly opposite the zenith.

26. (*a.* temporary, ***b.* porous**, *c.* impenetrable, *d.* permanent) : IMPERMEABLE :: COMMENCE : COMPLETE

    (b) Porous and impermeable are antonyms, as are commence and complete.

27. PHILE : (***a.* love**, *b.* hate, *c.* trust, *d.* distrust) :: PHOBE : FEAR

    (a) *-phile* is a suffix denoting love for something, while *-phobe* is a suffix denoting fear of something. Both suffixes are derived from the Greek language.

28. SOCRATES : (*a.* dagger, *b.* suffocation, *c.* noose, ***d.* hemlock**) :: GARFIELD : BULLET

(d) Socrates died from drinking hemlock, Garfield from being shot with a bullet.

29. OCHLOCRACY : MOB :: AUTOCRACY : (*a.* intellectual elite, *b.* rich, ***c.* dictator**, *d.* senate)

(c) Ochlocracy is rule by a mob; autocracy is rule by a single dictator.

30. MOOR : PIN :: ROOM : (*a.* cue, ***b.* nip**, *c.* swim, *d.* thread)

(b) Room is moor spelled backward; nip is pin spelled backward.

31. FIREWATER : (*a.* acid, *b.* fire, ***c.* liquor**, *d.* lye) :: POTLATCH : FESTIVAL

(c) Potlatch was an Indian name for a winter festival; firewater was an Indian name for liquor.

32. (*a.* voluble, ***b.* mum**, *c.* lively, *d.* deaf) : MUTE :: SILENT : TACITURN

(b) Mum and mute are synonyms, as are silent and taciturn.

33. ATOM : MOLECULE :: CELL : (*a.* DNA, *b.* cytoplasm, ***c.* tissue**, *d.* ectoplasm)

(c) Atoms combine to form molecules. Cells combine to form tissue.

34. AZURE : (***a.* blue**, *b.* red, *c.* yellow, *d.* brown) :: MAGENTA : PURPLE

(a) Azure is a shade of blue; magenta is a shade of purple.

35. (*a.* quail, *b.* turkey, ***c.* duck**, *d.* pheasant) : DRAKE :: CHICKEN : ROOSTER

(c) A drake is a male duck; a rooster is a male chicken.

36. CIRRHOSIS : LIVER :: NEPHROSIS : (*a.* gallbladder, *b.* lung, *c.* pancreas, ***d.* kidneys**)

(d) Cirrhosis is a disease that usually strikes the liver; nephrosis is a disease of the kidneys. In cirrhosis, scar tissue replaces the healthy tissue in the liver impairing normal functioning of the liver. There are many causes, for example, alcoholism or hepatitis. Nephrosis is a non-inflammatory disease that may manifest itself, for example, in low albumin level and high cholesterol level in the blood. *A disease of the gallbladder is gallstones; gallstones are crystalline bodies that form when the fluid in the gallbladder hardens. The pancreas stores digestive enzymes; therefore, it may be very difficult if it gets injured or punctured. A disease of the lung is asthma, whereby the airways constrict and become inflamed, leading to wheezing and troubled breathing.*

37. IMPEACH : HOUSE :: (*a.* protect, ***b.* convict**, *c.* rebut, *d.* remand) : SENATE

(b) The House has the power to impeach the President, while the Senate has the power to convict him or her. Impeachment is the first stage in the process of removing a government official. It is a legal statement of charges. The second step is conviction, in which the Senate tries the accused. A two-third majority is required for conviction.

38. (*a.* metabolism, ***b.* anabolism**, *c.* menabolism, *d.* atabolism) : CONSTRUCTION :: CATABOLISM : DESTRUCTION

(b) Anabolism is constructive metabolism, while catabolism is destructive metabolism. Anabolism constructs molecules from smaller units and requires energy. Catabolism breaks down molecules into smaller units and releases energy. *Metabolism is the process by which living cells absorb nutrients and convert them into living substance.*

39. GALAHAD : (*a.* size, *b.* cowardice, ***c.* nobility**, *d.* lechery) :: GRISELDA : PATIENCE

(c) Galahad was the most virtuous knight in the Arthurian legend and was distinguished for his nobility. Griselda is a character from folklore who stands for patience.

40. INDUCTION : DEDUCTION :: (***a. synthetic***, *b.* inferential, *c.* a priori, *d.* a fortiori) : ANALYTIC

   (a) Induction is a synthetic form of thinking, while deduction is an analytic form of thinking. Synthetic thinking involves the combination of several ideas into one whole. Analytic thinking involves the separation of a whole into its parts. *Inferential thinking is reasoning that is based on circumstantial evidence (rather than observations) in order to make a logical judgment.* A priori *means that something is derived by logic without need of observed facts.* A fortiori *means "for a stronger reason."*

41. FLOOZY : DISREPUTABLE :: FLIBBERTIGIBBET : (*a.* immoral, *b.* unintelligent, *c.* mentally unbalanced, ***d.* flighty**)

   (d) A floozy is disreputable, while a flibbertigibbet is flighty.

42. RED : LONGEST :: (*a.* blue, *b.* yellow, ***c.* violet**, *d.* green) : SHORTEST

   (c) Red light waves are the longest in the spectrum; violet waves, the shortest. *The order from the shortest to the longest wavelength is violet, blue, green, yellow, orange, and red.*

43. STABLE : TABLE :: START : (*a.* motion, *b.* horse, *c.* stop, ***d.* tart**)

   (d) The word table is the same as the word stable, but without the initial *s*. Similarly, the word tart is the same as the word start, again without the initial *s*.

44. IN VIVO : (***a.* in vitro**, *b.* in moribus, *c.* in extremis, *d.* in vacuo) :: LIVING ORGANISM : TEST TUBE

   (a) Something grown *in vivo* is grown inside a living organism. Something grown *in vitro* is grown inside a test tube. In vacuo *means "in an empty space";* in moribus *means "in a dead object";* in extremis *means "to the furthest degree."*

45. f'' : f' :: (*a.* speed, *b.* distance, *c.* time, ***d.* acceleration**) : VELOCITY

   (d) The second derivative of a function, f'', can be used to determine acceleration. The first derivative, f', can be used to determine velocity.

46. UNICYCLE : BICYCLE :: BICYCLE : (*a.* locomotive, *b.* dirigible, *c.* motorcycle, ***d.* automobile**)

   (d) A bicycle has twice as many wheels as a unicycle. An automobile has twice as many wheels as a bicycle.

47. SPELUNKER : (*a.* deserts, ***b.* caves**, *c.* glaciers, *d.* forests) :: ALPINIST : MOUNTAINS

   (b) A spelunker explores caves; an alpinist climbs mountains.

48. APOTHECARY : (*a.* doctor, ***b.* pharmacist**, *c.* drug addict, *d.* patient) :: LAWYER : ATTORNEY

   (b) An apothecary is a pharmacist; a lawyer is an attorney.

49. (*a.* Daniel Boone, *b.* The Headless Horseman, ***c.* Paul Bunyan**, *d.* Tonto) : BABE :: LONE RANGER : SILVER

   (c) Babe was an animal (ox) belonging to Paul Bunyan. Silver was an animal (horse) belonging to the Lone Ranger. Paul Bunyan was a legendary lumberjack who embodied frontier vitality in American folklore. *Daniel Boone (1734–1820), a pioneer and hunter, was one of the first American folk heroes. The Headless Horseman is a character from Washington Irving's short story "The Legend of Sleepy Hollow." Tonto was the Native American assistant of the Lone Ranger, both of whom are fictional characters who were created by George Trendle and Fran Striker.*

50. SCULPTOR : STATUE :: (***a.* composer**, *b.* politician, *c.* psychiatrist, *d.* blacksmith) : FUGUE

   (a) A statue is a work of art created by a sculptor; a fugue is a work of art created by a composer.

51. JOURNEYMAN : APPRENTICE :: ASSOCIATE PROFESSOR : (*a.* professor, *b.* research associate, ***c.* assistant professor**, *d.* teacher)

(c) In craft guilds, a journeyman is one step above an apprentice. In colleges and universities, an associate professor is one step above an assistant professor.

52. HOLMES : (*a.* Baker, *b.* Bond, ***c.* Watson**, *d.* Moriarty) :: CRUSOE : FRIDAY

(c) In their respective exploits, Holmes was assisted by Watson, Crusoe by Friday. James Bond is a fictitious British agent in a series of novels (later made into films) by Ian Fleming. 221B Baker Street is the street address at which Holmes' office was located. Moriarty was his mortal enemy, a mathematics professor but also a villain.

53. FILLY : MARE :: GIRL : (*a.* adult, *b.* human, *c.* mother, ***d.* woman**)

(d) A filly grows into a mare; a girl grows into a woman.

54. IMPECUNIOUS : (*a.* generous, ***b.* poor**, *c.* wealthy, *d.* greedy) :: OBESE : CORPULENT

(b) Impecunious and poor are synonyms, as are obese and corpulent.

55. WAR BETWEEN THE STATES : CIVIL WAR :: WAR TO END ALL WARS: (*a.* American Revolution, *b.* Hundred Years War, ***c.* World War I**, *d.* World War II)

(c) The Civil War is often called the War Between the States. World War I is often called the "War to end all wars."

56. HISTOLOGIST : TISSUE :: GRAPHOLOGIST : (*a.* maps, *b.* weather, ***c.* handwriting**, *d.* earthquakes)

(c) A histologist studies tissue; a graphologist studies handwriting.

57. (***a.* to play**, *b.* will have played, *c.* playing, *d.* having played) : INFINITIVE :: WAITING : PARTICIPLE

(a) To play is an infinitive; waiting is the present participle of *wait*.

58. PEDOMETER : (*a.* breaths, ***b.* steps**, *c.* heartbeats, *d.* salivations) :: PROTRACTOR : DEGREES

(b) A pedometer measures numbers of steps; a protractor measures numbers of degrees.

59. ANGLE OF INCIDENCE : 45° :: ANGLE OF REFLECTION : (*a.* 0°, *b.* 22.5°, ***c.* 45°**, *d.* 90°)

(c) If the angle of incidence of a light ray is 45°, its angle of reflection is also 45°.

60. (*a.* professional, *b.* hireling, *c.* journeyman, ***d.* tyro**) : NOVICE :: AMATEUR : BEGINNER

(d) Tyro, novice, amateur, and beginner are all synonymous.

61. (*a.* novella, *b.* trial, *c.* soliloquy, ***d.* epic**) : POETRY :: NOVEL : PROSE

(d) An epic is a form of poetry; a novel is a form of prose. *A novella is a form of prose as well, being shorter than a novel but longer than a novelette. A soliloquy is a form of dramatic monologue where the speaker is addressing himself. The Trial is a novel by Franz Kafka.*

62. CONGLOMERATION : AGGLOMERATION :: CLUSTER : (***a.* heap**, *b.* dispersion, *c.* hierarchy, *d.* aggrandizement)

(a) A conglomeration is a cluster; an agglomeration, a heap.

63. (***a.* Jackson**, *b.* Jefferson, *c.* Howe, *d.* Taylor) : DAVIS :: SHERMAN : LINCOLN

(a) Stonewall Jackson was a Confederate general under Jefferson Davis, while William Sherman was a Union general under Abraham Lincoln. *Thomas Jefferson (1743–1826) was the third president of the United States. Both Albion Howe (1818–1897) and George Taylor (1808–1862) were generals in the Union Army.*

64. UMBRAGE : (**a. offense**, b. defense, c. innocence, d. responsibility) :: GUILT : CULPABILITY
(a) Umbrage and offense are synonymous, as are guilt and culpability.

65. PERFECT : PREFECT :: FLAWLESS : (a. caretaker, **b. government official**, c. refectory, d. preface)
(b) Something that is perfect is flawless. A prefect is a government official.

66. DOZEN : 12 :: BAKER'S DOZEN : (a. 8, b. 11, **c. 13**, d. 16)
(c) There are 12 objects in a dozen, and 13 objects in a baker's dozen. The expression of a baker's dozen comes from 13th century England, where bakers could be severely punished if they were found to gyp their customers. Therefore, they often preferred to bake more items to ensure they would not betray their customers.

67. (**a. tawdry**, b. dehiscent, c. seraphic, d. edacious) : GAUDY :: NADIR : BOTTOM
(a) Tawdry and gaudy are synonyms, as are nadir and bottom.

68. PLUTO : (**a. Hades**, b. Thanatos, c. heaven, d. purgatory) :: SATAN : HELL
(a) According to Roman mythology, Pluto resided in Hades. According to certain Christian doctrine, Satan resides in hell. *Thanatos was the Greek personification of death. Heaven is the abode of God, angels, and the souls who received salvation. Purgatory is a Roman Catholic concept of a place for those who are ultimately destined to go to heaven but who need to be purged of their imperfections.*

69. DEMONSTRATE : SHOW :: FORSWEAR : (a. promise, b. curse, **c. renounce**, d. conceal)
(c) Demonstrate and show are synonyms, as are forswear and renounce.

70. SHEEP : SHEEP :: (a. rhinocerii, b. rhinoceres, **c. rhinoceroses**, d. rhinocerae) : RHINOCEROS
(c) Sheep is the plural form of sheep; rhinoceroses is the preferred plural form of rhinoceros.

71. PRETEND : PORTEND :: FEIGN : (a. fain, b. act realistically, **c. presage**, d. look back on)
(c) Pretend and feign are synonyms, as are portend and presage.

72. UNIVERSAL DONOR : (a. A, b. B, **c. O**, d. Rh⁻) :: UNIVERSAL RECIPIENT : AB
(c) People with blood type O are called universal donors because people with all blood types can receive their blood; people with blood type AB are called universal recipients because they can receive every blood type.

73. (**a. landscape**, b. portrait, c. madonna, d. still life) : CLAUDE LORRAIN :: CARICATURE : HONORÉ DAUMIER
(a) Claude Lorrain (ca. 1602–1682) is best known for his landscapes, Honoré Daumier (1808–1879) for his caricatures.

74. BRUNET : DARK BROWN :: HOARY : (a. red, **b. white**, c. black, d. blonde)
(b) Brunet coloring is dark brown, while hoary coloring is white.

75. POINT : LINE :: LINE : (a. solid, **b. plane**, c. hypersphere, d. polygon)
(b) An infinite collection of consecutive points forms a line. An infinite collection of consecutive lines forms a plane.

76. LA BOHEME : PUCCINI :: LA TRAVIATA : (a. Berlioz, b. Menotti, **c. Verdi**, d. Rossini)
(c) *La Boheme* is an opera composed by Puccini (1858–1924); *La Traviata* is an opera composed by Verdi (1813–1901).

77. PESETA : SPANIARDS :: SHEKEL : (*a.* Chinese, ***b.* Israelis**, *c.* French, *d.* Indians)

   (b) A peseta is a coin that was used by Spaniards; a shekel is a coin used by Israelis. The French used francs as currency; the Indians use rupees as a currency; the Chinese use yuans as a currency.

78. (*a.* Declaration of Independence, ***b.* Articles of Confederation**, *c.* Declaration of Rights and Grievances, *d.* Townshend Acts) : U.S. CONSTITUTION :: LEAGUE OF NATIONS : UNITED NATIONS

   (b) The U.S. Constitution replaced the Articles of Confederation. The United Nations replaced the League of Nations. *The Townshend Acts were passed by the British Parliament in 1767 to establish that Britain had the right to raise revenue and to tax the colonies. In 1774, the British Parliament passed the Coercive Acts in response to which the First Congress drafted the Declaration of Rights and Grievances, which declared that taxes imposed on British colonists were unconstitutional lest British colonists had consented. The Articles of Confederation (completed in 1781) were the first attempt at establishing a constitution of the alliance of the 13 independent states.*

79. MILLIMETER : CENTIMETER :: CENTIMETER : (***a.* decimeter**, *b.* meter, *c.* decameter, *d.* kilometer)

   (a) There are 10 millimeters in a centimeter, and 10 centimeters in a decimeter.

80. ENSIGN : NAVY :: (*a.* private, *b.* sergeant, ***c.* second lieutenant**, *d.* colonel) : ARMY

   (c) An ensign is the lowest ranking commissioned officer in the Navy; a second lieutenant is the lowest ranking commissioned officer in the Army.

81. COLT : REVOLVER :: NOBEL : (*a.* A-bomb, *b.* tear gas, *c.* rifle, ***d.* dynamite**)

   (d) Colt invented a type of revolver; Nobel invented dynamite.

82. HYDRATED : WATER :: ORGANIC : (*a.* hydrogen, *b.* nitrogen, *c.* oxygen, ***d.* carbon**)

   (d) A hydrated substance contains water; an organic substance contains carbon.

83. (*a.* doctors, *b.* officers, *c.* clergymen, ***d.* saboteurs**) : FIFTH COLUMN :: SPIES : INTELLIGENCE

   (d) During a war, saboteurs comprise a network that is often called a fifth column. Spies work in an intelligence network.

84. PING-PONG : BADMINTON :: TENNIS : (***a.* lacrosse**, *b.* football, *c.* handball, *d.* soccer)

   (a) The games of Ping-Pong, badminton, tennis, and lacrosse are all played with rackets.

85. (*a.* Aegisthus, ***b.* Priam**, *c.* Agamemnon, *d.* Theseus) : PARIS :: DAEDALUS : ICARUS

   (b) Priam was the father of Paris; Daedalus was the father of Icarus and tried to escape to Crete by flight. *Aegisthus was the son of Thyestes and of his daughter, Pelopia. Agamemnon was the the son of King Atreus of Mycenae and Queen Aerope. He was eventually murdered by his wife Clytemnestra. Theseus was a king of Athens.*

86. BLACKSTONE : (*a.* medicine, *b.* politics, ***c.* law**, *d.* teaching) :: ROBERTS : PARLIAMENTARY PROCEDURE

   (c) Blackstone is known for his work on law, Roberts for his work on parliamentary procedure.

87. WIFE OF BATH : (***a.* Chaucer**, *b.* Milton, *c.* Wordsworth, *d.* Spenser) :: BELINDA : POPE

   (a) The Wife of Bath is a literary character created by Geoffrey Chaucer for *The Wife of Bath's Tale*. Belinda is the name of a fictional character in Alexander Pope's *The Rape of the Lock*.

88. SHAARA : CIVIL WAR :: (*a.* Plutarch, ***b.* Thucydides**, *c.* Herodotus, *d.* Pliny the Elder) : PELOPONNESIAN WAR

(b) Shaara is known for his historical writing on the Civil War, particularly for his pulitzer-winning piece *The Killer Angels*, which was the inspiration for the 1993 film "Gettysburg"; Thucydides is known for his historical work on the Peloponnesian War (431–404 B.C.). *Plutarch was a Roman historian and wrote* Parallel Lives *and* Moralia. *Herodotus was a Greek historian who was the first to have a "scientific" approach to history. His most famous work is* The Histories. *Pliny the Elder was a Roman writer who wrote* Naturalis Historia.

89. JEHOVAH'S WITNESSES : RUSSELL :: MORMONS : (*a.* Young, ***b.* Smith**, *c.* Thomas, *d.* Kirby)

(b) The Jehovah's Witnesses sect was founded by Charles Russell; the Mormons were founded by Joseph Smith. *Brigham Young continued the movement following Smith's death.*

90. 10 : OCTAL :: (*a.* 1, ***b.* 1000**, *c.* 111, *d.* 101) : BINARY

(b) 10 in octal is equal to 1000 in binary; both are equal to 8 in conventional decimal notation.

91. NEW JERSEY : THIRD :: (*a.* Virginia, *b.* New York, ***c.* Delaware**, *d.* New Hampshire) : FIRST

(c) New Jersey was the third state to join the Union; Delaware was the first. *New Hampshire was the 9th state to join the Union, Virginia was 10th, and New York 11th.*

92. URIAH HEEP : HYPOCRITICALLY HUMBLE : WILKINS MICAWBER : (***a.* poor but optimistic**, *b.* poor and pessimistic, *c.* rich and optimistic, *d.* rich but pessimistic)

(a) In Charles Dickens' *David Copperfield*, Uriah Heep is a character who is hypocritically humble, while Wilkins Micawber is poor but optimistic.

93. ABBOTT : FLATLAND :: DANTE : (*a.* China, ***b.* Purgatory**, *c.* Never-Never Land, *d.* Moonland)

(b) Abbott wrote a narrative describing his travels in Flatland; Dante wrote *The Divine Comedy*, describing in the second part of the trilogy his travels in Purgatory.

94. (*a.* catharsis, *b.* tragedy, *c.* bathos, ***d.* ethos**) : UNIVERSAL :: PATHOS : PERSONAL

(d) Ethos describes universal elements in a work of art, while pathos describes personal ones.

95. CANTOR : RABBI :: MUEZZIN : (*a.* minaret, *b.* guru, *c.* Brahmin, ***d.* imam**)

(d) A cantor and a rabbi are both religious functionaries in the Jewish religion, while a muezzin and an imam are both functionaries in Islam. *Gurus are commonly found in the religions of Hinduism, Buddhism, and Sikhism. A minaret is the spire of a mosque. Brahmin is the highest of the four traditional social castes in India. The term today is used more broadly to refer to a charismatic leader with many followers.*

96. ORPHEUS : RETURN OF EURYDICE TO HADES :: WIFE OF LOT : (*a.* transformation into a star, *b.* return to Sodom, ***c.* transformation into a pillar of salt**, *d.* return to Canaan)

(c) As a result of Orpheus's looking back when he went to fetch her from the underworld, Eurydice was forced to return to Hades (Greek mythology). As a result of Lot's wife's looking back on Sodom, she was transformed into a pillar of salt (Book of Genesis in the Bible).

97. CENTIGRADE : 100 :: KELVIN : (*a.* 132, *b.* 100, *c.* 0, ***d.* 373**)

(d) The boiling point of water is 100° Centigrade, and (to the nearest unit) 373 Kelvin. Centigrade is an old-fashioned name for *Celsius*.

98. LA GIACONDA : (*a.* **Mona Lisa**, *b.* La Pietà, *c.* Madonna, *d.* Venus de Milo) :: ARRANGEMENT IN BLACK AND GRAY : WHISTLER'S MOTHER

(a) *La Giaconda* and *Mona Lisa* refer to the same painting by Leonardo da Vinci. *Arrangement in Black and Gray* and *Whistler's Mother* refer to the same painting by Whistler.

99. EMPIRICIST : UTILITARIAN :: HUME : (*a.* Spinoza, *b.* Leibnitz, *c.* Kant, **d. Mill**)

(d) Hume was an empiricist philosopher; Mill, a utilitarian philosopher. *Spinoza and Leibniz were rationalists. Kant tried with his work to build a bridge between empiricists and rationalists.*

100. BLOOMFIELD : SURFACE STRUCTURE :: (*a.* Whorf, *b.* Sapir, *c.* Skinner, **d. Chomsky**) : DEEP STRUCTURE

(d) In their respective linguistic analyses, Bloomfield theorized on the basis of surface structure, while Chomsky has theorized primarily on the basis of deep structure. *Benjamin Whorf was an American linguist who developed the theory of linguistic relativity. Together with Edward Sapir who was his teacher, he proposed that language affects thoughts (the Sapir-Whorf hypothesis). Burrhus F. Skinner was a psychologist who is known for his work on operant conditioning.*

101. GERMANIC : EUROPE :: (*a.* Swahili, **b. Bantu**, *c.* Zulu, *d.* Nigerian) : AFRICA

(b) Germanic languages are found throughout Europe. Bantu languages are found throughout Africa.

102. EVAPORATE : (*a.* **freeze**, *b.* melt, *c.* dehydrate, *d.* condense) :: VAPOR : SOLID

(a) To evaporate is to become vapor. To freeze is to become solid.

103. POSITION : VELOCITY :: VELOCITY : (*a.* speed, **b. acceleration**, *c.* torque, *d.* jerk)

(b) The measure of the rate of change of position is velocity just as the measure of the rate of change of velocity is acceleration.

104. TESTOSTERONE : HORMONE :: NEURON : (*a.* brain, *b.* dendrite, *c.* tissue, **d. cell**)

(d) Testosterone is one of many different types of hormones just as a neuron is one of many different types of cells.

105. 1066 : BATTLE OF HASTINGS :: 1588 : (*a.* defeat of Napoleon, *b.* King Philip's War, **c. defeat of the Spanish Armada**, *d.* establishment of Jamestown)

(c) The year 1066 was when the Battle of Hastings was fought, and 1588 was the year of the defeat of the Spanish Armada. *Napoleon's failed invasion of Russia took place in 1812. King Philip's War took place from 1675 to 1676. Jamestown, the first permanent English settlement in North America, was established in 1607.*

106. PSYCHOSOCIAL STAGES : (*a.* **Erickson**, *b.* Freud, *c.* Chomsky, *d.* Lewin) :: DEVELOPMENTAL STAGES : PIAGET

(a) This analogy is about theories of psychological stages. A series of psychosocial stages was proposed by Erickson. A series of developmental stages was proposed by Piaget. *Freud is famous for the development of psychoanalysis. Chomsky developed a theory of generative grammar; Lewin is considered one of the founders of social psychology.*

107. HIP : PELVIS :: (*a.* shoulder blade, *b.* kneecap, **c. jaw**, *d.* cranium) : MANDIBLE

(c) The name of the hipbone is the pelvis just as the name of the jawbone is the mandible.

108. TANTALUS : SUSTENANCE :: SISYPHUS : (*a.* food, *b.* mobility, *c.* oxygen, **d. rest**)

(d) In classical mythology, Hades denied Tantalus of sustenance and Sisyphus of rest.

109. (**a. tsetse fly**, *b.* snail, *c.* roundworm, *d.* housefly) : SLEEPING SICKNESS :: MOSQUITO : MALARIA

(a) The tsetse fly is known to spread sleeping sickness, while the mosquito passes malaria.

110. RICE : CHRISTOPHER :: (**a. Kissinger**, *b.* Christopher, *c.* Shultz, *d.* Baker III) : EAGLEBURG

(a) Rice and Kissinger were both political scientists who became Secretaries of State. Christopher and Eagleburg were both diplomats who became Secretaries of State. *Shultz was an economist, and Baker III was a lawyer.*

111. (**a. Mussolini**, *b.* Carbonari, *c.* Ciampi, *d.* Virgil) : ITALY :: HIROHITO : JAPAN

(a) During World War II, Mussolini was the leader of Italy while Hirohito was the leader of Japan. *The Carbonari were a secret brotherhood founded in the early 19th century in Italy to overthrow the government. Carlo Ciampi was President of Italy from 1999 to 2006. Virgil was a Roman poet (70 B.C.–19 B.C.).*

112. VIRILE : FERAL :: ENERGETIC : (*a.* potent, *b.* tame, *c.* angry, **d. wild**)

(d) Virile means energetic, while feral means wild and undomesticated.

113. EVA PERON : ARGENTINA :: IMELDA MARCOS : (*a.* Indonesia, *b.* Portugal, **c. The Philippines**, *d.* Spain)

(c) Eva Peron was a world-famous first lady of Argentina, and Imelda Marcos was a world-famous first lady of The Philippines.

114. (**a. Rudyard Kipling**, *b.* Salman Rushdie, *c.* Chinua Achebe, *d.* Graham Greene) : INDIA :: JOSEPH CONRAD : THE CONGO

(a) Rudyard Kipling was born in and wrote fictional literature set in British Colonial India. Joseph Conrad traveled to and wrote fictional literature set in The Congo. *Salman Rushdie is a British-Indian writer who faced death threats by Muslims after the publication of* The Satanic Verses. *Chinua Achebe is a Nigerian writer best known for* Things Fall Apart. *Graham Greene is an English writer whose works often revolved around Catholicism.*

115. MARY ANN CROSS : (*a.* Jane Eyre, *b.* Sense and Sensibility, *c.* Virginia Woolf, **d. Middlemarch**) :: SAMUEL CLEMENS : TOM SAWYER

(d) Mary Ann Cross used a pen name (George Eliot) in writing her famous novel, *Middlemarch*. Samuel Clemens used a pen name (Mark Twain) in writing his famous novel, *The Adventures of Tom Sawyer*.

116. TITANIC : ATLANTIC OCEAN :: EDMUND FITZGERALD : (*a.* Pacific Ocean, **b. Lake Superior**, *c.* Lake Michigan, *d.* Indian Ocean)

(b) The *Titanic* was a ship that sank in the Atlantic Ocean, and the *Edmund Fitzgerald* was a ship that sank in Lake Superior. A song by Gordon Lightfoot has immortalized the latter.

117. MURINE : RODENT :: (*a.* ursine, *b.* lupine, *c.* equine, **d. vulpine**) : FOX

(d) The word murine describes something that is in some way like or relating to a rodent and the word vulpine describes something that is in some way like or relating to a fox. *Ursine describes something that is like a bear. Lupine describes something that is like a wolf, and equine describes something that is like a horse.*

118. (**a. Sancho Panza**, *b.* Tuesday, *c.* Don Quixote, *d.* Candide) : CERVANTES :: FRIDAY : DEFOE

(a) Sancho Panza was the loyal friend of the title character in Cervantes's novel *Don Quixote*. Friday was the loyal friend of the title character in Defoe's *Robinson Crusoe*.

119. SAILING: (*a*. trim, *b*. batten, *c*. **jibe**, *d*. turnbuckle) :: SKIING : SLALOM

(c) To turn back and forth in a zigzag through the water while sailing is called to jibe. To do the same motion while downhill skiing is called to slalom.

120. NaCl : SALT :: NH_3 : (*a*. bleach, *b*. pepper, *c*. baking soda, *d*. **ammonia**)

(d) NaCl is the chemical formula for household salt, while NH_3 is the chemical formula for household ammonia.

ANSWER SHEET
Practice Test 11

1. Ⓐ Ⓑ Ⓒ Ⓓ
2. Ⓐ Ⓑ Ⓒ Ⓓ
3. Ⓐ Ⓑ Ⓒ Ⓓ
4. Ⓐ Ⓑ Ⓒ Ⓓ
5. Ⓐ Ⓑ Ⓒ Ⓓ
6. Ⓐ Ⓑ Ⓒ Ⓓ
7. Ⓐ Ⓑ Ⓒ Ⓓ
8. Ⓐ Ⓑ Ⓒ Ⓓ
9. Ⓐ Ⓑ Ⓒ Ⓓ
10. Ⓐ Ⓑ Ⓒ Ⓓ
11. Ⓐ Ⓑ Ⓒ Ⓓ
12. Ⓐ Ⓑ Ⓒ Ⓓ
13. Ⓐ Ⓑ Ⓒ Ⓓ
14. Ⓐ Ⓑ Ⓒ Ⓓ
15. Ⓐ Ⓑ Ⓒ Ⓓ
16. Ⓐ Ⓑ Ⓒ Ⓓ
17. Ⓐ Ⓑ Ⓒ Ⓓ
18. Ⓐ Ⓑ Ⓒ Ⓓ
19. Ⓐ Ⓑ Ⓒ Ⓓ
20. Ⓐ Ⓑ Ⓒ Ⓓ
21. Ⓐ Ⓑ Ⓒ Ⓓ
22. Ⓐ Ⓑ Ⓒ Ⓓ
23. Ⓐ Ⓑ Ⓒ Ⓓ
24. Ⓐ Ⓑ Ⓒ Ⓓ
25. Ⓐ Ⓑ Ⓒ Ⓓ
26. Ⓐ Ⓑ Ⓒ Ⓓ
27. Ⓐ Ⓑ Ⓒ Ⓓ
28. Ⓐ Ⓑ Ⓒ Ⓓ
29. Ⓐ Ⓑ Ⓒ Ⓓ
30. Ⓐ Ⓑ Ⓒ Ⓓ

31. Ⓐ Ⓑ Ⓒ Ⓓ
32. Ⓐ Ⓑ Ⓒ Ⓓ
33. Ⓐ Ⓑ Ⓒ Ⓓ
34. Ⓐ Ⓑ Ⓒ Ⓓ
35. Ⓐ Ⓑ Ⓒ Ⓓ
36. Ⓐ Ⓑ Ⓒ Ⓓ
37. Ⓐ Ⓑ Ⓒ Ⓓ
38. Ⓐ Ⓑ Ⓒ Ⓓ
39. Ⓐ Ⓑ Ⓒ Ⓓ
40. Ⓐ Ⓑ Ⓒ Ⓓ
41. Ⓐ Ⓑ Ⓒ Ⓓ
42. Ⓐ Ⓑ Ⓒ Ⓓ
43. Ⓐ Ⓑ Ⓒ Ⓓ
44. Ⓐ Ⓑ Ⓒ Ⓓ
45. Ⓐ Ⓑ Ⓒ Ⓓ
46. Ⓐ Ⓑ Ⓒ Ⓓ
47. Ⓐ Ⓑ Ⓒ Ⓓ
48. Ⓐ Ⓑ Ⓒ Ⓓ
49. Ⓐ Ⓑ Ⓒ Ⓓ
50. Ⓐ Ⓑ Ⓒ Ⓓ
51. Ⓐ Ⓑ Ⓒ Ⓓ
52. Ⓐ Ⓑ Ⓒ Ⓓ
53. Ⓐ Ⓑ Ⓒ Ⓓ
54. Ⓐ Ⓑ Ⓒ Ⓓ
55. Ⓐ Ⓑ Ⓒ Ⓓ
56. Ⓐ Ⓑ Ⓒ Ⓓ
57. Ⓐ Ⓑ Ⓒ Ⓓ
58. Ⓐ Ⓑ Ⓒ Ⓓ
59. Ⓐ Ⓑ Ⓒ Ⓓ
60. Ⓐ Ⓑ Ⓒ Ⓓ

61. Ⓐ Ⓑ Ⓒ Ⓓ
62. Ⓐ Ⓑ Ⓒ Ⓓ
63. Ⓐ Ⓑ Ⓒ Ⓓ
64. Ⓐ Ⓑ Ⓒ Ⓓ
65. Ⓐ Ⓑ Ⓒ Ⓓ
66. Ⓐ Ⓑ Ⓒ Ⓓ
67. Ⓐ Ⓑ Ⓒ Ⓓ
68. Ⓐ Ⓑ Ⓒ Ⓓ
69. Ⓐ Ⓑ Ⓒ Ⓓ
70. Ⓐ Ⓑ Ⓒ Ⓓ
71. Ⓐ Ⓑ Ⓒ Ⓓ
72. Ⓐ Ⓑ Ⓒ Ⓓ
73. Ⓐ Ⓑ Ⓒ Ⓓ
74. Ⓐ Ⓑ Ⓒ Ⓓ
75. Ⓐ Ⓑ Ⓒ Ⓓ
76. Ⓐ Ⓑ Ⓒ Ⓓ
77. Ⓐ Ⓑ Ⓒ Ⓓ
78. Ⓐ Ⓑ Ⓒ Ⓓ
79. Ⓐ Ⓑ Ⓒ Ⓓ
80. Ⓐ Ⓑ Ⓒ Ⓓ
81. Ⓐ Ⓑ Ⓒ Ⓓ
82. Ⓐ Ⓑ Ⓒ Ⓓ
83. Ⓐ Ⓑ Ⓒ Ⓓ
84. Ⓐ Ⓑ Ⓒ Ⓓ
85. Ⓐ Ⓑ Ⓒ Ⓓ
86. Ⓐ Ⓑ Ⓒ Ⓓ
87. Ⓐ Ⓑ Ⓒ Ⓓ
88. Ⓐ Ⓑ Ⓒ Ⓓ
89. Ⓐ Ⓑ Ⓒ Ⓓ
90. Ⓐ Ⓑ Ⓒ Ⓓ

91. Ⓐ Ⓑ Ⓒ Ⓓ
92. Ⓐ Ⓑ Ⓒ Ⓓ
93. Ⓐ Ⓑ Ⓒ Ⓓ
94. Ⓐ Ⓑ Ⓒ Ⓓ
95. Ⓐ Ⓑ Ⓒ Ⓓ
96. Ⓐ Ⓑ Ⓒ Ⓓ
97. Ⓐ Ⓑ Ⓒ Ⓓ
98. Ⓐ Ⓑ Ⓒ Ⓓ
99. Ⓐ Ⓑ Ⓒ Ⓓ
100. Ⓐ Ⓑ Ⓒ Ⓓ
101. Ⓐ Ⓑ Ⓒ Ⓓ
102. Ⓐ Ⓑ Ⓒ Ⓓ
103. Ⓐ Ⓑ Ⓒ Ⓓ
104. Ⓐ Ⓑ Ⓒ Ⓓ
105. Ⓐ Ⓑ Ⓒ Ⓓ
106. Ⓐ Ⓑ Ⓒ Ⓓ
107. Ⓐ Ⓑ Ⓒ Ⓓ
108. Ⓐ Ⓑ Ⓒ Ⓓ
109. Ⓐ Ⓑ Ⓒ Ⓓ
110. Ⓐ Ⓑ Ⓒ Ⓓ
111. Ⓐ Ⓑ Ⓒ Ⓓ
112. Ⓐ Ⓑ Ⓒ Ⓓ
113. Ⓐ Ⓑ Ⓒ Ⓓ
114. Ⓐ Ⓑ Ⓒ Ⓓ
115. Ⓐ Ⓑ Ⓒ Ⓓ
116. Ⓐ Ⓑ Ⓒ Ⓓ
117. Ⓐ Ⓑ Ⓒ Ⓓ
118. Ⓐ Ⓑ Ⓒ Ⓓ
119. Ⓐ Ⓑ Ⓒ Ⓓ
120. Ⓐ Ⓑ Ⓒ Ⓓ

Time: 60 MINUTES

> **Directions:** In each of the following questions, you will find three initial terms and, in parentheses, four answer options designated *a*, *b*, *c*, and *d*. You are to select from the four answer options the one that *best* completes the analogy with the three initial terms. To record your answers, use the answer sheet provided.

1. GRAY : ELEPHANT :: (*a.* white, *b.* brown, *c.* green, *d.* gray) : GRIZZLY BEAR

2. (*a.* ratatouille, *b.* vermouth, *c.* lemonade, *d.* gin) : EAT :: MANHATTAN : DRINK

3. EARTH : PLANET :: (*a.* asteroid, *b.* sun, *c.* comet, *d.* Orion) : CONSTELLATION

4. JOHN : (*a.* Jackson, *b.* Adams, *c.* Pierce, *d.* Garfield) :: ANDREW : JOHNSON

5. 1 + 2 : MARCH :: 12 – 3 : (*a.* September, *b.* October, *c.* November, *d.* December)

6. CANNON : CANNON :: STIMULI : (*a.* stimulation, *b.* stimuluses, *c.* stimulate, *d.* stimulus)

7. GRAPES : WINE :: (*a.* alcohol, *b.* hops, *c.* alfalfa, *d.* kemp) : BEER

8. SCROOGE : GREEDY :: (*a.* Antony, *b.* Portia, *c.* Cassius, *d.* King Lear) : TREACHEROUS

9. (*a.* hurricane, *b.* hail, *c.* sleet, *d.* thunder) : RAIN :: BLIZZARD : SNOW

10. BLANC : ALPS :: EVEREST : (*a.* Andes, *b.* Himalayas, *c.* Jungfrau, *d.* Caucasus)

11. i : e :: (*a.* $-\infty$, *b.* π, *c.* 1, *d.* $\sqrt{-1}$) : 2.71828

12. (*a.* Na, *b.* Al, *c.* O_2, *d.* N) : SALT :: H : HYDROCHLORIC ACID

13. UROLOGIST : (*a.* bladder, *b.* urine, *c.* heart, *d.* ears) :: OPHTHALMOLOGIST : EYES

14. A : C :: ALPHA : (*a.* lambda, *b.* kappa, *c.* omicron, *d.* gamma)

15. (*a.* coin, *b.* bullion, *c.* currency, *d.* check) : CASH :: PROBABLE : CERTAIN

16. SKINNER : ENVIRONMENT :: (*a.* Galton, *b.* Locke, *c.* Sagan, *d.* Spence) : HEREDITY

17. DOG : NOUN :: (*a.* newspaper, *b.* at, *c.* the, *d.* is) : ARTICLE

18. IRISH : (*a.* setter, *b.* Guernsey, *c.* mutt, *d.* St. Bernard) :: LABRADOR : RETRIEVER

19. PERSHING : (*a.* French, *b.* U.S., *c.* English, *d.* Canadian) :: WELLINGTON : ENGLISH

20. MORNING STAR : EVENING STAR :: VENUS : (*a.* Mercury, *b.* Mars, *c.* Jupiter, *d.* Venus)

21. HYPERBOLE : HYPERBOLA :: STATEMENT : (*a.* statements, *b.* curve, *c.* exaggeration, *d.* ellipse)

22. X̄ : SAMPLE :: (*a.* μ, *b.* σ, *c.* λ, *d.* ρ) : POPULATION

23. METHYL : ETHYL :: GRAIN : (*a.* turpentine, *b.* alcohol, *c.* rain, *d.* wood)

24. SHORTEST : (*a.* February, *b.* August, *c.* April, *d.* December) :: LONGEST : JUNE

25. (*a.* nadir, *b.* zenith, *c.* summit, *d.* hilt) : BOTTOM :: APEX : TOP

26. PERCENT : 100 :: PROPORTION : (*a.* 0, *b.* 1, *c.* 0.1, *d.* 0.01)

27. RATIONAL : $\sqrt{100}$ :: IRRATIONAL : (*a.* $\sqrt{1}$, *b.* $\sqrt{-4}$, *c.* $\sqrt{50}$, *d.* $\sqrt{0}$)

28. ENORMITY : (*a.* great wickedness, *b.* great largesse, *c.* great goodness, *d.* great passion) :: SLANDER : VILIFICATION

29. VANILLA : TEA :: (*a.* stem, *b.* root, *c.* flower, *d.* bean) : LEAF

30. NOON : EVE :: 12:21 : (*a.* 8:34, *b.* 10:01, *c.* 7:54, *d.* 11:29)

31. (*a.* soap, *b.* aspirin, *c.* base, *d.* litmus) : ACID :: LYE : ALKALINE

32. SAM : AIR :: ABM : (*a.* sea, *b.* land, *c.* ballistic, *d.* missile)

33. STEP : STAIRCASE :: (*a.* notch, *b.* support, *c.* poles, *d.* rung) : LADDER

34. OCHER : (*a.* yellow, *b.* green, *c.* blue, *d.* gray) :: LAVENDER : PURPLE

35. MARE : EWE :: HORSE : (*a.* goat, *b.* sheep, *c.* pig, *d.* deer)

36. RAVIOLI : (*a.* spaghetti, *b.* linguine, *c.* cannelloni, *d.* enchilada) :: MANICOTTI : TORTELLINI

37. (*a.* bacteria, *b.* viruses, *c.* fungi, *d.* rickettsiae) : TYPHUS :: MYCOBACTERIA : TUBERCULOSIS

38. TWO : IMPEACH :: (*a.* zero, *b.* one, *c.* three, *d.* four) : CONVICT

39. 0 PROOF : 0% :: 50 PROOF : (*a.* 10%, *b.* 25%, *c.* 75%, *d.* 100%)

40. BENEDICT : ALFREDO :: EGGS : (*a.* oeufs, *b.* clams, *c.* ziti, *d.* fettuccini)

41. INDUCE : INDUCT :: (*a.* adduce, *b.* reason, *c.* persuade, *d.* deduct) : ADMIT

42. (*a.* maroon, *b.* crimson, *c.* pink, *d.* scarlet) : RED :: GRAY : BLACK

43. STOP : POT :: STOOL : (*a.* feces, *b.* toilet, *c.* chair, *d.* loot)

44. PICASSO : (*a.* Bosch, *b.* Daumier, *c.* Tintoretto, *d.* Dali) :: GUERNICA : GARDEN OF EARTHLY DELIGHTS

45. $3x^2 : 6x :: 5y : (a.\ 5,\ b.\ 10,\ c.\ 5y^{1/2},\ d.\ 10y^{1/2})$

46. UNICORN : (*a.* mythical beast, *b.* duet, *c.* zebra, *d.* union) :: SINGLETON : BICYCLE

47. (*a.* Holland, *b.* Yugoslavia, *c.* Denmark, *d.* Switzerland) : ALPINE :: GREECE : MEDITERRANEAN

48. M.D. : EARNED :: (*a.* D.D., *b.* Ph.D., *c.* D.D.S., *d.* O.D.) : HONORARY

49. (*a.* Don Juan, *b.* Pablo, *c.* Sancho, *d.* Dulcinea) : DON QUIXOTE :: WATSON : HOLMES

50. SONATA : (*a.* movement, *b.* sonatina, *c.* coda, *d.* solo) :: NOVEL : NOVELLA

51. NOVICE : EXPERT :: (*a.* teacher, *b.* apprentice, *c.* journeyman, *d.* layman) : MASTER

52. CLUB : (*a.* diamond, *b.* heart, *c.* spade, *d.* ace) :: LOWEST : HIGHEST

53. GOSLING : GOOSE :: SHOAT : (*a.* goat, *b.* sheep, *c.* horse, *d.* hog)

54. C : LEMON :: A : (*a.* liver, *b.* lettuce, *c.* orange, *d.* cake)

55. PACIFIC : OCEAN :: (*a.* Mercury, *b.* Jupiter, *c.* Uranus, *d.* Neptune) : PLANET

56. ICHTHYOLOGIST : (*a.* sentences, *b.* algae, *c.* insects, *d.* fish) :: ZOOLOGIST : ANIMALS

57. ELECT : SELECT :: TIE : (*a.* lose, *b.* win, *c.* sty, *d.* rope)

58. MALLET : (*a.* hunting, *b.* rugby, *c.* cricket, *d.* croquet) :: BAT : BASEBALL

59. BAROMETER : AIR PRESSURE :: TACHOMETER : (*a.* speed of descent, *b.* speed of rotation, *c.* acceleration, *d.* inertia)

60. EMERALD : GRUE :: (*a.* ruby, *b.* sapphire, *c.* amethyst, *d.* diamond) : BLEEN

61. MARTIN : DAVID :: (*a.* Dombey, *b.* Micawber, *c.* Magoun, *d.* Chuzzlewit) : COPPERFIELD

62. (*a.* 2:00, *b.* 3:00, *c.* 5:00, *d.* 6:00) : SEATTLE :: 4:00 : CHICAGO

63. VENUS : (*a.* Uranus, *b.* Mars, *c.* Saturn, *d.* Pluto) :: LOVE : THE DEAD

64. SUBORN : (*a.* give birth to, *b.* prove, *c.* bribe, *d.* demand) :: SUBORDINATE : INFERIOR

65. A : O :: (*a.* E, *b.* OA, *c.* B, *d.* RH) : AB

66. (*a.* coal, *b.* petroleum, *c.* black opal, *d.* uranium) : BLACK GOLD :: PYRITE : FOOL'S GOLD

67. MALACHITE : GREEN :: LAPIS LAZULI : (*a.* blue, *b.* red, *c.* yellow, *d.* amber)

68. LONGITUDE : LATITUDE :: (*a.* 110°, *b.* 90°, *c.* 70°, *d.* 50°) : 20°

69. VALENTINE : SECOND :: NICHOLAS : (*a.* first, *b.* sixth, *c.* tenth, *d.* twelfth)

70. MARK : (*a.* Lisbon, *b.* Berlin, *c.* Zurich, *d.* Basel) :: FRANC : PARIS

71. (*a.* biology, *b.* chemistry, *c.* physics, *d.* astronomy) : HERSCHEL :: SURGERY : LISTER

72. METER : KILOMETER :: 10 : (*a.* e, *b.* 10, *c.* 10^3, *d.* $\sqrt{10,000}$)

73. (*a.* Ash Wednesday, *b.* St. Bartholomew's Day, *c.* Maundy Thursday, *d.* All Saints' Day) : EASTER :: FIRST : LAST

74. GHOST : SPIRIT :: GHOUL : (*a.* body, *b.* vampire, *c.* nightmare, *d.* grave robber)

75. GERUND : (*a.* adverb, *b.* pronoun, *c.* conjunction, *d.* noun) :: PARTICIPLE : ADJECTIVE

76. N.Y. : N.J. :: N.H. : (*a.* N.D., *b.* N.C., *c.* N.M., *d.* N.W.)

77. (*a.* Abelard, *b.* Aquinas, *c.* Erasmus, *d.* Eusebius) : HELOÏSE :: TRISTAN : ISOLDE

78. GOBI : (*a.* Africa, *b.* Asia, *c.* South America, *d.* Central America) :: SAHARA : AFRICA

79. X : X^2 :: STANDARD DEVIATION : (*a.* mode, *b.* median, *c.* variance, *d.* chi square)

80. LEONINE : (*a.* vulpine, *b.* porcine, *c.* supine, *d.* bovine) :: LION : FOX

81. AUGUST 8 : LEO :: (*a.* January 8, *b.* April 8, *c.* October 8, *d.* December 8) : SAGITTARIUS

82. CHESS : CHESSMEN :: GO : (*a.* cards, *b.* stones, *c.* pegs, *d.* balls)

83. CIPHER : NAUGHT :: (*a.* zero, *b.* all, *c.* most, *d.* one) : NONE

84. SEVENTH-DAY ADVENTIST : (*a.* Friday, *b.* Saturday, *c.* Sunday, *d.* Monday) :: MUSLIM : FRIDAY

85. (*a.* 10, *b.* 11, *c.* 12, *d.* 13) : DUODECIMAL :: 13 : DECIMAL

86. (*a.* shawl, *b.* belt, *c.* cloak, *d.* sash) : BURNOOSE :: CAP : BUSBY

87. LEGHORN : (*a.* cattle, *b.* goat, *c.* sheep, *d.* fowl) :: ANGORA : GOAT

88. LISZT : HUNGARY :: MENOTTI : (*a.* U.S.A., *b.* Greece, *c.* Spain, *d.* England)

89. MELODY : (*a.* immediate, *b.* successive, *c.* retrogressive, *d.* momentary) :: HARMONY : SIMULTANEOUS

90. SINUSITIS : SINUS :: MENINGITIS : (*a.* liver, *b.* heart, *c.* artery, *d.* membrane)

91. APPROXIMATE : EXACT :: (*a.* analog, *b.* analogous, *c.* analogical, *d.* analogy) : DIGITAL

92. (*a.* is as, *b.* is almost, *c.* is virtually, *d.* is) : IS LIKE :: METAPHOR : SIMILE

93. CONGRESS : U.S.A. :: DIET : (*a.* Germany, *b.* Turkey, *c.* Japan, *d.* China)

94. MAYOR : (*a.* Montevideo, *b.* Sussex, *c.* Casterbridge, *d.* Marseilles) :: HUNCHBACK : NOTRE DAME

95. INDUCTION : DEDUCTION :: HUME : (*a.* Locke, *b.* Leibniz, *c.* Berkeley, *d.* Mill)

96. STOP : (*a.* h, *b.* j, *c.* t, *d.* v) :: FRICATIVE : F

97. (*a.* $^1/_2$gt^2, *b.* ra, *c.* $^1/_4$g^{2}k, *d.* pc) : D :: MA : F

98. FIDELIO : BORIS GODUNOV :: BEETHOVEN : (*a.* Rimski-Korsakov, *b.* Shostakovich, *c.* Prokofiev, *d.* Mussorgsky)

99. MISER : AVARICIOUS :: SYCOPHANT : (*a.* plutonic, *b.* veracious, *c.* unctuous, *d.* sybaritic)

100. (*a.* genitive, *b.* dative, *c.* ablative, *d.* vocative) : ACCUSATIVE :: INDIRECT : DIRECT

101. (*a.* wheat, *b.* barley, *c.* oats, *d.* rice) : SAKE :: JUNIPER BERRIES : GIN

102. A RAISIN IN THE SUN : THE GRAPES OF WRATH :: (*a.* Morrison, *b.* Hansberry, *c.* Miller, *d.* Hare) : STEINBECK

103. SHARP : TACK :: COOL : (*a.* cucumber, *b.* stone, *c.* stream, *d.* milk)

104. SASQUATCH : NORTH AMERICA :: YETI : (*a.* South America, *b.* Europe, *c.* Australia, *d.* Asia)

105. CRETE : (*a.* Turkey, *b.* Syria, *c.* Greece, *d.* Albania) :: SICILY : ITALY

106. $a^2 + b^2$: (*a.* hypotenuse squared, *b.* rectangular area, *c.* circumference cubed, *d.* spherical volume) :: $(y - y_1) / (x - x_1)$: SLOPE

107. (*a.* tomato, *b.* peanut, *c.* chestnut, *d.* ginger) : PARSNIP :: TURNIP : POTATO

108. KEEL : FRAMES :: BREASTBONE : (*a.* human, *b.* ribs, *c.* pectorals, *d.* backbone)

109. PUSILLANIMOUS : (*a.* brave, *b.* hungry, *c.* joyful, *d.* jealous) :: PERFIDIOUS : LOYAL

110. MARS : VENUS :: EARTH : (*a*. Jupiter, *b*. Saturn, *c*. Mercury, *d*. Neptune)

111. CACOPHONOUS : NOISOME :: SOUND : (*a*. sight, *b*. feel, *c*. smell, *d*. taste)

112. CAT : MOUSE :: (*a*. squirrel, *b*. bandicoot, *c*. lemur, *d*. mongoose) : SNAKE

113. ELEPHANT : (*a*. piano, *b*. tusk, *c*. table, *d*. hoof) :: WHALE : LAMP

114. (*a*. Padua, *b*. Siberia, *c*. Verona, *d*. Narnia) : OZ :: SHANGRI-LA : ATLANTIS

115. AURORA BOREALIS : (*a*. Northern Lights, *b*. Gulf Stream, *c*. Black Forest, *d*. El Niño) :: CRANIUM : SKULL

116. PUMMELO : CITRUS FRUIT :: (*a*. rutabaga, *b*. grain, *c*. lentil, *d*. artichoke) : LEGUME

117. KENNEDY : (*a*. House Representative, *b*. Senator, *c*. Mayor, *d*. Governor) :: CLINTON : GOVERNOR

118. ARGES : CYCLOPS :: MEDUSA : (*a*. gorgon, *b*. minotaur, *c*. siren, *d*. hydra)

119. I.E. : (*a*. English, *b*. Italian, *c*. Latin, *d*. Greek) :: RSVP : French

120. (*a*. weary, *b*. tenacious, *c*. harmonious, *d*. sprightly) : JOCUND :: VERITABLE : AUTHENTIC

1.	**B**	31.	**B**	61.	**D**	91.	**A**
2.	**A**	32.	**C**	62.	**A**	92.	**D**
3.	**D**	33.	**D**	63.	**D**	93.	**C**
4.	**B**	34.	**A**	64.	**C**	94.	**C**
5.	**A**	35.	**B**	65.	**C**	95.	**B**
6.	**D**	36.	**C**	66.	**B**	96.	**C**
7.	**B**	37.	**D**	67.	**A**	97.	**A**
8.	**C**	38.	**A**	68.	**A**	98.	**D**
9.	**A**	39.	**B**	69.	**D**	99.	**C**
10.	**B**	40.	**D**	70.	**B**	100.	**B**
11.	**D**	41.	**C**	71.	**D**	101.	**D**
12.	**A**	42.	**C**	72.	**C**	102.	**B**
13.	**A**	43.	**D**	73.	**A**	103.	**A**
14.	**D**	44.	**A**	74.	**D**	104.	**D**
15.	**D**	45.	**A**	75.	**D**	105.	**C**
16.	**A**	46.	**B**	76.	**C**	106.	**A**
17.	**C**	47.	**D**	77.	**A**	107.	**D**
18.	**A**	48.	**A**	78.	**B**	108.	**B**
19.	**B**	49.	**C**	79.	**C**	109.	**A**
20.	**D**	50.	**B**	80.	**A**	110.	**C**
21.	**B**	51.	**B**	81.	**D**	111.	**C**
22.	**A**	52.	**C**	82.	**B**	112.	**D**
23.	**C**	53.	**D**	83.	**A**	113.	**A**
24.	**D**	54.	**A**	84.	**B**	114.	**D**
25.	**A**	55.	**B**	85.	**B**	115.	**A**
26.	**B**	56.	**D**	86.	**C**	116.	**C**
27.	**C**	57.	**C**	87.	**D**	117.	**B**
28.	**A**	58.	**D**	88.	**A**	118.	**A**
29.	**D**	59.	**B**	89.	**B**	119.	**C**
30.	**B**	60.	**B**	90.	**D**	120.	**D**

In the following, explanations concerning the correct responses are in roman font. Explanations regarding distracters (incorrect responses) that are not self-explaining or could be misinterpreted are in italics in order to highlight the explanations of the answers that are correct.

1. GRAY : ELEPHANT :: (*a.* white, **b. brown**, *c.* green, *d.* gray) : GRIZZLY BEAR
   (b) An elephant is gray; a grizzly bear is brown.

2. (**a. ratatouille**, *b.* vermouth, *c.* lemonade, *d.* gin) : EAT :: MANHATTAN : DRINK
   (a) Ratatouille is something one eats; a Manhattan is something one drinks.

3. EARTH : PLANET :: (*a.* asteroid, *b.* sun, *c.* comet, **d. Orion**) : CONSTELLATION
   (d) Earth is a planet. Orion is a constellation of stars in the sky. *None of the other choices is a constellation.*

4. JOHN : (*a.* Jackson, **b. Adams**, *c.* Pierce, *d.* Garfield) :: ANDREW : JOHNSON
   (b) John Adams and Andrew Johnson were both U.S. presidents. The names of the other presidents were Andrew Jackson, Franklin Pierce, and James Garfield.

5. 1 + 2 : MARCH :: 12 – 3 : (**a. September**, *b.* October, *c.* November, *d.* December)
   (a) March is the third (1 + 2) month of the year; September is the ninth (12 – 3) month.

6. CANNON : CANNON :: STIMULI : (*a.* stimulation, *b.* stimuluses, *c.* stimulate, **d. stimulus**)
   (d) Cannon is the plural form of cannon. Stimuli is the plural form of stimulus.

7. GRAPES : WINE :: (*a.* alcohol, **b. hops**, *c.* alfalfa, *d.* kemp) : BEER
   (b) Wine is made from grapes; beer is made from hops.

8. SCROOGE : GREEDY :: (*a.* Antony, *b.* Portia, **c. Cassius**, *d.* King Lear) : TREACHEROUS
   (c) Scrooge (in *A Christmas Carol*) was greedy; Cassius (in *Julius Caesar*) was treacherous. *Portia is the wife of Brutus (Julius Caesar's famous assassin) in Shakespeare's* Julius Caesar. *Antony is a soldier and ruler of the Roman Empire in Shakespeare's* Antony and Cleopatra.

9. (**a. hurricane**, *b.* hail, *c.* sleet, *d.* thunder) : RAIN :: BLIZZARD : SNOW
   (a) A hurricane is characterized by strong wind and heavy rain; a blizzard is characterized by strong wind and heavy snow.

10. BLANC : ALPS :: EVEREST : (*a.* Andes, **b. Himalayas**, *c.* Jungfrau, *d.* Caucasus)
    (b) Mont Blanc is the highest mountain peak in the Alps; Mount Everest is the highest mountain peak in the Himalayas. *The Alps are a mountain range in Europe. The Andes are a mountain range in South America. The Himalayas are a mountain range in Asia. The Jungfrau is a mountain in the Swiss Alps and the Caucasus is the mountain range that separates the continents of Asia and Europe.*

11. i : e :: (*a.* –∞, *b.* π, *c.* 1, **d. $\sqrt{-1}$**) : 2.71828
    (d) The quantity i is equal to $\sqrt{-1}$; the quantity e is (approximately) equal to 2.71828. *The quantity of π is approximately equal to 3.14159. The symbol ∞ represents infinity.*

12. (**a. Na**, *b.* Al, *c.* O_2, *d.* N) : SALT :: H : HYDROCHLORIC ACID
    (a) Salt is a compound containing sodium (Na); hydrochloric acid is a compound containing hydrogen (H). *O_2 stands for oxygen, N stands for nitrogen, and Al stands for aluminum.*

13. UROLOGIST : (***a. bladder***, *b.* urine, *c.* heart, *d.* ears) :: OPHTHALMOLOGIST : EYES
    (a) A urologist treats the bladder; an ophthalmologist treats the eyes.

14. A : C :: ALPHA : (*a.* lambda, *b.* kappa, *c.* omicron, ***d. gamma***)
    (d) *A* is the first letter and *c* is the third letter of the Roman alphabet; alpha is the first letter and gamma is the third letter of the Greek alphabet. *Lambda is the 11th letter of the Greek alphabet, kappa is the 10th letter, and omicron is the 15th letter.*

15. (*a.* coin, *b.* bullion, *c.* currency, ***d. check***) : CASH :: PROBABLE : CERTAIN
    (d) A check has probable value in a financial transaction (it is not certain to clear). Cash has certain value. *A bullion is a pure form of a precious metal and therefore has a certain value. A coin is a metal disc usually issued by a government that is used as money. A currency is the form of money used in a country.*

16. SKINNER : ENVIRONMENT :: (***a. Galton***, *b.* Locke, *c.* Sagan, *d.* Spence) : HEREDITY
    (a) Skinner is known for his belief that environment largely shapes behavior; Galton believed that heredity largely shapes behavior. John Locke was an English philosopher and empiricist. *Carl Sagan was an American astronomer and astrophysicist. Kenneth Spence was an American psychologist who developed the theory of Stimulus Control.*

17. DOG : NOUN :: (*a.* newspaper, *b.* at, ***c. the***, *d.* is) : ARTICLE
    (c) Dog is a noun; the is an article.

18. IRISH : (***a. setter***, *b.* Guernsey, *c.* mutt, *d.* St. Bernard) :: LABRADOR : RETRIEVER
    (a) An Irish setter and a Labrador retriever are both kinds of dogs.

19. PERSHING : (*a.* French, ***b. U.S.***, *c.* English, *d.* Canadian) :: WELLINGTON : ENGLISH
    (b) Pershing was a U.S. general who led the American Expeditionary Force in World War I; Wellington was an English general who served in the Napoleonic wars.

20. MORNING STAR : EVENING STAR :: VENUS : (*a.* Mercury, *b.* Mars, *c.* Jupiter, ***d. Venus***)
    (d) Venus is known both as the morning star and as the evening star.

21. HYPERBOLE : HYPERBOLA :: STATEMENT : (*a.* statements, ***b. curve***, *c.* exaggeration, *d.* ellipse)
    (b) A hyperbole is a type of statement; a hyperbola is a type of curve.

22. $\bar{X}$: SAMPLE :: (***a.*** μ, *b.* σ, *c.* λ, *d.* ρ) : POPULATION
    (a) $\bar{X}$ is a symbol for a sample mean; μ is a symbol for a population mean. *σ stands for the standard deviation of a population. λ stands for eigenvalues and Lagrange multipliers. ρ stands for a correlation coefficient in statistics. Note that these Greek letters have additional meanings in other sciences.*

23. METHYL : ETHYL :: GRAIN : (*a.* turpentine, *b.* alcohol, ***c. rain***, *d.* wood)
    (c) Ethyl is methyl without the initial *m*; rain is grain without the initial *g*.

24. SHORTEST : (*a.* February, *b.* August, *c.* April, ***d. December***) :: LONGEST : JUNE
    (d) The shortest day of the year occurs in December. The longest day of the year occurs in June.

25. (***a. nadir***, *b.* zenith, *c.* summit, *d.* hilt) : BOTTOM :: APEX : TOP
    (a) The nadir is the lowest point, or bottom of something; the apex is the highest point, or top. *A zenith is the direction pointing directly above a particular location. A summit is the highest point of a mountain. A hilt is the handle of a sword.*

26. PERCENT : 100 :: PROPORTION : (*a.* 0, *b.* **1**, *c.* 0.1, *d.* 0.01)

(b) The highest possible percent is 100; the highest possible proportion is 1.

27. RATIONAL : $\sqrt{100}$ :: IRRATIONAL : (*a.* $\sqrt{1}$, *b.* $\sqrt{-4}$, *c.* $\sqrt{50}$, *d.* $\sqrt{0}$)

(c) $\sqrt{100}$ is a rational number; $\sqrt{50}$ is an irrational number. A rational number can be expressed as a ratio of two integers (which are natural numbers like 1, 2, 3, and their negatives). An irrational number is a real number that cannot be expressed as a fraction and therefore is not a rational number.

28. ENORMITY : (*a.* **great wickedness**, *b.* great largesse, *c.* great goodness, *d.* great passion) :: SLANDER : VILIFICATION

(a) Enormity is great wickedness; slander is vilification.

29. VANILLA : TEA :: (*a.* stem, *b.* root, *c.* flower, *d.* **bean**) : LEAF

(d) Vanilla comes from a bean, tea from a leaf.

30. NOON : EVE :: 12:21 : (*a.* 8:34, *b.* **10:01**, *c.* 7:54, *d.* 11:29)

(b) Noon and eve are both palindromes (they read the same spelled backward and forward), as are 12:21 and 10:01.

31. (*a.* soap, *b.* **aspirin**, *c.* base, *d.* litmus) : ACID :: LYE : ALKALINE

(b) Aspirin is acid; lye is alkaline.

32. SAM : AIR :: ABM : (*a.* sea, *b.* land, *c.* **ballistic**, *d.* missile)

(c) The second letter in the acronym *SAM* (surface-to-air missile) stands for air; the second letter in the *ABM* (anti-ballistic missile) stands for ballistic.

33. STEP : STAIRCASE :: (*a.* notch, *b.* support, *c.* poles, *d.* **rung**) : LADDER

(d) A staircase has steps; a ladder has rungs.

34. OCHER : (*a.* **yellow**, *b.* green, *c.* blue, *d.* gray) :: LAVENDER : PURPLE

(a) Ocher is a shade of yellow; lavender is a shade of purple.

35. MARE : EWE :: HORSE : (*a.* goat, *b.* **sheep**, *c.* pig, *d.* deer)

(b) A mare is a female horse; a ewe is a female sheep.

36. RAVIOLI : (*a.* spaghetti, *b.* linguine, *c.* **cannelloni**, *d.* enchilada) :: MANICOTTI : TORTELLINI

(c) Ravioli, cannelloni, manicotti, and tortellini are all stuffed pasta dishes.

37. (*a.* bacteria, *b.* viruses, *c.* fungi, *d.* **rickettsiae**) : TYPHUS :: MYCOBACTERIA : TUBERCULOSIS

(d) Typhus is caused by rickettsiae (parasitic bacteria), tuberculosis by mycobacteria.

38. TWO : IMPEACH :: (*a.* **zero**, *b.* one, *c.* three, *d.* four) : CONVICT

(a) Two presidents of the United States have been impeached (Andrew Johnson and Bill Clinton); no president has been convicted.

39. 0 PROOF : 0% :: 50 PROOF : (*a.* 10%, *b.* **25%**, *c.* 75%, *d.* 100%)

(b) Something that is 0 proof has a 0% concentration of alcohol; something that is 50 proof has a 25% concentration of alcohol.

40. BENEDICT : ALFREDO :: EGGS : (*a.* oeufs, *b.* clams, *c.* ziti, *d.* **fettuccini**)

(d) Eggs Benedict and fettuccini Alfredo are both food dishes.

41. INDUCE : INDUCT :: (*a.* adduce, *b.* reason, ***c.* persuade**, *d.* deduct) : ADMIT

(c) To induce is to persuade; to induct is to admit. *To adduce means to cite or to allege in order to support an argument; to deduct is to take away, as from an amount; to reason means to think logically.*

42. (*a.* maroon, *b.* crimson, ***c.* pink**, *d.* scarlet) : RED :: GRAY : BLACK

(c) Pink is red mixed with white; gray is black mixed with white.

43. STOP : POT :: STOOL : (*a.* feces, *b.* toilet, *c.* chair, ***d.* loot**)

(d) Pot is all but the first letter of stop reversed; loot is all but the first letter of stool reversed.

44. PICASSO : (***a.* Bosch**, *b.* Daumier, *c.* Tintoretto, *d.* Dali) :: GUERNICA : GARDEN OF EARTHLY DELIGHTS

(a) Picasso painted *Guernica.* Bosch painted *The Garden of Earthly Delights. Daumier is famous for his works depicting the life of Don Quixote; Tintoretto is known for his painting of the last supper (and da Vinci created a painting with the same title!); Dali is famous for his bizarre, surreal images, often of soft watches like in* The Persistence of Memory.

45. $3x^2$: $6x$ :: $5y$: (***a.* 5**, *b.* 10, *c.* $5y^{1/2}$, *d.* $10y^{1/2}$)

(a) The expression $6x$ is the first derivative of $3x^2$; 5 is the first derivative of $5y$.

46. UNICORN : (*a.* mythical beast, ***b.* duet**, *c.* zebra, *d.* union) :: SINGLETON : BICYCLE

(b) A unicorn and a singleton both refer to one of something; a duet and a bicycle both refer to two of something.

47. (*a.* Holland, *b.* Croatia, *c.* Denmark, ***d.* Switzerland**) : ALPINE :: GREECE : MEDITERRANEAN

(d) Switzerland is an Alpine country; Greece is a Mediterranean country. *Croatia is an eastern European country. Denmark is located in northern Europe, and Holland is located in western Europe.*

48. M.D. : EARNED :: (***a.* D.D.**, *b.* Ph.D., *c.* D.D.S., *d.* O.D.) : HONORARY

(a) An M.D. (Doctor of Medicine) degree is earned; a D.D. (Doctor of Divinity) degree is honorary. *A Ph.D. is a Doctor of Philosophy, a D.D.S. is a Doctor of Dental Surgery, and an O.D. is a Doctor of Optometry.*

49. (*a.* Don Juan, *b.* Pablo, ***c.* Sancho**, *d.* Dulcinea) : DON QUIXOTE :: WATSON : HOLMES

(c) Sancho was the sidekick of Don Quixote; Watson was the sidekick of Holmes. *Don Juan, the protagonist of a legend, is a rogue and likes to seduce women. Pablo is a character from John Steinbeck's novel* Tortilla Flat. *Dulcinea is a character who is referred to in* Don Quixote *but does not actually appear.*

50. SONATA : (*a.* movement, ***b.* sonatina**, *c.* coda, *d.* solo) :: NOVEL : NOVELLA

(b) A sonatina is a short sonata; a novella is a short novel. *A movement is a self-contained part of a larger composition. A coda is a musical passage that brings a piece to a conclusion. A solo is a (part of a) piece played or sung by one artist alone.*

51. NOVICE : EXPERT :: (*a.* teacher, ***b.* apprentice**, *c.* journeyman, *d.* layman) : MASTER

(b) An apprentice is a novice; a master is an expert.

52. CLUB : (*a.* diamond, *b.* heart, ***c.* spade**, *d.* ace) :: LOWEST : HIGHEST

(c) In bridge, the club represents the lowest suit and the spade represents the highest suit.

53. GOSLING : GOOSE :: SHOAT : (*a.* goat, *b.* sheep, *c.* horse, ***d.* hog**)

(d) A gosling is a young goose; a shoat is a young hog.

54. C : LEMON :: A : (***a.* liver**, *b.* lettuce, *c.* orange, *d.* cake)

(a) A lemon is a very good source of vitamin C; liver is a very good source of vitamin A.

55. PACIFIC : OCEAN :: (*a.* Mercury, ***b.* Jupiter**, *c.* Uranus, *d.* Neptune) : PLANET

(b) The Pacific Ocean is the largest of the oceans; Jupiter is the largest of the planets.

56. ICHTHYOLOGIST : (*a.* sentences, *b.* algae, *c.* insects, ***d.* fish**) :: ZOOLOGIST : ANIMALS

(d) An ichthyologist studies fish; a zoologist studies animals of all types.

57. ELECT : SELECT :: TIE : (*a.* lose, *b.* win, ***c.* sty**, *d.* rope)

(c) Elect is pronounced like select, minus the initial *s* consonant sound; tie is pronounced like sty, minus the initial *s* consonant sound.

58. MALLET : (*a.* hunting, *b.* rugby, *c.* cricket, ***d.* croquet**) :: BAT : BASEBALL

(d) Croquet is played with a mallet, baseball with a bat.

59. BAROMETER : AIR PRESSURE :: TACHOMETER : (*a.* speed of descent, ***b.* speed of rotation**, *c.* acceleration, *d.* inertia)

(b) A barometer measures air pressure; a tachometer measures speed of rotation.

60. EMERALD : GRUE :: (*a.* ruby, ***b.* sapphire**, *c.* amethyst, *d.* diamond) : BLEEN

(b) In Nelson Goodman's famous paradox, an emerald can now be construed as grue (green until the year 2000 and blue thereafter), whereas a sapphire can be construed as bleen (blue until the year 2000 and green thereafter).

61. MARTIN : DAVID :: (*a.* Dombey, *b.* Micawber, *c.* Magoun, ***d.* Chuzzlewit**) : COPPERFIELD

(d) *Martin Chuzzlewit* and *David Copperfield* are both titles of novels by Charles Dickens. Dombey and Son *is a novel by Charles Dickens; Wilkins Micawber is a character in* David Copperfield, *and Francis Magoun was a writer and professor at Harvard.*

62. (***a.* 2:00**, *b.* 3:00, *c.* 5:00, *d.* 6:00) : SEATTLE :: 4:00 : CHICAGO

(a) When it is 2:00 in Seattle, it is 4:00 in Chicago.

63. VENUS : (*a.* Uranus, *b.* Mars, *c.* Saturn, ***d.* Pluto**) :: LOVE : THE DEAD

(d) In Roman mythology, Venus was the goddess of love; Pluto was alleged to be the god of the dead. *Saturn was the god of agriculture and harvest, Uranus was the god of the sky, and Mars was the god of war.*

64. SUBORN : (*a.* give birth to, *b.* prove, ***c.* bribe**, *d.* demand) :: SUBORDINATE : INFERIOR

(c) Suborn and bribe are synonyms, as are subordinate and inferior.

65. A : O :: (*a.* E, *b.* OA, ***c.* B**, *d.* RH) : AB

(c) A, O, B, and AB are all blood types.

66. (*a.* coal, ***b.* petroleum**, *c.* black opal, *d.* uranium) : BLACK GOLD :: PYRITE : FOOL'S GOLD

(b) Petroleum is referred to as black gold; pyrite is fool's gold.

67. MALACHITE : GREEN :: LAPIS LAZULI : (***a.* blue**, *b.* red, *c.* yellow, *d.* amber)

(a) Malachite is green in color; lapis lazuli is blue.

68. LONGITUDE : LATITUDE :: (***a.* 110°**, *b.* 90°, *c.* 70°, *d.* 50°) : 20°

(a) Lines of longitude and latitude are at right (90°) angles to each other, as are lines at 110° and 20°.

69. VALENTINE : SECOND :: NICHOLAS : (*a.* first, *b.* sixth, *c.* tenth, ***d.* twelfth**)

(d) St. Valentine's Day occurs during the second month of the year; St. Nicholas Day occurs during the twelfth month.

70. MARK : (*a.* Lisbon, ***b.* Berlin**, *c.* Zurich, *d.* Basel) :: FRANC : PARIS

(b) The mark was the unit of currency in Germany, of which Berlin is the capital; the franc was the unit of currency in France, of which Paris is the capital.

71. (*a.* biology, *b.* chemistry, *c.* physics, ***d.* astronomy**) : HERSCHEL :: SURGERY : LISTER

(d) Herschel is famous in the field of astronomy; Lister is famous in the field of surgery.

72. METER : KILOMETER :: 10 : (*a.* e, *b.* 10, ***c.* 10^3**, *d.* $\sqrt{10,000}$)

(c) A kilometer is 1000 meters; 10^3 is 1000 times log 10.

73. (***a.* Ash Wednesday**, *b.* St. Bartholomew's Day, *c.* Maundy Thursday, *d.* All Saints' Day) : EASTER :: FIRST : LAST

(a) Ash Wednesday is the first day of Lent; Easter is the last day.

74. GHOST : SPIRIT :: GHOUL : (*a.* body, *b.* vampire, *c.* nightmare, ***d.* grave robber**)

(d) A ghost is a spirit; a ghoul is a grave robber.

75. GERUND : (*a.* adverb, *b.* pronoun, *c.* conjunction, ***d.* noun**) :: PARTICIPLE : ADJECTIVE

(d) A gerund is a verb form that can act like a noun; a participle is a verb form that can act like an adjective.

76. N.Y. : N.J. :: N.H. : (*a.* N.D., *b.* N.C., ***c.* N.M.**, *d.* N.W.)

(c) N.Y., N.J., N.H., and N.M. are all abbreviations for two-word states of which the first word is *New.*

77. (***a.* Abelard**, *b.* Aquinas, *c.* Erasmus, *d.* Eusebius) : HELOÏSE :: TRISTAN : ISOLDE

(a) Abelard and Heloïse were lovers, as were Tristan and Isolde. Abelard was a medieval philosopher and theologian. Tristan and Isolde are characters in a legend. *Desiderius Erasmus was a Dutch Renaissance humanist and Catholic theologian. Eusebius Caesarea was the bishop of Caesarea Palestine and through his work provided a basis for Church History. Saint Thomas Aquinas was an Italian Catholic priest and proponent of natural theology.*

78. GOBI : (*a.* Africa, ***b.* Asia**, *c.* South America, *d.* Central America) :: SAHARA : AFRICA

(b) The Gobi Desert is in Asia; the Sahara Desert is in Africa.

79. X : X^2 :: STANDARD DEVIATION : (*a.* mode, *b.* median, ***c.* variance**, *d.* chi square)

(c) A variance is a standard deviation squared.

80. LEONINE : (***a.* vulpine**, *b.* porcine, *c.* supine, *d.* bovine) :: LION : FOX

(a) Leonine means "like a lion"; vulpine means "like a fox." Porcine means "like a pig," supine means "lying on the back," and bovine means "like a cow."

81. AUGUST 8 : LEO :: (*a.* January 8, *b.* April 8, *c.* October 8, ***d.* December 8**) : SAGITTARIUS

(d) Someone born on August 8 is born under the sign of Leo; someone born on December 8 is born under the sign of Sagittarius. *Aries (March 21–April 20); Taurus (April 21–May 21); Gemini (May 22–June 21); Cancer (June 22–July 22); Leo (July 23–August 21); Virgo (August 22–September 23); Libra (September 24–October 23); Scorpio (October 24–November 22); Sagittarius (November 23–December 22); Capricorn (December 23–January 20); Aquarius (January 21–February 19); Pisces (February 20–March 20).*

82. CHESS : CHESSMEN :: GO : (*a.* cards, ***b.* stones**, *c.* pegs, *d.* balls)

(b) The game of chess is played with chessmen; the game of go is played with stones.

83. CIPHER : NAUGHT :: (***a.* zero**, *b.* all, *c.* most, *d.* one) : NONE

(a) Cipher, naught, zero, and none all refer to nullity.

84. SEVENTH-DAY ADVENTIST : (*a.* Friday, ***b.* Saturday**, *c.* Sunday, *d.* Monday) :: MUSLIM : FRIDAY

(b) Sabbath occurs on Saturday for a Seventh-Day Adventist and on Friday for a Muslim.

85. (*a.* 10, ***b.* 11**, *c.* 12, *d.* 13) : DUODECIMAL :: 13 : DECIMAL

(b) The number 11 in duodecimal (base 12) notation equals the number 13 in decimal (base 10) notation.

86. (*a.* shawl, *b.* belt, ***c.* cloak**, *d.* sash) : BURNOOSE :: CAP : BUSBY

(c) A burnoose is a type of cloak; a busby is a type of cap.

87. LEGHORN : (*a.* cattle, *b.* goat, *c.* sheep, ***d.* fowl**) :: ANGORA : GOAT

(d) A leghorn is a type of fowl; an angora is a type of goat.

88. LISZT : HUNGARY :: MENOTTI : (***a.* U.S.A.**, *b.* Greece, *c.* Spain, *d.* England)

(a) Liszt was a noted composer from Hungary; Menotti is a noted composer from the United States.

89. MELODY : (*a.* immediate, ***b.* successive**, *c.* retrogressive, *d.* momentary) :: HARMONY : SIMULTANEOUS

(b) Melody is successive; harmony is simultaneous.

90. SINUSITIS : SINUS :: MENINGITIS : (*a.* liver, *b.* heart, *c.* artery, ***d.* membrane**)

(d) Sinusitis is an inflammation of the sinus; meningitis is an inflammation of a membrane.

91. APPROXIMATE : EXACT :: (***a.* analog**, *b.* analogous, *c.* analogical, *d.* analogy) : DIGITAL

(a) An analog computer yields approximate results; a digital computer yields exact results.

92. (*a.* is as, *b.* is almost, *c.* is virtually, ***d.* is**) : IS LIKE :: METAPHOR : SIMILE

(d) A metaphor often uses the linking verb *is*; a simile links two concepts by *is like*.

93. CONGRESS : U.S.A. :: DIET : (*a.* Germany, *b.* Turkey, ***c.* Japan**, *d.* China)

(c) The main legislative body of the United States is the Congress; the main legislative body of Japan is the Diet.

94. MAYOR : (*a.* Montevideo, *b.* Sussex, ***c.* Casterbridge**, *d.* Marseille) :: HUNCHBACK : NOTRE DAME

(c) *The Mayor of Casterbridge* and *The Hunchback of Notre Dame* are both titles of books.

95. INDUCTION : DEDUCTION :: HUME : (*a.* Locke, ***b.* Leibniz**, *c.* Berkeley, *d.* Mill)

(b) Hume, an empiricist, used induction as his major mode of reasoning. Leibniz, a rationalist, used deduction as his major mode of reasoning.

96. STOP : (*a.* h, *b.* j, ***c.* t**, *d.* v) :: FRICATIVE : F

(c) The sound of *t* is a stop; the sound of *f* is a fricative. A fricative is a sound that is produced by forcing air through a narrow passage. A stop is a consonant produced by stopping the flow of air at some point.

97. ($a.$ $\frac{1}{2}$ $\mathbf{gt^2}$, $b.$ ra, $c.$ $\frac{1}{4}$ g^2k, $d.$ pc) : D :: MA : F

   (a) Distance fallen by an object equals one-half the force of gravity times the amount of time squared; force equals mass times acceleration.

98. FIDELIO : BORIS GODUNOV :: BEETHOVEN : ($a.$ Rimski-Korsakov, $b.$ Shostakovich, $c.$ Prokofiev, $d.$ **Mussorgsky**)

   (d) *Fidelio* is an opera by Beethoven; *Boris Godunov* is an opera by Mussorgsky.

99. MISER : AVARICIOUS :: SYCOPHANT : ($a.$ plutonic, $b.$ veracious, $c.$ **unctuous**, $d.$ sybaritic)

   (c) A miser is avaricious; a sycophant is unctuous.

100. ($a.$ genitive, $b.$ **dative**, $c.$ ablative, $d.$ vocative) : ACCUSATIVE :: INDIRECT : DIRECT

   (b) In Latin, the dative case is used for indirect objects; the accusative case is used for direct objects.

101. ($a.$ wheat, $b.$ barley, $c.$ oats, $d.$ **rice**) : SAKE :: JUNIPER BERRIES : GIN

   (d) Just as the beverage gin is made from juniper berries, so is the beverage sake made from rice.

102. A RAISIN IN THE SUN : THE GRAPES OF WRATH :: ($a.$ Morrison, $b.$ **Hansberry**, $c.$ Miller, $d.$ Hare) : STEINBECK

   (b) Lorraine Hansberry wrote *A Raisin in the Sun* and John Steinbeck wrote *The Grapes of Wrath*.

103. SHARP : TACK :: COOL : ($a.$ **cucumber**, $b.$ stone, $c.$ stream, $d.$ milk)

   (a) The phrases "sharp as a tack" and "cool as a cucumber" can both be used to describe people.

104. SASQUATCH : NORTH AMERICA :: YETI : ($a.$ South America, $b.$ Europe, $c.$ Australia, $d.$ **Asia**)

   (d) The myth of the existence of a hairy hominid called sasquatch originated in North America just as the myth of the existence of a hairy hominid called yeti originated in Asia.

105. CRETE : ($a.$ Turkey, $b.$ Syria, $c.$ **Greece**, $d.$ Albania) :: SICILY : ITALY

   (c) Crete is a large island that is part of Greece and Sicily is a large island that is part of Italy.

106. $a^2 + b^2$: ($a.$ **hypotenuse squared**, $b.$ rectangular area, $c.$ circumference cubed, $d.$ spherical volume) :: $(y - y_1) / (x - x_1)$: SLOPE

   (a) The expression $a^2 + b^2$ is equal to hypotenuse squared just as $(y - y_1)/(x - x_1)$ is equal to slope.

107. ($a.$ tomato, $b.$ peanut, $c.$ chestnut, $d.$ **ginger**) : PARSNIP :: TURNIP : POTATO

   (d) Ginger, parsnips, turnips, and potatoes are all edible root vegetables.

108. KEEL : FRAMES :: BREASTBONE : ($a.$ human, $b.$ **ribs**, $c.$ pectorals, $d.$ backbone)

   (b) The keel is the structural centerline of a ship, to which the frames are attached. The breastbone is a structural midline of the body, to which the ribs are attached.

109. PUSILLANIMOUS : ($a.$ **brave**, $b.$ hungry, $c.$ joyful, $d.$ jealous) : PERFIDIOUS : LOYAL

   (a) Pusillanimous means the opposite of brave, just as perfidious is the opposite of loyal.

110. MARS : VENUS :: EARTH : ($a.$ Jupiter, $b.$ Saturn, $c.$ **Mercury**, $d.$ Neptune)

   (c) Mars, Venus, Earth, and Mercury are all terrestrial or "rocky" planets. *Jupiter, Saturn, and Neptune are gas planets.*

111. CACOPHONOUS : NOISOME :: SOUND : (*a.* sight, *b.* feel, ***c.* smell**, *d.* taste)

    (c) Something cacophonous is an unpleasant sound. Something noisome is an unpleasant smell.

112. CAT : MOUSE :: (*a.* squirrel, *b.* bandicoot, *c.* lemur, ***d.* mongoose**) : SNAKE

    (d) Cats are frequently kept to ward off mice just as mongooses are kept to ward off snakes.

113. ELEPHANT : (***a.* piano**, b. tusk, *c.* table, *d.* hoof) :: WHALE : LAMP

    (a) The elephant was once poached so that its ivory could be used for keys on pianos. The whale was once poached so that its oil could be used to burn in lamps.

114. (*a.* Padua, *b.* Siberia, *c.* Verona, ***d.* Narnia**) : OZ :: SHANGRI-LA : ATLANTIS

    (d) Narnia, Oz, Shangri-La, and Atlantis are all fictitious places of literature. *Padua and Verona are cities in Italy. Siberia is a part of Northern Asia located in Russia.*

115. AURORA BOREALIS : (***a.* Northern Lights**, b. Gulf Stream, *c.* Black Forest, *d.* El Niño) :: CRANIUM : SKULL

    (a) Aurora Borealis is the term of Latin origin used for the Northern Lights. Cranium is the term of Latin origin used for the skull.

116. PUMMELO : CITRUS FRUIT :: (*a.* rutabaga, *b.* grain, ***c.* lentil**, *d.* artichoke) : LEGUME

    (c) A pummelo is a citrus fruit just as a lentil is a legume.

117. KENNEDY : (*a.* House Representative, ***b.* Senator**, *c.* Mayor, *d.* Governor) :: CLINTON : GOVERNOR

    (b) Before becoming president, Kennedy and Clinton were a senator and a governor, respectively.

118. ARGES : CYCLOPS :: MEDUSA : (***a.* gorgon**, *b.* minotaur, *c.* siren, *d.* hydra)

    (a) Arges was a cyclops just as Medusa was a gorgon. *The Minotaur is a mythical creature with the head of a bull and the body of a man. A siren is a mythical sea nymph that lures sailors to their demise. Hydra is a mythical monster with nine heads; when one head is struck off it is replaced by two new ones.*

119. I.E. : (*a.* English, *b.* Italian, ***c.* Latin**, *d.* Greek) :: RSVP : French

    (c) The commonly used acronym "i.e." is derived from Latin just as the commonly used acronym "rsvp" is derived from French.

120. (*a.* weary, *b.* tenacious, *c.* harmonious, ***d.* sprightly**) : JOCUND :: VERITABLE : AUTHENTIC

    (d) Jocund means sprightly just as veritable means authentic.

NOTES

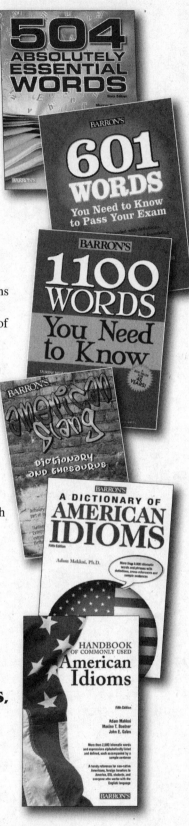

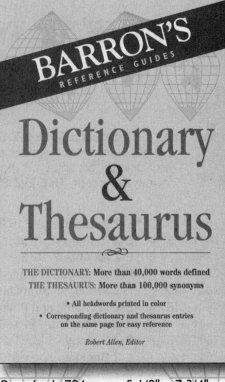

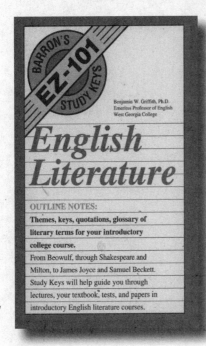